Most German of the Arts

PAMELA M. POTTER

Most German of the Arts

MUSICOLOGY AND SOCIETY
FROM THE WEIMAR REPUBLIC TO
THE END OF HITLER'S REICH

Yale University Press
New Haven &
London

To my parents

Printed in the United States of America.

Library of Congress Cataloging-in-Publication Data
Potter, Pamela Maxine.
    Most German of the arts : musicology and society from the Weimar
Republic to the end of Hitler's Reich / Pamela M. Potter.
      p. cm.
    Includes bibliographical references and index.
    ISBN 0-300-07228-7 (alk. paper)
    1. Musicology — Germany — History — 20th century.   2. Music and
society — Germany.   3. Nationalism in music.   4. National socialism
and music.   5. Denazification.   I. Title.
ML3797.P67   1998
780'.7'2043 — dc21   97-50585
               CIP
             MN

A catalogue record for this book is available from the British Library.

The paper in this book meets the guidelines for permanence and durability of the Committee on Production Guidelines for Book Longevity of the Council on Library Resources.

10 9 8 7 6 5 4 3 2 1

Contents

Acknowledgments

The research for this book was initiated under a grant from the Berlin Program for Advanced German and European Studies (Volkswagen-Stiftung and the Social Science Research Council). I am greatly indebted to this program for sponsoring my research in Europe for two years and for providing a stimulating atmosphere of scholarly interaction. Subsequent support was provided by a John F. Enders Research Assistance Grant, an Andrew W. Mellon Postdoctoral Fellowship in the Humanities, and a Hewlett Summer International Research Grant. A special debt of gratitude goes to the University of Illinois Campus Research Board for supporting this project at several stages and in numerous ways—providing funding for research assistants, equipment, database development, release time, and publication subvention.

I wish to thank the following libraries and archives and their personnel for their generous assistance and cooperation: Berlin Document Center (Mr. Simon, Dr. Marwell, and Herr Fehlauer); Bundesarchiv Koblenz (Frau Booms); Universitätsarchiv München (Frau Spin and Dr. Böhm); Universitätsarchiv Köln (Frau Schütz); Universitätsarchiv Berlin (Dr. Schulze); Universitätsarchiv Leipzig (Prof. Schwendler); Universitätsarchiv Freiburg (Frau Klaiber); Universitätsarchiv Bonn (Dr. Schmidt); Universitätsarchiv Heidelberg; Staatsbibliothek zu Berlin, Preußischer Kulturbesitz (Dr. Hertin-Loeser); Niedersächsisches Staatsarchiv Bückeburg (Dr. Poschmann); Zentrales Staatsarchiv

Potsdam; Geheimes Staatsarchiv Berlin-Dahlem (Frau Brandt); Archive of the Gesellschaft der Musikfreunde; Staatliches Institut für Musikforschung Preussischer Kulturbesitz (Prof. Reinecke); Archiv der Universität Wien; Archive of the University of Nebraska at Lincoln; and the Music Library, University of California at Berkeley (Judy Tsou). Special thanks go to Dr. Horn of the Bayerische Staatsbibliothek in Munich for taking the time to catalogue the papers of Adolf Sandberger and Otto Ursprung at my special request. I also wish to thank the University of Wisconsin School of Music and the departments of History and German for providing me with office space during summers and leave time, offering me a comfortable and quiet environment to think and to write.

Many colleagues have generously given their time to careful and critical readings of the manuscript at various stages. I am sincerely indebted to Joan Evans, Michael Kater, and Karen Painter for their thorough scrutiny of the manuscript in its entirety and their invaluable suggestions for improvements. Individual chapters additionally benefited from the expertise of Celia Applegate, Peter Fritzsche, and Bruno Nettl, whose insights have been enormously helpful. Doris Bergen, Geoffrey Giles, and Alan Steinweis called my attention to important research in their areas of expertise, Paul Heiser devoted countless hours to creating a data base to access archival information, and Patricia Sandler offered thoughtful criticisms on difficult passages. I am most grateful to my research assistant, Anna Schultz, who took on the unenviable tasks of proofreading, double-checking all references, and assisting in the final compilation of the manuscript.

My engagement with the musical environment in Nazi Germany was first inspired and motivated from working with Christoph Wolff and Reinhold Brinkmann during my studies at Harvard and in Berlin. My exploration of musicology's role reached its first stage of development as a dissertation for the Yale Department of Music under the direction of Reinhard Strohm, to whom I am indebted for his tireless encouragement and continued interest. I also wish to thank Harry Haskell at Yale University Press for his faith in this project and his helpful suggestions throughout the long process of writing, Eliza Childs for her meticulous copy editing, and Phillip King for his care and guidance in the final preparation of the book. My deepest gratitude is reserved for my husband, Robert Radwin. He has supported me in every way possible throughout the most stressful stages of this undertaking, and I thank him for his limitless patience and encouragement.

Introduction

In 1878, Richard Wagner proclaimed that the German essence was to be found in music. Sixty years later in 1938, at the opening of the largest musical gathering of the Third Reich, Propaganda Minister Joseph Goebbels reassured the crowd that music was the most glorious art of the German heritage. To this day, the legend of Germans as the "people of music" lives on worldwide. The catechisms of classical music require familiarity with the three "B's" (Bach, Beethoven, and Brahms), all of them Germans; concert halls perpetuate the names of the great German masters in their repertoires; music history is taught essentially as a progression toward German self-realization; and Germany and Austria continue to attract music connoisseurs and students as their governments invest in the preservation of impressive musical institutions, events, and projects. The popular perception of Western music assumes that Germans have always played a central role in the enrichment of the musical art. Musicologist Albrecht Riethmüller tells of an encounter in 1992 in which a young professor of technology inquisitively remarked, "Music is German, isn't it?"[1]

Music has indeed held a place of honor in German cultural history, and it has been a crucial component in shaping German identity. The idea of a German nation-state had to overcome a long history of political fragmentation and regional differences, but music represented a mode of artistic expression in which all Germans could share. The German-speaking aristocracy and state

patrons had long sustained lavish musical institutions and launched the careers of some of the most influential composers, conductors, and performers.
Left with this rich musical legacy, nineteenth-century writers, philosophers,
critics, and composers highlighted music as a central component in defining German character and identity. The idea of Germany's musical strength
gained momentum during the campaign for German unification, matured in
the first half of the twentieth century, and was exported abroad in the perception of the German nation as the "people of music."

Music has come to represent one of Germany's most important contributions to Western culture, impressing the rest of the world with a reputation for
superior achievement and serving as a source of national pride, especially in
times of low morale and insecurity. One such low point was reached at the end
of World War I, an era fraught with conflicts, contradictions, and insecurities.
The Weimar Republic had a violent start, punctuated by bloody uprisings,
assassinations, and the failings of a lax system of law and order. The Treaty of
Versailles in 1919, the occupation of the Ruhr in 1923, and the concurrent
hyperinflation further demoralized and angered large portions of the defeated
country, splintering the German electorate into numerous political factions
and lowering expectations for the survival of the Republic, even after conditions improved with the currency stabilization and a period of prosperity from
1924 to 1929. The Great Depression in 1929 brought social and political
conflicts to a head, creating a state of emergency and a rise in disorder and
unemployment and marking the beginning of the Republic's decline.

The conflicts and insecurities of Weimar society reached into cultural realms
as well. Reactions against Romanticism inspired wild and iconoclastic experimentation in art, music, and literature, making this one of the most exciting
and most stimulating eras in German cultural history. At the same time, the
emergence of a working-class culture demanded that the arts be accessible and
comprehensible, providing entertainment and pleasure rather than intellectual
challenge. The effects of urbanization on cultural life also proved to be both
inspiring and unsettling. The growth of cities led to new directions in architecture and new forms of popular entertainment, but urbanization forged ahead
so rapidly that it met with resistance. The modern lifestyle competed with nostalgia for simpler times, a neo-Romantic glorification of nature and emulation
of folk rituals, and the rejection of cosmopolitanism and "asphalt culture."

Technology was also a double-edged sword in cultural terms. It enhanced
the arts with advances in mass production and communication and opened the
door to foreign—and especially American—cultural trends. Although these
were eagerly consumed by many, alarmists condemned mechanical production and outside influences as part of an insidious conspiracy by Germany's

former enemies to infiltrate and destroy true German art. The perceived struggle between German *Kultur* and Western *civilisation* intensified during the war, and Germany's subsequent political and economic subjugation by "intellectually inferior" powers only sharpened the vitriolic wartime rhetoric. Additionally, the search for a scapegoat within Germany's borders gave a tremendous impetus to singling out the Jews as an all-purpose enemy. Jews were gradually held accountable for all contemporary problems, whether linked to capitalism or to communism.

In the face of so many unsettling conflicts, many Germans found solace in musical activity. Music offered a safe haven from daily tribulations and a reminder of Germany's cultural strengths. Despite the lost war and economic turmoil of the 1920s, Germany still boasted an enviable number of orchestras, functioning opera houses, chamber groups, and world-renowned conductors and soloists, presenting "musical strength" as Germany's most inexhaustible source of international recognition and national pride. Much faith was also invested in music's power to cure social ills. This faith spread as large sectors of the population took part in amateur music making, often setting aside their political and class differences and experiencing solidarity through music. Choral activities in particular grew at an unprecedented rate, and the fact that workers' choral societies welcomed the participation of middle-class singers and conductors proved that music could blur social and political distinctions. As the economy worsened, amateur music making provided an inexpensive source of entertainment.

In the midst of these developments, the field of musicology was coming into its own. Still a young discipline, the most significant advances in music scholarship prior to the war had emerged from German and Austrian schools. The war's damaging effects on international exchange alienated German scholars from their colleagues in other countries and encouraged more attention to Germany's own musical resources. The postwar economy, political upheavals, and changing demographics forced scholars to ponder the usefulness of their profession to modern German society. Immediately after World War I, German musicologists initiated projects to focus attention on German music and to bridge the gap between the academy and the public. They set up their own scholarly society and a central musicological institute with these nationalist and populist agendas in mind. Failing to exert any significant influence in music policy or education reform in the Weimar system, they found that by successfully cultivating a relationship with the amateur movement they could channel their work toward bolstering patriotism, stimulating the economy, and serving as educators to the general public.

Although the Weimar government did nothing to discourage developments in musical life and musicology, it lacked the resources to nurture them and managed to effect improvements only in music education. The regional idiosyncrasies of cultural administration in the Weimar years left many institutions to fend for themselves. By 1933, the struggling economy forced a number of opera houses and orchestras, as well as several musicological enterprises, to shut down.

The Nazi government, taking special notice of the historical centrality of music in reinforcing German pride, chose to capitalize on music's important functions toward a variety of ends. The Nazis took note of the growing popularity of amateur music making, integrated musical activities into their party and military organizations, and subsumed amateur associations under their administration. They also solved long-standing problems facing musicians since the breakdown of court patronage and made important advances in providing them with professional and economic security. Above all, Nazi leaders exploited Germany's international reputation as the "people of music" toward building an image of global strength. They pumped resources into struggling musical institutions of world fame in an effort to mitigate irate foreign accusations of Nazi atrocities and to downplay their image as barbarians.

Nazi ideologues, in promoting pseudoscientific notions of German racial superiority, saw the importance of highlighting music as incontrovertible proof of that superiority and, as such, explored the utility of music scholarship. In addition to assisting in sustaining musical activity, musicologists could promote the notion of German superiority through music and could help rationalize the suppression and eradication of "inferior" elements. Ambitious musicological projects initiated in the Weimar Republic and paralyzed by the economic crisis were reanimated and expanded by the Nazi Education Ministry. The Propaganda Ministry also supported musicological ventures, and the cultural organizations of Heinrich Himmler and Alfred Rosenberg enlisted the services of musicologists in research, propaganda, and special wartime assignments.

Musicology was not the only scholarly discipline to improve its lot with the help of the Nazi regime. Nevertheless, its story is special. First, musicologists were entrusted with unlocking the mysteries of the art deemed so central to German culture. Second, musicology can be described as an essentially German discipline, resting largely on the pioneer work of German and Austrian scholars. Finally, still a relatively young science in the 1920s and 1930s, musicology struggled to gain recognition in the academy, compelling musicologists to conduct a variety of side activities in the musical world. Their occupations in journalism and involvement in performance and composition put them in the unusual position of moving freely between the ivory tower and the community.

For this last reason, musicologists did not conform to the image of the postwar academic elite, who opposed the Republic and resisted change. Those ensconced in the safe haven of the university had enjoyed special privileges since the early nineteenth century: they enjoyed economic security as civil servants but wielded complete control over their own affairs. Weimar officials pressed universities to come closer to meeting the practical needs of the public at large, but conservative intellectuals at the universities balked at these perceived infringements on their autonomy. Musicologists, however, felt less threatened by the demands from both Social Democratic and National Socialist politicians to serve the needs of the nation. The following brief comparisons with related disciplines will illustrate how musicology, while sharing common experiences with all humanistic scholarship, differed from other fields in significant ways.

In both musicology and the study of German literature, the political upheaval did not bring any significant methodological changes.[2] Musicology followed methodological paths almost identical to those of literature: wavering between principles of *Geistesgeschichte* and neo-positivism, seeking theoretical models from the sciences, and, in the course of the 1930s, concentrating on defining a constant German essence in all periods of history.[3] Nationalism, racial theory, glorification of the *Volk,* and anti-Semitism, so prominent in the 1930s, had their roots in the eighteenth and nineteenth centuries in both German literature and musicology.[4] With the establishment of the Nazi state, the two fields recognized the opportunity to draw attention to themselves in a regime that aimed to reeducate the masses. In German literature, for example, the name of the scholarly journal changed from the humanistic title *Euphorion* to the nationalistic *Dichtung und Volkstum* in a gesture to address the needs of the German nation.[5] Musicologists then issued a completely new journal in 1936, *Deutsche Musikkultur,* that would bridge the gap between scholars and the public.

Both German philologists and musicologists continued long-standing practices of using the German language and German music, respectively, as parameters to define the German nation. Both gradually emphasized Germany's role as a cultural leader among nations and promoted their respective subjects as the source of the German essence.[6] Germanists, however, were restricted to the German language and at most could extend their campaign beyond the borders of Germany to embrace the lands where Germanic tongues were spoken. Musicologists had the ability to imbue the language of music, especially untexted absolute music, with imagined manifestations of Germanness that could cross language barriers.

Musicologists and Germanists also reacted to similar sociological factors, offering to serve the nation as educators, demonstrating an interest in politically pertinent topics and methods out of career opportunism, and rejoicing in the government's attention to their contributions.[7] Unlike other disciplines, however, musicology had a greater claim to fulfilling the educational mission because it had a direct link to a living practice. Musicologists maintained strong ties to amateur musical activities both within and outside the university that drew them into the pulse of activity. They were not only the keepers of the flame for Germany's legendary musical past, they also ventured out beyond the walls of the academy, offering guidelines in the proper use of music, providing editions of old German music and German folk songs that could be used in everyday activities, and, during World War II, looking ahead toward becoming active leaders of musical life in an expanded sphere of German power that would extend over most of Europe.

Musicologists had not only the means to serve the nation and state, but also the desire, as many of them demonstrated a true commitment to the tasks set before them. The increased interest in folk music research in the 1930s emerged from a generation of scholars trying to resolve a conflict between their dry philological training and their experiences outside the university — in the military and the youth movement — that allowed them to witness the "community-building powers" of music firsthand. They observed that folk song research, mostly in the hands of Germanists, consisted of a dry and detached armchair analysis of its material, not to mention a myopic focus on the text and complete neglect of the music. These musicologists insisted that new methodologies in folk music research involve intimate contact with the communities preserving the living practice. Their task was not merely to collect texts and transcribe melodies, but also to immerse themselves in folk rituals and lifestyles and use their knowledge toward educating the Volk.[8]

Musicologists' eagerness to understand the Volk and their special commitment to spreading German culture to the common people comes through most clearly in a comparison with folklorists. Studies of the folklore discipline in the Third Reich regard this field as most susceptible to "nazification" because of the interest it attracted from Nazi ideologues. Nevertheless, folklorists did not display the same brand of sincerity as musicologists in their dealings with Nazi heads. Himmler contracted scholars in several humanistic fields to work in occupied areas and in northern Italy, not only to plunder cultural treasures but also to establish a working relationship with indigenous populations and to "educate" ethnic Germans to the National Socialist worldview. Folklorists, it seems, ignored the latter part of their assignment and paid far more attention to hoarding material objects.[9] Musicologists, by contrast, showed themselves to be far more serious about their "cultural-political" instructions. Their extensive work for Himmler involved a feverish documentation of folk practices and brought them into close contact with the native population. Throughout the region, they organized educational lectures on folk music, folk dancing courses, and folk music retreats.[10]

One purpose of this book, then, is to explore the relationship between musicology and German society, a relationship that in many ways eluded other academic disciplines. This is not a general history of German musicology, nor is it a survey of the significant German contributions to music scholarship during this period. While such a survey might be useful, testimonies to the notable achievements of scholars of the period can be gleaned elsewhere: from later scholarship that relies on their work, from reference works that carefully accentuate the positive accomplishments of these scholars, and from the Festschriften that honored them later in their careers. Instead, my purpose is to look beyond the standard musicological literature and uncover the relationship musicology cultivated with the state, the party, and the German people. Its prominence is not immediately apparent in the scholarly writings but comes through forcefully in the plethora of literature penned by some of the most respected musicologists and directed to a nonscholarly public — a body of literature that usually goes unnoticed. In addition, a rich documentation in state archives, university archives, and collected papers vividly reconstructs the activities of musicologists within and beyond the academy. All these resources provide a glimpse into musicologists' actions and preoccupations in light of economic, political, and social developments during one of Germany's most tumultuous periods. They also help us to understand some of the more celebrated scholarly achievements of the period in a new light, explaining, for example, the reasons why German folk music research made such impressive advances in the 1930s.

Another purpose of this book is to place musicology of the Third Reich in a historical context. For many years, historians of the Nazi era avoided dealing with music and music scholarship, despite — or perhaps because of — the centrality of music in German culture and society. Those who did discuss musicology in any systematic or comprehensive way isolated it from its historical context by designating it as "Nazi musicology" and illustrated it through the polemical writings of a collection of music critics and other nonspecialists all designated as "musicologists." In this book I begin with 1918 — when the German musicology research institute, the scholarly society, and two scholarly journals got started — and conclude with the late 1950s. Looking at the Nazi period in the context of what preceded and followed allows us to see that trends, regardless of how ideologically induced they may appear, did not originate in the charged atmosphere of 1933, nor did they evaporate in 1945.

This book also looks exclusively at the writings and activities of trained musicologists, without straying into other related professions. While the language of bona fide musicologists might be less extreme than those of critics and dilettantes writing on music, the sentiments are by no means dry and detached from the political and ideological climate. Such leading figures of international repute as Heinrich Besseler, Friedrich Blume, Karl Gustav Fellerer, Helmuth Osthoff, Heinrich Husmann, Arnold Schering, and Hans Joachim Moser often rose to the occasion to work enthusiastically for the Nazi regime and to endorse its program to strengthen the German Volk-identity through music.

The organization of chapters is not chronological, save for the final chapter on denazification, but is topical. Such an organization helps to elucidate the continuities from the Weimar era through the Hitler regime. The changing role of music in German society following World War I is the subject of chapter 1. This provides the backdrop for understanding the new challenges to musicology and the needs to reassess and redefine its function in postwar Germany, which are examined in chapter 2. The following three chapters reconstruct the institutional and professional developments that redefined the tasks of the musicologist. Chapter 3 is a survey of the creation of institutions following World War I, their nationalist agendas, their attempts to secure financial support from the Nazi regime, and the negative effects their nationalism had in cutting German musicology off from the rest of the world. In chapter 4 I examine the German university in the postwar and Nazi eras, the transformation of higher education, and musicology's place within it. Chapter 5 is an investigation of nonacademic career opportunities for musicologists, especially after 1933, with a special focus on the research and wartime opportunities offered by the cultural branches of Himmler's and Rosenberg's organizations.

The subjects explored in the next two chapters focus more closely on writings of musicologists. The methodological crisis felt in all humanities disciplines after the war and the experimentation with new models, the attempted application of racial theory and "the Jewish Question" to music, and the inducements to concentrate on developing German folk music research are discussed in chapter 6. Commentators on the goals of musicology in the Nazi state all seemed to agree on the urgent need to explore the German essence in music, giving credit to the Nazi leaders for encouraging German music, but this, too, was a growing preoccupation that can be traced back to the eighteenth century, as examined in chapter 7. Vague generalizations, such as that

German strength lies in the ability to adapt foreign models, persisted without much change, despite attempts to find more tangible German musical traits in folk music, regional studies, and Gregorian chant. Territorial gains during World War II then inspired musicologists, in a sense, to "annex" the musical achievements of subjugated countries and claim them as German.

Musicology reaped substantial benefits from the support of the Nazi government and party, laying the foundations for large-scale undertakings that would outlive the Hitler regime. Initiatives such as the multivolume reference work *Die Musik in Geschichte und Gegenwart* and the development and expansion of the editions of early German music known to this day as Das Erbe deutscher Musik can be traced to Nazi government sponsorship. In the postwar era of denazification it was necessary to downplay these and other benefits. This is the subject of chapter 8: how leaders of postwar musicology managed to resurrect Nazi-sponsored enterprises and singled out a few individuals to represent all that was truly "Nazi," in order to detract attention from the continuing prominence in postwar Germany of individuals, ideas, and methodologies that all thrived under Hitler.

German musicology has had a profound influence on musicology worldwide. Yet its emergence and development in a political and cultural climate that encouraged an emphasis on the German nature of music cannot be ignored, especially given musicology's general tendencies to emphasize the German component, often to the detriment of other national traditions. Musicology — not just German musicology — has been slow to accept such non-German subjects as nineteenth-century French and Italian opera, English music, and American popular music as serious research topics. Also, examining how a discipline responded to a period rife with political, economic, and social upheavals brings the moral obligations of scholarship into sharp focus and indicates the challenges and pitfalls it might encounter under similar circumstances. Although the Nazi period provides a scenario of extremes, it illustrates how, in periods of intellectual and political transition, academic pursuits must respond to antiintellectualism, budgetary restrictions, and the encroachment of popular ideologies into scholarly discourse. The issues explored in this book show how such factors can distort scholarship and pervert its mission.

Abbreviations

AfMf	*Archiv für Musikforschung*
AfMw	*Archiv für Musikwissenschaft*
DASB	Deutscher Arbeiter–Sängerbund (German Workers' Singers' League)
DAF	Deutsche Arbeitsfront (German Labor Front)
DDT	Denkmäler Deutscher Tonkunst (Monuments of German Music)
DGMW	Deutsche Gesellschaft für Musikwissenschaft (German Society for Musicology)
DMG	Deutsche Musikgesellschaft (German Music Society)
DTB	Denkmäler der Tonkunst in Bayern (Monuments of Music in Bavaria)
DTÖ	Denkmäler der Tonkunst in Österreich (Monuments of Music in Austria)
EdM	Erbe deutscher Musik (Heritage of German Music)
GDR	German Democratic Republic
IMS	International Music Society/International Musicological Society
ISCM	International Society for Contemporary Music
KdF	NS-Gemeinschaft "Kraft durch Freude" (National Socialist Community "Strength through Joy")
M	Mark

MGG	*Die Musik in Geschichte und Gegenwart*
NSDAP	Nationalsozialistische deutsche Arbeiterpartei (National Socialist German Workers' Party)
RKF	Reichskommissar für die Festigung des deutschen Volkstums (Reich Commissioner for Securing German Nationhood)
RM	Reichsmark
SA	Sturmabteilung (Storm Division)
SD	Sicherheitsdienst (Security Service)
SS	Schutzstaffel (Protection Staff)
ZfMw	*Zeitschrift für Musikwissenschaft*

The Background: Music and German Society, 1918–1945

Before the musicology profession could find its niche in German society, it had to come to terms with the new role of music in post–World War I Germany and with the shifts in musical hierarchy. Noting how Germany's historically potent musical culture had withstood the challenges of the war and economic crises, contemporaries imbued music with the powers to heal the wounds of a demoralized and divided German population. The unprecedented growth of amateur music making — through the formation of choral societies and the activities of the youth movement — was a testimony to the belief that music could create national and social solidarity.

But amateur participation, along with new forms of entertainment (radio, phonograph records, vaudeville, cabaret, and jazz) and a growing interest in folk music, gradually drew audiences away from the musical legacies of the era of court patronage. Such venerable institutions as the symphony orchestra and the opera house were threatened with extinction, and the careers of concert musicians were jeopardized. The Weimar government supported amateur activities and improved conditions for music education, but a serious effort to address the interests of the professional realm and the institutions of high culture had to wait for the Nazi regime. The Nazi government placed a high priority on introducing safeguards for professionals and subsidizing struggling orchestras and opera houses. Despite its antimodernist rhetoric, it did relatively little to enforce an ideologically conceived policy for controlling musical taste. Its greatest impact on German musical life took the form of massive personnel purges directed mainly against Jews, but the complexity of musical proliferation in an industrial society rendered any censorship of "undesirable" music impracticable. Rather than seizing complete control, the Nazi regime allowed changes in musical production and consumption to proceed, while exploiting the effectiveness of music for its ideological purposes whenever possible. Thus the transition of musical life from the Weimar Republic to the Third Reich displays more continuities than caesuras.

German Music after World War I: An Eyewitness Account

The Weimar period is often romanticized as the heyday of artistic experimentation and progressive thinking. Peter Gay, in his 1968 retrospective of Weimar culture, reinforced the belief that the Republic facilitated the liberation of expressionism and modernism and gave the impression that their counterparts in musical composition — atonality, dodecaphony, neoclassicism, primitivism, and musical expressionism — dominated the musical tastes of the era.[1] A closer examination of musical life, however, reveals that outlets for musical activity and consumption spread far beyond the reach of contemporary composers, experimental or otherwise, and that conservative musical tastes arose from all social and political factions to resist experimentation.

The effects of rapid industrialization, urbanization, an unstable economy, and a lost war conjured up a host of demons in the forms of technology, the working class, encroaching foreign capitalist interests, and not least among them, the increasingly threatening image of the Jew. Living in a society split into numerous political and social factions and degraded by the military defeat, many Germans wallowed in nostalgia for simpler times. According to some contemporaries, music, too, had allegedly fallen victim to all the negative forces in postwar society, but it also offered solutions to contemporary problems. The musicologist Hans Joachim Moser, an often-cited eyewitness to the state of musical life in the shadow of World War I, voiced many of these concerns. Moser (b. 1889) was the son of the violinist Andreas Moser and the godson of Joseph Joachim. He studied singing and composition alongside musicology and frequently presented himself as a soloist, composer, and even novelist, while producing a staggering number of publications on musicological subjects. After World War I, Moser held academic positions in Halle, Heidelberg, and Berlin, where he became director of the National Academy of Church and School Music (Staatliche Akademie für Kirchen- und Schulmusik) in 1927. Moser limited his research almost exclusively to German music, but his knowledge of that subject was vast, encompassing all periods of art music and folk music.

Concluding his lengthy and detailed survey of the history of German music, Moser observed how, on the one hand, German music had suffered from the political, social, technological, and economic changes of the postwar era. On the other hand, it still offered the potential to lift his distressed countrymen out of confusion and disarray.[2] The new industrial economy and expanded foreign exchange had, according to Moser, seriously compromised Germany's musical strength. The age-old struggle between German *Kultur* and French *civilisation* (in his words, a present-day version of the struggle between God and the devil) was compounded by the newer dangers of capitalism and technology, or the "Americanization" (*Amerikanisierung*) of German musical life.[3] These problems could be traced back to the beginnings of "art for art's sake," when music started to stray from the public, and worsened with urbanization. The growth of cities allowed folk culture to disappear and opened the door to the "negroization" (*Vernegerung*) of popular song and dance. Moser was also greatly concerned over the decline of church music, attributable to the separation of church and state and far more destructive than the more blatant social divisions between worker and employer. He blamed American businessmen, in collusion with Jews, for turning music into capital. The Jewish problem, however, would cease once a healthy German musical culture could be restored.[4]

Moser also noted the growing insecurity among the music professions. The dissolution of court-sponsored cultural institutions threw professionals at the mercy of a fickle economy. In the absence of any quality-control standards in the freelance market, where professionals now competed with amateurs for teaching and performance opportunities, Moser feared that accomplished orchestral musicians had turned into "proletarians." In addition, technological breakthroughs—radios, piano rolls, and recordings—allowed for the enjoyment of performances without having to enlist the services of performers. Some musicians sought protection from professional organizations, but concert artists could still fall victim to unscrupulous agents. Given the diversity and sheer volume of musical activity in Germany, Moser called for the establishment of an umbrella organization, a form of "Reich Music Chamber" (*Reichsmusikkammer*).[5] This term was later employed by the Nazi Propaganda Ministry when it restructured cultural administration and brought it under Reich jurisdiction. Moser probably borrowed the concept from the recent corporatist endeavors of such professions as law and engineering to form professional "chambers" to address their concerns on a Reich-wide basis.[6]

In spite of these problems, music held great promise to revive patriotism in the wake of military defeat. Moser proposed that music was and, as he tried to demonstrate throughout his work, had always been central to German culture. This unique German strength became even more visible in the current state of crisis. It was a great source of pride for him that Germany had managed to maintain more musical institutions per capita than any other country in spite of the war and hyperinflation. Moser boasted the existence of approximately 50 opera houses and "perhaps 150 orchestras of rank" that the state had helped to preserve, a clear indication of the importance of music for the German nation. In addition to state-supported groups, world-famous conductors were "rebuilding our value as a nation since 1918," and freelance musical offerings from 100 string quartets, 50 piano trios, 25 chamber music groups with winds, at least 15 oratorio quartets and madrigal groups, smaller vocal groups, and countless solo singers together provided an "accurate measure of German music culture."[7] Music was the best means for defeated Germany to earn its place in the sun, "for if Germany possesses *one* area and *one* profession that wield absolute influence, despite all of the enmity and distance we face in the world, these are German music and the composer (second only [in influence] to our sciences); one must not allow this noble, truly peaceful weapon to rust from lack of use."[8]

Music also had the potential to smooth over class and political divisions. Amateur choral societies experienced rapid growth in the years after the war, along with collegium musicum organizations, amateur orchestras, and military music corps, none of which, he assured his reader, threatened professional orchestras. Moser saw the greatest potential for healing the wounds of a divided society in music education, in the broadest sense of the word. If every German citizen could be musically literate and musically active, then a true feeling of community and belonging could be restored to its preindustrial level. Education would keep German music healthy, and the current musical initiatives of the youth movement and of composers of "music for use" (*Gebrauchsmusik*) could perpetuate a thriving amateur musical culture that would remedy Germany's social problems.[9]

Music as a Cure for Social Dissent: The Amateur Revolution

Although Moser's overall assessment was colored by his middle-class apprehensions about democracy and the working class, many of his observations accurately outlined prominent trends. By the late 1920s, amateur orchestras, chamber music, and especially choral singing had become immensely popular pastimes, crossing all political and class barriers. At a time when Germany seemed ever more politicized and disjointed, communal music making promised to promote solidarity. Participation, it was hoped, would not only instill community spirit and goodwill but would also restore music's power to unify, which had been lost in the bourgeois era.

Amateur music making had already served the mission of strengthening a sense of German identity when the agenda of German unification encouraged feelings of belonging to a larger German nation and downplayed regional loyalties. From the 1870s through the 1920s, a number of umbrella organizations for amateur music groups devoted themselves to the promotion of German music and sponsored festivals both at home and abroad.[10] The amateur choral movement was particularly committed to strengthening German identity. Church and secular choral singing had become almost exclusively an amateur activity early in the nineteenth century,[11] outgrowing its predominantly liturgical function as oratorio societies gained in popularity. In 1862, the German Singers' League (Deutscher Sängerbund) was formed to unify the growing number of German male choral groups all over the world. Its charter stated the nationalist goal of "the proliferation and refinement of German male choral singing and the promotion of German feeling. . . . Through the unifying power of German song [the organization] hopes to preserve and enhance the German national consciousness and a feeling of solidarity among German tribes."[12]

By 1929, the Sängerbund encompassed more than 13,000 choirs in the German Reich alone and accounted for at least 1.3 million members. Other choral unions soon followed: the German Choral Society (Deutsche Sängerschaft), representing German choral groups in universities around the German Reich, Austria, Danzig, and Czechoslovakia, was formed in 1896; the Union of German Teachers' Choirs (Vereinigung deutscher Lehrer-Gesangvereine) formed in 1909; and the Reich Association of Mixed Choirs of Germany (Reichsverband der gemischten Chöre Deutschlands), representing the economic and artistic interests of unaffiliated mixed, women's, and children's choirs, was formed in 1924. A separate organization for male choirs dedicated to German folk song was also established in the 1920s, even though most of its groups also belonged to the Sängerbund.[13]

Amateur participation in choral singing increased significantly when groups loosely affiliated with the Social Democratic party and Communist party adopted the activity as a suitable means to instill a distinct working-class consciousness. Between 1892 and 1900, membership in the loose federation of workers' singing groups increased from nearly 10,000 to nearly 100,000, and in 1908 a national organization known as the German Workers' Singers' League (Deutscher Arbeiter-Sängerbund or DASB) was founded. Despite a drop during the war, the DASB recovered rapidly, accounting for 230,000

members in 1920 and 440,000 in 1928. Workers' groups provide one illustration of how musical participation succeeded in erasing social boundaries.
Since the 1890s, the Social Democratic party sought to promote a workers'
culture distinct from that of the bourgeoisie, but unlike some of its other
activities, like sports, its choral groups gradually gave higher priority to musical goals than to class solidarity. By the late 1920s, many of them had become
virtually indistinguishable from their bourgeois counterparts and, in an attempt to raise their musical standards, enlisted professional conductors and
non-working-class members. The musical repertoire consisted mainly of popular and folk songs along with more ambitious works from the classic and
Romantic German choral repertoire, much to the dismay of socialist and
communist purists who rejected the compromising nature of the DASB and
encouraged a more ideologically suitable repertoire.[14]

From the statistics in Leo Kestenberg's *Jahrbuch der deutschen Musikorganisationen 1931*, one can estimate that the number of German citizens participating in choral activities approached two million, and the number of non-
church-affiliated choral groups (designated as oratorio societies, mixed choirs,
male choirs, female choirs, children's choirs, madrigal societies, Liedertafel,
workers' choirs, and groups associated with unions, professions, and factories) came to a total of approximately 19,000 organizations.[15] Participation in
choral singing spread so quickly throughout the Reich that between 1927 and
1929 four organizations of choral groups banded together into the Interest
Group for German Choral Singing (Interessengemeinschaft für das deutsche
Chorgesangwesen) as a forum to deal with the financial concerns of choral
societies.[16]

The amateur revolution also had an impact on instrumental music, but
actual participation is more difficult to measure. Kestenberg's *Jahrbuch* lists
approximately fifty amateur orchestras and chamber music groups throughout the Reich (nine orchestras in Berlin alone) that belonged to the Reich
Union of German Orchestras (Reichsbund deutscher Orchestervereine), but it
names only a handful of military or uniformed corps (Kapellen), though many
more probably existed. There is also no way of estimating the number of
citizens who took part in music making at home (*Hausmusik*), which was
clearly growing in popularity, given the establishment of over a dozen Hausmusik periodicals between 1918 and 1932.[17]

Choral singing was by far the fastest growing amateur musical activity in
Germany for obvious reasons. It required less training and technical skill than
other musical activities; it could be adapted to a wide range of ability levels, from unison singing of familiar tunes to full-scale oratorios and contemporary compositions; and it offered a nonthreatening environment for social

interaction that could blur political and economic differences. Consequently, choral singing became the central focus for the music activities of the German youth movement.

The German youth movement (*Jugendbewegung*) made its first appearance around the turn of the century as a group known as the Wandervogel. This was a loosely organized band of middle-class youths who roamed the countryside, conjured up nostalgic fantasies of Germany's medieval past, and sought camaraderie through after-school hikes, retreats, and cultural activities. The spontaneous emergence of a youth culture around this time is commonly linked to rapid industrialization and urbanization. Bourgeois youth were disillusioned with the absence of a political consensus, the constraints of Wilhelmine culture and the bourgeois family ideal, an old-fashioned education system, and the failure of the technological age to provide outlets for self-expression. The youth movement strove for a new identity and sense of community (*Gemeinschaft*) through nonconventional dress, an appreciation for nature, and a new educational philosophy. The last of these ultimately inspired educational reforms that incorporated more music, art, and cultural activities into the general curriculum.[18] The youth cult spread beyond the middle class, and in the course of the 1920s and early 1930s, virtually all major political parties and organized religions sponsored their own youth groups.[19]

Music was always an integral part of youth movement activities.[20] In August 1923, a loose federation of youth groups known as the Bündische Jugend formed,[21] and two separate musical factions emerged out of this development: the Musikantengilde, under the guidance of Fritz Jöde, and the more nationalistic and folk-oriented Finkensteiner Bund under Walter Hensel. Generically referred to as the "youth music movement" (*Jugendmusikbewegung*), these organizations promoted an alternative musical culture to foster the Gemeinschaft ideal. They eschewed anything they regarded as musical manifestations of bourgeois individualism, art for art's sake, and the cult of genius. Instead they pursued an "objective" sort of music that could bond the entire community, something that could be found neither in bourgeois conventions nor in the emerging workers' culture, and set out to discover a "communal music culture" (*Gemeinschaftsmusikkultur*) that would exploit the "community-building power of music" (*gemeinschaftsbildende Kraft der Musik*).[22]

The leaders of the Jugendmusikbewegung developed their own rigid categories of acceptable and unacceptable music. Acceptable forms, those which exploited the community-building power of music, included folk songs and choral music, preferably pre-1700 polyphony, and modern works written explicitly for the youth movement. Unacceptable were all types of music conceived as commercial and alienating. Leaders railed against jazz, the

"American-Jewish money sensation," the "demonry" of modern music, the virtuoso "industry" sustained by American dollars, and all forms of entertainment music (operetta, jazz, and popular hits were condemned as the "downfall of our people"). Any technology-based means of music reception robbed music of its educational value by eliminating direct participation, and the traditional concert was similarly denounced as a passive musical experience that suppressed self-expression and had grown into a profit-making industry. Even Hausmusik fell out of favor because it was rooted in the isolated bourgeois family unit and because much of the music required a piano, thereby limiting its enjoyment to specific locations and social classes. The Jugendmusikbewegung cast its net even wider to reject the entire concept of professionalism in music. The distinction drawn between professional and amateur had allowed music to stray from the Volk. The virtuoso, the ultimate symbol of bourgeois individualism, used music as a means to display technical mastery, to acquire fame, and to make money.[23]

The Jugendmusikbewegung emphasized direct participation regardless of levels of ability, thus choral singing formed the core of its organized activities. The movement sponsored week-long singing retreats (*Singwochen*) and evening convocations to accommodate city-dwellers (*Abendsingwochen*). The Finkensteiner Bund sponsored informal singing societies (*Singgemeinde*) to promote camaraderie. Fritz Jöde directed public sing-alongs (*Offene Singstunde*) to bring together individuals from all social backgrounds and developed a system of hand signals so as not to alienate those who could not read music. Sometimes practices were not entirely consistent with stated ideals, however. Jöde expanded the Singstunden to radio broadcasts (*Rundfunksingstunden*), although the movement formally rejected technologically produced music. Also, for many of the larger choral activities, leaders discovered that a complete eradication of the concert format of performers and audience was virtually impossible, even for their own musical activities.[24] There was also some inconsistency between theory and practice when it came to repertoire. The Jugendmusikbewegung formally rejected all art music since the classical period that was alleged to widen the gap between music and the people. Instead, it encouraged *Gemeinschaftsmusik*, including a wide range of early music from classless eras or contemporary works composed with the ideals of the movement in mind.[25] Yet art music of the eighteenth and nineteenth centuries made its way into the movement's repertoire,[26] chamber and orchestral music was acceptable as long as it did not exceed an intermediate level of technical mastery, and even music for the much criticized piano gained acceptance.[27]

The popularity of the youth movement alerted the state to the importance of education and led to broad-based reforms. As music consultant for the Prussian Ministry of Science, Art, and Education (Preußisches Ministerium für Wissenschaft, Kunst, und Volksbildung), Leo Kestenberg, a close associate of Fritz Jöde, undertook a total revamping of music education in the public schools and achieved what was perhaps the Weimar Republic's most significant and longest lasting contribution to Germany's musical life. Kestenberg was a practicing musician-turned-bureaucrat and a Social Democrat committed to the idea of the Republic and to the ideal of making music widely accessible, but he was more realistic than those who simply put their faith in music's divine power to cure social ills. He recognized the school as the best leveling institution for carrying out "musikalische Volksbildung," a higher appreciation of music throughout the population. Kestenberg met with opposition from conservatives who wanted to retain the strong ties between school and church music, but by 1922 he managed to effect massive reforms. These raised the occupation of music educators to a profession by standardizing their qualifications and redefined the music curriculum in the schools from kindergarten all the way up to postsecondary education.[28]

The State and Music Professions in the Weimar Republic and the Third Reich

In 1928 Moser expressed grave concerns over the "proletarianization" of professional musicians, and following the depression Kestenberg warned of the pressing need to deal with their uncontrollable rise in unemployment.[29] The German notion of the "professional" was not as uniformly accepted as in other cultures, taking hold at various rates and with varying degrees of success among different professions in Imperial Germany and the Weimar Republic.[30] Musicians were especially slow to develop a uniform identity as a profession, and the ambiguity over the status of "amateur" and "professional" left those expecting to make a living as full-time musicians or music educators in competition with less qualified performers and instructors. With the exception of musicians employed in state institutions and enjoying the securities of civil servants, most had an undefined status after World War I, despite many decades of campaigning for representation and economic protection.[31]

In addition, the collapse of court patronage left open the question of musical sponsorship. The central government of the Weimar Republic assumed virtually no responsibility for protecting musical institutions, leaving much of the organization of musical life to the whims of local bureaucrats and private enterprises. The only branch of the government playing any kind of role in cultural affairs was the Reich Ministry of the Interior. One of its funds provided money to Reich musical organizations, and another was set aside to "guarantee" events and enterprises of national importance and occasionally to provide subsidies "in limited measure," but the support it provided to musical concerns was "relatively small."[32] Other than that, a small, semi-official Central Institute for Education and Instruction (Zentralinstitut für Erziehung und Unterricht) coordinated Reich officials and private groups in organizing national festivals, conferences, and commemorative events and publishing their proceedings.[33]

Otherwise, most cultural institutions came under the jurisdiction of the individual provinces (*Länder*) and cities. In most cases, provincial theaters, opera houses, orchestras, and conservatories received around one-third of their government subsidies from the province and the rest from municipal coffers.[34] Despite the Reich government's designs to minimize regional autonomy, the diversity in economic resources and attitudes among the provinces created a variegated landscape of cultural policy,[35] inevitably creating gross inequities for the professional musician from one location to another. Some provincial governments might entirely neglect musical institutions, while others might take a keen interest in funding musical and musicological projects to promote culture of a local flavor or to build up unique attractions.[36] Policies regarding private music instruction also varied, making it difficult for qualified teachers to compete with amateurs who demanded lower instruction fees in states that had no strict regulations.

These precarious circumstances paved the way for various special interest groups to lobby for the legal and economic protection of the music professions. Kestenberg, in his 1931 *Jahrbuch,* enumerates approximately thirty organizations, most of them founded since 1919, representing all aspects of musical activity. There were societies for church musicians, music critics, private teachers, composers, orchestra musicians, conductors, educators, soloists, theater professionals, agents, and even an organization to protect the interests of former military musicians. The goals of most of these organizations were purely practical: to secure economic protection, set up health and unemployment benefits, announce job openings, standardize wage scales, set professional standards (some organizations required proof of training to qualify for membership), facilitate training, and mediate between employees and employers in recruitment and labor disputes. Performers' and composers' organizations also addressed copyright issues, complicated in recent years by the mechanical reproduction of musical performances. The splintered character of professional interest groups was just one more manifestation of the divisiveness of Weimar society. Memberships ranged from several hundred to more than twenty thousand,[37] but many organizations shared almost identical agendas, resulting in competition as well as redundancy.

With Hitler's rise to power in 1933, the Nazi government immediately recognized these problems and paid more attention than its forerunner to regulating musical activity on a Reich-wide basis. A landmark development toward this end was the establishment of the Reich Culture Chamber (*Reichskulturkammer*) under the authority of Propaganda Minister Joseph Goebbels, the genesis and development of which has been thoroughly investigated by Alan Steinweis. The first cultural task of the Nazi government was to obliterate regional discrepancies. The issue of centralization and uniformity was of great importance to Hitler, who insisted that there was "no Anhältisch or Hessisch culture, but only a universal German culture, which is determined not by ministries, but by the ideology."[38] Propaganda Minister Joseph Goebbels worked to devise a national umbrella organization for cultural professions and sold Hitler — a self-proclaimed artist — on the idea of creating the Reich Culture Chamber, over which Goebbels would preside. Its establishment furnished the means to bring cultural activities under the supervision of one Reich body devoted exclusively to a wide range of cultural matters. The Reich Culture Chamber comprised seven subchambers: music, theater, visual arts, literature, film, radio, and the press. These became the obligatory unions for all practicing cultural professionals in the broadest sense. The Reich Music Chamber (*Reichsmusikkammer*), for example, encompassed departments for composition, soloists, orchestras, entertainment music, music education, choral music, church music, concert agencies, copyright questions, music and instrument vendors, financial and legal matters, and thirty-one regional offices.[39] No longer the stepchild of the Ministry of the Interior and no longer subject to the inconsistencies of regional administration, cultural affairs could, at least in principle, flourish under uniform practices and promises of financial support.

The second task was to address the demands of the special interest groups. A primary objective of Nazi cultural policy was to enlist the cooperation of cultural professionals by allaying their fears of threats to their existence and by giving in to a number of their demands for financial and professional security. Goebbels worked closely with existing professional organizations, allowing them a certain amount of autonomy by retaining the former professional associations (*Berufsverbände*) and special interest groups (*Interessengemeinschaften*) as "Fachverbände" functioning within each chamber. This eliminated the competition that existed in the Weimar Republic among splinter groups with similar goals and appealed to a large number of prominent artists who would otherwise feel no attraction to the Nazi movement.[40]

The Music Chamber could take credit for an impressive number of practical measures within a relatively short amount of time: the setting of wages for professional musicians, regulations for professional certification, restrictions on amateurs performing for money (initially controlled by police raids on places of entertainment and later relaxed when it was discovered that the biggest offenders were SA musicians), the introduction of exams and training courses for private music instructors, and an old age pension plan. The social insurance system created in Bismarck's time had not extended to artists, but the authoritarian structure of the Nazi regime could effectively introduce coverage for artists by making it compulsory.[41]

Amateur Music in the Nazi State

Although the government directed new resources into securing the status of cultural professionals, the massive involvement of German citizens in amateur music making did not escape the notice of Nazi administrators, who immediately saw an opportunity to cash in on its popularity. The Music Chamber was conceived as an exclusively professional entity, but it took over both the Deutsche Sängerschaft and the Reichsverband der gemischten Chöre Deutschlands and demanded eight pfennigs from each amateur member per year, which, given the huge membership, provided 80,000 marks annually toward the operation of the Chamber.[42] Amateur orchestras and other ensembles also came under the jurisdiction of the education division of the Music Chamber, as did a special Hausmusik task force.[43]

The German Labor Front (Deutsche Arbeitsfront or DAF), a contender for controlling cultural professionals before the Reich Culture Chamber's powers were fully consolidated,[44] also planned to capitalize on the amateur music scene. In 1935, it became the sponsor of the National Socialist Reich Symphony Orchestra, which had been founded in 1931 to occupy unemployed Nazi musicians and was called upon to perform at various high-profile political events.[45] An impetus to encourage adult education, particularly of the working class, had gained momentum over the course of the 1920s, and the DAF managed to incorporate the existing educational activities of labor unions and night schools into its National Socialist Community "Strength through Joy" (NS-Gemeinschaft "Kraft durch Freude" or KdF).[46] In addition to its division "Schönheit der Arbeit" ("beauty in work"), which concerned itself with the aesthetics and safety conditions at the workplace, the KdF division "Kulturgemeinde" ("culture community") oversaw a wide range of cultural activities in its offices for after-hours recreation (Amt "Feierabend"), adult education ("Deutsches Volksbildungswerk"), military liaisons (Amt "Wehrmachtheime"), sports (Sportamt), and vacation planning (Amt für Reisen, Wandern, und Urlaub).[47]

Several of these offices incorporated musical activities into their programs. The Feierabend division stated its musical objectives as both music participation (open sing-alongs, musical retreats, radio programs) and exposure to the masterworks. It arranged recreational gatherings to bring together amateurs and professionals, to encourage the proliferation of folk music and dance, and to heighten awareness of the musicality of the "race."[48] It also furnished stipends for young talent and was best known for its subscription service for theater and concerts, which provided admission to cultural events, including the Bayreuth festival, at reduced rates.[49] The adult education division similarly advocated a heightened racial solidarity through adult education and provided guidelines for music instruction on all levels.[50] It offered lectures and music lessons at its own music schools and in other adult education facilities, recruiting musicians for party and civic ceremonial music corps and identifying talent for advanced study.[51] In addition, KdF sponsored concerts of major orchestras in large cities, remote communities, and factories (arranging performances during breaks).[52]

The military and paramilitary organizations of the Third Reich also sponsored musical activities. The SA and SS organized their own orchestras and chamber groups that gave public concerts of new and standard repertoire, and the Waffen-SS and the Wehrmacht set up music conservatories.[53] Much of this activity was aimed to counteract the growing influence of popular music, advocating music's ceremonial functions and encouraging the use of certain timbres over others, especially brass and organ. Promoters of brass bands urged youth groups and adult amateur musicians to take up brass instruments and to participate in mass gatherings, such as the party rallies, in the hope that they would be inspired to emulate military music and would shun the "misuse" of brass in jazz bands.[54] The organ also took on new significance as a ceremonial instrument. As an outgrowth of the organ revival, a campaign by a relatively small groups of organists, composers, musicologists, and organ builders, the organ came to be regarded the most German of all instruments and thus most appropriate to accompany German political functions.[55] It was featured in the Nuremberg Party Rally of 1936 and at the official memorial ceremony for World War I veterans in 1938.[56] Its potential for ceremonial functions became the focus of a special task force of the Reich Youth Leadership (Reichsjugendführung).[57] Including the organ in political events could capitalize on the devotional powers associated with its use in the church and serve as an antidote to its more popular uses in the cinema and other entertainment venues.[58]

The Jugendmusikbewegung as such disappeared in 1933, but the work of its leaders continued, albeit in a different guise. The youth movement started to disintegrate in 1933 when the Hitler Youth (used here to refer to all youth activities under the Reich Youth Leadership) became the only legal youth organization.[59] By the end of that year, most preexisting youth groups either ceased to exist or pledged their allegiance to the Hitler Youth, whose voluntary membership reached 5.4 million by 1936. With 4 million German youths remaining outside the organization, membership in the Hitler Youth became compulsory in 1939.[60]

Hitler Youth differed from the youth movement in its size, its centralized organization, and its commitment to one party ideology and to the goal of molding ideal citizens for the Third Reich.[61] After 1945, some scholars tried to depict a historical break between the youth movement of the 1920s and the Hitler Youth[62] and play down any similarities as mere "outward trappings."[63] Still it is impossible to ignore their shared fundamental goals. The youth movement displayed strong features of nationalism, antirepublicanism, anti-Semitism, and authoritarianism that would be carried on in the Hitler Youth.[64] The youth movement grew out of bourgeois youth's disappointment with an earlier generation's failure to achieve political stability, and the Bündische Jugend unified youth groups under the principles of commitment to community, faith in the leadership of charismatic figures, altruistic acts for the Fatherland, and belief in a new type of man, modeled more on the soldier-hero type than on the medieval wandering scholar ideal of the Wandervogel.[65] Similarly, the Hitler Youth strove to rectify the political failures of the recent past; to create a "new man" based on the soldier-hero persona; to promote duty to the Fatherland; and to trust in leaders who possessed charisma rather than knowledge or ability.

The musical components of the youth movement display an unmistakable continuity into the Hitler Youth, perhaps more than other youth movement activities. These continuities exist not merely in the "outward trappings" of similar performance practices and repertoire, but rather in the Hitler Youth's obvious commitment to the musical philosophy espoused by the Jugendmusikbewegung. To be sure, many of the differences between the two reflect the Hitler Youth's unwavering commitment to National Socialism and clear focus on ideological training, but other differences simply represent a more advanced stage in the development of Jugendmusikbewegung ideas.

The most obvious difference between music practices of the pre-1933 youth movement and the Hitler Youth is the degree of organization. Whereas the Jugendmusikbewegung suffered from a practical and ideological rift between the Musikantengilde and the Finkensteiner Bund, the Hitler Youth encompassed a large, uniform system of special musical units throughout the Reich. By 1944, each regional division (*Bann*) of the Hitler Youth had music units of some sort, in the form of choral groups, singing troops (*Singscharen*), orchestras, instrumental ensembles, brass units (*Bläserkameradschaften*), ceremonial units of a more military character (*Musikzüge, Spielmannszüge, Fanfarenzüge*), and theatrical and puppet show music troops (*Laienspielscharen, Puppenspielscharen*), totaling more than nine hundred music units throughout the Reich.[66] One other significant difference was the Hitler Youth's attention to instrumental music making. The Hitler Youth, like the Jugendmusikbewegung, promoted singing, especially the singing of folk songs, as its central musical activity. Singing was favored by both movements for its accessibility and its capacity to promote feelings of camaraderie and national identity.[67] But unlike the Jugendmusikbewegung, music units of the Hitler Youth paid just as much attention to instrumental activities, especially brass bands.[68] Hitler Youth leaders highlighted the band's ceremonial functions (*Feiergestaltungen*), declaring ceremony as "the first function of music."[69]

Otherwise, the Hitler Youth followed the same path as the Jugendmusikbewegung in developing its attitudes toward concerts, Hausmusik, and radio. At first the Jugendmusikbewegung rejected these forms of musical activity, but eventually it accepted their inevitability in modern society and made use of them. The Hitler Youth carried this one step further: leaders regarded Hitler Youth music units as good training grounds for Hausmusik and amateur orchestras; they organized trips to the theater, opera, and concerts; and they formed a close collaboration with radio programmers, making sure that special Hitler Youth radio groups (*Rundfunkspielscharen*) were featured regularly, because they recognized radio as a powerful medium that allowed youth to participate in and be exposed to folk music and the works of German masters.[70]

More important, the Hitler Youth and the Jugendmusikbewegung shared a common philosophy of music education. Pedagogical writings from the Jugendmusikbewegung established goals that would be pursued by Hitler Youth pedagogues: healing the rift between music and the Volk, purifying and recreating a new type of person, and instilling feelings of national solidarity.[71] Both movements conceived of education as taking place outside the classroom and involving both youth and adults. The strongest links between the two movements were the plans for building extracurricular music schools and specially training music educators to run them.[72] Jöde had elaborated such plans in his book *Musikschulen für Jugend und Volk,* from which Hitler Youth music leaders borrowed not only their terminology but also their blueprints. Jöde had already developed a separate curriculum for training instructors for Jugendmusikbewegung institutions in his faculty position at the Akademie für Kirchen- und Schulmusik.[73] Although caught up in accusations of Marxist leanings, political volatility, and sexual indiscretions leading to his dismissal from the academy in 1936, Jöde was rehabilitated in 1940,[74] and his educational goals continued to approach their full realization under Hitler. He was eventually able to take an active part in forming the curriculum for training Hitler Youth music instructors and was invited to contribute a chapter to the second edition of the Hitler Youth music handbook, *Musik im Volk.*[75] This was no mere coincidence: Wolfgang Stumme, head of the music division in the central headquarters of the Reich Youth Leadership and editor of the handbook, was a student of Jöde's in the above-mentioned seminar.[76] By 1944, Hitler Youth's Musikschulen für Jugend und Volk numbered around 160 and loyally adhered to Jöde's earlier plans, right down to the details of the curriculum, even though they were publicized as arising completely out of the political education of the Hitler Youth.[77]

The music education philosophy of the Hitler Youth deviated from that of the Jugendmusikbewegung only in its view of German society, adopting the National Socialist concept of the "people's community" (*Volksgemeinschaft*) and idealizing the German race. Consequently, the Hitler Youth emphasized notions of racial purity, constantly harping on the evils of Judaism and the need to eradicate its musical manifestations (such as jazz and the "Jewish" school of composition) from German musical life.[78] The Hitler Youth also made a clear distinction between the education of the public and the cultivation of a leadership class. Jöde had wanted to use his music schools to make music education available to all, but Stumme additionally pointed to the importance of music in training the Nazi elite. In the Adolf Hitler schools, where the most promising and racially pure youths were handpicked, educated, and groomed for leadership, learning an instrument was required (unlike in the Jugendschulen where it was optional) because of its usefulness in building character and reinforcing discipline.[79]

Nazi Musical Ideals in Theory and Practice

Various government and party organizations in the Third Reich idealized music as a vehicle for strengthening the nation and the race, recognizing its ceremonial, educational, and disciplinary value. When it came to specifying which music could best serve these functions or, better yet, which music was to be shunned, however, musical leaders proved rather evasive. At best, they issued occasional proscriptions against music deemed undesirable, but effective methods for identifying and eliminating such music were never refined in the twelve years of the Nazi regime. The Nazi government failed to establish any consistent aesthetic criteria for good or bad music, and despite the loud outcries against Judaism, bolshevism, and Americanism in music, the system largely failed to implement effective measures to suppress even the more easily identifiable strains of jazz and atonality. It did, however, succeed in weeding out and silencing large numbers of "degenerate" musical personnel, especially Jews, targeting prominent figures and systematically depleting the numbers of "undesirables" active in Germany by means of their emigration, deportation, or murder.

The most coherent public display of any sort of Nazi musical aesthetic was the "Degenerate Music" (*Entartete Musik*) exhibition of 1938. The exhibit was part of a large national music festival, the Reich Music Days (*Reichsmusiktage*) in Düsseldorf, a joint project of the Reich Music Chamber and KdF. The stated purpose of the event was to foster communication between the creators of music and the public, providing a forum for composers, performers, bureaucrats, educators, and scholars to present their achievements to the "people's community," for "there is no musical culture that is not the people's culture."[80] The festivities lasted eight days and were spread over the city, featuring KdF-sponsored concerts at local factories and hosting the music camps of the Reich Youth Leadership and the Nazi Student League (Nationalsozialistischer Deutscher Studentenbund), the special conference on "Singen und Sprechen," and the first musicology conference in the new Reich.[81] High points of the festival included a production of Richard Strauss's opera *Arabella* under the composer's direction, the premiere of his *Festliches Vorspiel* composed for the event, an address by Goebbels, a performance of Pfitzner's *Von deutscher Seele,* and the Berlin Philharmonic's rendition of Beethoven's Ninth with the Kittel Choir. The Reichsmusiktage were to be an annual event that would honor Düsseldorf as the official "Reich Music City," but it lasted only two years.[82]

The Reichsmusiktage should have been able to illustrate sharp distinctions between "good" and "bad" music, as the parallel art exhibits in Munich on "German Art" and "Degenerate Art" had accomplished the previous year. Yet music was far more elusive in character than the visual arts, one reason why Goebbels remained aloof from musical matters and focused his energies on dictating policy in other arts and media.[83] It is doubtful that anyone would have left the festival with a clear understanding of how to implement a National Socialist music policy. Even Goebbels, the masterful orator, was strikingly vague in his announced "ten commandments" for German musical creation. He proclaimed that "the nature of music lies in melody" rather than in theoretical constructs; "all music is not suited to everyone"; music is rooted in the folk, requires empathy rather than reason, deeply affects the spirit of man, and is the most glorious art of the German heritage; and musicians of the past must be respected.[84] The accompanying Degenerate Music exhibit, a potential tutorial in recognizing and rooting out destructive musical influences from the new state, consisted merely of haphazard attacks on a hodgepodge of trends and individuals and was full of contradictions.

The exhibit's printed catalogue consisted of a lengthy essay by Hans Severus Ziegler, the director of the National Theater in Weimar, and reproductions of some of the panels that hung in the exhibition hall. Its cover features a caricature of a black saxophonist against a red background wearing a Jewish star on his lapel, an image that neatly suggests the collusion of all the symbolic enemies of German culture (American jazz, subsidized by Jewish promotion, with bolshevism and internationalism lurking in the background). Most of the other illustrations served to ridicule prominent Jewish composers, conductors, and critics and their associates, and to vilify jazz, operetta, and atonal composition. Ernst Krenek, although not a Jew, is featured prominently for his "jazz opera" *Jonny spielt auf,* whose main character clearly served as a model for the cover illustration. A photograph of Anton Webern, also not a Jew, bears the caption that this " 'master student' of Arnold Schoenberg outdoes his training even in the length of his nose." Franz Schreker and Ernst Toch are featured as "two Jewish scribblers," and despite Schreker's great popularity, he is cited here for his "sexual-pathological confusion." Even operetta, a consistently popular form of entertainment, merits mention by virtue of the success of Jewish composers Leo Fall and Oscar Straus, illustrated here in unflattering portrait caricatures but warranting no further explanation. The illustrations also feature excerpts from two Brecht-Weill collaborations, *Die Dreigroschenoper* and *Mahagonny,* presented as proof of their promotion of greed and capitalism but completely missing the intended sarcasm of their work. The Jewish conductor Otto Klemperer is highlighted as a "Jew against Wagner" for his recent controversial Wagner productions at the Kroll opera. The catalogue closes with a seemingly unrelated epilogue: a photograph of Hindemith and his "Jewish wife" and a mildly reproachful review of the 1929 premiere of the Hindemith-Brecht collaboration *Lehrstück* in Baden-Baden.

Ziegler, musically uneducated, relied heavily on the Degenerate Art exhibit of the previous year in formulating his commentary. Admitting in his essay that degeneracy is much easier to detect in visual arts than in music,[85] Ziegler tried to relate the two art forms whenever possible. The catalogue reproduces portraits of "two prominent early campaigners for musical bolshevism," the critics Heinrich Strobel and Adolf Weissmann (the latter designated here as a Jew), taking care to mention that both portraits were by Jewish artists. Another illustration shows Bauhaus designer Oskar Schlemmer's stage design for Schoenberg's "insane-asylum fantasy" *Die glückliche Hand,* exploiting the prominent theme of the 1937 art exhibit that linked expressionist art with insanity and juxtaposed expressionist paintings and sculptures with allegedly indistinguishable attempts by mental patients. Finally, an illustration with the caption "Degenerate Art and Degenerate Music Hand in Hand" features two expressionist paintings with musical subjects: Carl Hofer's "Jazz Band" and Paul Klee's "Musical Comedy."

All these images receive little or no explanation in the accompanying text, nor does the essay try to establish guidelines for identifying unacceptable music. Ziegler states outright that the intention is not to "write prescriptions or circumscribe laws for the new formation of German musical life," but rather to educate youth.[86] Owing to Ziegler's obvious reluctance and lack of competency in discussing musical issues, the essay indulges in polemics against democracy, bolshevism, and Jews, with more emphasis on Jewish literary figures than musicians. Any discussions of actual music are superficial, and the only significant overlap in text and illustrations lies in the references to Schoenberg. A less than flattering portrait of the composer is captioned with a description of his work by another Jew, characterizing him as an explorer who "uses sounds of anguish, hysteria, and turns it into music." Corresponding passages in the text name Schoenberg as the inventor of atonality who tried to undermine the essence of German musical expression, the triad.[87]

The Degenerate Music exhibit neither provided guidelines for music practice nor reflected current or future music policy. As shocking as the consistent attacks against Schoenberg's experiments may seem, it is unlikely that such character assassination would have aroused much surprise at the time, certainly not in 1938 but probably not even prior to 1933. Before World War I Schoenberg had made a name for himself with the successes of *Pelleas und Melisande* (1910), *Pierrot lunaire* (1912), and *Gurrelieder* (1913), but by the late 1920s the critical reception of his works was less than enthusiastic. Many younger composers had successfully turned their attention to Gebrauchsmusik and *Zeitopern* in an effort to forge a better relationship with general audiences, overshadowing Schoenberg's latest creations. Even the musically sophisticated critic Alfred Einstein cast doubt on Schoenberg's effectiveness by describing his recent works as "a secret closet to which only he has the key."[88] At the 1930 premiere of *Von heute auf morgen*, Einstein criticized Schoenberg for his half-hearted attempt to compose a work for the masses, choosing a story with broad appeal but setting it to a twelve-tone score displaying "fanatical seriousness and an overwhelming lack of humor," resulting in a work of "pure self-gratification" that was "unsocial and inhumanly difficult."[89] Leo Kestenberg had appointed Schoenberg to direct the prestigious composition master class at the Prussian Academy in 1925, and Schoenberg's public humiliation and resignation in 1933 attracted much attention. The fact that Schoenberg was a Jew and had recently declined in popularity provided a convenient coincidence that racist propagandists exploited for ideological purposes.

The other prominent target in the exhibit was jazz, but this, too, had a recent history of rejection by the Jugendmusikbewegung and conservative critics. As Michael Kater observes in his exhaustive study of jazz in Nazi Germany, an intense anti-jazz campaign during the depression was fueled by German musicians' fears of competition from the influx of foreign jazz musicians following the currency stabilization in 1923. By the end of the Weimar Republic, the public had lost interest in jazz and gravitated toward older styles of entertainment music.[90] Part of this decline may be attributable to the fact that, with the exception of a small number of connoisseurs, the German public and German composers were exposed to only a watered-down version of jazz. Isolated from the United States and parts of Europe immediately after World War I, Germany cultivated a very distorted, second-hand notion of American jazz, having access only to imported sheet music, a few recordings of white dance bands (e.g., Guy Lombardo), and home-grown "text books" by German authors explaining methods for "jazz" performance and composition.[91] Ironically, jazz enjoyed increasing success during World War II.[92] It is therefore feasible that once Germans had access to the more varied and livelier products of genuine jazz, its popularity quickly caught on.

Many of the other attacks featured in the exhibit and its catalogue were similarly ineffectual. Ziegler's list of individual compositions by Jews and non-Jews that had "insulted German audiences" includes a passing reference to the work *Histoire du soldat* without naming its composer, Igor Stravinsky.[93] At the time of the exhibit, Stravinsky's music was enjoying a brief period of rehabilitation, following pre-1933 attacks on his "musical bolshevism" and outrage over a 1934 performance of *Le Sacre du printemps*. In 1936, an improved economy and calmer political climate allowed Stravinsky's works to enjoy considerable success until the outbreak of the war.[94] Furthermore, despite the more focused criticism against the "destroyers" of "Germanic" tonality, atonal and twelve-tone works continued to be heard and created in the Third Reich.[95]

While an eradication of undesirable music proved an ill-advised, if not impossible, program to pursue, the eradication of undesirable individuals forged ahead. The Nazi purge of artistic personnel affected gypsies; nonwhites; and political, social, and sexual "deviants," but Jews remained the central target.[96] Richard Wagner's 1850 polemic on Judaism in music had challenged German composers to suppress "Jewish music," but the failure to identify any such body of music or its traits turned Wagner's aesthetic challenge into a policy of physical exclusion of "musical Jews." In the years before Hitler's accession, anti-Semitic rhetoric in musical discourse turned to political and economic stereotypes rather than to elusive musical generalizations. Characterizations reminiscent of the *Protocols of the Elders of Zion* suggested that Jewish capitalists, driven by their race, had come to control the music business while Jewish music critics steered public taste. At the same time, middle-class fears of the growing workers' movement linked Jews with bolshevists through the figure of Karl Marx. Representing Jews as both capitalists and communists led to inevitable contradictions. In his writings in the 1920s, Moser might praise Mendelssohn as a great German composer in one context, only to castigate him in another by linking him with Mahler, Schreker, Schoenberg, and Satan.[97] Moser also promoted the common image of the Jew as capitalist entrepreneur, but elsewhere labeled developments in music education as destructive "Jewish-communist experimentation."[98]

The proliferation of racial theories soon furnished "scientific findings" that determined that Jews constituted a biological race and thus were incapable of full assimilation. The "dejewification" (*Entjudung*) of musical life in the Nazi state proceeded first in a series of high-profile acts to ostracize prominent Jewish figures and their friends, and then through bureaucratic exclusion of all Jews from the Reich Music Chamber. In the first stage, Schoenberg was compelled to resign his post at the Prussian Academy, Bruno Walter was threatened and coerced into canceling his German engagements, and Richard Strauss, an Aryan composer and president of the Reich Music Chamber, temporarily became a pariah for refusing to break off his collaboration with Jewish author Stefan Zweig. Dejewification then affected less prominent cultural professionals, as admission into the Reich Culture Chamber came to require documentation of Aryan lineage. The Jews who had managed to join the Music Chamber earlier were systematically expelled starting in 1936, and in 1937 the government started to ban Jews from attending public cultural events, a measure that became fully enforceable only in 1941 when Jews were required to wear yellow Star of David badges. Though impossible to achieve a complete purge of all Jewish artists, since many exceptions were made for political reasons, the removal of all Jews from the cultural sphere was nevertheless the Nazi government's highest cultural priority.[99]

The dejewification of culture industries undoubtedly increased job opportunities for "true Germans," but it also created a sizable class of unemployed Jewish musicians. Apprehensive of the serious economic implications of this sudden increase in unemployment, and also acknowledging the public relations value of giving an impression of providing for the Jewish community, the Nazi government decided to allow Jews to conduct their own cultural programs. The Jewish Culture League (Jüdischer Kulturbund) started in Berlin, where it grew to include three theater ensembles, an opera ensemble, two symphony orchestras, a chamber theater, numerous choral groups and chamber music groups, and also sponsored lectures, exhibits, film programs, cabaret, and dances.[100] Deportation and emigration quickly depleted its personnel, and by 1941, operating on a shoestring, the league was dissolved by the Gestapo.

The workings of the Jewish Culture League further illustrate the impossible task of establishing criteria for acceptable and unacceptable music. Attempts at drawing distinctions between German and Jewish music dated to Wagner's polemical writings, but even he vacillated on the procedures for removing Jewish influences from German composition. Nazi officials overseeing the Jewish Culture League ran into similar dilemmas. They encouraged the performance of works by Jews, permitted foreign works as long as their content was not anti-German, and placed restrictions on German works. At the beginning, the prohibition of German works was not very strictly enforced, but it tightened as the regime sought to widen the gap between so-called German art and Jewish art: Beethoven was banned in 1937, and Mozart followed in 1938 after the annexation of Austria. Yet even when pressures to concentrate exclusively on Jewish music increased, Nazi censors ran into difficulties. On one occasion they rejected the league's request to perform Mahler because an inexperienced official insisted that the composer of "The Wayfarer's Song" must have been Aryan. At a national Jewish Culture League conference in 1936, held in the presence of Music Chamber and Gestapo representatives, musicians, critics, educators, and scholars debated the parameters for defining Jewish music. They reached a consensus on synagogue cantillation and Jewish folk music, but as cultured bourgeois Germans, the Jews in the league felt that such music did not belong in a concert hall. In the end, the league's programs consisted mostly of art music from the nineteenth century, allowing for many hearings of the "racially" Jewish Mendelssohn, Meyerbeer, Offenbach, and Mahler, with some attention also to contemporary Jewish composers.[101]

The Limits of Censorship

Even if authorities had been able to develop clear guidelines for acceptable and unacceptable music, it is not certain that such guidelines could have been implemented. First of all, German officials had learned from recent experience that censorship had to be handled with extreme caution. Until 1918, German theaters were required to submit all scripts to the police to screen them for obscenity, blasphemy, or lese majesty, but in most cases the police were surprisingly lax. The authorities recognized, on the one hand, that political satire and risqué entertainment provided a harmless release of tension for discontented citizens. On the other hand, the scandal of censorship could backfire by drawing undue attention to a performance.[102] Furthermore, music censorship was rendered ever more impractical, if not impossible, by the variety and abundance of musical outlets lying beyond government or police controls. Amateur music activities had spread beyond churches and schools into the youth movement, amateur organizations, and adult education. Hausmusik, an activity that thrived in the unfavorable economic conditions of the Weimar Republic and continued to prosper into the Third Reich, was ideally carried out in the privacy of the home. Rapid developments in recording and radio technology, including access to foreign broadcasts, were making music consumption an increasingly private matter beyond the control of censors.

Steinweis has described arts censorship in the Third Reich as improvised and "amorphous," and music censorship as especially difficult to enforce owing to the decentralized nature of musical activity.[103] On the local level, commissioners appointed by the Reich Music Chamber functioned primarily as coordinators of the local concert season; they approved bookings and resolved schedule conflicts but lacked the authority to control programming decisions.[104] Other agents were equally limited as censors. Hitler had commissioned Nazi ideologue Alfred Rosenberg as "deputy to the Führer for the supervision of the entire intellectual and ideological training and education of the Nazi party" (Beauftragter des Führers für die Überwachung der gesamten geistigen und weltanschaulichen Schulung und Erziehung der NSDAP). Rosenberg used this authority to keep a vigilant eye on cultural and educational events and mobilized the Nazi press to stir up trouble whenever he or his staff perceived ideological transgressions. The Rosenberg Bureau (Amt Rosenberg) had its own Music Bureau (Amt Musik), headed by the musicologist Herbert Gerigk. This division may have wielded more power than other departments under Rosenberg, but its censorship authority extended only to the musical activities of the Deutsches Volksbildungswerk in the KdF.[105] The centralized structure of church administration might have facilitated closer controls over church music performance, but even among the German Christians (Deutsche Christen), the Lutheran movement devoted to "purifying" the liturgy and becoming the official church of the Nazi state, attempts to purge hymns of Hebrew words and alleged Jewish melodies met with open resistance from congregants unwilling to part with familiar tunes.[106]

In the case of jazz, Third Reich policy followed the principle that it was better to be lenient than to impose restrictions and risk defiance. Despite some harsh punishments imposed by local authorities, central government measures against jazz performance were notably tentative,[107] and although radio came under government supervision, jazz ultimately thrived on the German air waves. Radio broadcasting had become an instrument of the state during the depression, and regulating reforms under von Papen enabled Goebbels to effect a complete takeover of all radio companies. Initially jazz was banned by Nazi authorities, but in the course of the war it became evident that listeners who were attracted to jazz would search for it on foreign stations and inevitably would hear foreign news broadcasts. This led the authorities to curtail any radio bans on jazz. Radio programs started to include works by jazz artists Louis Armstrong, Duke Ellington, and Benny Goodman but concealed their names, insisting that this was not "Negro and Jewish jazz" per se but rather the "relaxed, strongly rhythmic music" that soldiers desired.[108]

The recording industry managed to circumvent government controls more effectively than broadcasters could, allowing for surreptitious consumption of banned music in the privacy of one's home. The German recording industry suffered significant setbacks during the depression but made an astounding comeback under the Nazis. The government made no gestures to take over the industry, and German companies ostensibly complied voluntarily with racial policies. They eliminated Jewish composers and performers from their domestic catalogues and flooded the German market with marches, light classics, and film music. In their foreign trade, however, they continued to sell "degenerate" products.[109] International commerce also allowed for the continued supply of jazz recordings into Germany. Kater documents a fairly continuous influx, first legally and then illegally through smuggling. International trade was important for German record companies, especially when foreign currency was in demand. When Goebbels banned all recordings featuring non-Aryans in 1938, many forbidden items could still be obtained legally because it was not known which American and British artists were Jewish or black. Despite tightened constraints when the United States entered the war, German soldiers stationed in occupied territories would purchase forbidden recordings and bring them home.[110]

The night club scene was another entertainment medium that was difficult to control, partly because it spread to a wide variety of performance spaces. Controls on nightclubs had been bothersome for Wilhelmine censors; entrepreneurs would evade licensing and censorship by staging risqué performances in closed clubs by invitation only.[111] In Nazi Germany, banned forms of music similarly managed to thrive in nightclubs. Many jazz clubs had doormen to screen suspected spies and set up elaborate warning mechanisms and foils in case of raids by Music Chamber officials. Some of these nightclubs were frequented by SS and SA officers who were jazz enthusiasts.[112]

Cabarets, which often featured politically charged sketches, dances, and songs, came under closer surveillance than other performance spaces: Goebbels was particularly averse to cabaret, and the Gestapo carefully scrutinized its political content. But even Goebbels's explicit restrictions on political cabaret could not be easily implemented. In 1937, he issued a ban on any references to politics, religion, and the state in theaters, variety shows, and cabarets, but his own ministry allowed so many exceptions to the measures that Goebbels had to reissue the order again in 1939 and 1940, still without success. The controversy continued until a final decree of March 1941 essentially transformed cabaret shows into variety shows with a string of unrelated and inoffensive musical numbers.[113]

For many years following World War II, music in Nazi Germany was commonly perceived as a strictly controlled regimen of march music, Wagner operas, and Beethoven symphonies, devoid of any atonal music, jazz, or any other remnants of "Weimar culture." This totalitarian conception of Nazi cultural policy, a by-product of early historiographic trends that tried to draw parallels between Nazi Germany and the Soviet Union, has only recently been challenged.[114] Even pre-Stalinist Soviet musical policies demonstrated an initial open-mindedness to musical criteria in the fifteen years following the revolution, going so far as encouraging experimentation and exposure to Western modernism.[115] Similarly, there is no evidence that total control over musical production was ever a priority for Nazi cultural policymakers in the twelve years of the Reich. Even when the Reich Culture Chamber imposed more direct measures on the arts after 1935, the Music Chamber's censorship consisted of little more than a few published and unpublished lists proscribing certain non-Aryans (Mendelssohn was not among them) and a ruling that dealers and publishers receive permission before disseminating the works of émigrés. The implementation of such measures, however, would exceed the means of the four-person staff of the Reich Music Examination Office (Reichsmusikprüfstelle), a branch of the Propaganda Ministry created in 1935.[116] Certain restrictions on music of enemy countries became more well defined as the war progressed, but these were motivated by economic boycotts and copyright laws and were probably not unique to Germany.[117]

Popular Entertainment and the Fate of High Culture

Even in a system like the Nazi regime intent on controlling public opinion, the choice of musical offerings ultimately had to concede to the public's wishes. Since the turn of the century, musical taste had been gravitating away from Romantic trends of monumentality and cultivated artistry. Wider exposure to foreign cultures inspired a taste for the exotic, audiences eagerly sought out new forms of popular entertainment, and technology completely transformed the nature of musical consumption. All these factors set off shifts in the hierarchy of musical institutions through the years of the Weimar Republic and the Third Reich, influencing policy as well as musical production and creating profound changes in the relative importance of popular culture and high culture.

The best illustration of policy conceding to public taste and the growing importance of popular music can be found in the music programming of radio broadcasts. From radio's beginnings, promoters emphasized its potential to educate the public to appreciate art music and contemporary works,[118] yet over the course of the 1920s music programs came to consist increasingly of popular fare.[119] The rising proportion of entertainment music (*Unterhaltungsmusik* or *U-Musik*) over serious music (*ernste Musik* or *E-Musik*) continued from one regime to the next. Nazi policymakers and program directors also set out to educate the masses through radio, but they eventually had to concede that radio's primary function was and remained diversion. In 1942, the committees overseeing radio programming split into six different categories of popular music and only two categories of serious music (the latter designated as "serious but generally understood music" and "classical music, difficult owing to its unfamiliarity"). Popular music was referred to as the "black bread" or staple diet of music broadcasting, and classical music as the "cake."[120] The public simply wanted more popular and fewer classical offerings, and a statement in the official publication of the Reichs-Rundfunk-Gesellschaft rationalized in 1934 that "it would not be National Socialist [behavior] for German radio, from an exalted vantage point of 'education,' to presume to invade the free time of productive human beings."[121]

Radio not only effectively proliferated popular music but also siphoned off attendance at concerts and operas. As the economy fluctuated, more alternative — and often cheaper — forms of diversion caught on, including radio, recordings, Hausmusik, vaudeville, cabaret, and cinema. Large vaudeville houses had posed the biggest threat to opera and concert attendance in the early 1900s. Critics even suggested that creators of high culture change their ways in order to attract the public they had alienated with recent esoteric experiments: "If opera houses and concert halls continue to deny the public what it desires and demands, then it turns to vaudeville or to operettas."[122] Cinema grew in popularity in the the 1920s, replacing vaudeville as the major form of entertainment and compelling impresarios to stage more elaborate shows to attract audiences.[123]

Opera directors and composers were well aware of the impact of popular entertainment on ticket sales, and a handful of composers met the challenge of reforming opera in order to win back audiences. Strauss constructed his opera

Intermezzo out of short, filmlike sequences, while Kurt Weill emulated silent film in *Der Protagonist* and *Royal Palace* by incorporating pantomime.[124] The biggest event to rock the opera world in the 1920s was the "jazz opera," Krenek's *Jonny spielt auf,* which reached an audience estimated at a half million in nearly five hundred performances between 1926 and 1929.[125] Some questions arose as to whether the austere opera house was the appropriate forum for works like *Jonny,* "motion-picture operas" like Max Brand's *Maschinist Hopkins,* and revue-type works like Weill and Brecht's *Der Aufstieg und Fall der Stadt Mahagonny,* but their successes proved otherwise.[126]

Competition from popular entertainment was not the only problem facing opera houses and orchestras. Most institutions of high culture in the Weimar Republic depended on financial support from provincial and municipal governments. But often economics and politics dictated giving priority to social programs rather than to entities that most regarded as luxury enterprises. When the Berlin Philharmonic appealed to the city parliament for support, for example, it faced the most resistance from members of left and center parties. They opposed lavishing funds on an institution with a high snob-factor, inaccessible to the middle and working classes, and argued that the money could be better used for social services.[127]

Even in states known for their generous support for cultural enterprises, economic strains proved too serious during the depression to maintain cultural subsidies. In Prussia, the highly organized Ministry for Science, Art, and Public Education had supported a wide variety of musical activities for many years. The Prussian state provided large subsidies to major conservatories and music education institutes and contributed almost eight million marks in 1929 to the Prussian State Theaters. It ran the prestigious composition seminar in the Prussian Academy of the Arts, as well as satellite schools for training composers, the folk song commission, the music history commission (responsible for the publication of the Denkmäler Deutscher Tonkunst), a committee to supervise the copyright and publication of music, and formal training courses for choral conductors.[128] Yet even in Prussia, economic pressures brought on by the depression made it impossible to continue support for its three opera houses, forcing the least financially viable one, the Kroll Opera, to close in 1930.

The grim outlook for institutions of high culture changed when Hitler came to power. Determined to counter an image of barbarism and project themselves as bearers of culture, Nazi heads of state made a special effort to preserve struggling cultural enterprises. As the first regime to establish any type of extensive, Reich-based cultural bureaucracy, the Nazi government had the infrastructure to absorb institutions into the state support system (a process commonly referred to as *Gleichschaltung* or "coordination"). Without such intervention, some of the most famous musical enterprises may have ceased to exist.

The situation of Berlin orchestras is a prime example. The Berlin Philharmonic, a private corporation since 1882, had dodged financial difficulties throughout its existence. These reached threatening proportions in 1922, after which the orchestra had to rely heavily on the city government for aid. Burdened with not one but two struggling orchestras (the Philharmonic and the municipal Berlin Symphony Orchestra), the city council made several unsuccessful appeals to the Reich and Prussian governments for additional help, but it was forced to dissolve the less celebrated Berlin Symphony Orchestra in 1932 and could not guarantee the further existence of the Philharmonic. The establishment of the Propaganda Ministry would prove fortuitous: in 1934, after a series of negotiations, the Propaganda Ministry assumed full financial responsibility for the Philharmonic. Each member of the orchestra received 600 marks for his share of the corporation and became a civil servant, the Philharmonic earned the designation of official Reich Orchestra, and Hitler specified that its members be placed in a special wage category in consideration of its "artistic achievements and special cultural-political importance."[129] Despite the loss of fiscal autonomy and the requirement to participate in some official functions, the orchestra's new role as a government entity had no noticeable effect on its repertoire. The orchestra had long favored a conservative symphonic diet with Beethoven as its staple, and it had shown no more initiative to promote experimental repertoire before the Gleichschaltung than after.[130]

Bayreuth was another struggling enterprise salvaged by Nazi interests. The Wagner mania had been waning before 1933; stagings of Wagner's works in German opera houses dropped dramatically after 1926, lagging far behind those of Verdi, Puccini, Mozart, and Lortzing, and attendance at the Bayreuth festival steadily declined. Passages from a few Wagner "hits" were used as background music for the propaganda films of Leni Riefenstahl, news reels, and radio announcements, but this failed to revive interest in Wagner's music.[131] But Hitler, an avid Wagnerian since his youth, became not only an honored guest at Bayreuth but also a benefactor. Each year he purchased tens of thousands of marks worth of tickets, provided half a million marks for each new production, extended the festival from an annual to a biennial event starting in 1936, and contributed an additional half a million marks to keep the festival running in 1940.[132] Hitler also averted the festival's closure during the war by opening performances to soldiers and making government funds available.[133] This was not a gesture of goodwill toward culture-starved soldiers, but rather a concerted effort to keep the legacy of Richard Wagner alive and to cultivate the image of Nazi leaders as patrons of high culture.

In addition to direct government support of struggling artistic institutions, centralized subscription organizations such as the NS-Kulturgemeinde and KdF also had an impact on their prosperity, having grown far beyond the size of agencies in the Weimar era. By buying up blocks of tickets for popular and serious cultural events and selling them at discount prices to their large membership,[134] these mass organizations provided these institutions with much-needed capital and sometimes used this power to influence artistic decisions. In Munich, for example, the opera houses and orchestras came to depend heavily on the Kulturgemeinde and KdF organizations, which then tried to force a popularization of the repertoires to render them more accessible to their subscribers.[135]

The Nazi government saw the resuscitation of struggling cultural enterprises as beneficial to both foreign and domestic relations. It would counter the claims of detractors abroad that Nazi leaders were philistines, and it would reinforce national pride by preserving the German musical legacy. As Moser proclaimed in 1928, music was Germany's greatest source of national pride and most potent weapon against other nations. The centrality of music in German culture was not without its tragic ironies: the inability of the cultured Jewish bourgeoisie in the Jewish Culture League to part with their music, mainly German music, and, more perversely, the ubiquity of music in the concentration camps, where musical ensembles entertained SS troops with waltzes, lieder, and symphonies, accompanied grueling labor, taunted inmates, and drowned out screams during executions.[136]

Rather than viewing Nazi musical life as a total departure from that of the Weimar Republic, as notions of a distinct "Weimar culture" and "Nazi culture" might suggest, it is important to recognize the seamless transitions in musical life from one system to the other. Nazi propagandists fueled existing negative stereotypes of Americans, communists, and Jews rather than creating new ones. The goals of bringing music closer to the public, eliminating "intellectualisms" and virtuosity, encouraging mass participation, and giving in to the forces of technology and popular entertainment had gained momentum in the Weimar Republic and persisted after 1933. In the end, Nazi cultural administrators did more than their predecessors to appease the entire spectrum of the music community, from the orchestra musician to the Louis Armstrong fan.

The purpose here is not to mitigate the crimes of the National Socialist regime, but rather to provide a background for examining the responses of artists and intellectuals to Nazi objectives. One must modify the images of totalitarian repression, censorship, and coercion — offered up in the panicked postwar testimonies at denazification trials — with the evidence that many Germans active in musical life continued to thrive, even prospered, under Hitler. What emerges instead is the image of a cultural climate that was not so intolerable as one might imagine for those who managed to escape political and racial persecution. The Nazi government proclaimed the importance of music for the German race and channeled resources into its preservation. Those active in the music professions, music education, music businesses, and even the noble intellectual pursuit of musicology could find some aspects of the Nazi cultural agenda that resonated with their own beliefs. This apparently also made it easier for them to overlook the fanaticism and atrocities brought down on their persecuted neighbors and colleagues.

2

Musicologists on Their Role in Modern German Society

The transformation of musical life following World War I was bound to affect the musicology profession. For one thing, many musicologists divided their time between music scholarship and music practice and thus had first-hand knowledge of issues that affected amateur music making, education, production, consumption, and administration. But even those who restricted their activities to academic pursuits were faced with rising criticism of ivory tower elitism and pressures on universities to demonstrate their usefulness in the new democracy. Academic opportunities for musicologists continued to expand during the Weimar Republic, but academics as a whole were expected to take a more active part in society.

Perceiving a crisis in their profession, musicologists called for a reassessment of the discipline. While continuing to establish themselves in the academic world, they investigated new ways to serve the public. Some became expert commentators on current musical and political issues, but as such they had no impact on Weimar policies. Others realized that their combined experiences as music scholars and practitioners gave them a unique opportunity to serve the community of amateur musicians as agents of *Volksbildung*, education in the broadest sense of the word. This social role enabled musicologists to make a comfortable transition from the Weimar system to the Nazi system as educators with the task of enlightening the German Volk about its musical heritage and musical strength. Despite the grander political ambitions of some individuals, musicologists never managed to assume the role of architects of either Weimar or Nazi music policy, even though some became well known for their fervent endorsements of governmental agendas.

Musicology's Ambiguous Identity

In 1918 musicology was a relatively new academic discipline, but Germans had already made their mark. In the second half of the nineteenth century, German and Austrian scholars distinguished themselves as path breakers in research and methodology, making important contributions to both historical and systematic branches of the field. They set standards for creating catalogues and indexes for research purposes and for undertaking critical editions of musical works. The most ambitious of their editorial projects were the multivolume scholarly editions of early music from German-speaking regions, the so-called monuments (*Denkmäler*) series, the largest among them dating to the last decade of the nineteenth century (Denkmäler Deutscher Tonkunst began in 1889, Denkmäler der Tonkunst in Österreich in 1888, and Denkmäler der Tonkunst in Bayern in 1900). German musicologists also devoted energy to establishing scholarly societies and periodicals. By the end of the nineteenth century, Germans had established three major scholarly journals and had organized the first international musicological society. Toward the end of World War I, the prospect of peace prompted a surge of organizational activity with the founding of the German Music Society (Deutsche Musikgesellschaft or DMG) and the Royal Institute for German Music Research (Fürstliches Institut für deutsche Musikforschung), along with their respective scholarly journals and publishing projects.

Despite these initiatives, musicology as a profession remained somewhat loosely defined. No one was more aware of this problem than someone like Friedrich Blume. Born in 1893, Blume had to interrupt his studies when called to serve in World War I. He finally finished his studies in the 1920s and rose to prominence in academe as an expert in Protestant church music, despite the precarious circumstances for musicologists in the Weimar period. Blume was ever vigilant of the practicality of remaining in the public eye and positioned himself to assume important tasks in the Third Reich through his activities within and beyond the university. A combination of shrewdness and luck enabled him to continue to lead musicological enterprises after World War II as well, winning distinction as founder of the German musicology society; general editor of the reference work *Die Musik in Geschichte und Gegenwart* (*MGG*); and leader in several organizations, including the International Musicological Society (president, 1958–61). In a 1969 article, Blume traced the origins of the modern musicologist or musicology professor to the practicing music director. An older scientific study of music, developed by music theorists in the Middle Ages and the Renaissance, had died out in German universities by the eighteenth century. Thereafter the university music director or *Kantor* assumed responsibility for systematic training in musicianship and music history. Owing to this mixed academic pedigree, modern musicology's status in the university remained ambiguous well into the twentieth century: the first two generations of noted scholars (August Wilhelm Ambros, Friedrich Chrysander, Philipp Spitta, and Hermann Abert) received their training in other humanities disciplines or practical music, and universities took their time in acknowledging musicology as a reputable discipline (Riemann, for example, never achieved the rank of full professor). As musicology gained more scholarly credibility, a split developed between those who remained close to music practice and those who promoted the study of music as a science and required mastery in related disciplines. In Blume's assessment, this ideological split was never resolved, and the role of music in the German university was never clearly defined.[1]

Musicology's relative novelty and lack of professional definition accounts for the fact that many prolific authors and respected scholars worked mainly outside the academy, that a long tradition of music criticism continued to supplement the income of even the most famous university professors, and that professors of musicology kept up their activities as practicing musicians and composers. These activities allowed them to interact with the music public and to relate more sympathetically with the utilitarian demands under the Weimar Republic and the Third Reich than scholars in other fields. When the war ended and the Weimar Republic was established, university professors were apprehensive of the new political environment. They generally opposed democratic principles, thriving in their own spheres of influence as a small oligarchy, and feared that the flourishing industrial-based economy would diminish their importance as bearers of culture. Fritz Ringer convincingly designates Weimar professors as a degenerating class of "mandarin intellectuals," who attained a high social position from educational achievements rather than from inherited land or acquired capital and, as such, were able to thrive only in the transitional period between agrarian and industrial economies. During that transitional period they had wielded the power to define the nation and the state in terms of its intellectual and spiritual life and portrayed themselves as the spiritual nobility of Germany. This had enabled them to resist any interference from ruling parties and to insist on the academic freedom and self-government granted to them.[2]

In the Weimar Republic, most university professors resented the new system that had grown out of a lost war and longed for the glorious days of the Kaiser. They were silent in their opposition, especially since the most powerful among them were civil servants and carried on a long-standing tradition of loyalty to governmental superiors. They did, however, associate the Republic with the current overcrowded universities, a perceived decline in scholarship, and the economic disaster of hyperinflation that accompanied the Republic's early years and reduced their standard of living.[3] Their hatred of the current system formed an impenetrable armor, making them determined to hold firmly to their remaining stronghold — the university — and to fight any government intrusions. Although the Weimar government succeeded in executing sweeping reforms in elementary and secondary education, it failed to introduce any change in the university because of the professors' exaggerated fear of losing control of university administration.

Prussian Minister of Culture C. H. Becker, overseeing more than half of the universities in the Reich, tried to introduce reforms that might have smoothed over recognizable problems in the universities. He suggested that faculties address students' needs for professional training and, alongside research, pay attention to issues of career and citizenship. Becker, as a professor himself, understood the university's problems and wanted only to modernize the oligarchy without dismantling it, but the majority of professors saw his suggestions as an unacceptable mixing of scholarship with politics and a reprehensible attempt at democratizing the university. As one historian argues, Becker's suggestions never came close to undermining academic freedom or self-rule, but universities were so staunchly reactionary as to thwart even those measures that might have improved the functioning of the institution.[4] Becker also piqued the anger of his colleagues by recommending curricular reforms. He suggested that sociology receive more formal recognition as a discipline and that interdisciplinary studies could offer a remedy to overspecialization and alienation from the public. This met with criticisms from the right, which accused him of promoting Marxism, materialism, and positivism and of seeking to undermine German Kultur.[5]

Musicologists, however, were not the typical Weimar professors. The immaturity of the discipline kept it from being fully accepted into the academy, and musicologists' activities outside the university made them less apprehensive of government interference and more open to some of the changes proposed by Weimar reformers. Having cultivated contacts with communities in their multiple roles as scholars, practitioners, and journalists, they were more comfortable with the Social Democratic ideals of forging ties outside the university. They were also more receptive to Becker's suggestions about interdisciplinary studies and methodologies derived from sociology and psychology, as they had initiated similar practices in the development of systematic and comparative musicology.

Although a comparatively large number of musicology departments and research institutions sprang up in Germany in the first decades of the twentieth century, numerous uncertainties lurked behind this expansion. World War I, for one, had had devastating effects on scholarship. Travel restrictions, a shortage of funds, and the dissolution of the International Music Society in 1914 and its *Sammelbände der Internationalen Musikgesellschaft* hampered research and stopped the flow of international scholarly exchange. The harsh realities of the Weimar economy set in soon thereafter: the costs of war, the inflation, and the job shortages caused by the return from the front of large numbers of unemployed musicologists. Dwindling state resources resulted in the disappearance of stipends and the suspension of such vital government-sponsored projects as the Denkmäler Deutscher Tonkunst. As Weimar officials attempted to bring higher education closer to the needs of the nation by expanding more practical research areas in universities,[6] the need to make the public aware of musicology's potential contribution to modern German life was felt with increasing urgency. If there was any consensus among the community of musicologists, it was that the discipline had entered a state of crisis after 1918. This feeling pervaded discussions about career options in the post-war economy, ruminations on the goals of newly established research and educational institutions, and methodological debates. In all these discussions, the same questions were raised: what was the role of musicology in modern German society, and how could musicologists address the economic, social, cultural, and political changes going on around them?

Musicologists frequently invoked the name of their predecessor Hermann Kretzschmar in these debates. In his well-known *Musikalische Zeitfragen* of 1903, Kretzschmar regarded the musicologist not only as a scholar but also as a commentator on current musical questions. In his view, it was the goal of the musicologist to bring a deeper understanding of music to the practicing musician and to the public at large rather than to serve other sciences.[7]

Some found it increasingly difficult to rationalize their research interests with the needs of society and were critical of ivory-tower isolation. Moser urged the public not to force scholars to compromise their talents but at the same time admonished his colleagues to pay more attention to issues of the day and find a middle ground between "dry specialization" and "cheap global aesthetics."[8] Two eminent scholars in Berlin, Arnold Schering and Johannes Wolf, had similar advice. Schering (b. 1877) had headed the university's musicology department since 1920 and was an expert on a variety of early music topics, including performance practice. He chided musicology for burying itself in the past and losing contact with modern composition. Johannes Wolf (b. 1869), director of the state library's early music collection and foremost expert in source studies and the history of notation, similarly stressed that musicology in the university needed to make itself more accessible to practicing musicians.[9]

Others held opposing views. Kretzschmar's successor at the University of Berlin, Hermann Abert, felt musicology had gone off in the wrong direction when it started to cast doubts on its philological orientations and defined its sole purpose as service to music performance. Without philology, Abert declared, musicology "would lose its honorable name as a science."[10] His insistence that the musician and musicologist "dwell in separate domiciles" and that musicology should evolve into an independent liberal science earned him credit for raising musicology to its incontestable position as a university discipline, worthy of chairs in Halle, Heidelberg, Berlin, and Leipzig.[11] Theodor Kroyer was similarly enraged that the purpose of musicological work be called into question. He complained that although detailed research work may appear "incomprehensible and useless for the Volksgemeinschaft" and less important than technology and material sciences, the power of music to bring salvation or misfortune justified even the most minute details of musicological scholarship. He concluded "that even musicology has a part in the obligatory common task of all university sciences to raise humanity from the present dissipation to a unified, whole being. State and municipality have given us this workshop — we too work for the state and the Volk!"[12]

Those seriously concerned with expanding the reach of the discipline filled the pages of the popular and music trade media with their views on a variety of topical issues. Their writings appeared in substantial numbers in journals for professional and amateur musicians and educators (*Deutsche Tonkünstlerzeitung, Die Musik, Allgemeine Musikzeitung, Melos, Deutsche Militär-Musiker Zeitung, Zeitschrift für Musik, Die Musikpflege, Collegium Musicum/Zeitschrift für Hausmusik, Deutsche Musikkultur, Völkische Musikerziehung, Musik in Jugend und Volk*), as well as many nonmusic journals (*Der Friede, Österreichische Rundschau, Deutsche Zeitschrift, Volk und Welt*, and *Nationalsozialistische Monatshefte*, to name a few). The press provided a forum for opinions and, potentially, suggestions in solving many of the problems in musical life. Some scholars used these avenues to seek a working relationship with other music professionals by taking an interest in the plight of musicians, education, modern music, and music technology, often offering advice to the government on how to reform cultural policy. The initiation of a new political order in 1918 and again in 1933 inspired a handful of scholars to concern themselves with music policy and recommend the creation of new institutions that would offer employment for musicologists. Both the Weimar Republic and the Third Reich, at least at the outset, showed interest in cultural reform, and musicologists welcomed these opportunities. In the end, however, they had little impact on actual policy.

Attempted Alliances with Musicians, Composers, and Educators in the Weimar Republic

Musicologists flaunted their expertise to try to instruct the state, making such recommendations as state support for music schools on the German borders ("the most important cultivators of Germanic culture"), minimal copyright guarantees for composers during their lifetimes, and distribution of music materials to students and amateurs through a better system of lending libraries.[13] The regional inconsistencies in cultural support jeopardized the careers of music professionals and guaranteed employment only for certain orchestra musicians, and Moser, in particular, championed the cause of musicians, private instructors, and composers by supporting the efforts of the Reich Association of German Composers and Music Teachers (Reichsverband deutscher Tonkünstler und Musiklehrer, which Moser called "the new Reich music guild").[14] Others came to the state's defense: the government could not be expected to rescue musical life from its current crisis single-handedly. The state had already made unprecedented advances in music education, improving the working conditions for private music teachers and delegating responsibilities of reform to practicing musicians rather than to bureaucrats.[15] One musicologist even proposed that the state should reduce its subsidies for musical events, since too many concerts were poorly attended and too many performances were of questionable quality. Instead of indulging the mere "exhibitionism of the bourgeoisie gone wild," the state should invest more selectively in education and publishing subsidies for "important" composers.[16]

Scholars tried to embrace the community of composers and to address their concerns about copyright and audience reception, but they failed to forge a strong alliance largely because of their lack of familiarity with contemporary music. In his keynote speech to the DMG in 1925, Arnold Schering encouraged a healthy relationship between the two professions, criticizing scholars who were more familiar with minutiae of the remote past than with dominant features of the recent past and imploring his colleagues to learn to approach modern music on its own terms.[17] As musicologists offered their views on the situation of modern music, however, they found themselves entangled in wider debates, and often political rhetoric crept into their statements.[18] Theodor Kroyer's views of modern music displayed an unabashed nationalism and alarmist conservatism; he warned against "the heralds of 'new music,' the most evil despisers of the old generation, who stir up confusion in a Bolshevist manner in order to speed up the violent collapse and set up *their* culture on the rubble of the old."[19] Schering, too, lapsed into political metaphors, describing the harmonic aspects of expressionist music as a "democratization" of concordances and a dissolution of earlier "class distinctions" among tones.[20] Nationalism and racial sentiments also left their mark on musicological interpretation of modern music. Ernst Bücken's *Führer und Probleme der neuen Musik* focused heavily on late German Romanticists and regarded impressionism and expressionism as regressive and the racial mixing in Saint-Säens's school of exoticism as severely limited.[21]

Musicologists made some isolated attempts to quiet the politicized controversies over modern music by looking at it in a broader historical context. Johannes Wolf drew a comparison between the resistance to some music during the Renaissance due to its use of mathematical techniques and the problems faced by Schoenberg and his school, hoping to illustrate that one must come to terms with seemingly radical musical techniques in all eras.[22] Hans Mersmann similarly declared the modern era as the beginning of a new musical epoch, comparable to the epochs dominated by monophony, polyphony, and tonality.[23] But even those who advocated patience and tolerance could not overlook the difficulties most modern music posed to the general public. If such music did possess an inner beauty, they could not immediately perceive it. One could blame the public's alienation on a gap in education, such as in the training of music teachers, in which early music skills were stressed and contemporary works were ignored.[24] One could also blame the recalcitrance of the bourgeois concert audiences,[25] but modern music still posed problems for some musicologists who tried to confront it systematically. Austrian musicologist Alfred Orel criticized the artificiality of atonal music, the predominance of theory over evolution of form and harmony, and, above all, the absence of "humanity in music."[26] Reactionaries such as Karl Blessinger, later renowned as the author of the notorious anti-Semitic tract, *Judentum und Musik,* attacked modern music as a national affront and condemned the invention of new scales as exemplified in the work of the Slav Alois Haba as meaningless for the German psyche and too far removed from the collective musical feeling of the Volk.[27] Those who championed modern music were also frustrated by their inability to comprehend newer trends: Mersmann lamented the decline in the emotional content of music—even in the works of Strauss and Mahler—and Schering sadly admitted that the musical meaning of expressionist composition eluded him and failed to provide him with the "joy of living" music offered.[28]

Even before the Nazis came to power, musicologists were losing interest in the burning issues of modern music, probably because such issues had already been extinguished.[29] In the 1920s, Mersmann had explained Schoenberg's alienation from the public as "the burden of the prophet": Schoenberg was a visionary whose message would be fully appreciated in the future but who had to endure ridicule until then, yet one could look forward to the creations of his followers Alois Haba and Ernst Krenek.[30] But by 1932, Moser was labeling Schoenberg and his school zealots whose time had passed. They had been surpassed by more promising younger contemporaries and the growth of amateur performance. Krenek, one of the up-and-coming, had matured from a "cacaphonist in the good graces of atonality" to show a "fortunate return to 'comprehensible' music."[31]

Musicologists continued to offer suggestions and criticisms throughout the late 1920s and 1930s, but they acted more in the role of social commentators. They were especially vocal about the state's reforms of music education. Around the turn of the century, scholars such as Kretzschmar and Abert were influential in shaping school and conservatory curricula, but this changed drastically after 1918.[32] In the postwar wave of educational reform, younger musicologists hoped to inherit some of this influence, or at least to preserve the spirit of Kretzschmar's program by retaining singing instruction as the central component in elementary education.[33] Some even suggested that musicologists exclusively supervise music teachers' certification and instruction in elementary schools, middle schools, and adult education.[34]

But as music education gained the status of an independent profession under Kestenberg's guidance, the input of musicologists became less welcome. Strains of nationalism and anti-Semitism crept into musicological responses to the new reforms: Moser referred to the special duty of Germans to take music seriously, because they were and always would be the "Volk der Musik," and criticized Kestenberg's "Jewish-communist educational experiments."[35] All musicologists could realistically hope for was to convince bureaucrats and pedagogues of the importance of both historical and systematic musicology for music education. Georg Schünemann, Bruno Stäblein, and Joseph Müller-Blattau made separate, simultaneous pleas urging music educators to look specifically to musicology when forming a curriculum and to consider all new developments in popular music and technology.[36]

Left out of the policy-making procedures in music education, musicologists turned to noncurricular education or Volksbildung, a movement that had its roots in the bourgeois notion of *Bildung* and spread during the Weimar years to encompass the duty to educate all social classes. The state's conception of Volksbildung relied on the socialist ideal that encouraged and even required high culture to become the common property of all classes. One way the government proposed to do this was to provide reduced-price tickets to cultural events for workers and to sponsor after-hours classes and lectures.

Volksbildung in music went far beyond the schools and aimed to bridge the gap between music and the Volk. Musicologists believed themselves capable of participating in this process, first by explaining the historical roots of the problem to the general public, and second by enlightening the masses to the subtleties of the musical art. In interpretations of music history appearing in the nonscholarly press, scholars explained that social class had always been reflected in different categories of music,[37] that the music of the nineteenth century had become too subjective and alienated from the Volk, and that this alienation could be linked to the many ills of modern society. Additionally, some blamed technology for setting off a spiritual decline and inspiring a reverence for flashy technique,[38] while others blamed materialism, which allowed artists to be subjective and egocentric and lose their connection with the public.[39] Despite the attempts by the Weimar Republic to bring music closer to the people, the virtuoso continued to thrive on a snobbish elitism carried over from the Wilhelmine age.[40]

Musicologists began to espouse the belief that music should return to serving the Volk and saw a role for themselves in this process. As early as 1918, Johannes Wolf described the musicologist as fulfilling the "noblest task, that of public education (*Volkserziehung*)."[41] Others offered suggestions to educators, composers, and the state, counseling the cultivation of folk music, encouragement of amateur participation,[42] and a reshaping of the goals of modern composition.[43] Hans Mersmann asked the state to implement a system of public education by setting up programs to cultivate folk music, to organize public concerts in urban centers and smaller towns and villages, and to provide lectures and workshops in music appreciation.[44] Egon Wellesz offered similar suggestions, proposing that the state appoint committees to organize and promote concerts for workers and to make music a part of everyday life through education.[45]

Weimar politicians considered music an effective means of mitigating the divisiveness in post-war German society.[46] Musicologists, too, believed that music was a crucial leveling device in the new democracy and a means to unify the German nation. Georg Schünemann, Wilibald Gurlitt, Leo Schrade, and Joseph Müller-Blattau, to name a few, echoed the belief that music could smooth over differences, that communal music making could heal the wounds dividing German society, and that general music education was the means toward this end.[47]

Scholars not only wrote about but also actively participated in Volksbildung by taking part in workers' adult education programs. Some quickly learned, however, that the realization of their ideals was more difficult than they imagined. Kretzschmar had already admonished that despite the good intentions of the socialists, the growing gap between the music of the bourgeoisie and the music of the worker could not be bridged simply by reducing the prices of tickets.[48] Egon Wellesz similarly warned against force-feeding culture to the proletariat.[49] Indeed, scholars emerged from the academy poorly prepared for the responses of an uneducated public. Moser complained bitterly of the low honoraria he received giving lectures for the purpose of "Bildung zum Volke" and the frustrations of putting his proletarian audiences to sleep with his scholarly lectures. He endorsed Volksbildung in principle but criticized its application, insisting that audiences receive more preparation and rejecting the myth of the "education-hungry" common people.[50]

Musicology and the Amateur Movement, 1918–1945

Fortunately for them, musicologists had skills other than lecturing with which to reach out to the public. Taking note of the huge growth of amateur musical activities, they responded with their usual learned commentaries but also made more tangible contributions to this movement. In the end, musicologists wielded far more influence in the amateur arena than in education, professional issues, or politics. With their historical knowledge, experience as music directors, and skills as editors of early music, musicologists were well equipped to highlight the important function of amateur music making throughout German history, advise on performance practice, and furnish amateurs with performable repertoire from lesser-known German composers. Their growing mastery of German music history served a variety of nationalistic ends, and their contributions to the amateur movement became their most successful ventures outside the academy, living on beyond the Weimar Republic into the Third Reich as their most valuable service to the "people's community."

The emergence of the amateur movement allowed musicologists to enlighten the public to historical precedents and to interpret the amateur's significance for modern society. Moser, as part of his campaign to defend the rights of professional musicians, published a mildly polemical historical survey of the distinctions between amateur and professional, attempting to show that Northern Europe always cultivated the professional more than Southern Europe, where amateurs prevailed, and concluding that the professional and amateur spheres must acknowledge who they are, must not try to traverse their boundaries, and must learn to respect one another.[51] But the amateur revival fit in well with a socialist perception of the history of music as well.

Music historians noted a marked decline in Hausmusik in the late nineteenth century that coincided with a bourgeois admiration for virtuosi, and they attributed its recent rebirth to the growing awareness of the needs of the masses for musical expression.[52] This depiction of Hausmusik as a prebourgeois phenomenon was in harmony with the ideals of the Weimar leaders.[53]

Musicologists also offered practical advice to the state and music industries. As a relatively informal and an inexpensive way to enjoy music, Hausmusik thrived in the Weimar Republic when the depression severely reduced normal concert attendance and created a demand for home entertainment.[54] Musicologists, citing Hugo Riemann's early contributions to its promotion,[55] considered themselves authorities in this area and offered practical suggestions for its further development. Johannes Wolf, illustrating the importance of Hausmusik through the ages, proposed that a healthy cultivation of Hausmusik in the home, school, and youth movement was the only antidote to the mechanization of music and a sure way for German music to preserve its leading position in the world.[56] Eugen Schmitz recommended economic measures to encourage Hausmusik, suggesting that cheaper instruments, such as the guitar and the clavichord, be mass produced to replace the more expensive lute and piano, and that the state circumvent the paper shortage by driving up the prices of "useless" entertainment music and keeping the prices of art music at a minimum.[57] These suggestions resonated with those of Jugendmusikbewegung leaders, who also tried to promote the revival of such early instruments as the recorder, the viola da gamba, and the harpsichord and encouraged using alternate instruments, such as the guitar instead of the lute, for music otherwise considered obsolete.[58] In 1932, Schünemann reiterated the need to encourage Hausmusik, not only because its long history demonstrated German musical superiority, but also because it benefited the music and publishing industries.[59]

For the most part, however, Weimar-era musicologists directed their energies toward approaching amateurs directly, publishing information for wider audiences, and sometimes taking an active part in their organizations. A number of prominent musicologists (Schering, Schünemann, Max Friedländer, Moser, and Fritz Stein) appeared at the first conference of the independent Task Force for German Choral Societies (Arbeitsgemeinschaft für das Deutsche Chorgesangwesen) in 1928. In the presence of state officials, many of them expressed their concerns that choral societies needed to be promoted as a community-building activity and supported by the state and municipalities to counteract the public's exaggerated enthusiasm for sports and cinema.[60]

The Jugendmusikbewegung also had long-standing links with musicologists, deriving many of its ideas from the writings of Ernst Kurth and August

Halm and drawing a few scholars into some of its more controversial issues, such as the problems of leadership and criticism of its "pseudoaesthetic."[61] Younger scholars in particular (those born after 1890) were active in the youth movement. A number of musicologists who would make names for themselves as scholars in Germany and abroad, including Hans Joachim Moser, Joseph Müller-Blattau, Hans Mersmann, Walther Lipphardt, Friedrich Blume, Wilibald Gurlitt, Heinrich Besseler, Manfred Bukofzer, and Wilhelm Ehmann, played prominent roles in conferences, performances, retreats, and publications.[62] Mersmann served as coeditor of *Das Neue Werk,* a collection of contemporary works, along with Fritz Jöde, the founder of the movement, and Paul Hindemith; and Moser and Müller-Blattau served on the editorial board of the periodical *Die Singgemeinde.*[63] Some of these same scholars, trained in the old-fashioned philological tradition of historical musicology, later redirected their work toward folk music research and traced this interest to their experiences in the youth movement.[64]

At the onset of the Third Reich, many more musicologists joined the continued effort to cultivate a relationship with the amateur. In contrast to the youth movement, only a few assumed prominent roles in Nazi amateur musical organizations: Gotthold Frotscher served served as music consultant for the Reich Youth Leadership and editor of its journal, and Siegfried Goslich was music consultant in the Deutsches Volksbildungswerk division of KdF.[65] But musicologists continued to peddle their wares to the public as historians, music directors, and editors of early music.

Periodicals dedicated to amateur music begun in the late 1920s and early 1930s had already offered opportunities for musicologists to reach the amateur. In addition, the year 1932 marked the first national Hausmusik celebration ("Tag der deutschen Hausmusik") and the establishment of a new Hausmusik periodical (originally entitled *Collegium Musicum,* its name was changed to *Zeitschrift für Hausmusik* in its second year). The first issues featured articles by Müller-Blattau on early music performance practice and the history and repertoire of string instruments.[66] Later volumes, especially those from 1937 to 1942, included contributions by musicologists Moser, Gurlitt, Ehmann, and others, guiding readers to sources for repertoire, outlining the history of amateur music making, and teaching basic elements of music.[67] The same was true of the choral journal *Die Musikpflege,* founded in 1930 but including contributions from well-known musicologists (Wolf, Blume, Bücken, and others) only after 1934, when it became subsumed under the Reich Music Chamber.[68]

Singing the praises of the noble amateurs, musicologists continued to focus attention on their needs and limitations, advising educators and composers to help cultivate amateur music in their instruction and works.[69] The only differences between Weimar-era and Nazi-era statements was a modification in language that paid homage to Nazi leadership. Fritz Stein, for example, stressed the importance of choral singing as a communal activity, but he claimed that only after the National Socialist revolution could choral groups transcend class division,[70] even though the so-called bourgeois and proletarian choral societies had long since ceased to uphold any class identity in their membership or repertoire. Such statements try to portray the growth of the amateur movement as a National Socialist phenomenon, but in fact they echo practices and principles established during the Weimar Republic and continue to highlight the socialist goals of the amateur movement.

The continued reliance on socialist ideals into the Nazi era came out in the discussions of the term "Hausmusik." Friedrich Blume set out to disassociate the term from its bourgeois connotations, redefining it as a practice that stretched back to the time of Luther — a time in which music's accessibility, feelings of community, and religious emotion were more important than expressions of individuality — and drawing comparisons to the contemporary function of Hausmusik.[71] Hausmusik in its narrower, bourgeois-era connotation had clearly outlived its purpose with the decline of the bourgeoisie, the economic crisis, and the proliferation of radio and recording technologies. Hausmusik in the broader historical sense, however, could apply to the increase in amateur participation taking place since World War I, could embrace vocal as well as instrumental music, and could move in any direction, whether in the form of a revival of early Baroque and pre-Baroque works or in developing new types of musical expression.[72]

Blume's suggestion to amateurs to turn to classical and preclassical music was part of a broader musicological initiative to promote music of the past as the mainstay of amateur repertoire. This music could serve as the model for contemporary Hausmusik in the broader, nonbourgeois sense, because much of it had been intended as a type of Gebrauchsmusik,[73] and acquaintance with music from Germany's past, in particular, could strengthen pride in national identity. Hausmusik was presented as an all-encompassing activity of the entire community and a central component of unique German proclivities for community spirit and hospitality. Old German Hausmusik dating to the Middle Ages could serve as a rich source for capturing the true spirit of German communal music making.[74] One could turn to some lesser-known, easier works of Bach and sons and even to the formerly spurned bourgeois composers Mozart, Haydn, Beethoven, and the Romantics to see that the amateur-friendly character of Hausmusik was never lost in German music.[75]

Musicologists undoubtedly harbored ulterior motives in promoting this music, having invested heavily in its proliferation in their research and music editing. Since the turn of the century, and more so since the end of the war, the public had exhibited an unprecedented interest in early music, imploring musicologists to pay attention to the performance needs of amateurs in their production of editions and in their studies on performance practice.[76] The loudest wake-up call to musicologists came when the Denkmäler Deutscher Tonkunst was forced to suspend its publication in 1919 for lack of funding, after thirty years of uninterrupted activity that yielded nearly sixty volumes of works by German masters. Scholars had complained that the Denkmäler were never fully appreciated or utilized by practicing musicians,[77] but the suspension of their publication caused the editors to realize that they had to meet the public halfway. A joint task force of musicologists and Prussian officials sponsoring the project resolved that the Denkmäler would resume publication only after undergoing significant changes: future editions would publish their critical commentary as a separate volume and would be designed in a performance-ready format with the amateur market in mind. Musicologists additionally stepped up their activities in producing other performable editions of early music in such series as *Das Chorwerk, Nägels Musik-Archiv, Kammersonaten, Organum, Das Chorbuch des Musikanten,* and *Musikalische Formen in historischen Reihen,* and in initiating a number of regional Denkmal projects.[78]

On the eve of the Nazi takeover, musicologists were already deeply engaged in publicizing early music. In 1929, Blessinger was lauding his colleagues' efforts in providing resources for the amateur movement, although he feared that the amateurs' heavy reliance on early music might have grown out of contemporary composers' failure to produce effective Gebrauchsmusik.[79] Moser reached out to amateur orchestras, praising their community-building benefits but emphasizing that such groups required special repertoire, much of which could be found in early music and in the works of lesser-known composers of the nineteenth century.[80] As editors of early music repertoire, musicologists recognized the opportunity to turn a scholarly preoccupation into a useful enterprise. In the promotion of early music performance they found the most tangible and convincing demonstration of their service to the community without abandoning their research initiatives. Scholars encouraged early music performance, drew attention to newly discovered works of long-forgotten masters, and exposed the community to the fruits of their labors by facilitating local performances with the collegium groups many of them directed. A revival of early music performance gave musicologists the opportunity to maintain their standards of scholarship, secure government funding for the continuation of editing projects, gain a foothold in the music publishing industry, and demonstrate their connection to the Volk by reaching out to the growing community of amateurs.

Musicologists' Role in the Nazi State

The promise of sweeping cultural reforms in 1933 encouraged musicologists to renew their efforts to increase their political influence in the new system, efforts that had proved futile in the Weimar Republic. The younger generation especially showed great enthusiasm in the first few years of Hitler's Reich, adopting a variety of slogans about bonding musicology with the Volk to argue for the creation of government posts for musicologists. The implicit hope was that the new state would allow musicologists to influence the course of music policy. The unasked questions, however, were what the state would gain from investing in this relatively small and unknown discipline, and what musicology's service to the Reich would entail.

In an effort to address these concerns, the Deutsche Gesellschaft für Musikwissenschaft (or DGMW, the name given to the DMG after 1933) focused its June 1935 meeting on musicology's function in the new state. The establishment of the Propaganda Ministry and the Reich Culture Chamber and the resulting Gleichschaltung of numerous existing organizations gave members of the society reason to wonder about the fate of the organization. In order to clarify the society's position on its role in the new state, president Arnold Schering asked three prominent members (Ludwig Schiedermair, Ernst Bücken, and Rudolf Steglich) to give short presentations on musicologists' responsibilities in public music events, in lecturing activities, and in propaganda. Schiedermair (b. 1876) had headed the musicology department in Bonn since 1915, was founder and director of the internationally known Beethoven Archives, and was active in the administration of both the DGMW and the music section of the Deutsche Akademie. Bücken (b. 1884) had established the musicology department in Cologne; distinguished himself as the general editor of the multivolume *Handbuch der Musikwissenschaft,* as well as the *Handbuch der Musikerziehung* and the biography series Die grossen Meister der Musik; and had published several commentaries on the state of musicology. Steglich (b. 1886), head of the musicology department in Erlangen, was a key player in the Handel revival in the 1920s, served as editor of the *Händel-Jahrbuch,* and was about to assume the editorship of the society's journal. The central concern of all three contributors was that, on the one hand, musicology needed to convince the state of its necessity but, on the other hand, any regulations recommended by the government should be kept under the control of the musicologists themselves.

Owing to time constraints, the presentations could not be made at the annual meeting but were published in the journal instead. Steglich addressed the question of the society's potential role as an agent of propaganda ("Zum Propagandawesen der Deutschen Gesellschaft für Musikwissenschaft"). Since, according to Steglich, musicology was already a form of propaganda, any kind of regulation of its *Propagandawesen* could consist of only a few additional precautions to clarify the purpose of musicology to the public: keeping close communication with the daily press and popular journals; maintaining ties with critics and other writers on music; encouraging cooperation with musicians, music educators, and the general public; and thereby demonstrating "that musicology exists, that it is necessary, that it is vital."[81] Bücken also supported the notion that musicology should make itself available for propaganda purposes. Addressing the question of musicologists as lecturers ("Das musikwissenschaftliche Vortragswesen"), he recommended that musicology focus more on "current questions" (*Zeitfragen*) in Kretzschmar's sense, confronting new problems with "the sharp weapon of the spoken word," the most urgent of the new Zeitfragen being the questions of racial research and music policy. He believed in regulating public lectures to make discussions of pressing issues accessible to both expert and amateur. As lecturers, musicologists should offer their services to student organizations, subscription services (specifically the NS-Kulturgemeinde), radio, and cultural exchange with ethnic Germans in outlying regions (by working with the Propaganda Ministry and the Deutsche Akademie). These activities, however, had to be carried out within the scholarly society, which would regulate — but not censor — musicological lectures.[82]

The most sweeping statements came from Schiedermair, who would later succeed Schering as president of the society and bring the organization into closer cooperation with the Nazi Education Ministry and the Propaganda Ministry. In his statements on musicologists' participation in musical events with historical significance ("Beteiligung der deutschen Musikwissenschaftler an öffentlichen Musikfeiern historischen Gepräges"), he stressed the responsibility of musicology to overcome its inferiority complex, to emerge "conscious of Volk and full of strength" and attach itself to the larger cultural framework, and to prevent the new Reich from excluding it from taking part in the reorganization of musical life. This should be done, of course, by directing historical research toward reinforcing the national consciousness and by initiating an active involvement in musical life. Such involvement had, in the days of Kretzschmar, been a primary force in musicology but weakened as the discipline became more specialized and lost its connection to the Volk.[83] From these statements one can detect that musicologists were still trying to find their niche in society, still striving to influence the course of music policy, but also fearing state interference in their internal affairs.

The avenues of influencing music education policy remained closed as before. Despite its overhaul of cultural administration, the Nazi regime did little to reform music education, and the professionalization of music educators continued along Kestenberg's guidelines after 1933, although officially he was discredited because he was a Jew.[84] Only in Austria, where musicologists started dealing with German bureaucracy after the *Anschluss* in 1938, were there any attempts to influence music education policy. Erich Schenk, head of the musicology department at the University of Vienna, drafted a lengthy proposal to the Reich Education Ministry in December 1940 suggesting that a new curriculum for music educators be subsumed under his own musicology department, but his proposal was summarily rejected by the ministry.[85] Otherwise, there was no need to undo Kestenberg's beneficial work, especially since the Nazi state promised to continue to stress education as one of the most powerful means of shaping the thinking and insuring total commitment of current and future generations. As a gesture to the ostensible commitment to education, the journal of the Reich Association of German Composers and Music Teachers changed its name from *Deutsche Tonkünstlerzeitung* (German Composer's Newspaper) to *Der Musikerzieher* (The Music Educator), turning from the bourgeois notion of music as an expression of the free artistic spirit (symbolized by the composer) to the educational function of music in service to the community (symbolized by the music teacher).

For the most part, musicologists continued merely to offer advice and promote more emphasis on musicological skills in education, adding up-to-date political and ideological rhetoric to bolster their suggestions. Karl Gustav Fellerer, director of the musicology department in Cologne since 1939 and a distinguished scholar of Catholic church music, insisted that music educators be well versed in all branches of musicology, both historical and systematic, to refine their understanding of biological processes, talent types, and racial differences and to present early music to students as a living art and an "indication of the intellectual creative strength of the Volk."[86] Alfred Quellmalz additionally demanded that educators have a command of the minutiae of folk music research and use their acquired knowledge of racial differences to determine the acceptable or degenerate traits of art music to convey to students the elements of German essence.[87] When Erich Valentin argued for a more stringent music history requirement for music educators, he relied on the adage that "the education ideal of the new state is the same as that of its political goal: totality."[88] Praise of the new state could also cushion the blow of criticizing the government. Fritz Stein (b. 1879) held a professorship in Kiel, where he was also active as a conductor. He became director of the Berlin conservatory in 1933 and worked for the Reich Music Chamber to promote choral activity in the Third Reich. Extolling the National Socialist regime's emphasis on education, Stein bemoaned the fact that more money went into theater productions than into educating the next generation of musicians. To add insult to injury, he claimed, this money was not going to promote German music, but rather the cost for one state-subsidized production of a *foreign* opera could have supported twenty German music students for three years.[89]

Musicologists still publicized their commitment to Volksbildung but here, too, adapted its parameters to the new ideology. The designation Volk no longer referred to the proletariat but rather to the German nation. Scholars confounded the distinction between high and low culture by insisting that the music of the Volk correspond to indigenous German music, including serious music,[90] and that entertainment music (Unterhaltungs- und Gebrauchsmusik), which would have been considered low culture and hence the music of the masses, was in fact mostly the work of alien races, was degenerate, and was to be excluded from any program of Volksbildung. From that point on, musical Volksbildung would have to be directed toward "forming humanity out of the given *völkisch* inheritance and racial make-up" and strengthening the "biological organism of the völkisch structure."[91]

The continued interest in Volksbildung enabled musicologists to make another smooth transition from socialism to National Socialism. The nineteenth-century cultivated bourgeoisie (*Bildungsbürgertum*) remained the common enemy, for it had outgrown its usefulness either for a proletarian society or for the new German nation. In an article that first appeared in the Nazi party organ, the *Völkischer Beobachter,* in 1934, Gotthold Frotscher echoed the sentiments of music pedagogues of the 1920s that music education could bind the disparate social classes and that bourgeois conventions should yield to the needs of Volksbildung, but he framed his statement in terms of new possibilities offered by the Nazi state.[92] Frotscher advanced in academe in the Third Reich, gaining a position on the Berlin faculty and receiving acclaim for his history of organ music, while keeping his hand in the musical activities of the Hitler Youth. Werner Korte (b. 1906), head of the musicology department in Münster since 1932, also juxtaposed pure socialist sentiments with the stated goals of Hitler and Rosenberg, attacking the bourgeois concert hall as a superficial institution and suggesting that these facilities be exploited for their educational potential, teaching the public how to distinguish between music emanating from the German essence and degenerate charlatanism of Jews and virtuosi. Anti-Semitism merged neatly with attacks against the bourgeois cultural legacy, since it was already commonplace to link nineteenth-century individualism and the alienation of music from the Volk with the chicanery of Jews allegedly dominating cultural life, and to blame Schoenberg and Jewish critics for confusing value judgments.[93]

A new term "Volksmusik," referring to the musical education of both the youth and adult populations, became more widely used to distinguish a National Socialist version of musical Volksbildung from earlier agendas. This National Socialist concept of "Volksmusik" could allegedly be traced to Hermann Kretzschmar, and there were even attempts to imbue Kretzschmar's character with National Socialist leanings. Hermann Halbig claimed that Kretzschmar had a philosophical bond with Walther Schultze-Naumburg, a pioneer in racial theory, because both were present at a conference on education; he highlighted Kretzschmar's noble lineage, "Germanness," and "unshakable *völkisch* roots"; and he promoted the Nazi state as providing the best circumstances for realizing Kretzschmar's goals.[94] But the term also had deep roots in the youth movement, where it referred to the music of the entire nation and encompassed both high and low culture.[95] The Jugendmusikbewegung, despite having fallen into disrepute due to its alleged "Marxist Weltanschauung,"[96] continued to serve as a source of inspiration for musicologists interested in Volksbildung. The concept of Volksmusik was modified only slightly to claim it as a National Socialist directive. Fritz Stein alluded to Hitler's requirement of fanaticism toward learning among artists and saw this as a prerequisite for achieving the goal of "Volksmusikkultur" [quotation marks are his],[97] and Goslich acknowledged the influence of the pre-1933 youth movement in outlining the methods and goals of Volksmusik but nevertheless gave most of the credit to the Nazi state.[98] He derived the Nazi party's intention to broaden the concept of music education from Paragraph 20 of the party program (the item addressing educational reform that expresses aims closely resembling those of the Weimar reformers) and listed the contribution of various party and government organizations.[99] He described the replacement of private instruction with "work groups" and the establishment and successes of Volksmusik schools as a goal which could only be realized after Hitler's rise to power,[100] and he reported huge successes throughout the Reich since 1937 in cultivating activities in villages, factories, and schools, often in collaboration with local Hitler Youth. Goslich (b. 1911) earned a doctorate in musicology in Berlin in 1936 but soon focused his career on service to the state and party. As music consultant for the Deutsches Volksbildungswerk in the KdF, Goslich directed its energies toward educating workers through daily musical activity at the workplace; instruction and participation in music groups; and introductory lectures on symphony, chamber music, opera, and music history delivered by musicologists and others. He envisioned a future quasimilitaristic workday filled with music that would accompany waking, flag-raising, working, eating, recreation, and retiring.[101]

In reality, musicologists had little impact on setting standards for music practice, music policy, or music aesthetics. In Nazi Germany, as in the Weimar Republic, musicologists offered suggestions for educational and political reform but did not have an active role in establishing policy. To the extent that they addressed issues of music and politics (*Musikpolitik*) at all, they tended to focus on its philosophical and historical meanings, leaving the actual decisions and implementations of policy to bureaucrats.

A few musicologists had begun to reflect on the implications of linking music with politics after the stock market crash in 1929, observing that freelance music professions belonged to an era of liberalism and were doomed in a country intent on socialization.[102] In 1932, Karl Blessinger wrote that music had become powerless to resist attaching itself to political parties, despite the risk of becoming a signboard for a party's cultural interests. Blessinger saw the postwar period as a time of unfulfilled promises to renew musical life and an era fraught with the nagging problem of music's inaccessibility to the Volk. His only suggestion to liberate music from political powers was to fortify it through public education.[103]

Musicologists expounded a bit more on the concept of Musikpolitik with Hitler's ascendancy, despite isolated warnings of partisan exploitation of the term and growing disregard for the creative essence of music.[104] In 1933, two musicologists came forth as early apologists for the new order and its policies. One was Peter Raabe, the Liszt scholar and conductor in Aachen who later rose to prominence as Richard Strauss's successor as president of the Reich Music Chamber. Raabe was better known as an administrator and performer than as a musicologist. He received his doctorate at age forty-four, served on the board of the Allgemeiner Deutscher Musikverein from 1920 until its dissolution in 1937, and considered himself anything but an educator despite his part-time appointments in Aachen and Königsberg.[105] His numerous essays and speeches on music policy predate his appointment to the Reich Music Chamber by at least seven years[106] and came to outweigh by far his contributions to music scholarship.

The other musicologist to emerge as an early apologist for the Nazi state was Karl Gustav Fellerer, a German scholar who worked in Switzerland until his return to Germany in 1939. Unlike Raabe, Fellerer was a highly respected researcher with a specialization in Catholic church music, thus his interest in Musikpolitik is somewhat more surprising than that of Raabe, the organizer and public figure. Within months of Hitler's seizure of power, Fellerer issued an impassioned statement in the *Deutsche Tonkünstler-Zeitung,* hoping to explain to skeptics why the current political developments in Nazi Germany should be welcomed. He simultaneously published a lengthier version of this apology in the *Schweizerische Rundschau,* a Swiss monthly journal for cultural issues, defending some of the shocking steps already taken by German censors and inviting Swiss Germans to share in the benefits of a strong German national identity.

The language of the two articles clearly indicates that Fellerer was speaking from true conviction. He identified a gradual dissolution of German art in the recent past at the hands of the "art for art's sake" doctrine and in the toleration of all styles. The new Nazi state, in Fellerer's view, would effect an "equalization" (using the terms *Gleichordnung* and *Gleichorientierung,* similar to the term Gleichschaltung) and direct art toward expressing the thoughts and feelings of the nation, as in ancient Greece and in Eastern cultures. In music, this could be accomplished only through isolation and protection from outside influences; this would allow German music to find its inner strength. Even the Nazis' controversial prohibition on jazz radio broadcasts jibed with Fellerer's views on aesthetics and cultural history. Just as the ancient Greeks recognized the power of music to change society and the need to regulate music closely, the Nazi state was justified in imposing restrictions on jazz and foreign musical influences toward developing national art and education.[107]

In the Swiss version of this article, Fellerer further explained that the Nazis' early restrictions on jazz in radio and in certain locales were not police actions, but rather had deeper meaning for "inter-German relationships"; the Nazi state was not a "police state," but rather a "destiny-community rooted in the *Volkstum.*"[108] Such steadfast support of the goals of the Nazi state, which extended to defending censorship and exhorting Germans living both within and outside the Reich to support the cause, reveal his strong feelings toward the preservation of German Kultur, perhaps a symptom of living in the multicultural state of Switzerland. It comes as no surprise that Fellerer gladly accepted the opportunity to return to Germany in 1939 when he succeeded Kroyer as head of the musicology department in Cologne.

Fellerer's rationalization was followed by other musicologists' enthusiastic endorsements of Nazi music policy. Heinrich Besseler (b. 1900) had distinguished himself with his extensive scholarly work on the music of the Middle Ages, the Renaissance, and J. S. Bach. On the Heidelberg faculty since 1928, he had also participated in the music activities of the youth movement. In the course of the Third Reich, he became increasingly involved in extracurricular services to promote the interests of the Nazi state in the field of musicology, yet he rarely published any politically charged statements. Thus his speech to the philologists' conference in Trier in 1934, published in the form of a second-hand summary, is noteworthy. It cites events in which a strong connection between music and the nation engendered "inner strength," tapped into "creative primal strengths," allowed musically strong nations to "follow internally ruled biological necessity," and let "original musical talent" arise from the "people's community" in a protected environment of "internal isolation." Besseler strongly approved of the situation in Nazi Germany and regarded nascent music organizations and festivals as "potential frameworks for a new high art, which in its highest self-realization grows organically out of the whole."[109]

Others drew further parallels between ancient Greece and modern Germany. This tendency can be traced to the Bismarck era in such disciplines as archaeology, when the state invested heavily in excavations of ancient Greek sites and built opulent museums to house their treasures. Linking Nazi Germany with ancient Greece also served as a counterbalance to Mussolini's claims of reviving the glory of the Roman Empire. Although musicologists had used ancient Greece as a standard for assessing modern musical life as early as the 1920s,[110] the Platonic state took on special significance as a model for the Nazi coordination of cultural life.[111] As part of the 1938 musicological conference that took place at the Düsseldorf Reichsmusiktage, the first organized musicological event in the new Reich,[112] one session was dedicated to the topic of "State and Music" and drew significantly on the theme of Platonic ethos. The session was chaired by Besseler and featured his paper entitled "Music and State" (probably the same talk he delivered in Trier in 1934), along with papers by Rudolf Steglich and Gerhard Pietzsch, both of which (at least in their published versions) exploited the Platonic connection.[113]

Many of these musicological discussions used Plato's blueprints for a closed and highly regulated society as a basis for formulating vague guidelines for a Musikpolitik for the Nazi state, but they usually fell short of offering concrete suggestions. Fellerer, for example, described the ancient system in such a way as to make an unmistakable connection between Plato's admonitions about the power of music and the Nazis' rejection of jazz,[114] but he failed to offer specific parameters for acceptable music in the Nazi state. Similarly, Pietzsch found parallels between the Platonic ideal of education and the accomplishments of Nazi party organizations and cited Plato's instructions to composers, but he could arrive at nothing more than vague recommendations for the types of music the Nazi state should encourage, suggesting only that rhythm builds community but melody and harmony do not.[115] Steglich went one step further in attempting to assign specific roles to such musical elements as melody and rhythm in the new state, producing a theoretical model for setting standards for acceptable music, but again to no real avail. He managed to conclude only that the repertoire of patriotic songs and Nazi "songs of struggle" (*Kampf-lieder*), especially the Horst Wessel Song (the SA march adopted as a Nazi national anthem), somehow fulfilled his highly ambiguous criteria.[116]

A few other musicologists struggled to find criteria for musical standards in the Nazi state. Werner Korte attributed the problems of modern music to the bourgeois institutions of the nineteenth century, which extolled virtuosity and genius regardless of comprehensibility, to the point where modern music had become a "museum" enterprise, but he admitted to failing to find any contemporary music that could bear the "National Socialist stamp."[117] Otherwise, musicologists generally retreated from such discussions. They had, up to that point, shown little interest in any of the objects of Nazi derision — such as jazz and popular music — and had only commented sporadically on the problems of modern music. Overt challenges to a Nazi musical ideal from the avant-garde ceased to be a problem by 1933, by which time the prominent, defamed atonal composers had emigrated. Any other discussions of degenerate music rarely came from the ranks of trained musicologists, with the exception of Herbert Gerigk and a few others.[118] Gerigk, an ardent National Socialist, head of the music department of Alfred Rosenberg's operation, and editor of *Die Musik,* occasionally aired his view on modern art music and popular music, frequently attacking Schoenberg, jazz, and other such degenerate musical manifestations and employing elaborate racial arguments to justify his rejection,[119] but he was merely elaborating on Rosenberg's ideological extremism rather than providing aesthetic criteria that could be used as a basis for policy.

Historian Michael Meyer has, on several occasions, claimed that musicologists in the Third Reich determined music policy and guidelines for censorship. In doing so, however, he consistently draws on the writings and activities of journalists, general historians, and attorneys rather than on musicologists.[120] Creating a true Musikpolitik for the Nazi state was not going to be the work of musicologists. First, musicologists in both the Weimar and Nazi regimes had gravitated more toward educational concerns or other outlets that could make better use of their acquired skills. Second, few had ever shown much interest in jazz and entertainment music, and by this time few wanted to venture into the thorny issues of modern music because they, as well as the public, had lost interest in it. Any standards that did exist, such as the ban on most Jewish composers and, after the outbreak of the war, various foreign composers, came from the suggestions in works on race by nonmusicologists or were dictated by foreign policy.

Musicologists never completely abandoned their role as learned commentators, and throughout the 1930s they occasionally addressed issues of current concern in the popular press, such as the problems posed by technology: the emergence of a "mechanical" approach to performance and composition as an effect of a negative influence of technology;[121] the practical and aesthetic problems posed by film music and its worthiness as a subject of musicological inquiry;[122] and the new possibilities of applying technology to organology, music perception, and an understanding of racial differences.[123] An awareness of technological advancements could also expose musicologists to new audiences. Radio had become a popular source of entertainment as well as public education and propaganda, raising a number of issues regarding the importance of responsible broadcasting. Müller-Blattau made musicological knowledge useful to radio technicians and enthusiasts by publishing a five-part series on "the beginnings of music" in the radio weekly *Die Sendung*,[124] while others commented on the responsibility of radio to educate and uplift the public through its musical broadcasts[125] and warned against radio's potential to turn good music into disturbing noise when used inappropriately.[126]

Nevertheless, by the late 1930s, the perception of musicology's role in society was still difficult to articulate, and the debate surrounding Kretzschmar's challenges of 1903 continued. Friedrich Blume attempted to put these to rest, judging Kretzschmar's expectations unreasonable and contending that music research can neither direct music practice nor be subservient to it, but instead has an obligation to serve the needs of general historical knowledge. Blume essentially sided with those who wanted musicology to maintain its sovereignty, even though he employed catchphrases that linked musicology to the goals of National Socialism and embellished his claims with declarations of the field's contribution to an understanding of the historical and biological, völkisch-racial composition of the German and European musical spirit.[127]

There were others, however, who used similar language to argue the opposite: that musicology needed to respond to the needs of the Volk and that much work remained to be done. A mere handful practiced what they preached by participating actively in such organizations as the Hitler Youth, the SA, and cultural branches of the DAF. In 1938, Gotthold Frotscher called for an "organic" union of musicology, education, and music practice, much in the same spirit as Kretzschmar, to create a "völkisch" musicology that could contribute to the history of the Volk and the race.[128] Yet as late as 1944, he could still write of the crisis caused by musicology's isolation, its reluctance to take a stand on current burning issues, and its lack of concern for Germany's musical heritage.[129] In the same Hitler Youth publication, Ehmann proposed that musicologists supervise the amateur music making of Nazi party organizations housed in the university and closed his remarks with an appropriate quote from Kretzschmar's *Musikalische Zeitfragen*.[130] Ehmann (b. 1904) received his musicological training in Freiburg, where in 1935 he designed a position for himself as music director for all political ceremonies at the university. In 1940, he advanced to become head of the musicology department in Innsbruck.

The debate had not ended, and Kretzschmar was still at the center of the controversy. Despite these frustrating ruminations, however, musicologists managed to make significant progress in their service to the Nazi state, not by assuming influential roles in the state bureaucracy, but by channeling their research skills toward the nation's needs. For instance, many had a more lasting — if less obvious — impact on the amateur movement than such active leaders as Frotscher or Goslich merely by continuing to unearth and process unknown works of early German composers for performance. When Friedrich Blume contributed a chapter on musicology to the Festschrift in honor of Hitler's fiftieth birthday, he focused almost exclusively on Denkmal editions and Gesamtausgaben as musicology's greatest contribution to the Nazi state. Blume opens the chapter with the following:

> German musicology has to preserve one of the noblest commodities of German culture. Music has always been one of the liveliest and most characteristic expressions of the German spirit. The German Volk has for centuries erected for itself and for its destiny a "victory boulevard" of great monuments. Given this fact, the direction of any music research that takes its obligations to the Volk and state seriously has become clear. The heritage of German music dictates its duties. Even if earlier research often went off in several futile directions and sacrificed a living bond with the ordinary for a pursuit of the extraordinary, a National Socialist musicology can only proceed from the living core of German music, laying the periphery around it, orienting remote problems around this center.[131]

When other musicologists were called upon to describe the discipline to the general public, they, like Blume, frequently depicted the field's main activity as the rediscovery of old German music through the editing of Denkmäler and Gesamtausgaben. Hans Engel (b. 1894), head of the musicology department and the institute for church and school music in Königsberg since 1935, summarized musicology's accomplishments for a general readership in the journal *Geistige Arbeit* by giving a detailed account of Denkmälerausgaben and Gesamtausgaben activities and reporting that "the Third Reich has recognized the necessity of promoting and compiling musical Denkmal editions."[132] Rudolf Gerber (b. 1899, headed the musicology department in Giessen since 1928, lectured in Frankfurt, and took over the department in Göttingen in 1943) also featured the Denkmäler as musicology's highest duty to society, imploring musicologists to heed the call of the nation and make the fruits of their scholarship accessible to the public.[133] This emphasis came not only from scholars feeling most comfortable in this activity, but also because it was an enterprise which the state had always financed, it had an impact on the musical activities of amateurs, and it offered tangible evidence of musicology's contribution toward strengthening German identity by uncovering Germany's rich musical past.

The large body of musicologists' contributions to the nonscholarly media reveals how they attempted to redefine their purpose in German society by addressing contemporary issues. The uncertainty of the times called for such a response: the changeover in regimes; the precarious position of musicology departments in universities; and the drastic changes taking place in musical organization, tastes, and means of proliferation. The contemporary social, political, and cultural changes also had a profound impact on dynamics within the discipline, on musicologists' activities outside the university, and on the focus of their scholarship. Although many of their ideas about their potential to influence German musical life remained unfulfilled, they succeeded in serving the political and ideological goals of both regimes from their home base of musicological research, reshaping methods, areas of interest, and activities as circumstances required. They may have indulged in the hope that such scholarly work would eventually open up opportunities for them to exert more influence outside the academy. Following World War I, German musicologists emerged from the academy, seeking ways to apply their skills to the needs of the nation. The discipline would show no signs of retreating for many years to come.

3

The Organization and Reorganization of Musicological Scholarship

Musicology made great strides in establishing itself as a professional and national entity during the Weimar Republic, gaining a presence in universities throughout the Reich and enjoying an international reputation. Simultaneously, German scholars were inspired to create two important organizations at the end of World War I: a research institute and a professional society, each with its own scholarly journal. In an atmosphere of ever-changing economic, political, and social demands, however, it was no small challenge for these two organizations to define their missions. From their very beginnings, both tried to navigate the often conflicting political currents of internationalism, nationalism, democratization, and conservatism.

The research institute adopted the nationalist and populist goals of promoting an understanding of German music and serving the general public. It became a valuable research facility with vast holdings and a sophisticated system of cataloguing, but the hyperinflation in 1922 crippled its operation, and by 1927 it existed in name only. By contrast, the professional society set out to foster international scholarly exchange, hoping to replace the International Music Society (IMS), which disbanded at the outbreak of World War I. But strained international relations, combined with growing nationalist sentiment and the economic restraints on international travel and communication, compelled the founders to abandon their international mission.

Faced with serious financial hardships, both organizations sought to attach themselves to the new bodies of cultural administration established by the Nazi government. The Nazi Education Ministry took a special interest in the research institute, making it more powerful by moving it to Berlin and expanding it with the Gleichschaltung of existing archives and publishing projects. The professional society was ultimately overshadowed by the enlarged research institute, despite energetic attempts to demonstrate its potential service to the Nazi program. In the end, musicological enterprises gained from the Nazi authorities' unprecedented attention and support, but they suffered great losses in the emigration of important scholars, the gradual breakdown of international communication, and isolation from the non-German and exiled community of musicologists.

The Founding of a German Music Research Institute

The Royal Institute for Musicological Research at Bückeburg (Fürstliches Institut für musikwissenschaftliche Forschung i.E. zu Bückeburg) grew out of a 1914 speech by the musicologist Max Seiffert on the need for a central musicological archive.[1] Seiffert's ideas materialized as a full-scale institute, established on 21 June 1917, with an endowment from Prince Adolf of Schaumburg-Lippe. Administered primarily by German university professors appointed by the patron, its original plans called for seven departments: a research library; a collegium musicum; a department for experimental musicology; a lending library; a division for Bückeburg local music history; a special collection of sixteenth-century music; and a collection and bibliography of all current musicological works coming out of German, Austrian, and Swiss-German universities.[2] In 1918, an archive and a division for provincial affairs (Abteilung für Landesangelegenheiten) were added, the latter upon special request of Prince Adolf to provide musical expertise to the state, church, schools, and municipal organizations and to improve the cultural life of the community.[3]

The Bückeburg Institute's mission, at least on paper, reflected the prevailing concerns of German musicologists during the postwar period: how to contribute to a strong German national identity in the wake of World War I and how to cultivate a relationship with the general public. In a speech at the first annual meeting of the institute in 1919, Max Seiffert, serving as secretary, stirred up nationalist and anti-Republican sentiments, noting how the war had destroyed the IMS and created an atmosphere of name-calling at international conferences, and how the November Revolution had endangered the fledgling institute as it "destroyed the proud structure of the German Reich."[4] The institute's active membership was limited to German scholars, its publications concentrated on German subject matter, and its prizes were reserved for works by Germans that contributed to a better understanding of German culture.[5] Its most important publication, the scholarly journal *Archiv für Musikwissenschaft* (*AfMw*), was established in 1918, with editorial board members Max Seiffert, Johannes Wolf, and Max Schneider, to "further the entire field of musicology and its subdisciplines and related disciplines through new research."[6] Its underlying agenda, however, was to capitalize on the strengths of German scholarship and to pay more attention to Germany's musical legacy. The editors clearly distinguished the journal's purpose from that of the earlier IMS journal, the *Sammelbände der Internationalen Musikgesellschaft,* by focusing more on "Germanness" (*Deutschtum*). This was needed, they claimed, because Germany's much-envied musical superiority, a product of the fusion of foreign artistic ideas and German mastery over the centuries, had recently met with much resentment. Although realizing it would be counterproductive to ignore all foreign ties out of "misguided patriotism," the editors believed the cultivation of German music history should be the major task of the journal and hoped that old friends and colleagues abroad would eventually become loyal working partners.[7]

The institute's publication of scholarly monographs and editions reflects similar prejudices. In choosing works, the institute tended to favor studies that dealt with German music history and chose exclusively from the output of leading German scholars and occasionally included some highly recommended doctoral dissertations. During the Weimar years, the institute published three reference works as part of its series named after its patron, the Fürst-Adolf Ausgabe (facsimiles of Mozart manuscripts, edited by Schiedermair; Max Schneider's *Ganassis Regola Robertina;* and Wolf's tables of the history of notation); two dissertations (Ernst Bücken's on heroic style in opera and Irmgard Leux's on the eighteenth-century German composer Christian Gottlob Neefe); three local music histories (on Bautzen, the Wettiner, and Zeitz); and music editions (ten volumes of the complete works of Friedrich Bach, the "Bückeburg Bach," edited by Schünemann; and six volumes of Seiffert's edition of music at the court of Ernst von Schaumburg).[8] The German focus sharpened even more in 1920 with the creation of a new task force for regional German music history (Fachausschuß für die Musikgeschichte deutscher Landschaften und Städte).[9] This initiative had the practical component of involving regional authorities and seeking their help for financing the institute's publications. The city of Zeitz donated 1,000 marks toward the publication of its local music history, and a publication on Danzig was approved by the task force with the recommendation that "the Danzig senate should be approached again for a subsidy, with an emphasis on the political importance of the work."[10]

Seiffert also advocated strong ties with the general public, emphasizing musicology's patriotic duty to enhance general education and musical practice. In a speech on the duties and goals of the institute delivered at the second annual meeting, he outlined Germany's glorious music history up to the fatal decline of the current times, a decline which could be reversed only by educating German youth to distinguish between good and bad, between "elevating, fulfilling, valued art of past and present masters and shallow pseudo art of [recent] changing times." The institute would contribute toward that end through a "living union of music practice and science," not only with the works of the great masters but also through the rediscovery of local heroes or *Kleinmeister*.[11] The institute was unexpectedly thrust into the position of making good on its promises after the November Revolution. When court institutions, among them the court music ensemble (*Hofkapelle*), were dissolved, the concerts arranged by the institute's division for provincial affairs became the only outlet for art music and early music performance in Bückeburg.[12]

The strongest feature of the Bückeburg Institute was its research facilities. The library included the valuable collection of music owned by the prince's family with large holdings of scores, piano reductions, and musicological writings.[13] The archive became a center for systematically compiling all sources of German music history.[14] Seiffert had emphasized the urgent need for such a project because of the careless handling of valuable documents in smaller cities and the ever-increasing risk of their disintegration.[15] The archive was the basis of what later became a Reich-wide collaboration with the Prussian Music History Commission (Musikgeschichtliche Kommission), the body that oversaw the publication of the Denkmäler Deutscher Tonkunst, and a similar entity in Bavaria (Gesellschaft zur Herausgabe der Denkmäler der Tonkunst in Bayern). Both were eager to cooperate with the institute: all research trips were suspended during the war, and rising travel costs after the war exceeded the Prussian commission's budget allowance, thus an agreement with the Bückeburg Institute would enable them to carry on their research and bear only part of the financial burden. All three parties signed a general agreement,[16] and by 1933 the archive had recorded and photographed the inventories in Bückeburg, Stadthagen, Silesia, and other local collections. More important, it was able to collect copies of German music manuscripts and rare printed editions in London, Brussels, Zürich, Uppsala, Paris, Padua, and Vienna,[17] a mission Seiffert had described as partial "reparations for the cultural losses incurred over several decades."[18]

Despite the original plans to incorporate all branches of musicology, the institute ultimately concentrated exclusively on historical musicology. By the end of 1918 there was no one to direct the department for experimental musicology, as the single candidate for the position had turned down the offer. Instead, the historical departments grew and diversified into three-member committees (*Fachausschüsse*) for specific periods, musical genres, and methodologies.[19] The impressive list of committee members included virtually every leading or up-and-coming German scholar in the field. One of the tasks of the Fachausschüsse was to evaluate works for publication in its three publications series: Practica (music editions), Theoretica (reference works, monographs, bibliographies) and the Fürst-Adolf-Ausgabe.[20]

Although its reputation as a research facility was growing, the institute was beset by financial difficulties from the very beginning. The revolution of November 1918 forced the abdication of its patron and brought on huge financial losses.[21] The prince managed to save the institute by assuming partial financial responsibility,[22] but by 1921 the dissolution of other court operations necessitated a new charter that made the institute dependent on private and government contributions.[23] Director C. A. Rau made a successful appeal to the local authorities to guarantee a regular yearly subsidy, and he urged the Reich Ministry of the Interior to follow suit, noting the institute's rise to international prominence despite the obstacles facing all German sciences,[24] but Rau's sudden death delayed the negotiations.[25] Supporters and members of the institute set up a Friends' Society (Gesellschaft der Freunde des Fürstlichen Institutes für musikwissenschaftliche Forschung zu Bückeburg) in 1921 to raise money for the institute's projects, but all of its income in the first year was spent on inflated costs for advertising.[26]

The institute never completely recovered from the dissolution of the Schaumburg-Lippe court holdings in 1919 and the hyperinflation of 1922–24. In the 1923 report, Theodor Werner expressed in poignant terms the predicament of all scholars involved in the difficult economic "war after the war": "it is not so much that they cannot buy butter, but that they cannot buy a book — this is the sign of the lowest desperation of those who, in cultivating scholarship, are aware of its priceless goods and the surest weapons against the sneering spirit of materialism."[27] In 1922, institute members considered suspending all publication projects except for the journal, but the institute weathered the inflation by repeatedly soliciting emergency assistance from the local Schaumburg-Lippe government. After the mark was stabilized in 1924, it averted total collapse through private contributions, a small subsidy from the Reich, and a publication subsidy for the journal from the Notgemeinschaft der deutschen Wissenschaft.[28] The Notgemeinschaft was founded in 1920 by a consortium of colleges and universities as a private source of funding for scholarly activities in all fields, and eventually it secured the bulk of its subventions from the Reich Ministry of the Interior. It provided subsidies for journals, series, and monographs; purchase of materials, equipment, and laboratory animals; acquisition of foreign-language publications; and research travel.[29]

These measures were not sufficient to ward off the necessary reduction in activities and gradual retreat into oblivion in the years that followed. The institute renewed its appeals to the Reich Ministry of the Interior in 1925, with an endorsement from the local government highlighting the institute's international stature, and the Reich ministry honored the request with a one-time subsidy of 3,000 marks.[30] But simultaneous appeals to the Prussian Ministry of Science, Art, and Public Education, following Rau's precedent of 1921,[31] failed despite an impassioned plea from the Prussian Academy of Sciences to make the Bückeburg Institute a central resource for the entire Reich. By this time, the effects of the inflation had terminated all ongoing publishing projects except for the journal and threatened the very existence of the establishment.[32] The institute had lost its earlier income, which it hoped to regain through general economic reforms, but showed no signs of recovery one year later, as its tenth anniversary approached.[33] The provincial government made a contribution for the anniversary celebration, noting the international importance of the institute and encouraging it to carry on its mission "to improve its reputation and to contribute to the struggle to win further world recognition for German scholarly work."[34] But these amounts did not approach the sum needed to keep the journal alive, and the 1926 volume of the *AfMw* was the last.

By this time the institute was already fading into oblivion: in the journal's final volume, Theodor Werner complained of poor public relations after having received a letter from someone who had "discovered" the *AfMw* and asked how to get hold of it. If this widely circulated journal was unknown, Werner argued, "how must it look for the institute itself, tucked away in a little town in northern Germany, even more inaccessible to visitors than its journal!" In 1926, Seiffert, who became acting director after Rau's death, had invited professors from all German musicology departments to Bückeburg to become acquainted with the institute's activities and resources, but in the face of widespread financial hardships only two were able to visit.[35] Werner took it upon himself to publicize the institute in Germany's other scholarly musicological journal, *Zeitschrift für Musikwissenschaft,* using the space usually devoted to the institute's annual report to provide a basic description of its history, structure, and activities.[36]

The German Music Society

Unlike the institute, which focused expressly on the cultivation of German music research, the Deutsche Musikgesellschaft (DMG) had the potential to become an international scholarly society, but its founders showed great ambivalence toward putting aside wartime animosities. At war's end, the possibilities for renewed communication seemed limitless, but the scars of war were not quickly healed. While some regarded peacetime as an opportunity to initiate a new international society, others felt betrayed by their foreign colleagues during the breakdown of the IMS in 1914 and argued for an organization that focused more on indigenous resources.

In December 1917, Hermann Abert sent a confidential appeal to scholars and friends of musicology and serious music. Hoping to draw on the same energy Germans had spent on forming the IMS, he proposed a German music society to take its place. With the war still raging, Abert's tone was hardly conducive to reconciliation: "The labor of peace which had been supported by thorough German efforts and by economic means offered selflessly by Germany has been destroyed through that war that was forced upon Germany, since as early as the last years before its outbreak, and indeed originating from the non-German side, political tension penetrated even the life of the IMS in an unpleasant manner." World War I had forced musicologists to realize that scholarship could continue without an international society, and in Abert's view, the new organization should encourage more interest in German musical culture.[37]

The document announcing the founding of the DMG on 19 December 1917 omitted Abert's observations of the victimization of Germany by enemy nations and stressed instead the mission of resuming the tasks of the IMS. While it reiterated the need for further research into German music, the announcement deemphasized the national exclusivity of Abert's original proposal.[38] The society was to reach beyond the German Reich to involve scholars from Austrian, Swiss-German, Czech, and Hungarian schools, and the first board of directors included Guido Adler (Vienna), Karl Nef (Basel), Peter Wagner (Fribourg, Switzerland), and Hermann Rietsch (Prague). This international emphasis may have originated from Hugo Riemann. In the preface to the 1919 revised edition of *Handbuch der Musikgeschichte*, Riemann welcomed peacetime as an opportunity to remove those obstacles to international cooperation that had been so detrimental to musicological research. He cited the founding of the DMG explicitly, along with other national organizations in England and France, as a preliminary step toward a new international society, for Germany had no need to close itself off or cultivate nationalist interests.[39]

The society was thus founded on dual and sometimes conflicting principles of fostering both nationalism and internationalism.[40] Its official organ, the

Zeitschrift für Musikwissenschaft (*ZfMw*), came into being at a meeting on 20 January 1918, and first appeared in October 1918, the same month that the *AfMw* made its debut. The two journals rivaled each other in their high scholarly standards, but the *ZfMw* promised to further the international cause more than the *AfMw*, as its founders meant for it to replace the defunct journal of the IMS. In spite of this, editor Alfred Einstein's introduction to the first issue was more aggressively protective of national interests than the opening remarks in the *AfMw*. Einstein bluntly questioned the practicality of the IMS's earlier visions of internationalism, when the French, Italians, and English had been producing their own journals while the Germans were expending all their energies on the international society: "the International Music Society had its nucleus and its emphasis in the work of its German members: they were the ones who quantitatively and — why not say it? — also qualitatively gave the greatest service and made the most sacrifices to the discipline." Einstein felt that the new journal could justifiably limit its scope to German scholarship because "our musical past is so rich in substance and so rich with creative heroes, that our cupboard would certainly not be bare." Although ignoring non-German scholarship completely might be contrary to the "German spirit," Einstein promised to give priority to German scholarship, especially in view of the unfortunate experience of the war years, when certain non-German scholars had no misgivings about directing "one hate-book after another" against Germany.[41] In the seventeen years of the *ZfMw*'s existence, from 1918 to 1935, the number of contributions from non-Germans remained small.

The 330 members of the DMG came from Germany, Austria-Hungary, Switzerland, Holland, and Sweden, but when Hugo Riemann died in 1919, the most vocal spokesperson for international cooperation was gone, and the society moved further into isolation. In 1921, the board of directors recognized the need for an international conference to be held in Leipzig but planned to reserve the meeting's six public lectures for Germans and for scholars from "neutral foreign countries."[42] When the meeting took place in 1925, Abert reported: "Our conference has become primarily a German rather than an international one. We invited only certain individuals from our former enemy countries whom we could trust to know enough to separate politics from scholarship, and, to the extent that they accepted, extended our hand to them without hesitation. However, we want to continue working and waiting to see if the outside world can get along without German scholarship. For this is an area that knows neither war nor peace, neither reparations nor guarantees, but rather the constant flood of competition of all in the service of scholarship."[43] The list of papers of the 1925 meeting shows that it was international only in the narrowest sense of the word. The only non-German to deliver a paper was Higini Anglès of Barcelona, whose strong ties to Germany later made him the champion of German causes in predominantly anti-German circles.

When an international society was finally established in 1927 (the International Musicological Society), the DMG could justifiably relinquish its self-imposed responsibility to foster international cooperation, but other factors, mainly financial, were already starting to limit its ambitions. The 1925 Leipzig meeting caused the first wave of serious financial setbacks: all arrangements had been made for the conference to take place in October 1923, yet at the last moment the entire plan had to be dropped because of the hyperinflation, and when the meeting finally did take place, it burdened the society with a huge deficit.[44] In 1931, in the depths of the depression, the society had to postpone another planned conference indefinitely.[45]

By the time Hitler came to power, the society had fallen into serious financial straits. As the Nazi government showed interest in furthering German culture, the DMG saw the possibility of new sources of government assistance and resolved to demonstrate its commitment to the goals and standards of the Nazi state before approaching the authorities. The first step in the DMG's internal Gleichschaltung was securing the allegedly voluntary resignation of Alfred Einstein, a Jew, as editor of the *ZfMw* in June 1933. This happened behind closed doors, and most of the musicology community were never quite sure of the circumstances of Einstein's departure. Ludwig Schiedermair, writing to Adolf Sandberger in July 1933, welcomed the change of editors, hoping not only that the "unbearable boredom" and "colorlessness" of the journal of the last years would come to an end, but also that the DMG could entertain more fundamental reforms.[46] In his response to Schiedermair, Sandberger implied that there was more to Einstein's resignation than met the eye. Both he and Johannes Wolf were opposed to the outcome, Sandberger wrote, but Schering, the president of the society, had informed Sandberger that nothing was to be done; knowing Sandberger's standpoint, Schering neglected to invite him to the board meeting.[47]

Einstein never actually resigned; rather, the board dismissed him after deciding that, in order to seek support from the new government, the society could not keep a Jew in such a prominent position. Einstein received his official notice of dismissal from Johannes Wolf on 24 June with the explanation that "conditions are stronger than we are and force us, in the interest of the DMG's future, to execute a change in the editorship of our journal by the end of the fiscal year (September 1933)."[48] Wolf clarified in a personal note that "what you already feared, and what I naively thought impossible, has come to pass: they have demanded your termination as editor of the journal. The board had to deal with the question a few days ago and came to the conclusion that it is impossible to run against the current, especially since the enterprise must request a subvention from the state." Wolf revealed that he, too, was resigning from his seat on the executive board out of protest against Einstein's treatment and frustration with the internal politics of the organization.[49]

Other factors also influenced the board's, and particularly Schering's, action against Einstein. Since fall 1932, Einstein had been caught in the middle of a bitter conflict between Schering and Theodor Kroyer, Einstein's former professor and close friend. The conflict centered on an article by Kroyer on *a cappella* performance of early music, which Einstein had accepted for the journal and which took issue with theories that Schering held dear. The apparently tactless language in the original version compelled Einstein to urge Kroyer to tone down his attacks on Schering,[50] but the conflict escalated to the point where Schering threatened, among other things, to resign his post in the society if the article appeared.[51] Einstein tried desperately to mediate the conflict, but rivalries between Kroyer and Schering were too deep. Kroyer's article did not appear in *ZfMw,* but a similar piece came out in the international journal *Acta musicologica* in 1934.

The next step in the Gleichschaltung of the society came in late September 1933 at a special meeting called by Schering for the "new formation of the DMG." His stated reasons were to expand the activities of the society, which had been limited to producing the journal and lacked any "external influence" beyond that.[52] Schering was elected president of the new society, henceforth known by the slightly revised name, German Society for Musicology (Deutsche Gesellschaft für Musikwissenschaft or DGMW), and announced shortly thereafter in a mailing to all members his commitment to winning for German musicology its "appropriate rank in the new state," to strengthen its "bond with the people," and consequently to shape its achievements "for the culture of the German soul." This announcement also proclaimed the "unanimous recognition of the *Führerprinzip,*"[53] a hierarchical concept practiced in the Nazi party and superimposed on the Nazi state. As spelled out in the new charter, the DGMW was modeled on this "leader and management principle," the directives of the president were to be "binding for all work of the society," and complaints against the decisions of the president were not permitted.[54] Schering adhered to this principle to the end of his term: when he stepped down in 1936, he chose Ludwig Schiedermair as president and would not allow an election because it would go against the Führerprinzip.[55]

The tasks of the Bückeburg Institute were discontinued one by one in the lean years following the inflation, and the new DGMW saw the opportunity to resurrect some of those projects and subsequently reorganized itself into divisions called *Fachgruppen* along the same lines as the institute's *Fachaus-schüsse*. The Fachgruppen were each headed by a group leader (*Gruppen-führer*) rather than a committee of three and represented a wide range of concerns as well as an honest attempt to make the new organization more than just the publisher of a journal. Each group was headed by a prominent scholar and addressed such areas as local history, preservation, university issues, publishing, publicity, folklore, comparative musicology, radio and recording industries, bibliography, church music, criticism, conference management, and conference planning.[56]

The internal Gleichschaltung was thus complete: the Jewish editor of *ZfMw* was gone, the society was renamed without actually ever dissolving the old organization, the new society was restructured on the Führerprinzip model, and the expansion into Fachgruppen demonstrated its new agenda to serve the state and to encourage the scholarly application of folk and racial research. Schering was now ready to call this transformation to the attention of the authorities and, depending on their response, to pursue the question of financial assistance. In late November 1933, he addressed a letter to the Propaganda Minister Joseph Goebbels announcing the restructuring of the society, its "joyful will to work together to build a new German culture with all of its strength" and its consciousness of the "high responsibility placed upon it for its part in the administration and proliferation of the immortal musical culture of our people."[57] All he received in response, however, was a terse acknowledgment from one of Goebbels's assistants.[58]

The Nazi Education Ministry and the Resurrection of the Research Institute

The DMG may have been snubbed by the Propaganda Ministry, but Education Minister Bernhard Rust soon showed a keen interest in resurrecting the severely reduced Bückeburg Institute. The Prussian Ministry for Science, Art, and Public Education was expanded in 1934 to serve the entire Reich when Prussian minister Bernhard Rust was appointed to head the Prussian and Reich Education Ministry (Reichs- und Preußisches Ministerium für Wissenschaft, Erziehung, und Volksbildung).[59] Rust was ultimately responsible for breathing new life into the all-but-defunct Bückeburg Institute and using it as a base for bringing all musicological enterprises under his control.

The first steps of Gleichschaltung of the institute were already underway when local authorities began to supervise its financial operations and required detailed information on the racial lineage of newly appointed personnel and their spouses.[60] The Reich government started to take notice of the institute in

September 1933, when the local Reich representative (*Reichsstatthalter*) offered to discuss its future, review its files, and pay a visit. During that visit, Seiffert made his first plea to expand the institute and move it to Berlin, where it would be able to work with other scholarly institutions.[61] He followed up early in 1934 with a detailed proposal to Reich officials for the transformation of the Bückeburg Institute into the Reich Institute, stressing the urgency of the matter if projects in progress were to continue.[62] The proposal contained a brief history of the institute, an overview of its possessions, an enumeration of its future plans, and suggestions for its reorganization. Seiffert cited three events that hampered the development of the institute: the death of the director, C. A. Rau; the abdication of Prince Adolf after the events of November 1918; and the hyperinflation. In addition to curtailing the institute's publications in 1927 and its yearly meetings in 1931, financial setbacks left acting director Seiffert with minimal resources to perform his duties.

Seiffert's proposal acknowledged the pros as well as the cons of a reorganization: although a move to Berlin had been under consideration since 1931, it would mean losing the spacious quarters in Bückeburg as well as the quiet of Bückeburg's "pristine German landscape." It could also mean a loss of independence with the annexation of other institutes; uprooting the possessions from their "home"; and watering down the "thoroughly German nature" of the establishment by bringing it into the metropolis. Nevertheless the advantages far outweighed the inconveniences, and Seiffert pressed for establishing a central institute by playing on nationalist and populist sentiments. First, one could not forget the countless valuable musical treasures sold to foreign customers because local governments did not have the means to retain them, and while the Reich and provincial governments had made efforts to preserve art treasures, museums, and architecture, German music, the most important contributor to "the cultural standing of our nation," had been left by the wayside.[63] Second, Seiffert portrayed the planned central institute as meeting the needs of the Volksgemeinschaft by collecting and preserving German musical treasures—scores, books, instruments, manuscripts—and making them accessible to the public. In addition to continuing its archival and bibliographic services, the institute would pursue new directions in research with a nationalistic orientation (research on German music and musicians "according to race and tribe, regional origins, national-German essence, and significance for the German cultural totality") and would publish both scholarly and popular works on those subjects.[64]

Accompanying Seiffert's proposal was an endorsement by Fritz Stein, director of the Hochschule für Musik in Berlin. The plan to transform the institute was a notion which pleased his "musicological heart" and would fulfill "an old dream of German musicology." Reiterating Seiffert's points, he further stated the need for more folk emphasis, that is, more research into folk instruments, folk dances, and musical ritual, with the purpose of cultivating a "feeling toward homeland and tribe" among young musicians and the public. Stein also implied that the DMG's failure to unify the discipline made the creation of a central institute necessary, especially since musicology was falling behind other fields.[65]

The Reich representative in Schaumburg-Lippe forwarded Seiffert's proposal to the appropriate officials — the Reich Ministry of the Interior, the education minister, the propaganda minister, and even Hitler's deputy Rudolf Hess — calling attention to the institute's importance for the "cultivation of German musical culture" and to Seiffert's personal sacrifice and record of "true German idealism."[66] The Propaganda Ministry, consistently ambivalent toward the fate of musicology, delayed taking any steps until its jurisdiction was ascertained,[67] but the proposal apparently struck a chord in the Education Ministry. Rust contacted the Reich representative immediately, and in July 1934 he sent a delegate, Werner Weber, to Bückeburg along with Fritz Stein. They discussed the transferral with Seiffert and local authorities, and all agreed that the move was highly advisable: the institute had demonstrated its national importance, and in Berlin it would be better situated to work with other scholarly establishments.[68] Rust recognized the loss that Bückeburg would suffer and offered to help the local authorities set up a music school in its place.[69] The transferral took place in the following months,[70] and by November 1934 the institute formally came under the jurisdiction of the education minister with the new name of State Institute for German Music Research ("Staatliches Institut für deutsche Musikforschung"), with Max Seiffert as permanent director.[71]

Plans for the State Institute called for five departments, but only three actually materialized. The music history department (Department I) managed the archives and library; worked on periodicals (*Archiv für Musikforschung* and *Deutsche Musikkultur*), bibliographies (*Bibliographie des Musikschrifttums* and *Verzeichnis der Neudrucke alter Musik*), monographs, and music editions (Denkmäler and Gesamtausgaben); and awarded two prizes for outstanding musicological works of younger scholars. The folk music department (Department II) collected and catalogued transcriptions; worked on its own edition and collaborated on editions with other organizations; and offered information and counsel to the general public. Department III maintained the instrument collection and the *Generalkatalog* of the DDT; published catalogues of the collection and monographs on musical instruments; and arranged guided tours, lectures, and loans of instruments. A department for "music and race" (Department IV) and one for experimental musicology (Department V) never advanced beyond the planning stages.[72]

The Centralization of Musicological Activity

The Education Minister assumed far more authority over the operation of the new institute than had either Prince Adolf or the Bückeburg government. While entrusting much of the daily business of the institute to Seiffert, the minister made final decisions on all appointments and assigned an administrative inspector to supervise office management and bookkeeping.[73] Bringing the institute under government management enabled the moribund institution to resume and expand its activities, but it also allowed the Reich Education Ministry to influence the scholarly discipline of musicology, thereby staking a claim in cultural administration alongside its competitors (the Propaganda Ministry, Rosenberg, and the DAF).

Seiffert was undoubtedly the driving force in publicizing the institute's predicament and urging its transferal to Berlin. His vision of 1914 called for a national facility, and the Bückeburg setting, although quaint, did not to fulfill his dream. Furthermore, Seiffert was a well-connected faculty member in Berlin, whereas in Bückeburg his power was limited: he was appointed acting director after Rau's death in 1921 and never advanced to a permanent position there. His political ambitions may have also played a role in the move to Berlin. In 1932 he was turned down for a position as secretary in a government ministry,[74] and an enigmatic document among Fritz Stein's papers suggests that Seiffert may have had very large-scale plans for reforming German musical life that went beyond running the institute.[75] Seiffert oversaw the move to Berlin in 1934 and continued at the institute as director, although he restrained his enthusiasm for assuming full responsibility for the institute and initially recommended Moser as director instead.[76]

Yet even Seiffert's ambitions did not measure up to those of the Education Ministry. In his 1934 proposal, Seiffert called for an intensified collaboration between the new institute and other musicological operations to be carried out through committees. He recommended that the director of the institute be a member of the Prussian Music History Commission and have close ties with the Bavarian and Austrian counterparts, as well as with the Deutsche Akademie in Munich, the Prussian Academy of Arts, the Folk Song Commission of the Prussian Academy of Sciences, and the DGMW, "for the purpose of a division of labor."[77] The Education Ministry, however, had grander notions of a centralized musicological facility. The minister dictated that the new institute incorporate the Hochschule's instrument collection and the German Folk Song Archive in Berlin.[78] It was also to take over the folk song archive in Freiburg, but the adamant refusal of the Freiburg director, John Meier, prevented this.[79] The institute then absorbed the German, Bavarian, and Austrian Denkmäler editions (the last following the *Anschluss*); assumed responsibility for the one remaining musicological journal, the *Zeitschrift für Musikwissenschaft,* from the DGMW; and, with the argument of reaching out to the Volksgemeinschaft, initiated the bimonthly magazine, *Deutsche Musikkultur,* which soon incorporated the periodical *Musik und Volk.*

The transformation of the Royal Institute for Musicological Research at Bückeburg into the comprehensive, pan-German State Institute for German Music Research involved not only a cultural loss to Bückeburg but also a loss of independence among the numerous entities swallowed up in the name of centralization. Prince Adolf offered his timid objections and, not satisfied with the mere establishment of a music school in its place, asked that the ministry and the Reich Music Chamber compensate the city's loss with some institution of comparable importance.[80] Fritz Stein raised stronger objections to the take-over of the Hochschule's instrument collection. In a lengthy correspondence with the Education Ministry in the early months of 1935, he urged officials to leave the collection alone so that he could develop an early music performance program. The ministry turned down Stein's request but agreed to leave a small part of the collection in the Hochschule for teaching purposes and required the new director of the instrument collection to teach part time at the Hochschule, replacing a faculty member Stein had lost in the transfer. Stein was still not satisfied, but in the end he was granted only the part-time instructors he needed.[81]

The largest centralizing effort was the creation of Das Erbe deutscher Musik (EdM), a Gleichschaltung of all preexisting musical Denkmäler editions. Most Denkmäler editions were independent enterprises, some having operated more than four decades. The Austrian historical music editions (Denkmäler der Tonkunst in Österreich or DTÖ) had existed since 1888, the German editions (Denkmäler Deutscher Tonkunst or DDT) since 1889, and the Bavarian editions (Denkmäler der Tonkunst in Bayern or DTB) since 1900. The DDT and DTÖ had parallel histories: each began with an edited volume of compositions by ancestors of the respective ruling family (an edition of Frederick the Great's compositions for flute was a forerunner of the DDT, and the two-volume "Kaiserwerke" preceded the DTÖ). These were presented to the reigning heirs to flatter them and at the same time draw their attention to the need to preserve musical treasures in published editions. This tactic succeeded in both cases, and the Prussian and Austrian rulers, impressed with the "patriotic and artistic goals" of the undertakings, provided the necessary funds to secure future volumes.[82]

The plans to combine all Denkmäler editions into EdM under the auspices of the State Institute were conceived as early as January 1935, when Weber and von Staa, both of the Education Ministry, headed a committee of musicologists to reassess the goals of the Denkmäler. In February, the committee concluded that a composite Reich enterprise (*Reichsdenkmalunternehmen*) under the institute "should correspond to the meaning and standards of musicology in the National Socialist Volk order."[83] They dictated new guidelines to Heinrich Besseler, director of the institute's Denkmäler division, who started to assign duties to others even before the institute came to Berlin.[84] The new series was to reach the Volksgemeinschaft through a standardized format that met the needs of both scholars and amateur musicians. This new format would eliminate all archaic clefs, provide translations of Latin and Italian texts, give full realizations of figured basses, and — perhaps an unforeseen sacrifice on the side of scholarship — reduce the length of introductions and critical commentaries.[85]

Besseler described these guidelines in the Education Ministry's official newsletter in 1935 and outlined the overall conception of the enterprise. Changing the title from "Denkmäler Deutscher Tonkunst" to "Erbe deutscher Musik," he noted, was significant. First, replacing the term *Denkmäler* (monuments) with *Erbe* (inheritance) represented a fundamental break with tradition. The new series would produce musical editions not for exhibition as museum pieces but for use in live performance. This was a realization of German musicology's new responsibility to grow in the "living space of the Volk" by preserving the musical heritage and promoting it as a living practice.[86] Besseler similarly explained the abandonment of the term *Tonkunst* (composition). This term, with its implied emphasis on *Kunst* (art), threatened to exclude all forms of "life-related music making," such as folk music and dance, ceremonial music, and German renditions of Gregorian chant.[87] The new editions would encompass the entire "musical heritage" (*musikalisches Erbe*), including folk music and "nonartistic functional music" (*nicht-kunstmäßige Gebrauchsmusik*) and extending its geographic boundaries to include all former Reich provinces (*losgetrennten früheren Reichsgebieten*) and, eventually, German communities abroad (*Auslandsdeutschtum*).[88]

The EdM, unlike its predecessors, came out in two separate series, the national (*Reichsdenkmale*) and the regional (*Landschaftsdenkmale*). This differentiation was very pragmatic; it provided a way to weed out less important works without rejecting them entirely and controlled all regional operations without stripping them of their local significance. The national series continued the work of the DDT, including only items that "represent the highest level of German music in their respective periods [that] should be accessible to the general German musical life."[89] The regional series was to include everything else, ending the old procedure of juxtaposing important works with "mediocre [ones] bearing only local significance."[90] While the national series depended on Reich subsidies and publishers' investment, the regional series drew heavily on financial support from local governments. Each of the regional headquarters (*Landschaftstellen*) was to make its own arrangement with a publisher, produce its own series, and receive a subsidy or guaranteed subscription from local authorities. The institute was on hand to standardize their editorial practices, collect data and photocopies from the regional task forces for its archive, and determine the number and type of editions that the local groups were allowed to produce. The Reich government would match the local government's contribution.[91]

This centralized decentralization of the Denkmäler editions solved some problems while creating new ones. It solved the long-standing problem of the DDT's regional imbalance. Critics had long contended that the DDT concentrated too heavily on Saxony-Thuringia, apparently because of general editor Hermann Kretzschmar's personal preference (three-quarters of the volumes focused on music from the area between Eisenach and Dresden). But the incorporation of preexisting Denkmäler editions into the EdM did cause new friction, especially with Adolf Sandberger, director of the DTB. Sandberger held complete control over DTB's planning and administration. He was not willing to share this authority and conform to new editorial standards, and the matter could be settled only after his death.[92] In contrast, Germany's political expansion in 1938 facilitated a very smooth takeover of the DTÖ and the introduction of a regional edition in the Sudetenland. It was announced that "the establishment of Greater Germany [*Großdeutschland*] has brought the much-longed-for merger with Austrian and Sudeten-German research," which meant the official end of the old DTÖ and its new affiliation with the institute.[93] By the end of World War II, the EdM had produced twenty-four volumes of Reichsdenkmale out of a projected total of forty-three, and eighteen volumes of Landschaftsdenkmale, coming from Bavaria, Hessen, Rhine-Main, central Germany, Alps and Danube regions, Schleswig-Holstein, Mecklenburg-Pomerania, East Prussia–Danzig–West Prussia, and Sudetenland-Bohemia-Moravia, with plans for editions from the Rhineland, Berlin-Brandenburg, and Swabia.

The second most important publishing venture of the State Institute, the scholarly journal *Archiv für Musikforschung* (*AfMf*), also involved the takeover of an existing enterprise from a weaker organization, in this case the DGMW. Still unable to find a government sponsor in spite of Einstein's expulsion as editor, the *ZfMw* encountered mounting financial difficulties from 1933 to 1935. Following Schering's attempt to replace Einstein with his protégé Rudolf Steglich, which brought protests of nepotism and Steglich's alleged incompetence,[94] the *ZfMw* did not appear in fall 1933. An issue came out January 1934 under the editorship of Max Schneider, but the journal could not guarantee the regular honoraria because many Jews and foreigners had canceled their memberships, thus reducing the funds available from dues.[95] It was necessary for the State Institute to step in and cosponsor a new journal as a continuation of the *ZfMw*. The last issue of volume 17 of the *ZfMw* appeared with the date of December 1935, and in 1936 the new *AfMf* appeared with a title page that bore the words "first volume" (erster Jahrgang) in large print and "volume 18 of the *Zeitschrift für Musikwissenschaft*" in small print.[96]

Besseler, in his other position as coordinator of periodicals in the State Institute, portrayed the establishment of *AfMf* as a resurrection of the old Bückeburg journal, the *Archiv für Musikwissenschaft*.[97] Its scope was to "expand" and to "serve the great solidarity of music research in the entire German-speaking region and in culturally related countries,"[98] and Schneider hoped that the support from the institute would effect higher honoraria for contributions and thereby encourage higher quality submissions.[99] The journal did show a few signs of change, but they were more ideological than qualitative: starting with the second volume, its featured articles and book reviews paid increased attention to racial studies, folk music research, and genealogy.

The *AfMf*, despite its new identity, served as Germany's primary scholarly journal for musicology, continuing the functions of the *ZfMw*. In the interest of demonstrating musicology's service to the public, Besseler stated the need for a second periodical "which would forge a connection between scholarship and [everyday] life in National Socialist Germany." The new "musicologically directed, cultural-political German music journal" would appear bimonthly and would be directed to a readership of "practical musicologists" (serving "as a natural link between research and life") and music lovers "disappointed with the present low standards of music periodicals." It would enable musicologists to address musicians and amateurs on all questions of the musical heritage and to take part in the tasks of the present "in the spirit of scholarly responsibility."[100] The outcome of this proposal was the journal *Deutsche Musik-kultur,* which appeared in 1936 and incorporated the periodical *Musik und Volk* in October 1937.[101] In an effort to solicit more input from amateur concerns, Besseler later tried to involve representatives from the Wehrmacht, the SA, the Hitler Youth, DAF, and others toward improving the journal.[102]

The creation of *Deutsche Musikkultur* was just one more example of how German musicology could make an easy transition from Weimar to Hitler by focusing on musicology's educational potential. It was in keeping with the Bückeburg Institute's original intentions to foster a healthy relationship with the community, a goal it had virtually abandoned in favor of serving the needs of scholars. The State Institute renewed the objectives of reaching out to the public, first in the reorientation of the Denkmäler editions and then in the creation of this less scientific journal to complement the *AfMf*. At the institute's 1934 annual meeting, the Reich representative highlighted the institute's ability "to serve the goal of National Socialism: the new forming of man and his art and culture."[103] The institute thus adapted its original agenda to the Nazi program, preserving and reviving old issues to further German culture and to serve the public.

The institute also revived one of its original initiatives of improving the education of young musicologists, a priority which also conformed to the National Socialist stated policy of encouraging and providing for the younger generation of professionals (*Nachwuchsförderung*). One of the original Fachausschüsse of the Bückeburg Institute had served higher education by offering advice on musicology curricula at German universities and offering retreats for professors.[104] The new State Institute likewise realized its dedication to musicological training shortly after its relocation by sponsoring a retreat exclusively for "younger colleagues and the new generation of scholars" (*wissenschaftlichen Nachwuchs*) in Frankfurt/Oder in October 1936.[105] Participation was strictly limited to thirty-three younger German scholars, most under forty years of age,[106] and a select number of foreign scholars known to be sympathetic to "the new Germany"[107] (as opposed to the considerable number of non-Germans finding fault with the Third Reich and canceling their DGMW memberships).

The Education Minister also lent his support to encouraging younger scholars. As a gesture of goodwill at the first general meeting in Berlin, Rust donated a bust of Hitler and endowed two prizes for the best doctoral dissertations in musicology, to be awarded on Hitler's birthday.[108] No one received the prize in the first year because no dissertation came up to the presumed National Socialist standards.[109] But even when a dissertation did finally win approval in 1939, Besseler, a member of the selection committee, complained to the Education Ministry about the decision. As the "only party member" on a committee including Schering, Schünemann, Max Schneider, Marius Schneider, and Blume, he protested that a dissertation by a Sudeten-German (his student Karl Michael Komma) on a politically provocative subject had been overlooked, despite the political significance of the recently annexed Sudeten-German region of Czechoslovakia. Besseler argued that the winning dissertation had not been subjected to "political evaluation" or judged for its service to "the new direction of the discipline in the National Socialist spirit." He railed against the committee's lack of political insight and blindness to "the National Socialist will for renewal of scholarship" and urged the ministry to clarify that the prize is not awarded for mere diligence but rather for demonstration of a plucky National Socialist spirit.[110]

The institute abandoned some of its older publishing projects after moving to Berlin, although it started to cooperate with other organizations in supporting similar enterprises: the complete works of Gluck, Haydn, Schein, and Fux; a series of editions of medieval music; piano reductions of Baroque opera in Lower Saxony and of other opera selections; facsimile editions of writings on music; and picture books on composers and music iconography. Some important research publications were taken over from other organizations or newly established: the *Bibliographie des Musikschrifttums,* edited by Kurt Taut, began in 1936 and took over the task formerly carried out by the *Jahrbuch der Musikbibliothek Peters.* The institute also started the *Verzeichnis der Neudrucke alter Musik* in 1936, edited by Walter Lott. Most important, the institute laid the foundation for the most comprehensive music reference work of post–World War II Germany, *Die Musik in Geschichte und Gegenwart* (MGG), and appointed Friedrich Blume as general editor, a job he held until 1968.[111]

The Decline of the DGMW

The DGMW, in the meantime, was feeling increasingly threatened. The establishment of the State Institute rendered its elaborate departmentalization of Fachgruppen superfluous, and an announcement in the last volume of the ZfMw read: "Since the former Bückeburg Institute has been raised to be designated the 'State Institute for German Music Research' (Berlin), thereby relieving the German Society for Musicology of a number of tasks, the future cooperation of both facilities should be realized."[112] The society was still searching for an appropriate government agency to serve as a sponsor. The ostensible snub from Goebbels in November 1933 was probably due to uncertainties in the partitioning of responsibilities between the Reich Culture Chamber, established in that same month, and the Education Ministry, but Schering was eager to settle the question.[113] Rust must have appeared more approachable than Goebbels as a potential sponsor because of his close involvement with the institute. Thus when Schering stepped down as president in 1937, his successor, Ludwig Schiedermair, actively pursued sponsorship from the Education Ministry.

Schiedermair's appointment initially incited a controversy among members. Schering enforced the Führerprinzip by not permitting an election, but according to Schiedermair, other members, especially Hellmuth von Hase of the publishing house of Breitkopf & Härtel, contested the appointment and challenged Schering's authority.[114] After accepting the post, Schiedermair claimed to have found the society in a state of internal turmoil, with each group doing what it wanted and showing no interest in working together.[115] He also reported that Schering had signed an unfavorable contract with the publishers of the *ZfMw,* Breitkopf & Härtel, and that he intended to cut all ties with Breit-kopf & Härtel in order to save the society from further exploitation. This, he claimed, could be carried through only by dissolving the society.[116]

Whether this was an accurate assessment of the situation or an outgrowth of personal rivalries with von Hase is open to speculation, but it marked the first step toward bringing the society under the influence of the Education Ministry in 1938. Schiedermair resigned as president in March 1938 and dissolved the DGMW with the intention of reestablishing it under the auspices of the minis-try, rationalizing that the dissolution would quell internal conflicts and above all wrest the monopoly of the journal from Breitkopf & Härtel. He had al-ready confided to Sandberger that the education minister was prepared to endorse a musicological conference.[117] The conference in question can be none other than the meeting held at the Reichsmusiktage in Düsseldorf in May 1938, running alongside the notorious Degenerate Music exhibit. The con-ference was publicized as the first musicological gathering in the new Reich, and its focus was the problem of "Music and Race," a theme supposedly suggested by Goebbels and elaborated on by Friedrich Blume in a keynote address.[118] The DGMW was not the only organization to hold a meeting at the Reichsmusiktage, but it was one of the few that adopted a central theme complementing the Degenerate Music exhibit. As the exhibit vilified the Jew-ish or Jewish-influenced "musical charlatans" of the Weimar period, the musi-cologists at the meeting focused their attention on aspects of racial research that could potentially support such vilification scientifically.

Participants at the Düsseldorf meeting gave serious consideration to the topical questions of music and race, German musical style elements, and music and the state. The program consisted of twenty-four individual papers, a sa-lutatory by Schiedermair, and Blume's keynote address.[119] The list of partici-pants is impressive, and the paper titles reflect most of the major trends in research that had risen to political importance.[120] A session devoted to Ger-man music (entitled simply "Deutsche Musik") included Hans Joachim Ther-stappen's paper "Music in the Greater German Realm" ("Die Musik im groß-deutschen Raum"), a timely study that rationalized the recent annexation of Austria with music-historical evidence. Another burning question, that of de-fining Germanness in music, was the subject of Müller-Blattau's paper ("Das Deutsche in der Musik"), which does not survive but, judging from his other works, probably employed characteristics of folk music to identify German elements in art music throughout the ages. The session "German Masters" ("Deutsche Meister") featured a rare appearance by the aging Theodor Kroyer, who delivered a paper on German style characteristics ("Deutsche Stileigentümlichkeit in der Musik"), and a paper by Rudolf Gerber on his racial and psychological analysis of Brahms's personality and works ("Volkstum und Rasse in der Persönlichkeit und Kunst von Johannes Brahms"). Walter Vetter's paper "National Characteristics in Mozart's Operas" ("Volkhafte Wesensmarkmale in Mozarts Opern," published in the *Zeitschrift für Musik* in the same year) attempted to derive German traits from Mozart operas, not from the obvious examples of the Singspiele, but rather from the Italian operas. Vetter used this opportunity to pay homage to Nazi ideologue Alfred Rosenberg and to deny Mendelssohn his German identity.[121]

Besseler led the session "Music and the State," which addressed current musical policy and how to bring musicology closer to the world of the music performer and public. Gerhard Pietzsch ("Staat und Musik") articulated the need to counteract the gradual alienation of music from society and to encourage music "written by the community, for the community of the National Socialist Volk." Steglich, like Pietzsch, drew on references to the Platonic state, commonly cited as a prototype for the Third Reich, especially in the area of education. The titles of papers in the session "Questions in Music Research" ("Fragen der Musikforschung") reflect once more the self-conscious evaluation of the field and its relevance: Theodor Werner's "The Music Scholar and Reality" ("Der Musikgelehrte und die Wirklichkeit"), E. Kirsch's "The Perspective of Music History in Transition" ("Musikgeschichtsbetrachtung am Wendepunkt"), and Werner Korte's anti-Semitic attack on humanistic musicology, "The Tasks of Musicology" ("Die Aufgaben der Musikwissenschaft").

Blume's keynote address set the stage for the final, and longest, session on music and race. He praised German musicology for its healthy situation, in spite of some postwar deviations, and restated the conference's goals of bringing musicology in touch with the people and addressing the questions of race that were plaguing both music practitioners and scholars.[122] In Blume's speech, as in his other works on racial musicology,[123] he gives the appearance of critiquing the methodology but not without obsequiousness toward the prevailing ideology; still his murky conclusions may be subtly condemning the interference of nonspecialists in the realm of musicology. The papers in the final session "Music and Race" offered a wide variety of interpretations of the concept. For example, Werner Danckert's "Folk, Tribe, and Race in the Light of Folk Song Research" ("Volkstum, Stammesart, Rasse im Lichte der Volksliedforschung") presented a meticulous comparison of the folk music styles of various German tribes (*Stämme*) and related them to the styles of various historical periods, while Frotscher's "Tasks and Problems of Musical Race-Style Research" ("Aufgaben und Probleme der musikalischen Rassenstilforschung") extrapolated aimlessly on deriving racial style from all the arts and using the results to dictate music education and policy.

Although the Düsseldorf meeting showed that the DGMW was serious about engaging musicology in questions central to the National Socialist worldview, it was to little avail in securing the future of the society. Schiedermair failed to disengage the society from its exploitive publisher, as the title pages of subsequent issues of the journal prove. Not only was Schering's plan to make the society more than just the producer of the journal never realized, but the society's functions became even less significant after 1933. First, the establishment of the State Institute rendered the society's elaborate new system of task forces superfluous. Second, since the *AfMf* came under joint editorship with the institute, the DGMW lost its role of producer of the journal and was demoted to a mere coproducer.

One year after the Düsseldorf meeting, Schiedermair stepped down as president and was replaced by the relatively unknown Alfons Kreichgauer, director of the institute's instrument collection, adjunct instructor at the Hochschule from 1935 to 1938, and a lecturer at the University of Berlin thereafter.[124] By summer 1940, the DGMW had come to a virtual standstill and was eventually dissolved by the Education Ministry.[125] With the Education Ministry's permission, Blume and Erich Schenk of Vienna called a meeting in the summer of 1941 to organize a new society — provisionally named the Reich League of German Musicologists (Reichsbund der deutschen Musikwissenschaftler) — to replace the DGMW, but nothing came of this plan.[126] The State Institute, in contrast, thrived by virtue of its large operations and collaboration with other Nazi cultural organizations before it was shut down on 1 January 1945.[127]

The Isolation of German Musicology

In many respects, German musicology in the interwar years thrived as never before, establishing organizations, projects, and publications during the Weimar period and attracting unprecedented recognition and government support in the Nazi years. Accompanying this domestic prosperity, however, was a gradual retreat from the non-German scholarly community, the negative effects of which would ultimately outweigh the benefits gained at home. Since the beginning of World War I, festering animosities among musicologists from warring nations motivated many to channel their energies into national rather than international causes, some from feelings of resentment, others because of frustration with the lack of cooperation. In the course of the Nazi years, the mistreatment and emigration of Jewish scholars and the disapproval from non-German colleagues contributed to the breakdown of the fragile foundations of international cooperation, and German scholars pushed themselves further into isolation as the years progressed.

Just as the DMG started out in 1918 with a pledge to renew international ties and plans to organize international conferences, so too did scholars from other German-speaking countries take steps to reverse the breakdown in communication brought on by the war. The first signs of international cooperation came out of a 1924 conference in Basel, which grew into a large international gathering with participants from Belgium, Denmark, Germany, England, Finland, France, Italy, Austria, Spain, and Czechoslovakia.[128] A more formal attempt to unite musicologists from several countries came shortly thereafter. The Union Musicologique, based in The Hague, set out to form a confederation of existing musicological societies. An organizational meeting took place in Lübeck in 1926, but it was attended by only three representatives from Germany, three from Denmark, two from Holland, and one from Austria; other invited countries sent no representatives. Abert, who attended as one of the German representatives, judged their absence as an indication that the time was not ripe for former enemy nations to work together with Germany and Austria, at least not on a formal scale, and he advised his colleagues to accept this passive resistance from Germany's former enemies. "Let us not take this too sentimentally or tragically; the last thing we want is to force ourselves on anyone. . . . The conference gave us the desired opportunity to recognize our position all too clearly and showed us unequivocally our future marching route. Therefore, for us it was not a disappointment." The outcome of this meeting was the resolution that the DMG would be ready to enter the Union as soon as "mainly the former war-waging states, at least France or England" joined.[129]

It took the energy and organizational skills of Austrian musicologist Guido Adler to exploit the interests of the Basel participants and successfully realize a revival of the IMS. Adler (b. 1855) cofounded one of the earliest musicological journals (*Vierteljahrsschrift für Musikwissenschaft*) in 1884 with two of the pioneers of German musicology, his elders Spitta and Chrysander. One year later he was appointed to the faculty in Prague and soon initiated the series Denkmäler der Tonkunst in Österreich, serving as general editor from 1894 to 1938. He succeeded Hanslick at the University of Vienna and founded its prestigious musicology department, while establishing style history as an important approach to the writing of music history. He continuously influenced the development of musicology on a broad scale through his early writings on defining the discipline, his publication of important collaborative works, and his organization of conferences. Adler had been a strong advocate of international cooperation and had warned against the dangers of nationalism in his public lecture at the 1924 Basel conference.[130] In 1927, he hosted a Beethoven centennial conference in Vienna that attracted an even wider international attendance than the Basel meeting and included participants from the United States, the Soviet Union, Portugal, and Hungary. Adler used the event to begin organizing the new International Musicological Society, with a board of directors drawn from the four leading nations in musicological research (Germany-Austria, England, France, and Italy) and with Basel as its central headquarters.[131] Basel's municipal authorities provided office space for the society and approved a yearly subsidy, as did the German Reich, the first national government to lend support to the organization.[132]

Although German scholars played prominent roles in the new IMS (the organizational meeting had more representatives from Germany than from any other country), their self-image as unappreciated outcasts from the international community never entirely disappeared. Such feelings arose not solely out of German nationalism, but also out of other countries' refusal to accept German scholars back into the fold. In the communications section in the first volume of the *ZfMw*, Einstein expressed resentment that Germany had "naturally" been excluded from an international conference of intellectuals in Paris.[133] Non-German scholars in several fields had drawn lines between "Allied science" and "Teutonic science" and maintained the two to be incompatible.[134] Such experiences in the scholarly community made German musicologists particularly cynical about the future of international cooperation. Following the well-attended Basel meeting in 1924, Einstein aired his doubts that the show of interest in international exchange would have any long-term effect in unifying the musicological community because each national group had become more involved in its own concerns since the beginning of the war and had gone off in its own direction.[135] Similarly, when the DMG attempted to organize an international conference in Leipzig, it, not surprisingly, approached the international community with great caution and sought out only its closest allies.

The tensions between the new IMS and its German members grew steadily in the years after its formation and reached a climax at the 1936 meeting in Barcelona. By that time, a number of prominent musicologists had left Germany to escape political and racial persecution. The Nazi government had officially encouraged tendencies toward nationalist isolation by warning scholars in all disciplines against cultivating contacts with Jewish or Jewish-influenced scholarly circles and instructing them to sever ties with German-Jewish émigrés. The scholarly community outside Germany simultaneously viewed intellectual developments in Germany with great skepticism.

In preparation for the Barcelona meeting, Heinrich Besseler, appointed by the Education Ministry to head the German delegation,[136] handpicked only those colleagues who would present a strong and unified front against a perceived enemy alliance of Jewish émigrés and their sympathizers. Besseler seems to have planted the idea of an anti-German conspiracy in the minds of other participants. Otto Ursprung, for example, insisted on the basis of information from Besseler that it was necessary to attend the conference in order to pose a counterweight to the émigrés in attendance.[137] The German delegation came to envision an enemy camp consisting of Jews (Guido Adler, Otto Gombosi), German-Jewish émigrés (Curt Sachs, Alfred Einstein, Leo Kestenberg), and their supposed sympathizers, most notably the English president of the IMS, Edward Dent. They counted among their allies the Spanish musicologist Higini Anglès, the organizer of the conference. Anglès was always active in promoting German causes in Spanish musicology and would later spend time in Germany while escaping the Spanish Civil War. He was working on the IMS front to encourage a strong German representation. When the German delegation had to be drastically reduced, he expressed his disappointment to his friend Ursprung, noting that the conference would be very well attended, "especially by Jews who no longer live in Germany," and regretting that more musicologists from Germany would not be able to attend.[138] He ultimately demonstrated so much pro-German support at the conference in the face of perceived anti-German sentiments that the German consul in Barcelona personally thanked him.[139]

In forming the ideal "German front," Besseler recommended delegates to the Education Ministry on the basis of political reliability as well as scholarly reputation. He believed that Johannes Wolf, for instance, had "looked after German interests badly," something Besseler found "all the more regrettable" given the impending "considerable opposition from Jews and émigrés" the Germans would have to face in Barcelona.[140] Besseler proceeded to use a variety of tactics to block Wolf's influence. Wolf was currently the German representative to the IMS board and vice president, but Besseler hoped to remove him from the IMS inner circle and promote Kroyer instead. Kroyer would not agree to offer his services if it meant insulting Wolf, so Besseler asked Georg Schünemann to urge Wolf to step down from his offices, adding that the Education Ministry and German colleagues had disapproved of Wolf's behavior as former board member of the International Society for Comparative Musicology. Doubtful that this warning would suffice, Besseler also urged the ministry to make approval for Wolf's attendance at the conference contingent upon his stepping down. Besseler wished to ensure that Wolf's resignation not be publicized until the delegation reached Barcelona, since "certain interests could exploit this resignation to gain votes," or a "counter-campaign" could be attempted. The scheme succeeded, and Wolf stepped down.[141]

Besseler also urged the ministry to block Wilibald Gurlitt's attendance because he was married to a "full Jew" and, as Besseler speculated, had laid great importance on cultivating contacts abroad because his university position in Freiburg was not secure. Besseler deduced that Gurlitt had personally elicited an invitation from Edward Dent and felt that Gurlitt's attendance would not benefit the German delegation, which ideally would present a group of scholars "who now and in the future will carry on work within Germany."[142] The ministry followed Besseler's advice and withheld permission from Gurlitt to attend the meeting, much to the surprise and dismay of both Higini Anglès, a Gurlitt student, and the German consulate in Spain.[143] In contrast, Besseler eagerly endorsed the participation of Marius Schneider as specialist in musical ethnology and urged Kurt Huber, currently head of the State Institute's folk music division, to join his forces, especially since "the émigré Curt Sachs will probably speak in French on 'musical prehistory.'"[144]

Despite Besseler's energetic efforts, the German delegation remained small because of government restriction on taking hard currency out of the country, making it impossible for many to afford the trip even though the Education Ministry had approved their participation. In the end, only Besseler, Huber, Hans Engel, Hermann Keller from the Musikhochschule in Stuttgart, and Kroyer and his assistant Walter Gerstenberg were allowed to go, while Wolf, Schneider, and Ursprung stayed behind. According to Besseler's detailed report to the Education Ministry, the conference ran smoothly, and with the help of Anglès, Kroyer was elected vice president of the society. But Besseler also complained of the Spanish government's anti-German and allegedly Masonic political stand (Freemasons were one of the groups declared enemies of National Socialism) and Edward Dent's anti-German influence on the organization. Besseler believed that Dent had consulted with Guido Adler and Leo Kestenberg before the meeting and conspired to recommend "the Jewish émigré Alfred Einstein, now living in Vienna," to replace Wolf as German representative.[145]

The Barcelona situation set a precedent for the Education Ministry to involve itself directly in international musicological conferences. The ministry considered setting up a permanent, central planning committee for international musicological conferences to include Schiedermair, Blume, Schenk, and possibly Müller-Blattau and Engel.[146] Furthermore, following an exemplary execution of his responsibilities as delegation head, Besseler was called on to represent Germany at a number of international conferences and to furnish the Education Ministry with full reports, paying special attention to the political climate at each event. The ministry gave Besseler orders to take special note of the German presence and assess the degree of anti-German sentiment, in order to determine the success of the ministry's "reform of international scholarly collaboration in the international scholarly societies," the immediate goal of which was the "preparation and guarantee of a strong German influence in international cooperation." This concern for German influence in international scholarship was part of a larger political responsibility for the future leaders of Europe — the Germans — who would be just as accountable "for guiding scholarly collaborations in their sphere of power" as "for rebuilding the economic and political order of Europe."[147]

All Besseler's reports dutifully address the ministry's concerns. In his report on the Third International Music Conference that took place as part of the annual music festival in Florence (the Maggio Musicale Fiorentino), Besseler noted the unsatisfactory state of the "Fascist spirit" among the Italians; a "dominant art rhetoric colored by liberal individualism"; the "prominence" of Darius Milhaud and Henri Prunières ("French Jews who came to be known through the postwar international music enterprise"); the absence of German émigrés, who, he found out confidentially, had been warned to stay away; and the need for a stronger German presence and a "thorough purge" of the influence of "old internationalists and Freemasons" from the Maggio Musicale Fiorentino.[148] In his 1938 remarks on the upcoming IMS conference in New York, Besseler once again described the organization as "under Jewish-Masonic influence" and saw the decision to move the conference to New York as "an act which, given the situation described, can not leave the German members of the society indifferent."[149] His final report on the New York meeting lists the attending European representatives, carefully singling out Jews (Fernando Liuzzi, Dragan Plamenac, Otto Gombosi), a Catholic clergyman (Albert Smijers), a "Freemason and friend of Jews" (Edward Dent) and his "accomplice" (Knud Jeppesen), as well as the Jewish émigrés then living in the United States (Curt Sachs, Alfred Einstein, and Manfred Bukofzer).[150]

The tensions surrounding the Barcelona meeting persisted long after all participants had gone home. The IMS, dissatisfied with the German firm Breitkopf & Härtel as publishers of its journal *Acta musicologica*, had decided to give the journal over to a Danish publisher. Besseler urged his colleagues to withhold any contributions to the periodical and cease collaboration with the president of the IMS for this "unfriendly act" against Germany, with which several complied.[151] This boycott not only created more bad sentiment in an already unfavorable climate, but also cut musicologists off from one more publishing outlet during a time of dwindling opportunities. The Ministry of the Interior and the Education Ministry had already reduced publishing options with new ordinances. In August 1934, the Ministry of the Interior proscribed submissions to foreign journals which had been started by recent émigrés from Germany.[152] In January 1935, the Education Ministry then issued an order to scholars to limit the scope of their journals, to reduce the number of dissertations reprinted in them (dissertations were usually short and were often published as long articles rather than as books), and to reduce fees for editors and honoraria for contributors. German scholars, it stated, should learn to do with less for the good of German scholarship.[153]

Such sacrifices only compounded the difficulties for German scholars trying to get their work published: on the one hand, they were already experiencing rejection from non-German periodicals on political grounds,[154] and on the other hand, very little was done to create new outlets at home. What appears as a rash of new music journals created after 1933 is deceptive, since many were simply renamed, reorganized, and combined with other journals. Between 1934 and 1938, several journals underwent Gleichschaltung in the same manner as the *ZfMw,* having been dissolved (often involving a purge of unacceptable personnel), reestablished under the auspices of a government or party organization, and given a new name. The frequency of this process conveys the false impression of a broadening of intellectual activity under the Nazis. A second process then took place in the war years, when financial constraints forced numerous periodicals to merge into one journal with a completely new title. On the whole, the number of music periodicals declined between 1933 and 1945.

Gleichschaltung and wartime merger affected numerous music journals. *Melos* became *Neues Musikblatt* in 1934 and merged with *Zeitschrift für Musik, Allgemeine Musikzeitung,* and *Die Musik* to form *Musik im Kriege* in 1944 (*Die Musik* and *Musik im Kriege* were edited by Herbert Gerigk and came under the auspices of the Rosenberg Bureau). *Musikalische Volksbildung* became subsumed under the Education Ministry and the NS-Lehrerbund as *Völkische Musikerziehung* in 1934, which merged with *Deutsche Tonkünstler-Zeitung* in 1944 to form the *Zeitschrift für völkische Musikerziehung. Der Kreis* and *Die Singgemeinde* merged into *Musik und Volk* (under the Reichsbund Volkstum und Heimat), which was then incorporated into *Deutsche Musikkultur* (under the State Institute) in 1937 and finally included in *Musik in Jugend und Volk* in 1938, under the Reich Youth Leadership and the DAF. In 1936 the *Bundeszeitung des deutschen Mandolinen- und Gitarrenspielers* became part of *Die Volksmusik* (under the Reichsverband für Volksmusik in the Reich Music Chamber) and then merged with *Gut Ton, Die Handharmonika,* and *Zupf- und Balgmusik* to become *Musik am Feierabend* in 1944. A few new journals appeared in the 1940s but were, for obvious reasons of war constraints, very short-lived. Two volumes of the Propaganda Ministry's *Jahrbuch der deutschen Musik,* edited by von Hase, appeared in 1943 and 1944 and included contributions from a few musicologists.[155] Also, a select number of old journals were revived in new guise, such as Abert's *Mozart-Jahrbuch,* which had appeared in 1923 and 1929 and reappeared as the *Neues Mozart-jahrbuch* in 1941 (the 150th anniversary of Mozart's death), brought out by the Mozarteum and edited by Erich Valentin.

Reviewing the balance sheet of gains and losses to German musicology in the Hitler years, it becomes necessary to sort out the qualitative from the quantitative. The pointless exclusion of valued non-Aryan colleagues and the growing isolation from international communication resulted in qualitative losses from which German scholarship could hardly recover after World War II. Even ostensible gains are tempered by the fact that "new" organizations, facilities, and publications such as the State Institute, the DGMW, EdM, and a long list of journals were essentially only renamed and reorganized, not newly created. Their emergence, linked with the establishment of numerous party and government interests, gives the appearance of a burst of innovation, creativity, and support in the twelve-year period of Nazi rule, when in fact most ventures simply reorganized themselves in order to enjoy government or party sponsorship.

In the final analysis, the Nazi regime was more in the business of salvaging old musicological enterprises than creating new ones, but the overall financial and organizational backing it offered the field far exceeded support from prior administrations. The Weimar government had been ill-equipped to respond to pleas for assistance when cultural enterprises faced fiscal vulnerability. The Nazi government, however, with its complex infrastructure of numerous cultural committees, chambers, and party organizations heeded more cries for help, particularly from organizations that could demonstrate shared goals with its cultural agenda. Organizations shed their former identities, purged their personnel, recast their bylaws, and announced their commitment to serving the Volksgemeinschaft in accordance with National Socialist principles. For musicologists, this meant building on their earlier commitments to focusing on German music history, encouraging the work of German scholars, and breaking down barriers between scholarship and the public. It also meant betraying colleagues who were Jewish or married to Jews, paying lip service to questionable areas of "scientific" inquiry such as racial research, and cutting themselves off from the scholarly community in the rest of the world.

4

Musicology in the University

The German university, a venerable institution dating to the early nineteenth century, served as a model for university systems in other countries. During the Weimar Republic, however, its infrastructure for guaranteeing academic freedom by concentrating power in the hands of full professors came under criticism. Professors resisted any attempts at university reforms, remaining mistrustful of the Weimar Republic and its democratizing motives. Musicologists, however, were of a different mind. Facing difficulties establishing a foothold in the university system, they were motivated to preserve close ties to the community as music directors, and faculties placed great value on the quality of their early music ensembles as a means of keeping musicology in the public eye.

The Nazi takeover of universities was less disruptive than one might assume. An overwhelming conservatism had made the university a fertile breeding ground for anti-Semitism, especially since 1918. Musicology faculties in Germany had always kept their doors closed to Jewish candidates, with the exception of those few qualified in innovative areas. Thus when National Socialism started to infiltrate the universities, the purge of Jewish faculty barely changed the profile of musicology departments. Nazi university reforms did, however, strip full professors of their influence and leave internal disputes open to personal and political intrigue. But, if anything, this power shift placed musicology in a stronger position in the university. Obligatory ceremonies and political rituals made the musicologist–music director indispensable and gave musicology departments leverage in securing faculty positions.

Military conscription threw universities into complete disarray during World War II, and musicology was a vulnerable discipline, as it was hardly considered crucial for the war effort. Nevertheless, musicologists offered their services beyond the academy, conducting courses for soldiers and maintaining an active schedule of wartime lectures to demonstrate the indefatigable spirit of German scholarship. Throughout the war, the university community remained as conservative and politically aloof as ever, and instances of protest, such as the martyrdom of musicologist Kurt Huber, were rare.

The University and the Weimar Republic

By 1918, the German university had come to be regarded as an antiquated institution intent on upholding a proud German intellectual tradition. The nineteenth-century reforms of Wilhelm von Humboldt that guaranteed academic freedom in a totally self-governing environment had made it a model for many Western university systems. Although financed by provincial ministries of culture with curators serving as government representatives at the universities in some provinces, faculties were privileged by law to run their own affairs, with most of the power concentrated in the hands of the full professor (*Ordinarius* or *ordentlicher Professor*).[1] Each Ordinarius headed a department and dealt directly with the ministries. A rector presided over the senate of the university, a body consisting of the four newly elected deans of the four *Fakultäten* (the university consisted of the law, medicine, theology, and philosophy divisions or "faculties," the last of which, the Philosophische Fakultät, included musicology and all other arts and sciences); the four previous deans; the current and outgoing rectors; and five elected *Ordinarien*.[2]

All other instructors were considerably less privileged than the Ordinarien. Ranked below the Ordinarius were the *Extraordinarius* or *außerordentlicher Professor,* who held a tenured civil service position but was not an official member of the university faculty; the *Privatdozent,* who had earned a doctorate and had achieved the scholarly credentials of the *Habilitation* granting permission to hold lectures at the university (*venia legendi*); and the *Lektor* or *Assistent,* who had earned the doctorate, was working on the Habilitation, and was permitted to assist in teaching.[3] These last two categories were traditionally not salaried, but rather earned their income from lecturing fees collected directly from the students. Within these basic categories were further subcategories. The designation *planmäßig* or *etatsmäßig* could indicate that a professor's salary was drawn from the ministry's regular budget, as opposed to those positions designated as *außerplanmäßig, nichtetatsmäßig,* or *persönlich.* When an individual was promoted nominally without becoming a civil servant and functioned mainly as an instructor, the designation *titular* or *nichtbeamtet* was used. Finally, the *Honorarprofessor* was unsalaried, although technically at a higher rank than the Extraordinarius, and was usually an older scholar specially appointed to instruct on a part-time basis.[4]

This system protected the self-governing powers of the universities and guaranteed academic freedom by preventing the interference of the state, but it functioned best on a small scale. A sharp rise in the student population before World War I created a need for more instructors, and the increase in junior faculty and lecturers led to a serious imbalance of power. The Ordinarien, retaining their control even as the lower ranks swelled, were unwilling to grant any more authority to their subordinates. Junior faculty members banded together in a number of national organizations to demand more influence in the university administration, but built-in safeguards protecting the powers of the Ordinarien hindered any changes. The result was an unhealthy atmosphere of competitiveness, abuses of power in determining promotions, and a stalemate over finding a solution.[5]

When the war ended, the professorial class found themselves in an awkward position, having in a sense outlived their usefulness in an industrial society.[6] Professors were generally mistrustful of the new democracy, and while a few supported the Republic, most of the academic elite considered themselves above politics, resisted change, and accepted the new system — if at all — only out of necessity. Most academics assumed the persona of the apolitical esthete, characterized by Thomas Mann in his *Reflections of a Nonpolitical Man (Betrachtungen eines Unpolitischen,* 1918): culture bearers of the German nation who held themselves above the workings of politics, dedicated themselves to scientific objectivity, and defended German Kultur against the invasion of Western *civilisation.*[7] From the time of the Enlightenment, Germans had held themselves at arm's length from intellectual developments in England and France, understanding *Aufklärung* as something quite different from a shallow and utilitarian "Enlightenment" in the Anglo-French sense. Bildung and Kultur were conceived as antiutilitarian and much deeper than "education" and "civilization."[8] World War I served to sharpen the perceived distinctions between the Germans and the Western allies who fought against them.

To the extent that Weimar professors articulated any political views, most blamed Germany's military defeat on industrial conspirators at home, adhering to the so-called stab-in-the-back legend. Those who did associate with organized political parties mainly gravitated toward the German Nationals

(Deutschnationalen) or the right wing of the German People's Party (Deutsche Volkspartei). The leading parties — the Democrats and Social Democrats — had only a modest representation among professors, and the small number of socialists and pacifists kept a low profile at the universities. The more politically engaged "republicans of reason" (*Vernunftrepublikaner*), those who were resigned to the republic as the only feasible option at the time, were also small in number.[9]

The university community seemed to feel that the best way to guarantee successes in the future was not to tamper with successes of the past and strongly resisted change, even when the government suggested reforms that could benefit the institution. In addition to urging the universities to pay more attention to the broader needs of society, Prussian minister of culture C. H. Becker had attempted to take steps toward improving the contentious climate among faculty members. He proposed measures that would minimize income inequities by guaranteeing salaries for lecturers and promoting Extraordinarien to Ordinarien; and he hoped to diminish abuses of power (without entirely removing them) by setting up a neutral committee to review hiring and promotion decisions.[10] Professors rejected these and other suggestions as invasive and found Becker's reforms particularly distasteful because, unlike his predecessors in the ministry who were not academics, Becker was a renowned scholar of oriental studies and was condemned for "fouling [his] own nest."[11]

Musicology within and beyond the Academy

The Weimar era ushered in a growth spurt for musicological activity at universities that included the establishment of full professorships in at least nine institutions, but a general reluctance to create full-fledged departments kept musicology from gaining a firm footing. For example, the department in Bonn was established in 1919, but its director, Ludwig Schiedermair, did not secure a state-funded full professorship until 1942.[12] The university in Freiburg/Breisgau also set up a musicology department in 1919 but appointed only a Lektor, Wilibald Gurlitt, as its head. By the end of the first year, Gurlitt had demonstrated his ability to run the seminar efficiently and "in strict scientific form," such that the university promoted him to keep him from accepting a position at Heidelberg, but it was not until 1929, ten years after the establishment of the department, that Gurlitt was promoted to Ordinarius.[13]

In Heidelberg, the university's resistance to promote its musicologists led to a rapid turnover in personnel and long stretches of time without a professor in musicology. Kroyer arrived in Heidelberg in 1920 and was promoted to Ordinarius in 1922,[14] but he remained only one more year before moving on to

Leipzig in 1923. Moser then took over at the Extraordinarius level but left in frustration in 1927 after his application for promotion was turned down because the administration refused to set a precedent by promoting professors after only two years.[15] Heinrich Besseler, appointed in 1928 to succeed Moser, tried repeatedly to be promoted to Ordinarius and, despite his scholarly reputation and political conformity in the Nazi years, failed to achieve that rank until after World War II.

Such procrastination caused even more difficulties in Cologne. Ernst Bücken established the musicology department in 1920 and functioned as its director from 1921 to 1932 without ever achieving the rank of Ordinarius. In 1922 he asked for a promotion, emphasizing the need for a strong, well-established musicology institute in Cologne, especially since the discipline had already been recognized in all other German universities, but all he gained was a promotion to Extraordinarius in 1924, and then not even in the permanent, civil service category.[16] Even if the university's decisions were based on its dissatisfaction with Bücken the individual rather than a reluctance to acknowledge musicology, it showed no interest in recruiting an Ordinarius any time in the first decade of the department's existence. The absence of a senior scholar caused serious problems for students when in 1928 the Prussian Ministry of Education prohibited the writing of dissertations in departments that had no permanent senior professors.[17]

The depression retarded the establishment of musicology even more. In Leipzig, home of one of the oldest and most famous musicology departments, the university had hesitated to give full recognition to musicology for some time. Hugo Riemann (b. 1849) is acclaimed as one of the most important musicologists of his time, known for his mastery in music theory, history, acoustics, aesthetics, performance practice, editing, lexicography, and the brilliant synthesis of several of these areas of knowledge. He became a professor in Leipzig in 1901 and director of the Saxon Research Institute for Musicology in 1914 but never held a position as Ordinarius, despite his illustrious and productive career. After Riemann's death, the dean raised his position to Ordinarius and appointed Hermann Abert in 1919 and Kroyer 1923, but Kroyer was ultimately so frustrated with the limitations imposed by cutbacks during the depression that he left for Cologne in 1932.[18] The university at first tried to keep him from leaving, but when his decision seemed irreversible, the authorities used his departure as an opportunity to save money by terminating the Ordinarius position.[19]

The university tried to solicit funds from a private source, the publisher H. Hinrichson, to make up the difference between the cost of an Extraordinarius and an Ordinarius.[20] Hinrichson offered 20,000 marks to cover the difference for approximately four years, but the Saxon education ministry declared that it was "not in a position to accept such a gift."[21] The university failed to find a successor for Kroyer until summer 1933, when it appointed Helmut Schultz to the lower-ranked Extraordinarius position. Despite the lower classification, Schultz carried all of the responsibilities of an Ordinarius — heading the department, the instrument museum, and the Saxon Research Institute for Musicology — in addition to the increased teaching load caused by Hermann Zenck's departure in October 1932.[22] The demotion of the position prompted outrage not only among the Philosophische Fakultät but also among scholars outside the university.[23] Many musicologists were unimpressed with Leipzig's choice of a young man who had produced little more than an average dissertation, and they made accusations of nepotism.[24] In subsequent years the ministry rejected other proposals to reinstate the Ordinarius and further reduced the musicology department's staff and financial resources.[25]

The immaturity of musicology as a scholarly discipline kept it from gaining a firm footing in the university, owing to a certain amount of mistrust from other fields. But because the musicology profession was far less ensconced in the university culture than other academic professions, musicologists held a rather unusual position of freely moving within and beyond the academy. They compensated for their tenuous university status by channeling their energies into performance groups that served both the university and the non-academic community. This flexibility allowed them to respond more favorably than other academics to the growing pressures after World War I to contribute to the nation's commonwealth.

As the permanence of musicology in universities proved unpredictable, scholars drew on their heritage as music directors to move beyond the academy. Karl Gustav Fellerer suggested in 1928 that the old combination of musicologist–music director be reinstated so that young scholars could find opportunities in the conservatory and not be limited to the university.[26] Shortly thereafter, Willibald Nagel reported on his success with such an experiment in the conservatory in Württemberg.[27] Musicologists in universities also extended their duties beyond research and classroom instruction. Leipzig was an important center for musical activity, and the head of the musicology department there was expected to work with the Thomaskirche, the State Conservatory, the Gewandhaus Orchestra, and the city orchestra, as well as playing an important role in music education in all of Saxony.[28] After Hugo Riemann revived the institution of the collegium musicum shortly after the turn of the century,[29] the Leipzig faculty placed a high priority on seeking experienced collegium directors for their musicology positions. When it proposed promoting Schering from Privatdozent to Extraordinarius in 1915, its endorsement called attention to his collegium performances.[30] Before appointing Abert in 1919, the selection committee praised his direction of the collegium, an institution that had become "traditional and indispensable" in Leipzig.[31] Direction of the collegium was reserved for the Ordinarius starting with Kroyer, whose performances were cited not only for their scholarly and educational value but also for their "unmistakably favorable effects on wider circles."[32]

The collegium musicum drew even more attention to musicology departments in smaller cities, where its performances were a significant component of the local musical fare. Herbert Birtner established a collegium in Marburg in 1930,[33] and Hans Engel's collegium in Greifswald was part of an initiative to promote an interest in local music history,[34] allowing scholars to uncover and edit works of regional composers and perform them with the collegium. Müller-Blattau's collegium in Königsberg drew its participants from the community as well as the student body and involved its audiences in educational dialogues on the historical meaning of the pieces performed.[35] In its first year, the musicology department in Bonn reported that its historical performances of early operas and church music "received notice far beyond Bonn."[36] Gustav Becking's collegium at the university in Erlangen similarly received praise for its successes in Bayreuth, Würzburg, Coburg, Munich, and other cities.[37]

The collegium eventually took on the function of promoting German culture within and beyond the Reich by reviving masterpieces of Germany's past. Gurlitt was one of the pioneers in this venture; he earned praise for instilling in his Freiburg group a true dedication to reviving old German masterpieces, insisting on the use of early instruments, and highlighting rarely heard works.[38] Gurlitt envisioned the collegium movement of the 1920s as an opportunity for musicologists to demonstrate a merger of "the best tradition of our German music history with the healthy spirit of our present-day youth and amateur music movements." It allowed musicologists to demonstrate their sincere efforts to break away from overspecialization in their scholarship as well as to preserve Germany's national treasures of early music.[39] Müller-Blattau, inspired by Gurlitt, gave his repertoire the same German emphasis. He took his group on a Baltic tour in 1932 to perform a German baroque program and a program of "Hausmusik [in the time of] Goethe," fulfilling the important political function of encouraging German culture in Eastern Europe.[40] The preservation of German culture in the "detached" East was also Gotthold Frotscher's reason for starting a collegium in Danzig in 1926.[41]

The noteworthy cultural-political function of the collegium gave musicologists a strong argument for funding their activities, particularly in outlying "culturally endangered" regions. It was argued that German music and its scholarship should be cultivated in such regions to ward off foreign cultures. Cologne, for example, lay within the occupied Rhineland in the western part of Prussia, close to the French border. Bücken emphasized the department's important role in strengthening Rhenish-German interests (especially by challenging Belgian claims that Beethoven had Belgian lineage); the importance of cataloging music performance in the Rhineland in the past century in order to study the "musicality of the Rhineland Germans"; and its valuable service of providing public lectures and performances.[42] His nationalistic emphasis struck a chord with the authorities, who placed great value on "the strengthening of German musicological aspirations in the Rhineland" and promised to provide state funding for "musicological cultural activities" that included public lectures and "surveillance of foreign propaganda."[43]

Jews in the University before 1933

The combination of a nationalistic, antiliberal atmosphere with unchecked self-rule made the university fertile ground for anti-Semitism. Under the Kaiser, university teaching had provided more openings for Jews than other professions because faculty hiring had to conform to stricter qualifications and was presumably less vulnerable to nepotism and prejudice. For a brief period in the late nineteenth century, Jews had opportunities not only to enter the university ranks but also to become Ordinarien. Still, converts to Christianity had a definite advantage over practicing Jews, and objective sciences were more open to Jews than such areas as literature, classics, and other ideology-prone disciplines. These opportunities diminished during World War I: the total percentage of Jews appointed at universities declined from 2.8 percent in 1889 to 1.2 percent in 1917.[44]

After 1918, the situation worsened; stronger constitutional measures to ensure equal opportunities for all religions were overriden by the sharp rise in anti-Semitic feelings that emerged from military defeat, the economic crises, and the rise of National Socialism. Prospects for Jews turned especially bleak as students gravitated toward the political right and professors openly defied measures proposed by the Republic. Contemporary statistics show that the percentage of Jewish Ordinarien (including baptized Jews) declined during the Weimar Republic from 6.9 percent in 1909–10 to 5.6 percent in 1931–32.[45] Whether justified or not, Jews were assumed to have liberal leanings and therefore were held responsible for the current ills of society. Jewish instructors could lose their teaching privileges on the mere suspicion of their harboring antinational thoughts,[46] and because professorial appointments were usually political, it was extremely difficult for Jews to rise to the level of Ordinarius.

Anti-Jewish sentiment among German intellectuals came to full fruition by the mid-1920s. Up to that time, anti-Semitism was rampant but not openly articulated.[47] Then in 1925 the German Academic Convocation issued a proclamation stating: "The alienation of German colleges performed at the hands of Jewish instructors and students must be barred. No more teachers of Jewish extraction are to be hired. Jewish students will be limited to a quota."[48] It is not hard to imagine that eight years later, in 1933, universities were ready and willing to implement the legal exclusion of Jews from higher education. The removal of Jews from academic posts in 1933 was, in effect, little more than a legitimization of long-standing practices and deep-seated prejudices.

Musicology faculties were hardly free of anti-Semitism and may have surpassed other disciplines in their discrimination against Jewish colleagues. The study of music was by its very nature not a value-free intellectual exercise, and like other disciplines prone to ideological and national influences, musicology offered far fewer opportunities to Jews than, for example, mathematics, medicine, and other more objective sciences.[49] When large numbers of Jewish musicologists started to leave Germany in 1933, only two of a group of approximately one hundred and fifty[50] — Curt Sachs and Erich von Hornbostel — held positions as university professors, and neither one would have come so far had he not possessed unique qualifications for developing new areas of musicology. The newness of the discipline and its openness to social sciences and interdisciplinary studies may have thus allowed for the only window of opportunity for Jewish scholars.

That both Sachs and Hornbostel were active in Berlin is significant. Berlin strove to have the most prestigious university in the Reich, and its close ties with the Reich government gave it exclusive access to funding for new areas of research. From the days of Hermann von Helmholtz and Philipp Spitta in the late nineteenth century, the musicology curriculum at Berlin always required training in both music history and systematic musicology. Carl Stumpf and his students Hornbostel and Sachs had nurtured the areas of acoustics, music psychology, and comparative musicology into thriving fields. Hornbostel additionally built up a renowned archive of sound recordings from all over the world.[51] Sachs was the foremost scholar in organology, had proven himself in studies in ancient music and other areas,[52] and was director of the instrument collection at the Staatliche Hochschule für Musik. Both were sole experts in their fields, but they would have encountered difficulties entering the musicology faculty without Stumpf's guidance and intervention, and undoubtedly they would have faced further obstacles in trying to advance. In a letter he wrote after World War II, Sachs alluded to Stumpf's important role in getting him onto the faculty; however, "in a Fatherland where anyone exhibiting the slightest mediocrity could achieve Ordinarius rank," Sachs was unable to achieve that rank in his fourteen years at the university.[53]

Although German-Jewish émigrés had a considerable impact on musicology outside Germany, the notion that a brain drain resulted from the Nazis' racist policies must be qualified by the fact that most Jews who fled Germany were unlikely to penetrate the ranks of German universities even if Hitler had not come to power. Many who became leading figures overseas were either students in 1933 or had just finished their degrees (e.g., Manfred Bukofzer, Willi Apel, Edward Lowinsky, and Erich Hertzmann). Most other Jewish musicologists never held positions as professors in Germany before 1933. Some managed to remain close to academic life by working in libraries, archives, and small institutes (Robert Lachmann, Käthi Meyer-Baer, and Georg Kinsky), while others turned to journalism and editing, limiting their scholarly work to their spare time (Alfred Einstein, Hugo Leichtentritt, Paul Nettl, and Otto Gombosi).

Alfred Einstein (b. 1880) was well known as the foremost expert on the Italian madrigal and the works of Mozart, and his skill and productivity were so widely respected that he was entrusted with the responsibilities of editing *ZfMw*, revising Riemann's *Musiklexikon,* and enlarging and correcting Köchel's catalogue of Mozart's works. Despite these outstanding scholarly achievements, he was systematically excluded from securing an academic position from the time he earned his doctorate in 1903 until his forced emigration in 1933. He was not allowed to proceed with his Habilitation because his doctoral adviser, Adolf Sandberger, refused to endorse him. Einstein was convinced that Sandberger was motivated by anti-Jewish feelings,[54] and he believed that Sandberger recommended him as general editor of the *ZfMw* only to ease the guilt he felt over ruining his student's career.[55] Einstein was not alone in his assessment of Sandberger's anti-Semitism, which was generally known throughout the musicology community.[56] Other musicology students complained of similar acts of discrimination by their professors. In 1930, one complained that professors in Cologne were hindering Jewish students from receiving their degrees, and he urged the Jewish community to refrain from contributing funds to the university's building expansion project.[57]

Despite initial setbacks, Einstein persisted in pursuing an academic post on the strength of his scholarly recognition and applied to succeed Moser in Heidelberg in 1927.[58] Moser assessed Einstein's chances as good, given his publications and the respect he enjoyed from the scholarly community, but had other reservations: "first of all, he doesn't have his Habilitation, and then, his Judaism—this has nothing to do with the politics of the faculty, on the contrary we're all very liberal here. But the fact is that there are already so many Jews here that the ministry would hesitate to increase the number."[59] Moser's logic was typical of "enlightened" anti-Semitism among academics. When he claimed that Heidelberg was liberal but already had its share of Jews, he spoke as one who could remember a time when Jews had no chance of holding university positions. Heidelberg was liberal, relatively speaking, but there was only so much change a community could tolerate. The entry of the Nazis sealed Einstein's fate in Germany. A 1950 interview with Einstein in *Time* magazine concluded: "by chasing him out of his rut and back to work as a master mason in music scholarship, Adolf Hitler, [Einstein] says, became 'my greatest benefactor.' "[60]

The situation for Jews was quite different in Austria and above all Vienna, where the musicology faculty grew to rival the best in Germany under the direction of Guido Adler, a Jew. Adler had succeeded Edward Hanslick as Ordinarius in 1898, and by the time he retired in 1927, the five-member faculty included two other Jews, Egon Wellesz and Wilhelm Fischer.[61] When their systematic musicologist Richard Wallaschek died in 1917, they considered trying to recruit the Austrian-born Hornbostel in order to sustain the balance of historical and systematic musicology on a level competitive with Berlin but, lacking the means to attract Hornbostel, hired Robert Lach as Privatdozent instead.[62] On other occasions as well, the university seemed to give more consideration to national origins than to religious affiliation, favoring Austrians over German nationals. In the search for Adler's successor in 1927, the committee rejected most of the candidates Adler recommended, ignoring all the non-Austrians on his list except for Abert. They gave top priority to Lach, who stood out as the best Austrian candidate.[63] On the question of anti-Semitism, the Vienna faculty was in fact known to take a stand against perceived anti-Jewish actions. Lach had to be called to task when he opposed bestowing an honorary degree on Richard Strauss because of Strauss's collaboration with "the Jew" Hugo von Hofmannsthal.[64] This is not to say that anti-Semitism was taboo in Vienna, on the contrary, it was probably more blatant than in Germany by virtue of the larger number of influential Jews there; rather it was not institutionalized to the same degree as in German universities.

The Nazification of Universities

The universities on the eve of the Nazi takeover displayed several traits that inclined them toward agreeing with many aspects of Hitler's agenda: mistrust of the Republic, a desire for strong leadership, institutionalized anti-Semitism, and a tendency to sympathize with right-wing political movements.

Perhaps more crucial for Nazi infiltration were the growing ranks of discontented students hoping to change their lot. Their disillusionment could be traced to the end of the war when they blamed older generations for the military defeat and the Treaty of Versailles. Much more radically anti-Republican than Weimar professors, university students became increasingly disenchanted with an older generation that offered no concrete suggestions for building a new state. Universities were overcrowded, families had lost money during the war, and students for the first time were compelled to work to support themselves. They fared relatively well during the inflation as a source of cheap labor but lost their edge in the workplace when it ended, comprising one of the few groups that suffered more after the economy stabilized between 1924 and 1929.[65]

As students became more impoverished and more utopia-minded in the late 1920s, many were drawn to the nationalist idealism of Hitler and to the more socialist-oriented elements of the Nazi party. To counter the Nazis' initial mistrust of intellectuals, Baldur von Schirach, as head of the Nazi Student League (founded in 1926), managed to convince Hitler that students would be a useful tool in wooing the educated bourgeoisie. Under von Schirach's guidance the Nazi Student League grew rapidly, with members winning elections in student government, gaining influence with local party administration and SA organizations, and ultimately penetrating the official student body organization, the German Students' Union (Deutsche Studentenschaft).[66]

The Nazi student movement proved effective in dismantling the university power structure, partly because of the unusual energy and dedication of its members. Some of them devoted more time and money to the political cause than to their studies, spending their earnings on elaborate posters and publications and registering for the minimum number of courses required for matriculation.[67] The first few months after Hitler's seizure of power saw a culmination of student unrest in a series of virulent public denunciations of Jewish professors and Jewish scholarship: in Berlin, students issued their "Twelve Theses against the Un-German Spirit of the University," which included a provision that Jewish professors henceforth publish only in Hebrew; in Kiel, students demanded the dismissal of twenty-eight professors under threat of violence and seized publications by "untrustworthy" scholars from the library; in Breslau, students were reported to have seized books by Jewish authors from bookstores; and the Nazi Student League announced a general boycott of lectures by Jewish professors. These early public acts of protest reached their climax in May 1933 with the infamous book-burning ceremonies in Berlin.[68] Students were also instrumental in the witch-hunts that led to the expulsion of faculty members and acted throughout the Reich as agents of the SA in random street violence against Jews, which sometimes resulted in murder.[69] Student violence eventually forced administrators to give in to student demands to dismiss "undesirable" professors in order to quell the disturbances.[70]

Musicology students were also involved in creating trouble for faculty and used their National Socialist ties to defend or harass individuals. Several of Bücken's students went directly to the Reich Education Ministry on his behalf with a lengthy report enumerating the injustices against him during his tenure at Cologne. In 1929, the university had once again turned down Bücken's request for promotion, but it did consider appointing an Ordinarius and solic-ited evaluations of Bücken and other candidates from leading musicologists.[71] The inquiry took an unexpected turn when Theodor Kroyer offered his ser-vices, expressing his interest in "building" once more, as he had done in Mu-nich, Heidelberg, and Leipzig, and his desire as a Catholic to work in a Cath-olic region.[72] The university jumped at the opportunity to gain Kroyer and to silence Bücken's campaigns, especially since the latter had enlisted influential friends to plead his case.[73] Kroyer moved to Cologne with his entourage in 1932, but he refused to work "under the same roof" as his former student Bücken, criticizing Bücken's "exceptionally superficial" training of students and his utter neglect of the library.[74]

Because the university had delayed establishing a chair and allowed Bücken to function as director for twelve years, Bücken felt justified in fighting for his rights as founder of the department. Students rallied behind him, report-ing to the ministry of alleged intrigues by the allegedly Jewish director of the Musikhochschule (Braunfels) to thwart his first attempts at promotion in the 1920s, and, upon Kroyer's arrival, his "brutal" removal from the depart-ment he had single-handedly founded.[75] Two students who belonged to Na-tional Socialist organizations registered a complaint against Kroyer after he expelled them from the department for telling the local Nazi press, the *West-deutscher Beobachter,* that Bücken had been mistreated by the university. The press noted Bücken's recent election to the Deutsche Akademie and referred to it as "reparations for an injustice of many years" caused by the "Braunfels system," overthrown only recently by the "National Socialist revolution."[76] This notice compelled Kroyer to insist upon a formal investigation of the students' behavior.[77]

In Heidelberg, students lodged complaints against Besseler that ultimately led to a full-fledged party investigation and trial. The Reich Student Leader-ship (Reichsstudentenführung, established in 1936 to resolve conflicts be-tween the Nazi Students' League and the Germans Students' Union)[78] cited Besseler for retaining Jewish works in the library. Besseler, they alleged, also frequently recommended works without pointing out that their authors were

Jewish. One of the informants was a musicology student whom Besseler had removed from his seminars and who went on to work for the Rosenberg Bureau. This student supplied Gerigk with information later used to compile the list of accusations that led to the party trial.[79] According to the postwar testimony of the Munich professor who arbitrated the party trial, the rector had decided that, considering the indispensability of some scholarly works by Jewish authors, books should not be removed entirely but must nevertheless be marked.[80] Besseler complied by setting aside all the books in the musicology library by Jewish authors and labeling them accordingly.[81] He also presented documentation at the party trial in his defense to prove that he purchased for the library the anti-Semitic directory of Jews in music (*Judentum und Musik,* compiled by Christa Maria Rock and Hans Brückner) as soon as its second edition became available in 1937.[82]

Students may have stirred up substantial unrest to the point of intimidating university administrators, but the attitudes of faculty members also contributed to the Nazi infiltration of universities. Hitler's ideas held a certain attraction for downtrodden junior faculty members as well as for the older anti-Republican professorial elite. Several declarations of support for Hitler emanated from faculty organizations and spokespersons, starting before 1933 and increasing during the early years of Nazi rule. The Hochschulverband, an independent organization that lobbied for the interests of academic professionals, supported the Nazi students in their campaign to expel the alleged pacifist professor Emil Gumbel in 1931. It quickly declared its allegiance to Hitler in 1933, stressing the importance of making the university a political institution, dissolving class antagonisms, and focusing on the unity of the German people. In March, before the Reichstag election, 300 professors published an appeal to vote for Hitler; in April the Hochschulverband protested the "gruesome propaganda" in the foreign press launched against racial purges; and in June it declared full adoption of a National Socialist ideology. A number of academic luminaries gathered in November 1933 and endorsed a "Call to the Educated of the World" to appreciate Hitler and the aims of the party, while 700 professors offered their official "recognition of Adolf Hitler and the National Socialist state."[83]

The change in government proved most promising to disenfranchised junior members, especially when the Reich Education Ministry established the German Lecturers' Union (Deutsche Dozentenschaft) in 1934 as a lobbying group for junior faculty.[84] Furthermore, many of the well-established university professors found themselves attracted to Hitler's ideas and persona out of their disillusionment with the Weimar government, their nostalgic longing for a strong leadership that would return Germany to its former glory, and their latent anti-Semitism. Otto Proksch had stated in his speech at the university in Greifswald in 1924: "If German essence and Christian belief join together, then we will be saved. Then we will want to work with our hands and wait for the day when the German hero comes, [when] he comes as prophet and king."[85] The most famous example of support for Hitler was Martin Heidegger's inaugural address as rector at the university in Freiburg, in which he declared: "Your lives will no longer be regulated by dogmas and ideas! The Führer himself and he alone is the present and future reality for Germany and its law."[86]

Established musicologists also exclaimed enthusiasm for Hitler's accession. Karl Gustav Fellerer gave his impassioned defense of Nazi cultural policy in the German and Swiss press.[87] Munich professor Alfred Lorenz had joined the Nazi party in 1931 and actively encouraged younger musicologists to adopt racial sciences in their research. He published two simultaneous pleas in December 1938, each emphasizing one of two different approaches to the field: ancestry and the Jewish Question.[88] Gustav Friedrich Schmidt, also on the Munich musicology faculty, had been head of the organization "Kulturwacht" (Culture Watch) in 1931, an organization dedicated to "the intellectual struggle against the destruction of our Western culture."[89] He joined the Nazi party in 1933 and composed "Der Führer rief! Ein deutsches Kampf- und Treuschwurlied," ("The Führer Calls! A German Song of Struggle and Pledge"), dedicated to Adolf Hitler and acknowledged by the Reich Chancellery.[90]

The Racial and Political Purge of Musicology Faculties

While such positive response to Hitler can be understood in the context of the political climate and internal tensions in the universities, the most troubling aspect of the professorial reaction to the first stages of the Gleichschaltung was the inertia in the face of the widespread expulsion of colleagues. Not only did most professors fail to raise any objections as scores of Jewish and politically suspect colleagues lost their positions, but some used the situation to their advantage.

In musicology, the loss of Jewish personnel was not overwhelming in pure numbers because of the relatively small size of musicology faculties and the ubiquitous exclusion of Jews from academic positions in this field. But in addition to the anti-Jewish measures, the loose wording of some of the laws gave faculties a powerful tool to oust any individual by trumping up charges of political unreliability or citing the need to make room for younger scholars in the interest of Nachwuchsförderung. The loss of even one individual from such small departments could change its entire character and scholarly orientation.

The purging of university faculties occurred in two phases: the implementation of the civil service law of 7 April 1933, which allowed for the removal of a large number of Jews and political undesirables; and the Nuremberg laws of 1935, which allowed for the removal of the remaining Jews, half-Jews, and all others defined by the law as Jewish. Three items of the "Law for the Restoration of the Professional Civil Service" (Gesetz zur Wiederherstellung des Berufbeamtentums) were implemented to remove personnel: Paragraph 2 required the removal of civil servants who attained their status after 9 November 1918 and allegedly lacked the usual qualifications (loosely defined to extend to political reliability); and Paragraph 3 called for the removal of non-Aryans (later defined as those with at least one non-Aryan grandparent and those married to Jews), with the exception of anyone who was appointed before 1 August 1914, who fought for Germany or its allies in World War I, or who lost a father or a son in the war. The loosely worded Paragraph 6 allowed for the retirement of individuals "for the purpose of rationalizing the administration even if they are not yet unfit for service" and whose positions could not be filled thereafter.[91]

Universities constitute one of the realms in which the civil service act could be applied to non–civil servants, affecting Privatdozenten and Extraordinarien as well as Ordinarien and resulting in the release of an estimated 1,684 academic personnel in 1933.[92] The anti-Jewish measures of the civil service law effected the immediate dismissal of the only two Jewish musicologists holding faculty positions, even though neither of them was a civil servant (both were nichtbeamtet). In September 1933, Sachs and Hornbostel received letters announcing the withdrawal of their teaching privileges, citing Paragraph 3.[93] Wilibald Gurlitt, married to a Jew and himself identified as one-quarter Jewish, was spared because of his veteran status.[94]

The civil service law was followed by numerous measures that gradually excluded Jews from university participation: they could not join the German Students' Union, were excluded from Prussian teachers' colleges, could legally lose their doctoral degrees if their German citizenship was revoked, and were excluded from positions as Assistenten in Prussia and from Habilitation in general by December 1934.[95] The Nuremberg laws of 15 September 1935, and specifically the "Law for the Protection of German Blood and German Honor," which made it illegal for Germans to marry or have sexual relations with Jews,[96] eventually provided an impetus to force such musicologists as Schrade and Gurlitt from their faculty positions.

Wilibald Gurlitt (b. 1889) had been on the Freiburg faculty since 1920, established its scholarly reputation, and earned national acclaim as a pioneer in the activities of the collegium musicum and the organ movement. That

Gurlitt's wife was Jewish became an issue only late in 1936 when Joseph Müller-Blattau, a former student of Gurlitt's, expressed an interest in coming to Freiburg. Müller-Blattau was invited to speak at an Alemannic cultural festival in Freiburg in October. The Freiburg rector reported to the Education Ministry of the "shameful situation" that no one on the faculty was as well versed in Alemannic music and suggested that Müller-Blattau be brought in to replace Gurlitt.[97] Gurlitt, it was argued, could not be trusted with the responsibility of preserving German culture in a border region like Freiburg, which was in need of warding off "invasive western powers," and he would be best placed in an interior region like Saxony.[98] A 1936 pamphlet had called special attention to the accountability of border universities to recognize their responsibilities to the nation as a whole, to come out of isolation, and to function as the cultural soldiers of Germanness,[99] and authorities took the importance of music professors in fulfilling these tasks very seriously. Müller-Blattau, "rooted in the Alemannic realm," was not only an established scholar but also a member of the party and the SA.[100]

This interest in Müller-Blattau was presumably the incentive to suddenly call attention to Gurlitt's Jewish wife. Although Gurlitt had been exempted from the civil service law, the authorities, backed by the new Nuremberg laws, raised the question of his racial suitability. Long before assuming the position in Freiburg, Müller-Blattau was giving advice behind the scenes on the question of Gurlitt's removal, suggesting as early as October 1936 that the university in Freiburg retire Gurlitt or send him to another university.[101] In June 1937, Gurlitt was dismissed, effective the following September, technically on the grounds of the civil service law's Paragraph 6, but actually because of his marriage to a Jew ("jüdische Versippung").[102] Gurlitt, at age forty-eight, was devastated by the dismissal. Not only was he thrown into severe financial hardships, he was also banned from public speaking and publishing and removed from examination boards, committees, and organizations; his family endured Gestapo surveillance; and his children were denied entry into schools and universities.[103]

After Gurlitt's ouster, Müller-Blattau's appointment was swiftly executed. In light of the "special cultural-political tasks in Freiburg," the rector recommended Müller-Blattau as the only appropriate candidate for Gurlitt's position.[104] The faculty opted to forego the normal procedure of assembling a short list of three candidates and recommended Müller-Blattau on the strength of his Alsatian origins, his folk music research, and his potential for future collaboration with the Folk Song Archive in Freiburg.[105]

Another indirect victim of the Nuremberg laws was Leo Schrade. Schrade

(b. 1903) came to Bonn from Königsberg to finish his Habilitation in 1932, and in 1935 he became an instructor in music history with a specialty in German medieval music.[106] Schrade sensed the authorities' disapproval in 1935 when the Education Ministry denied him permission to work at the Warburg Library in London because the library, which had moved from Germany, had been in "Jewish hands" (probably a reference to Manfred Bukofzer) and so was out of bounds for German scholars.[107] It is possible that contact with Jewish scholars abroad would have been reason enough to remove Schrade from the faculty in 1935, but an investigation revealing his wife's Jewish lineage did not begin until spring 1937.[108] Schrade was released in June of that year on grounds of "jüdische Versippung," but the clause invoked in his case was the 1934 ordinance that invalidated the Habilitation of Jews and withdrew their teaching privileges.[109] Unlike Gurlitt, Schrade received continued financial support until he could find another position because he was "otherwise personally and intellectually irreproachable."[110] He pursued an eminent career outside Germany, building up a musicology program at Yale University, where he taught until 1958, then becoming director of the musicology institute in Basel, Switzerland.

Schiedermair, as head of the Bonn musicology department, did little to protect Schrade. Schiedermair was a rising star under the Nazis and probably did not want to jeopardize his success by harboring a "Jewish" scholar on his faculty. In addition to directing the Beethoven house and archive and the Task Force for Rhenish Music History (Arbeitsgemeinschaft für rheinische Musikgeschichte), he was appointed to the Bonn city council in 1936 and was the first recipient of the *Kulturpreis* in Bonn and the Beethoven medal. He was also showered with honors outside Bonn, appointed chairman of the German music division in the Deutsche Akademie in Munich in 1928, made an honorary member of the International Mozarteum foundation in 1937, and appointed president of the DGMW in 1937. After Schrade's dismissal Schiedermair went on to become a permanent member of the State Institute in 1940 and received the Gold Mozart Medal in 1941 from the Mozarteum in Salzburg and the Silver Mozart Medal in 1942 from the City of Vienna.[111]

The civil service law was also invoked to remove faculty on political and other grounds. Moser and Wolf received identical letters from the ministry in June 1933 stating that because of the need to set aside funds for junior faculty (specifically Privatdozenten), their teaching contracts would be suspended at the end of 1934.[112] Named Honorarprofessor in music history at Berlin in 1927, Moser lost his teaching privileges and his contract on the grounds of

Paragraph 6 in September 1934,[113] a particular hardship since he had just been forced to retire as director of the Staatliche Akademie für Kirchen- und Schulmusik because of its merger with the Hochschule für Musik. Moser was at a loss to comprehend his sudden change in circumstances because he viewed himself as politically flawless: a pure Aryan, a war veteran, and never a Marxist.[114]

Although the civil service and Nuremberg laws affected only a handful of musicologists, their departure contributed to significant changes in the scholarly orientation and status of the departments they left behind. The removal of faculty members in Berlin resulted in a complete overhaul of the musicology staff, whose composition was significantly altered by the promotion of young National Socialists. Erich Schumann, for example, a close associate of Herbert Gerigk in the Rosenberg Bureau, was named Ordinarius at age thirty-five in September 1933 in the fields of systematic musicology and physics. His main scholarly activity was in the latter, and during the war he was chief of the science division of the Military High Command (Abteilung Wissenschaft im Oberkommando der Wehrmacht) and engaged in research on explosives for the Reich Research Council (Reichsforschungsrat).[115] Fritz Bose, also only in his thirties, took over Hornbostel's courses while working for the SS in the Race and Resettlement Office (from 1935 to its dissolution in 1939) and the personal staff of the Reichsführer SS (from 1935).[116] Werner Danckert, born in 1900 like Bose and a party member since 1937, became außerplanmäßiger Professor in 1939 while holding several auxiliary positions in the Rosenberg Bureau.[117] Postwar investigations traced Danckert's appointment to the Rosenberg Bureau's intervention, in opposition to Schering's wishes.[118]

Schering, too, was instrumental in giving priority to young National Socialists like Gotthold Frotscher. Frotscher had solid ties with Nazi organizations: he became a member of the Nazi party in 1933 and held several offices in the party and the Reich Youth Leadership.[119] Later he became editor of the music journal issued by the Reich Youth Leadership, *Musik in Jugend und Volk*, and his list of publications included several works on race and folk music, in addition to the area for which he is known, the history of organ music and the use of the organ in contemporary political functions.[120] When Frotscher's appointment in Berlin was turned down in 1935, Schering came to his aid. In his endorsement of Frotscher, Schering referred to an unprecedented shortage of faculty members in musicology: Wolf could not be counted as a member of the faculty because he already exceeded the age limit, and Schumann and Kreichgauer, as representatives of systematic musicology, should not really be counted either. Schering asserted that the number of musicology students would "certainly increase" in the following semesters, therefore more musicologists were needed.[121]

Schering also used the argument of Nachwuchsförderung to push out Wolf, but in doing so he completely contradicted some of the arguments he was using to promote Frotscher. When the dean recommended Wolf for promotion from Honorarprofessor to Ordinarius, even though he was about to turn sixty-five,[122] Schering objected. Instead of projecting a growth in enrollment, he cited declining numbers in musicology from sixty-nine students in spring semester of 1933 to approximately thirty-five in spring semester of 1935 and reported the need to eliminate certain lectures. He stated that the faculty was *overrepresented* by himself, Wolf, Schünemann, Osthoff, Schumann, and Kreichgauer, with two Ordinarius positions, his and that of Erich Schumann. A third Ordinarius would not only be unique among German musicology faculties but would also be superfluous given the current enrollment. Finally, Wolf's promotion would, in Schering's opinion, limit growth possibilities for junior faculty and ignore the dire need to promote the work of "talented and culturally-politically reliable young forces" who could easily cover the areas taught by Wolf. Schering also let it be known that he and Wolf had personal differences, that Wolf had overstepped his authority as Honorarprofessor by giving exams, and that his promotion would only lead to more friction.[123] The dean was inclined to oppose Schering and endorse Wolf's promotion specifically because of Schering's personal objections, and the Education Ministry suspected that Schering desired to keep a monopoly in the University of Berlin.[124] In the end, however, the ministry refused to allow Wolf to continue lecturing under the prior conditions, and ultimately Wolf withdrew from the faculty and declared his "academic teaching activities as terminated."[125]

Gurlitt's removal from the Freiburg faculty led to significant changes in the intellectual orientation of that department. The one reservation regarding hiring Müller-Blattau was his noticeable weakness in the area of general music history and its significance for intellectual history (*geistiggeschichtliche Entwicklung*), implying that his appointment would break with the successful intellectual orientation of Freiburg musicology established since the war.[126] Müller-Blattau carried on the *Orgelbewegung* activities started by Gurlitt by expanding the national organ conference, but during his tenure the direction of the musicology department turned to a cultivation of folk music research that persisted after his departure. The Education Ministry's 1941 order to annex the Freiburg Folk Song Archive to the musicology department deepened this commitment, as did the suggestion that Walter Wiora receive a joint appointment in both institutions.[127]

The scholarly orientation of the faculty in Bonn also changed significantly, owing more to the Nazi seizure of power than to the departure of Schrade. Although Schiedermair seems to have supported Schrade throughout his ordeal, Schiedermair's plans for the scholarly direction of the department changed after 1933. He had welcomed Schrade to Bonn not only for his ability to cover the Middle Ages, but also because of his scholarly interest in the music history of the Rhineland.[128] In the year following Hitler's accession, however, Schiedermair started to pay additional attention to racial and genealogical questions in dissertations, research projects, and lectures.[129] Such questions fell within the interests of another Bonn faculty member, Joseph Schmidt-Görg, who published several studies on the genealogy of famous composers, and it is possible that the new ideological directions adopted by Schiedermair left no room for a musicologist with broader interests.

The department in Vienna, with its high proportion of Jewish faculty members, was ironically unaffected by both the civil service and Nuremberg laws, simply because all of its Jewish musicologists were gone for one reason or another by the time of the Anschluss in March 1938. Adler had retired in 1927, Fischer had gone to Innsbruck in 1928, and Wellesz fled to England in March 1938. A document written by Schenk addressed to the Education Ministry gives the impression that Adler's library was seized by the Gestapo after his death in 1941. Schenk asked the Education Ministry to have the library transferred to his institute, giving no indication of a willingness to purchase the material.[130]

The Anschluss affected prominent Jewish musicologists outside the university, many of whom went on to lead successful careers after their emigration, most notably Karl Geiringer. Born in 1899, Geiringer earned his doctorate in Vienna in 1922, served on the DTÖ commission and produced several editions, and became museum curator and librarian at the Gesellschaft der Musikfreunde in 1930. Days after Hitler's march through the streets of Vienna, most of the staff of the Gesellschaft der Musikfreunde was dismissed, and Geiringer was suspended because he was "a full Jew, and since his reinstatement is out of the question and his function is by no means indispensable, he will be fired in April."[131] His letter of dismissal, dated 31 March, cited the Nuremberg laws explicitly, and two weeks later he was additionally barred from using the archive for his own research.[132] Yet he had used his time there to advance research in classical and Romantic music and after emigrating to the United States continued in this vein, developing musicology programs at Boston University and at the University of California in Santa Barbara.

Nazi University Reforms

University professors in the Weimar Republic have been described as "midwives to Nazism," a colorful metaphor suggesting that although they contributed little to the creation of the Third Reich and should not have to bear parental responsibility, they assisted in the birth of the Nazi regime and nurtured the newborn state.[133] Professors generally showed little reaction to the Nazi takeover, and their failure to take a stand against it may have been their biggest mistake, for the beginning of the Third Reich marked the end of their age of self-rule.

The antiintellectual stand of the Nazi party, evident in the early writings of Hitler and Rosenberg, persisted throughout the Third Reich. The university as an autonomous entity would undermine the principle of a total state, academicians were suspected of opposing a National Socialist victory, and academic disciplines were regarded as overspecialized and irrelevant. One cannot ignore the similarities between the reform agendas of the Weimar era and those of the National Socialists: the criticisms against overspecialization in "alienated" (*lebensfremd*) sciences, the desire to bring scholarship closer to the needs of students, and the need to grant more privileges to junior faculty members were all part of C. H. Becker's unsuccessful 1918 proposal.[134] The Nazis, however, succeeded in penetrating the inner workings of higher education far beyond the modest reforms attempted in the Weimar Republic. Although they fell short of their ultimate goal of replacing the university with a system of National Socialist training colleges, they managed to dismantle the oligarchic structure of the German university, even if in a disorganized and haphazard manner.

The first fundamental change was the imposition of the Führerprinzip on university administration, a measure which wrested power from the hands of the Ordinarien. Rectors, formerly figureheads elected by the faculty senate, became Education Ministry appointees and took over the power of appointing deans, formerly elected by faculty members. Rectors and deans, answering only to the education minister, held most of the decision-making powers, and faculty governing bodies were reduced to an advisory capacity and to distributing funds to individual departments. Promotions and appointments, all previously determined by the faculties, came under the direct control of the Education Ministry in order to keep out politically and racially "undesirable" elements.[135]

Professors, and particularly Ordinarien, relinquished power not only to their superiors but also to their subordinates: students, junior instructors, and any party members among those groups. The Hochschulverband, the only representative body of university instructors, was dissolved, and instructors of all ranks were lumped together in the Lecturers' Union (Dozentenschaft), which was politically equivalent to the Student Union under the control of the Education Ministry. Each of these had a leader, who was always a party member and usually lacked seniority or academic stature. Two other corresponding bodies associated with the Nazi party gained influence: the newly formed Nazi Lecturers' League (NS-Dozentenbund) and the older Nazi Student League, both of which came under the jurisdiction of the minister of party affairs (Rudolf Hess).[136] These party branches of the academic community had control over assessing the political reliability of candidates for academic positions.[137]

The new system, in which the party, various student and faculty organizations, and the Education Ministry struggled for power, afforded a new recourse to individuals on all levels to advance their careers. University personnel, regardless of rank, could use Nazi party connections to further their personal causes. Ordinarien could no longer rely on their status to protect them from the harassment of party officials, appointments could be held up by the Nazi Lecturers' League, and internal rivalries could be complicated by party intervention.

The loss of respect experienced by senior musicologists was particularly evident in Munich, where the faculty came under closer scrutiny than elsewhere, probably because of the concentration of Nazi party operations in that city. In 1935, Rudolf Ficker had to answer for a statement made by his wife that was overheard and reported to the Bavarian prime minister. While in Tyrol, Frau Ficker allegedly said to a lawyer from Innsbruck: "National Socialism? Ridiculous — in Munich it's passé — at most only the dumb Tyroleans believe in it!"[138] This prompted an investigation, but the outcome apparently was not serious enough to hinder Ficker's appointment as dean a few years later. A similar embarrassment happened to Sandberger while on a lecture tour in Lörrach. The secretary of the IMS, a party member, reported that Sandberger responded to the "Heil Hitler" greeting with the words: "What's that supposed to mean? Get away from me! I don't want to have anything to do with that!"[139] Sandberger had to submit a lengthy explanation to the university, and the rector decided not to take action against him only because he was retired.[140]

Professors were also required to take part in various exercises, ceremonies, marches, and student performances; to give to charities; and to subscribe to certain journals.[141] In Munich, individuals had to submit written excuses for not attending flag-raising ceremonies and marches,[142] and there were consequences for not contributing to the required charities. When Sandberger failed to give to the Winter Aid Campaign (*Winterhilfswerke*) in 1941, the rector launched an investigation because he was the only university affiliate who had not fulfilled this "patriotic duty."[143] Sandberger explained that his daughter's illness had strained his finances. Nevertheless, the university refused him funds for a trip to Italy, denied him a visa for a trip to Paris, and strongly advised him to pay the remainder of the yearly contribution.[144]

These were only minor annoyances when compared with the effects of party influence on faculty appointments. When Schering died in 1941, the Berlin faculty sought a suitable replacement to preserve the "humanistic side of musicology" and coordinate university activities with those of the State Institute. Friedrich Blume seemed the perfect candidate. He was a student of Abert, he was secretary of EdM and therefore had strong ties with the institute, he was respected by his colleagues, and he had called attention to himself as politically engaged through his publicized preoccupation with racial research. The dean extolled his "series of intelligent, clear and well-written works, including *Das Rasseproblem in der Musik* (1939), which must be specially praised."[145]

Blume stood well above the other candidates, and his appointment might very well have succeeded had the Lecturers' Union and the Nazi Lecturers' League not expressed reservations. The Lecturers' Union resurrected an old rumor that Blume had been involved in a plagiarism scandal.[146] Blume explained this as a case of a publishing house "in Jewish hands" (Max-Hesse-Verlag, publisher of the Riemann lexicon edited by Alfred Einstein) making accusations in order to maintain its monopoly on the publishing of a standard music lexicon. According to Blume "Hermann Abert tried to break through this Jewish monopoly by producing a competing music lexicon with a more popular appeal." The Hesse Verlag naturally saw this as a threat and, with the help of an "extremely shrewd Jewish lawyer," accused Abert and his assistants (which included Blume) of plagiarism, an allegation which was never proven.[147]

Objections from the Nazi Lecturers' League originally emanated either from the Rosenberg Bureau or from the Propaganda Ministry, which favored the appointment of Georg Schünemann.[148] These political objections, masqueraded as scholarly appraisals, took issue with appointing a specialist in Protestant church music because such music was of "impure origins" and conflicted with the cultural-political needs of the position.[149] The league also questioned Blume's scholarly originality: they accused him of posing as an "ideological prophet" in his racial investigations when all he did was borrow ideas from others, and they considered his work on the history of the orchestral suite a mere compilation of facts. As alternatives, the league recommended Helmuth Osthoff, Hermann Zenck, and Hans Engel.[150] Helmuth Osthoff (b. 1896), best known for his important contributions to research on Renaissance music, had been a protégé of both Johannes Wolf and Arnold Schering and was currently a Privatdozent in Berlin. The Nazi Lecturers' League judged him as first-rate in the "ethical tasks of musicology" to "place the völkisch-conscious German element in the foreground" and praised his work as "culturally-politically valuable," reflecting his "exemplary behavior as National Socialist and teacher."[151] Osthoff may have had support from higher places, judging from a 1944 letter from the Party Chancellery (the central administration of the Nazi party) to the Education Ministry asking why Ost-hoff had not yet been appointed to the Berlin chair.[152] The position remained vacant until after the war, when it was more difficult to attract scholars to Berlin, and Walther Vetter was finally appointed in 1946.

Minor internal conflicts could take on exaggerated political dimensions when the party was called on to settle disputes, as in the case of the continuing feud between Bücken and Kroyer. The tensions between the two prompted the university to look for a position for Bücken in another university. After Kroyer called for an investigation of Bücken's students in November 1933 for making accusations against the department in the local Nazi press, Bücken went over the heads of the administration and insisted on a party-run investigation.[153] Bücken had already revealed himself to be a political chameleon. He had used his earlier ties to the Catholic Center party for advancement and was sus-pected of using connections to the Social Democrats to further his career before 1933.[154] This time he appealed to a comrade from his pre-Nazi days in the German-National party who now held the rank of Nazi party area leader (NSDAP Kreisleiter) and was one of the university's curators.[155] A party inves-tigation was carried out by Walter Trienes, the district deputy of the Staats-kommissar in the NS-Kulturgemeinde and author of the book *Musik im Gefahr* (*Music in Danger*).[156]

Trienes drew up lengthy reports based on selected files that the university surrendered to him and concluded that Bücken had been treated unfairly.[157] The dean protested that the Trienes report was based on information predat-ing the current disagreement, and that as an outsider Trienes had no right to make such strong accusations against the university administration.[158] The university held to its original position despite Trienes's conclusions,[159] but Trienes continued to interfere in university affairs and after Kroyer retired in 1938 endorsed Bücken as Kroyer's successor. He submitted a list of candidates for Kroyer's replacement based on suggestions from the Rosenberg Bureau and, following an order from the party's district leader, went directly to "the most prominent representatives of German musicology" for evaluations of Bücken.[160]

The Education Ministry's Influence

That the Nazi government was far more successful than the Weimar government in imposing reforms was not the result of a carefully devised program. University affairs, nominally assigned to the Ministry of the Interior but largely left to provincial jurisdiction in the first year of Nazi hegemony, became a Reich concern with the formation of the Reich Education Ministry in May 1934 under Bernhard Rust. But beyond issuing his Guidelines for the Simplification of College Administration in April 1935, followed by a series of pointless individual decrees, Rust preoccupied himself with protecting his authority from competing interests.[161]

The Reich Education Ministry issued a flood of ordinances toward achieving uniformity among universities in curricula, daily routines, and academic and nonacademic activities, but it met with limited success. It had the potential to effect fundamental changes in curricula but lacked the imagination and organization to exploit the restructuring of the university hierarchy toward a total overhaul of academic programs. The Education Ministry's numerous communiqués were often too vague to be taken seriously. A directive of December 1934 stated the tasks of higher education to "establish as close a relationship as possible to the National Socialist needs of our people" and encouraged field trips that would contribute to "national-political education" and promote camaraderie among students from various disciplines.[162] Early on, such fields as folklore, military sciences, and political pedagogy prospered, as did the integration of racial and National Socialist topics into natural sciences, social sciences, humanities, and theology, but these initiatives tapered off by 1939.[163]

In the humanities, there were a variety of attempts to interpret the spirit of National Socialism and enhance curricula with ideologically inspired courses and requirements. In Cologne, the dean tried to require Nordic studies as a secondary field for doctoral exams in all humanities disciplines but especially in German philology.[164] The university in Rostock similarly proposed establishing an Institute for Nordic Culture, which would include a musicology division and would meet the demands "which National Socialism must pose on research and teaching" by uncovering common Nordic traits and strengthening the Nordic awareness of the pan-German Volk sentiment.[165]

Curriculum reform reflected some of the ministry's suggestions to an extent but was largely left to the whims of individual departments. As the new director of the musicology department in Munich, Rudolf Ficker highlighted his own interest in the role of the Nordic race in Western music history, an interest he had pursued since 1924, by proposing a musical instruments museum in conjunction with a research institute for comparative musicology to study musical development of individual nations and races.[166] Furthermore, the university made special concessions to Alfred Lorenz as he approached retirement age, by virtue of his having joined the Nazi party in 1931 and his lectures on "Race and Music," which he held as early as 1933. The university repeatedly extended his teaching privileges for cultural-political reasons and allowed him to lecture exclusively on his Wagner research because "in these

matters Lorenz is indispensable and of greatest importance for National Socialist arts policies."[167] The Munich faculty also showed the most interest in
exploring folk music's relation to art music and to racial groupings, especially
in Kurt Huber's courses from 1939 until his dismissal and execution in 1943
(Huber's courses included "German Folk Music: The German Folk Ballad" in
1939–40 and 1942–43; "Research in Musical Talent" and "Proseminar in
Bavarian Folk Music" in 1940; and "Proseminar in German Folk Music: Nordic Folk Music" in 1941–42).

In Berlin from 1935 to 1940, at least one and sometimes two courses were
offered on folk music (by Schünemann, Frotscher, or Danckert), military music (by Schumann in 1938 and 1939), and personality types in music (by
Danckert in 1939–40). In Freiburg, Ehmann directed a special study group
entitled "The German Music Movement Today" in 1938 and a course on folk
song in 1939. Müller-Blattau, despite the university's expectations in appointing him, never gave a course on Alemannic music or even folk music until his
last semester there, adhering more to standard offerings (opera, Bach, Handel,
classic and Romantic German music) during most of his tenure. Bonn increased course offerings on folk music research and performance; Schrade was
scheduled to teach a course on regional music research in 1938; and Schiedermair explored "Current Questions in German Music" in 1941.

In Heidelberg, Besseler seems to have deviated from his Renaissance and
classic-Romantic areas immediately after Hitler's accession, offering a course
entitled "Music in the Intellectual Life of the Nation" in 1933; "Folk Song,
Amateur Music, and Music Education" and "Essence and Goals of German
Music and Art" in 1933–34; and "German Music and Its Neighbors, Past and
Present" and "Musical Questions Today" in 1934–35.[168] Bücken had tried to
maintain a synthetic, style-criticism orientation in Cologne,[169] but when Fellerer took over the department in 1938 he promoted regional culture and
systematic musicology, claiming that comparative musicology and musical
racial studies were now his personal areas of interest.[170]

The Education Ministry was also unable to impose uniformity because of
the persistence of regional policy discrepancies, despite Hitler's attempts to
coordinate all provincial governing bodies under one state administration. In
spring 1940, Rust issued a revised law for the uniformity of administration of
scholarly institutions, with the aim of tightening his grip on universities and
colleges under provincial control. Noting that he had been able to exert direct
authority over schools in Prussia, Austria, and other annexed and occupied
territories, he hoped to gain influence in all regions but timidly recommended
not to change the status quo dramatically. He realized that standardization
would never lead to uniformity of scholarly activity, but it might allow for

more comprehensive planning and distribution of tasks to appropriate institutions. He was well aware of the futility of trying to suppress the regional independence of these institutions and tried instead to reinforce their ties with their local communities by establishing auxiliary "Friends' Societies" to support the universities.[171]

The decentralization left the humanities disciplines, above all, at a disadvantage, and the Party Chancellery complained to the Education Ministry in 1944 about the sorry state of humanities departments in German universities due to underfunding. This deficiency, they claimed, had not been remedied since the Weimar years and threatened to force these disciplines, at one time world leaders, to lapse behind those of America and England.[172] The Education Ministry's response implied that, aside from the difficulty of enlisting qualified personnel, the problem lay mostly with the decentralization. Improvements had been possible in Prussia, where the ministry had direct control, but little could be done to influence the funding practices in other provinces.[173]

Rust claimed to have succeeded in bringing Austrian universities under his control, and this holds true at least for the musicology department in Vienna. After 1930, economic conditions forced the Extraordinarius position in musicology to remain empty, but in December 1938, the Education Ministry expressed its desire to reestablish the position and initiate a search.[174] The university was grateful for this opportunity afforded by the good fortune of the Anschluss,[175] and the musicologists respectfully accepted the education minister's rejection of their final choice of Robert Haas and recommendation to hire Schenk.[176] Political assessments now played just as important a role in the department's decision-making process as scholarly suitability. During the search, the faculty decided that Lach, due to retire in January 1939, should be allowed to extend his stay in order to receive a better pension, out of respect for his having joined the Nazi party in 1933 when it was illegal in Austria.[177] The faculty no longer gave priority to the balance between historical and systematic musicology as it had done in 1927. The committee euphemistically declared the dwindling of scholarship in those areas "since Carl Stumpf and Erich von Hornbostel are dead" (von Hornbostel died in England in 1935) and acknowledged the futility of searching for anything but a music historian to replace Lach after his retirement.[178]

In choosing Haas as their top candidate, they drew attention to his victimization as a National Socialist under the former system in Austria before the Anschluss. A party member since 1933, Haas's political convictions allegedly kept him from advancing at the Vienna National Library and from securing academic appointments in Vienna, Graz, and Innsbruck, although he was a top candidate. He had also waged a difficult battle with "Jewish business interests" for his Bruckner edition, a situation which "was decided in his favor . . . by our Führer Adolf Hitler." Appointing him in Vienna would furnish an opportunity to compensate for all he suffered from his unwavering devotion to National Socialism.[179]

The ministry prevailed in appointing Schenk instead, but its favoritism toward Schenk is not so clearly documented. The ministry wished to bring him to Vienna because of his expertise in Mozart and Gluck research, just as Haas was attractive to an Austrian university for his Bruckner work,[180] but whether Schenk's political activity influenced the decision remains a mystery. The university archive no longer contains a personnel file for Schenk, and it is likely that Schenk, serving as Ordinarius after 1945, removed his documents after the war, perhaps to conceal his political involvement. His seizure of the entire contents of files is noted elsewhere in the archive's holdings, and several files regarding politically sensitive issues are missing entirely.[181] What is known of Schenk's political activity from other sources is that he was closely affiliated with the Rosenberg Bureau and offered his services on several occasions, including providing details of the racial affiliation of Jews who had received their doctorates in Vienna.[182] When the musicology department in Vienna came under Schenk's direction, he tried to arrange a collaboration with Himmler's SS-"Ahnenerbe," proposing a large research project investigating the "Germanic remnants in the Italian cultural sphere," focusing on the Middle Ages and the Renaissance and requiring thorough archival work in Italian libraries.[183]

Within those universities more or less under Rust's direct control, the Education Ministry could keep a close watch on the political activities of personnel. In Berlin, it reprimanded Frotscher for his "lack of camaraderie" when he criticized a member of the Nazi Student League in the published "Kulturpolitisches Arbeitsblatt" for not knowing any ceremonial or familiar folk songs.[184] In Vienna, Haas and Orel were reprimanded for jeopardizing the chances of a German to be hired in a musicology department in Switzerland by providing positive evaluations of the only Swiss candidate. It was noted that they failed to contact the appropriate officials in the Reich before proceeding with their evaluations.[185]

The Role of Musicology in the National Socialist University

The university reforms after 1933 succeeded in dismantling the power monopoly that Ordinarien had enjoyed for generations. Professors were thrown together in one pool with instructors of all levels, had the same amount of influence as the student organizations, and lost most of their decision-making powers to the rectors, the Nazi Lecturers' League, and the Education Ministry. The hierarchy among university disciplines, a phenomenon which placed musicology at a disadvantage in its early stages, became irrelevant as all university personnel were reduced in status. If anything, the position of musicology in the university was strengthened in those years.

Musicologists continued to make their discipline more accessible and relevant to a wider sector of the population, as they had done before 1933. The National Socialist summons to scholars to come out of isolation and heed the practical needs of the nation resonated well with musicology's already strong ties between scholarship and practice. The ability of musicologists to serve a public function gave them more capital within the university than ever before and could be used as an argument to add new positions, to retain faculty members, and to establish new departments. In 1935, for example, a new musicology department was established in Frankfurt by Müller-Blattau and was given the responsibility of overseeing all musical activities of the university and of catering to the cultural needs of the community.[186]

Musicology became a more valued commodity in border districts in the late 1930s and 1940s. In Königsberg, the rector urged the authorities not to separate the musicology department from the conservatory because neither could survive on its own and because "the separation of art and science in higher German education facilities is an action which does not abide by the National Socialist idea of education."[187] In a later effort to expand the institute, the rector further argued that as the only musicological outpost in the east, Königsberg could not afford to ignore the discipline, thus its expansion had cultural-political significance.[188]

Much of a musicology department's value in border districts was gauged by the activities of the collegium musicum, which came to represent a stable fixture of German culture and a central component of musical life. When Friedrich Blume had an opportunity to leave Kiel for a position in Frankfurt in 1937, the rector wrote to the Education Ministry that losing him would strike "a heavy blow to the cultivation of Germanness in the northern realm," especially if it meant losing his collegium musicum. Blume's collegium was, in the rector's opinion, indispensable for the cultural life of the region and was essential for the university's "struggle for folk identity" (*Volkstumskampf*). The rector offered to promote Blume to Ordinarius to keep him, since "up here a music professor with a collegium musicum can and must carry out a pressing, völkisch-political task."[189] The Education Ministry heeded this request and informed the mayor of Frankfurt that Blume was not available, being engaged in "the cultural defensive struggle against the Danes," and within months Blume was promoted to Ordinarius.[190]

The collegium continued to reach out to the public and, working with local Denkmäler projects, drew recognition for acquainting lay audiences with Germany's musical heritage.[191] Collegium directors broadened their duties to encompass more public service and to aid the propaganda of the state. Besseler put together a collegium program of an overture by Johann Kaspar Ferdinand Fischer (a local early eighteenth-century Kleinmeister) followed by a communal singing of "Wohlauf Kameraden," a Bach concerto, a song by a Nazi Student League member set to a text by Neidhart von Reuenthal, and an original "Soldiers' Cantata" by a Heidelberg student.[192] Erich Schenk, while in Rostock, supplemented his collegium activities by directing other concerts, radio performances, and academic ceremonies.[193] In 1938 Herbert Birtner fulfilled another cultural-political task by taking his Marburg group on tour to perform for ethnic Germans living in Yugoslavia.[194]

Collegium programs also assisted in reinforcing patriotism and wartime optimism and applauding the territorial gains of German troops. Wartime collegium concerts in Cologne under Fellerer included a program of historic military music, a special program of Franco-Flemish music in commemoration of the German-Flemish cultural festival shortly after German troops invaded Belgium, and an abundance of programs dedicated to the accomplishments of local Rhenish composers.[195] Collegium groups were also sent out to entertain troops, but they sometimes encountered a rather chilly reception from the soldiers and had to abandon their high-brow music programs in favor of more informal sing-alongs.[196]

The introduction of ceremonies and political events as regular university activities gave musicologists additional responsibilities and raised their status. The university in Freiburg tried to enlist Gurlitt's collegium for official university ceremonies in order to save money, but Gurlitt resisted. He maintained that his group was meant for scholarly exercises and, lacking a brass ensemble, was in any case not equipped to perform the obligatory national anthem and the Horst Wessel Song.[197] Wilhelm Ehmann, a Privatdozent in musicology, proposed establishing a new position for a director of practical music, owing to the changing relations between "musical knowledge" and "musical activity" and their political connection to the "life of the people." He flaunted his achievements in merging university musical life with the activities of party and state organizations (e.g., the SA, SS, Hitler Youth, and the Nazi Student League).[198] Gurlitt heartily endorsed Ehmann's proposal. Such a position would, in Gurlitt's opinion, complement the collegium musicum and fulfill the new tasks of the "Volkstum work of the National Socialist movement" by someone who had "a sense of music that corresponds to the political needs of the present day" and understood the "new type of singing in the camaraderie of the National Socialist movement."[199] The faculty appointed Ehmann as "reader for practical musical tasks" to take charge of music at university ceremonies. His appointment was justified by the perceived importance of ceremonies in the National Socialist university and Freiburg's need to reinforce cultural strength as a border region.[200] Gurlitt's endorsement backfired when his collegium musicum was ordered to come under Ehmann's direction as part of the cultural sciences division of the Student Union. The Student Union also barred Gurlitt from participating in a scheduled concert because he was not a Nazi party member.[201]

Musicology's role in the university would naturally change over the course of the war, when the authorities shut down entire university programs without any guarantees of reopening them.[202] Musicology may have gained status in the 1930s, but it was hardly considered crucial for the war effort. For the total war mobilization, Rust authorized the release of students and teachers from a variety of vocational schools (including music schools and conservatories) to work in the arms industry; suspended the matriculation of new students; and ordered all students not enrolled in selected sciences and war-related technologies and all female students to be available to serve in home-front tasks.[203]

Military service, as in the last war, forced students to interrupt or delay their studies indefinitely, but the military offered incentives to keep soldiers interested in their studies through a number of university extension programs.[204] Georg Schünemann participated in such a program, traveling to four different air force bases in the spring of 1944 to deliver lecture-demonstrations on the songs of German farmers in Russia.[205] In addition, the district lecturers' leader (*Gaudozentenführer*) in Bonn and the rector of the university issued a special publication series of "war lectures" (*Kriegsvorträge*), the list of which suggests that musicological research had not been hindered by the war. Those contributing included Schiedermair ("Beethoven"), Osthoff ("Johannes Brahms und seine Sendung"), Schenk ("Beethoven zwischen den Zeiten"), and Hermann Unger ("Anton Bruckner und seine 7. Sinfonie"). Schiedermair tried to withhold his Beethoven lecture from this series, hoping to reserve it for a more prestigious publishing venue, but he ultimately gave in to the rector's repeated requests and earned rave reviews from Herbert Gerigk for demonstrating Beethoven's Germanness in an easily accessible format.[206]

The continuity of programs of study was further endangered by the conscription and reshuffling of faculty. Musicology faculties had to undertake elaborate exchanges of personnel, sometimes relying on instructors to double their duties by helping out at a neighboring university, sometimes undergoing less convenient transfers as ordered by the Education Ministry. Helmut Osthoff, for example, had been transferred back and forth even before the war began, and when Müller-Blattau left Frankfurt for Freiburg in 1937, the education minister ordered Osthoff to go from Berlin to Frankfurt as a substitute. It then promoted him to Extraordinarius in January 1939 at his home university and ordered him back to Berlin in mid-semester in December 1944, but he continued to teach one week per month in Frankfurt for the remainder of the semester.[207] Danckert, called in to substitute for Osthoff, was sent to Graz to fill in for Birtner and shuttled between the two cities.[208] Frotscher also filled in at the university while conducting his lectures at the Hochschule für Musikerziehung, until bomb damage forced him to hold instruction in his apartment.[209]

Cologne and Bonn, neighboring cities, could easily arrange exchanges of faculty for a time during the war. Fellerer was called up for military service in spring 1943 but ran the Cologne musicology department from the front for most of 1943 and 1944, reading dissertations, coordinating substitute lecturers, and keeping up a daily correspondence with the dean. In April 1943, Schiedermair agreed to come once a week from Bonn to run some of the lectures, but he had to stop in February 1944 for health reasons. Fellerer suggested that Osthoff (Frankfurt) or Gerber (Göttingen) might come every two weeks to lecture, but both declined (Gerber was already shuttling between Giessen and Göttingen). Ultimately Schmidt-Görg, a younger member of the Bonn faculty, took over Schiedermair's lectures in June.[210] The University of Cologne finally issued an urgent appeal to military authorities to release Fellerer from at least part of his service to take care of the large number of neglected students at the musicology institute.[211]

In the province of Baden, Müller-Blattau's voluntary move from Freiburg to Strasbourg in 1941 left a serious shortage of musicologists. The Education Ministry called upon Besseler to fill in at Freiburg in the academic year 1941–42 while continuing his duties in Heidelberg, but Besseler stopped after one year and was called up himself for military service in September 1943. The two universities were left with a large number of students and no replacement, and military authorities refused Heidelberg's requests to release Besseler from service.[212] Hermann Zenck, the only musicologist left in the south-west area, was also called up as part of the total war mobilization in November 1944, but Besseler was finally relieved of his military service and allowed to return to Heidelberg in January 1945.[213]

The Rarity of Protest

As the war progressed and Germany's defeat seemed inevitable, the university became a forum for isolated attempts to defy the Nazi regime. The most legendary action was carried out by the group known as the White Rose

(*Weisse Rose*) based in Munich. Through a series of flyers distributed to groups throughout the Reich, a core of students and one professor, musicologist Kurt Huber, warned of the Nazis' destruction of the German nation and implored German citizens to throw off their shackles and crush the dictatorship. In 1943 Huber and several of the students were arrested, tried, and executed. Their saga has been told and retold in historical studies, popular literature, films, poetry, and an opera.[214]

The White Rose, however, was an exceptional phenomenon. Academe for the most part continued to shun politics or to tend toward conservatism, and aside from Huber's bold actions, protest was rare among musicologists. One of the few to protest racial policies, both openly and discreetly, from the earliest days of the Third Reich was Johannes Wolf. Wolf was approaching retirement in 1933 and so was perhaps less intimidated by political pressures than his mid-career colleagues, but his outspoken independence caused him continuous harassment in the Nazi years, not only from the authorities but especially from other musicologists. Even before he had resigned from the DMG board out of solidarity with Einstein, Wolf was cited by the Education Ministry for his close associations with Jews like Robert Lachmann, noted by the ministry as his "right-hand man."[215] While scheming to force Wolf off the board of the IMS, Besseler voiced his misgivings to the ministry about Wolf's promotion to Ordinarius in Berlin because of close ties with émigrés.[216] This allegation prompted an investigation involving interrogations of Max Seiffert and Wolf's ex-wife.[217] Thereafter the Education Ministry kept a close watch on Wolf, particularly in his activities abroad. It went so far as to reprimand him for publishing an article in an issue of *The Musical Quarterly* that included articles by "Jewish émigrés and anti-German foreigners" (Kestenberg, Einstein, Paul Rosenfeld, and Romain Rolland).[218]

Wolf nevertheless persisted in expressing his disapproval of the regime, including a thinly disguised criticism of Nazi anti-Semitic measures in his 1942 contribution to Peter Raabe's Festschrift. Wolf had not published much in a long time, and it is surprising that he broke his silence to honor Peter Raabe, who had never really earned much acclaim as a scholar (as Strauss's successor to the presidency of the Reich Music Chamber, Raabe devoted the last part of his life to the cause of National Socialist music policy). But Wolf probably saw the Raabe Festschrift as an opportunity to voice his dissatisfaction with the effects of the government's racial policies in a publication of high political profile. His essay dutifully affirms the importance of music to the German race and Volk and the importance of racial research in musicology, but sandwiched in between these statements is a brief summary of musicological activity that opens with the following: "Musicology, like other humanities disciplines, had not yet completely recovered from the damages of the great war, when the duty for new defense first arose, and the strengthening of racial feeling led to the departure of personnel who were not easily replaceable."[219] This fleeting remark can only be referring to the forced emigration of Jews as a result of racial fanaticism.

Kurt Huber's brand of protest was quite different from that of Wolf. Huber was of a generation that was initially captivated by the nationalist idealism of the Nazi party and came to recognize the perversity of the regime only much later, as the war appeared to be lost. In 1942, a small number of students who had attended Huber's philosophy lectures approached him convinced him to help in their distribution of subversive flyers. Huber contributed to one of their documents and was the sole author of the sixth, and last, flyer.[220] As reported in the judgment of the Volksgerichtshof, Huber had shared with the students his concern that northern Germany was tending toward bolshevism, while southern Germany appeared to be tending in a positive direction toward democracy. At first opposed to the idea of distributing flyers, for it would not reach a large enough mass, Huber eventually agreed to help write them for distribution in southern Germany. Only there, he felt, would his ideas for a more democratic form of government find sympathy. In his defense to the Nazi court, Huber futilely maintained that in the two flyers to which he contributed, he chose to play down what he believed were the students' communist sentiments and instead reinforce the need for students to continue to fight in the Wehrmacht. He had merely wanted to put the nation back on the right course and had always been an opponent to communism.[221]

Huber's martyrdom stands out as one of the few acts of courage and conviction among German musicologists, and his tragic end has become a point of departure for assuming that his experience with the Nazi regime was a constant struggle. But Huber enjoyed a reputation as one of the most qualified representatives of scholarship in the Third Reich. Besseler had singled him out as a crucial participant in Barcelona and a powerful weapon against Jewish émigré scholars. Huber was appointed as the first director of the State Institute's folk music department, judged as the best candidate by both the Education Ministry (Weber) and the institute (Besseler).[222] Nevertheless even the most authoritative account of the White Rose continually emphasizes Huber's anti-Nazi feelings and explains his departure from the institute as the result of intrigues, even when acknowledging that he joined the Nazi party a few years earlier.[223] Another account represents him as a musicologist who was "barely noticed" in Munich and describes his years in Berlin as a "disaster": "the university administration and the Nazi student organization expected him to produce blood-and-soil marching songs based on folk tradition.

He refused to cooperate; he was a scientist, not a propagandist. The situation became tense and almost unbearable. At the end of the year, his contract was not renewed, and the Huber family, more reduced in circumstances than ever, returned to their spartan life in Munich."[224]

There is no documentary evidence to support such accounts of Huber's steadfast opposition to the Nazis or to his victimization in Berlin. Rather, it seems that Huber agreed to come to Berlin if he could combine his position at the institute with a teaching position at the university and applied for a formal transfer (*Umhabilitierung*).[225] The university was unable to accommodate him, however, because the psychology institute, with which he would be associated, currently had no director or senior professor, and he would have to wait until that position was filled.[226] Huber accepted the job at the institute provisionally for six months and took a leave of absence from the University of Munich. He impressed his superiors with his work at the institute, but as the question of his transfer was put off repeatedly,[227] he complained to the Education Minister that he would have to leave if the situation were not remedied, since maintaining households in both Munich and Berlin was too much of a financial strain.[228] The ministry denied Huber's claim that a university transfer had been a precondition for his taking the position at the institute or that it was ever promised to him.[229]

Huber was not hounded in Berlin but rather left the institute and returned to his former position voluntarily, as indicated in the 30 August 1938 memo from the education minister to the institute.[230] Upon his return to Munich, he requested help from the university, but the Philosophische Fakultät was disinclined to bail him out after his "Berlin adventure." The party, however, interceded, requesting the rector to find the means to assist Huber and his family.[231] One year after his return, Walther Wüst, the dean of the Philosophische Fakultät and a high-ranking official in SS cultural divisions, wrote a glowing recommendation for Huber's promotion. It mentioned his assistance to party organizations on questions of folk music practice and his eagerness to join the party, putting to rest any doubts about his political reliability.[232] Huber entered the Nazi party in 1940.[233]

After examining Huber's own experiences leading up to his execution, a picture emerges that is much more three-dimensional and human than those portrayals striving to present him as a long-standing opponent of National Socialism and a paragon of resistance. Like many of his colleagues, Huber had no reason to protest for most of the regime's duration. A committed German nationalist, a member of the Bavarian Peoples' party before 1933, an acclaimed scholar of folk music who acknowledged the usefulness of racial applications, Huber was encouraged by the serious attention the new regime paid to preserving folk culture, strengthening national identity, promoting music participation on all levels, and offering a bulwark against communism. He turned to the White Rose only after hearing reports of atrocities at home and in occupied territories and observing the compromising of nationalist ideals and the sacrifice of the German people and German culture in a bloody war that could not be won.[234]

Seen in this light, Huber's reasons for protesting against the Nazi regime seem somewhat more consistent with the idealistic nationalism prevalent among intellectuals and particularly among musicologists. The Nazi regime showed promise of making good use of many of the activities musicologists were pursuing out of necessity. It placed value on their dual roles as scholars and practitioners, on their recent concentration on research in German music history, and on their attention to music education, youth activities, and the cultivation of folk music. Musicology in its current state could be used to boost national pride and promote ideas of German superiority. The regime could regard musicology as a valuable partner, and musicologists could find a common cause with the Nazi cultural agenda and direct their research and curricula toward nationalist and contemporary issues. When the Nazis dismantled the university's power structure, musicology gained in stature within the academy, and the benefits for musicology extended beyond the confines of the university.

The saga of universities capitulating to the Nazi program starts with the arch-conservatism of professors during the Weimar Republic and culminates in the terrorist tactics of students instigating such events as the book burning ceremony in Berlin. Professors' failure to resist Nazi reforms seems inconsistent with their adamant refusal to allow the Weimar government to infringe upon their autonomy, but their passiveness could be explained by the combination of fear inspired by recent events on campuses and a misconception that the Nazi students had support from high places.[235] It could also be explained by academe's latent anti-Semitism and sincere attraction to the Nazi program, as well as to the bold swiftness with which Nazi authorities infiltrated and restructured the entire system of higher education.[236] In any event, the daring actions of the White Rose generally failed to shake the conservatism of university campuses. When the execution of Huber and the students was announced, the Munich students cheered the university porter who had caught them. Similar acts of protest at the university of Hamburg led to arrests and the trial and execution of three students, but any planned acts of sabotage never came to completion because of a lack of cooperation.[237]

New Opportunities outside the University, 1933–1945

World War I and its aftermath drastically altered the career paths of a generation of musicologists. Studies were interrupted, students had to support themselves with odd jobs, and the scarcity of academic positions drove significant numbers into less prestigious occupations. Many of the problems confronting the war veterans and their younger colleagues found solutions after Hitler came to power. The government and the party found creative ways to engage musicologists in projects that fit well with the Nazis' broader social and ideological aims, easing the burden of academic unemployment and winning enthusiastic support from the age groups most affected by World War I. The organizations of Heinrich Himmler and Alfred Rosenberg were especially active in providing research and publishing opportunities, involving musicologists in large-scale educational plans, and enlisting their services in the plunder of musicological treasures in occupied territories. The multiplicity of government and party agencies supporting musicological ventures sometimes cooperated with each other but more often worked at cross purposes.

Musicologists' reasons for wanting to serve the state and party varied. The war veterans, paranoid from the experiences of interrupted studies, economic hardships, and limited career prospects, gravitated toward external opportunities as a safeguard, even after they had secured academic posts. The younger cohorts, those born too late to serve in World War I, approached these opportunities with far more ideological conviction and pragmatism, having received much of their education under Hitler's regime and seeing work for the state as a chance to gain experience and secure a strategic edge in the academic job market. The eastward expansion of the Reich promised to open up more opportunities for musicologists to control music policy and education, spheres of influence that had been closed to them at home. In all these enterprises, musicologists displayed an earnestness in spreading German culture that far outshined the determination of academics from other fields.

The Employment Situation for Musicologists after World War I

In his original proposal for the DMG, Abert pointed to the need to ease the reentry of scholars returning from war as one of the most serious problems facing the profession.[1] While World War I had caused inconveniences for established scholars by isolating them from their colleagues and cutting off their access to foreign archives, it posed far more serious obstacles to those just starting out in the field. Military conscription had disrupted studies, and the end of the war brought an influx of continuing students and employable musicologists all returning home at once. Those hoping to complete their studies faced obstacles from certain Weimar policies that made it difficult to finish dissertations.[2] The postwar period brought on an unprecedented need for students to support themselves with nonacademic work, and many even had to resort to all varieties of manual labor during the hyperinflation of 1922–23.[3] Besseler at age twenty-three, for example, had to support himself as a music critic until he could procure a position as Assistent and then as Privatdozent.[4]

With degrees in hand, this group realized they had to look beyond academe for permanent employment, sometimes discovering that they were overqualified for most nonacademic occupations. Those with training in acoustics turned to jobs in radio, film, recording, and any area where such knowledge could be applied,[5] but others began to consider a doctoral degree in musicology a liability, especially for employment in criticism and opera dramaturgy.[6] Musicologists had traditionally worked part time as music critics for newspapers, but turning criticism into a full-time career presented certain professional complications. For one, factions of the musicology establishment looked down on the activity. Some older scholars, such as Abert, denounced the profession as unworthy for musicologists.[7] Younger colleagues echoed his indignation, engaging in such work begrudgingly and considering dependence on the press for employment a mockery of the "liberal science" in which they received their training.[8]

Another problem in music criticism was the absence of quality control: anyone could be a critic, and musicologists who devoted most of their time to criticism felt increasingly threatened by untrained competitors. In an attempt to limit music criticism to trained musicologists and weed out dilettantes, scholars and educators proposed rigorous qualification standards. Hugo Leichtentritt, a musicologist active mainly as a critic, maintained that a doctorate in musicology was a bare minimum for attaining the knowledge needed to approach music criticism as a "science."[9] Schering also advocated the benefits of such qualifications, regarding a musicology prerequisite as a salvation from the chaos of the late nineteenth century, when music criticism was overrun with dilettantes.[10]

The overriding desire among young musicologists, however, was to pursue an occupation in academe, just as their teachers had done. Theodor Kroyer received numerous appeals from former students for assistance in finding academic positions in the years following the hyperinflation, each expressing the frustrations of having to leave one's dreams unfulfilled. Theodor Werner complained: "I am, like everyone else who could still make a living in 1919, a poor wretch today, living mercifully from time-consuming journalistic activity and from a satisfactory position at the conservatory, however I (perhaps foolishly) long for the university."[11] A similar appeal came from Alfred Einstein, forced to work in a publishing house during the inflation but longing for the academy: "I'm now in my sixth year of this slavery. In my most productive hours of the day, I waste my time with publishing matters that don't interest me in the least and take me away from what's really important to me; it is simply an unworthy preoccupation. . . . I have to escape from these conditions. . . . So please tell me if you think I would have any prospects [at the University of Heidelberg], and since you know the situation there all too well, please give me some indication of what steps I should take in approaching the department and the Education Ministry."[12]

When veterans were lucky enough to secure academic posts, universities had to make special concession for those who, because they were forced to interrupt their studies, were entering the field at a more advanced age. In 1925, the University of Königsberg allowed Müller-Blattau to go up for a promotion before the usual six-year period following the Habilitation,[13] and in 1923, Friedrich Blume asked the University of Leipzig for written confirmation of his intention to finish his degree in 1915 before being drafted, in the hope of acquiring a higher ranking in an academic post. He added: "you will certainly understand that in the current economic situation one has to strive to recognize any advantages that present themselves, in order at least to retrieve a part of those years lost during the war."[14] Although many of these individuals went on to lead high-profile academic careers, they never forgot those early years of insecurity and would, in the future, be inclined to maximize their chances for professional survival through their work both within and beyond the university.

New Opportunities in the Nazi State

In the first years after the Nazi takeover, the prospects of reform raised hopes. Younger scholars, encouraged by promises of Nachwuchsförderung, were brimming over with suggestions for how the state could use their skills. In 1933, a youthful Heinrich Husmann recommended the establishment of a central agency, staffed by young musicologists, who would use their scholarly expertise to advise adult education organizations on putting together success-ful concert programs.[15] In his 1935 report on a study carried out by the German Students' Union at the University of Berlin, Siegfried Goslich opened with a quote from Hitler and then declared: "the penetration of the entire life of our Volk with National Socialist ideology has awakened the feeling of obligation to come to terms with the new situation among the younger genera-tion of musicologists." The group suggested that new careers for musicologists include a position of "Musikführer" in National Socialist organizations, as well as jobs in dramaturgy, journalism, radio, and film. The group also drew up a plan for coordinating the obligatory work service for students (*Arbeits-dienst*) and service in the SA with fields of study, demonstrating the student body's intention to reach a synthesis of "artistic training, scholarly maturity, and the feeling of unconditional bonds to Volk and Fatherland."[16]

Fellerer came up with additional suggestions, such as the creation of the "Musikkonservator" to supervise the preservation of musical treasures on a regional level; the expansion of teaching opportunities beyond universities in accordance with the new system of music education; activity in theater, con-cert agencies, radio, the recording industry, publishing, and instrument and music sales; and the application of training in systematic fields to radio tech-nology, mechanical music, recording, and instrument building. Fellerer argued that if musicology were to be "bound to the Volk," it must apply itself to prac-tical areas and not leave them open to dilettantes.[17] Less focused propositions also abounded, such as creating the contrived profession of "music politician" or "music policymaker," designed for an individual with knowledge of music history acquired at the university level and qualifications in "music, scholar-ship, the National Socialist movement, and administration,"[18] in other words, some sort of government position tailor-made for a trained musicologist.

The professionalization of music criticism continued to warrant serious consideration, but the earlier visions of restricting its practice to trained musi-cologists were slipping away. Nine months after the Nazis came to power,

Erich Valentin (b. 1906, lecturer in Magdeburg and at the Mozarteum in Salzburg) pointed to the Nazis' attention to the importance of criticism, citing the task force for German music critics (Arbeitsgemeinschaft deutscher Musikkritiker) established by the Kampfbund für deutsche Kultur (Fighting League for German Culture). He proposed that a state-subsidized formal degree program in music criticism be set up at the conservatory as a means of imposing quality control and establishing music criticism as a recognized profession.[19] The Kampfbund, founded by Alfred Rosenberg in 1929, was an elitist group of artists and intellectuals who adhered to the ideal of a pure German culture for the German nation. A contender with Goebbels for control of cultural affairs in the early years of the Third Reich, the Kampfbund was more concerned than most other Nazi organizations with establishing aesthetic criteria and means for purifying German culture.

The problem of corruption and dilettantism in music criticism appeared headed for obsolescence after Nazi Propaganda Minister Joseph Goebbels formally abolished all arts criticism in November 1936 and replaced it with objective reportage or "arts observation" (*Kunstbetrachtung*). The reasons for, as well as the effects of, Goebbels's *Kritikverbot* are not fully understood,[20] but it is clear that the ban was seldom enforced. Rather lax in its formulation, the ban stipulated that authors exercise self-censorship, and it applied only to newspapers, not to trade journals.[21] The apparent restrictions on the critic were so vague that Valentin did not think it inappropriate to propose his "Seminar für Musikkritik" in 1937, as he had done in 1933, stressing that high quality music criticism would fulfill the critic's noblest duty to work for the "art and culture of the people."[22] Gerigk expressed his disappointment with the Kritikverbot, because "bourgeois" journals did not adhere to it and "National Socialist" journals that complied were thus muzzled and robbed of the chance for counterattack.[23] A 1942 doctoral dissertation, for which musicologist Rudolf Ficker served as codirector, assessed that the ban had only slowly and sporadically begun to take hold and had caused much confusion regarding the duties of the so-called music observer (*Musikbetrachter*).[24] In any event, music criticism never became the exclusive domain of musicologists, and other journalistic alternatives were limited: one could write concert programs, but even there a less scientific style became more desirable, especially since the Nazi subscription program of KdF had brought lay audiences into the concert hall for the first time, and program notes had to meet their needs.[25]

Many more work options arose out of the creation of new state and party facilities that could make use of musicological expertise. The expansion of the State Institute was only one of several developments that broadened the potential application of musicological training, with other opportunities within the Propaganda Ministry, the SS, and the Rosenberg Bureau.

Musicologists must have viewed the creation of the Propaganda Ministry and especially the Reich Music Chamber as an administrative breakthrough. It indicated that the state was prepared to take cultural concerns seriously, particularly the standardization of arts professions and elimination of amateur competition. Alfred Morgenroth, the musicology consultant in the Reich Music Chamber, responded directly to the Student Union suggestions, listing jobs that the chamber could provide for those with musicological training and endorsing a state examination that would qualify students for additional careers.[26] In addition to the Music Chamber, the Propaganda Ministry had a separate music department, headed by Heinz Drewes, through which Goebbels sponsored a number of musicological publishing projects: the edition of Bruckner's complete works, Gluck's complete works, and a multivolume collection of folk songs.[27] This office commissioned a collection (never published) of historical essays by musicologists, edited by Moser and including contributions by Fellerer and Engel, that used historical evidence to demonstrate Germany's long-standing musical presence in countries annexed or under German occupation by 1944.[28] The Propaganda Ministry also sponsored lecture tours, especially by older scholars: Sandberger twice received assistance to promote his lecture-concert programs on his discovery of new Haydn works, and Schering was invited to give four radio broadcasts in Stockholm on his latest Beethoven research.[29]

Moser managed to secure a full-time position in the Propaganda Ministry when Drewes appointed him to run the Reichsstelle für Musikbearbeitungen (Reich Office for Music Arrangements), established in 1940 on an order from Hitler (a *Führerauftrag*) to replenish the dwindling opera and concert repertoires.[30] The prohibition of Jewish and foreign works had reduced the supply of available repertoire, while the addition of "German" musical establishments resulting from military expansion gave rise to a demand for acceptable German repertoire. The Reichsstelle was to commission new works, especially operettas, and to rework old compositions to render them more appropriate. By 1943 it had commissioned revised librettos for operettas set in Poland that would change the setting to German or German occupied locations. Further plans included reworking Handel oratorios deemed undesirable because of their Old Testament subjects and Bach cantatas rendered "intolerable" (*un-leidlich*) by their Pietist texts.[31] Drewes first appointed Moser as general secretary, then promoted him to director with a 33 percent pay increase in recognition for his outstanding work and because of Hitler's personal interest in the project.[32]

The Propaganda Ministry enlisted a number of other musicologists as part-time consultants. Georg Schünemann, director of the music division of the State Library and Extraordinarius in Berlin from 1939, served as director of the German Music Institute for Foreigners under the aegis of the Propaganda Ministry.[33] Gotthold Frotscher held several consulting positions alongside his appointment to the Berlin musicology faculty, such as musicology consultant in the Chief Cultural Office of the Propaganda Ministry and music consultant for the Reich Youth Leadership.[34] Siegfried Goslich served as a folk music consultant in the Reich Music Chamber,[35] but he was more active in his capacity as the music consultant in the Deutsches Volksbildungswerk of the DAF. He provided accounts of the division's activities in both editions of Stumme's *Musik im Volk,* and he edited a substantial handbook for teachers issued by the Volksbildungswerk, entitled *Musikalische Volksbildung.*

The Education Ministry initially was a more willing patron of musicology than the Propaganda Ministry, spearheading the transformation of the Bückeburg Institute and promising support to the DGMW prior to the Reichsmusiktage, but its interest proved tentative as the years went by. Schiedermair had secured some vague promise of sponsorship from Rust when he dissolved and reestablished the DGMW in 1938, but the society was thereafter allowed to languish until it ceased to exist by 1941. Rust had focused more attention on the State Institute, university departments, and other independent research facilities. But as the war progressed, he withdrew his support even from the institute, left it to struggle with competing interests, and considered decentralizing or disbanding it in the future. In terms of variety of opportunities and recruitment of large numbers of musicologists in projects and tasks, Himmler's SS and Rosenberg's cultural organization proved to be the most interested in enlisting musicologists' expertise for their goals.

Musicology in the SS-"Ahnenerbe"

The name of the SS is usually associated with concentration camps, police terror, and genocide, orchestrated with ruthless efficiency by the authoritarian Heinrich Himmler, but the SS was more than just a police organization. Historians have found it convenient to use the term "SS state" to convey the complexity of the organization as a state within a state, immune to the legal and judicial system of the Reich.[36] The SS was formed with the dual purpose of cultivating a Nazi leadership class and exterminating those designated as racially and biologically inferior or politically recalcitrant. Established in 1929 to serve as Hitler's bodyguard staff, the SS in its early years aimed to recruit membership from aristocrats and intelligentsia who could trace their pure

German lineage to 1750. SS membership thus had an air of prestige, but the organization also accepted lower-class elements eager and willing to bully its opponents.

In 1934, Himmler profited from the purge of the heads of the SA and took over many of its police functions and terror tactics. Thereafter the SS grew in power and numbers and changed dramatically: Himmler consolidated his power through a complex network of intelligence, known as the Security Service (*Sicherheitsdienst,* or SD); and in 1936, the SS took over all police divisions (except for such services as fire, traffic, and sanitation) and consolidated them into the secret police (*Gestapo*) and related divisions. It continued to expand its corps of SS guards into a vast army of special troops, ultimately wielding full control over the concentration camps.[37]

As it grew and changed character, the SS persisted in its mania to cultivate a Nazi elite, imposing its own physical, mental, and ideological standards on its members and developing its own science, education, and quasi religion. Himmler had long fancied himself a historian and took a keen interest in furthering a general knowledge of Germanic prehistory. He shared such interests with the architect of the "blood and soil" mythology and Nazi agrarian policies, Richard Walther Darré, and the two supported an amateur historian Herman Wirth in the formation of the "Deutsches Ahnenerbe" (German Ancestral Heritage) in 1935. This was to be a "scientific" society dedicated to studying the history of the Germanic race. It was attached to the SS Race and Resettlement Office (Rasse- und Siedlungshauptamt) and was funded largely by Darré's agricultural office.[38] The Race and Resettlement Office was concerned with both theoretical and practical issues of resettling formerly estranged ethnic Germans into the Reich.[39]

Most of the active participants in the "Ahnenerbe" were required to be inducted into the SS and its Race and Resettlement Office at various ranks,[40] as was the case with the two musicologists most active in the organization — Fritz Bose and Alfred Quellmalz.[41] In an effort to raise scientific standards, Himmler eventually pushed out his cofounders Darré and Wirth and absorbed the "Ahnenerbe" into his personal staff, surrounding himself with more legitimate scholars (for example, the folklorist Joseph Otto Plaßmann and the highly regarded Munich professor Walther Wüst, whom he named president) and leaving the administrative tasks to an SS officer, Wolfram Sievers.[42] When Himmler absorbed the "Ahnenerbe" from the Race and Resettlement Office, he brought with it most of the Race and Resettlement Office's other scientific subdivisions.[43]

The "Ahnenerbe" strove to be a multidisciplinary undertaking, involving natural sciences, social sciences, and humanities disciplines in a collaborative setting to achieve a complete understanding of the Germanic race.[44] Thus any musicologists who could demonstrate an interest in musical issues related by any stretch of the imagination to the Germanic race were in a position to receive financial backing from the SS. As a source of research funding, the "Ahnenerbe" held many advantages over more conventional sources because the SS had a special legal status and so could circumvent visa and currency complications often encountered by scholars applying for travel abroad.[45] Such was the experience of Johann Wolfgang Schottländer, who was working on the seemingly unrelated research area of ancient Greek notation. He successfully appealed to Himmler for money to travel to Greece, Switzerland, and Italy after being turned down by the Deutsche Forschungsgemeinschaft on the grounds that his plans were too ambitious. The SS was willing not only to fund his travel, but also to consider publishing his results as part of an "Ahnenerbe" series.[46]

The first musicologist to receive long-term benefits from the SS was Fritz Bose. Born in 1906, Bose earned his doctorate in 1934, and after World War II he enjoyed success as head of the Institut für Musikforschung and faculty member of the Technische Hochschule in Berlin. Bose was a very enterprising young man who, like others of his generation, hoped to maximize his potential in academe by forging strong political connections. He first entered the political arena by capitalizing on new research angles and offering his unique skills to state and party officials. In a 1934 issue of *Unser Wille und Weg,* a Nazi Party organ edited by Joseph Goebbels, Bose publicized the usefulness of an interdisciplinary approach in musicology that would consider music in racial-biological terms.[47] At the time he was employed as an assistant in the musicology division of the Berlin Acoustics Institute (Institut für Lautforschung). This was moved from the State Library to the University of Berlin after its director was expelled in accordance with Paragraph 6 for alleged Social Democratic leanings and discrimination against National Socialists.[48] Bose, then twenty-eight and having just received his doctorate, sent an unsolicited letter of application to the Education Ministry suggesting that he be entrusted with expanding the archive's music division to include a center for comparative folk music and musical race research. He listed among his qualifications his Aryan lineage, his membership in the Nazi party and the Nazi Students' League, and his attempts to join the SA. He also pointed out that he was the only German student of Erich von Hornbostel, the only younger representative of the field besides Marius Schneider (Hornbostel's successor as director of the Berlin Sound Recording Archive), head of the DGMW Fachgruppe for comparative musicology, and the only researcher applying "exact, scientific" (*naturwissenschaftlich*) methodologies to the study of music and race and to comparative folk song research.[49]

Bose simultaneously attached himself to the SS-"Ahnenerbe," seeing this as

a way to establish ties with influential people and advance his career in academe. In its quest to accumulate a comprehensive knowledge of the Germanic
race, the "Ahnenerbe" defined Germanic music as broadly as possible, including all aspects of Nordic musical culture, past and present. Bose's first project
for the SS was a research trip to Finland in summer 1936 to evaluate folk
music materials.[50] In 1940 he stated that he could assess the music's usefulness
for understanding prehistoric Nordic culture only through comparative studies with the folk music of such regions as Iceland and the Faroe Islands.[51]
Accordingly, in 1943 the "Ahnenerbe" contacted Wilhelm Heinitz for copies
of his recordings of folk music from the Faroe Islands.[52]

The musical agenda of the "Ahnenerbe" also had broad historical parameters, and Bose received a second assignment to conduct research on the lur, a
Bronze Age instrument usually found in pairs and thus presumed to point to
Germanic origins for polyphony. In both scholarly and popular literature the
lur had come to symbolize the cultural advances of Germanic tribes: both
Alfred Einstein and Hans Joachim Moser had addressed the debate over the
early existence of the lur as a possible testimony to early Germanic polyphony,
a claim largely dismissed because ancient instruments — including the Jewish
temple instruments — were often found in pairs.[53] Oskar Fleischer was the
main advocate of the lur's importance in understanding Germanic ingenuity,
and he even had the instrument reconstructed and used in demonstrations.
Fleischer insisted that the lur provided evidence of the German "invention" of
the major triad and polyphony and, most of all, that it weakened the assumptions that ancient Germans were barbarians who were civilized by the Greeks
and Romans.[54] The influential amateur musicologist Richard Eichenauer
perpetuated Fleischer's claims, and the instrument came to represent concrete proof of a Germanic racial trait dictating a preference for consonance
and an inborn aversion to the alleged atonalism of the Jewish race.[55] The
"Ahnenerbe" entrusted Bose with the task of researching and reproducing
models of the lur and with refuting those who claimed that it was not used as a
musical instrument or that it was fashioned after an oriental prototype.[56] They
were ultimately disappointed by his inability to complete the project, and
Sievers criticized his lack of experience, his laziness, and his opportunistic
objectives to advance himself in the field by attaching himself to Himmler's
organization. Alfred Quellmalz took over the project in 1941, terminating
Bose's affiliation with the "Ahnenerbe."[57]

While still in the good graces of the SS, however, Bose exploited these
influential ties. He complained to the "Ahnenerbe" of difficulties he had at the
Acoustics Institute while working on the lur project and requested full-time
employment by the SS. Bose wanted to preserve his university ties by perform-

ing his functions at the institute on a voluntary basis, giving lectures, proceeding with his Habilitation, "and — if it please the gods — some day become a real professor." He was also awaiting approval from the Education Ministry to teach courses in "Musical Race Studies" and hoped that Himmler might put in a good word for him.[58] The "Ahnenerbe" considered this request important enough to pass it on to Himmler via Sievers, stressing Bose's unique qualifications to carry out the lur project and issuing veiled threats of an investigation of Bose's employer: "Whether these measures on the part of the director of the Acoustics Institute are directed against the work of the SS and harbor ideological opposition to the matter, or whether it is a question of competence, cannot be determined here."[59] Wüst decided that Bose should be retained for the project, but because of his youth and lack of a Habilitation, he should not be given a full position, nor should Himmler approach the Education Ministry on his behalf. Bose could, however, be affiliated with the existing but unstaffed SS research center for musicology with special emphasis on Nordic music (Forschungsstätte für Musikwissenschaft [Mit besonderer Berücksichtigung der Nordischen Musik]).[60]

In its first years, the "Ahnenerbe" established its own publishing house in Berlin-Dahlem and a publication series of monographs in the humanities. It coproduced several scholarly periodicals as well as issuing three journals of its own: the monthly *Germanien,* dedicated to a variety of topics on prehistory, Germanic history, and folklore; and two journals dedicated to genealogy, *Zeitschrift für Namenforschung* and *Das Sippenzeichen.*[61] These publishing ventures benefited a number of musicologists. Müller-Blattau's study *Germanisches Erbe in deutscher Tonkunst* was accepted as part of an "Ahnenerbe" publication series after a rejection from Bärenreiter and came out simultaneously in a Hitler Youth series.[62] This study uses examples of folk music, lullabies, and children's songs to reconstruct Germanic prehistoric music and to derive melodic gestures that can be found throughout German art music. Himmler requested that Müller-Blattau be persuaded to work for the "Ahnenerbe," but the discovery of his pre-1933 connections to Jews, democrats, and communists, his support of atonality and "Jewish" methods of music psychology, and his characterization as a political chameleon worked against him.[63]

The scholar who benefited most from "Ahnenerbe" publishing opportunities was Hans Joachim Moser.[64] From 1938 through 1940 Moser was a regular contributor to *Germanien,* edited by the folklorist J. O. Plaßmann. Moser supplied a steady stream of articles on the history of military music, on folk songs, on fundamental elements of German music, as well as timely essays on the music history of recently annexed and occupied lands.[65] Moser was skillful in quickly furnishing contributions to reinforce Germany's military advances with evidence of an early German musical presence in relevant regions. In September 1938, the same month as the Munich agreement which allowed Germany to annex the Sudetenland, Plaßmann accepted Moser's offer to write an article on Sudeten-German music history.[66] By October 1939, one month after the invasion of Poland, Moser had submitted a similar article on Danzig.[67] Two of Moser's *Germanien* articles — the Sudeten-German essay and another on Austria that praised the events of the Anschluss — were reprinted in a special "Ahnenerbe" publication, entitled *Deutsches Land kehrt heim: Ostmark und Sudetenland als germanischer Volksboden,* celebrating the "homecoming" of Austria and the Sudetenland into the German Reich.[68] Moser agreed to write a series of articles on the history of German military songs in spring 1939, but as military gains rapidly increased, he suggested to Plaßmann: "would *you rather have in the meantime a more politically topical essay on the Flemish-Dutch-German musical connection?* Also one on the musical *culture-bridge* to Scandinavia would certainly be feasible" (Moser's emphasis).[69] This letter was written shortly after the occupation of Denmark in April 1940 and preceded the offensive on Belgium and Holland by five days, and Plaßmann responded favorably, urging Moser to proceed immediately in accordance with the "official position."[70]

Moser, like Bose, sought permanent employment from the "Ahnenerbe," but for different reasons. Moser, a casualty of Paragraph 6, was retired from the directorship of the Staatliche Akademie für Kirchen- und Schulmusik in 1933. He left his position on good terms and drew a comfortable pension until 1936, when the government reopened a 1930 case accusing Moser of adultery, found against him, and reduced his pension by 40 percent.[71] This left Moser to supplement his income with freelance writing in order to support his large family. The mutually beneficial collaboration with the "Ahnenerbe" prompted him to submit a book manuscript to the "Ahnenerbe" publishing house, to ask for travel funds, to seek an endorsement for his pending appointment with the Propaganda Ministry, and ultimately to request appointment as a permanent consultant.[72] Unfortunately for him, the SD discovered positive representations of Jewish composers in the 1934 edition of his *Musiklexikon,* rendering him an unacceptable collaborator.[73] But because of his productivity and important contributions to the journal, Plaßmann urged that the collaboration to continue in secret, with Moser penning his articles under an alias.[74]

SS-"Ahnenerbe" Wartime Projects beyond the Borders of the Reich

In the course of the war, scholars from various fields worked with the "Ahnenerbe" in the occupied territories in handling issues of cultural property, both in the form of seizing valuable items and surveying activities. The musicologists among them, however, were far more interested in studying and educating the ethnic German populations than in plundering their possessions. Beginning with the Anschluss, Himmler redirected the goals of the "Ahnenerbe" toward becoming the most influential cultural administrator in newly acquired regions of the expanding Reich. After the war broke out, its actions in Poland, Russia, South Tyrol, and parts of Yugoslavia concentrated on "securing," that is, seizing, all cultural property deemed relevant to the study of the Germanic race. (Such seizure was a direct violation of the Hague Convention.) In Norway, Holland, Denmark, and Belgium, it also set up facilities for imposing German culture on these "Germanic" populations. The "Ahnenerbe" intensified its activities in the humanities more than in the natural sciences in these years, and because of the special status of the SS, many humanities researchers were able to avoid military service through "Ahnenerbe" activities that Himmler designated "war essential" (*kriegswichtig*).[75]

Within a few months of the invasion of Poland, Himmler used his position as "Reich Commissioner for Securing German Nationhood" (Reichskommissar für die Festigung des deutschen Volkstums, or RKF) to assume control over the seizure of arable land, and in December 1939, he extended his jurisdiction to the seizure of Polish cultural property.[76] One SD man informed Himmler of the existence and importance of the Warsaw Sound Recording Archive, containing folk songs collected since 1935 by the Austrian-trained musicologist Julian von Pulikowski and deemed useful for an understanding of Polish and Ukrainian "tribes" and crucial to musicological research. Because the collection was too fragile to be seized and transported, it was hoped that Himmler would allow Pulikowski, who was "well grounded in German work methods," to carry out the study and write up the results.[77] Musicologists were consulted: Pulikowski had contacted German colleagues on his own, but any collaboration with a Pole would require special permission from the German occupying command (the *Generalgouvernment*) in Poland.[78] Quellmalz attested to Pulikowski's reliability and the importance of the collection, and the SS approved its continued maintenance under Pulikowski's supervision.[79]

It is important to note that the idea to seize or at least monopolize the Warsaw Sound Archive came from a member of the intelligence, not from a musicologist working for the SS. Although most "Ahnenerbe" wartime initiatives consisted of seizing and transporting "Germanic" artifacts into Germany, most of the musicologists involved understood their task as collecting data and literally preserving a cultural legacy in danger of disappearing. They concentrated their efforts on recording and transcribing the folk music of surviving ethnic German communities in occupied territories and those selected

for resettlement rather than on seizing physical property (by contrast, musicologists working with Rosenberg spent most of their energy plundering as the
war progressed).

Fritz Bose, ever vigilant of new opportunities, wrote Sievers in February
1940 only days after the war terminated his work in Finland[80] and recommended that the SS extend the notion of "cultural property" to the performance realm. German military advances were opening up the possibility of
recording folk music and folk dances of Volhynian and Baltic ethnic Germans in resettlement camps, and of ethnic Germans residing in former Poland,
Galicia, the Carpathian Mountains, and South Tyrol. Bose stressed the urgency of such a project owing to the risks of resettlement disrupting the lives of
the subjects; the need to make the project the domain of the "Ahnenerbe"
rather than a university, where it might be neglected; and, because of his access
to recording equipment, the expediency of assigning the project to him.[81]

Coincidentally Alfred Quellmalz, Huber's successor as director of the State
Institute's folk music division, had applied to the Ethnic German Transit
Agency (Volksdeutsche Mittelstelle) ten days earlier and, in early March, carried out such a project in the resettlement camps of Volhynian and Galician
Germans, apparently without "Ahnenerbe" involvement.[82] Immediately after
the completion of the Volhynian-Galician project, Quellmalz approached the
"Ahnenerbe" and embarked on what was to become the largest scale musicological venture under its supervision: the collection of folk materials from
ethnic Germans in the South Tyrol. Quellmalz's work with the "Ahnenerbe"
facilitated a fruitful collaboration between the SS and the State Institute. This
collaboration raised the status of the institute through its involvement in an
activity of cultural-political importance and through the addition of new material to both its folk music and historical archives.

Following a 1939 agreement between Germany and Italy, German-speaking
inhabitants of the South Tyrol region of Italy were given the option to resettle
in the German Reich. An overwhelming majority voted in favor of resettlement, and Himmler, overseeing its execution, appointed Sievers director of a
cultural commission to supervise the transport of the settlers' cultural property into the Reich. Sievers set up headquarters in Bozen and gathered a group
of experts from various disciplines to work with him, coordinating the transport of property owned by the settlers and zealously photographing, transcribing, or otherwise documenting all relevant materials that the Italians
would not let out of the country. This endless task of documenting allowed the
commission to stay in the South Tyrol longer than necessary, enabling the
German government to justify the presence of the "Ahnenerbe" and to secretly
penetrate parts of the region officially closed to them by the Italian authorities.

For this reason, scholars were discouraged from publicizing their activities back home.[83]

The musicological work in the South Tyrol was the most prolonged and most thoroughly documented of all "Ahnenerbe"-sponsored musicological projects, but it was also a carefully guarded secret. Seiffert, aware of the political prestige of the SS and the gains to the institute's collection, was naturally in favor of offering full cooperation to the "Ahnenerbe" and allowed Quellmalz to be absent from Berlin to organize and supervise the field research.[84] Assisted by Bose and Gertraud Wittmann (an institute employee), Quellmalz orchestrated a tight schedule of recording, interviewing, filming, and transcribing, all the while encountering difficulties with Italian bureaucrats.[85] The volatile political situation forced Quellmalz to turn down Walter Wiora's offer to publish a report on the South Tyrolean project in *Das Reich*, transmitting a warning from Sievers that any such publications might land the author in a concentration camp.[86] The project dragged on much longer than anticipated, and Quellmalz had to justify his prolonged absence to Seiffert and the Education Ministry.[87] In the end, the South Tyrol project lasted from June 1940 until December 1942. By that time, Quellmalz's staff had grown to include eight collaborators working on such diverse areas as folk songs, instrumental music, folk dances, children's songs and games, and music history. They scoured the South Tyrolean countryside, making sound recordings of vocal and instrumental music, photocopies of manuscripts and printed songbooks, transcriptions, and silent films of folk dances, games, plays, and instrumental techniques, as well as photographing and collecting biographical data from the population in order to learn more of its racial and sociological composition.

Quellmalz also reported on a program of Volksbildung in the South Tyrol: he and Bose delivered lectures on folk music to capacity crowds throughout the region, another staff member led folk dancing courses, and the entire group ran a week-long folk music retreat in summer 1941.[88] The musicologists' interaction with the native population for the purpose of educating and reinforcing German identity was not typical for all scholars working for the "Ahnenerbe" in the South Tyrol. Just as musicologists in the university distinguished themselves with their community service, those working for Himmler seemed more dedicated than other academics to establishing contacts with indigenous populations and spreading German culture.

The special duty of musicologists comes across clearly when their activities are compared to those of scholars from other fields. According to its list of objectives, the SS strove not only to collect artifacts but also to establish a working relationship with indigenous populations, carrying out the cultural-political tasks of fostering cooperation and educating ethnic Germans to the

National Socialist worldview. But Anke Oesterle's description of folklorists who worked for the "Ahnenerbe" indicates that they paid far more attention to hoarding material objects, rationalizing their greed with alleged scholarly pursuits.[89] Musicologists, by contrast, were more attentive to the cultural-political tasks. In addition to the feverish collection and documentation of melodies and folk practices, which in itself brought them into close contact with the natives, musicologists spread the gospel of Germanization to the South Tyroleans with their lectures, workshops, and retreats.

The South Tyrol project not only expanded the knowledge of folk culture, but it also yielded significant gains for historical musicology. The wealth of archival material compelled Quellmalz to request that the "Ahnenerbe" engage another assistant, Walter Senn, to document these sources exclusively. This information would enhance the State Institute's *Generalkatalog* as well as assisting Quellmalz in the preparation of a volume for the Reichsdenkmale and in the research for his Habilitationsschrift.[90] The SS presence in Italy also inspired other German musicologists to pursue similar projects that could exploit SS privileges. In 1942, Erich Schenk proposed a collaboration between his department at the University of Vienna, along with its research center in Florence, and the "Ahnenerbe" to investigate "Germanic remnants" in Italian music from the sixth century to the sixteenth century, a project that would require thorough archival work in Italy.[91]

Schenk was aware of the Germanic focus of the "Ahnenerbe," and so he framed his proposal in terms that would appeal to Himmler's objectives. By this time scholars were familiar with Himmler's idiosyncratic musicological interests. Plaßmann once relayed to Moser Himmler's query regarding the origins of a particular folk song, and his interest in Gregorian chant was well known among musicologists.[92] Sievers was thus initially intrigued by Schenk's proposal, given Himmler's "special interest in questions of Gregorian chant,"[93] but he ultimately rejected it after consultation with Quellmalz, who felt that Schenk's proposal covered too long a time span to be appropriate for the purposes of the "Ahnenerbe." Furthermore, the personnel Schenk recommended (himself, his institute, and Walter Senn) were experts in seventeenth- and eighteenth-century music and were ill-prepared to undertake a serious comparative study of Gregorian chant (Quellmalz suggested instead that a third party, Beichert from Freiburg, receive a stipend from the "Ahnenerbe" for such a project). Finally, the project was not as urgent as the collection of folk music from disappearing German cultures and could wait until after the war. Although not wishing to dismiss Schenk entirely, since the "Ahnenerbe" could make good use of his Florence center's photography equipment and his access to Italian archives otherwise blocked by Italian bureaucracy, Quellmalz confided to Sievers "out of SS camaraderie" his mistrust of Schenk. Schenk was known to take on large projects and then fail to complete them, and Quellmalz was opposed to distracting Senn from his more important research in the South Tyrol.[94]

The situation turned into a contest of mutual exploitation. Schenk obviously had little interest in Gregorian chant and wanted only to forge a relationship with the SS and to promote Senn, and the "Ahnenerbe" wanted only to make use of Schenk's Florentine connections. Because Schenk had approached the "Ahnenerbe" with a portfolio of positive recommendations from other SS officers, Sievers respectfully suggested he consider a smaller-scale operation involving the collection of photocopies from sources dating only through thirteenth century.[95] Schenk countered that Senn would soon be finished with his South Tyrol project and could conduct full-scale work on Gregorian chant, but Sievers held firm to his decision.[96]

Quellmalz, for his part, had also exploited Schenk's proposal to widen his sphere of influence into chant research and to gain the services of another assistant — Beichert — without the involvement of Schenk.[97] Eight months later, however, Quellmalz could not report much progress and suggested that the work requiring access to Italian and French archives wait until after the war. Other scholars were pursuing chant projects, most notably the editions by Ewald Jammers and Bruno Stäblein for the Reichsdenkmale, Fellerer's *Deutsche Gregorianik im Frankenreich* and his continuing research into the German elements in Gregorian chant in Holland and Flanders, and, especially, Jammers's completed manuscript *Die völkische Zugehörigkeit des gregorianischen Chorals*.[98] Quellmalz directed his energies toward ensuring the publication of Jammers's book, which was intended for a series edited by Blume entitled "Schriften zur musikalischen Volks-und Rassenkunde" but was held up by paper shortages. He sought the intervention of the Sicherheitshauptamt and the "Ahnenerbe" to push the project through, all under the premise of addressing Himmler's special concern for Gregorian chant.[99]

Quellmalz developed additional projects beyond the South Tyrol, but they scarcely came to fruition. He drew up plans for an all-encompassing research project on "Germanic-German" folk music in Holland, Flanders, Normandy, and Walloon; French folk music; and the folk music of Germanic peoples in Scandinavia and the Baltic states, but all he managed to realize was one research trip to Brussels in August 1942.[100] The "Ahnenerbe" was also at work in the province of Laibach-Gottschee, a German enclave in the Hapsburg empire ceded to Yugoslavia in 1919. When Laibach-Gottschee was annexed by Italy after the Axis powers devastated Yugoslavia, the Italian and German governments reached an agreement similar to the South Tyrolean formula, authorizing Himmler to set up RKF and "Ahnenerbe" outposts in those areas.[101] The

"Ahnenerbe" tried to release Quellmalz from his obligations in the South Tyrol for at least four months to work in the Gottschee resettlement program in July 1941, but almost a year later he had still not started there.[102] The Nazi party district leader (*Gauleiter*) responsible for the resettled Gottschee Germans authorized researchers in Graz to carry out the project instead. Quellmalz angrily attributed this move to vengeful political intrigues on the part of Werner Danckert, since Quellmalz had written a negative review of Danckert's book. Quellmalz tried to reverse the decision with the aid of SS intervention.[103]

The SS-"Ahnenerbe" served as a useful springboard for young scholars embarking on new careers or older scholars at loose ends. Although it provided mainly limited funding for individual research projects, for many this was enough to enhance their qualifications for career advances. Moser used his SS connections to earn political credibility and move on to a position in the Propaganda Ministry, and Quellmalz used his extensive work with the "Ahnenerbe" essentially to define the working areas of the nascent folk music division of the State Institute. Bose, although unsuccessful, attempted to use his SS affiliation to make a good impression on the education minister and to improve his chances of securing academic employment.

Musicologists as "Cultural Watchdogs": The Rosenberg Bureau

The ultimate goals of the "Ahnenerbe" — to create a Germanic secular religion, to supervise research on the Germanic race, and to establish guidelines for the education of the elite — overlapped considerably with those of the Rosenberg Bureau.[104] Rosenberg, as author of the nebulous and barely read Nazi treatise *Mythus des 20. Jahrhunderts,* had been the only leading figure in the early years of the Nazi party to display any interest in ideological questions in any concrete way and so became the chief National Socialist ideologue by default.[105] In January 1934, in an attempt to quell the disturbances that broke out in summer 1933 over religious and art policy, Hitler handed Rosenberg a vaguely worded order to supervise the ideological education of the party. Rosenberg used this symbolic gesture as an excuse to create an entire office, coining his own title of "deputy to the Führer for the total intellectual and ideological education and training of the NSDAP" out of the cumbersome wording of Hitler's order. He built a power base out of this questionable authority to compete with other high-ranking party and state officials, hoping to impose a uniform ideology (*Weltanschauung*) on all German citizens (unlike Himmler, who focused only on the intellectual elite). Rosenberg's success was constantly impeded by financial insecurity, rival forces, and his uncompromising personality.[106]

On the whole, Rosenberg had limited impact on cultural life beyond posing constant annoyances to Goebbels and others, but in the area of music he and his staff had a considerable degree of effectiveness. In his first year as "deputy to the Führer," Rosenberg successfully challenged Goebbels's authority on a handful of musical issues, including the famous cases of Strauss, Furtwängler, and Hindemith. Rosenberg brought attention to Strauss's collaboration with a Jewish librettist, ultimately bringing about Strauss's resignation as president of the Reich Music Chamber and the failure of the opera in question. He also objected to Wilhelm Furtwängler's promotion of the works of Hindemith, a composer who, Rosenberg claimed, had been decadent in his earlier years. The ensuing complications led to Furtwängler's temporary retreat from public life (including his resignation from the Music Chamber vice presidency) and a public apology, as well as to Hindemith's emigration.[107]

The Music Bureau, under the direction of the musicologist Herbert Gerigk, was the most active division in the Rosenberg Bureau and exerted its influence through a variety of publishing enterprises. In its first two years, its workers reviewed compositions and books on music, attended every major concert and opera in Berlin and environs, and submitted reports to Gerigk for the reviews of music events he published in the press. After the Rosenberg Bureau assumed control over *Die Musik* in 1937, the once respected journal became a vehicle for Gerigk to expose perceived deviations from National Socialist principles and occasionally to compile lists of "undesirable music" (*unerwünschte Musik*).[108] Gerigk soon recruited his musicologist friends to supply book reviews and involved the Reich Student Leadership to gather information from students regarding the political conformity of university professors.[109] As Rosenberg's influence on cultural affairs dwindled, the Music Bureau still exerted some limited powers of censorship. Gerigk supervised both the Music Bureau and the Cultural-Political Archive (Kulturpolitisches Archiv), which contained detailed records on some 60,000 individuals, and he obtained the power to approve and censor the music activities of the Deutsche Volksbildungswerk of the DAF.[110]

The Music Bureau's most notorious achievement was the compilation of the *Lexikon der Juden in der Musik*, edited by Gerigk and Theophil Stengel and published in 1940 by Hahnefeld, one of the two directories of Jews active in cultural life to come out of the Rosenberg Bureau.[111] The *Lexikon* followed Theodor Fritsch's 1934 *Handbuch der Judenfrage*, which included a haphazard list of Jews active in music and other fields (it mistakenly designated Hans Joachim Moser as a Jew), and *Judentum und Musik: mit dem ABC jüdischer und nichtarischer Musik*, edited by Christa Maria Rock and Hans Brückner and published in 1935. Although this, too, was rife with inaccuracies, listing Hugo Riemann as a Jew but omitting Paul Bekker and Alexander Zemlinsky, revisions by Brückner appeared in 1936 and 1938,[112] indicating that there was a demand for such items. The Nazi party leadership was impressed with the potential practical use of the *Lexikon,* which took care to alert readers to the business-minded nature of Jews in music and documented the aliases they used, and it urged the publisher to aim for a broad market.[113]

The thoroughness of the *Lexikon* had much to do with Gerigk's control over the Cultural-Political Archive, which gave him access to a plethora of data on individuals. His contacts with other musicologists added to its accuracy. When Gerigk approached Schenk for information about suspected Jews who had received their doctorates in Vienna, Schenk responded thoroughly and promptly. Gerigk thanked him for his cooperation, adding that "a careful scrutiny of the names of Viennese doctorates would probably bring to light many more fat Jews."[114] Schenk's willingness did not help him when he appealed to Gerigk to help a talented student who, he had discovered, was part Jewish. Gerigk instead pointed to this episode as an indication that the Nuremberg laws needed to be changed to prevent such students from entering the university.[115] Blessinger also helped Gerigk achieve accuracy. While preparing a review of the *Lexikon* for *Die Musik,* he expressed to Gerigk his concern that although preparing a flawless list of all Jews in music would be an impossible task, nevertheless for "practical use" accuracy was crucial. The omission of Jews from the *Lexikon* might lead to contact with those individuals on the mistaken assumption that they were Aryan. He offered his contribution toward comprehensiveness by alerting Gerigk to individuals he knew in Munich who, he was sure, were Jewish.[116]

Gerigk also supervised publications of a more serious musicological nature but played down the involvement of the Rosenberg Bureau in them. A series entitled Klassiker der Tonkunst in ihren Schriften und Briefen (Classic Composers in Their Own Writings and Letters) offered a research stipend and a publishing contract to prospective contributors.[117] Another series under Gerigk's general editorship was entitled Unsterbliche Tonkunst (Immortal Composition), a series of biographies of mostly German composers, penned by Fellerer, Engel, Gerber, Korte, Müller-Blattau, Schenk, and others. With the aid of the Rosenberg Bureau's Literature Office (Hauptamt Schrifttum, formerly Abteilung Schrifttumspflege), Gerigk oversaw their publication, although their title pages never revealed any connection to the Rosenberg Bureau.[118] By 1940 the Klassiker series had produced four volumes and prepared two more for publication, while Unsterbliche Tonkunst boasted eleven volumes. The intent of both series, as Gerigk reported to Rosenberg, was to "undertake for the first time an attempt to present the life and works of important musicians in the context of our ideology."[119]

The Music Bureau had an indirect hand in evaluating other publications for their adherence to the Nazi Weltanschauung. In his capacity as a preliminary reader for the Literature Office,[120] Gerigk involved musicologists in evaluating the works of their colleagues. Volunteers included his assistant Wolfgang Boetticher, Werner Korte, Ernst Bücken, Werner Danckert, Erich Schenk, and Rudolf Gerber.[121] The Literature Office had grown out of a preexisting division of the Kampfbund, and although its influence is debatable,[122] it was extremely active, employing as many as 1,700 reviewers by 1942 and evaluating up to 10,000 books and 1,000 magazines per year for their ideological and factual content. These evaluations appeared in such periodicals as *Die Bücherkunde,* were used for compiling recommended reading lists for party members (*NS-Bibliographie*), and provided data for the office's index of Jewish authors. Reviewers received no salary for their evaluations, only an honorarium if a review appeared in *Die Bücherkunde.* The office's overall effectiveness was hampered by Hess's creation of a competing organization (the Parteiamtliche Prüfungskommission zum Schutze des NS-Schrifttums), probably devised to contain Rosenberg's influence in the publishing industry.[123]

The musicologists' reports evaluated works from a variety of angles. Although most assessed scholarly merit, some rejected works precisely because they were directed to a musically sophisticated readership and therefore useless for the general education of Nazi party members.[124] In contrast, even the most ardent works of Nazi propaganda could be judged negatively on the basis of scholarly criteria.[125] In cases where the reviewer was well versed in the subject matter, such as Danckert's review of a study by Wiora, a report might scrutinize methodology more than political integrity. Danckert's only ideological caveat was that the study, published in Blume's series on race and music (Schriften zur musikalischen Volks- und Rassenkunde), contributed little to the field of racial research.[126] Some reviews similarly focused on scholarship and fulfilled their ideological duties only by noting an author's "indiscriminate" reliance on the work of Jews or the failure to designate Jews appropriately with a "J" or and asterisk.[127] Other reviews, however, notably those by Gerigk, focused exclusively on the treatment of Jews, émigrés, and the Jewish Question as the only measure of a work's acceptability, and failure to handle these areas appropriately in one work could condemn an author's entire output in the eyes of ideological arbiters.[128]

The Music Bureau performed a variety of other miscellaneous tasks, serving as a clearing house for any number of cultural-political questions. It serviced other Nazi organizations, such as the Deutsches Volksbildungswerk and the Propaganda Ministry, by handling requests to the Cultural-Political Archive to clear the names of prospective performers, lecturers, and other participants in their cultural programs.[129] It addressed inquiries into the party's attitude toward such contemporary composers as Hans Pfitzner and Wolfgang Fortner, and it even fielded such questions as the appropriateness of performing Bach's religious music in light of Nazi opposition to the Church and the German lineage of Franz Liszt.[130] In 1940 the Music Bureau undertook the task of providing theater directors with lists of appropriate operas and operettas.[131]

The Music Bureau interfered in university affairs to a certain degree. Rosenberg's strategy was to reach out first to intellectuals, who then could influence the public at large, and got their attention through the periodicals under his control.[132] He then surreptitiously infiltrated the workings of higher education through his Science Department (Abteilung Wissenschaft), established in late 1934. The aim of this department was to keep a close watch on all activities in higher education by attending university meetings, keeping files on personnel, reviewing books used in research and instruction, and, after the war broke out, approving faculty appointments. The Education Ministry would send names to the Party Chancellery, which forwarded them to Science Department and the Nazi Lecturers' League. If either of these two offices lacked information, they would recommend a politically reliable expert in the candidate's field to provide an evaluation. The Party Chancellery, after collecting all evaluations, passed its recommendation on to the Education Ministry.[133]

Gerigk had much to offer this department because of his control over both the Cultural-Political Archive and the Music Bureau. In 1940, he urged the Science Department supervisor to use any influence he might have to promote Rudolf Gerber, a trusted colleague in both scholarly and ideological capacities, for a position in Strasbourg.[134] In 1944 alone, Gerigk provided the department with judgments on more than a dozen musicologists either being considered for positions or recently appointed. Most of his assessments were negative, such as those of Marius Schneider, Willi Kahl, Heinrich Besseler, Friedrich Blume, Arnold Schmitz, Friedrich Noack, Wilhelm Heinitz, Georg Schünemann, and Fritz Stein. Husmann, Müller-Blattau, and Engel got mixed reviews, while any positive assessments were mostly reserved for his close collaborators: Korte, Blessinger, and especially Danckert. One exception was Schünemann, with whom Gerigk had worked closely but whom he revealed as having past "Marxist-liberal" leanings.[135]

Gerigk's criteria for evaluating colleagues fell roughly into three categories: scholarship, personality, and political reliability. He judged scholarship on its ideological merits, its position on the Jewish Question, and any negative manifestations of scholastic methods or dilettantism. Personality assessments considered relationships to students (i.e., attitudes toward National Socialist students), signs of being overly ambitious, and sexual orientation. In judging political reliability, Gerigk frowned upon apolitical behavior, which could not be corrected by mere membership in the Nazi party; any ties to either Catholic or Protestant churches; evidence of switching political allegiances before and after 1933; and any ties to remotely suspect organizations, such as the Rotary Club.[136] Gerigk had wanted to open up an investigation on Blume, who, he claimed, joined the Rotary Club after January 1933.[137] Blume had, in fact, still belonged to the Rotary Club as of 1937, but the party's position had never explicitly proscribed membership up to that point.[138]

The Spoils of War: Musicologists in the Sonderstab Musik

In 1938, just before the war broke out, Rosenberg had secured an independent budget after years of failed attempts at extracting funding from the party and the KdF.[139] The war severely reduced his personnel and, after the order for total mobilization, diminished the bureau to nothing more than a name, but it also opened up unexpected opportunities for some of the remaining departments. The "Hohe Schule der Partei," a planned elite school for training party leaders, was Rosenberg's attempt to control National Socialist education at the university level. Hitler authorized him to draw up plans for a massive complex to be built on the Chiemsee that would include its own Adolf Hitler School, a research center and training institute for party members, and facilities for training party education officers. Apparently ignoring these plans, Rosenberg proceeded to erect individual research institutes throughout the Reich. Hitler decreed in January 1940 that the actual operation of the Hohe Schule would have to be postponed until after the war, but he allowed Rosenberg to proceed with preparations for research facilities and in setting up a party library.[140]

Gerigk, like Rosenberg, loosely defined the duties of the Hohe Schule and used it frequently as an excuse to fund Music Bureau publications. The *Lexikon der Juden in der Musik* was labeled a Hohe Schule project, as were the series Klassiker der Tonkunst and Unsterbliche Tonkunst,[141] and Gerigk secured Rosenberg's approval to underwrite Danckert's study on German song and dance in Bohemia and Moravia as a Hohe Schule publication.[142] Gerigk also involved Schenk, Gerber, Fellerer, Danckert, and Helmut Osthoff in plans for a large-scale music lexicon, allegedly for the Hohe Schule, which would be "newly compiled in the sense of our Weltanschauung" and would "counteract" the "dangerous false opinions" contained in existing scholarly reference works.[143] Some of Gerigk's suggestions for appointments at other universities were also supposedly formed out of consideration of their future effects on the musicology department of the Hohe Schule.[144]

Plans for the elusive Hohe Schule and its library were used to justify Rosen-berg's most successful venture, the large-scale seizure of cultural property in occupied territories known as the "Einsatzstab Reichsleiter Rosenberg." Ro-senberg had limited financial resources for acquiring books for the party li-brary, and he could not count on access to materials seized by Himmler, who disapproved of Rosenberg's encroachment into the realm of research. Instead, Rosenberg reached an agreement with the SD and the foreign ministry in dividing up the spoils of occupation. After the Foreign Ministry and the SD had seized all relevant documents on foreign policy and security, they agreed to let Rosenberg sort out what was left and transport it home for use by the Hohe Schule. The "Einsatzstab Reichsleiter Rosenberg" consisted of a main operation division for each country and a number of "Sonderstäbe" (including a "Sonderstab Musik"), special task forces for each field of expertise staffed by specialists who carried out the actual examinations and confiscations of items.[145]

The Einsatzstab gave Rosenberg a means to defy international law as Himm-ler had done. It extended its plundering activities to include Masonic lodges; Jewish homes; state, community, and organization libraries; schools; univer-sities; museums; and academies. With regard to seizing private property from Jewish citizens under occupation, it was argued that no cease fire agreements had been made with Jews. Rosenberg managed the large-scale seizure of art works, books, and other valuable cultural property, justifying the action as "retrieving" objects taken from Germany over the course of history. In Novem-ber 1940 he gained a strong ally in Hermann Göring, who authorized the Einsatzstab to seize property for Hitler, for Göring's private collection, and for German museums, as well as for the Hohe Schule.[146]

The goals of the Sonderstab Musik were first to seize, evaluate, and trans-port objects useful for musicological research and for the Hohe Schule, and then to assess the conditions of musical life under the occupation and the feasibility of establishing German cultural institutions. In the seizure of cul-tural property, musicologists were instructed to seek out music manuscripts and old printed matter in libraries and monasteries; musical documents and instruments in Jewish possession; and Jewish recordings in record stores and radio stations.[147] Gerigk's assistant Boetticher was the most active: he went to Warsaw in 1940 to pack up and transport material seized for the Rosenberg Bureau, to search the Warsaw branches of Columbia Records and His Mas-ter's Voice for "Jewish-undermined" and "treasonous" material, and to seize and transport all such material for the Hohe Schule. When he was called up for military service, the Rosenberg Bureau requested that he be excused because of his excellent musicological qualifications, command of foreign languages, and prior work in Cracow, Warsaw, Belgium, France, and Holland. Boetticher was allowed to have a dual assignment with the Einsatzstab and the Waffen-SS and was sent to the Baltic states early in 1942.[148]

While Rosenberg made a pact with Göring to supply him with art treasures,[149] Gerigk and the Music Bureau reached a separate agreement with Rosenberg's rival, Propaganda Minister Goebbels. Gerigk had made such a positive impression on the higher authorities that Goebbels appointed him director of the music commission for the retrieval of music documents of supposed German origin in France and Belgium.[150] A list of expenses indicates that Fellerer and Schünemann were sent to Paris in March and April 1941, and Gerigk ordered Gerber and Fellerer again to Paris on Einsatzstab assignments to seize German printed music in fall 1942.[151] Gerigk also used contacts with other musicologists to seek out valuable holdings. He asked Hellmuth Osthoff, stationed with the occupying troops in Belgium, to assess the collection of music manuscripts in Brussels, and Schiedermair alerted Gerigk to the existence of Beethoven manuscripts in the Brussels Royal Conservatory.[152] In his work for Goebbels, Gerigk located numerous manuscripts, letters, and rare printed music dating from the Middle Ages through the nineteenth century that would fill important gaps in the holdings of the Prussian State Library.[153] This work was deemed kriegswichtig because the material they were viewing — unica prints of works by Germans from 1750 to 1830 — would not be accessible under normal peacetime circumstances.[154]

The zeal with which musicologists cooperated in the illegal plundering was undoubtedly fueled by mounting resentment over the loss of German musicological resources to the West during the last decades. Immediately following World War I, Einstein chastised the Vienna Library for handing over five original Petrucci prints to Italy, calling the act "shameless art theft of the Italians" carried out "in the name of 'justice' and 'righteousness.'" He was especially incensed that Vienna had originally acquired the items in 1835 through exchange rather than seizure, that Italy possessed identical exemplars, and that Italian researchers would probably not use the materials.[155]

The threat of loss hit close to home in the 1920s as musicology departments found themselves financially strapped and unable to purchase music libraries. After losing the use of the Heyer collection when it was sold to the musicology department in Leipzig, the new department in Cologne had eyed the Wolffheim library, up for sale in 1926. Both Wolffheim and his dealer acted "with burning ambition" to keep the collection in German hands because many German libraries had been sold to American and other foreign buyers since the inflation, "adding insult to injury" at a time when Germany was obliged to pay reparations,[156] but they were unsuccessful. Max Seiffert, in his 1935 proposal to consolidate the Bückeburg Institute, pointed to the dire need for Reich subvention especially "when one considers how much of the irreplaceable German musical goods have wandered abroad — the private music libraries of Prof. Wagener (Marburg) to Brussels, A. Schatz (Rostock) to Washington, W. Wolffheim (Berlin) mostly to Italy and Switzerland, as well as large portions of the Royal Library of Wernigerode."[157]

The middle-aged musicologists active in the Sonderstab Musik must have felt a degree of satisfaction in helping themselves to the spoils of valuable library materials and other musical artifacts, especially in the Western occupation, after years of fuming over what they had lost to their former enemies in years of economic hardship. Some of them also enjoyed intellectual advantages by gaining exclusive access to previously inaccessible source materials and benefiting from subsidized research travel under the guise of war-related assignments.

Otherwise, working for the Rosenberg Bureau offered little in the way of compensation, since Rosenberg's coffers were usually empty. Most of the musicologists working with Gerigk — Erich Schenk, Karl Gustav Fellerer, Georg Schünemann, Werner Danckert, Rudolf Gerber, Werner Korte — already held secure positions and could afford to volunteer their services. Such labor-intensive duties as evaluating books for the Literature Office brought no compensation, and only the Einsatzstab activities were well funded, thanks to generous support from Goebbels. Many of them had vivid memories of the uncertainties of the post-war period. Their association with the Rosenberg Bureau may have been no more than a cautious investment toward potential political influence and security in the future.

For younger musicologists, working for Rosenberg offered relatively few prospects, especially when compared with opportunities offered by the well-heeled SS-"Ahnenerbe." Wolfgang Boetticher was the only one who benefited significantly from an association with Rosenberg.[158] As a member of a generation educated under Nazi dictatorship, Boetticher, born in 1914, had been involved in Nazi organizations from a young age and continued to move up through the ranks. He became a task force leader in the University of Berlin chapter of the Reich Student Leadership in 1934, advanced to the national organization as official musicology expert in 1937, and joined the Waffen-SS in 1941.[159] He was first summoned into Rosenberg's service in 1937, came on the payroll as a full-time employee in early 1939, and was promoted in late 1942 when Hitler appointed him as a bureau director (Reichshauptstellenleiter der NSDAP).[160]

Boetticher may have joined Gerigk's ranks in the hope of promoting his academic career. Unlike his older colleagues, he could make himself available to the Rosenberg Bureau at any time, and even if the Rosenberg ties proved politically useless, his labor paid off in scholarly advances. The Music Bureau published some of his work on Schumann as part of the series Klassiker der Musik,[161] and his activities with the Einsatzstab allowed him to complete his Habilitationsschrift and other important projects by bringing him to several occupied territories during the war and enabling him to use their libraries. In evaluating his Habilitation, Schünemann wrote that "the war initiative led him on a mission from Minister Rosenberg to Paris, Brussels, Warsaw, Cracow, Amsterdam, and other cities, where he was required to assess the German musical treasures. [Boetticher] exploited this rare opportunity for scholarly study in the area of lute music. . . . The Habilitationsschrift comes out of earlier research which he supplemented significantly with war-time visits to foreign libraries."[162] Boetticher used his time in Vilna to research and write about the German influence on Latvian folk song, the results of which he published in 1944, and used his time in occupied Paris to write a study on a newly discovered Mozart autograph in the Bibliothèque Nationale,[163] publishing his findings in the 1944 *Neues Mozart-Jahrbuch*. The advantages of working with Gerigk paid off indirectly in research and publishing opportunities, and in September 1944 he was appointed to the Berlin faculty.

But, on the whole, association with Rosenberg yielded few long-term benefits for musicologists. Rosenberg's overall effectiveness in cultural affairs paled in comparison to that of Himmler, and his multiple responsibilities as head of the foreign office in the Nazi party and later as minister of the Occupied Eastern Territories distracted him from investing time and energy into his cultural ambitions. Rosenberg's operation further failed to define its goals and cooperate with other interests, and its lack of a stable financial base made it impossible to support much staff or many long-term research initiatives. Within the Rosenberg Bureau, the achievements of the Music Bureau were exceptional, succeeding in attracting the attention of Joseph Goebbels, but they were insufficient to broaden and sustain its operations through the war.

Musicologists and the Germanization of the East

The goals of the Sonderstab Musik in Eastern Europe were quite different from the mission of retribution motivating the actions in the West. The entire war campaign was driven by a desire to colonize eastward, pushing into Russia and exploiting its land for German "living space" (*Lebensraum*). Military aggressions in the West aimed only at weakening any European counteroffensives that might prevent Germany from invading and occupying Russia and all that lay in between. The final objective of the war was to resettle the growing German population in the vast expanses of land to the east and exploit its agricultural resources.[164] Scholars specializing in the history, literature, linguistics, anthropology, and geography of Eastern Europe enthusiastically advised the government on resettlement and Germanization of cultural and educational institutions. They used their scholarly rationalizations to justify the occupation of the East by demonstrating that Germany had ancient rights to these territories and was now merely "reclaiming" them.[165]

For musicologists, too, it was important to determine that Germany had some historical claims on the eastern territories stemming from a centuries-old German influence in the musical cultures of countries under occupation. Such rationalizations had pervaded musicological literature since the Anschluss, and one of the tasks of Sonderstab Musik was to substantiate theories of German presence in the musical history of the occupied East with physical evidence. In the document detailing Boetticher's assignment in the Baltic states, Gerigk instructed him to identify "available music manuscripts and prints in public and scholarly libraries. Most important are those documents that are of German origin and that indicate the political significance of the eastern territories."[166]

The Sonderstab Musik went beyond the mere seizure of materials in the East; it proceeded to assess the conditions in occupied territories for the future takeover of musical life. As outlined in Boetticher's assignment, the mission was to include investigating activities of concert agencies with special attention to their foreign contacts; compiling a list of Jewish musicians and composers for the *Lexikon der Juden in der Musik;* and evaluating the political reliability of non-Jewish musicians with a view toward encouraging them to work for the German cultural cause: "it would be advantageous to make close contact with resident Aryan composers and performing artists. It is important to determine the present and past political orientations of these non-Jewish musicians. In appropriate cases you should try to win over these artists for the cultural tasks of the German Reich. In this way it will be possible to create optimal conditions for cultural institutions and scholarly organizations to be founded in the future."[167] Such work was considered so important by the Nazi government that Gerigk was exempted from military service as late as May 1942 because Rosenberg acknowledged his actions in the East as essential for the war effort, facilitating a "recognition of and defense against the destructive Weltanschauung of the enemy."[168]

Although these tasks represent only preliminary steps, they nevertheless gave musicologists an unprecedented opportunity to have concrete input into the control of musical life and musical policy in the East. These experiences could have led to more important assignments after the war. The tasks of resettlement and cultural Germanization would involve not only filling university positions but also establishing or reforming music education, concert life, amateur music making, music publishing, and other aspects of musical life and industry. Having been excluded from these tasks at home, despite the emergence of two regimes since the end of World War I, musicologists saw another chance to have an impact beyond the narrow realm of teaching and scholarship.

Even before the war, musicologists had begun to offer unsolicited practical advice on musical Germanization in the East.[169] As Hitler began to exert pressure on Czechoslovakia to cede its German-populated provinces and Czech troops mobilized in response to rumors of a German invasion in May 1938, Gustav Becking publicized the desperate situation of the region's musical life. In an issue of the *Zeitschrift für Musik* dedicated to Sudeten-German music, he stressed the need to enhance German musical culture and to preserve folk music traditions among the Sudeten-Germans.[170] He also insisted that the state step in to improve music education.[171] Two months after the invasion of Poland, both Moser and Frotscher suggested measures for Germanizing musical life in Poland and incorporating music education into Hitler's proposed resettlement of Germans in newly acquired Polish territories.[172]

Musicologists continued to contribute to a conceptualization of the East as a German musical and cultural terrain and reported on steps toward Germanization. Moser and Frotscher referred to a "German East" as a vast area in which Germans had a profound cultural influence in music as well as in other arts and sciences.[173] The October 1939 issue of *Musik in Jugend und Volk*, dedicated to the Germanization of Poland, included Guido Waldmann's article "German Cultural Achievements in Poland" ("Deutsche Kulturleistungen in Polen") and a related article by Frotscher on folk music. In 1943 Walther Vetter reported on the advances of German music in Posen in the periodical *Wartheland* (dedicated to the "rebuilding and culture in the German East"),[174] and Hans Heinz Stuckenschmidt, heralded after 1945 as a defender of modern music and a victim of Nazi censorship, was active in Czechoslovakia as late as 1941, reporting on German musical activity in Prague for the SS-sponsored journal *Böhmen und Mähren* and for the Berlin-based periodical *Ostland: Halbmonatsschrift für Ostpolitik*.[175]

Others exploited the Germanization process for their own advancement in publishing projects, lectures, and university politics. In 1943, Schünemann took the initiative to work directly with the Generalgouvernement to plan a Chopin Gesamtausgabe, despite the judgment of many musicologists that such an edition was unnecessary.[176] Then, while he and Boetticher delivered lectures in Holland and France, respectively,[177] Moser and Valentin propagated Germanization with lectures in Cracow in 1944, the former on Richard

Strauss and the latter on German music and poetry in the East. Both lectures were regarded as so important for the Germanization of the East that they were published by the Buchverlag Deutsche Osten in the series "Blätter für deutsche Kultur." Universities likewise used the campaign of eastern Germanization to gain support for their musicology departments: administrators in Königsberg argued that, as the only musicological outpost in the East, its musicology department had to be preserved and allowed to grow out of consideration of *Ostpolitik*.[178]

Moser took an active part in the Germanization of the East from his post in the Propaganda Ministry. A letter dated 21 March 1941, addressed from "Leiter M" ("Director M," i.e., head of the music division of the Propaganda Ministry, Heinz Drewes) to "the Minister" (Goebbels), with corrections in Moser's hand, emphasized the need for "musical-cultural reforestation" of the German East, a goal achieved not just with financial resources but with a thorough investigation of historical evidence of German musical influence in these regions. Moser cites examples of German musical hegemony dating as far back as the thirteenth century and suggests scholarly inquiries into the history of German musical cultivation in Hungary, Poland, Czechoslovakia, and the Baltic countries. His suggestions went well beyond research, emphasizing that these areas needed to be investigated and publicized "in order that out of this cultural-geographic picture of music history it will be possible to develop the cultural-political tasks and possibilities for the present and the future in these vast regions that are once again entrusted to us."[179]

Austria, the first eastern region to be annexed and referred to thereafter as the "Ostmark," was the earliest testing ground for musicologists to wield some influence in cultural policies. The Anschluss in 1938 brought about the immediate termination of DTÖ and its replacement with a Landschaftsdenkmale commission under the State Institute. In 1940, the education minister converted existing folk song archives in Austria into "district archives for folk music" (*Gauarchive für Volksmusik*) that came under the supervision of the institute's folk music department and reported directly to Quellmalz.[180] In addition, the Propaganda Ministry reportedly contributed 10,000 marks to the Bruckner Gesamtausgabe, formerly funded by the Schuschnigg government.[181]

Several state and party sponsors took an interest in preserving Salzburg as an important music center and appointed German musicologists in administrative capacities. The Propaganda Ministry financed the Salzburg festival, the theater, and the orchestra of the Mozarteum; the Education Ministry took over the music school of the Mozarteum and turned it into a state conservatory; and the Reich Youth Leadership established a Musikschule für Jugend und Volk at the Mozarteum. Hitler also commissioned a new Mozart Gesamtausgabe, and in response to Gerigk's protests against the Propaganda Ministry's "interference," authorized a branch of the Hohe Schule to counteract the intrigues of Goebbels.[182] German musicologists from the Reich edged out their Austrian colleagues and assumed prominent positions. Erich Valentin became director of the Central Institute for Mozart Research and established and edited the *Neues Mozart-Jahrbuch* in collaboration with the Deutsche Akademie. Schiedermair headed the academic council of the Mozarteum and was showered with honors from Salzburg government and party officials, receiving the Gold Mozart Medal in 1941 from the Regierungspräsident and the Silver Mozart Medal in 1942 from Baldur von Schirach.[183]

The invasion of German scholars and bureaucrats held some advantages for Austrian musicology. The decisive influence of the education minister on the University of Vienna made it possible to fill the Extraordinarius position that had been empty since 1931, and an Extraordinarius was also made available in Innsbruck.[184] The University of Graz also welcomed its "fortuitous incorporation" into Reich university system as an opportunity finally to establish a chair in musicology.[185] Still, Austria narrowly escaped a free-for-all plundering of musicological resources. Hitler's decree to keep all cultural property within the borders of former Austria thwarted plans to transport music archives of Austrian monasteries to the Prussian State Library.[186]

Cooperation, Competition, and Coercion

Rivalries among Himmler, Goebbels, Göring, Rosenberg, Rust, and Ley are often linked to a grand scheme by Hitler to divide and conquer, but they have also been identified as a symptom of the chaos lying at the core of the Nazi system. These rivalries also penetrated musicology. Setting out with good intentions to work together, nonuniversity musicological enterprises lapsed into countless acts of sabotage, libel, and intrigue that only impeded the successful attainment of common goals. The stakes were relatively meager, mainly involving control over certain publishing projects, archives, and other minor operations, but the rivalry was fierce, especially as the war progressed and competition for funding and personnel heightened. The ruthlessness of the competition can be explained by a combination of shrinking resources, a survival mentality carried over from the Weimar era, and a fervent desire to take advantage of the chaos of war and wrest control over large operations to guarantee a strong position in peacetime within the Reich and in the new territories.

Ideally, the State Institute should have served as the headquarters for musicological activity in all facets of Nazi society. Its individual departments were directed to communicate with the German Foreigners Institute in Stuttgart, the folk song archive in Freiburg, the Volk-Union for Germans Abroad, the Music Research Society in Switzerland, the Berlin conservatory, and the Deutsche Akademie in Munich.[187] In 1939, the institute set up a unit in the German Foreigners Institute in Stuttgart to study and organize the musical life of ethnic Germans.[188] As a result of this collaboration and the cooperation of the Austrian Gauarchive and the folk song archive in Freiburg, the institute built up a huge collection of folk music materials in the early 1940s. At one point the institute even worked with a division of the Rosenberg Bureau in the collection of folk materials from Volhynian and Galician Germans in resettlement camps.[189]

The Deutsche Akademie, established in 1925 with the purpose of promoting German culture at home and abroad, operated German language schools in foreign countries, administered scholarly exchanges, and sponsored a variety of projects. Its administration was purged in 1936–37, and it came under the authority of the Propaganda Ministry in 1941.[190] Several well-known German and Austrian musicologists (among them Schiedermair, Schering, Bücken, Huber, Moser, Lach, Lorenz, Haas, Engel, Sandberger, Schmitz, Müller-Blattau, and Ursprung) were inducted into its music division, and the academy sponsored such large-scale musicological projects as "Das Wesen der deutschen Musik," "Deutsche Musik im Ausland," the Weber Gesamtausgabe (in collaboration with the institute), a catalogue of printed music, a catalogue of Reger's works, Sandberger's *Neues Beethoven-Jahrbuch,* a collection of German folk songs (in collaboration with the Folksong Archive in Freiburg), and the *Neues Mozart-Jahrbuch* (with the Mozarteum).[191]

The institute was also mandated to work together with the SA, the SS, the Reich Youth Leadership, the Rosenberg Bureau, KdF, the Wehrmacht, the Nazi Teachers' League, the Reich Music Chamber, the Reich Women's Leadership, the Reich Agricultural Society, and the Arbeitsdienst.[192] In 1939, Besseler tried to involve the Wehrmacht, SA, Hitler Youth, DAF, and Arbeitsdienst toward improving the journal *Deutsche Musikkultur,*[193] and the South Tyrol project enabled Alfred Quellmalz to forge a fruitful cooperation with the SS-"Ahnenerbe." This cooperation expanded, as Quellmalz proposed a collaboration between the "Ahnenerbe" and the institute's instrument collection on the lur project.[194] Himmler's appointment of Quellmalz as director of the Research Center for Indogermanic-German Music in December 1943 strengthened the collaboration, aiming to pursue a research project on German folk music in Scandinavia, Holland, and Belgium and granting Quellmalz release from military service and permission to return to the institute.[195] These two organizations also worked with the Reich Youth Leadership and the Nazi Party Head Cultural Bureau on a multivolume folk song anthology edited by

Hans Engel, Joseph Müller-Blattau, and H. P. Gericke, with additional assistance by Guido Waldmann, Walter Wiora, and Gotthold Frotscher.[196]

Such collaborative ventures were not common, but this project drew support from all four organizations because of its practical use as a party or school song book. Unfortunately, the project also piqued the anger of John Meier, director of the Folksong Archive in Freiburg, who saw it as rivaling his own multivolume folk song edition, despite the entreaties of Quellmalz and Albrecht that their project was directed more toward practical than toward scholarly use.[197] This was just one of many counterproductive disagreements between Meier and the institute. The Freiburg Folksong Archive, which gathered only the texts of folk songs and not the music, was supposed to come under the control of the institute, but Meier never succumbed and continued to vie with the institute over the jurisdiction for regional archives, especially those lying outside the old Reich. With the education minister serving as mediator, it was agreed in 1944 that the two independent archives would share their materials, while provincial archives would submit materials on folk songs and children's songs to Freiburg, and materials on adult folk dances and instrumental folk music to Berlin (the Austrian Gauarchive were to send all of their transcripts directly to Berlin).[198] In the meantime, however, Meier, had also attempted to beat out the institute for control of Pulikowski's sound archive in Warsaw by circumventing the education minister and dealing directly with the Generalgouvernment, prompting Quellmalz to set off immediately to Warsaw to thwart his attempts.[199] Meier also dealt directly with the Education Ministry on the Gottschee folk music project, without including Quellmalz.[200]

The institute had to contend not only with competition from Meier but also with the waning support and occasional sabotage from its sponsor, the Education Ministry. When Quellmalz argued against closing the folk music department during the war, he noted that the Freiburg archive would gain an unfair advantage since it would continue to operate.[201] At the same time, Martin Miederer, the Education Ministry official in charge of the institute, visited Meier's archive and told him of his plans to set up a "Reich Institute for German Music Research" made up of individual departments throughout the Reich, "with their own budgets and their own directors." Each institute would concentrate on subjects of local significance, such as an institute for Beethoven research in Bonn, a Bruckner research institute in Linz, and a Spohr institute in Kassel. Miederer's plans for an institute for folk song research in Freiburg involved dissolving the State Institute's folk music division and moving it to Freiburg, presumably under Meier's supervision and in collaboration with the musicology department at the University of Freiburg.[202]

The most persistent attacks on the institute emanated from the Rosenberg Bureau, specifically from Gerigk. Gerigk attempted to undermine its appointments at every opportunity and schemed to establish a separate institute, under his control, in Leipzig that would eventually take over the State Institute's functions. Had it not been for the institute's alliance with Himmler, Gerigk might have succeeded. When Huber was appointed head of the institute's folk music department, Gerigk connived to have his contract revoked because Werner Danckert had not been considered for the appointment.[203] From information gathered from students, Gerigk ascertained that Huber had warned against the influence of the Rosenberg circle while on a research expedition in Yugoslavia, and he further accused Huber of "consciously or unconsciously" thinking along the lines of "political Catholicism."[204] This prompted the Education Ministry to investigate Huber's political reliability, with inconclusive results. The office of Rudolf Hess not only confirmed Huber's ties to Catholicism and his warning against Rosenberg but also cited him for renting an apartment from a Jew. They hesitated to say whether Huber could be expected to "step forward without reservation and at any time for the sake of the National Socialist state."[205] This event did nothing to harm Huber's career, and in 1940 the same office endorsed his promotion to Extraordinarius at the University of Munich.[206]

In the same year as his campaign against Huber (1937), Gerigk launched an investigation of Besseler by seeking out reports from the Reich Student Leadership to learn of his relationship to students and whether a bookcase in his department library still bore the name of its Jewish donor.[207] Gerigk broadened his attack with accusations of Catholic ties; of studying with Jews and advising Jewish students; and of defending Ernst Krenek, jazz, and cabaret. Ever suspicious of ambition, Gerigk claimed that Besseler considered himself the "Führer" of German musicology, that he hindered the careers of Werner Korte and Erich Schenk, that he purchased the library of the Jewish émigré Curt Sachs, and that he retained books by Jewish authors in the musicology library at the university.[208]

At Besseler's request, these matters came before a Nazi party tribunal that ultimately cleared his name. Yet he insisted that his coincidental change of position in the institute and failure to be promoted to full professor in Heidelberg resulted from Gerigk's accusations, and he demanded compensation.[209] Neither the institute nor the Education Ministry honored this request. Seiffert explained that Besseler's removal as head of the Denkmäler department resulted from a reorganization of committees dictated by the Ministry. He was reappointed as editor of the *AfMf,* thus the change constituted a lateral transfer rather than a demotion.[210] The Education Ministry also decided that Besseler's situation at the university bore no connection to his political trial but was due to the absence of an available chair.[211] Besseler never recovered from his feelings of victimization and referred frequently to these events during his denazification trial, maintaining that he was persecuted at the hands of Rosenberg.[212]

Gerigk kept a close watch on all institute personnel. He constantly contemplated ways to remove Seiffert as director,[213] and after Hans Albrecht took over in 1941, Gerigk turned his attention to others. He scored his first success in 1944 by hindering the appointment of Marius Schneider. The Berlin Sound Archive, under Schneider's direction, was to be moved from the State Museum to the institute. Schneider's employer endorsed his supervision of the project, praising his knowledge, congeniality, racial purity, heroic military record, and commitment to National Socialism.[214] When his name was submitted to the Science Department in the Rosenberg Bureau as a matter of course, Gerigk pounced on his devout Catholicism, "contested" research methods, professional pettiness, lack of commitment to Nazi ideology, and a lack of a clear position toward the Jewish Question and successfully blocked his appointment.[215]

Gerigk meanwhile envisioned his own institute—a Leipzig branch of the Hohe Schule devoted to music research, which would render the bulk of the State Institute's activities obsolete. The Party Chancellery informed the Education Ministry that Gerigk had, with Hitler's approval, secretly drawn up "generous plans" that would "revolutionize musicological work in Europe." Gerigk drew attention to the institute's recently proposed Gesamtausgaben and multivolume reference work (*MGG*) and questioned the wisdom of planning such large-scale projects in a time of war, leaving the young scholars on active duty out of consideration.[216] Although the Education Ministry was disinclined to allow Gerigk or the Nazi party any authority in musicological activities, Gerigk's criticism nevertheless prompted it to raise these issues with the institute's director. He countered that these projects needed intensive advance preparation and, to the contrary, would guarantee employment for returning soldiers. He saw no reason why the institute and Gerigk's Hohe Schule outpost could not work together, but he seriously doubted that there would be enough musicologists available after the war to staff two such closely related operations.[217]

Gerigk's intrigues were not limited to undermining the institute. He was relatively unknown as a researcher, having earned his doctorate in Königsberg in 1928 with a dissertation on the music history of the city of Elbing. Before his appointment by Rosenberg, he had worked as a music director in a radio station and became director of the Provincial Chamber of Culture in Danzig in 1934.[218] By 1937 he had already made a name for himself in musicological circles for his intrigues. Hans Engel wrote to Sandberger that he thought Gerigk wielded control over Schering and therefore regarded him as a threat to the DGMW as well as many other musicological outlets. Gerigk had already taken control of the publishing houses of Hesse and Athenaion and, given the opportunity, would eagerly seize the *AfMf*, having already attacked *Deutsche Musikkultur* as "reactionary" and the institute's officials — Besseler, Huber, Engel, and Weber — as "Catholics." Engel hoped that Schiedermair, the new president of the DGMW, would not invite Gerigk and his cohorts into the DGMW leadership.[219] True to form, Gerigk made a scene the following November at the DGMW meeting: he marched in with Korte, Schenk, and Erich Schumann and declared the organization illegal, prompting only laughter from those present.[220] Gerigk also admitted that he hoped to gain influence in the music division of the Deutsche Akademie.[221]

Sandberger responded to Engel's observations, admitting that he knew little of Gerigk's scholarship, but recalled Gerigk's resentment when his Verdi research was not suitably praised in the *Beethoven-Jahrbuch,* which Sandberger edited.[222] Soon thereafter Sandberger became all too familiar with Gerigk's tactics. In the September issue of *Die Musik,* Gerigk accused Sandberger of praising the work of Jews in the *Beethoven Jahrbuch*. Sandberger had to explain himself to the university officials and the president of the Deutsche Akademie, defensively proclaiming his own anti-Semitic credentials by stating his well-known opposition to "Mahler propaganda," his victimization at the hands of Jewish critics, and his disapproval of Paul Bekker's "Jewish arts policy."[223]

Gerigk also repeatedly attacked Moser, using his objections to Moser's political character as an excuse to question the ideological integrity of the organizations that employed his services, namely, the SS-"Ahnenerbe" and the Propaganda Ministry. Gerigk was probably responsible for jeopardizing Moser's continued collaboration with the "Ahnenerbe." He started a rumor that Moser was Jewish and then accused the organization of ideological impropriety for employing Moser. Gerigk also criticized the Propaganda Ministry for hiring Moser in spite of his dismissal from academic positions, the disciplinary action that reduced his pension, and the ideological laxity in his writings.[224] He then tried to monopolize Moser's Reichsstelle assignments by carrying them out independently, accusing Moser and the Propaganda Ministry of being ideologically underqualified. In 1940, Gerigk took on the task of translating Mozart libretti, "made urgent as a result of the renewed one-sided preoccupation of the Propaganda Ministry," and of examining opera and operetta repertoire and compiling data in a handbook to be distributed to theater directors. Illustrating the Propaganda Ministry's inability to do the job, Gerigk related the anecdote of an operetta composer "who submitted a Singspiel to us and explained that he had been asked in the Metropol Theater whether his work contained nude dancing and jazz. When he said no, he was told that it could not be considered, because the minister required both."[225]

Gerigk also tried to compete in the Reichsstelle's scholarly projects. He was critical of each of Moser's projects and schemed to create his own versions. Moser had undertaken to edit a large-scale history of Germany and its neighbors that would demonstrate Germany's musical presence back to the Middle Ages in the lands under occupation or in alliance with Germany. Drewes, his superior, described this project as "a collaborative work suggested by me . . . which summarizes the influence of German music on neighboring lands; finally giving honor to the truth, it will present quite a different picture of European music history from anything ever attempted."[226] Drewes invited Gerigk to contribute a chapter on the Baltic states and Finland, but Gerigk declined because he believed that a lack of research would make the project unmanageable.[227] The invitation nevertheless alerted Gerigk that such an approach to European music history was in vogue, and three months later he invited Rudolf Gerber to join him in exploiting the current interest in German musical influence. The two traveled to Paris late in October 1942, allegedly to investigate "the influence of German musicians on the musical culture of France."[228] Simultaneously, the Deutsche Akademie expressed a desire to initiate a similar publishing project. Ludwig Schiedermair sought collaborators for the project and submitted their names for approval to Gerigk and the Nazi Lecturers' League. In 1943, he met with academy members to discuss the book, projected for 1944 and provisionally entitled "The Influence of German Music Abroad" ("Einfluß deutscher Musik auf das Ausland"), and noted that negotiations regarding the "competing project" in the Propaganda Ministry were still underway.[229] Negotiations may have been deemed necessary because the academy had come under the auspices of the Propaganda Ministry in 1941.

Musicologists' Motivations and Musicology's Duty

In a 1945 essay commemorating the tenth anniversary of the Bückeburg Institute's move to Berlin, referred to as the founding of the State Institute, Fritz Stein praised the insight of the Nazi leaders for acknowledging the importance of music and musicology, which had been ignored by earlier administrations: "The National Socialist state created a central headquarters for music research through which it can direct and organize the tasks of this research. But it also gave expression to its cultural will in that it created a focal point for a science which, hardly comparable to any other, is a fruit of the

German spirit; which serves the research of an art that is a life's necessity for an entire people and up to now always has been a stepchild of public cultural policy."[230]

The Nazi leadership showed an unprecedented interest in musicology's potential. As Stein implied, their motivations may have been to "direct and organize the tasks of this research," but the new attention to the "stepchild of public cultural policy" must have caused considerable excitement in the field of musicology. Certainly at the beginning of the Third Reich, the possibilities to pursue music research outside the academy and to increase musicology's influence in German society and in the expanding Reich seemed limitless. Ironically, while Stein was praising the administration for its foresight, the Education Ministry was plotting the demise of the institute. The outcome of World War II caused most of these dreams to evaporate, but one cannot ignore the legacies of Nazi government initiatives that survived the war, such as EdM and *MGG,* to name only two.

The party and state presented new options for applying musicological training outside the academy, and those who cooperated did so for scholarly, monetary, political, and career benefits. Some of the more experienced scholars, such as Sandberger and Schering, took advantage of government sponsors to publicize their work and collect substantial fees. Others were seduced by the rare research privileges, even when these involved illegal activities. Many who worked with Rosenberg were already secure in academic positions and had nothing to lose by offering their services for free. Their compensation came in the form of rare opportunities to view, evaluate, and occasionally take possession of coveted musicological treasures in libraries and monasteries under German occupation.

Younger scholars like Bose and Boetticher threw themselves into government- and party-sponsored initiatives wholeheartedly, recognizing the potential benefits to their future careers as scholars. Both Bose and Boetticher entered these collaborations with the goal of attaining university positions, and the scholarly advantages of their tasks enhanced their academic qualifications and catapulted them into careers that flourished beyond 1945. Moser, too, used such opportunities to serve a secret desire to return to academe. He fulfilled his Reichsstelle tasks with enthusiasm and earned the praise of Nazi leaders, but his heart belonged to the academy. In 1941, when the death of Arnold Schering prompted a search for his successor, Moser wrote to a friend: "I am carrying out a commission from the Führer to have treasured classical and nineteenth-century operas reworked for the repertoire — but this lies on the edge of my real interests, and although this in combination with my pension as academy director would presumably pay me more than the Schering Ordinarius position, nevertheless I strive to return to the university, my real home."[231]

The participation of other mid-career musicologists can only be described as pure ambition. The musicology community was aware of the polarization of the field between the competing "Besseler camp" (or "institute clique") and the "Gerigk camp" (or "Rosenberg circle"). Besseler was a reputable scholar and could have succeeded in the academy solely on the strength of his work. He was entrusted with such important projects as the Denkmäler operation and periodicals, but he went beyond these tasks to ingratiate himself with the authorities. Besseler voluntarily submitted regular reports to the Education Ministry on German musicological activity abroad, joined the SA, and went to great lengths to clear his name with the party, insisting on challenging Gerigk's accusations within the jurisdiction of a Nazi party tribunal. His drive can only be explained by a need for power and influence, an ambition his archrival Gerigk had accurately identified. Gerigk, unlike Besseler, had achieved little recognition as a scholar. Motivated by ambition alone, he devoted all his energies to seeking out and destroying his enemies, thwarting and co-opting the plans of rival organizations, and wresting as much influence from others as possible. He was in many ways a personification of the Rosenberg Bureau's mission.

Beyond the petty motives of individuals, the nature of musicological participation in government and party ventures took on a character of its own. The authorities took special note of music's centrality in German culture and recognized the potential of the music scholar to assist in fulfilling the greater goals of the Nazi state, especially beyond the borders of the old Reich. Music was central to any program of cultural Germanization in newly acquired territories, and plans for reshaping musical life in the occupation had to emerge from a thorough understanding of local musical traditions among a team of experts.

Musicologists, for their part, regarded a foothold in the development of musical *Ostpolitik* as one way of gaining status and support in the Nazi cultural and educational hierarchy. The Sonderstab Musik went beyond mere pillaging to assess the climate for Germany's future takeover of musical life. As Gerigk instructed Boetticher, the mission was to include evaluating the political reliability of Aryan musicians with a view toward encouraging them to work for the German cultural cause. Musicologists were to seek out cooperative inhabitants and assess their receptiveness to the future establishment of German institutions.

The "Ahnenerbe" similarly sought not only to plunder but also to establish a working relationship with indigenous populations, carrying out the cultural-political tasks of fostering cooperation and educating ethnic German natives to the National Socialist worldview. Musicologists were more than just diligent scholars who could lend intellectual credibility to Himmler's operation. The SS must have recognized in them a commitment that extended beyond detailed research and into the realm of employing their expertise as consultants and administrators in the Germanization of the expanding Reich. Musicologists working for Himmler distinguished themselves with their dedication to the cultural-political aspects of their assignment, placing it over the mere seizure of artifacts and fostering German culture among the South Tyroleans with lectures, workshops, and retreats.

With their willingness to contribute to the broader political aims of the Nazi state, these musicologists hoped to demonstrate their potential to take even greater responsibility in the expanded Reich. Although these preliminary tasks represented only a beginning, they gave musicologists a rare opportunity to have concrete input into the control of musical life and musical policy in the countries under occupation.

6

The Shaping of New Methodologies

Musicologists, like all intellectuals at the beginning of the twentieth century, were witnesses to a crisis in German thought. The perceived challenges to all humanities disciplines from the forces of materialism, natural science, and technology left musicologists to ponder possible applications of scientific methods, ways to liberate musicology from its dependence on other humanities, and means to render music scholarship more useful for practicing musicians. Noteworthy developments in previously ignored areas of systematic musicology — including acoustics, psychology, and the study of folk and non-Western music — caught the attention of music historians, who were intrigued by the scientific applications and the potential for revealing clues to prehistoric music by comparing the practices of societies designated as "primitive" and "cultured."

After the Nazis came to power, the leading minds in systematic fields — most of them Jews — were driven out of Germany, leaving further research to underqualified students and poorly trained colleagues. Concurrently, an interest in the connection between race and music became fashionable. In the absence of qualified scholars who could critically assess the validity of "racial musicology," those left to the task relied heavily on the pseudo-scientific premises established by popular racial theorists at the turn of the century. Their pursuit of a racial methodology yielded nothing of use.

A musicological confrontation with the Jewish Question, promoted for its potential political benefits, failed to inspire much interest. By contrast, the study of German folk music advanced significantly during this time. Although government and party encouraged folk music research with monetary incentives, it was fueled primarily by the enthusiasm of a generation of historical musicologists impressed in their student days by the youth movement and intent on bridging the gap between theory and practice. Folk music research served the multiple purposes of contributing to a Germanic ideology, serving the needs of amateurs, and potentially leading to a deeper understanding of German character and identity.

The Limits of Geistesgeschichte and Emergence of Neo-Positivism

Shortly before the turn of the century, the study of history underwent a methodological crisis that had an especially profound impact on the history of arts and literature. The prevailing tradition of historicism drew a clear distinction between the laws of man and the laws of nature. Grounded in the writings of Wilhelm von Humboldt and Leopold Ranke, historicism maintained that history unfolds as a result of unique acts of human volition and cannot be compared with the recurring, predictable laws of nature that lack purpose or will. History, therefore, can provide the deepest understanding of all things human.[1] The growing influence of positivism at the end of the nineteenth century promoted rational thinking and threatened to undermine religious, irrational, or metaphysical views of the world. In the epistemological discussions that followed, two camps emerged. The Neo-Kantians (Wilhelm Windelband, Heinrich Rickert, and Max Weber) upheld a distinction between the methods of natural science and those of history and cultural sciences, but they were open to the possibility of an objective, rational approach to history. In the other camp was Wilhelm Dilthey, who had more influence on literature and the arts than on historical method, especially after World War I. Dilthey tried to be more rigid than the Neo-Kantians in opposing a rational approach, proposing that human beings can only know the social and human world through their own experiences and can never really know the physical world. Dilthey's writings on the methods of *Geisteswissenschaft* (science of the intellect or consciousness) hearken back to the ideas of Hegel and German Idealism but are full of contradictions. Dilthey tried, on the one hand, to assert the possibility of objective knowledge and the scientific study of history and society, but on the other hand adhered to the conviction that human experience was of a highly personal and subjective nature.[2]

Subscribing to the writings of Dilthey and his followers, scholars of the arts and literature in the early twentieth century succumbed to the same contradictions observed in Dilthey's writings. They adopted the concept of an "objective intellect" (*Geist*) that expresses itself in the philosophy, religion, law, art, music, and literature of an era, and they concentrated their activities on studying the history of the intellect (*Geistesgeschichte*). The writing of Geistesgeschichte demanded that a scholar follow certain basic principles. First, one must attempt to understand the culture and ideas of a historical period as living contemporaries did, trying to "experience" and "feel" the subject matter (*verstehen* as the result of *erleben* and *einfühlen*). One must also preserve the unity and totality of the subject under study (*Einheit* and *Ganzheit*), implying that cultural objects must be studied as a single entity and may not be broken up into smaller components through analysis. Finally, one must keep in mind that the Geist can be understood only after examining several areas of thought, thus all of the Geisteswissenschaften are interdependent.[3]

The advocates of Geisteswissenschaft eschewed anything they considered *naturwissenschaftlich,* positivistic, analytical, biographical, and empirical, and laid much of the blame for a perceived crisis of learning on the rise of materialism and technology and on the decline of German Idealism.[4] Yet they were unable to remain rigid in their convictions. In his examination of art history and literature, Jost Hermand noted that around 1900, these two fields adopted the battle-cry of "Free us from positivism!" (*Los vom Positivismus!*), although they gradually allowed many positivistic approaches, such as analysis, to enter their work. In the 1920s, cultural historians became fascinated with the notion of recurring patterns in history and devised elaborate schemes to explain them, while nationalism gave rise to the increased focus on the "German essence," defined as something in the blood which determined one's perception of the world. Methodological discussions criticized Dilthey's reliance on philosophy, and individual Geisteswissenschaften grew more independent from one another, ignoring Dilthey's interdisciplinary dictum of understanding the Geist through the "mutual illumination of the arts" (*wechselseitige Erhellung der Künste*). In the 1930s, interest in the hypotheses and constructs of Geistesgeschichte were replaced by more positivistic principles. With the rise of National Socialism, those two disciplines of art history and literature redirected their activities toward complete immersion in all things German.[5]

The patterns observed by Hermand bear striking resemblance to developments in the writing of music history. Methodological discussions were lively in the first half of the century, but differing positions were not always easy to identify. Positivism often infiltrated resolute antipositivist positions, and trends came in and out of fashion. Musicologists became embroiled in a debate over the virtues of Geistesgeschichte, exploring the parameters of form, style, and nationality that had been employed in art history; reconsidering the more "positivist" branches of musicology (e.g., acoustics, psychology, comparative musicology); and assessing the specific needs of musicological research and the problems associated with borrowing too heavily from related disciplines. Dilthey's rules proved too restrictive; in order to establish musicology as a self-sufficient science on equal footing with the other humanities, one had to transcend the limits of Geistesgeschichte to accommodate the special requirements of music research.

One of the earliest methodological debates after World War I revolved around the status of musicology as a Geisteswissenschaft. In the decade that followed, several musicologists had something to say on the issue but could not agree on how to proceed. At the heart of the debate lay the problem that music, owing to its sensual and transitory nature, could not be studied as one might study a painting, a building, or a document. Questions arose as to whether musicology should divorce itself from the philosophical precepts of Geistesgeschichte. Music could not be subjected to the same philosophical criteria as visual art, and music research needed to derive a methodology from music's own internal structure. The field needed to establish its independence from history, philosophy, and philology and address its own set of questions and problems.[6]

Immediately after the war, in the first volume of *AfMw*, Egon Wellesz pointed to the pressing need to develop a sound methodology for musicology, particularly with the establishment of a new journal, and to free musicology from its dependence on art history without completely discarding beneficial approaches successfully derived from it.[7] In the same volume, Curt Sachs proposed a heavier reliance on art history and suggested studying the artistic styles of a culture and period and looking for corresponding parallels in music (e.g., a penchant for ornamentation, for repeating patterns, for linearity or spatial forms).[8] While Bücken held the middle ground, stating that only certain periods could be understood in a *geistesgeschichtlich* manner, Schering recommended looking beyond the humanities to sociology for new methodological models.[9]

These scholars agreed that musicology needed to reevaluate its methods, become less dependent on borrowed concepts, and find its own tailor-made approaches, but few were ready to abandon the principles of Geistesgeschichte altogether. Instead, they continued to observe their sister disciplines and experiment with some of the approaches used by them. The history of style, already in use in other humanities, was adapted to musicology by Guido Adler in 1911. It was revolutionary for its time because it broke away from strictly biographical-aesthetic studies in music and focused instead on the work of art.[10] History of style, especially as executed by Hugo Riemann, won more favor among younger scholars than other approaches, such as the history of genre or form.[11] Riemann's style history approach was regarded as an important breakthrough because it accommodated two sides of a musical work: its function as "an expression of the spiritual life of an epoch, a nation, a personality" and its function as the "solution to a purely musical problem."[12]

It was also crucial to devise a music-specific periodization, as Riemann had attempted, making it unnecessary to force music history into the period classifications used by other arts.[13] To this day, the imposition of style periods borrowed from art history (e.g., Renaissance, Baroque) poses problems in interpreting the history of musical style, compelling musicologists to envision stylistic shifts at points where art historians found them. Riemann began to devise a music-specific periodization by coining such terms as "figured-bass era," used as a substitute for "baroque."

Geistesgeschichte was challenged on other fronts as scholars in the humanities began to perceive the impact of science and technology on the world around them. This encouraged historical musicologists to open their minds to the branches of the discipline that relied on the natural and social sciences, but it also manifested itself in an almost slavish emulation of what was perceived as scientific inquiry. Many "new" perceptions of history borrowed models from the sciences, and although these were often founded on old ideas, the inclusion of statistics, elaborate charts and graphs, and metaphors appropriated from natural sciences gave the impression that the humanities were changing with the times.

Part of the motivation for seeking new schematic models for illustrating the flow of music history was to escape from the teleological assumptions prescribing that all objects constantly improve on themselves and strive for perfection. This old-fashioned conception, which had dominated the writing of music history, showed up in metaphors of social Darwinism and sometimes persisted subconsciously. Alfred Einstein, while recovering in a military hospital during the war, wrote a concise history of music without access to his library, resulting in his widely read *Short History of Music* (*Geschichte der Musik*). Left to recreate music history purely as he remembered it, his natural inclination was to base it on the central idea of a constant struggle — among nations, generations, genres, and individuals, and within the soul of the artist — striving relentlessly for a higher form of art. Einstein's use of Darwinian metaphors of struggle and progress persists throughout his book. He describes the entire sixteenth century as an era of struggle (*Kampfzeit*), the movement toward monody as a "struggle against counterpoint," and the nineteenth century as a complex web of struggles and contradictions that carry over into the twentieth century. Einstein also regarded struggle as a necessary experience for the true artist: Mendelssohn, a master of external form, lacked the "real inner struggle in his life and work," while Schumann reached his musical maturity after experiencing "external struggles and internal instabilities."[14]

Einstein's reliance on Darwinian metaphors apparently raised some voices of protest: in the preface to the second edition, Einstein commented that he had not meant to imply that music history always proceeds in a straight line and that earlier artworks are necessarily inferior to later ones, still he emphasized that the history of Western music can only be seen as a unified development, with innovations that necessarily derive from preexisting materials.[15] But Einstein was not alone: Darwinian metaphors had become so much a part of the vocabulary that they could hardly be suppressed. Mersmann portrayed the music history of a culture as an organism subject to the laws of evolution, and Adler described the momentary musical hegemony of one nation as "a matter of natural selection, a process similar to that of selective breeding in Nature."[16] The overuse of such metaphors prompted a stern warning from the influential music critic Paul Bekker, who advised music historians to divorce cultural history from the potential dangers of social Darwinism and advocated understanding music history as a metamorphosis rather than as a progressive development. He also warned against subjective value judgments of other periods and, by implication, of other cultures.[17]

In an effort to escape from the teleological trap, music historians looked for alternative schemes for presenting music history in cyclical terms. Bekker perceived music history as a fluctuation between the predominance of "cult music" and of "profane music."[18] Mersmann adapted the Renaissance-Baroque principle from the art historian Heinrich Wölfflin, where "Renaissance" represented the unified, constructive phase of a period and "Baroque" the diffuse, dissolution phase.[19] Schering arrived at a similar model for tracing the history of musical texture and timbre (*Klangstil*), described as fluctuating between a tendency toward "homogenous style" (*Tonverschmelzung*, a term borrowed from Carl Stumpf) and the "split sound complex" (*gespaltener Klang*).[20]

The most elaborate cyclical schematization was Alfred Lorenz's *Western Music History in the Rhythm of Generations* (*Abendländische Musikgeschichte im Rhythmus der Generationen*), which proposed that history falls into recurring patterns at precise intervals of three hundred years. His basic unit for historical analysis is the generation of musicians, each spanning thirty years and each reacting against the creations of the preceding generation. Basing the broad sweep of musical development on the two conflicting principles of "homophonic-rhythmic" (*homophone Rhythmik*) and "polyphonic-introspective" (*polyphone Innenschau*) and noticing that any great ideas in history require three hundred years (ten generations) to take hold, he reduced music history to a pattern of alternating influence of one principle over the other, climaxing every three centuries. Thus the period from approximately 400 to 700 A.D. saw the rise of the homophonic influence, reaching its peak in Gregorian chant; the next three hundred years moved in the polyphonic direction, culminating in organum; 1000 to 1300 moved back toward homophony with the troubadours and Minnesingers; 1300 to 1600 became the age of polyphony as we know it; and 1600 to 1900 became the age of homophony in the common usage of the term.[21]

Alongside the attraction to principles of natural sciences was an attraction to social sciences, growing out of an awareness of class and the creation of a new social-historical approach to musicology.[22] Such scholars as Moser, Fellerer, and Schünemann investigated the history of music festivals, music education, Hausmusik, military music, and folk music, posing such timely and provocative questions as whether musicians in the past could be considered proletarians.[23] Stephen Hinton has discovered similar tendencies in the early works of Besseler, who, in the midst of an emerging concept of Gebrauchsmusik and under the influence of Heidegger's teachings in the early 1920s, sought a new paradigm for music history that would focus less on concert music and more on everyday music practices.[24] A social history approach came to be especially favorable in histories of German music, forming the basis of Paul Bekker's 1916 study that traces music in Germany from the French Revolution to 1916 as a communal activity; a 1933 study of German musical life by Walther Berten; and Ernst Bücken's 1941 book on the music of the Germans.[25]

The social history approach can be detected in much of the historical literature in the 1920s and 1930s, owing undoubtedly to the increased awareness of class differences, the interest in amateur music, and the pressures on musicologists to address the needs of the public. This approach allowed musicologists to acknowledge the importance of the amateur movement, treating it as a historical subject and using the tools with which they were equipped, rather than venturing into commentary on contemporary issues of musical life. These historical guides were also useful aids for the early music revival and instructive supplements to the large number of editions coming out at the same time.[26]

Unlike most other humanities scholars, musicologists had to balance their duties inside and outside the realm of scholarship, leading some critics to judge that musicologists' side activities as journalists, composers, and conductors were obstacles to "scientific objectivity" and to total dedication to scholarly work.[27] But musicology could not ignore its responsibilities to music practice. The pressures for musicology to develop its own methods and terminology came not only from within the discipline but also from amateur musicians' demands for less philological or art historical analysis of early music and more guidance in how to perform it. Professional musicians and composers also pressured musicology to pay more attention to musical issues of the present.

The musicologist's relationship to the practicing musician became the topic of another debate, with scholars divided on the question of who should concede to whom. Should musicology be more sensitive to the needs of practitioners, or should practitioners take a more earnest interest in music scholarship? The major advocate for encouraging musicology to reach out to the music-making population was Hermann Kretzschmar. In both his polemical writings and in his presentation of music history, Kretzschmar attempted to build a bridge between musicology and performance practice. In keeping with arguments set forth in his *Musikalische Zeitfragen,* Kretzschmar stressed the importance of music history for the performance of early music, treating the historical topics strictly by performance genre in order to make them more accessible to the performer. He published a brief introduction to music history (*Einführung in die Musikgeschichte*) as the seventh volume of the series he edited consisting of handbooks on music history organized by genre (*Kleine Handbücher der Musikgeschichte nach Gattungen*). Kretzschmar's history turns out to be a brief source study, intended to serve as a handbook for the musician (as should all musicological works, in his opinion).[28]

Others assumed the opposing position, that musicians must make an effort to understand musicology. Promulgating an essentially geistesgeschichtlich conception of the goals of musicology and placing its home in the university, Johannes Wolf encouraged stronger relationships with practicing musicians but placed the burden of change on the musician rather than the musicologist.[29] Arnold Schering's opening remarks at the Leipzig meeting of 1925 also found fault with practicing musicians, who had taken far too little interest in musicology. He conceded that musicology had to take the first step in making amends, and he praised his colleagues for their recent efforts in approaching music through form and style history, but he held firm to the benefits of a synthetic geistesgeschichtlich orientation.[30] In the end, the principles of Geistesgeschichte were not easily shaken, but all seemed to agree that the field was in need of far-reaching changes that would solve the problems of intellectual stagnation and outline a greater purpose for musicology.

The Interrupted Development of Comparative Musicology

For historical musicologists grappling with the problem of establishing methodological independence from other Geisteswissenschaften, one solution was to look to the nonhistorical subdisciplines of musicology in order to explore the unique characteristics of music. The classification of musicology as a Geistesgeschichte had implied adhering to history and resisting the positivism of exact sciences, but as musicologists became aware of the limitations of Geistesgeschichte, they began to take other areas of musicology more seriously. In 1885, Adler had divided musicology into two large categories: historical and "systematic," the latter containing the subdisciplines of aesthetics, pedagogy, analysis, and the study of non-Western music (*Musikologie*).[31] Hugo Riemann, a skilled master in many of these branches, acknowledged acoustics, music psychology, aesthetics, and theory as independent musicological fields and had already opened the door to their interaction in developing a synthetic approach.[32] By 1918 one could turn to Riemann as a model, reaffirming the validity of synthesizing history with the other branches of musicology rather than planting musicology more firmly within the confines of antipositivistic Geisteswissenschaften.[33]

The study of non-Western musical cultures, Adler's Musikologie, had been a topic of interest since the early nineteenth century, but it was not until the beginning of the twentieth century that it started to develop its own methodology. Its early goals were to use the information gathered from non-Western, so-called primitive sources to arrive at clues to the origins of music and to acquire insights into music psychology. By comparing findings from Musikologie with knowledge of Western music history, it was hoped that common denominators among music systems and music perception could be isolated, hence the designation of the emerging discipline became "comparative musicology" (*vergleichende Musikwissenschaft*), the predecessor of modern ethnomusicology.[34]

Research in comparative musicology took its greatest strides in the first three decades of the twentieth century at centers in Berlin (under the guidance of Stumpf, Hornbostel, and Sachs) and Vienna (under Wallaschek and Lach). Comparative musicology in Germany was a small operation at the end of World War I, housed within Stumpf's Psychology Institute, but it showed rapid signs of growth with the expansion of its well-known recorded sound archive. It soon developed into a broad interdisciplinary complex, drawing on ethnology, music theory, psychology, biology, and physics. Stumpf's collaborators included Erich von Hornbostel (with a doctorate in chemistry), Otto Abraham (a physician), Erich Fischer, Max Wertheimer (an authority in Gestalt psychology), and later Curt Sachs, one of the few with training in the humanities (art history and historical musicology). Sachs was later joined by others trained in musicology: Georg Schünemann and Marius Schneider, who pursued the course of synthesizing comparative and historical musicology, and Johannes Wolf, who remained more a supporter of the research than a practitioner.[35]

While still standing by the merits of Geistesgeschichte, historical musicologists took notice of comparative musicology, particularly in the ways it could serve the aims of music history. The Berlin school's work in collecting and analyzing data for studies of cognition, tonometrical measurements, and methods of transcription lent the field of comparative musicology the outward characteristics of an objective science. Nevertheless certain subjective cultural biases lay at its foundation, despite the equal application of analytical methods to both non-Western and European folk music. Stumpf and Hornbostel emphasized the goals of discovering the origins and nature of music by combining music psychology with the comparative analysis of scales, harmony, and rhythm of various cultures, but their underlying interest focused on determining which musical features were uniquely European and therefore represented a "higher" stage of development.[36] Intrigued by the idea that studying primitive cultures could unravel some of the mysteries of prehistoric and early Western music, Georg Schünemann suggested investigating the connections between Gregorian chant and Asian music along with the music of similar "peoples . . . who are not yet acquainted with harmony," tracing the emergence of consonances among primitive peoples, looking for the origins of polyphony in the heterophony and parallel organum-like singing in Asia and Africa, and determining similarities between Asian and early medieval notation.[37]

Wilhelm Heinitz, one of the purists among systematic musicologists, protested such biases, declaring that "our European adherence to triadic harmony is not the only inspirational system."[38] He envisioned comparative musicology some day eliminating the prejudices inherited from historical musicology and saw the incorporation of scientific methods as even "helping to construct a secure foundation for a forthcoming philosophy of music history [relying on] demonstrable data."[39] All the same, in the introduction to the first issue of the *Journal for Comparative Musicology* (*Zeitschrift für vergleichende Musikwissenschaft,* established in 1933), cofounder Johannes Wolf acknowledged that the study of non-Western music had to be taken seriously because knowledge of the Orient could contribute to knowledge of the primitive stages of the Occident, and because the rush to westernize the East threatened to destroy these valuable links to the past.[40]

After Hitler came to power, an emphasis on race and folk culture drew more of music historians' attention to the potential usefulness of systematic fields for understanding the Germanic race and the German Volk. There was increased concern among musicologists in all branches to bring systematic musicology out of its isolation and to pay closer attention to what it had to offer. Fritz Bose made a plea to his fellow musicologists in 1934 to stop neglecting systematic fields and to consider their useful application in studying European and German folk music, in determining the race factors in music, and even in understanding music history.[41] Fellerer provided a brief history of the dominance of historical musicology, the split between the two areas, and the recent attempts at synthesis toward aiding music history, folk music research, regional studies, and organology (Fellerer blatantly omitted the names of the Jewish pioneers in systematic musicology, Erich von Hornbostel and Curt Sachs).[42] Bücken similarly lauded the development of comparative musicology and folk song research in the work of Fritz Bose and Kurt Huber, and Blume suggested that one needed to explore how systematic musicology could positively affect music practice.[43]

Only a few dissenters spoiled this spirit of cooperation. Alfred Lorenz was interested only in determining the musical superiority of the German race, and music psychology and especially the detailed study of "exotic music" had, in his opinion, been overestimated. He deemed the music of inferior races as inherently bad and called for an end to this fascination born of the false assumption that all races were equal.[44] Müller-Blattau took such prejudice one step further, claiming that the interest in world music had been a distraction from the important task of concentrating on the German folk element. It was time to put an end to the preoccupation with non-European subjects. In a veiled allusion to the dominance of Jews, such as Hornbostel and Sachs, in comparative musicology, he stated that "we were not masters of this area and had to leave it in the hands of a few, mostly of an alien race."[45]

By the time systematic fields attracted so much attention from the mainstream for its potential usefulness to contemporary research and music practice in the Nazi state, the scholarly infrastructure of comparative musicology had been all but dismantled. The forced emigration of Sachs and Hornbostel left the operation at the University of Berlin in the hands of a few inexperienced students and colleagues. Hornbostel's teaching responsibilities went to the twenty-eight-year-old Fritz Bose, while the thirty-year-old Marius Schneider assumed the direction of the Berlin Sound Archive. The instrument collection, built up over many years by Curt Sachs, was eventually handed over to the State Institute, to be supervised by Alfons Kreichgauer. The physicist Erich Schumann was appointed Ordinarius in systematic musicology at the university in 1933, a rank neither Sachs nor Hornbostel had been able to achieve in all of their years in Berlin. Schumann, who offered valuable service to the Wehrmacht in weapons research, acquired the rank immediately after their expulsion, although he had little to contribute to the field in terms of research.

In addition to losses at the Berlin faculty, the Nazi takeover forced the dissolution of the Society for Comparative Musicology (founded in 1930 as the Gesellschaft zur Erforschung der Musik des Orients and renamed Gesellschaft für vergleichende Musikwissenschaft in 1933). Its journal, the *Zeitschrift für vergleichende Musikwissenschaft,* had to terminate publication when its Jewish editor-in-chief, Robert Lachmann, emigrated to Israel in 1935. Psychologists such as Wolfgang Köhler and Max Wertheimer who had collaborated with the Berlin musicologists also left Germany upon Hitler's accession, as did a large proportion of the younger generation trained in comparative musicology: Mieczylaw Kolinski, Walter Kaufmann, Hans Hickmann, Manfred Bukofzer (all students of Sachs and Hornbostel), Klaus Wachsmann, Ernst Emsheimer, and Edith Gerson-Kiwi.[46] Many of these émigrés went on to make important contributions to the development of musicology outside Germany. Lachmann and Gerson-Kiwi, for example, are credited with establishing modern musicology in Israel; Bukofzer became widely known as a respected scholar and developed a comprehensive program in musicology at the University of California at Berkeley; and Kolinski found the Society for Ethnomusicology in the United States and went on to become a professor in Toronto.

Ironically, many of the directions initiated by Jews were perceived as holding promise for establishing research projects that would serve the aims of the Nazi state. The Propaganda Ministry, the SS-"Ahnenerbe," and the Rosenberg Bureau, to name a few, actively encouraged research and publication in German folk music and race studies, and a vocal campaign called for the redefinition and expansion of musicology to include ancestry research and biological methods leading to an understanding of the musical features of the Germanic race. Comparative musicologists had already made large contributions to the collection and analysis of folk music, and their expertise in ethnology, biology, and psychology qualified them to assess the validity of the proposed directions in race and ancestry. The only ones left to take on these tasks after 1933, however, were the few students remaining at the Berlin school and a host of ill-equipped historical musicologists, most of whom sought refuge in folk music research rather than confronting racial and biological issues.

The Political Resurrection of Racial Studies in Music

Even if the pioneers of systematic musicology had been allowed to continue working in Germany, it is doubtful that they would have been taken seriously. The popular mentality had gravitated away from rational thinking and found solace in the irrational, emotional, and mystical. By the end of the Weimar Republic, emotionally charged terms like *Volk, Gemeinschaft, Blut, Rasse,* and *organisch* defied definition or analysis. Rather, they stirred feelings of longing for an ideal, unified German nation in an era of political and social fragmentation.[47]

The notion of racial components in music was not restricted to German thought, yet the concept of race in German intellectual history had been exploited by demagogues and had taken on a distinct anti-Semitic focus. Furthermore, some of the most widely read literature harboring an anti-Semitic political agenda was the work of dilettantes but wore the guise of scientific inquiry. One of the shrewdest anti-Semitic propagandists at the turn of the century was Theodor Fritsch. Fritsch realized that carefully crafted propaganda was the surest way to spread feelings of anti-Semitism and strengthen the position of the faltering anti-Semitic political parties. Through numerous pamphlets, he successfully spread distorted images of the Jewish religion, character, and mentality to a wide audience. His *Handbook of Anti-Semitism,* published in 1894 and reissued in thirty-six editions by 1933, appealed to a more educated readership by quoting extensively from alleged authoritative sources that disparaged Judaism. The widely read *Foundations of the Nineteenth Century* by Richard Wagner's son-in-law, Houston Stewart Chamberlain, similarly drew extensively on historical and scientific data. Chamberlain arrived at a somewhat more refined schematization of racial hierarchy than the common crass differentiation between "inferior" Semites and "superior" Aryans, but he still aimed to denigrate the Jews. Merging religious and racial conceptions of the Jew, these early theorists arrived at a multitude of reasons why the Jew represented all that was evil in society.[48]

German racial theorists in the 1920s similarly portrayed their musings as scientific but moved even farther away from data and physical anthropology and deeper into the metaphysical realm, regarding physical traits only as superficial indicators of the racial beauty inherent in the "racial soul" (*Rassenseele*). Hans F. K. Günther, one of the most respected and widely read among the theorists of the racial soul (his 1922 book on the racial composition of the German people was reprinted fifteen times), embellished his carefully phrased prose with footnotes and supporting evidence that accorded him recognition as a serious thinker and won him a chair at the University of Jena. Günther presumed to be even more sophisticated than Chamberlain in his theory of race, eliminating the possibility of a pure race, but nevertheless creating a racial hierarchy according to degrees of purity. He considered the Aryan race to be the most "pure" and superior to all others, while the Jews were the least pure and therefore inferior to all others. Günther was countered by rival theorists, such as L. F. Clauß (*Die Nordische Seele,* 1930), who all but discounted physical traits for identifying race, and Siegfried Passarge (*Das Judentum als landschaftskundliches und ethnologisches Problem*), who emphasized the importance of environment on racial typology, especially for identifying the Jew. These conflicting theories did not cast doubt on the scientific validity of racial theory or undermine its attraction, but rather they appealed to the irrational and allowed for completely subjective criteria for identifying races and especially for determining who was a Jew.[49]

The lack of a tradition of intellectual rigor in racial theory allowed musicologists and others engaged in its application to indulge in eccentric methods derived from the works of these early racial theorists. In terms of serious scholarly investigation, however, the racial question in musicology had already been answered — negatively — long before the Nazis came to power. In 1923, the leading figure in the Viennese school of comparative musicology, Robert Lach, attempted to put an end to dilettantish digressions on race and music by demonstrating the incompatibility of racial concepts with musical style. Lach complained that although the nonspecialist assumes that a correspondence must exist between races and their respective musical styles, the comparative musicologist is simply incapable of determining such a correspondence through the scientific means available. Lach demonstrated the futility of trying to designate racial style in such musical parameters as scale systems, rhythmic and formal constructions, performance, and the psychological roots of musical expression. Musical elements thought to be characteristic of one particular nation or race could be found among many races, whether "primitive" (*Naturvölker*), "intermediate" (*Halbkulturvölker*) or "civilized" (*Kulturvölker*). These stylistic features could appear at any stage of a culture's musical history, thus "what comparative musicology can demonstrate regarding musical phenomena of human cultural history and ethnology are merely symptoms of development," not of racial makeup.[50]

Lach's sound invalidation of the correspondence between music and race seemed to have rung the death knell for the application of racial theories in serious music research: the scholarly literature in the ensuing years showed very little interest in confronting the issue in any systematic way. But the term "race" did not disappear from discussions of music. Rather, music critic Adolf Weissmann's 1926 essay "Race and Nation in Music" ("Rasse und Nation in der Musik") reported the incessant overuse of the term. Weissmann predicted that any detectable traces of race in music would soon disappear because of extensive racial mixing throughout Europe, although certain racial proclivities (the rhythm of Negro jazz, the "irony" of French music, and the "unshakable racial feeling" in Eastern European music) might still exist.[51] Weissmann further emphasized the difficulty in designating not only a German race but also a German nation, a plurality of foreign influences being the only unique feature of German "racial expression" (*Rasseausdruck*). Most important, Weissmann accurately identified Germany's peculiar preoccupation with the racial question, observing that "where racial purity is most controversial, one tries to demonstrate it most ardently."[52]

Musicologists were also known to indulge in the indiscriminate use of the term "race" and allusions to biological and hereditary parameters. As a component of his Klangstil theory, Schering proposed that an individual was powerless to choose his preferred Klangstil but rather was subject to an inborn "sound ideal" (*Klangideal*), described as "völkisch, racial, cultic, social, i.e., something beyond the individual."[53] Alfred Lorenz also made some references to race in his *Abendländische Musikgeschichte im Rhythmus der Generationen* (although not with the same ideological conviction that would later motivate him to promote racial studies). He paid homage to the work of his father, Ottokar Lorenz, by conceding that race could influence the intellectual make-up of an individual, but he would not concede that race had much relevance in studying the arts.[54]

By the time the Nazi government and party started to encourage a racial direction in scholarship, the only existing comprehensive exposé on race and music was the work of the dilettante Richard Eichenauer. A Nazi party member since October 1932 and an SS officer active in the Race and Resettlement Office,[55] Eichenauer had no formal training as a musicologist. He studied German, modern languages, and music in Munich and Leipzig and was certified to teach languages and singing at the high school level. He modeled his 1932 book *Music and Race* (*Musik und Rasse*) on analogous attempts in art history and literature, focusing on the "racial soul" — rather than on exclusively on inherited physical characteristics — to gain an understanding of the racial aspects of musical style.

Eichenauer's aim was to isolate the racial features of a composer's soul through study of physical characteristics and some biographical data, but primarily by looking at the composer's works. Tracing the roots of the Nordic racial soul back to India, Persia, and especially ancient Greece (he finds the strongest ties between Greek and Germanic civilization in their common mission for music "to achieve the training of humanity in the direction of a Nordic model"), Eichenauer attributes the origins of polyphony and the triad to northern lands, based on the existence of the lur; traces a preference for triadic motion and major mode in the chant from Nordic lands (similar to modern Kampflieder); and ascribes an inborn Nordic racial tendency to Leonin's and Perotin's innovations in polyphony.[56]

Eichenauer characterizes the growth of polyphony from 1400 to 1600 as a struggle between the "alien non-European" (*europafremd*) and the Nordic-Germanic races. He even tries to assert that Palestrina, the Italian master of counterpoint, was racially of Nordic-Dinaric extraction. (Nordic and Dinaric strains together constituted a highly desirable Aryan combination in the eyes of racial theorists.) Similarly, since opera "most clearly betrays the influence of the Nordic spirit," he attempts to prove that Rameau possessed physical Nordic traits and displayed the Nordic elements of harmonic strength, sophisticated counterpoint, and straightforward structure in his music.[57]

Eichenauer subjects many more individual composers to racial examinations, coordinating their physical and musical traits. According to Eichenauer, Bach's physical features correspond with his Nordic "passionate soul" (*leidenschaftliche Seele*) and with his skill in writing counterpoint, which is the realization of a Nordic idea. Handel is physically one of the "purest representatives of the Nordic race," thus Eichenauer downplays any Italian influence in his music or hints of glorification of the Old Testament in his English oratorios. Gluck, like the ancient Greeks, imbued Nordic feeling into Greek dramas and employed "Spartan" rhythm, while Haydn displays yet another exclusively Nordic strength, that of melody. Mozart, racially Dinaric-Nordic like Haydn, bears all of the qualities of the Nordic soul despite an alleged Italian "influence." Ironically, the towering figures of German Romanticism pose the most problems for Eichenauer's racial analysis: Beethoven's appearance betrays certain eastern influences mixed in with the Nordic, while Schubert's "soft" features resulting from racial mixing come across in his shifts from major to minor, his "harmonic weakness," and his preference for small forms, all manifestations of oriental genes. The same problems arise with Schumann and Wagner, although the latter's music is the quintessence of Nordic-Dinaric racial mixture.[58]

Eichenauer saves most of his anti-Semitic diatribe for his discussion of the nineteenth century and the present. He believed that Gregorian chant, of Jewish origins and therefore essentially un-German, should not be condemned out of anti-Semitic blindness, because the Jews of the nineteenth century, to whom most anti-Semitism is directed, pose a special case.[59] In his final chapter, Eichenauer enumerates the counterproductive forces that threaten Germanness in music: verismo in opera, the East Baltic gypsy influence (which has had its effects on Max Reger), and above all the Jewish influence since the nineteenth century. The Jewish Volk, Eichenauer claims, is not a Volk at all but consists of a mixture of many races, thus the term "Jewish" implies an absence of racial identity. The Jews Meyerbeer and Offenbach both abused their musical abilities, and Mahler was frustrated by his love for German folk song in conflict with his racial limitations. Finally Schoenberg and all other Jewish progressives "are obeying a law of their race when they seek to destroy harmonic polyphony, which is totally foreign to them."[60]

In 1933, the interest in racial matters became fashionable as never before, and the application of racial theory, or at least the adaptation of a racial perspective, received a second chance in scholarly circles. Lacking any other comprehensive works on the subject of music and race, musicologists raised Eichenauer's book to the status of a reference work and subsequently cited it as the authoritative study, despite its author's lack of credentials and essentially trite and logically flawed conclusions. The few remaining comparative musicologists and some ambitious historians lunged forward into a murky and methodologically shaky area of inquiry, but the motives for their undertaking came through clearly in their prose: to validate their own work and the field of musicology as a whole, and to address the challenge from Nazi leaders to arrive at conclusions about the musical superiority of the German race.

Fritz Bose was one of the first to make a public statement on the racial question in 1933 in an issue of the *Deutsche Tonkünstlerzeitung*. Bose noted with some surprise how *Rassenkunde* had suddenly become a focus of interest, but he agreed that such attention was long overdue, after years of neglect from "official scholarship" that left the subject at the mercy of dilettantes. Careful not to insult Eichenauer, he claimed that "all sciences begin with dilettantes," but nevertheless promoted the combination of comparative musicology with experimental psychology as the only means of isolating aspects of music determined by race. Eichenauer did not have access to such methods, making his work far removed from "exact science." Bose recommended the comparative study of non-Western "primitives," whose music reveals a much truer manifestation of the race, and a closer study of the purer manifestations of European races found in folk music, and he stressed the practical significance of such activities for contemporary musical life.[61]

Bose persisted in promoting the practical and political usefulness of comparative musicology. A second article, "Das Rassische in der Musik," which appeared in the Nazi party organ *Unser Wille und Weg*, emphasized the application of biology: that music, as the language of both body and soul, needs to be considered in racial-biological terms when analyzing the performance of rhythm (which involves bodily motion) and vocal timbre (which involves inherited physical characteristics of the larynx and oral cavity). Bose also proposed close scrutiny of melodic motion, musical structure, and musical symbolism, "through which the racial elements in music are expressed."[62] Irmgard Leux-Henschen, a student of Adolf Sandberger, further endorsed the marriage of musicology and biology, urging musicologists to overcome their "antipathy against the exact experimental biological mode of perception" and to offer their expertise to biological research on musical ability, music psychology, and the heredity of musical talent.[63]

Incentives to Explore the Race Problem and the Jewish Question in Musicology

For the most part, this show of interest in racial research, particularly among younger musicologists, failed to lead to serious inquires into race within musicological circles, perhaps owing to the pitfalls already revealed by experts many years before. It was only after persistent encouragement and artificial political inducement that more respectable scholarly venues entertained the questions of race and music. In 1937, *AfMf* published a lengthy discourse on racial methodology. The article was not the work of a renowned musicologist, but rather of a school teacher in Berlin, Siegfried Günther.[64] Still, the editors of the journal hoped the article would serve as a catalyst for more serious inquiries.

In stark contrast to Bose, Günther downplays the need for exact scientific inquiry. Citing attempts by American scholars to understand the connection between music and race through experimental psychology, Günther surmises that not only were Americans under political pressure to reject the notion of a connection between race and music, but that their purely scientific methods were useless for the purposes of German scholarship. A German approach must integrate the National Socialist Weltanschauung and principles of National Socialist–influenced sciences, which incorporate the irrational, rather than restricting itself to outmoded "Jewish rationalism." Günther recommends an examination of the "style" of races rather than examining only musical materials, as comparative musicologists had done. Most important for him, however, is that methodology be guided by the teachings of Hitler and Rosenberg, and that researchers keep in mind that the undeniable dominance of Nordic music throughout the Western world is not merely a result of imperialism but rather testimony to the "power of the Aryan race."[65] The 1938 volume of the *AfMf* included another contribution by Günther,[66] designed to stimulate further serious inquiries into racial matters. An editor's note preceding Günther's article indicated that it would be the first of a series of racial-musicological contributions investigating the characteristics of Germanic races, the racial manifestations of personal styles, and the racial implications of German style. But aside from a few related book reviews, only one substantial article on the subject ever appeared in the *AfMf*, and that not until 1944.[67]

In 1938, the incentives to address the ideological questions of race and the role of the Jew in German musical culture were stepped up, both from within the discipline and from Nazi leaders. In that year, Ernst Bücken promoted racial research as one of the "tasks and goals" of German musicology and stressed the importance of developing a methodology, since initial attempts had not yielded the "expected results."[68] And in December, Alfred Lorenz, perhaps the most outspoken promoter of racial research because of his "spiritual" ties to Wagner and familial ties to Ottokar Lorenz, published two simultaneous pleas to apply racial methods to ancestry research and to the Jewish Question. He recommended a new format for music biographies, which would include a detailed ancestry table and reveal the sources of genius. Beethoven, he claimed, was not great because he stood above the "music midgets" of his time, but rather because he inherited certain superior traits. He also used this opportunity to reject the Geisteswissenschaft method as "the leveling system which originated from the Jewish spirit" and underestimated true genius.[69] Lorenz further expressed the need to update Wagner's analysis of the Jewish Question and to distinguish between real Jewish music (i.e., emanating from the racial soul) and imitations of non-Jewish music, since the Jews supposedly had no originality. He also claimed that some of his conclusions about Jews' lack of originality and "Jewish musical traits" were actually first noticed by nineteenth- and twentieth-century Jewish scholars and critics.[70]

The most important incentive for engagement with racial issues, though, was Goebbels's invitation to musicologists to hold a conference at the Reichsmusiktage in Düsseldorf, their first since the founding of the Third Reich. In his opening address, Schiedermair expressed gratitude to Goebbels and acknowledged musicology's obligation to address the needs of the music public; the central theme chosen for the meeting, "Music and Race," was a problem that "dominated music practice as well as research."[71] A session devoted to music and race, along with Friedrich Blume's keynote address on the subject, were, according to newspaper reports, expected to attract the most attention.[72]

The papers in the session on music and race, to the extent that they can be reconstructed through separate articles and reports, tended to skirt any serious confrontations with devising a racial methodology. Werner Danckert's talk entitled "Nationhood, Tribal Manner, Race in the Light of Folk Song Research" ("Volkstum, Stammesart, Rasse im Lichte der Volksliedforschung") was most likely a very tame attempt to compare the styles of folk music among several German groups without ever referring to race.[73] Similarly Helmut Schultz's "Folk Characteristics of Instrumental Timbres" ("Volkhafte Eigenschaften des Instrumentenklangs") made some vague connections between instrument groups and national differences, but completely avoided race issues.[74] A published version of Gotthold Frotscher's "Tasks and Problems of Racial Style Research in Music" ("Aufgaben und Probleme der musikalischen Rassenstilforschung") merely reiterated the catechisms of racial theories: that music and race are inseparable, that musical style should be analyzed according to principles of racial theory, and that the best approach is a comparative study of folk music.[75] Folk music studies, he added, could form a basis for contrasting the works of German masters with those of the racially foreign (Mahler, Mendelssohn, and popular song writers of the postwar period), liberating German music from Jewish domination and fulfilling Hitler's ideal of finding inspiration through race and blood.[76]

Blume's keynote speech, while dutifully proclaiming that questions of race were indeed worthy of careful consideration, came closest to dealing with the feasibility of a racial methodology, but in the end it posed more problems than solutions.[77] In his close scrutiny of the problems of finding a workable methodology, Blume was careful never to accept or reject prior racial methods outright. He continued to develop his ideas in a lecture series for the Schleswig-Holstein University Society and published his results as a separate monograph.[78] His masterful fence-sitting also allowed him to enjoy the praise of contemporary Nazi critics, while feeling no pressure to conceal the speech or its enhanced monograph version after 1945.[79]

What Blume did conceal after 1945, however, was the extent to which he profited from this opportunity. The fact that he should take an interest in the racial question at all is striking because it bears no relation to his other research interests. But the honor of delivering the keynote speech in Düsseldorf and the lecturing and publishing opportunities that would follow would have provided enough motivation for him to take on the challenge. Recognized hence as the expert on racial methodology, he went on to edit a series of music-historical studies dealing with race.[80] He was also invited to contribute the chapter on German musicology to the Festschrift for Hitler's fiftieth birthday, which appeared in 1939, and in which he singled out racial studies as a central task of National Socialist music research.[81]

In both the Düsseldorf address and the book entitled *The Problem of Race in Music* (*Das Rasseproblem in der Musik*), Blume pointed to weaknesses in prior methods and proved the futility of some of their basic assumptions. Through it all, however, he never missed an opportunity to heap respectful adjectives upon the "fathers" of racial research (including Eichenauer), to acknowledge the timely importance of such inquiries, and even to ignore his own criticisms of their work. A careful reading of *Das Rasseproblem* reveals many redundancies, tautologies, and contradictions, concealed behind lengthy and often byzantine argumentation, unnecessarily complex vocabulary, and multiple terms referring to the same ideas.

Blume opens his discussion with the political parlance that the relation between music and race is important for the "German Volk's relation to its own music and to music in general," but one should not leave it to the careless conjectures of dilettantes.[82] To find a "scientific" approach one has to broaden the scope of the inquiry so that it can truly include the entire race, "not just the Volk, nation, tribe or other unit," and all music, "not an arbitrary category such as high art music of the last few centuries, or German folk music, or other complexes of musical objects."[83] To be truly scientific, one should avoid concentrating on one race but rather must look at the nature of race in general, and above all one should not limit one's scope to a particular composer or work in search of an expression of the individual's racial character in his music, because such an inquiry could lead to the *false* assumptions that certain elements of biological race correspond to concrete musical phenomena.[84]

Blume raises some very important methodological questions in his introduction, and he attempts to answer whether there were elements in music that could potentially reveal racial characteristics in the next two chapters. In the first chapter he addresses the question of "fundamental characteristics and components of music" (tonal systems, rhythm, and performance practice), and in the second chapter the "empirical objects of music" (such as folk music, art music, specific genres and forms, polyphony). One by one he dismisses these musical parameters as potential indices of race, but throughout the study he raises hopes that something might be salvaged out of the pile of discarded approaches.

Blume categorically rejects the elements of tonal systems, scales, and tonality as objects for understanding race because all are theoretical deductions derived from melody and because none could be associated exclusively with any specific race; rather, one could find many different scales or tonal systems within one racial group and could find tonality present among many races.[85] These observations echo one of the warnings issued by Lach in his 1923 article, but Blume does not cite him anywhere. The similarity in the titles of Blume's book (*Das Rasseproblem in der Musik*) and Lach's article ("Das Rassenproblem in der vergleichenden Musikwissenschaft") could suggest that Blume was familiar with Lach's work. But since Lach completely discredits racial methodology, it was probably not in Blume's best interest to call attention to the article; Blume clearly wished to avoid a categorical acceptance or rejection of racial methods.

Having cast doubt on almost all musical parameters for failing to harbor racial traits, Blume cautiously proposes that a comparative study of melody might be the best way to reveal differences between races. He then immediately undermines this proposal with references to prior attempts showing that melodic differences do *not* necessarily follow along racial lines, but rather reveal differences among "peoples" (*Völker*). In addition, melody often reflects common economic systems, such that triadic melody is not so much a Nordic trait as it is a trait of hunting cultures. Is melody a potential source for racial study or not? The author hesitates to take a firm stand: "As we see, the entire question of melody structure is a very intricate problem, which nevertheless seems promising for racially oriented music research."[86]

The reason for such vacillation is that in later pages he would ignore all his own warnings against depending on melody in order to promote his plan to find racial characteristics in the study of Gregorian chant. Having somewhat discredited melody as a potential racial parameter, he nevertheless regards a comparative melodic analysis of Gregorian chant as a fruitful enterprise for music historians interested in racial research. Blume's "new approach" would involve looking not at musical elements or objects for racial consistency, but rather at the processes of musical transmission. This could reveal much about the talents, inclinations, and abilities of a race.[87]

Having ruled out virtually all types of music believed by others to have racial qualities and guiding the reader to look not at musical objects themselves but rather at the processes of transmission, Blume draws attention to the notion that Germans reveal a certain talent for adopting and reworking styles to create something "unmistakably German." Such talent, he concludes, grew out of racial traits of efficiency, creative energy, productivity, and growth potential. His supposed revelation actually revives the very old idea that the Germans' talent lies in their ability to rework foreign elements, such that the result is "thoroughly German." But unlike such predecessors as Riemann, who identified this talent as the outcome of a German tradition of thorough musical training, Blume regards it as a sign of "the musical ability of the race" ("das musikalische Leistungsvermögen der Rasse").[88]

But what exactly constitutes this German race? This unresolved problem plunges Blume into a quagmire of contradictions. The problem of racial mixing, Blume admits, is particularly acute among the Germans: "The central position of Germany and the constant confrontations — in war and peace — of the Germanic and its environment have resulted in the continuous adoption of foreign musical values."[89] The ability to improve upon foreign models could be observed in other countries, but Blume resolves this apparent contradiction by identifying the populations of those countries as "Germanic." These include the English, the Flemish, the Dutch, and possibly the Italians ("partially Germanic-based").[90]

Yet how could such groups comprise a race? In the first few pages, Blume had clearly established the importance of drawing clear distinctions between what is meant by "race" and what is meant by Volk or nation. "Nordic" designated a race, whereas "Germanic" designated a Volk that could be subject to racial mixing. In the absence of either demonstrable racial traits or any pure race, how could Blume hope to derive racial elements from either Gregorian chant or the history of German reception? Even if he were to succeed in isolating "Germanic" talents, how could he automatically attribute these to a particular race? Would he not be ignoring his own warning against confusing race with Volk and nation? Blume ostensibly resolves this contradiction by resting his entire racial evidence on the flimsy supposition of Hans F. K. Günther that, even in circumstances of extensive racial mixing, Nordic features always come to the fore, like a dominant gene: "Since, according to H. F. K. Günther, the Germanic (*Germanentum*) is the predominating expression of the Nordic race, it may be regarded as [the equivalent of] the Nordic race within the historical limitations we have set for our understanding of the Germanic in music and therefore can apply to other peoples [i.e., Völker that are not Germanic but belong to the Nordic race] as well."[91]

Leaving that question open to debate, he then violates other taboos he had established at the beginning of the study. Having stated that it is absurd to look for racial traits in the works of a single composer, since, for example, Bach's *Musical Offering* and *Wachet auf* were so radically different from one another, he then locates certain historical exceptions, such as Buxtehude, in whose work one can find evidence of pure race. He declares, without any attempt at justification, that Buxtehude is "purely or almost purely of the Nordic race," and supports this with the fact that Bach was eager to study with him.[92] He even goes so far as to extrapolate on the "Nordic moments" in a single work, Bach's B-Minor Mass.[93] Also, after rejecting the idea that a style characteristic such as polyphony might be linked to a specific race, he nevertheless goes on to claim that the creative use of polyphony is unequivocally Nordic, and that the individuals of the Notre Dame school and the Franco-Flemish composers were Nordic and "of Germanic blood."[94]

In *Das Rasseproblem in der Musik*, Blume managed to appease both skeptics and advocates of racial research by simultaneously undermining the basic assumptions of prior attempts and applying those same assumptions to his own investigations. Blume avoided offending his readers by addressing the founders of the discipline with little more than gentle rebukes, paying obsequious respect to Eichenauer, Günther, and Clauß even when he disagreed with them.[95] In his final chapter, meant to be a summary of his findings and suggestions for the future role of musicology, he ignores all his earlier painstaking criticisms and emphasizes instead the Eichenauer-like suppositions that music reflects the racial soul as well as the physical race, and that modern society could develop a "racial feeling" (*Rassegefühl*) and cultivate it through education.[96]

Blume's book contained several pragmatic agendas for the future course of musicology in the Nazi state. His closing remarks conclude that racial research was the domain of natural scientists (biologists and psychologists), and "musicologists should not be measuring skulls."[97] He saw a solution for the racial problem in music as attainable only through the cooperation of all branches of musicology (perhaps this was the only tangible point he wished to make), and only by drafting a new "platform" for combined musicological disciplines will scholars gain new perspectives and ask new questions.[98] There was also a pragmatic element in Blume's persistent promotion of research on Gregorian chant as the key to an understanding of the race, despite the pitfalls he indicates elsewhere in the study. He was very likely aware of Himmler's special interest in Gregorian chant, and it is probably no coincidence that one of the studies in Blume's series on race, that of Jammers, was to be funded by the SS-"Ahnenerbe."

Blume's solution to the race problem was sufficiently vague and open-ended to permit further methodological inquiry. Wolfgang Boetticher's assessment of the racial aspects of music combines the promotion of interdisciplinary work with random anti-Semitic attacks. He suggests borrowing certain elements of both natural sciences and Geistesgeschichte, but he uses graphic biological metaphors to describe the phenomenon of degeneracy at the hands of Jewish-dominated salons.[99] Hans Engel also tried his hand at racial methodology, ignoring the warnings of Blume and Siegfried Günther by promoting somatic as well as psychological biological investigations of individual composers. Responding to the "outbreak of natural sciences in the Geisteswissenschaften," Engel suggests analyzing the physical, psychological, and musical attributes of individual composers to arrive at generalizations of national styles. Relying on the investigations of scientists who found links between body types and mental illnesses and relating these types to the temperaments of individual poets, he illustrates how, for example, Weber, Chopin, and Liszt all possessed similar physical constitutions and expressed a similar brand of Romanticism in their music. More important, Engel makes sure that the broader implications of his claims for the future of the discipline, for its "scientification," do not go unnoticed. He predicts that "in the future music research will no longer be able to limit itself to philology and history," since the "application of scientific psychological typology" will prove indispensable.[100]

The Düsseldorf meeting sent a message that musicologists were serious about the application of racial science and inspired more works on the topic. Aside from the publication of the Düsseldorf conference papers in periodicals and Blume's monograph series, the following years witnessed the output of a collection of essays edited by Guido Waldmann entitled *Race and Music* (*Rasse und Musik*), dedicated to the application of racial theories to music education and including contributions by Gotthold Frotscher, Richard Eichenauer, and Joseph Müller-Blattau. References to race pervaded larger-scale works in music history and folk music research to an unprecedented degree, but the term never received sufficient clarification or refinement, and its indiscriminate use, so harshly criticized in the 1920s, resumed. "Race" became a buzz word, thrown into any context as a political validation or as a foil to the reviewers in the Rosenberg Bureau. Even Johannes Wolf's subtle condemnation of racist policies published in the Festschrift for Peter Raabe is sprinkled with references to the importance of racial research, yet Wolf's message clearly criticized the extent to which racial hysteria had depleted musicological brain power in Germany.

The Düsseldorf conference, however, showed any astute observers that musicologists could not provide satisfactory answers to the racial question. Musicologists proved to be equally ineffective on the Jewish Question. For all the encouragement and attention it received, this area generally failed to capture the interest of musicologists, with only a few exceptions: Gerigk and Stengel's *Lexikon,* and Karl Blessinger's *Judentum und Musik,* a graphic and anecdotal polemic on the destructive influence of nineteenth-century Jews. A student of Sandberger, Blessinger received his doctorate in 1913 with a dissertation on the music of Ulm in the seventeenth century. In subsequent years he published articles on the crisis in modern music, entered the Nazi party in 1932, was named Extraordinarius in 1935 at the Staatliche Akademie der Tonkunst in Munich, and achieved the rank of Ordinarius at the Staatliche Hochschule für Musik in Munich in 1942.[101] His monograph on Judaism in music, entitled *Mendelssohn, Meyerbeer, Mahler: Three Chapters of Judaism in Music as a Key to the Music History of the Nineteenth Century* (*Mendelssohn, Meyerbeer, Mahler: Drei Kapitel Judentum in der Musik als Schlüssel zur Musikgeschichte des 19. Jahrhunderts*), appeared first in 1939 and was reissued in 1944 with the more Wagneresque title *Judaism and Music* (*Judentum und Musik*).

Following from Eichenauer's claim that it was only the nineteenth-century Jews who exerted a destructive influence, Blessinger focuses almost exclusively on the nineteenth century, despite the inconsistency of extending the positive racial traits of the Germans back into prehistoric times while limiting the Jewish racial destructiveness to the nineteenth century. The focus on Jewish composers of the nineteenth century by both Eichenauer and Blessinger obviously took its cue from the nineteenth-century phenomenon of racial anti-Semitism and the polemics of Richard Wagner.[102] Blessinger's vindictive tone, surpassing that of Wagner or Eichenauer, exploits colorful biological metaphors, but his approach makes no attempts to apply any earlier methods of the racial science in any systematic way. Blessinger labels the Jew as a "cultural parasite" that attacks its "host" in three stages: the "atomization" of European culture into small components that have lost their inner connection ("the Mendelssohn era"); the mixing of elements of various origins into a "colorful patchwork" ("the Meyerbeer era"); and the false posing of "Talmudic sophistry" as the highest achievement of Nordic philosophy in order to steer development toward Jewish goals ("the Mahler era"). The three main composers come to represent three distinct Jewish types: Mendelssohn is the "assimilation Jew," Meyerbeer the "unscrupulous business Jew" and Mahler the fanatic type of "Eastern Jewish rabbi."[103]

Blessinger's interpretation of nineteenth-century history essentially turns basic principles of the Enlightenment and Romanticism into Jewish plots. The French Revolution, according to Blessinger, gave Jews and Freemasons the opportunity to infiltrate aristocratic circles and to use the salon to enable Jewish women to employ a "tactic that was already typically Jewish in the Book of Esther" — using perverse eroticism to entice young men and influence their artistic tastes.[104] The following century saw the rise of the Singspiel, but Blessinger regards the lighter nature of the genre as an effect of Jewish behind-the-scenes manipulation, culminating in the success of Offenbach.[105] Blessinger points to the important role of the Jewish-dominated press in putting a positive spin on all new "Jewish" trends, thereby dictating the tastes of the public. He even insists that the New German School up to Wagner came under the influence of Jews, as indicated by their heavy dependence on program; that the emphasis on the genius of the individual served the advancement of Jews; and that the idea of art for its own sake was "of Talmudic origin."[106] He describes the final onslaught on German music in the Jew's use of the exotic to entice the public: the use of Eastern rhythms, jazz, quartal harmonies, and oriental scales (Mahler), along with such perversities as a fascination with hermaphrodites (in the films of "the Jew Chaplin" and the odd gestures of Jewish conductors) and the exhausting and narcotic effects of "Jewish rhythm" in jazz and dance music.[107]

Blessinger's book gave him an entree into the public lecture circuit and, like Eichenauer, won the him the acclaim of some musicologists by virtue of its uniqueness.[108] Despite Blessinger's momentary successes, however, no musicologists went on to develop a methodology for detecting "Jewishness" in music. The reluctance to take on the Jewish Question can be explained in a number of ways. First one could and did argue that thanks to Hitler the Jewish threat had been removed,[109] hence the discussion was outdated. Furthermore, attempts to define any race, including a Jewish race, proved impossible, and characterizing Jewish music was even more slippery, as Wagner had already discovered.[110] Adding to Wagner's *ad hominem* attacks on his Jewish contemporaries, Nazi propaganda (such as the "Degenerate Music" exhibit) blamed twentieth-century Jews for poisoning German culture by introducing dazzling virtuosity, superficiality, pseudo-intellectual charlatanism, and American degeneracy, thereby complicating any definition of Judaism in music. In order to describe what made music "Jewish," one would have to find common denominators in the works of Mendelssohn, Meyerbeer, Offenbach, Mahler, and Schoenberg; synagogue cantillation, Yiddish folk song, and American jazz, an impossible task even for the most imaginative propagandist.

Advances in German Folk Music Research

In contrast to the limitations of race and the Jewish Question, German folk music was a research area that held great promise for musicologists to meet the needs of the Nazi state. Relatively unexplored by music scholars, German folk music research allowed them to apply their skills toward pragmatic ends. Those who outlined the tasks, goals, and achievements of musicology in the new state all emphasized the importance of folk music. In his 1935 article "The Tasks of Musicology in the Third Reich," Rudolf Gerber stressed the importance of including folk music in Denkmäler editions and of making them available to the general public.[111] In "Tasks and Goals of German Musicology" (1938), Bücken expressed high hopes for future collaborations among comparative and historical musicologists on European folk music research and resulting publications that could meet the intellectual needs of the German community.[112]

German folk music was an attractive area of research for musicologists for a variety of reasons. First and foremost were the growing needs of newly formed amateur, military, and party organizations for everyday folk song repertoire. The folk music that musicologists made available might also influence the works of contemporary German composers. The establishment of a folk music department in the State Institute consolidated resources, facilitated research, and promised state support for musicological work in that area, in addition to incentives from the SS-"Ahnenerbe." Most of all, völkisch thought, incubating over the last several decades, had shaped a romantic image of the German Volk by indulging in the irrational and enjoyed its moment of glory with the rise of National Socialism. Consumed by pessimism and a burning desire for the German Volk to overthrow its perceived oppressors, this ideology sought solutions in metaphysical, spiritual, and racial venues, rather than in devising any pragmatic economic, political, or social programs.[113] Folk music was an important component in the irrational conception of the Volk. Folk songs, both real and invented, were a favorite preoccupation in the literature of German Romanticism and were long regarded as a symbol of German national identity and unity. A serious interest in German folk music would be a powerful signal that musicology could serve the spiritual needs of the German nation.

The scholarly study of folk song was not new, but for more than a century it had remained in the hands of linguists, who paid far more attention to text than to melody. The German Folk Song Archive in Freiburg, established in 1914, initially collected and organized vast numbers of folk songs in text form, without their melodies. Archive founder John Meier began to extend folk song research beyond the methodological limitations of German philology (*Germanistik*) and into the realm of folklore (*Volkskunde*). He proposed studying the objects more as part of a social system, relating folk songs to rituals, customs, and other sociological parameters, but he was still ill equipped to deal extensively with the music. A serious study of melody had to wait for the establishment of the Archive of German Folk Songs in Berlin in 1917 under the direction of Max Friedländer.[114] The growth of the Jugendmusikbewegung along with a widespread singing movement (*Singbewegung*) in the 1920s and 1930s fueled the interest in folk melodies, and the Berlin archive became active in collecting and organizing tunes into a comprehensive catalogue. Under Hans Mersmann's direction, the aims of the collection expanded, broadening the archive's definition of folk music to include music from these contemporary amateur movements.[115]

Up to 1933, folk music research had been concentrated in the hands of only a few musicologists in Berlin, but thereafter it caught the attention of musicologists from all branches of the discipline. A considerable number of historical musicologists, regardless of their areas of expertise, had many reasons to be attracted to folk music research. It was a politically relevant subject area but was less problematic and more accessible than, for example, the racial problem or the Jewish Question. It could be approached from a variety of angles: the positivistic gathering of data, the geistesgeschichtlich study of its history or relation to the history of art music, and even the treatment of folk music as a pure manifestation of the music of the Germanic race. There was also the potential for historical musicologists to apply their skills as editors in planned critical editions of German folk songs.

The motivations of trained music historians may have had some deeper emotional roots as well. Although their enthusiasm might initially give the impression of pure opportunism, exploiting a politically important and heavily funded research area, this was not always the case. By their own admissions, some of these musicologists felt frustration in their student days, constrained in their traditional historical training while witnessing the widespread impact of folk music on the amateur movement. Kurt Huber, in outlining his plans for the folk music division of the State Institute, designated the development of folk music research as the task of a new generation, one that was inspired by the Jugendmusikbewegung and eager to explore "national music research" when their time came.[116] As a member of that generation, Müller-Blattau confessed in the Reich Youth Leadership publication *Musik und Volk* that as a student of the "strict science" of historical musicology before World War I, he was baffled by the gap between scholarship and practice. His experience as a soldier reawakened in him the importance of communal singing of folk songs for building camaraderie, nostalgia, and patriotism. His generation, he observed, thereafter resolved to reform musicology, bridging the gap between scholarship and music making and raising folk music to a respectable subject worthy of study. The National Socialist revolution, he concluded, finally made this possible.[117]

Comparative musicologists also saw ways to channel their research toward a deeper understanding of German folk music. When the Acoustics Institute in Berlin was transformed from a division of the library to an institute within the university, Fritz Bose saw this as a great opportunity to exploit its sound recordings for musicological research, rather than continuing to use them mainly for phonetics studies. But he conceptualized the goals of the institute as not to gain an understanding of the music of exotic and primitive peoples, but rather to apply methods of comparative musicology to gain an understanding of the differences among Germanic tribes and the influence of race on folk music, tasks appropriate for "the altered orientation of scholarship in the National Socialist state."[118]

German folk song research was wide open for musicologists. Not only was the neglect of the "song" factor in the hands of Germanists an embarrassing lacuna, but their laborious classifications and dry analysis had alienated them from the "folk" factor as well. Philologists had engaged in pedantic debates over folk song authorship, reception, form, function, transformation, and the validity of nonrural songs as a subject of research. Two leading influential theories emerged in the 1920s: Meier's notion that folk songs were composed by educated musicians and were then adopted by the common people (*Kunstlied im Volksmund*), and Joseph Pommer's proposal that folk song originated with the folk and continued to live on in their practices. Julian von Pulikowski, a student of Lach, harshly criticized all such armchair analysis. He complained that scientific collection and analysis were meaningless unless one fostered an intimate relationship with the communities producing the music, such as Kodaly and Bartók had done.[119] Furthermore the exclusive focus on folk songs and their texts led scholars to overlook instrumental music and folk dance practices.

In the years that followed Hitler's seizure of power, a greater number of musicologists entered the arena, infusing the debates with a new fervor and energy inspired by völkisch thought. Their views appeared in a variety of specialist and nonspecialist publications. The central figure in promoting new approaches was Kurt Huber, who would serve as director of the folk music division in the State Institute from March 1937 to October 1938. Before his appointment, Huber was known for his passionate participation in the methodological debate, insisting on reforms in folk music research for the good of the nation. In a 1934 critique of current methods published in the *Deutsche Zeitschrift,* Huber blamed the influence of the Enlightenment and humanism for the perversion of Herder's goals of understanding the German Volk through its folk songs. According to Huber, the goal of folk music research was to reveal the "spirit of the German Volk" (*deutsche Volksseele*). Trained in psychology, he proposed a "psychological typology" of German folk music and folk dance that would broaden traditional categories, and the application of a geographic-statistical comparison as used in linguistics.[120]

Although these suggestions offered some feasible methodological recommendations, including a rather liberal interpretation of folk music that was not restricted to rural sources or to traditional geographic divisions, one cannot help noticing Huber's preference for the irrational, emotional, and anti-Enlightenment paths toward a true understanding of German folk song through true German methods. As with current thoughts on the racial soul, Huber's preoccupation with revealing the Volksseele as the ultimate goal of folk music research concentrates on the process of music making rather than on actual musical materials.

Huber revealed even more passionate conviction in a 1936 article appearing in *Deutsche Musikkultur,* where he stressed the need to make folk music research accessible to the public. His suggestion to create a network of regional folk music archives (*Landschaftsarchive*) was aimed at reacquainting German youth with their own folk music traditions, rather than continuing to provide them with the inaccurate, idealized folk song collections that had flooded the marketplace. Each archive would be run by a staff of musicologists, Germanists, and folklorists, all of whom would maintain close connections with the rural practitioners of "true" folk music, when possible, or with the youth movement, if nothing else existed in the region.[121]

Here Huber's conception of folk music had become much more conservative, falling back on the traditional geographic classifications of folk song he had rejected earlier and on the notion that "pure" folk music existed only in regions where urbanization had not destroyed its indigenous roots. Moreover the scholar, in his view, bore the primary responsibility of transmitting folk song in its purest forms and had to weed out all destructive, "parasitic" obscenities and sentimentalities (e.g., ballads, cabaret songs, and popular hits) from folk song collections and archives.[122] The system of regional archives formed the basis of his organizational plans when he assumed control of the institute's folk music division in 1937.[123]

The new breed of folk music researchers split off into two directions thereafter, one theoretical and one practical. One group continued the detailed methodological debates on the parameters for defining folk music, on classification, and on interpretation of findings. Discussions were prompted by the appearance of new studies by Pulikowski (*Geschichte des Begriffs Volkslied im musikalischen Schrifttum*, 1934), Mersmann (*Volkslied und Gegenwart*, 1937), and Danckert (*Das europäische Volkslied* and *Grundriss der Volksliedkunde*, both 1939).[124] The other group concerned itself with the practical application of folk music research toward educating and strengthening the German Volk. Because of their own involvement in musical activities, Frotscher (music consultant for the Reich Youth Leadership), Goslich (consultant in the Reich Music Chamber and the DAF), Ehmann (music director and liaison with state and party music activities at the University of Freiburg), and Quellmalz (Huber's successor) were most interested in "applied" folk music research, that is, involving musicologists in education and in the everyday music making of state, party, public, and private institutions. This latter group all understood folk music as an indigenous cultural product inextricably linked to the life and customs of the Volk and believed that dances as well as songs had to be understood in their sociological context and evaluated for what they could reveal about race and ideology.[125] Musicologists, educators, and state and party functionaries involved in music were responsible for guiding practice away from the degeneracy of popular music and toward music emanating from the true German Volkstum. The ever-growing number of amateur music groups, augmented by the creation of state, party, and military music organizations, justified a careful screening and supplying of new repertoire.[126]

What is striking in all of these discussions, both the theoretical and the practical, is a subtle shift in terminology. One increasingly refers to the developing field as "musical folklore" (*musikalische Volkskunde*) rather than folk song or folk music research (*Volksliedkunde, Volksliedforschung, Volksmusikforschung*). In some cases the preference can be attributed to a desire to distance the new musicological methods from those of earlier Germanist *Volksliedforscher*, who focused primarily on text and on source studies, and to apply the methods of folklore (Volkskunde) to music research and practice. A new, expressly musicological methodology was sought by drawing on traditional musicology (classic works from Forkel to Riemann which paid attention to "folk" music) or by developing a new sociological approach.[127] In the other contexts, however, musikalische Volkskunde clearly conveys the broader cultural-political responsibility of musicologists to strengthen German national consciousness by purifying its folk music repertoire,[128] a musikalische Volkskunde that is, in Huber's original conception, a revelation of the "Volk soul" through music. The preference for the term "musikaliche Volkskunde" may have also represented an effort to bring folk music research closer to the folklore discipline and its organizations and thereby maximize chances for research and funding opportunities, since the field of folklore was enjoying more special treatment from Himmler and Rosenberg than musicology was.[129]

The "Nazification" of Musicology?

Historians of German folklore scholarship have represented that field's concessions to Nazi ideology as an all-encompassing "nazification" of the discipline. Yet although musicology engaged in topics that the Nazis held dear, one cannot really speak of a wholesale nazification of musicology, certainly not to the same degree that folklore transformed itself. Even if musicological literature of the 1930s and 1940s reveals new, revived, or heightened interest in issues of race, anti-Semitism, or folk culture, a closer examination shows that not all these areas received the same treatment, and that the attractions did not all derive from one source, such as Nazi policy or ideology. The attention to racial methodology is perhaps the only trend that can be traced more or less directly to a recommendation from the government, since Goebbels reportedly suggested it as the central theme for the musicology conference in Düsseldorf.[130] Still, the engagement with race was inconclusive and never led to a bona fide research program, and the topic of Judaism received little if any serious attention. Folk music research, in contrast, was one of the few areas where serious engagement advanced both research and music practice. The reasons for such changes have less to do with specific doctrines of National Socialism, and more to do with broader developments in German intellectual history, involving the recent crises in methodology, the intensification of völkisch thought, curiosity regarding scientific methods, and fascination with the popularization of folk music.

Just as new research interests are not direct proof of nazification, the existence of political and racist rhetoric in contemporary writings of musicologists does not necessarily reveal a comprehensive brainwashing or nazification of the discipline. Such rhetoric was used indiscriminately, often in feeble attempts to lend credence to a particular position. For example, in the course of the 1930s, the Geistesgeschichte debate became so riddled with rhetoric that opposing positions were ultimately indistinguishable from one another. When

Werner Korte decided to attack Geistesgeschichte in 1935, he freely exploited anti-Semitic and anti-Weimar rhetoric. He blamed Gurlitt for moving musicology in a Geistesgeschichte direction, thereby exposing the discipline to the "dangers which were increased by the alien-race industriousness in the period of the inflation of the German spirit." This trend, however, was now "dead, dead for the new Reich," and musicology would henceforth dedicate itself to understanding the German "Volk and race."[131] Korte's renewed attack in 1938 similarly attributed the "fundamental errors" of Geistesgeschichte to the "not insignificant percentage of Jews" working in the area before 1933 and singled out Curt Sachs as the perpetrator of its Jewish intellectualisms.[132] Lorenz, too, attacked Geistesgeschichte as "the 'milieu' theory which arose in the liberal era."[133]

Political and anti-Semitic rhetoric could be used just as effectively to argue the opposing point of view. Siegfried Goslich used a model from Geistesgeschichte to envision the renewal of German culture under the guidance of the National Socialist state. Historical interpretation was a necessary step beyond the collection of material and production of editions of early music, and along with the "new life and new state" would come a new form of art that drew on the treasures of the past to gain insights into the essence of the German nation and race.[134] Goslich equated the role of musicology as a Geistesgeschichte with the National Socialist state's expectations of the discipline. Boetticher, proposing a middle ground, also exploited anti-Semitic rhetoric. He promoted a synthesis of natural science with certain elements of Geistesgeschichte for the study of race, but he rejected the idea of progress in history by attributing it to Curt Sachs (a popular target after his emigration) and ruled out the notion of "objective Geist" because it denied the element of personality in a musical work and because it was prominent in the writings of the Jew Heinrich Schenker.[135] Thus while individuals may have held a variety of positions, each claimed to have the blessing of the Nazi program.[136]

The turn toward German subject matter, although predating Hitler, was similarly distorted by political rhetoric and attributed to the National Socialist revolution. Gerber emphasized the need for musicology to become a "political" science, to forge a connection with the practicing musician, and to serve the general public by revealing to it the musical heritage of the German spirit. He praised musicology for taking on a "lofty cultural-political task" in exploring "German national character, the structure of the German soul in the products of its musical imagination" and the "tribal and racial idiosyncrasies found in German music history."[137] Friedrich Blume, in his contribution to the Hitler Festschrift, also noted the growing attention in musicological scholarship to German topics and to an understanding of the German musical essence and "persistent characteristics" of German music, and he designated the central task of musicology in the new Reich as the preservation of the German musical heritage.[138]

Political rhetoric in musicological writing cannot be attributed to Nazi publication guidelines or censorship, for criticism of such politically favored trends also found its way into print. In 1939, Wilibald Gurlitt, already ousted from his academic post in Freiburg, published a retrospective summary of musicological achievements of the preceding decade. Reduced in status and financial security, he apparently felt he had nothing to lose in drawing attention to the weaknesses of certain fashionable trends, regardless of their political usefulness. For instance, he had no qualms about pointing to the inconsistencies in Müller-Blattau's book *Germanisches Erbe in deutscher Tonkunst,* although he was aware of its illustrious sponsor, the SS-"Ahnenerbe," and its inclusion in the NS-Bibliographie. He cast further doubt on the recent urgency to discover Germanness in music, an element far more elusive than one might wish, despite the current "new significance" that the German question had been accorded. Gurlitt also cautioned that Eichenauer's work had not yet proven itself capable of drawing real parallels between racial categories and musical reality.[139] With regard to the folk music craze, Gurlitt remarked that "even if folk music research is justifiably taken on with such intensity today," it is "indeed not always to the advantage of furthering the depth of its scholarship."[140] Finally, Gurlitt saw no reason to purge the names of Jews or émigrés from his retrospective, mentioning the work of Hornbostel, Sachs, Hindemith, Schenker, Gradenwitz, and Geiringer.

Pro-Nazi rhetoric in musicological writings is not the result of editing or censorship, nor is it simply an attempt to flatter the powers that be. Rather it reveals varying degrees of opportunism mixed with genuine enthusiasm. Musicologists celebrated recent political developments that allowed them to pursue research that was meaningful to them, particularly in folk music and in the nature of German music. Government and party incentives aside, musicology reached this state of scholarship largely on its own. The methodological shifts that occurred after the war arose, on the one hand, from an intellectual malaise and an overall sense of crisis among intellectuals, and, on the other hand, from a sense of renewal and a need to articulate German musicology's mission. The perceived crises at the turn of the century, the intensifying debate over musicology's relationship to musicians and to the public, the appeal of presenting musicology as a serious science, and the establishment of new organizations and journals all inspired scholars to reassess the state of the discipline and map out its future. The less tangible forces of völkisch ideology, nostalgia, the desire to resurrect the German spirit from the ashes of the war, and a romantic fascination with folk culture, to which so many were attracted in their student days, beckoned them toward new directions previously off limits. Race studies had been constrained, justifiably, by the scientific rigor demanded by leading scholars of comparative musicology, and folk music research, largely the domain of linguists, had lain beyond the reaches of traditional musicology.

The new regime managed to locate some common ground between musicologists and Nazi ideologues. Nazi party and state functionaries channeled resources into the already growing area of German folk music, in the hope that scholars would enrich the repertoire of songs for use in schools, political functions, and the Wehrmacht. But this was only a small part of a grander mission to solidify national identity after World War I, calling on music historians and folk music experts to feed the public consciousness with reasons to be proud of and to preserve Germany's past and present musical strengths. Rather than generalizing this confluence of aims as musicology's wholesale conformity to Nazi ideology, one must keep in mind the intellectual, social, and political forces that had already been leading the field in these directions.

7

Attempts to Define "Germanness" in Music

By the late 1930s, proclamations of the primary tasks in musicology in the Nazi state pointed to the importance of understanding the German essence in music. Yet far from representing a break with the past, the subject of musical Germanness had preoccupied critics, composers, and musicians for more than two centuries. Although such attempts rarely yielded any conclusive results, musical commentators persisted in their search for the "German" in German music, always fearing that Germany's musical strength was about to fade into oblivion.

Following Germany's defeat in World War I, the interest in musical Germanness intensified and became the domain of musicologists. Not only was it necessary to rekindle German pride, it was crucial to recognize and drive out "destructive" cultural influences brought on by modern society. The political developments after 1933 encouraged musicologists to view the future of German music with greater optimism, but they came no closer to identifying what made it German. Despite energetic attempts to isolate tangible German musical traits through race research, comparative studies of folk music, regional studies, analysis of Gregorian chant, and close investigations of individual composers and their lives, musical Germanness remained elusive. Musicologists kept returning to conclusions reached over the past two centuries, such as the notion that German strength lay in the ability to adapt foreign models.

During World War II, Germany's territorial gains inspired musicologists, in a sense, to annex the musical achievements of subjugated countries and broaden the definition of German music and to increasingly portray developments in European music history as German accomplishments. Musicologists' contributions to this and other wartime propaganda often led to collaborative ventures with state and party agencies, but their interest in musical Germanness went far beyond mere Nazi-era career opportunism. Rather, it formed part of a long process, mapped out decades earlier, of vindicating German musical superiority.

Early Interests in Musical Germanness

The question of German peculiarities in composition can be traced at least to the end of the Thirty Years' War, when Athanasius Kircher attempted to describe German "tendencies" in composition (*Musurgia universalis,* 1650). In the first half of the eighteenth century the question of national differences in music emerged as a topic of lively discussion, especially in the new music periodicals appearing in Germany. Contemporary commentators were confused by the variety of German compositional practices and were frustrated by their inability to pin down German musical traits with the same ease that they could single out Italian, French, and Polish styles. Johann Adolf Scheibe, for example, could describe Italian music as having predominating melodies, often embellished, which overshadowed harmony; French music as "short and very natural" with clear rhythmic and metric articulation; and Polish music as happy and satirical. Scheibe observed that German music had mostly borrowed from foreign prototypes, but he nevertheless regarded German composers as having distinguished themselves by improving on these foreign models with their diligence, regularity of phrases, sensitive use of harmony, and, most important, "good taste." Scheibe went so far as to assert that "the so-called Italian music as we now know it in the works of our greatest German composers could even be of German origin."[1] His motivation was to encourage German composers to overthrow the blind admiration for destructive foreign influences, especially the Italian, and to recognize and cultivate their own, superior talents.[2]

Most eighteenth-century critics complained of the same problem: excessive admiration for foreign imports had led Germans to ignore their own musical accomplishments, and only foreigners fully appreciated German strengths.[3] Pinpointing Germanness in music, however, or even defining "German" music, was problematic: Germany's central location and its long history as a cultural crossroads made it one of the most cosmopolitan musical landscapes on the continent. This phenomenon probably accounted for Germany's musical strengths over the centuries, but it was also an obstacle to anyone hoping to isolate specifically German elements in the works of German composers.

The internationalism of German music became especially problematic in the course of the nineteenth century. Composers of German birth were singled out as giants in music history, but much of their acclaim was due to their composing in essentially non-German musical idioms. Most of Bach's works were based on French and Italian models, and Handel made his reputation as a composer of Italian operas and English oratorios. The same was true of Haydn and Mozart, Austrians inducted into the German pantheon, both of whom started out composing Italian operas. The symphonies, piano sonatas, and chamber music of the Viennese classicists were outgrowths of the works of Italian forerunners, and the classical style usually regarded as the hallmark of German musical achievement could be traced to Bohemian roots. Beethoven, considered to express musical Germanness in its purest form, modeled his only opera on the French rescue opera. Even after the legendary fall of Italian music and rise of German — or at least German-speaking — figures to the hegemonic position of Europe's musical giants by the nineteenth century, any distinguishable Germanness in music remained elusive, largely because of the continued receptivity of German composers to foreign compositional practices.

After Beethoven's death, many simply assumed that German musical greatness had peaked and now was on the verge of fading away: Beethoven exuded Germanness, regardless of what that meant, and now he was dead with no successors.[4] German musical life was perceived as vulnerable once again to foreign infiltration. Schumann, for instance, established the *Neue Zeitschrift für Musik* in 1834 partly to address his concerns over a decline of standards in German musical life. He expressed his frustration over the absence of a successor to Beethoven. He proposed to wage war against the degraded musical tastes of his country exhibited in the cult of the piano virtuoso, and he planned to use the journal to expose mediocrities in contemporary music, all of which were of foreign origin.[5]

At the same time, Germany's notable accomplishments in music played an important role in shaping national identity in the era leading up to unification in 1871, preoccupying philosophers and novelists, not to mention those directly involved in music.[6] Although musical commentators struggled to formulate a positive conception of musical Germanness, they nevertheless had faith that such a thing existed, and they feared its impending extinction at the hands of over-rated foreign imports. Wagner insisted that such threats loomed despite contemporary political developments leading toward German nationhood, and despite proclamations of German freedom, German spirit, German essence, and German nation. Wagner placed the blame on the German population itself.[7] Even in his most xenophobic digressions, namely his anti-Semitic polemics, Wagner never blamed the Jewish "outsiders" as perpetrators set on deliberately destroying German culture, but rather attributed their success to the inherent weakness of the German spirit. This needed to be corrected, Germans needed to become reacquainted with their own strengths, and, as eighteenth-century critics had also urged their countrymen, Germans needed to praise the creativity of their native artists.[8]

Wagner also perpetuated the notion that Germans were distinguished by their talent for reworking foreign models, but he extended that idea far beyond the boundaries of music. Germans, he claimed, had the ability to unlock the meaning of all foreign intellectual products, musical and nonmusical, and render them universal. He credited the Germans with elucidating for all others the writings of antiquity, the essence of Christianity, and non-German works of literature. He also regarded music as the ultimate refuge for preserving the German essence in the core of its expression, even when that music superficially emulated foreign habits, such as in the works of J. S. Bach. But when it came to defining this essence, Wagner was baffled. In 1878, thirteen years after drafting the original essay "What Is German?" ("Was ist deutsch?") and seven years after a unified German Reich had become a reality, Wagner added a postscript, admitting that he found the question to confuse him more and more and confessing: "I consider myself incapable of answering the question 'what is German.' "[9]

Music persisted in asserting itself as a central characteristic of the German nation, especially after World War I. For many Germans, the war had highlighted the cultural and spiritual differences between Germany and its enemies, as expressed in Thomas Mann's widely read *Reflections*. This refueled the desire to understand the depth of German character in order to contrast it with the perceived superficiality and spiritual poverty of Germany's enemies, especially the French. The military defeat additionally created a longing for a lost national pride and solidarity, and music making was imbued with supposed powers of healing the wounds of a split society and promoting feelings of camaraderie. The spread of amateur music making, the survival of an impressive number of state-funded musical institutions despite the war and inflation,[10] and the emphasis placed on music education through Kestenberg's reforms were all testimony to the importance of music to the German state and its citizens.

This postwar health of musical activity only reinforced the Germans' reputation as the "people of music," both at home and abroad. More than ever, music was coming across as Germany's most important cultural commodity, and musical talent came to be regarded as a distinguishing feature of the German nation. Understanding Germany's musical past and present, it was believed, could lead to a deeper understanding of the German character and help define the German nation. One needed only to reveal the secrets of what made the German so musical and to discover the "German" in German music.

The German Focus in Writings on Music after World War I

The most likely candidates to carry out this investigation were musicologists, but they were not very well prepared for the task. The question of Germanness in music had been a concern more among composers and critics than among musicologists. As musicology initially strove to be taken seriously and had sought a scholarly foundation, focusing its research on the philological treatment of early musical sources from all over Europe — not just Germany — scholars found themselves ill prepared to take on a question that had haunted the domains of criticism, literature, and philosophy.[11]

It was not until the aftermath of World War I that musicologists sharpened their focus on the history of German music and confronted the question of musical Germanness. A variety of factors brought them to this point: wartime travel restrictions had drawn their attention to their own musical resources out of necessity; contributing to German national pride and boosting morale in the postwar era gave them a way to meet the needs of society; and isolation from the international scholarly community fueled their feelings of nationalism. The major German scholarly organizations were founded immediately after the war on grounds of promoting German music scholars as well as work in German music, and the record of publications clearly indicates an ever-increasing engagement with German topics from 1918 to 1945 and a gradual acknowledgment of the Germanness question. At least in quantitative terms, a survey of the listings of works on music published annually in the *Jahrbuch der Musikbibliothek Peters* reveals a heightened concentration on German music history, especially in the 1930s. The tables of contents of the major scholarly journals yield even more striking statistics. The *Archiv für Musikwissenschaft* ran only from 1918 to 1925, but in those years at least half of its articles focused on German music history. In the *Zeitschrift für Musikwissenschaft,* there were usually at least 50 percent more studies on Germany than other studies in the volumes from 1920 to 1933.

Beyond German subject matter, however, musicology was initially somewhat reserved in tackling the problem of Germanness, addressing the question mainly in the context of general histories. In time, however, such studies presuming to be surveys of Western music came to resemble little more than epics of German musical self-realization. The earliest scholarly attempts to understand Germanness in the context of larger studies of the history of Western music generally defined German music by what it was not, that is, by distinguishing it from music thought to be typical of other nations. Hugo Riemann, in his *Music History Handbook (Handbuch der Musikgeschichte)*, concluded that German musical output could not be identified by specific musical characteristics but rather by a distinctly German approach to composition that involved the adoption and reworking of foreign elements.[12] The international exchange among musicians and the training of Germans abroad served to enrich German composition without detracting from its strengths, thanks to the North German tradition of organists and cantors, who were so isolated that they remained virtually untouched by the new trends that posed "the threatening danger that the healthy core of true German essence could be destroyed."[13]

After Riemann's death in 1919, as voices in the musicological community encouraged an isolationist attitude and more attention to German music history, the impetus to reinforce German identity and to mold an enviable image of German musical accomplishment increased. Riemann had determined that German music achieved a status of world hegemony only in the nineteenth century, following a long period of Italian domination, but scholars after him felt compelled to search for indications of consistent musical superiority stretching back into prehistoric times. Einstein attempted to trace a German musical spirit, finding hints of it in the "kernel of Nordic music feeling," in a musical "Germanic hegemony" within the Roman Empire, in the "Alemannic flowering" of the sequence, and in the "joy of harmonic consonance" dating back to the use of the lur among Germanic tribes before Caesar.[14]

Einstein acknowledged Germans' talent for reworking foreign models but presented it as a spiritual phenomenon rather than an outgrowth of a pedagogical tradition in Riemann's sense. Schütz, for example, warned against the danger of dilettantism in Italian monody while also "enthusiastically and contemplatively" taking on the new forms and trying "to melt them together with the spirit of the German language and with German introspection."[15] Einstein maintained that Franco-Flemish international musical hegemony managed to suppress national traditions in Spain and Italy, but not in Germany, where Konrad Paumann and Adam von Fulda had cultivated native organ music and vocal music, respectively. Then, while Italy gradually rose to prominence in the course of the sixteenth century, Germany was cultivating its "quietly blooming little garden" of secular vocal music.[16] Bach, above all, had the ability to nurture everything he touched to reach its ultimate greatness, growing "like a strong, healthy tree trunk, rich, sprawling, necessary for the branching-out of polyphony as well as for the most delicate branches and flowers of melody."[17] Haydn carried on this German greatness, his quartets and symphonies signifying "great deeds of the German spirit," and from the nineteenth century on, the popular choral music movement served as a barometer for the "musical health of a Volk totality."[18] Einstein's history taken as a whole pays much more attention to Germany than to any other country, striving to isolate a constant, immutable German spirit throughout music history, which reached its full expression in Germany's musical hegemony in the eighteenth and nineteenth centuries.

Another general survey weighted heavily toward the German component is Müller-Blattau's small 1932 volume for a pedagogical series ("Musiklehre— Musikerziehung"). Despite a title of *Introduction to Music History* (*Einführung in die Musikgeschichte*), it is essentially a history of German music with a focus on the relation between folk music and art music. Müller-Blattau concentrated on activities in Germany in each period of music history, giving relatively brief mention to developments in other countries. Looking at specific composers, or pairs or groups of composers that exhibit polarities, he compared Lasso with Palestrina, Praetorius with the "three Sch" composers (Schein, Scheidt, and Schütz), and Bach with Handel, and he isolated Haydn, Mozart, and Beethoven as the major representatives of three different periods. He then looked at Schubert and Wagner individually, and only in the last pages did he briefly consider the contributions of other countries.[19]

The wave of postwar nationalism called attention to the absence of a comprehensive musicological treatment of the history of German music. There were only a few attempts, such as Arnold Schering's forty-page summary of German music history for a general readership, published in 1917. This offered some sweeping generalizations about German feeling, passion, sincerity, thoroughness, and ties to folk music and education, but Schering intended to provide only an overview of musical events in German-speaking lands rather than an investigation into German music per se.[20] In response to the need for a scholarly history of German music, Hans Joachim Moser produced a three-volume study (*Geschichte der deutschen Musik,* published in the early 1920s). Hoping to arrive at positive conclusions about the Germanness of German music by looking at what it was, rather than what it was not, Moser focused on the compositions of secondary figures, or Kleinmeister. They were the ones, he believed, who appealed most to German audiences and whose music could offer better insight into Germanic taste and Germanic creativity.[21]

Moser's study sought to single out musical features as specifically German, particularly in the earlier chapters where he could afford to be more speculative because of sparse evidence. For example, in discussing medieval repertoire that would be unfamiliar to his readers, Moser can claim to demonstrate a Germanic preference for tonality and major mode.[22] He assumes certain features of early music to be typically German, such as the employment of a four-beat pattern with a strong downbeat (*Vierhebigkeitsprinzip*), a racial preference for bold leaps rather than timid step-wise motion,[23] a preference for tonality growing out of the Germanic use of the natural horn, and a harmonic conception of melody, a quality shared with Celts and Slavs.[24]

As Moser's survey progresses, however, he lapses into vague descriptions that are more poetic than technical. The stylistic features proposed as German in the earlier chapters soon unravel with contradictory evidence as he ventures into more familiar repertoire. He makes claims of German strengths in counterpoint and a decided weakness in song composition and recitative but disproves them by his own demonstration of Gluck's contrapuntal weakness, Handel's talent for writing vocal melody, and the undeniable prominence of lied composition as an explicitly German preoccupation. When describing the more familiar repertoire from the Baroque on, he resorts to such vague properties as "masculinity" (*Männlichkeit*) and "depth" (*Innigkeit*) as characteristics common to composers of various eras.[25]

Moser also escapes to the realms of mythology, religion, and sociology, offering a variety of aesthetic generalizations that can neither be proven nor disproved with musical evidence. He cites the importance of music in German folklore and mythology (e.g., the fact that the god Wotan is a musician); the central function of Hausmusik in German musical life as early as the fifteenth century; and a racial proclivity toward the "Gothic," as opposed to the "Renaissance" tendencies of the Italians, which embodied an irrepressible religious devotion that can be detected in all German masterpieces.[26] He also confidently points to the German talent for reworking foreign models, stressing the benefits of international exchange for helping Germans to unleash their creativity.[27]

Although many were impressed with Moser's thoroughness and recognized the importance of the monumental undertaking, his vagueness disappointed readers who had hoped that he would finally unlock the mystery of Germanness. He responded to his critics with an article intended to provide a more precise definition by comparing German music with that of the "greatest competitors *in musicis*," the French and Italians. Falling back on the comparative approach he had formerly rejected and describing musical Germanness in terms of what it was not, he attempted to illustrate in numerous descriptions (and no musical examples) that the Italians and French are satisfied with the superficial, while the Germans desire depth and substance. The coup de grace was a chart comparing the three nations according to nine criteria (major conception, major goal, mode of presentation, temperament type, worldview, attitude toward object, form of growth, form of cheerfulness, and musical-dramatic result), which only served to weaken his prior inconclusive conclusions.[28]

While trying to devise a positive description of German music, Moser's arguments harbor the contemporary sentiment that German music was close to extinction, an opinion already voiced by Wagner as well as Scheibe. Moser and his contemporaries elaborated on older fears while conjuring up new ones. They blamed bourgeois individualism and "art for art's sake" for creating an ever-increasing gulf between musicians and the public. These tendencies, for which Jews were regarded as partly accountable, were bound to poison a healthy German musical environment. Moser regarded Mendelssohn as a "unique product of the rare combination of foreign origins with cultivated traits of the German bourgeoisie" and his Jewish heritage as the reason for the lack of German passion and the trite use of rhythm and meter in his works. Moser refers to Leo Blech's "clever consciousness of his tribe" in knowing the limits of his talents, denigrates Mahler as a Jewish farce, and indulges in a farfetched anti-Semitic interpretation of the songs of Mahler, Schreker, and Schoenberg, linking them to Asia or Africa but not to Germany.[29]

With the exception of Moser, most of these pessimists were not the more serious scholars but generally music critics, composers, conductors, and some of the less academically engaged musicologists, who increasingly targeted such modern dangers as jazz and other American "grotesqueries," along with atonality, internationalism, and comparative musicology.[30] Composer Hans Pfitzner, who at the turn of the century had vehemently criticized Busoni's challenge to composers to explore new realms as a direct affront to German art, broadened his attacks in the 1920s to include "Bolshevist" atonality, the "jazz-fox-trot" craze of musical Americanism, and the omnipresence of Jewish internationalists.[31] The *Neue Zeitschrift für Musik,* under the editorship of Alfred Heuss, a musicologist by training and critic by profession, continued to fulfill Schumann's mission of preserving the integrity of German music but in the 1920s began attacking Jews, atonalists, and foreigners in the German music scene.[32] Peter Raabe issued a strong warning regarding the future of German music in a 1926 article entitled "German Musical Essence and German Manner" ("Deutsches Musikwesen und deutsche Art"). Although the title seemed to promise a definition of Germanness, Raabe merely complained that German character was in more danger than ever before. He was worried by the popularity of Negro dance bands to whose music Germans danced the Charleston and predicted that the next generation would be ashamed that their parents had acted like American apes. American films brainwashed Germans with grotesque humor, while German opera and theater languished. In words reminiscent of Wagner and Scheibe, Raabe wrote that he still believed that a strong German character could adopt and improve on foreign influences But instead, German character had revealed itself as weak and had raised the foreign to a higher stature than it deserved.[33]

In addition to Americanization and other foreign influences, several forces operating within Germany were perceived as threats to German culture: the working class, the amateur movement, technology, and materialism. According to Hermann Unger, true Germanness in music had finally emerged triumphantly in musical Romanticism, but this type of musical expression was being attacked as egotistical by advocates of folk culture.[34] He further denounced the contemporary "proletarian" and technological era as a cultural nadir. Standards had been lowered, anything foreign-sounding received praise, music was valued only for entertainment purposes and not for moral education, dilettantism had been elevated to the status of "folk art" and "art of the youth," and Germans had Americanized themselves by making art a dispensable commodity. Reiterating Wagner's conclusions, he suggested that Jews played a role in creating the current free-for-all. Nevertheless, he blamed German Christians for allowing Jews to finance and dominate cultural life and urged them to regain control of their culture.[35]

Musicologists on the Germanness Question after 1933

It was not until Hitler's rise to power that some of the more prominent musicologists expressed their views on the state of German music. Theirs was a more positive prognosis, and they loudly proclaimed their support for the political change and its relevance for music, music education, and music scholarship. Taking the cue from Moser's attempts to define musical Germanness in positive terms, musicologists in the Nazi state put a decidedly optimistic spin on the musical health of German culture and arrived at more assertive, if more vague, characterizations of musical Germanness. Immediately in 1933, Gurlitt and Fellerer hastened to offer encouraging words. Gurlitt paid homage to Hitler's proclamation of the duty to learn the essence of Germanness and rebuild the nation and society. This Germanness, Gurlitt claimed, was not to be sought in specific musical elements, but rather to be experienced as a broad, multifaceted musical phenomenon with a long history of variety and imagination.[36] Fellerer, for his part, emphasized the importance of Volkstum as the source of German musical strength and found it to be expressed most effortlessly in folk songs and best illustrated by the Horst Wessel Song.[37]

Full-length histories of German music did not necessarily pursue the Germanness question. A survey by Mersmann and another by Walther Berten paid little attention to it, while Otto Schumann's popularly oriented history turned its spotlight on the Jewish problem.[38] The Germanness question continued to prompt discussions of German diligence, talent for transforming borrowed models, and German harmonic proclivities (as distinguished from the French talent for rhythm and Italian talent for melody), but with a racial twist inspired by Eichenauer.[39] In addition, German music was observed to maintain an ever-present tie to the Volk throughout the ages, not simply in terms of borrowing from folk music but rather in being accessible to the public, despite pressures to explore virtuosity and experimentation at various times in music history.[40] Such an assertion may have run counter to the conservative assumptions of the critics who regretted the "lowering" of musical standards to appeal to amateurs, but it was symbiotic with the forces of the amateur movement that contributed to shaping Nazi music policy.[41] Elaborating on Moser's poetic generalizations, German music was further described as exhibiting Gothic features,[42] or as being obscure and complex, like the weather in Germany, but nevertheless meaningful to all Germans. This very obscurity, the fact that expressly German elements could be understood only by other Germans, was what made that music truly German.[43]

Ernst Bücken was the first to explore the Germanness question exclusively in expanded book form (*Deutsche Musikkunde,* published in 1935),[44] but despite his attempt to sharpen the focus of the discussion, he failed to reach any new conclusions. His opinions differ from earlier assertions only in their tone of confidence and defiance. He colors all aspects of developments in German music history as triumphant struggles of the German spirit and takes issue directly with Riemann's more equitable treatment of the music of other nations.[45] For example, Bücken presents the Germans' tendency to write in foreign idioms not as a manifestation of their openness and flexibility but rather as a response to a situation forced on them, out of which they emerged triumphant. Germans who wrote Italian opera were like "colonists" forbidden to speak their own language, but whose Germanness shone through particularly in death scenes and representations of nature. German composers, he concludes, never had their hearts set on imitation, even when they flocked to southern and western regions; instead they utilized such opportunities to become more conscious of their own German essence. Bücken also puts a positive spin on the fact that Germans were not known for inventing musical forms, seeing this as an advantage, for Germans were then free to allow their "form feeling" to turn non-German forms into German forms. German "creation," then, consists of a racial proclivity toward "rebellion against the forces of form."[46]

Bücken's assumptions are purely subjective, casting all alleged German tendencies in a positive light. Any musical tendencies, once established as creations of some descendent of Germanic racial stock, automatically excel beyond parallel tendencies in the hands of non-Germanic representatives. For example, once Bücken establishes that the Mannheim composers were German rather than Slavic, he can assert that the famous Mannheim crescendo was not a superficial sleight of hand (as he may have described it had he decided to designate them as Slavs), but rather an outbreak of their Dinaric folk temperament.[47] Such subjectivity succeeds only when one is preaching to the converted. In the end, Bücken fails to arrive at any generalizations of Germanness in music and, instead, closes with practical suggestions for rescuing German musical life from the degenerative influences of urban culture by enhancing music education.[48]

Thereafter, many studies simply accept musical Germanness as a given without defining it. Müller-Blattau's history of German music (*Geschichte der deutschen Musik,* 1938) assumes musical Germanness more or less as a given set of racial proclivities and as the ubiquitous drive to preserve folk song, culminating in the triumph of music for the Volk facilitated by the National Socialist state. Germans, for example, resisted the church by developing the "folk-like" sequence, they resisted feudalism when the cantors closed the social gap between art music and folk music, they responded to the invasion of foreign instrumental music and opera by incorporating folk melodies into their own instrumental and operatic creations, and they placed great importance on Hausmusik, choral singing, and music education.[49]

In Moser's abridged history of German music of the same year (*Kleine deutsche Musikgeschichte*),[50] the only features of Germanness mentioned are a greater attention to folk elements in German art music and the passionate depth of individual composers. But despite his frequent reliance on trite generalizations about German character, in his final pages Moser warns against the pitfalls he had encountered in both his lengthier *Geschichte der deutschen Musik* and the subsequent article responding to his critics. His brief comment on the essence of German music (under the promising chapter heading "Constant Characteristics of German Music") is an even broader generalization about the German approach to arts, not just music, concluding with a summation that hearkens back to the eighteenth-century diagnosis of "good taste" with Romantic overtones:

> We have little use for—indeed we scorn and despise—all that is licked smooth, flat beautification, cheap and understood by all; we seek *the* beauty, which does not reveal itself easily, which has been piously entombed and will only be experienced spiritually; a beauty from the soul, from the spirit, graced by virtue of an intellectual struggle, radiated from the world beyond, bedewed

by the supernatural; a chaste, secret, circuitous magnificence, not cheaply exposed, which can even border on ugliness under certain conditions, which distinguishes itself from common reality through the intricacy of its essence, through the elevation of its criteria. In art we do not desire the physical, but the metaphysical; not comfortable proximity, but the remote idea; not clever alertness, but the childlike dream; not the skillful sleight of hand of the faithless conjurer, but a bitter seriousness for ultimate meaning that remains in the form of artistic play.[51]

The shortcomings in these works did not go entirely unnoticed, but contemporary criticisms reveal some surprises about the general expectations from studies of Germanness. Walther Vetter, for instance, found the recent works of Bücken, Müller-Blattau, and Moser to be far too timid in addressing central ideological issues. Noting the increased interest in German music and admiring their efforts, he singles out problems common to all three: their confusion over whether Germanness is racial, geographic, or völkisch, and their insufficient attention to the Jewish Question. Vetter regards the essence of Germanness as a force that comes through when confronted with foreign challenges, and he would have liked to see more studies following Blessinger's model and demonstrating how German composers triumphantly drowned out Jewish voices.[52] Bücken, Müller-Blattau, and Moser are, in fact, surprisingly reticent on the Jewish Question, particularly in their works appearing *after* 1933. Moser even went so far in his 1938 *Kleine deutsche Musikgeschichte* as to redeem Mendelssohn and Joseph Joachim (his own godfather), reintegrating them into German music history and explaining their excision from the repertoire since 1933 as a matter of politics rather than a judgment of their contribution to German music. He was, however, in full agreement with the rejection of other Jews, regarding Mahler as the "father of atonality" and castigating Schoenberg and Bekker.[53]

Assumptions about Germanness continued to dominate large portions of the histories of Western music written thereafter by these same authors. Bücken's *Music of the Nations* (*Die Musik der Nationen*) barely got beyond the notions about musical Germanness he had presented in *Deutsche Musikkunde*. Because this was a general music history survey, he had to pay more attention to periods earlier than the nineteenth century than he had done in his other works, which only resulted in further breaches of logic and consistency.[54] Moser's *Lehrbuch der Musikgeschichte,* published by Max Hesse to replace Riemann's *Handbuch* as a rudimentary survey for musicology students, is also weighted toward Germanic accomplishment.[55] But having established himself as the pioneer in German music history, Moser could assume a more critical stance and even qualify some of his earlier generalizations. He offers quite a few warnings and disclaimers regarding many of the assumptions about the Nordic proclivity for major mode and polyphony, the importance of the lur, stylistic continuities in folk music over several centuries, and the inherent good and superiority of all traits identified as Nordic.[56] He also gives due acknowledgment to Jews, both composers and scholars, yet leaves their names out of his index. Such editorial quirks may reveal the author's concerns about censorship, particularly as fellow musicologists actively scrutinized such pedagogical literature for the Rosenberg Bureau. A reviewer might evaluate a book only by glancing at the table of contents, introduction, conclusion, and index. These would give the false impression that Moser focused on German music, relegated foreign music to one small chapter, and purged his text of non-Aryans.

Regional Studies, Folk Music, and the Discovery of German "Inventions"

The unsuccessful attempts to arrive at a definition of musical Germanness inevitably ran up against one fateful question: had there ever been a culturally coherent German nation, given the long history of fragmentation and disunity among the German states? One way of avoiding this question was to focus on studies of the musical traditions of individual regions and municipalities, ostensibly with the long-term goal of forming a composite picture of musical Pan-Germanness.

The 1925 Leipzig meeting, by dedicating an entire session to "Musikalische Landeskunde," signaled that regional studies should become a major focus of musicological work.[57] Regional studies bore many practical benefits. They enabled researchers to limit their studies to manageable proportions and a minimum of travel (an optimal situation for doctoral students with few resources) and to take advantage of so-called local patriotism by publicizing the field of musicology and by bringing musicologists in contact with local patrons and media.[58] The message of the 1925 meeting reverberated in the creation of organizations and editorial projects, including the Denkmäler der Musik in Pommern (1930), the Verein zur Pflege Pommerscher Musik (1932), the Arbeitsgemeinschaft für rheinische Musikgeschichte and the Arbeitsgemeinschaft zur Pflege und Forschung thüringischer Musik (1933), and the Denkmäler der Tonkunst in Württemberg (1933).[59] In addition, a new chapter of the DMG was founded in Frankfurt am Main, which pledged to deemphasize the scientific side of the society and promote interdisciplinary research on local history.[60] Ludwig Schiedermair later tried to attribute the cultivation of local music history research to the National Socialist revolution,[61] but this was a politically motivated exaggeration. In fact, the output of regional studies showed no substantial increase after 1933.[62]

While the musicological establishment encouraged regional studies in the 1920s as a means of understanding Pan-German music, Gustav Becking astutely questioned whether local music history was a valid historical problem or merely something which "grows out of the current interest in national types."[63] It was impossible to ignore the regional varieties that came under the name of German music, and these varieties only further inhibited arriving at any basis for a concept of German musical unity.[64] In his *Deutsche Musikkunde,* after hastily presenting some unsubstantiated examples of typical German rhythmic and melodic patterns and Nordic approaches to improvisation and form, Bücken concluded by stressing the importance of the countless regional variations. Carrying through his struggle metaphor, he asserted that the Volkstum expressed itself most forcefully in regions where it was most threatened, such as in border districts, and he focused somewhat more attention on those areas in examining regional variation.[65] Moser also encountered difficulties with the long-standing differences between the north and the south that resulted from religious wars, but he tried to see this in a positive light rather than as an obstacle to gaining a sense of German unity.[66] Albert Wellek's Habilitationsschrift of 1936 on the typology of musical talent among the Germans used methods of experimental psychology to acknowledge regional differences, in order to categorize them and refine them as a variety of manifestations of German talent. Gathering data from ear-training tests on subjects from different parts of the German-speaking area, he interpreted his findings as showing a pattern of "linear" music perception in the north and "polar" music perception in the south. These, he claimed, accounted for northern composers' tendencies to write "polyphonic" (contrapuntal) music and a homophonic inclination among the Vienna classicists, findings which could be further refined according to racial criteria.[67] In the end, however, the regional approach conveniently skirted the issue of defining Germanness in music and complicated it even more, revealing more variety than uniformity.

The quest for specific musical characteristics bearing the label of Germanness continued, with attention focused on the relatively new resources in folk music. The glorification of folk culture in nineteenth-century German literature had gradually led to a large-scale effort to collect and preserve folk music, and the fruits of these labors, housed in the folk music archives in Freiburg and Berlin, were a potential source for uncovering the mysteries of Germanness. It was assumed that folk music, unlike art music, was pure and sheltered from foreign influences, since scholars worked on the now discredited assumption that folk music was stagnant and therefore could represent the closest approx-

imation to some sort of "original" German music. On closer scrutiny, however, most of the specific musical gestures derived from folk music research
and proposed as uniquely German proved inconsistent. A legendary German
drive toward polyphony, love of counterpoint, and preference for tonality and
major mode were shown not to be exclusively German, were inherent in the
physics of musical sounds, or were contradicted by numerous counterexam-
ples in German music. Furthermore, as an oral tradition, folk music posed
serious obstacles in reconstructing musical Germanness as a constant throughout music history.

Folk music research had been the domain of a small number of comparative
musicologists, most notably Friedländer, Mersmann, Schneider, and Lach,
with a few others, such as Müller-Blattau, Schünemann, Fleischer, and Moser,
examining it as a historical subject or as a component of art music. It attracted
more attention as a research area after 1933 and sparked the interest of many
others trained in music history, including Fellerer, Huber, Ficker, Ehmann,
Frotscher, Vetter, Bücken, Danckert, Engel, and Goslich. Müller-Blattau's *Germanic Inheritance in German Composition* (*Germanisches Erbe in deutscher
Tonkunst*) was issued in two separate editions by the Reich Youth Leadership
and by the SS-"Ahnenerbe" in 1938, yet he had already established the groundwork for this study in 1926 and 1932.[68] As in the case of Moser's *Geschichte
der deutschen Musik,* however, Müller-Blattau is more successful at applying
his theories to lesser-known repertoires of early music. By relying on medieval
German texts, early English and Scandinavian musical sources, and German
examples of folk songs and children's songs, Müller-Blattau establishes a tem-
plate for Germanic melody, consisting of verses with four stresses and melodies
falling within a five-note range with a central tone of D or F (not to be confused
with major-minor tonality or with corresponding church modes). Müller-
Blattau designates this melodic outline, somewhat arbitrarily, as an "inheritance" (*Erbe*), passed down to the German Volk from its Germanic forebears
and tenaciously preserved in the songs and rituals of subsequent ages. He
proceeds to present examples of secular and liturgical song that fall into his
established pattern and, where relevant, to compare those to current-day vestiges in children's songs. But the consistency of his pattern begins to break
down as the Middle Ages come to a close. Müller-Blattau must concede that
the old patterns become harder to detect, and he must substitute them with
new ones. Folk music, he conjectures, probably preserved the "inheritance"
more faithfully, but no folk music sources from the seventeenth and eighteenth
centuries survived to support his theory. His new standard for Germanness,
derived necessarily from art music, is the ever-present bond between the composer and the Volk: Bach's reliance on Lutheran chorales and on secular folk

songs in his suites, variations, Passions, and cantatas; Handel's great success in composing popular oratorios; the use of authentic folk melodies in dance suites; and the use of theme and variation as a way of merging folk material into art compositions. All in all, however, Müller-Blattau concludes that the Germanic inheritance had fallen victim to foreign influences in the eighteenth century and had to wait for a grass-roots renewal in the song literature of the nineteenth century, in the Jugendmusikbewegung, and especially in the National Socialist Kampflieder.[69]

Folk music research drew special attention because of its potential to illuminate certain legends of German invention of tonality and polyphony. The elder scholar Oskar Fleischer, having lost some credibility after expounding on Gregorian chant as a source for the music of the Germanic race,[70] grew extreme in his convictions that the Germans invented tonality. In the tense climate of postwar international relations, he held fast to his belief in the musical superiority of the Germanic race and its invention of music as we know it. As a regular contributor to the noted völkisch monthly (*Die Sonne: Monatsschrift für nordische Weltanschauung und Lebensgestaltung,* alongside the racial theorist Hans F. K. Günther and the blood-and-soil ideologue, and later head of the SS Race and Resettlement Office, Richard Walther Darré), Fleischer denounced the Social Democratic nonsense of internationalism and asserted the superiority of German music. He maintained that 80 percent of the music heard throughout the world was German and not international, and that the German nation needed to shake off age-old assumptions that their ancestors were barbaric. Fleischer used the archeological evidence of the lur to demonstrate that the Germanic race must have invented diatonicism as well as polyphony, but he went one step further to assert that German folk music is overwhelmingly major: "Minor is a non-Germanic, weak mode, that does not correlate with our direct, powerful, upright nature. When we look at our folk music, it is almost exclusively in major, and—characteristically—from the first few beats one can usually recognize an almost military-sounding signal that could have been blown on the lur."[71]

Moser attempted to show more scientifically that tonality, or the "idea of major" (*Dur-Gedanke*), developed exclusively among the Germanic race in the folk music of the early Middle Ages, independently of the church modes. Referring to the writings of Houston Stewart Chamberlain, Moser designated the Germanic race (the Slavic, Germanic, and Celtic language groups) as uniform in physical appearance and exhibiting a nationalist ideology, revealed in the figures of Luther and Bismarck. This Germanic race was different from the peoples of the Mediterranean, characterized by physical diversity, "internationalist" drives (in the persons of Pope Innocent III and Napoleon), and "demographic chaos" (*Völkerchaos*). In musical terms: "that very struggle between church modes and popular-harmonic music is nothing other than that struggle between internationalism and nationalism, between communism and individualism, between demographic chaos and Germanness (Germanentum)."[72]

In the 1920s and 1930s, a number of interested parties put Fleischer's and Moser's assertions to the test. They scrutinized the folk music they associated with the Germanic or Nordic race, but all they found was a wide array of features that defied any convenient racial classification. In the early 1920s, the Icelandic researcher Jón Leifs attempted to locate the roots of the musical style of the Germanic race in Icelandic folk music, simultaneously drawing attention to his country as a potential source for understanding the Nordic race. Uncovering prominent features of Icelandic folk tunes that he considered to be "doubtless characteristics of primal Germanic masculinity,"[73] he declared Icelandic rhythmic features of freely changing meter and accent to bear a resemblance to the rhythms of Beethoven and Brahms. Furthermore, the pronounced preference in Icelandic music for singing in parallel fifths was echoed in the parallel motion of Brahms and Reger, albeit in thirds and sixths, which nevertheless can be a "representation of parallel fifths."[74] Ironically, Leifs seems to be most interested in demonstrating the ties between Icelandic "free tonality or atonality," observed in the scarcity of leading-tone and dominant functions, and Germanic "atonality," which held the key to progress[75] — ironic, since atonality would later be described as the Jewish "poison" that was destroying German music.

Similar comparative studies of Nordic folk music in the 1930s also failed to vindicate Fleischer's and Moser's theories. In his search for the oldest traces of Germanic folk music and early Nordic music, Werner Danckert examined folk songs from Scandinavia and the Swiss Alps but found no strong indications of tonality. Many of his examples exhibited chromaticism, a free use of the tritone, and a reliance on a pentatonic scale with no half steps. While rejecting the theory that the lur provided evidence of Germanic invention of polyphony, he did contend that music from the Alps and Iceland represented older Germanic music and the earliest evidence of polyphony, but in parallel fifths.[76]

The question of tonality received so much attention as to warrant a collection of musicological essays entitled *On the Tonality of German Folk Song* (*Zur Tonalität des deutschen Volksliedes*), edited by Wolfgang Stumme and Guido Waldmann and published by the Reich Youth Leadership in 1938. It is noteworthy that such a publication of fairly probing and technical discussions should find sponsorship by the youth organization. As the editors explain in the introduction, a problem had developed from misconceptions in the popular literature that only music in the major mode could be truly Germanic. This was prejudicing educators and youth group leaders against folk music harboring any hints of minor mode, leading to confusion in popular music practice over how to select pure, racially German folk music for performance. The editors warn that the essays will not answer any questions, but they will illuminate the difficulties in making connections between art and race.

Indeed, the essays in this collection show quite clearly the wide variety of conflicting opinions on how to deal with folk music, tonality, and race altogether. Opinions range from the purely racial biological approach in the first essay by the novice Fritz Metzler, to Kurt Huber's outright rejection of any attempts to correlate biological race with intellectual phenomena such as music. Metzler, who had recently explored this issue in his 1938 doctoral dissertation "Tonality and Melodic Structure of Nordic Folk Song,"[77] attempted to construct a racial map of the world according to the preferred scale types used by various cultures. Whereas Nordic folk music shows a preference for minor mode, church modes, and even chromaticism, German folk music remains steadfastly major and harmonic. Metzler attributes this difference to the fact that the Nordic race of Scandinavia is "long-skulled" (and prefers scales similar to those by other long-skulled races in Persia, India, and Arabia) and the Dinaric race populating most of Germany is "short skulled" (showing similarities to other short-skulled Mongoloid races in the preference for pentatonic scales and triadic melodies).[78]

Almost one-third of the work is given over to Metzler, followed by shorter contributions by better-known scholars who mostly contradict one another. Schünemann offered an evolutionary model, starting with the pentatonic features of fifteenth-century folk song, to the gradual influence of church modes on developing a seven-tone scale, to the influence of dances and instrumental music toward major-minor tonality, asserting that the ancient features can still be found in the outlying areas of the German world (Alsace, Lorraine, East Prussia, Upper Silesia, and in ethnic German enclaves).[79] Müller-Blattau and Frotscher both countered Schünemann with the inappropriateness of imposing art music criteria of church and major-minor modes on folk music, insisting instead that folk music must have its own criteria. Müller-Blattau insisted that folk music's strength comes from its resistance to exterior arbitrary rules, as evidenced by the unique features of the Horst Wessel Song.[80] Waldmann noted that despite the similarities between church modes and the music of ethnic Germans, these groups should nevertheless be regarded as cultivating the purest manifestations of Germanness by virtue of their struggles to fend off foreign influences.[81]

Huber's final statement alone lays bare the fundamental flaws of logic in the preceding excursions. First, he tackled the problem of his colleagues' misuse of historical evidence. Church modes were not rules but rather theoretical constructs designed to make sense out of current practice; pentatonic melodies existed throughout Northern Europe in both folk and liturgical repertoires, hence they represent no mode of "resistance" against any liturgical canon of seven-tone modes; and even though early German pentatonic melodies showed a preference for the intervals of the major and minor third and the fifth, this should not be misinterpreted as a precursor to tonality, since all tones are equal in this pentatonic practice. Huber then essentially attacked the entire racial approach in folk music analysis, rejecting attempts to compare early folk music practices with modern day practices and to ascribe their similarities to racial heredity. Later triadic features stemmed from the influence of instrumental dances and the use of horns, and the trend toward tonality was an outcome of the influence of art music. In conclusion, Huber pointed out the flaws of racial arguments in their attempts to relate intellectual developments in music with biological constants of race.[82]

Huber, who only a few years earlier had advocated a folk music research agenda to uncover the German "folk soul" and eliminate all undesirable elements from the folk music repertoire, had had the opportunity to observe, on the one hand, that in practice his warnings had gone too far, causing an aversion among practitioners to any folk music exhibiting the "un-German" or "Slavic" minor. On the other hand, he had witnessed how his colleagues had fumbled the task of clearing up the confusion because of their stubborn adherence to racial doctrine. One may even see in the obvious frustration expressed in this essay his first twinges of disillusionment with the racist and nationalist extremes fostered by the Nazi state. Huber's warnings probably fell on deaf ears, however. Walther Wiora praised the book in a review, highlighting the cooperative spirit motivating scientists to confront a practical problem and overlooking their obvious conflicts. Wiora molded the arguments into a consensus on the goals of folk music research and practice, goals not unlike those of Himmler's "Ahnenerbe": to record the disappearing remnants of "prehistoric and ancient" folk music among ethnic Germans; to analyze collected evidence toward achieving a better understanding of the origins of tonality and their meaning for race, nation, and region; to avoid the imposition of art music criteria on folk music analysis; to reconstruct the natural evolution of folk music toward tonality; and to recognize the strength of the Germans in their struggle with foreign influences and their ability to overcome them, adapt them, and make them truly German.[83]

To a lesser extent scholars also strove to credit the Germans with the invention of certain genres and repertoires of art music. This would have posed no problems had they restricted themselves to the incontestably German Minnesang and lied, but they probably would have considered these alone to underrepresent Germany's rich musical legacy. A comparison of the presentation of genres in Riemann's *Handbuch* and its successor—Moser's *Lehrbuch*—provides one example of how important this challenge had become. While Riemann focused on the lied and such small-form offshoots as Mendelssohn's *Lieder ohne Worte* as explicitly German innovations,[84] Moser gave far more credit to German ingenuity either by designating certain genres as German inventions or by failing to acknowledge non-German contributions. He focused on the German contribution to lute music and omitted any references to Spain, he presented the suite as Froberger's innovation, and he traced the roots of the lied back to monody but failed to acknowledge the existence of Italian monody.[85] He downplayed Bach's use of Italian styles and forms, and while acknowledging the Italian contribution to the development of sonata form, he nevertheless schematized its evolution as an idea introduced by Bach in his inventions and further developed by Haydn.[86]

Another potential source for defining Germanness was Gregorian chant. Blume had advocated chant as a fruitful subject for racial methodology, and Fellerer heeded these suggestion in a study of the development of Gregorian chant, seeking to derive racial musical traits from it and to demonstrate the ultimate victory of the Germanic version of chant over Roman practices.[87] Using the familiar metaphors of struggle and conquest, Fellerer describes how the German and Roman cultures confronted each other in the Frankish empire; how "the strength of Germanic musical feeling proved itself" by virtue of "recognition of its own racial approach" and set out to reform rather than adopt Roman practices;[88] and how the Germanic race ultimately created the version of Gregorian chant that was to prevail thereafter.[89] The Nordic proclivity for clearly articulated individual tones, syllabic text settings, and melodic leaps differed from the "Oriental" or Roman tendency toward the elision of tones, melismatic melody, and stepwise motion. These alleged racial differences came through in the varieties of notation (as demonstrated by Peter Wagner) and could still be observed in present-day singing styles.[90] Fellerer speculated that the Nordic preference for distinct pitches and the desire for organization led to advances in theory and laid the groundwork for tonality.[91] The study of chant held many strategic advantages, both political and intellectual. In addition to Himmler's reputed fascination with chant and the accompanying potential for research funding, the subject left itself wide open to bold speculations such as these because of the general lack of familiarity with medieval music and the difficulty in disproving such claims.

The Germanization of Composers: The Case of Handel

Following World War I, the writing of composer biographies for a general readership represented a sizable industry, with a number of ongoing music-biography series produced by several German publishing houses.[92] Yet despite the apparent popularity of such literature, musicologists were noticeably underrepresented as authors of biographers in these series until the 1930s. Biographical studies had for a time fallen out of favor among Geisteswissenschaftler as a manifestation of positivism. In 1920, Hermann Abert criticized the low standards to which biographies had fallen, and called for a serious scholarly approach that would draw on principles of Geistesgeschichte without entirely rejecting the glorification of genius.[93]

Abert's suggestions had some reverberations in the increasing attempts to popularize German composers of the past: perpetuating the mystical elements of genius, musicologists started to consider individual masters in a historical context and highlighted their bonds to the Volk. One motivation here was to reacquaint the German Volk with its lustrous musical legacy, in the hope that a greater appreciation of the masters would lure the public away from the dance halls. For instance, in a popular periodical for record enthusiasts Moser went to great lengths to demonstrate that the great German composers could harbor popular appeal, for "this is the German manner." This was an unabashed attempt to make these composers less intimidating to a musically uneducated public, drawing special attention to lesser-known works and recordings that could be enjoyed by all.[94] In the same vein, the Jugendmusikbewegung rediscovered Bach as a symbol of German greatness and love for education.[95] Musicologists tried to personalize his daunting and cerebral image by emphasizing Bach's relevance to the German nation and urging the public to incorporate his works into education and Hausmusik repertoire.[96]

The writing of book-length biographies soon regained importance for musicologists as a component of their duty as public educators, especially in the Third Reich. Ernst Bücken designated biographies as a "task dictated by the new times" and commented on their importance not only for scholarship but also for modern life.[97] Indeed, in the years following 1933, the output of biographical studies doubled, compared to the number produced in the Weimar Republic. More significantly, they showed a much higher contribution from trained musicologists as well as a decided emphasis on German masters. The increase was due in part to the launching of two new biographical series, both from the Athenaion Verlag in Potsdam. Great Masters of Music (Die grossen Meister der Musik), under the general editorship of Ernst Bücken, ran from 1932 to 1939 and produced volumes on Bach, Handel, Haydn, Mozart,

Beethoven, Schubert, Weber, Wagner, Bruckner, Reger, and Richard Strauss, and only one on a non-German — Verdi. Unsterbliche Tonkunst, under Herbert Gerigk's editorship, ran from 1936 to 1942 and published biographies of Schumann, Brahms, Gluck, Liszt, Lortzing, Johann Strauss, Hugo Wolf, and Pfitzner, a volume on Dvořák, which appeared after the annexation of the Sudetenland, and one on Grieg, which came out after the invasion of Norway.[98] Both Bücken and Gerigk relied almost exclusively on fellow musicologists to contribute to their series.[99] The opportunities offered by these new series, combined with the occurrence of several commemorative years for German masters, turned a few musicologists into biography "specialists" who churned out volumes on a wide range of composers. Contributors included Gerber, who wrote a book on Brahms and a book on Gluck, both for Herbert Gerigk's series; Korte (a Bach book for the NS-Kulturgemende, a Schumann book for Gerigk, and a Beethoven book); Müller-Blattau (Bach, Handel, Brahms, and Pfitzner); Vetter (Bach and Schubert); and Moser (Schütz, Bach, Handel, Gluck, Weber, and Schubert). Alfred Orel tended to concentrate his large output on composers who had a special significance for Austria (Beethoven, Brahms, Bruckner, Mozart, and Schubert).

Emphasizing the German character of these composers became the focus of many biographical studies, particularly when the subject was known for composing in non-German idioms (e.g., Mozart's Italian operas) or had an international reputation. Handel, who made his name as a composer of Italian operas and English oratorios and spent most of his life in England, was an especially perplexing specimen of a German composer, and the question of his Germanness had long challenged musicologists. Riemann and Johannes Wolf, whose general histories of music otherwise showed far less Germanocentric prejudice than other contemporary surveys, were intrigued by the challenge of isolating Handel's German essence. Riemann insisted on an unadulterable Germanness stemming from Handel's early musical training. Handel's sojourn in Italy allowed him to develop the Italian side of his style without affecting the "central German foundation of his vigorous genius," while the English choral tradition "corresponded to his natural inclination and his original German training."[100] Wolf similarly gave Handel special treatment. Throughout his *History of Music in Understandable Form* (*Geschichte der Musik in allgemeinverständlicher Form,* published originally in 1925), he consciously avoids Germanocentrism.[101] Yet after setting up a format of discussing eighteenth-century composers according to their places of activity rather than their countries of origin, he makes an exception for Handel. Wolf devotes his entire section on Germany to Handel, making special mention of his disciplined training and "German solidity."[102] The rest of Wolf's history, it should be noted, exercises sober objectivity, and despite the 1935 publication date of the third volume, Wolf pays as much attention to non-German musical developments as to the German and gives Jewish composers their due recognition.[103]

The Handel renaissance of the 1920s triggered the establishment of a Handel Society in 1925 and the *Händel-Jahrbuch* in 1928. While a few musicologists followed Abert's suggestions for a Geisteswissenschaft approach and painted a picture of Handel in more human proportions,[104] the Handel revival as a whole had overt political tones which transformed noticeably in the course of changing political circumstances. Although a central component of the movement was the revival and successful staging of the operas, more attention turned to the oratorios, which were also staged as full productions for the first time.[105] The intent of many Handel enthusiasts in the 1920s was to highlight the composer's importance as a populist and to focus almost exclusively on the oratorios. Their duty was to revive his forgotten oratorios, works which not only dignified the masses but would also meet the growing need for choral repertoire. Biographers like Leichtentritt attempted to offer insights on Handel's relevance for contemporary and future generations, seeing his works as a key to the desired liberation from Romanticism,[106] and Steglich promoted Handel's music as the most effective vehicle for building a sense of community.[107]

The fact that Handel spent most of his life away from his native country served as a useful allegory for the pessimism of the 1920s, warning that the sorry state of German musical culture might once again drive away its native sons. This led some to portray Handel as a frustrated German, alienated from his country by its unhealthy craze for foreign music, a situation comparable to present conditions. Steglich and others portrayed Handel's Germany in a state of national dissolution, lacking the sort of national musical consciousness that was so strong in Italy and England. They concluded that Handel could only be a true German outside Germany, and this allowed him to create a musical Germanness so fundamental that it outlived him.[108]

The comparisons between Handel's time and the present took on a more fervent tone after the National Socialist "revolution." Alfred Heuss, eager to express his enthusiasm over the Nazi takeover, chose not to wait for Handel's 250th birthday in 1935, when most other musicologists paid their homage, and instead commemorated the 175th anniversary of his death in 1934. Heuss announced with great enthusiasm that thanks to Hitler, Germany had finally achieved a state of Volk-totality similar to that of England in Handel's time and so was finally ready to appreciate the powerful meaning of the oratorios. Heuss infused Handel's works with contemporary political meanings. He interpreted passages from *Judas Maccabaeus* as representing the "cleansing" of all "unhealthy, destructive foreign elements" at home following a war, a path Germany should have followed in 1918 but, thankfully, had now seen fit to carry out in the purges of the first year under Hitler's leadership.[109] In another contrived parallel to National Socialist dogma, he wrote that Handel's use of anonymous soloists representing "the people" was a stand against the parliamentary system, allowing the people to speak directly rather than through "parliamentary mediators."[110] Julius Kopsch claimed that Hitler himself had pointed the way to a Handel revival in his speech at the Nuremberg Party Rally when he stated that the new Germany should revive old art works representative of German heroism rather than attempting to produce new, inferior ones. According to Kopsch, Handel's oratorios, such as *Judas Maccabaeus,* were the perfect means for motivating the masses on the scale that Hitler envisioned.[111] The notion that Germany was only now ready to fully appreciate Handel revealed itself over and over again in the commemorative year 1935 in articles by musicologists (Blume and Gerigk, for example), albeit in more moderate terms.[112]

The year 1935 celebrated not only Handel but Bach (also born in 1685) and Schütz (born in 1585), rendering the task of identifying Handel's German traits all the more crucial. The commemorative year brought to light the stark differences between the lives and works of Bach and Handel, and one had to demonstrate that, these differences notwithstanding, both composers were consummately German. The most common approach was to pair them as "two sides of the German essence," refining this with a genealogical analysis that accounted for their different "northern" and "southern" proclivities, which together cover the entire spectrum of the German race.[113] Previously, biographers had not attempted to derive Germanness from Handel's persona or his works and had proclaimed that no country — not England, Germany, or Italy — had the right to claim Handel as its own.[114] Now, however, musicologists scrutinized the details of Handel's life to uncover the slightest hints of a romantic conception of "German character": elements of struggle, heroism, masculinity, intellectual depth, passion, and didacticism. The perception that Handel struggled in a foreign environment figured significantly in proving his Germanness, giving rise to the explanation that although he could have acquired a prestigious position in Germany, he remained in England not out of a sense of well-being, but rather because leaving England would have meant abandoning the struggle.[115] The German side of Handel's personality was further alleged to reveal itself in his decisions to resolve conflicts in an open, manly confrontation rather than in intrigue; in his role as an educator who could elevate the tastes of the English public; and in such superficial details as his hearty appetite, his passionate temper, "private" quotes of German chorales in his late works, the German marginalia in the manuscript of his last oratorio, and his "loving bequests" to his German relatives.[116]

It was more crucial to determine the German essence of Handel's works, which scholars generously imbued with various signposts of Germanness. Many focused exclusively on the oratorios, ignoring or rejecting the Italian operas as "primitive aria bundles" that could no longer be appreciated in an era that had experienced Wagner's music dramas.[117] Most agreed that the oratorios showed Handel's German side best, revealing "Germanic sensitivity to nature," straightforwardness, monumentality, fighting nature, heroism, piety, and even "the high ethos of Nordic men" to seize and retain political power.[118] The predominantly homophonic texture made the works no less German (going by the theory that counterpoint was an expression of Germanness) but rather more accessible to the public. This refuted Edward Dent's outdated "sociological" interpretation that Handel never wrote for the people.[119] The dramatic elements of Handel's oratorios linked him to Goethe and Schiller and ultimately rendered him a model for Beethoven.[120]

Still, Handel's portrayal of a heroic Hebrew nation in the Old Testament oratorios posed problems. In the 1920s, Arnold Schering had dismissed any links between the subjects of these works and the "alien Jewish race,"[121] and Hermann Stephani had completely retexted *Judas Maccabaeus* as *Der Feldherr* in 1909.[122] Steglich had pointed out that earlier German translators had insisted on the "disturbing use" of words such as Jehovah, Alleluia, and Israel, even when Handel had not used them in the original, and suggested that such terms could easily be purged.[123] By 1935 all agreed Handel's heroic characterization of the Hebrew nation to be allegorical, representing either England (a concession to the Puritans' habit of comparing themselves to the "chosen people") or any idealized nation, conceivably even the "heroic ideal of struggling Nordic peoples."[124]

The Reich Music Chamber gave express permission to perform these works in their original setting, and the performance of oratorios received another significant vote of confidence from a high source when Alfred Rosenberg delivered a speech at the anniversary festivities at Handel's birthplace in Halle. Rosenberg's speech comes across as surprisingly tame, even bland, considering his other writings and activities. With regard to the Jewish nature of the oratorios, he stated only that "the Messiah of Judaism and 'The Messiah' of Georg Friedrich Handel have essentially nothing in common, as his contemporaries who called him 'the great heathen' must have noticed."[125] Rosenberg was evasive on the Jewish dilemma, talking only about the Messiah and not the numerous Old Testament settings, but his statements were interpreted as blanket approval for performing all Handel oratorios, even those that seemed to glorify the Jews.[126]

Handel and the Second World War

Rosenberg's speech barely mentioned Handel's Germanness, and, in the presence of English representatives, he proposed that England and Germany should consider Handel their common property.[127] This congeniality evaporated four years later when England entered the war. Thereafter, Handel studies adopted the mission of denying Handel's affinity to England and rejecting English claims to him. As early as 1925, Handel's draw to England had been explained by a racial affinity or "tribal kinship" between the German and English peoples,[128] but the suggestion that Handel might have felt more English than German became increasingly unpopular. Although Müller-Blattau had indicated that Handel became an English citizen in his biography of 1933, later accounts either ignored or flatly denied it.[129]

The "de-Anglicization" of Handel received special attention in 1941. An issue of the Hitler Youth journal *Musik in Jugend und Volk* dedicated to Handel encouraged amateur performance of his works and demanded unconditionally that he be considered nothing but German. Opening with the phrase from Rosenberg's speech naming Handel the "Viking of music," the issue included excerpts from Johann Adam Hiller's Handel essay of 1784, a performance-oriented analysis by Rudolf Steglich of choral passages from the oratorios, a refutation of the Old Testament connection by Richard Eichenauer, and two items by Gotthold Frotscher (currently serving as general editor of the journal), which offer suppositions that Handel never felt at home in England.[130]

Frotscher announced that although the English presumed to claim Handel as their own, there was evidence in Handel's "life and suffering" proving "that these claims are nothing more than English rumors." Frotscher asserted Handel was hoodwinked by English publishers and impresarios, yet Handel managed to create his loftiest works despite this sullied atmosphere; that English audiences were more interested in the singers than in his works and turned against him when he failed to cater to their tastes; that English librettists provided him with inferior texts and never appreciated his talent; and that during all his years in England Handel never mastered the English language, although he had become fluent in Italian during a much shorter sojourn. Frotscher concludes: "Handel neither became English in England, nor did he become one of the greatest composers of his time and all time because of

England; rather much more in spite of England and in confrontation with the English."[131]

Moser's 1941 Handel biography also set out to de-Anglicize the composer. Moser tried to downplay Handel's decision to go to England, proposing that he went only as a "musical ambassador" of Kurfürstin Sophie, who hoped to secure the English throne for her son George. Moser applauded Edward Dent's "nationalist conviction" that Purcell rather than Handel was the quintessential English composer.[132] He also now regarded the oratorios as problematic not only for their Jewish content but also for their implicit praise of English imperialism.[133] In an unpublished essay written around 1943, Moser further claimed that what appeared as an English influence on Handel could actually have been Handel's influence on musical styles later identified as English, noting that "Rule Britannia" and "God Save the King" were the creations of two of Handel's pupils.[134]

The de-Anglicization of Handel was part of a grander wartime propaganda scheme to weaken the image of the enemy during the war. Musicologists contributed by subjecting the music history of the English to much poetic license and selectively dredging up evidence of cultural depravity and weakness. In a 1939 article "England's Racial Decline as Reflected in Its Music," Blessinger reassured his readers that the final measure of a nation's strength was not the momentary effectiveness of its power apparatus, but the longer history of its cultural integrity. He proceeded to demonstrate that England's "inner weakness" resulted from its openness to various racial influences. England's cultural decline came as a result of the destruction of "Merry Old England" (during the reign of James II) and led to a fascination with virtuosity, an overall dilettantism, and the popular cynicism exemplified by *The Beggar's Opera*, leaving England's musical life vulnerable to the invasion and rapid takeover of the "eternal Jew" and the "contamination of the musical daily fare" with jazz.[135]

Fellerer also alluded to the racial composition of the English as the basis for understanding their music history and for contrasting them with Germans. Whereas the Germans always maintained their Germanness despite foreign influences and never ceased to produce musical giants, the English could boast relatively few great names.[136] Even the English musicologist Edward Dent recognized a decline after Purcell, and Fellerer determined that Dent's notion of an English renaissance in 1880 was little more than an imitation of German Romanticism colored by a "not insubstantial" Jewish influence.[137] Finally, Moser's 1943 essay characterized musical taste in nineteenth-century England by a desire to be Germanic, demonstrated by the popularity of Beethoven and Goethe. Indeed, the influx of German musicians was so strong that sometimes

Jews were mistakenly welcomed as Germans (e.g., Joachim and Moscheles). Moser also criticized the superficiality of the English public, who aspired to being trendy and "smart" (Moser uses the English word) but were actually "strongly influenced by Negroes" (*stark vernegert*) and exercised no independent judgment or understanding of art music.[138]

The renewed interest in Handel in 1941 shed new light on the question of "dejudaizing" the oratorios, a question that weighed more heavily as Jews increasingly became objects of derision in Germany. Studies of German popular opinion have shown that although the *Kristallnacht* pogrom in November 1938 prompted initial outrage, especially among the educated, the German population generally remained passive to subsequent acts of terror against the Jews, opposing anti-Jewish policy only when it threatened to turn Jews into martyrs or to incite anti-German repercussions abroad, and successfully castigating Jews from German society.[139] Thus despite Rosenberg's reticence on the Jewish content in Handel's oratorios and the Music Chamber's sanctioning of their performance, Eichenauer's contribution to the same 1941 issue of *Musik in Jugend und Volk* shows that he and others were uncomfortable singing the praises of the Hebrews while internalizing the belief that the Jews were the enemy.[140] How, he complains, can one continue to rejoice in David's slaying of Goliath, when every Hitler Youth member has learned that the Philistines are racial kin to the Germans? The only solution was to rewrite the texts in the manner of recent *Judas Maccabaeus* revisions: *Freiheitsoratorium, Der Feldherr,* and *Wilhelmus von Nassauen*.[141] Moser, too, had some good things to say about this last reworking in his 1941 biography and reservedly encouraged careful revisions of the texts for the time being, but he hoped that once "we Germans have the Jewish problem far behind us," the original versions could be revived as something "exotic" and "ancient."[142]

Wartime Expansion and the New Definition of "German"

The wartime annexations and occupations had the unexpected effect of inspiring musicologists to broaden their definition of German music as the boundaries of the Reich expanded. A survey of musicological literature from 1938 through the end of the war shows a distinct pattern of heightened interest in the music history of territories recently annexed or occupied by German troops. This literature closely followed the military advances, momentarily focusing on the musical history of areas of the future Reich in an effort to demonstrate that German musicians had for centuries exerted a profound influence on them. Musicologists, inspired by the doctrine of *Lebensraum,* furnished a musicological justification for the concurrent military advances while greatly expanding their definition of German music to include most of Europe.[143]

In earlier literature there was a tendency to adopt certain groups or individuals as Germans. Einstein, for example, duly assigned "uncontested world dominance" of music to the Netherlands up to the middle of the fifteenth century, but he defined "Niederländer" to include northern French, Flemish, and Germans.[144] Bücken similarly observed the center of musical development during the Renaissance as moving north, to the "Germanic peoples — English, Dutch, German, Scandinavian," and he traced Dunstable's progress toward "the consummate breakthrough of an indigenous Nordic musical feeling through the art music style of the continent."[145] The interest in racial studies further inspired attempts to trace the genealogy of such composers as Franz Liszt and César Franck[146] in order to demonstrate their German blood-ties, and to declare that Berlioz, "blond and blue-eyed — a rare combination for his home in southern France," was certainly spiritually, if not physically, German.[147]

During the war, this practice spread to the music histories and folk music studies of annexed or occupied countries. Tracing a German presence in the music of these areas allowed for claims that some countries never had an indigenous musical culture but merely flaunted a cheap imitation of the German product, or that the masters credited with musical advancements were German-trained or even "racially" German. Musicologists also looked hopefully to folk music as a source for demonstrating Germany's musical influence in various regions.[148] Danckert, Wiora, and Frotscher all looked for the influence of German folk melodies in Bohemia-Moravia; Scandinavia; the Baltic, Slavic, and Hungarian regions; and Poland at the same time these regions became a focus of Germany's military aims.[149]

The annexation of Austria and the German-populated areas of Czechoslovakia had a special significance. If Germany could claim Austrian and Bohemian musical heritage as its own, one could dispel any speculations that the classical style was anything but German in origin. Robert Lach, who had advocated the political unity of Austria and Germany as early as 1930, rejoiced in the events of the Anschluss in 1938.[150] Simultaneously, a number of his Reich-German colleagues traced the musical unity of the two countries farther than he had dared attempt.[151] Gerber asserted that Austrian music was in fact the most German: first because its geographical situation on the borders of Germandom posed a constant need to ward off foreign influences; and second because the German spirit managed to persist and flower in the classical period, despite the Hapsburg taste for foreign culture and despite the domination of "international Judaism" later represented by "the Czech ghetto-Jew Gustav Mahler."[152]

The musicological Lebensraum campaign continued in full force thereafter. Once Germany annexed the Sudetenland in September 1938 and advanced on the rest of Czechoslovakia early in 1939, German musicologists celebrated the events with timely expressions of their approval, welcoming the "brother tribe . . . into our hearts" and into "the new, greater homeland," along with the musically "less productive" Czechs.[153] With Bohemia and Moravia under German control, musicologists could claim the past musical achievements of these regions as German property. Aware that some of the best-known composers of the late seventeenth and eighteenth centuries had Bohemian origins or were at least exposed to Czech folk music, historians now had to eliminate any subversive notions of Czech influences on the great masters and to emphasize the German nature of the classical style. A campaign ensued to prove the German cultural and familial roots of such figures as Biber, Dittersdorf, Stamitz, Gassmann, Wagenseil, and many others who might otherwise be identified as Czech, claiming that the names of many true Germans had been slavicized.[154] Karl Michael Komma, Besseler's Sudeten-German protégé, classified Germans as the true creators and Czechs as the virtuosi, despite "crude falsifications" spread by Czech and Jewish authors.[155]

The pattern of musicological literature appearing in response to military advances continued, but with much more attention to the eastern areas of occupation. The penetration of the East, the targeted area of German expansion and Lebensraum, prompted a few musicologists to offer practical suggestions for its musical Germanization and inspired many more to support the effort with their quasi-scholarly investigations into German influence on musical culture. When Germany tried to reclaim Danzig in March 1939, musicologists immediately showed a growing interest in the city and asserted Germany's historical rights to it, and while Germany prepared for the attack on Poland in April 1939 and overran it swiftly in the following September, musicologists highlighted Germany's musical presence there and questioned whether an indigenous Polish musical culture had ever existed.[156] In contrast, when German troops advanced on Norway, Belgium, and Holland in 1940, only a few musicologists acknowledged the event with music-historical justifications.[157] Fellerer's Grieg biography appeared in 1942 as part of the Unsterbliche Tonkunst series and emphasized his importance as a Nordic composer, and the Propaganda Ministry commissioned Gerigk to write a book on Sibelius on the strength of its potential to help reinforce the cultural ties between Germany and Finland.[158]

The expanding definition of German music that accompanied the expansion of the Reich culminated in a collection of essays that was never published, provisionally entitled *German Music and Its Neighbors* (*Die deutsche Musik und ihre Nachbarn*) and compiled around 1943.[159] Heinz Drewes took credit for the project, oversaw it under the aegis of his Reichsstelle für Musikbearbeitungen, and appointed Moser as general editor. The purpose of the work was to demonstrate Germany's profound influence on the musical cultures of its neighbors, all of whom were currently under German occupation or allied with Germany. Individual contributions covered Germany's music-historical ties with Flanders and Holland (both essays by Fellerer), Hungary, Denmark, Yugoslavia, France, Czechoslovakia, and Italy. The last of these is an incomplete essay by Hans Engel, which contains much of the same material as his 1944 book, *Germany and Italy in Their Music-Historical Relationships* (*Deutschland und Italien in ihren musikgeschichtlichen Beziehungen*).[160] With the exception of the Italian essay, all contributions either treat the neighboring populations as essentially Germanic (Flanders, Holland, and Denmark) or propose that neighbors claiming to have cultivated indigenous musical culture often possessed nothing more than a cheap imitation of German music (Hungary, Czechoslovakia, and France).

This collection brought the genre of musicological justification of foreign policy and military expansion to new heights. First, it filled in several geographical gaps in the literature, with Reinhold Zimmermann's essay on France, Fellerer's essays on Belgium and Holland, Bernhard Engelke's essay on Denmark, as well as an essay on Hungary and one on Yugoslavia. Moser's introduction also includes somewhat shorter but nevertheless substantial discussions of Spain, Portugal, and the Baltic states. The work thus makes a much broader claim of German musical influence throughout Europe than earlier literature had.

Second, the collection is unique in that all of the essays, with the exception of Engel's careful treatment of Italy, argue Germany's musical superiority in much stronger terms than before and make more references to alleged improvements in musical life since the German occupation, implicitly looking forward to institutionalizing German musical life in occupied territories. Fellerer heartily endorsed the recent German occupation of Holland, referring euphemistically to the increase in the "reception" of German music since 1940, further solidifying a "Germanic cultural unit."[161] Similarly, the unnamed author of the essay on Yugoslavia noted a "strong proliferation of German concert activity" since the occupation by German troops in 1941, which was "winning over many grateful friends of German music."[162] Reinhold Zimmermann's ruthless attack on "so-called" French musical culture closed with a particularly pernicious euphemistic commentary on the fate of French Jewry, describing how the German occupation of France in 1940 "aggressively held back" the spread of the "Jewish musical spirit," giving way to a thriving cultivation of German music.[163]

The concentrated effort to define Germanness yielded vast amounts of material and a painstakingly thorough knowledge of the history of music in Germany, but it brought no one closer to an understanding of what made German music German. As early as 1924, musicologist Gustav Becking had warned that any national approach to music would be problematic and suggested approaching European music history as a whole. But while Becking carefully outlined the shortcomings of a national approach, he also recognized that the desire to determine national characteristics was more prominent in Germany than elsewhere in Europe. He attributed this to Germany's precarious global situation in which Germans experienced the shock of "not being understood and not understanding" and were determined to clarify their own "opaque and cryptic" national type and to write history as if it were a realization of national will.[164]

The need to restore national pride intensified after World War I, but the desire to find a common denominator for the ever-growing, multifaceted population designated as "German" preoccupied thinkers long before German unification in 1871 and merely increased in the course of World War II, extending beyond the borders of the Reich into Austria, Czechoslovakia, Poland, Hungary, even France. Wagner had thrown up his hands in 1878 by admitting: "I have come up against this question with more and more confusion . . . it is impossible to answer."[165] No one before or after Wagner had any more success in determining "what is German" in German music, perhaps because the real question that concerned music critics and musicologists transcended musical style and ran up against the deeply rooted historical difficulties of defining the German nation. At the crossroads of Europe, Germany had been a receptor to outside influences from all directions. Political upheavals beginning with the Thirty Years' War successively unified and rent asunder the plurality of self-governing units, while German-speaking rulers built up rich musical entourages. After a time, German strength in the cultivation and proliferation of music and ideas about music may have developed to the point where musical prodigiousness was one of the few things that all German-speaking people had in common, whether or not they knew it.

Eventually musical strength came to define an otherwise obscure concept of Germanness better than anything else, and as such music came to be jealously guarded as the core of the German nation. The slightest incursions of new musical ideas from the outside, at one time eagerly integrated into the creations of German musicians, came to be regarded as threats to German musical supremacy and, therefore, threats to the one tangible element holding the patchwork German nation together. This may help to explain why for two centuries the Germanness question was posed under the imagined threat of German musical decline and foreign takeover and with a warning to German composers to put their talents to better use. Undertones of paranoia, defensiveness, and warnings to German composers of impending doom resounded as strongly in the words of Moser and Raabe as in the words of Scheibe, Mattheson, Schumann, and Wagner.

The enormous responsibility of describing German character by describing German music may also explain why so many commentators avoided pinpointing specific musical traits as German. When it came to defining musical Germanness, few could venture beyond vague approximations. The emphasis on regional studies, encouraged by the musicological community for reasons of practicality and for their contribution to an understanding of Germanness, was nothing more than a refuge from the Germanness question, bringing to light regional discrepancies throughout the German lands while dodging the question of Pan-German consistencies. Folk music, perceived as a pure manifestation of a culture's natural musical inclinations, received attention as potentially harboring definite German musical traits, as did the new and fashionable racial approach, the renewal of biographies, and other genre and period studies, but none came any closer to isolating common denominators of musical Germanness over the ages. As military gains increased in World War II, musicologists searching for evidence of a German presence in the music of occupied countries in effect watered down the definition of German music to encompass all of European music.

There can be little doubt that musicologists' contributions to wartime propaganda led directly to opportunities to work with government and party agencies. Many individuals who established a theoretical foundation for a Germanization policy in their writings went on to serve as expert consultants. Among those who contributed generously to the Lebensraum literature, Schünemann, Frotscher, and Moser were entrusted with lecture tours in Holland, Switzerland, and Poland; and Müller-Blattau, Moser, and Engel benefited from SS, Propaganda Ministry, and Hitler Youth sponsorship for their publications. The Rosenberg Bureau enlisted Gerber, Danckert, and Blessinger as ideological consultants; involved Gerber, Danckert, and Fellerer in plans for the Hohe Schule; and commissioned Gerber, Fellerer, and Schünemann to participate in the Sonderstab Musik. Musicology's visible contribution to addressing the questions of Germanness in music and to wartime propaganda thus not only rationalized its scholarly pursuits, it also opened up opportunities outside the university and helped to sustain the discipline through Germany's economic, political, and ideological upheavals between the two world wars.

But it would be far too facile to dismiss this phenomenon as pure opportunism, especially after examining the long history of the search for Germanness in music that predated the Third Reich. Musicologists undoubtedly had come to believe that their subject matter—German music—was one of the most valuable possessions of the German people, and this conviction must have struck a sympathetic chord with the Nazi authorities. One of the primary goals of the Nazi state was the restoration of German national pride after the defeat in World War I. Any rehabilitation of the German self-image would have been unthinkable without drawing attention to Germany's long history of musical achievements, and this was a task tailor-made for the musicologist.

8

Denazification and the German Musicological Legacy

The Allied program of denazification that followed World War II set out to remove all vestiges of Nazism from German society. Under such circumstances, musicologists felt compelled to downplay the advances made thanks to the Nazi regime and, at the same time, hoped to ensure the continuation of musicological enterprises generated by Nazi support. The denazification of individual musicologists — the dismissals, judgments, and reinstatements — was highly inconsistent and depended less on one's political past and more on the variables in the American, British, French, and Soviet interpretations of denazification, the time of the judgment, collegial support, and the current need for a person's special talents.

Beyond the denazification of individuals by the Allied occupying forces, the German musicological community attempted to demonstrate that it had intellectually denazified the discipline. This consisted primarily of castigating a few individuals but had little effect on the scholarly directions and underlying premises of German musicology. Many of the intellectual trends predominant in the Nazi era had a long history behind them, had established roots in musicological traditions in other parts of the world, and would live on in some form.

The State of Music Scholarship in 1945

There is no doubt that musicology flourished during the Nazi regime. In 1944, at the height of the war, Germany could boast more musicology departments than anywhere else in the world, an uninterrupted flow of productivity in the form of Denkmäler and Gesamtausgaben, and the continued proliferation of German folk music.[1] One can imagine that musicologists, especially those active in war propaganda and looting, became increasingly obsessed with the fantasy of establishing German music as the music of Europe, a mission that grew out of an exaggerated manifestation of the long tradition of Germanocentric scholarship. Even as the tables turned at Stalingrad, Goebbels used all available resources to sustain optimism, offering empty promises of victory, promoting relief programs, and successfully averting potential antiwar uprisings.[2] But despite musicologists' hopes, such musical dominance was not to be realized. Aspirations to become music czars in newly acquired territories were dashed by Germany's loss of its expanded Reich, and those struggling to create an image of a German nation unified through its music would eventually have to deal with a Germany divided into two distinct and often conflicting cultures.

Just as in 1918, the end of the war prompted musicologists to assess the damages after 1945. It was easy to bemoan the material losses to libraries, archives, and publishing houses.[3] It was somewhat more difficult to assess the effects of the Nazi years on the standards of scholarship. Criticisms of a perceived decline in scholarly standards had abounded during the 1930s, but these spoke more to intergenerational conflicts: elders disapproving of the activities of the newcomers, the younger generation critical of their predecessors' methods, and the conservatives generally shaken by any new trends. In 1931, Kroyer had expressed his frustration with modern scholarship's tendency to overspecialize; in 1933 Hans Engel regretted the awkward position of scholars his age, caught between an older and a younger generation with questionable qualifications that occupied most of the academic positions; and Hans Spanke and Otto Ursprung disapproved of the reemergence of Geisteswissenschaft in the course of the 1930s.[4] By the end of the war, however, a few perceptive observers could see how politics had had a particularly profound effect on scholarship and education, not just in the Nazi years but since the end of the previous war. Adam Gottron noted a serious decline in educational standards during the Nazi period,[5] and Besseler attributed Germany's problems to the politicization and loss of autonomy in higher education that began in 1919 and reached its fatal culmination in the Third Reich.[6]

The increased politicization of musicology could hardly be denied. At the Barcelona meeting in 1936 German representatives first revealed publicly their fierce loyalty to the National Socialist state and began to alienate themselves from the rest of the scholarly community. After the war, musicologists became aware of the effects of their isolation and the extent to which they had become dependent on state and party support.

Denazification set an agenda to eliminate any vestiges of National Socialism. Thus musicologists who hoped to continue their work needed to downplay the role of politics in the musicological achievements of the past decades. In a climate in which everyone claimed to be apolitical, it was necessary to present musicology's past gains as purely internal developments, the results of scholarly initiative alone, in order to deflect from the political engagement of prominent musicologists. By deemphasizing their Nazi involvement, musicologists could pave the way for the reestablishment of dismantled Third Reich institutions and the rehabilitation of those who were temporarily suspended because of their Nazi affiliations.

Friedrich Blume, as president of the newly formed scholarly society, the Gesellschaft für Musikforschung, opened the first issue of its organ *Die Musikforschung* in 1948 with an assessment of the current state of the discipline. Surveying developments in the recent past, he was careful to give the impression that they were not necessarily forced by political circumstances. He traced the isolation of German scholars from the international community to 1914 (rather than to 1936); acknowledged the accompanying concentration on German subject matter and its support from the amateur movement; and lauded the advances since 1914 in historical research, practical editions, and source catalogues, all focusing exclusively on German music. Blume noted the unprecedented organizational gains in the Nazi years: the State Institute, its periodicals *Archiv für Musikforschung* and *Deutsche Musikkultur,* its folk music division, and, above all, the consolidation of independent Denkmal series into EdM, but he never mentioned the Nazi government's support in these ventures. Blume made no attempt to defend or criticize either musicology's isolation or its concentration on German subjects: these were simply facts. Any criticisms from abroad that Germans concentrated too much on their own music ignored the fact that currency restrictions in the 1930s had precluded any exchange of publications and exacerbated German isolation.[7]

Leaders in the postwar German musicological community saw no reason to denounce the nationalistic impulses that flourished in the preceding decades nor to ignore accomplishments under the Nazi state, but they were careful to gloss over the political background of those developments in the hope that

Nazi-era initiatives could be resurrected. In 1949, Schiedermair published a plea in a Cologne newspaper, which briefly mentioned the outcome of isolation, the loss of important composers and scholars to emigration, and the tremendous growth of American musicology, but he stressed the need to rebuild the central institute for musicological research.[8] In 1952, Blume submitted a formal proposal to the various administrative branches and the central church bodies in the Federal Republic, highlighting the accomplishments of musicology in the 1920s and 1930s (making no mention of the Hitler regime) and emphasizing musicology's past contributions to German society and to the economy by enriching music education and the amateur industry. Blume asked for the reestablishment of the State Institute; legal ordinances to secure musicologists' collaborations with the radio and recording industries and to guarantee copyright protection for their work; regulations requiring musicological training for a variety of nonacademic professions; research stipends; and subsidies to rebuild libraries, archives, university departments, and instrument collections devastated by the war.[9]

Blume emphasized the concentration of musicological activity in the universities alone in the preceding decades (needless to say, he did not mention the extracurricular pursuits carried out under the aegis of the Propaganda Ministry, the SS, and the Rosenberg Bureau). He further insisted that all serious scholars had remained true to their moral convictions throughout the Third Reich, although they were not allowed to express them, and the only one who raised his voice — Kurt Huber — paid with his life.[10] Aside from Huber's martyrdom, Blume calls little attention to other victims of Nazi barbarity and is somewhat evasive on the loss of personnel to forced emigration. Blume detracted from the loss of scholars such as Hornbostel, Sachs, and Lachmann by arguing that the strength in exclusively German music-historical research compensated for a weakening in systematic fields brought on by the departure of leading German scholars and their replacement with underqualified juniors. He further expressed his "astonishment" at the rapid gains in American musicology in the past decade. Making no mention of the German and Austrian origins or the circumstances of emigration of "American" musicologists, Blume heaped praise on the accomplishments of Apel, Einstein, Bukofzer, Sachs, Deutsch, David, Lowinsky, Geiringer, and Schrade.[11] He completely suppressed the fact that they were driven abroad by the atrocities of racist hysteria, the same conditions under which he had thrived.

These assessments of recent developments in German musicology were not incorrect: musicology had worked successfully with the amateur industry at least since 1918 and had set its own course for concentration on native subject matter long before Hitler, and there was no reason, in and of itself, to criticize

German scholars for enhancing an understanding of their own musical culture. But they naturally fail to acknowledge publicly that the discipline's self-motivated interests fed into the political programs to instill the notion of German superiority and justify the elimination of those deemed inferior. They also fail to acknowledge that, owing to common goals, the Nazi regime lavished more support on the discipline than any other administration had. Blume had benefited personally from this overlapping of agendas, winning recognition with his keynote speech on music and race at the Reichsmusiktage, earning the honor of contributing to the Festschrift for Hitler's fiftieth birthday, rising to the rank of Ordinarius in 1938, and receiving the commission before the end of the war to oversee what was to become one of German musicology's most ambitious postwar achievements, the reference work *Die Musik in Geschichte und Gegenwart.*

The postwar attempt to depoliticize musicology's role in the Nazi state, the silence on the fate of victims of National Socialism, and the encouragement of continued work on German subject matter are all part of a complex web of feelings that prevailed in the era of denazification. Denazification was the most far-reaching and protracted process in the Allied program to reform German society after the war. The Allies took it upon themselves to punish the war criminals, weed out the lesser perpetrators, and reeducate the rest, but their division of the German population into rather simplistic categories of Nazis or non-Nazis of varying degrees, the gross inconsistencies in the judgments reached, and the unrealistic goals of removing all Nazis from positions of power while needing their expertise to rebuild Germany were destined to yield unsatisfactory results. The overall consensus was that the program failed miserably. Rather than confronting the past and its atrocities, most Germans subject to denazification lapsed into amnesia, self-pity, and defiance. It has even been argued that the circumstances of denazification actually provoked so much defensiveness among the German population that basic doctrines of National Socialism (anti-Semitism, anti-Communism, and militaristic nationalism) persisted, paving the way for an immediate reemergence of National Socialist sympathy in the 1950s and 1960s.[12]

The Denazification Mentality

At Yalta in February 1945, the American, British, and Russian leaders set down their plans to punish war criminals; dissolve the Nazi party, legal system, organizations, and institutions; and remove militarism and Nazism from public, cultural, and economic life. The first goal could be accomplished with relative efficiency at the Nuremberg trials, and the dissolution of the party and other structures could be carried out through directives of the Military Government, but the removal of Nazism, or "denazification," of German society would prove to be exceedingly difficult. How could one isolate "Nazism" as a self-contained behavior pattern or set of beliefs without underestimating the forces in German history that led to Hitler's victory and the complex workings of German society from 1933 to 1945?

Denazification policy was subject to a wide variety of interpretations among the Allies and the Germans they entrusted to assist in the process. The Western Allies, with the Americans taking the lead, emphasized the purge of personnel and the "reeducation" of the German population toward establishing a democracy and a capitalist economy, whereas the Soviets conceived of a denazification of the entire system that would lay the groundwork for a communist state. Following mass arrests and immediate release of the least suspect, all Germans over the age of eighteen were required to fill out a questionnaire (*Fragebogen*) of more than 130 questions to determine their degree of involvement in the Nazi party and other organizations and activities. Some musicologists, such as Helmuth Osthoff, were painstakingly honest on the Fragebogen, listing all memberships and actions, even those of dubious relevance, and providing additional information about activities that might have been politically compromising.[13] Others were much more selective in the information they provided: Gotthold Frotscher, for example, gave no indication of his involvement in the Reich Youth Leadership (he circumvented this question by answering "no" to the question of membership/rank specifically for the Hitler Youth) and listed only his books and music editions and none of his articles or other publications.[14] The Fragebogen determined an individual's initial assignment to one of five categories of culpability: (I) major offenders (*Hauptschuldige*); (II) offenders (*Belastete*); (III) lesser offenders (*Minderbelastete*); (IV) followers (*Mitläufer*); and (V) exonerated (*Entlastete*). The punishments for categories I through IV varied among the zones of occupation. Actions included imprisonment, forced labor, loss of employment, loss of property, and fines. Individual cases were then processed, mostly by German tribunals set up under the authority of the Military Government.[15]

At the trials, most testimonies were strikingly similar. Defendants tended to deny most of their actions of the preceding twelve years and exaggerated events they construed as demonstrating their resistance, persecution, or apolitical behavior. Robert Ericksen, in examining denazification documents from the theology faculty in Göttingen, noted a number of conceits employed by the theologians that closely resemble those used by musicologists. His subjects, for example, claimed to have delivered anticommunist lectures to the Luftwaffe as a tactic to weaken the regime, got involved in the Nazi church (Deutsche

Christen) in an attempt to oppose Hitler from the inside, joined the SS only to wear the uniform, and defied Nazi ideology by remaining devout and praying daily. Ericksen analyzed the psychological undercurrents operating in such testimonies, noting how the panic and trauma of the postwar situation gave rise to selective, distorted, and conflicting memories that were eventually internalized as truths.[16] Musicologists also used the strategies of claiming acts of resistance, providing affidavits from clergymen and Jewish acquaintances, exaggerating claims of victimization, and distorting facts.

Musicologists' claims of resistance against the Nazi regime took on a number of imaginative forms, many of them vague and questionable. Heinrich Husmann, a volunteer (*Hausgemeinschaftsleiter*) for the Nazi party since 1933 and member since 1937, was reported to have secretly been a "critic and opponent" of National Socialism.[17] Hermann Zenck, recommended to category III (lesser offender), was earnestly defended by the university officials in Freiburg, despite having joined the SA in 1933 "like all young lecturers in Göttingen" and subsequently being drawn into the Nazi party. Zenck's anti-Nazi stand was allegedly known to all, but the only action anyone could cite was his defense of a student performance of the St. Matthew Passion in 1943 "against the resistance of party authorities."[18] Hans Engel, searching for an academic position after the Soviet capture of Königsberg (soon to become Kaliningrad), presented himself in late 1945 as an "active opponent to National Socialism." Engel claimed to have "worked actively against Nazi propaganda," joining the party in 1941 only in the face of direct threats and doing so on the advice of his superiors.[19] When Robert Lach lost his pension after the war on account of his joining the party in 1933 while it was still illegal in Austria, he claimed to have resisted the Nazi regime by paying no membership dues until 1938 and refusing to take an active part in the movement.[20] Kreichgauer's claims of anti-Nazi political activity included his protest against the Education Ministry's dissolution of the DGMW, of which he was president.[21]

Almost everyone facing denazification insisted on having helped Jews, half-Jews, spouses of Jews, and the politically persecuted. Lach mentioned having written letters of recommendation to English and American scholars on behalf of Jewish students who emigrated, and having defended Leopold Nowak against attacks over his Catholicism. He naively added: "I mention both of these, because I've heard from many sides that only good deeds done on behalf of Jews or Catholics can be used as grounds for overturning the [denazification] classification."[22] Friendship with Kurt Huber emerged as a potential vehicle for proving anti-Nazi leanings and was exploited by Huber's musicology colleagues as well as by the composer Carl Orff.[23] Huber came to symbolize the moral integrity of musicology, and some of his former associates tried to capitalize on his martyrdom. Otto Ursprung seized the opportunity to publish some of Huber's writings after the war and became entangled in a legal battle with Huber's widow over the publication rights.[24] Besseler also tried to use his association with Huber to clear his name during his denazification proceedings and asked Ursprung, based on his personal friendship with Huber, to testify for him. Besseler claimed that Huber had experienced his "shared struggles" in Berlin at the State Institute, and surely a testimony from Huber himself would have carried much weight after the war, had he survived.[25] Besseler did, in fact, assist his Jewish students Edward Lowinsky and Ernst Hermann Meyer after 1933 but for some reason neglected to produce affidavits from them during his denazification.

More abundant were the claims of victimization during the Third Reich, but here the tendency was to inflate any interpersonal conflicts, budgetary restrictions, or actions considered unfair into incidents of political persecution. Engel claimed that he was forced out of his position as director of the local chapter of the Reich Association of German Composers and Music Teachers because he was considered a "cultural bolshevist,"[26] and Schiedermair attributed the fact that he ceased to be dean in 1933 to his resistance against the Nazis.[27] Such claims often belied selective memory or suppression of facts. Lach considered himself a victim of National Socialism because he was overlooked in the appointment of a dean in 1938–1939 (the year he retired); he was pensioned as soon as he reached age sixty-five (although the faculty actually chose to delay his retirement to maximize his pension, a gesture to reward him for his early party membership); he received fewer invitations to give public lectures after the Nazis came to power; and he lost his loge seats in the concert hall in Vienna, all of which he regarded as "damages" at the hands of the Nazi regime.[28]

Suppressing facts to enhance a picture of political persecution benefited Besseler the most. His exoneration rested on his perceived victimization from the repeated refusals to promote him to Ordinarius. Indeed, given his importance as a scholar, the strong endorsements from his university, and his ostensible political reliability in the eyes of Nazi officials, it is difficult to explain his failure to rise in rank. His claims after the war, however, overlooked some important details. Besseler's first attempt at promotion came in 1932, only four years after his appointment at Heidelberg, and the ministry responded in April 1933 that his request "could not yet be fulfilled,"[29] probably because of his young age (he was thirty-two). Immediately after Besseler's exoneration by the Nazi party tribunal against Gerigk's attacks, the campaign for his promotion resumed, and by late 1937, he had the endorsement of the dean, the Nazi Lecturers' League, and even the Education Ministry.[30] The request was once again turned down, this time because of an ordinance from the Reich Chancellery prohibiting any promotion directly from persönlicher Extraordinarius to persönlicher Ordinarius.[31] The dean resubmitted the proposal in 1941, again with the endorsement of the Nazi Lecturers' League, only to be rejected because the university lacked the funding to create the position.[32] In 1944, however, Besseler turned down an Ordinarius position in Graz because of a promise from the Reich Education Ministry that, although no Ordinarius positions could be filled during the war, the university would do everything in its power to secure a position for him.[33] The Education Ministry had in fact finally approved his promotion to Ordinarius in October 1944,[34] presumably to be realized after the war. The details of Besseler's earlier attempts at promotion and of the final assurance by the Education Ministry never came to light in his denazification.

Moser found many reasons to claim victimization, and in fact his career in the Nazi years was hardly free of problems, although the nature of his publications and his associations with people in high places managed to pull him through. Still, Moser resorted to suppressing facts to give the impression of relentless persecution during the Third Reich. Moser claimed that his removal in 1933 as a result of Paragraph 6 was politically motivated because he was out of favor with the National Socialists, especially Werner Weber in the Education Ministry. When he tried to protest his forced retirement in 1934, he was punished with a disciplinary measure based on a 1930 claim of adultery that came out during his divorce proceedings. Two years later, his pension and professor title were withdrawn, with the additional threat of revoking his doctorate. Moser explained that he joined the Nazi party in 1936 to strengthen his position in an attempt to protest the Education Ministry's disciplinary measures. A member of Rudolf Hess's staff advised him that he could try to challenge the measure only if he became a party member, but this, in the end, turned out to be useless.[35]

In actuality, the Education Ministry proved to be anything but an adversary a few years after the disciplinary measures, using every opportunity to try to secure a more respectable working situation for Moser. According to Moser's account in 1941, Martin Miederer (Weber's replacement) received an order from Hess's staff to find a new academic post for Moser and promised to secure the Ordinarius position in Vienna for him. Rather than wait for Miederer to come through, Moser accepted the presumably prestigious Propaganda Ministry position on a "commission from the Führer."[36] Miederer continued to look after Moser's best interests: in February 1945, upon the recommendation of the Party Chancellery, he forwarded a suggestion that Moser succeed Schünemann as director of the music division in the Prussian State Library, but the decision was to be put off until after the war.[37]

Moser's honesty in explaining his Reichsstelle position in the Propaganda

Ministry is also questionable. In his postwar defense, Moser stated that he had no choice but to accept the Reichsstelle post, seeing it as his only means to support two growing families. The position also enabled him to assist many Jews, half Jews, spouses of Jews, Freemasons, and Poles by giving them commissions.[38] Despite his alleged financial difficulties, however, in 1941 he expressed his willingness to give up the Reichsstelle position in favor of a lower-paying academic post. His desire to be considered for the Schering chair, he explained, was not motivated by financial hardships — on the contrary, the combination of his income from the Propaganda Ministry and his pension from the academy amounted to more than the university position would bring. Rather it was a question of reputation or, in his words, "personal rehabilitation."[39] As for his duties in the Reichsstelle, he claimed in his defense to have prevented the replacement of Heine texts set by Schumann and to have delayed the publication of retexted Handel oratorios.[40] This may be true, but a budget Moser submitted to the finance office in the Propaganda Ministry in 1943 specifically requested that 34,000 marks be allocated for the reworking of oratorios and lieder.[41] Whether he intended to use the money for the stated purpose is, of course, open to question.

Moser is justified in pointing out that in some of his writings he made positive statements about Mendelssohn and Joseph Joachim, but he may have exaggerated the degree of retribution he suffered thereafter at the hands of the Rosenberg Bureau, the Reich Youth Leadership, and KdF. Moser alleged that these party interests continually plagued him, such that he was prohibited from delivering a lecture in Magdeburg because the party deemed him politically unreliable.[42] His assertion that he was blacklisted by KdF may have been true; the Rosenberg Bureau did have influence on the programs of the Deutsches Volksbildungswerk in the KdF, but it did not hold a monopoly on sponsoring all lecture tours. Moser's unfavorable status with Rosenberg did not preclude him from conducting other lectures, for example, in the occupied territories. Victimization by the Rosenberg Bureau was in any case hardly a rare distinction, as we have seen from Gerigk's repeated attacks on members of the musicology community, and ultimately had limited lasting effects. Many of Gerigk's targets, such as Blume, Besseler, Schünemann, and Sandberger, escaped pretty much unscathed and went on to prosperous careers during the Third Reich. Moser's connections to Rudolf Hess's staff (whom he offered as a reference in jockeying for the Schering position), his ties to the SS-"Ahnenerbe," and his employment by the Propaganda Ministry put him in good standing with forces far more influential than the Rosenberg Bureau.

A comparison of the denazification testimonies by Besseler and Moser yields an interesting contradiction that clearly illustrates the fickleness of denazification and the uncertainties in determining who was a Nazi. In referring to the officials in the Education Ministry with whom both had dealings, each chose to highlight the Nazi credentials of the one who proved uncooperative. Moser's negative experiences with Werner Weber prompted him to label Weber a leading National Socialists, while Besseler, in his own denazification, regarded Weber as an ally and chose to describe him as one of the "old, pre-National Socialist brand of civil servants." Conversely, Moser prospered from his association with Weber's successor, Miederer, while Besseler, whose dealings with him were less congenial, took care to refer to him as "SS-Sturmführer Martin Miederer" in his testimony.[43]

Discrepancies in Denazification among the Zones of Occupation

Location and timing were crucial factors in the outcome of a denazification investigation. Denazification in the British zone was known to be the most lenient. Statistics show that about 10 percent of all cases tried in the British zone were relegated to category IV (followers) and almost 60 percent to category V (exonerated). In the American and French zones, by contrast, approximately 50 percent ended up in category IV and no more that 2 percent in category V.[44] The denazification at universities in the British zone appeared to be very congenial and problem free.[45] The British have been criticized for standing too far in the background, allowing the universities to carry out their own denazification with the result that very few faculty members were removed. The German faculties simply convened with British supervisors, conceded that Nazi principles were scientifically unsound, and were automatically exonerated.[46] The swiftness and ease of this process in the British zone may account for the postwar successes of Blume (Kiel), Fellerer (Cologne), and Boetticher (Göttingen). Blume was retained as Ordinarius and immediately took the lead in reorganizing the field by establishing the Gesellschaft für Musikforschung; Fellerer remained Ordinarius in Cologne until his death, serving as a president of the Gesellschaft für Musikforschung and as rector at Cologne; and Boetticher became a Privatdozent at Göttingen in 1948 and Ordinarius in 1956.

Denazification under the French has also been judged as extremely lax, possibly because of the long history of French mistrust of the Germans, which resulted in a cynical attitude toward the process. Unlike the British and Americans, the French did not adhere to the strict classifications of guilt and innocence, preferring instead to judge each case on its own merits. The amount of paperwork involved, however, made it clear that the most efficient way to handle denazification was to leave it to the Germans. The French also placed more importance on speeding up the process, ordering amnesty by the end of 1947 for all "followers" and for party members who had held no office.[47] More interested in embarking on education reforms, they had a vested interest in reopening the universities as soon as possible and dismissed only the former university officers and the most outspoken Nazis from the Freiburg faculty.[48]

Of the three powers in the west, the Americans were the most thorough in executing denazification, but this proved especially difficult in the case of universities. Widespread illness forced the immediate reopening of university clinics, opening the door for all other university departments to resume their operations. Although American officers would have liked to take a more active part in university denazification, the immediacy and lack of personnel in their Education and Religious Affairs Branch compelled them to leave much of the responsibility to committees of Germans, composed of individuals regarded as non-Nazi or known to have suffered under the Nazis. Not long thereafter, the Americans handed over more responsibility for all denazification to similarly composed German tribunals (Spruchkammern).[49]

Denazification was anything but uniform in the universities under American occupation. In Heidelberg, the process was long and arduous because of its early implementation and the high concentration of party members on the faculty, nearly causing the university to close its doors in February 1946 because of the extensive initial purge of personnel.[50] This close scrutiny accounts for the very thick file on Heinrich Besseler in the Heidelberg archive. Besseler was clearly a problematic case as an early advocate for the Nazi state, a member of the SA since 1934, and a Nazi party member since 1937.[51] He distinguished himself as a loyal representative of Nazi interests in musicological issues and as a devoted servant of the Education Ministry at home and abroad. In addition he was a trusted ambassador, lecturing to the Society for the Encouragement of Cultural Life in Switzerland in 1942, which was associated with a clandestine National Socialist movement.[52] Because of the delicate nature of dealing with neutral Switzerland, only those deemed politically reliable were allowed to lecture there. Thus Wilibald Gurlitt was explicitly discouraged in 1936, while Frotscher was allowed to go in 1938 and 1939 at the suggestion of the Nazi party.[53] Frotscher described this particular organization as a "counterweight" to the "very strong and active French cultural propaganda" that set out to oppose "the work of émigré circles."[54] Besseler reported to the Reich education minister that he was impressed by the courage of the pro-German inner circle who welcomed him, and he praised their political activities.[55]

Almost all of the details of Besseler's activities, including his trip to Switzerland, came to light in the denazification investigation. In his defense, Besseler explained that he joined the SA to avoid further attacks, following the difficulties he had had with National Socialist students, and claimed that he tried to leave the SA but was forced into the SA reserve during the war. Besseler made several allegations of political persecution, complaining again of losing his appointment as head of the Denkmäler commission and attributing it to the appointment of Martin Miederer in the Education Ministry; pointing to the hounding by Gerigk; and claiming that his requested release from military service was denied because of his bad relationship with the party. His most ardent claim of victimization was the fourfold rejection by the Nazi government to promote him to Ordinarius. He insisted that he never worked actively with the party, within either the university or the community. He further mentioned that he never contributed writings to the propaganda machine.[56] This last claim, of course, did not acknowledge that his responsibilities in Berlin took him away from his research for five full years, as did his temporary assignment to the University of Freiburg and his military service.

Initially judged in 1945 as an "offender" because of his party membership and SA ranking, Besseler's status was changed to "lesser offender" by the Heidelberg Spruchkammer in March 1947 on the strength of his minimal activity in the SA and his run-in with Nazi students and the Rosenberg Bureau, which they linked to his dismissal from the institute and repeated failures at promotions. He was judged as not harboring deep National Socialist feelings but behaving outwardly so. The judgment did, however, frown on his reports to the Education Ministry on conferences abroad and on his trip to Switzerland. They also discounted his claim of political discrimination when his release from military service was delayed, especially since they believed he tried to send his assistant into the service in his place. But given that he had already been suspended from his position for a year and a half, and owing to the "unpolitical character of his scholarly discipline," his sentence was limited to a fine of 1,000 marks.[57] This judgment was overturned in 1948 by the provincial appellate court in Karlsruhe, which changed his status to "exonerated," largely because of his failure to achieve the status of Ordinarius and the fact that he was called up for military service.[58]

Despite his exoneration, Besseler still experienced difficulties in the university, although several important colleagues attested to his indispensability for the future growth of German musicology.[59] In 1948, the university decided not to recommend his reinstatement because of his marking of books by Jewish authors in the musicology library and because of his alleged attempt to have his assistant sent up for military duty in his stead.[60] It was at this point that Besseler looked for employment elsewhere and started negotiations with universities in the Soviet zone (Jena and Leipzig), where denazification had ended in March 1948,[61] and where he eventually managed to establish himself as a leading musicologist of the German Democratic Republic.

The inequities among and even within the zones was further complicated by haste. The process of denazification dragged on too long, and pressures to end it mounted, especially after the Soviets announced an end to denazification in their zone. The Americans felt compelled to speed up the process and exonerated almost everyone, such that "offenders" tried in 1948 received lighter sentences than "followers" tried in 1946 and 1947.[62] Munich, also in the American zone, serves as a counterexample to Heidelberg; denazification there was much more lax because of time and personnel constraints. Because Munich suffered extensive war damage, it had to postpone denazification, resulting in much more lenient judgments. The leniency at the university went so far that a scandal broke when the American press exposed corruption, cronyism, and the retention of Nazis on the faculty.[63] In musicology, too, some of the most committed old National Socialists — those who had earned distinction during the Third Reich for joining the party before 1933 — were granted clemency posthumously so their families could benefit from their pensions. Musicologist Rudolf Ficker, dean of the Philosophische Fakultät, showed such mercy in the cases of Alfred Lorenz and Gustav Friedrich Schmidt, whom he deemed as " 'followers' at most" despite their party membership.[64]

A few older musicologists were judged politically unrepentant and forced into retirement, probably owing more to their relative dispensability for the future of the discipline or to personal politics than to the policies of local officials. Ludwig Schiedermair was declared unsuitable to resume his teaching activities at Bonn because of the concessions he had made to National Socialism, especially in the pro-Hitler and anti-Jewish emendations to the 1940 edition of his book, *Die Deutsche Oper*. Since he was sixty-nine years old, it was easiest just to retire him.[65] Ernst Bücken, assigned to category IV (follower) in Cologne, tried to regain his teaching position. The university, in reviewing his file, remarked on his upcoming sixty-fifth birthday and also noticed that in his long campaign to become Ordinarius he had used all political connections possible: the Center party and the Jewish community before 1933, and after he joined the NSDAP in 1933, the Nazi potentates.[66] The university recommended that he not be reinstated, and Bücken died a few months later.

The Soviets espoused a completely different conception of denazification, seeing it not as a process of reeducation but rather as a purge of National Socialists.[67] Rather than weighing the degrees of culpability among those affiliated with the Nazi party and its organizations, the Soviet aim was to purge all party members and fill important positions with returning Communists who had fled or were imprisoned under the Nazis.[68] The philosophical differences between East and West created much confusion, especially in Berlin, where denazification was distributed among the four powers. The University of Berlin was located in the Soviet sector of the city, and like the Americans, the Soviets allowed the faculty to vet itself. The faculty adhered to the Soviet agenda, removing all party members and retaining only 200 of the 700 teachers and professors.[69] The Soviet guidelines, however, allowed some outspoken Nazis to slip through the cracks, on the technicality that they had never entered the Nazi party. Thus Walther Vetter, who had chided the authors on Germanness for ignoring the Jewish Question and praised Rosenberg in his Düsseldorf presentation, was appointed in Berlin in 1946 to succeed Schering. Vetter blended in unobstrusively with those persecuted by the Nazis who assumed positions of power in East Germany. Eventually he was joined by two such victims who had emigrated to England as Jews and Communists at the onset of Nazi domination: Ernst Hermann Meyer, who joined the faculty in 1948, and Georg Knepler, who returned to Vienna in 1946 and joined the Berlin faculty in 1959.

Werner Danckert was one former party member who experienced substantial difficulties reestablishing his career after he was removed from the Berlin faculty. Knowing that he was being judged by the Communists, he declared his religious affiliation on the questionnaire as "atheist" (*konfessionslos*).[70] Nevertheless, the dean of the Philosophische Fakultät sized him up as a close friend of Gerigk and a protégé of the Rosenberg Bureau and attributed his work on European folk song ("too quickly completed") as a ploy to become the director of the German Folksong Archive.[71] Although Vetter enthusiastically endorsed Danckert's reinstatement, the German Administration for Public Education in the Soviet sector decided against it, on the basis of his "doubtful" political tendencies, contradictions in his scholarship, and a failure to acknowledge non-German literature.[72] Danckert, along with Moser and Frotscher, thereafter earned notoriety in the chronicles of East Berlin musicology as the conveyors of fascist thought during the Nazi years.[73]

Moser, who was not investigated by the university committee but rather by the denazification commission of the Berlin Magistrate's Chamber of Artists (*Kammer der Kunstschaffenden*), faced the problem of trying to outguess German, French, British, and Soviet officials all at once. In fall 1945, Moser accepted a position at the conservatory in Berlin-Reinickendorf, in the French sector, but he was fired because of his Nazi party membership. The French Commandatur allowed him to return pending a decision of the denazification commission, to which he filed an appeal in January 1946.[74] In August 1947, with the case still unresolved, he received an offer to join the faculty at the University of Jena and the conservatory in Weimar, both in Thuringia, under Soviet occupation. The director of the Weimar conservatory urged him to withdraw his denazification appeal in Berlin, explaining that he would not need to have his name cleared there to work in Thuringia, though a negative verdict would cause problems. Moser was unable to withdraw his appeal, and he received a negative judgment in Berlin on the basis of his Reichsstelle activities and certain publications. He attempted to deal directly with the Soviet officials in Thuringia, in the hope that they would disregard the judgment of the other Allies, especially since the Berlin commission had not followed the procedures of the Western zones but decided either "yes" or "no" rather than applying the five gradations of culpability.[75]

Moser was tentatively allowed to take up his positions in Weimar, but after two months he was suspended when the Soviet officials in Berlin-Karlshorst (in the Soviet sector) and in Thuringia judged him to be politically tainted.[76] This happened only two months before the Soviets officially declared the end of denazification. In the meantime, publishers in the English zone were not allowed to publish his works because of his party membership and his involvement in the Propaganda Ministry.[77] By late 1948, the Jena position was offered to Besseler instead.[78] In Moser's own assessment, he had miscalculated the degree of sovereignty among the different sectors and occupying powers. Following the negative decision in Berlin, he had written to the commission that with his departure to Weimar, he understood he was no longer under the jurisdiction of the Berlin commission. He heard indirectly that this angered the English officers, who allegedly vowed to show him how much the English influence could extend into the Russian zone. This happened at a time when the Allies were making a special effort to work together in the denazification process.[79]

The End of Denazification and the Rebuilding of German Musicology

Despite the apparent thoroughness of Soviet denazification, once the process ended in March 1948, it was possible for those with questionable political histories to be considered for positions there, especially since universities in the impoverished eastern regions had difficulties attracting scholars. Shortly after the German Democratic Republic (GDR) was established, new laws allowed for former Nazi party members not designated as war criminals to be appointed to public service, especially if they possessed the needed credentials.[80] Although the GDR cultivated the notion that denazification in the Soviet zone was more stringent than in the western zones of occupation, there appears to have been plenty of room for negotiation, especially once denazification was over.

In summer 1948, Besseler, after failing to regain his position in Heidelberg, appealed to universities in the Soviet zone. Like Danckert, Besseler listed his religion as "unaffiliated" (*freireligiös*) on the questionnaire. He described his departure from the State Institute as "political dismissal by the NSDAP" after "resisting the orders of the NSDAP," an action that also hindered his promotion.[81] More important, he called attention to his current works in progress and to the "threat of American competition" from projects carried out by the American Institute of Musicology in Rome and from the Americans' photographic reproduction and publication of his *Musik des Mittelalters und der Renaissance* (part of the *Handbuch der Musikwissenschaft* series published by Athenaion in the 1920s and 1930s).[82] Besseler was appointed to Jena in January 1949 as Ordinarius and named department head of the philosophy division (Fachrichtungsleiter für die Fachrichtung Philosophie) in 1951. The only concern expressed over his political history was that he had lived in Heidelberg until 1949 and might harbor strong ties to the West, but the judgment concluded: "his behavior toward the German Democratic Republic is loyal, one can consider him a pure scholar."[83] His Nazi past was completely overlooked.

In the meantime, the Leipzig faculty was desperate to fill the position left vacant by Helmut Schultz's death and considered a large number of candidates. Walther Vetter made a very strong case for Besseler's appointment in Leipzig, pointing to that city's historical importance for music research and publishing and the need to foster collaboration between the university's musicology department and the music publishing industry. Vetter also warned of the growing threat of the United States, not only in its competitive ventures but also in its "attempts to claim illegally the fruits of German musicological work." These included the American publication of photo reproductions of the Bach-Ausgabe, of the third edition of the Köchel-Verzeichnis, of the second volume of *Publikationen älterer Musik,* and of Adler's *Handbuch der Musikgeschichte* and Bücken's multivolume *Handbuch der Musikwissenschaft,* as well as planned projects of the American Institute to publish the *Corpus scriptorum de musica* prepared by Wolf and to preempt Besseler's Dufay edition. Vetter regarded Besseler as the best candidate to bring German musicological publishing back on its feet, not only by virtue of his international reputation as a scholar, but more so because of his experience working in the State Institute in the late 1930s and overseeing a wide variety of publishing projects (Denkmäler, periodicals, and bibliographies).[84] Besseler came to Leipzig in 1956 and remained there until his death.

The argument of foreign competition was also employed in the Federal Republic to spur interest in investing in musicology. In his 1952 proposal to the government to revive institutions and enterprises terminated at the end of the war, Blume complained that Germany lagged far behind accomplishments in other countries, even Austria. He pointed to the "appropriation" of German achievements in the reprinting of Gesamtausgaben, the "takeover" of German initiatives by the American Haydn Society and the American Institute of Musicology, and the continued advances in such projects as the planned Schubert and Mozart Gesamtausgaben.[85]

In the course of the 1950s, German musicology continued to grow as new departments emerged, and the need to fill positions allowed for considerable leniency in making appointments. There seems to have been no attempt, however, to fill these positions with the victims of National Socialism. Aside from the return of the exiled Communists to East Berlin and the reinstatement of Wilibald Gurlitt in Freiburg, none of the prominent musicologists driven out of Germany returned to assume academic positions that opened up after the war. Instead, many of those who distinguished themselves in the Third Reich went on to become central players in German musicology's growth. Müller-Blattau, who moved to Strasbourg in 1941 while it was under German occupation, was appointed at Saarbrücken in 1952 and named the first Ordinarius there in 1958. Werner Korte, despite his incendiary writings of the 1930s and the judgment of "offender" after the war,[86] became the first Ordinarius in Münster in 1946, and Hans Engel enjoyed the same honor in Marburg in 1946.

There was much more going on in the affairs of postwar rehabilitation than just scrutinizing one's service to the Nazi state. Indeed, many who fared well during the Nazi regime experienced relatively few career difficulties after 1945. In addition to regional inconsistencies, timing, and the possession of needed skills, collegial support carried much weight. With so much of denazification left to personal politics and connections, colleagues' assessments played a crucial role both in Besseler's successes and in Moser's difficulties. Although Moser attributed his bad luck to the shaky relations among the Allies, he lacked sufficient support from established colleagues. Moser appealed to Blume to assist him in 1948, because Blume was well positioned in a university in the English zone, but Blume hesitated to help, allegedly on the advice of the English university control officer.[87] Moser ultimately secured a position at the Berlin Hochschule, but clearly he had a harder time succeeding than others. He lacked the necessary degree of political savvy, but he also lacked the support of colleagues before and after 1945. As a scholar, Moser was highly productive but regarded by many as less than serious, conducting side activities as a singer and novelist, and at times less than diplomatic in his professional relationships. His reputation was, in a word, dispensable.

Gestures to Denazify Musicological Scholarship

The Allied doctrines of denazification and reeducation caused German musicologists to consider how they might "denazify" the teachings of musicology toward reeducating the next generation of scholars. This might involve purging the field of nationalistic implications, of pseudoscientific methods, of certain sensitive aesthetic questions, and above all of any racist ideas. But how was such a task to be carried out? How does one "denazify" a discipline? Furthermore, to what extent had the discipline been "nazified" in the first place? How could one separate Nazi ideology from longer intellectual trends influenced by nationalism, völkisch thought, race theories, folklore, social Darwinism, German Idealism, and positivism?

Some individuals reacted impulsively, simply destroying their earlier, questionable works. Ludwig Schiedermair, for instance, gathered the texts of his unpublished articles and speeches that contained anti-Semitic statements or pursued genealogical investigations into one file, and left a note in the file instructing that they be burned.[88] Others continued to do what they had always done, oblivious to the possibility of repercussions. In 1956, on the occasion of Mozart's two-hundredth birthday, Moser was asked to change a lecture title from "Mozart the German" to "Mozart Between the Great Music Nations" to deemphasize Mozart's national character and to focus more on outside influences on his composition.[89] Apparently not comprehending the message implied in this request, Moser then published a comprehensive study of the music of the German "tribes" that he had begun twenty years earlier. Moser had first proposed the project, provisionally titled "German Music by Tribe and Region" ("Deutsche Musik nach Stammen und Landschaften"), to the SS-"Ahnenerbe" in 1940 for consideration by their press. He conceived of it as a musical outgrowth of other studies of racial classifications and foresaw its wide appeal among music lovers and folklorists and its use in schools, seminars, and Hitler Youth and Nazi Teachers' League retreats.[90] Both Plaßmann and Sievers were excited about the project, but they had to reject it when Moser's work with the "Ahnenerbe" was terminated, and Cotta Verlag took it on instead.[91]

The completed work of more than one thousand pages, entitled *The Music of the German Tribes* (*Die Musik der deutschen Stämme*, Vienna: Wancura Verlag), appeared in 1957. In it Moser rather injudiciously discussed the Jews as a distinct "tribe," albeit now reintegrated as one of the "German tribes" but differing from the others in having no geographic parameters. His indiscretion placed him center stage in the musicology community's outward gestures to denazify research and publishing. Moser was publicly denounced by the field when Blume and the board of directors of the Gesellschaft für Musikforschung refused to publish a review of the book in its journal because of Moser's remarks about Jews.[92] The Gesellschaft's public distancing from the work prompted the periodical *Musica* to follow its example, returning a review it had commissioned from Fritz Bose.[93] The publicity compelled Moser to withdraw from a UNESCO commission headed by Mersmann,[94] and it also prevented him from contributing to a Festschrift for Richard Münnich (the East German publisher rejected the essay he wrote because of his book and also because of the essay's alleged anti-GDR and anti-Polish sentiments).[95]

Whether he liked it or not, this incident drew much attention to Moser as an example of an unrepentant Nazi as well as a champion, or at least father confessor, for those who harbored anti-Semitic sentiments. When Alfred Orel had offended Eva Badura-Skoda with his anti-Semitic remarks, Badura-Skoda asked Moser to confront him on her behalf. When Moser did this, Orel had no reservations in stating his position to Moser. The young woman, Orel claimed, could not possibly comprehend the difference between Nazism and anti-Semitism, the latter of which was second-nature to anyone with his old Austrian, military background. His father, a military doctor, even knew Jews who considered themselves anti-Semites: "We in old Austria, with its Galician infiltration, had every reason to take our nonaggressive position of defense. But I think we understand each other in this respect."[96] One other colleague felt comfortable confessing her anti-Semitic feelings to Moser, remarking on the "Jewish takeover" of the Bärenreiter publishing house and of *Grove's Dictionary* and the "unpleasant impression" left by Eric Werner's "Jewish monograph" on Mendelssohn.[97] The furor over Moser's book elicited a vote of confidence from none other than Moser's old nemesis, Herbert Gerigk. Gerigk reassured Moser that he was publishing a very positive review of the book in his *Ruhr-Nachrichten*, albeit under the pseudonym Herbert Albrecht.[98]

Singling out members of the community whose political activities were known and formally ostracizing them proved an easy and effective way to denazify German scholarship. The Moser incident seemed to reassure most of the scholarly community abroad that German musicology had mended its ways. By insinuating that Moser persisted in racist methodology, Blume focused international attention on his work and held him up as a rare example of an unredeemable racist and nationalist ideologue. Paul Henry Lang concurred in an extensive criticism (notably in the form of an editorial rather than a book review) of Moser's book in *The Musical Quarterly*. But Lang did not focus as much on Moser's representation of Jews as on his attempts to Germanize all great figures of European music. Lang was apparently unaware that this route had been pursued by many noteworthy musicologists over the past several decades and had reached a climax during the war. Lang labeled Moser an incorrigible renegade and praised the efforts of other scholars to deemphasize German nationalism and "to explore the specifically Germanic quality and nature of their music, . . . for insight and knowledge and not for self-glorification."[99]

The English press also presented a naively uplifting assessment of postwar German musicologists. An item in the 1947 *Music and Letters* lauded the Gesellschaft für Musikforschung for choosing Blume as its president and elaborated on his alleged resistance against the Nazis:

> Already in 1938, Mr. Ernest Newman, in an article on Blume's study "Music [sic] und Rasse," drew our attention to "one of the leading living German musical scholars. . . . He indulges in none of the too customary dithyrambs over Germanic and Nordic music." This noble and daring attempt of Blume's to replace the race nonsense of the Nazis by a sober scientific analysis of the facts was followed by the lecture "Wesen und Werden deutscher Musik," which he was asked to deliver by order of the higher authorities in 1944 as part of a series of public lectures on "Die Kunst des Reiches." Blume, aware both of the support of his anti-Nazi friends and also of possible serious consequences for himself attendant on his adherence to strictly scientific principles, decided to use this opportunity to aim a blow at the official Nazi music propaganda. He could not, of course, in 1944, in a public lecture attended by high Nazi officials, freely say what he really meant. He had to camouflage the true meaning of his words with a certain amount of current phraseology.

From the description of the lecture's content that follows, however, it is not at all clear what Blume's "blow at the official Nazi propaganda" consisted of. In the lecture, Blume rejected the notion of polyphony as a German trait, as others had already done, yet insisted on the Germanness of Haydn, Bruckner, and even Liszt, and summarized Germanness as "a very strong power of receptivity, an inner tension between the rational and irrational, and a striving toward universality,"[100] that is, in terms reminiscent of Wagner and his followers.

That Moser could be attacked for striving to find Germanness in music beyond the borders of Germany, while Blume could be praised for "resistance" in his "scientific" attempts to isolate the specific, inherent qualities of musical Germanness, highlights the futility of trying to denazify musicological scholarship. Moser and Blume shared the same goal of defining musical Germanness as a national characteristic, and both worked on the underlying assumption of its universal hegemony.

Presumptions of German musical superiority survived in the writings of other German scholars as well, albeit presented in somewhat more tempered tones. Although Hans Engel made the point that scholarship should not be nationally insulated (even when one's own cultural history lies closest to the heart), he insisted on the continued publication of EdM because: "This is an honorable duty. We Germans in our state of need have one consolation and one source of pride: that is the music given to us and the rest of the world by the masters of all time — past and present — who emerged from our paradoxical but richly bestowed Volk. To research their work and encourage its cultivation is a duty that will benefit not only Germany!"[101]

Blume more subtly asserted the preservation of Germany's noblest legacies of music and music scholarship, hoping that "a rejuvenated German musicology will preserve the old spirit of the German scholarly tradition."[102] He campaigned for the reinstatement of EdM by depoliticizing its origins and praised the EdM's consolidation of other Denkmäler projects. Blume went to great lengths to defend this consolidation against suggestions of totalitarianism. He also denied any "party-ideological" connotation in the name "Erbe" adopted under the Nazis, citing Curt Sachs's title of his book *Our Musical Heritage* as comparably innocuous.[103]

Nor were racist methodologies that came to fruition in the Third Reich ever formally rejected. Indeed, some of the most damaging literature continued to be cited as authoritative long after the war. In the entry "Musicology" that appeared in *MGG,* published in 1961, there is no mention of racial studies in the body of the text, but the bibliography includes the heading "Race and Folklore" ("Rassen- und Volkstumskunde") and lists the works by Blume, Wellek, and Engel discussed earlier, as well as a 1943 article by Bose ("Klangstile als Rassenmerkmale" from the *Zeitschrift für Rassenkunde*) and a postwar contribution by the same author — a 1952 article on "measurable racial differences in music" ("Meßbare Rassenunterschiede in der Musik"). The *MGG* entry "Germany," which appeared in 1954, contains a bibliographic subheading ("Bedingtheit, Wesen, und Organisation der deutschen Musik: Psychologische, stilistische, geistesgeschichtliche Aspekte") that consists almost entirely of works that appeared between 1933 and 1945 and mentions many works that relied heavily on race theory to define Germanness (see chapter 7). It even lists Vetter's literature review that criticized the lack of attention to the Jewish Question.

The symbolic gestures of purging German musicology of National Socialist thought or initiative ultimately succeeded in salvaging the reputation of postwar scholarship, but it consisted of little more than an ad hominem attack rather than an ideological conversion. In subsequent years, reputations of many individuals were protected in sanitized entries in reference works that simply omitted descriptions of their activities and publications between 1933 and 1945.[104] Moser, however, remained one of the most cited, singular examples of a "Nazi musicologist." He was joined in the early 1980s by Wolfgang Boetticher, when the latter was invited to participate in a conference in the United States and a *New York Times* article called attention to his activities in Nazi Germany, compelling him to withdraw from the conference.[105] Harvard musicologist Christoph Wolff followed this event with an editorial in the *Frankfurter Rundschau,* reminding the musicology community in Germany that the facts about Boetticher's involvement had been published two decades earlier and questioning their failure to deal with this knowledge.[106] Boetticher and Moser were still prominent symbols of Nazism in 1990, when Albrecht Dümling responded to a criticism by Moser's son in the *Neue Musikzeitung* and focused on determining the guilt of both Moser and Boetticher.[107] Willem de Vries, while preparing a study of the Sonderstab Musik in the Western occupation, corresponded with Boetticher and asked about his past activities. Boetticher assured him that he had never worked for Rosenberg but had merely conducted research as a "guest" of the Einsatzstab while in the military, a claim easily refuted by documentary evidence.[108]

Figures such as Blume, in contrast, simply evaded such scrutiny. Besseler, too, was protected, owing in part to the limited access to information in the GDR and in part to the ardent defenses of his former students, notably the Jewish émigré and eminent University of Chicago professor Edward Lowinsky. Lowinsky bestowed an honorary doctorate on Besseler and passionately defended his teacher in the obituary he wrote. Using all the arguments Besseler himself had put forth in his denazification, Lowinsky paid special tribute to Besseler's assistance in allowing him to circumvent anti-Semitic edicts of the Nazi government. Lowinsky conceded only that "If he thought in the beginning of the National Socialist Government as capable of constructive cultural action, he belonged to a large group of German intellectuals who did likewise — and he lived to regret his mistake bitterly."[109]

Besseler remained untouchable long after his death in 1969. When the editorial by Christoph Wolff mentioned Besseler's marking of books by Jewish authors, Wolff was compelled to retract his statement because he lacked access to supporting evidence. Unable to view Besseler's files in Heidelberg because of an alleged "fifty-year blocking period," Wolff reported, based on second-hand information provided by Ludwig Finscher in Heidelberg, that "Besseler can apparently in no way be regarded as having been an active Nazi; that his political situation in Heidelberg was very complicated; and that he was much less — if at all — incriminated than has often been assumed, also by me. In particular, there doesn't seem to exist documentation that he bears personal responsibility for the stamping of Jewish titles in the Heidelberg library."[110]

Moser and Boetticher were thus branded at home and abroad as two of the few identifiable Nazis, whereas the Third Reich origins of EdM and *MGG* were quickly forgotten, opening the door to further support for the enterprises, and East German musicologists made vocal claims of having resumed musicological scholarship exactly where it had left off in 1933.[111] Only recently have a few German scholars embarked on critical examinations of the presumed reforms of musicological research after 1945, especially with regard to the concentration on German music and the retention of race-centered concepts. Eckhard John, in a survey of musicology at Freiburg, noted that Müller-Blattau showed no indications of changing his views after 1945 and persisted in promoting the idea of heredity as the source musical greatness among German composers.[112] Albrecht Riethmüller, while not limiting his criticism to EdM but questioning the entire undertaking of national musical collections in all countries, noted that the project continues to this day without any thought given to the quality of the works that are preserved or to the purpose of the activity.[113]

Reverberations in the United States

The shock of the Holocaust notwithstanding, the international community for the most part seemed eager to reestablish contact with German colleagues after the war and content to forego investigating their roles in the Nazi state. But some German-Jewish émigrés in the United States had a different view of the situation in postwar Germany. Having lived in a climate of condoned anti-Semitism until their emigration, they possessed a sensitivity to current developments that eluded others. Willi Apel, for example, objected to Moser's *Die Musik der deutschen Stämme* for reasons quite different from those of Lang. While he found no explicit anti-Semitic sentiments in the book, he was troubled by the broader implications of the problematic insistence on designating the Jews as a separate group.[114]

Alfred Einstein compiled a much longer list of those he held responsible for aiding the Nazi regime. Closely following the progress of his former colleagues undergoing denazification, Einstein formed a very negative impression of postwar Germany and distanced himself as much as possible. In 1949, he turned down an invitation to speak at the Free University in West Berlin because he had no desire to visit "the Fourth Reich," and in the same year he declined the Golden Mozart Medal from the Austrian government.[115] By 1948 he had withdrawn from the ISCM and the IMS because of the growing influence of Germans in those organizations.[116] And he withdrew from any active involvement in British musical life because of England's favorable treatment of former Nazis.[117]

Einstein was particularly vexed by a lack of insight on the part of the non-German world in their relationships with German scholars. He reviled Blume for passing himself off as an opponent to Nazism and for receiving praise in *Music and Letters*, and he warned Americans not to fall for Blume's overtures.[118] He agonized over the reinstatement of individuals he regarded as particularly dangerous. He was upset that Robert Haas, forced to give up his position in Austria by virtue of his political record, was later rehabilitated apparently because an article of his appeared in *The Musical Quarterly* under Lang's editorship. Einstein also expressed sadness at the news that such individuals as Hans Engel and Joseph Müller-Blattau could continue to hold academic positions.[119]

Curt Sachs also did not single out Moser as "one bad apple," but placed responsibility on the entire discipline. He wrote to Moser in 1949 of the numerous letters he received from Germans pleading their innocence:

> These gentlemen don't see that there is a straight line between the ardent nationalist and the executioner in Auschwitz, even when a few posts stand in between. Do you know Goethe's *Sorcerer's Apprentice?* . . . You too, like so many other scholars, helped to prepare the mentality that ultimately led to the slaughterhouses and gas chambers of the national concentration camp. . . . Those who are to be the intellectual leaders of Germany must be confronted with the fact that the horrible misfortune that overcame the world and also caused you so much personal sacrifice was not the act of a few fanatics but the explosion of the incendiary material set down by the generation of deceitful pseudo-scholars like Chamberlain, Woltman or Günther (foreign scholars find them laughable) and nourished by generations of teachers and professors. Only when the German learns to love his homeland without screaming in everyone's ears about the German soul and the German man, only when he perceives that national exhibitionism is not a virtue but a depravity, only then can there be peace — for Germany and for the others.[120]

Curt Sachs, a survivor of the decimated field of German comparative musicology, could see perhaps better than others the futility of German nationalism and could envision the potential for growth of the discipline free from German scholarly traditions. At the same time, however, other victims of National Socialism living in the United States could not entirely abandon their respect for the German intellectual and musical legacy. Einstein, unlike Sachs, seemed to consider himself an heir to the long and fruitful tradition of German historical musicology. Despite his intimate acquaintance with his German colleagues' political behavior, even their blatant anti-Semitism, Einstein continued to hold a tempered respect for German scholarship, both past and present. His first reaction to the publication of *MGG* was basically positive, although he thought it overrun with Nazi language,[121] and his kudos for American musicology was reserved largely for the work of fellow émigrés and students of the German tradition. In his assessment of scholarship in the United States, he singled out the works of Bukofzer, Plamenac, and Hewitt (a Besseler student) as recent outstanding accomplishments in American musicology.[122]

Einstein's respect for the German intellectual tradition found resonance in the United States, where American colleagues had harbored a profound reverence for German scholarship even before the influx of German refugees. Since the late nineteenth century, German musicologists had stood at the forefront of the discipline as leaders in research, organization, and publication, and American musicology was built on German foundations in the early twentieth century. A small group of American-born scholars, most of them trained in Germany and Austria, eagerly adopted the practices of émigrés who arrived in the 1930s during the most significant growth spurt of the discipline in the United States.[123] A recently compiled bio-bibliography of the thirty-five individuals who had the greatest impact on American musicology in the first half of the twentieth century includes thirteen who were refugees from Hitler and thirteen others — American and European — who received some or all of their training in Germany and Vienna.[124] The arrival of German refugees led to an unprecedented surge of musicological activity in the United States and only enhanced the respect for German scholarship.

The legacy of German scholarship in the United States also helped to instill a high regard for German music and, arguably, a subconscious assumption of its superiority. In addition to establishing German methodologies as the basis for research in music of the Renaissance by such scholars as Lowinsky, strong convictions of German musical superiority made their way into the American musicological canon. Such émigrés as Einstein, Geiringer, and Schrade discovered not only room for growth in the discipline, but also a concert life supportive of European and particularly German art music of the eighteenth and nineteenth centuries, areas in which they specialized. Obviously émigré scholars are not to be blamed for promoting Nazi notions of German superiority. But they had no compelling reasons to abandon their German identity, their belief in the German intellectual tradition, or their internalization of a long-standing precept of German musical superiority, nor to hesitate to pass that ideology on to their students in the process of disseminating their knowledge and techniques.

It is easy to overlook the political nature of Germanocentrism for those, Germans and non-Germans alike, who have internalized the assumption of German musical superiority. This unconscious acceptance results from being trained in a discipline developed by German scholars, and from having such notions reinforced by a concert life that continues to highlight the accomplishments of German musicians and composers. American musicology has inherited a Germanocentric concept of music history without understanding its immediate political relevance for the times in which it was originally formed, and without critically assessing its ramifications for an American discipline. The German emphasis has been allowed to persist in the training of musicologists and continually manifests itself in the higher concentration in German subjects in scholarly conferences and publications, and in the higher proportion of space given over to German music in such basic venues as music history textbooks.

The Notion of Nazi Musicology

The shortcomings of denazification due to an oversimplification of categories and a confusion over how to define "Nazi" have been acknowledged for some time,[125] but they are nevertheless understandable given the combination of urgency, revulsion, confusion, and a desire for retribution following the war. The discovery of the Holocaust and its incongruity with a German society so long respected for its arts, letters, and sciences naturally produced shock waves throughout the Western world. For the intellectual community, a distancing from identifiable perpetrators and a simple amputation of those twelve years from Germany's otherwise culturally rich history was a convenient way to deal with this paradox.

Based on the assumption that postwar musicology had been sanitized, it seemed logical to isolate the Nazi period as a separate, unconnected episode in musicology's history. A notion of "Nazi musicology" emerged to describe errant tendencies in the twelve-year period of the Third Reich. Historian Michael Meyer, perhaps one of the first to use the term in the English language,[126] portrayed "Nazi musicologists" as ivory tower scholars forced to compromise their integrity, only to revert to pre-1933 standards after the war. He claimed to have found "nazification" in an unprecedented attention to Wagner; in lectures on folk song and Germanness; and in the creation of the State Institute, a "center for politicized musicology."[127]

The problems with Meyer's generalizations should be self-evident. Meyer was simply unaware of the interest in folk song and the Germanness question predating 1933, and his judgment of the State Institute indicates that he did not know about the Bückeburg Institute or the continuation of the institute's projects after World War II. Furthermore, Meyer draws his generalizations about Wagner scholarship from the writings of nonmusicologists, when in fact musicologists had been relatively reticent on Wagner,[128] with only a few exceptions (e.g., Alfred Lorenz, and the 1933 dissertation of the Jewish émigré Hans Nathan).

These minor criticisms aside, a concept of Nazi musicology is problematic because it hinders an honest assessment of the scholars that flourished and the research that was produced under Nazi patronage. Contemporary music scholarship still relies heavily on the work of those who were active in the Third Reich and frequently utilizes landmark studies produced in those years. On such occasions, a researcher may be confronted with unexpected and seemingly incongruous references to contemporary politics or even Nazi language in otherwise respectable scholarly works. Postwar readers of Third Reich literature have had to choose between ignoring such references or, as a more extreme reaction, renouncing the entire twelve-year episode as an isolated moment of temporary insanity and delegitimizing such "politically tainted" products as unscholarly and unworthy of attention.[129] Some may even feel morally obliged to dismiss all of the work, including pre-1933 and post-1945 publications, of musicologists who actively served Hitler, after learning of their involvement. The names of many scholars engaged in propagandistic writings and collaborative wartime activities are not unfamiliar to musicologists today, both in Germany and abroad, and it is understandably discomfiting to discover that some of them may be teachers of prominent musicologists or authors of works still consulted.

Attractive as it may be to isolate and dismiss the Nazi era, such treatment underestimates the deep roots of intellectual trends that found correspondence with aspects of Nazi ideology. As we have seen, scholarship could not be denazified because German musicology in the Third Reich was never really nazified per se, but was following a course set long before 1933. This course could continue in the Third Reich and benefit from state support owing to its potential service to Nazi goals. It did not start spontaneously during Hitler's rise, nor could it be drastically rerouted after his fall but continued in some form after 1945. As the bibliographic sections of the *MGG* entries indicate, much of the literature of the period remained accessible and was still regarded as authoritative long after World War II.

Accepting a notion of Nazi musicology also poses the danger of assuming that musicology in any other geographic or historical context bears no relation to the intellectual products of that twelve-year episode in German scholarship. Classifying a group of writings as Nazi musicology allows persisting intellectual trends to evade critical scrutiny. Classifying a small groups of musicologists as Nazis reinforces complacent feelings that everyone else, by contrast, is immune to ideological influences and opportunism. Thus it allows others to distance themselves from that scholarship, despite its position in the scholarly tradition, and to distance themselves from the way the "Nazis" chose to relate their scholarship to other aspects of their lives.

How, then, is one to treat the Nazi phenomenon in musicology? A more useful treatment would be to apply our knowledge about the episode toward understanding the nature of the discipline as a whole. By reexamining the history of German musicology in its broader context, keeping an eye out for continuities before 1933 and after 1945 rather than exaggerating the discontinuities, there is a chance that scholars can remain vigilant of their own responsibilities, their vulnerabilities, and their potential impact beyond the confines of the academy.

First, the Nazi phenomenon reveals the inherently political nature of musicology. To say that musicology was never nazified does not mean that it was never political. It is, in fact, very telling that Besseler's ultimate exoneration rested largely on the Spruchkammer's misguided assumption of the "unpolitical character of his scholarly discipline."[130] On the contrary, one may argue that musicology was a political discipline from its very beginnings, particularly with regard to its Germanocentric emphasis, and has never ceased to be a political discipline. The pioneer works of the nineteenth century arose in a political climate intent on formulating a German identity, and the field continued to grow under circumstances that repeatedly demanded a positive reinforcement of that identity: the campaign for unification in 1871, the demoralization following World War I, the promotion of German racial superiority and the elimination of inferiors under Hitler, and the mission to spread German culture throughout Europe during the war.

After 1945, shifts in methodology gravitated toward objective, positivist approaches, such as chronologies and the careful analysis of source materials. These shifts might have been regarded as a departure from Nazi musicology, in that they abandoned the irrational in favor of the rational. Nevertheless, the German emphasis remained intact. Methods may have become less subjective and therefore less politically suspect, but the favored objects of these methods were still the composers designated as pillars of German greatness, such as Bach, Beethoven, Mozart, and Wagner.

Second, once we accept the political nature of musicology, we can see how, as a political discipline, musicology can be vulnerable to exploitation by political forces. This vulnerability is especially acute in periods of intellectual and political transitions. During such times, scholars need to be especially wary of the seduction of politically fashionable modes of thought. The situation of musicology in Nazi Germany provides a striking example of how the uncritical acceptance of theoretical trends and catchphrases could get out of hand and unleash destructive forces. Musicology experienced a methodological crisis after World War I, scholars energetically sought new models and methods for understanding music, and the hasty adoption of racial theories and political rhetoric led to a chaotic mess of inconsistencies. But those who conformed were guaranteed acceptance and publishing opportunities, blindly following others without imagining the consequences. Uncritical acceptance and indiscriminate use of such terms as "racial soul," "folk soul," "Nordic," "Dinaric," "Germanic," "völkisch," "organic," "struggle," and "Volksgemeinschaft" created a plethora of literature accepted only on the merits of its subscribing to a fashionable set of assumptions, regardless of its flawed logic and subjective judgments. The innocuous effects of such window dressing were that one could easily dazzle readers and conceal a lack of original thought or intellectual rigor. The more pernicious effects were the empowerment of these subscribers to dictate the wholesale condemnation of anything or anyone simply by attaching the label of "Jewish" or "bolshevist."

Third, the saga of musicology between the two world wars also graphically illustrates the effects of socioeconomic conditions on the musicology discipline. From 1918 on, musicologists dedicated their studies to their own musical heritage, as a result both of having been cut off from international scholarly exchange during the war and of facing limited opportunities for research travel abroad. The field as a whole felt threatened by the economic turmoil, high unemployment, and educational reforms that encouraged technological and otherwise practical fields. Feeling the pressure to justify its existence within and beyond the academy, musicology concentrated on contributing to nationalist aims in order to publicize its service to musical practice, general education, and the Volksgemeinschaft. As the National Socialist party and state mechanism created research funding and employment opportunities, musicologists continued to direct their interests toward politically acceptable subject matter. In the process, they contributed to the theoretical foundations of anti-Semitic policies and benefited greatly from the execution of those policies.

German musicology in the Weimar and Nazi eras can provide an instructive antimodel, showing how scholarship in a period of transition can be easily led astray. This example is especially useful, given that the period following World War I shares a number of features with musicology at the close of the twentieth century. The field of musicology has recently experienced a number of methodological crises. Musicologists are acknowledging the extent to which music has been isolated as an object, and many perceive that the field has fallen far behind other disciplines by failing to contextualize its subject matter. In an attempt to bring music out of isolation and understand its broader ramifications beyond "the text itself," musicologists have turned to other disciplines for theoretical models and methodologies. The benefits of this process have been to open up and establish a wide variety of new approaches and to enable scholars to seek out entirely new directions. It has also alerted the field to the political nature of both music and music scholarship after a long period of indulging in the self-perception of immunity from politics.[131]

The search for and application of new theoretical constructs and political concepts in scholarship can be a double-edged sword, however, as the uncritical acceptance of race theory and political rhetoric in Nazi Germany so clearly illustrated. Although certain models can be very useful in leading scholars to view their subject in innovative ways, a misinterpretation of or an overreliance on such models can make them appear as panaceas that offer easy answers and neat classifications, and can lead to their uncritical acceptance. Such misuse of borrowed models can also serve as a smoke screen for faulty logic — concealed behind a meaningless vocabulary of specialized terms — and can facilitate the subjective condemnation of anything that challenges its assumptions. Although far less monodimensional and ultimately less harmful than the Nazi-era uses of "Jewish" and "bolshevist," such terms as "racist," "elitist," "fascist," "patriarchal," "feminist," "positivist," and "new musicology" have shown signs of exploitation as subjective pejoratives when used in an uncritical and indiscriminate manner.

The last decades of the twentieth century have also presented a socioeconomic climate that challenges the field to redefine itself and concern itself with career issues. Here again, the socioeconomic factors of the Weimar and Nazi eras and the responses of musicologists to those conditions serve as instructive examples. Times of economic hardship are often accompanied by antiintellectualism, and scholars in the humanities usually find themselves especially vulnerable in such circumstances. Under the pressure to demonstrate its relevance, either within the academy or in a broader social context, scholarship can easily succumb to political agendas or realign its focus to appeal to a dominant political, ideological, or intellectual trend. The risks of compromising scholarly standards and moral integrity run especially high in such volatile conditions. It is incumbent upon scholars to be wary of directions in scholarship that may gain in popularity because they serve the needs of a particular political agenda. Every new approach must undergo a critical examination, and scholars must resist subscribing to popular trends for the purposes of career advancement. Above all, scholarship must remain sensitive to the exploitation of such trends toward castigating a group arbitrarily designated as a nemesis, regardless of whether that nemesis is defined by race, ethnicity, gender, intellectual orientation, or a set of beliefs.

Notes

The following abbreviations for archival materials, organizations, and frequently cited publications appear in the notes. The locations of archival collections are listed in the bibliography.

AfMf	*Archiv für Musikforschung*
AfMw	*Archiv für Musikwissenschaft*
AMz	*Allgemeine Musikzeitung*
BA	Bundesarchiv Koblenz
BDC	Berlin Document Center
BSB	Bayerische Staatsbibliothek
CM	*Collegium Musicum*
DASB	Deutscher Arbeiter-Sängerbund
DGMW	Deutsche Gesellschaft für Musikwissenschaft
DJ	*Die deutsche Jugendmusikbewegung in Dokumenten ihrer Zeit von den Anfängen bis 1933*, ed. W. Scholtz and W. Jonas-Corrieri (Wolfenbüttel: Möseler, 1980)
DMG	Deutsche Musikgesellschaft
DMJb	*Deutsches Musikjahrbuch*
DMK	*Deutsche Musikkultur*
DTZ	*Deutsche Tonkünstler-Zeitung*
FA	Fakultätsakte
Gn	*Germanien*

GStA	Geheimes Staatsarchiv Preußischer Kulturbesitz
HJ	Hitler-Jugend
JbMP	*Jahrbuch der Musikbibliothek Peters*
MGG	*Die Musik in Geschichte und Gegenwart,* ed. F. Blume (Kassel: Bärenreiter, 1949–68; suppl. 1973–79)
MJV	*Musik in Jugend und Volk*
Mk	*Die Musik*
MPf	*Die Musikpflege*
New Grove	*The New Grove Dictionary of Music and Musicians,* ed. S. Sadie (London: Macmillan, 1980)
NSDAP	Nationalsozialistische deutsche Arbeiterpartei
NSLB	Nationalsozialistischer Lehrerbund
NSM	*Nationalsozialistische Monathefte*
NStA	Niedersächsisches Staatsarchiv Bückeburg
NSV	Nationalsozialistische Volkswohlfahrt
PA	Personalakte
Phil. Fak.	Philosophische Fakultät
PPK	Parteiamtliche Prüfungskommission zum Schutze des NS-Schrifttums
REM	Reich Education Ministry (referred to as Reichsministerium für Wissenschaft, Kunst, und Volksbildung; Reichs- und Preußisches Ministerium für Wissenschaft, Erziehung und Volksbildung; and Reichsministerium für Wissenschaft, Erziehung und Volksbildung)
RKF	Reichskommissar für die Festigung des deutschen Volkstums
RMK	Reichsmusikkammer
RSK	Reichsschrifttumskammer
RuSHA	Rasse- und Siedlungshauptamt
SA	Sturmabteilung
SIM	Archive, Staatliches Institut für Musikforschung
SS	Schutzstaffel
UAB	Universitätsarchiv Berlin
UABonn	Universitätsarchiv Bonn
UAF	Universitätsarchiv Freiburg
UAH	Universitätsarchiv Heidelberg
UAK	Universitätsarchiv Köln
UAL	Universitätsarchiv Leipzig
UAM	Universitätsarchiv München
UAW	Universitätsarchiv Wien
UNL	University of Nebraska, Lincoln
VME	*Völkische Musikerziehung*
ZfH	*Zeitschrift für Hausmusik*
ZfM	*Zeitschrift für Musik*
ZfMw	*Zeitschrift für Musikwissenschaft*
ZStA	Zentrales Staatsarchiv Potsdam

Introduction

1. "Die Musik ist doch deutsch, oder etwa nicht?" Quoted in Riethmüller, *Die Walhalla und ihre Musiker,* 23. See also idem, "Musik, die 'deutscheste' Kunst."

2. Voßkamp, "Kontinuität und Diskontinuität," 140–62.

3. Hermand, *Literaturwissenschaft und Kunstwissenschaft,* 11–15, 21–23, 34–42, 45–48.

4. Schnauber, "Introduction," vii–xxii.

5. Oellers, "Dichtung und Volkstum," 246–48.

6. Lämmert, "Germanistik — eine deutsche Wissenschaft," 76–91.

7. Schnauber, ix–xii.

8. See chap. 6.

9. Oesterle, "Office of Ancestral Inheritance," 211–12, 218–19, 225–27, 230–32.

10. See chap. 5.

Chapter 1. The Background

1. Gay, *Weimar Culture.*

2. Moser, *Geschichte der deutschen Musik,* 2d ed., vol. 3, pp. 513–14.

3. Ibid., 453.

4. Ibid., 474, 497–502.

5. Ibid., 453, 468–69, 476.

6. Jarausch, *Unfree Professions,* 48.

7. Moser, *Geschichte der deutschen Musik,* 2d ed., vol. 3, pp. 467, 469–70. ". . . so kann man schon daraus ablesen, was die Musik im geistigen Haushalt der Nation bedeutet" (Moser, 467).

8. "Denn wenn Deutschland heute in der Welt trotz aller uns begegnenden Feindseligkeit und Abneigung *ein* Gebiet und *einen* Stand von unbedingter kultureller Überzeugungskraft besitzt, so ist es neben unserer Wissenschaft die deutsche Musik, der deutsche Tonkünstler; diese edle, wahrhaft friedliche Waffe lasse man nicht ungenützt rosten." Moser, *Geschichte der deutschen Musik,* 2d ed., vol. 3, pp. 477.

9. Ibid., 453–54, 470–73, 499–513.

10. *MGG,* 1st ed., s.v. "Gesellschaften und Vereine."

11. *MGG,* 1st ed., s.v. "Gemischter Chor."

12. From the introductory paragraph of the 1927 charter, quoted in Kestenberg, *Jahrbuch,* 19. This and all other translations are the author's, unless otherwise noted.

13. Ibid., 19–28.

14. Guttsman, *Workers' Culture,* 4, 61, 155–76.

15. The *Jahrbuch* includes a section on Reich music organizations, followed by a chapter for each province, with a special chapter on the city of Berlin. The material on Reich organizations provides numbers for the total memberships of the DASB, the Deutscher Sängerbund, and the Reichsverband der gemischten Chöre Deutschlands. In each chapter thereafter, Kestenberg lists all church and secular choral groups individually and, where available, provides numbers for their memberships.

16. Kestenberg, *Jahrbuch*, 19.

17. These included *Die Laute: Monatsschrift zur Pflege des deutschen Liedes und guter Hausmusik; Die Gitarre; Zeitschrift zur Pflege des Gitarren- und Lautenspiels und der Hausmusik; Lauten-Almanach: Ein Jahr- und Handbuch für alle Lauten- und Gitarrenspieler; Muse des Saitenspiels: Fach- und Werbe-Monatsschrift für Zither-, Gitarren- und Schossgeigenspiel; Münchner Zither-Zeitung: Fachblatt für Zitherspiel; Die Volksmusik; Die Zupfmusik; Der Lautenspieler; Schallkiste: Illustrierte Zeitschrift für Hausmusik; Bundeszeitung des Deutschen Mandolinen- und Gitarrenspieler-Bundes; Der Blockflötenspiegel: Arbeitsblatt zur Belebung historischer Instrumente in der Jugend- und Hausmusik;* and *Collegium Musicum* (renamed *Zeitschrift für Hausmusik*).

18. Stachura, *German Youth Movement,* 13–21, 54–55; Laqueur, *Young Germany,* 12–14

19. Stachura, *German Youth Movement,* chaps. 3 and 4.

20. Laqueur states that while the artistic and literary products of the Wandervogel were seriously wanting, "there was one field in which great work was done. The youth movement did probably more than any other movement at the time to develop musical culture on a very broad basis" (*Young Germany,* 18–19).

21. Treziak, *Deutsche Jugendbewegung,* 12.

22. D. Kolland, *Die Jugendmusikbewegung,* 12–13, 29–32.

23. Ibid., 32, 38, 40, 51, 56ff., 65–69, 75, 86–87.

24. Ibid., 58–65, 75–76.

25. Walther Hensel, "Von Gregorianischer Melodien," *Frankensteiner Liederbuch* 1 (1928), rpt. in *DJ* 337–38; Fritz Jöde, "Alte Madrigale und andere A capella-Gesänge aus dem 16. und 17. Jahrhundert," *Hausmusik* 14/16 (1921), rpt. in *DJ* 329; Wilhelm Thomas, "Lied im Alltag," *Die Singgemeinde* 2/29, rpt. in *DJ* 352–54.

26. Jöde's multivolume collection of music for the movement, entitled *Der Musikant,* concentrated on early polyphony and included an entire volume of music by J. S. Bach, but one volume, constructed as a historical survey of vocal music, includes a section on "the classicists." D. Kolland, *Die Jugendmusikbewegung,* 87–98.

27. D. Kolland, *Die Jugendmusikbewegung,* 93–94.

28. Holtmeyer, "Schulmusik und Musiklehrer," chap. 6, 112–17, 120–30.

29. Kestenberg regarded this as the central problem in contemporary musical life: "Es ist ja nicht mehr ein freiwilliger Entschluß: die täglich größer werdende Not des Berufsmusikerstandes zwingt unerbittlich dazu, sich mit den ökonomischen Prozessen, mit den politischen Gegebenheiten, mit Angebot und Nachfrage auf dem Musikmarkt zu beschäftigen, der Musiksoziologie endlich eine Basis zu geben." *Jahrbuch,* ix.

30. Jarausch, *Unfree Professions,* chaps. 1, 2, and 3.

31. Newhouse, "Artists, Artisans, or Workers?"

32. "Das Reich gewährt Veranstaltungen und Einrichtungen von Reichswichtigkeit oder vorbildlicher Bedeutung von Fall zu Fall in begrenztem Umfang Beihilfen, die dem Fonds zur 'Förderung wissenschaftlicher und künstlerischer Zwecke' entnommen werden. Der Anteil, der auf musikalische Veranstaltungen und Einrichtungen entfällt, ist verhältnismäßig gering und kann zahlenmäßig nicht angegeben werden." Kestenberg, *Jahrbuch,* 3.

33. Ibid., 3–6.

34. According to Kestenberg's statistics of 1930–31, the Landestheater in Baden received 438,000 marks from the state and 779,000 from the city of Karlsruhe, while the Nationaltheater in Mannheim received only 23,000 from the state and 1.1 million from the city (1033–35). The government of Hesse similarly gave 540,000 to the Landestheater, while the city of Darmstadt contributed 650,000 (1131–32). The Bavarian government, however, provided more than 2 million marks to the Bayerisches Staatstheater, twice the figure that the city of Munich contributed, and it subsidized the Staatliche Akademie für Tonkunst and the Staatskonservatorium Würzburg exclusively (819–20), and the Saxon government provided twice as much money (2 million marks) to the Staatstheater as did the city of Dresden (907–10). Figures fluctuated, and government interests renegotiated their contributions informally as needs changed with each fiscal year, with the notable exception of Thuringia, which passed a law explicitly stating that municipal governments were to cover 20 percent of the deficits of state theaters and orchestras located in their municipality (1091).

35. Düwell, "Kultur und Kulturpolitik," 78–79.

36. The Pomeranian government contributed to the Pomeranian Folksong Archive at the university, the publication of the "Denkmäler Pommerscher Musik," and a Pomeranian Music Festival. The Saxon and Leipzig governments each provided approximately 60,000 marks to the musicology department at the university toward the purchase of the Heyer collection, and the Rhenish government gave money to the Beethoven archive in Bonn toward the purchase of archival materials and to the state and city library in Düsseldorf toward the acquisition of Schumann manuscripts (Kestenberg, *Jahrbuch,* 292, 685, 907–8). The wide discrepancies in regional policy were due to the size and degree of bureaucratic organization. Cultural affairs were traditionally tied to education and the church and came under the jurisdiction of the respective ministries. In states such as Baden, Bavaria, Hesse, Oldenburg, the Saar region, and Württemberg all cultural affairs were handled by such ministries, often with a designated music expert, while Mecklenburg-Strelitz and Thuringia established separate ministries for general education (Volksbildung) or arts, and Hamburg had its own senate committee for the arts. Sometimes these ministries were subsumed under a ministry of the interior, and in rare cases the economic ministry would take charge of a cultural sphere. But a greater number of provinces (Anhalt, Brandenburg, Bremen, Hanover, Hesse-Nassau, Lübeck, Mecklenburg-Schwerin, Mecklenburg-Strelitz, Lower Silesia, Upper Silesia, East Prussia, Posen-West Prussia, Schleswig-Holstein, and Westphalia) had no such administrative bodies, and local representatives of the board of education supervised some aspects of music education.

37. Kestenberg, *Jahrbuch,* 58–86.

38. Steinweis, *Art, Ideology, and Economics,* 42.

39. Hinkel, *Handbuch der Reichskulturkammer,* 95–123.

40. Steinweis, *Art, Ideology, and Economics,* 45–49.

41. Ibid., 80–88, 94, 98–102.

42. Hinkel, *Handbuch der Reichskulturkammer,* 101; Steinweis, 69–70.

43. Heinz Brandes, "Die deutschen Laienorchester," in Stumme, ed., *Musik im Volk,* 1st. ed., 152–64; Hinkel, *Handbuch der Reichskulturkammer,* 100.

44. See Steinweis, *Art, Ideology, and Economics,* 38–44.

45. Kater, *Twisted Muse,* 33–34.

46. Fischer and Scholtz, "Stellung und Funktion," 156–58.

47. Hübbenet, *NS-Gemeinschaft "Kraft durch Freude,"* 14–18.

48. Gerhard Nowottny, "Volksmusikalische Praxis in der NS-Gemeinschaft 'Kraft durch Freude,'" in Stumme, ed., *Musik im Volk,* 1st ed., 112–21; Gerhard Nowottny and Carl Hannemann, "Volksmusikalische Arbeit in der NS-Gemeinschaft 'Kraft durch Freude,'" in Stumme, ed., *Musik im Volk,* 2d ed., 174–83.

49. Maria Ottich, "Die Musikarbeit der NS-Gemeinschaft 'Kraft durch Freude,'" in Hase, *Jahrbuch der deutschen Musik,* 61–62.

50. Goslich, ed., *Musikalische Volksbildung.*

51. Ottich, "Musikarbeit der NS-Gemeinschaft," 63.

52. Hübbenet, *NS-Gemeinschaft "Kraft durch Freude,"* 16–18, 35–36.

53. Prieberg, *Musik im NS-Staat,* 256–59. See also Bunge, *Musik in der Waffen-SS.*

54. Wulf, *Musik im Dritten Reich,* 257–61.

55. Stumme, "Musik in der Hitler-Jugend," in Stumme, ed., *Musik im Volk,* 2d ed., 30–31. On the organ movement of the 1920s, see Williams, "Idea of *Bewegung.*" On its activities in the Third Reich, see Kater, *Twisted Muse,* 171–74.

56. Riethmüller, "Bestimmung der Orgel," 40–44.

57. Stumme, "Musik in der Hitler-Jugend," in Stumme, ed., *Musik im Volk,* 2d ed., 30–31.

58. Riethmüller, "Bestimmung der Orgel," 36, 50–51.

59. Nazi youth organizations were distinguished by an overabundance of terms (e.g., Deutsches Jungvolk, Hitler-Jugend, Jungmädel, Bund Deutscher Mädel) coined to describe the different age groups, genders, and levels of hierarchy in the organization. These organizations were spread all over the Reich in more than forty districts (called *Gebiete* for the boys' groups and *Obergaue* for the girls' groups). Each district encompassed approximately twenty subdistricts (*Banne* and *Untergaue,* respectively), and each subdistrict was subdivided into four to six large units that were further subdivided. For the precise terminology and organization, see Klönne, *Jugend im Dritten Reich,* 42–43.

60. Most right-wing and *völkisch* youth organizations voluntarily dissolved; the youth groups affiliated with political parties disbanded when those parties were declared illegal; and the confessional groups conceded when a Nazi sympathizer was elected Reich Bishop and handed over all Protestant groups to Reichsjugendführer Baldur von Schirach, and when the Concordat between Hitler and the Vatican won the sympathy of Catholic groups. Von Schirach gained wider control through the cooperation of other Nazi officials: youth groups affiliated with trade and industry, agriculture, and sports were handed over to Hitler Youth jurisdiction by the head of the German Workers' Front, the Reich Agriculture Minister, and the Reich Sport Leader, respectively. Stachura, *German Youth Movement,* 113–16, 122–34.

61. See Kater, *Twisted Muse,* 135–46.

62. Kater, "Bürgerliche Jugendbewegung," 127–29.

63. Laqueur, *Young Germany,* xii; Stachura, *German Youth Movement,* 59ff., 117.

64. Kater, "Bürgerliche Jugendbewegung," 133–44.

65. Stachura, *German Youth Movement,* 12–14, 45–51.

66. Stumme, "Musik in der Hitlerjugend," in Stumme, ed., *Musik im Volk,* 2d ed., 21.

67. D. Kolland, *Die Jugendmusikbewegung,* 130–40; Wilhelm Gößler, "Verantwortung und Aufgabe einer Jugendstimmerziehung," in Stumme, ed., *Musik im Volk,* 1st ed., 45–55, 2d ed., 53–62; Friedrichkarl Roedemeyer, "Deutsche Stimm- und Sprechbildung," in Stumme, ed., *Musik im Volk,* 1st ed., 176–82, 2d ed. 338–44.

68. Helmut Majewski, "Neugestaltung deutscher Blasmusik," in Stumme, ed., *Musik im Volk,* 1st ed., 31–45; idem, "Wesen und Formen der Blasmusik," in Stumme, ed., *Musik im Volk,* 2d ed., 31–43.

69. Stumme, "Musik in der Hitler-Jugend," in Stumme, ed., *Musik im Volk,* 2d. ed., 30.

70. Stumme, "Musik in der Hitler-Jugend," in Stumme, ed., *Musik im Volk,* 1st ed., 25–26; Stumme, "Musik in der Hitler-Jugend," in Stumme, ed., *Musik im Volk,* 2d ed., 23, 26, 30.

71. Fritz Jöde spoke of the creation of a "neuen Mensch" through education and stated "Das Ziel der Neuorganisation einer Musikerziehungsarbeit in diesem Sinne ist nichts Geringeres als die Wiederbelebung einer tätigen Teilnahme an der Musik aller Schichten unseres Volkes" (D. Kolland, *Die Jugendmusikbewegung,* 112); Götsch referred to the "Reinigung und Wiederherstellung" of the total person (D. Kolland, *Die Jugendmusikbewegung,* 113); Flitner emphasized "Die Überlieferung des Gefühls, ein Volk zu sein" (D. Kolland, *Die Jugendmusikbewegung,* 114).

72. Out of the *Jugendmusikbewegung* came the institutions of the Jugendmusikschule for schoolchildren, the Volksmusikschule for teens and adults, and such regional adult-education facilities as the Musikheim in Frankfurt/Oder. In 1922, Fritz Jöde established the first Volksmusikschule in Hamburg and the first Jugendmusikschule in conjunction with the "Seminar für Jugend und Volksmusik" in Berlin in 1925. D. Kolland, *Die Jugendmusikbewegung,* 117–18.

73. D. Kolland, *Die Jugendmusikbewegung,* 117–27; Fischer-Defoy, 47–48.

74. Kater, *Twisted Muse,* 146–50.

75. Fritz Jöde, "Die Musik im Kindesalter," in Stumme, ed., *Musik im Volk,* 2d ed., 79–92; Fischer-Defoy, *Kunst Macht Politik,* 99.

76. Fischer-Defoy, *Kunst Macht Politik,* 98; Prieberg, *Musik im NS-Staat,* 250. Prieberg learned from an eyewitness that Jöde actually urged his associates to enter the music organizations of the Hitler Youth, seeing this as "the only possibility for continuing our work in music." Letter from Herbert Napiersky to Prieberg, quoted on 244.

77. Stumme, "Die Jugendmusikschule," in Stumme, ed., *Musik im Volk,* 2d. ed., 53–62. Compare with Jöde's curriculum outlined in D. Kolland, *Die Jugendmusikbewegung,* 118–19.

78. Wolfgang Stumme, "Musikpolitik als Führungsaufgabe," in Stumme, ed., *Musik im Volk,* 2d ed., 11–12.

79. D. Kolland, *Die Jugendmusikbewegung,* 118–20; Stumme, "Musik in der Hitler-Jugend," in Stumme, ed., *Musik im Volk,* 1st ed., 23–24; 2d ed., 25–26.

80. Heinz Drewes of the RMK, quoted in Schwerter, "Heerschau und Selektion," 113.

81. Program rpt. in Dümling and Girth, eds., *Entartete Musik: Eine kommentierte Rekonstruktion,* 105–10.

82. Schwerter, "Heerschau und Selektion," 112, 122.

83. Kater, *Twisted Muse,* 189–90.

84. Joseph Goebbels, "Zehn Grundsätze deutschen Musikschaffens," *Amtliche Mit-*

teilungen der Reichsmusikkammer 5 (1938), facsimile in Dümling and Girth, eds., *Entartete Musik: Eine kommentierte Rekonstruktion,* 123; portions translated in Ellis, "Music in the Third Reich," 127.

85. Ziegler, *Entartete Musik,* 14–16.

86. Ibid., 6.

87. Ibid., 13, 22–24.

88. Alfred Einstein, "Opera in Breslau: Schönberg's *Die glückliche Hand [The Favoured Hand],* Handel's *Joshua,* and Ballet," *Berliner Tageblatt,* 26 March 1928, trans. in Dower, *Einstein on Music,* 50.

89. Einstein, "Arnold Schönberg: *Von heute auf morgen* (World première in Frankfurt)," *Berliner Tageblatt,* 3 February 1930, trans. in Dower, *Einstein on Music,* 104–5.

90. Kater, *Different Drummers,* 26–28.

91. Robinson, "Jazz Reception."

92. Kater, *Different Drummers,* chaps. 1 and 2.

93. Ziegler, *Entartete Musik,* 18–20.

94. Evans, "Rezeption der Musik Strawinskys."

95. Prieberg, *Musik im NS-Staat,* 126, 298–306; Kater, *Twisted Muse,* chap. 5.

96. Steinweis, *Art, Ideology, and Economics,* 126–32; Kater, *Different Drummers,* 30, 38.

97. Moser, *Geschichte der deutschen Musik,* 2d ed., vol 3, pp. 401.

98. Ibid., 501; idem, "Die Stellung der Musik im deutschen Geistesleben der Gegenwart," *DMJb* 2–3 (1925): 120–21.

99. Steinweis, *Art, Ideology, and Economics,* chap. 5; Kater, *Twisted Muse,* 75–85, 88–91.

100. Sponheuer, "Musik auf einer Insel," 111–12; Freeden, *Jüdische Presse,* 84–85; Steinweis, *Art, Ideology, and Economics,* 120–21; Kater, *Twisted Muse,* 97–101; Jelavich, *Berlin Cabaret,* 232–33.

101. Steinweis, *Art, Ideology, and Economics,* 122; Sponheuer, "Musik auf einer Insel," 115–31; Kater, *Twisted Muse,* 101–3.

102. Jelavich, *Berlin Cabaret,* 34–35.

103. The performing arts in state institutions could be more closely supervised than amateur activities, but Steinweis refers to cases where one official approved opera and concert performances of works of Mendelssohn and Offenbach, while another insisted that at least one new German opera be performed each season. Steinweis, *Art, Ideology, and Economics,* 132, 134–38.

104. Ellis, "Music in the Third Reich," 142–43.

105. Bollmus, *Amt Rosenberg,* 107–8.

106. Bergen, *Twisted Cross,* 164–71.

107. Kater, *Different Drummers,* 52, 104.

108. Drechsler, *Funktion der Musik,* 24, 33, 42, 131.

109. Elste, "Privatheit und Politik," 107–111.

110. Kater, *Different Drummers,* 49–51, 86–87, 138–46.

111. Jelavich, *Berlin Cabaret,* 86–95.

112. Kater, *Different Drummers,* 64, 101.

113. Jelavich, *Berlin Cabaret,* 230–57.

114. See Kershaw, *Nazi Dictatorship*, chap. 2.

115. Boris Schwarz, *Music and Musical Life*, 7, 41–140.

116. Steinweis, *Art, Ideology, and Economics*, 138–41, and Ellis, "Music in the Third Reich," 129–30.

117. Ellis, "Music in the Third Reich," 130–34.

118. Hailey, "Rethinking Sound"; Amzoll, "Zur Rolle des Rundfunks."

119. Amzoll, "Aufstieg und Verfall."

120. Drechsler, *Funktion der Musik*, 30, 35–36, 41–43, 86–95; Kater, *Different Drummers*, 47.

121. "Es wäre nicht nationalsozialistisch, wenn der deutsche Rundfunk sich anmaßen wollte, von einer erhöhten 'Bildungs'-ebene herab in die Freizeitgestaltung des schaffenden Menschen einzugreifen." *Mitteilungen der Reichsrundfunkgesellschaft*, 1 February 1934, quoted in Drechsler, *Funktion der Musik*, 121.

122. Jelavich, *Berlin Cabaret*, 22–26; Hugo Haan, "Oper und Brettl," *Signale für die musikalische Welt*, 13 March 1901, 322, quoted and trans. in Jelavich, *Berlin Cabaret*, 26.

123. Jelavich, *Berlin Cabaret*, 168.

124. Gilliam, "Stage and Screen."

125. Robinson, "Jazz Reception," 108.

126. In opera reviews for the *Berliner Tageblatt* from 1927 to 1930, Alfred Einstein gave backhanded praise to Krenek's attempt to meet the general public on its own terms and had great admiration for Reznicek's *Satuala*, although he condemned both to only short-term success. Although offering some praise for *Mahagonny* and *Maschinist Hopkins*, Einstein objected to their classifications as operas (reviews translated in Dower, *Einstein on Music*, 37–41, 54, 108–113).

127. City councillor Hoffmann-Gwinner refers to the fact that the well-known conductors never lead the popular concerts, admission prices are too high, and the "Philharmonie" concert hall does not allow radio broadcasts of the concerts held there. The Center party joined in the opposition for so-called nationalistic reasons, probably because of the high salary Furtwängler was to receive in spite of the depths to which the economy had fallen. *Stenographische Berichte*, mtg. of 1 December 1927, 998ff.; mtg. of 9 September 1929, 753ff. In 1931, C. A. Lange, a member of the city council and vocal advocate of the orchestra, expressed astonishment at a decision to cut back funding from the Philharmonic and offered as a possible explanation the belief that the orchestra was thought to be infested with National Socialists, but a more likely cause was disappointment of the left when Furtwängler refused to conduct the public concerts. Lange, *Groß-Berliner Tagebuch*, 164.

128. Most performing arts issues were addressed to the arts division; musicology and college music groups were supervised by the university division; music education, pedagogy, and adult education were distributed among three separate divisions; and the maintenance of church organs and bell towers came under the supervision yet another division of the ministry. Kestenberg, *Jahrbuch*, 115–20.

129. Potter, "Nazi 'Seizure.' "

130. A fairly complete list of concerts, from the establishment of the orchestra through its centenniel year, can be found in the third volume of Muck, *Berliner Philharmonisches Orchester*.

131. H. Kolland, "Wagner-Rezeption," 498–502; Bair, "National Socialism and Opera," 130.

132. Prieberg, *Musik im NS-Staat*, 307; Kater, *Twisted Muse*, 35–39.

133. Karbaum, *Bayreuther Festspiele*, 91–93.

134. Steinweis, *Art, Ideology, and Economics*, 75–76.

135. Ellis, "Music in the Third Reich," 203–8, 246–52.

136. John, "Musik und Konzentrationslager," 1–36.

Chapter 2. Musicologists on Their Role in Modern German Society

1. Blume, "Musicology in German Universities."

2. Ringer, *Decline*, 3–13.

3. Heiber, *Universität unterm Hakenkreuz*, 32, 35–39.

4. Bleuel, *Deutschlands Bekenner*, 162–66

5. Ringer, *Decline*, 228–29.

6. Ibid., 67–75.

7. Kretzschmar, *Musikalische Zeitfragen*, 79.

8. Hans Joachim Moser, "Die äussere und innere Krisis in der Musikwissenschaft," *Die Hochschule* 4 (1920): 42–46.

9. Arnold Schering, "Musikwissenschaft und Kunst der Gegenwart," in *Bericht über den I. Musikwissenschaftlichen Kongress, Leipzig*, 13; Johannes Wolf, "Musikwissenschaft und musikwissenschaftlicher Unterricht," *AMz* 45 (1918): 532, and *Festschrift Hermann Kretzschmar*, 178–79.

10. Hermann Abert, "Kunst, Kunstwissenschaft, Kunstkritik," *Mk* 16 (1923): 7–8.

11. Hans Boettcher, "Zum Gedächtnis Hermann Aberts," *DTZ* 25 (1927): 269.

12. Theodor Kroyer, "Die Wiedererweckung des historischen Klangbildes in der musikalischen Denkmälerpraxis," *Mitteilungen der Internationalen Gesellschaft für Musikwissenschaft* 2 (1930): 80.

13. Hermann Unger, "Musikprobleme der Zeit," *DMJb* 1 (1923): 36–39.

14. Hans Joachim Moser, "Die neue Reichsmusikzunft," *AMz* 49 (1922): 704–5.

15. Hans Joachim Moser, "Musik und Staat," *Mk* 22 (1929): 7–16.

16. Hermann W.v. Waltershausen, "Musikleben und öffentliche Mittel," *DTZ* 25 (1927): 107–8.

17. Schering, "Musikwissenschaft und Kunst der Gegenwart," 14, 18–20.

18. See Hans Mersmann, "Die Situation der deutschen Musik," *Deutsche Rundschau* 226 (1931): 77–80.

19. Kroyer, "Neue Musik," *Literarischer Handweiser* 56 (1920): 163.

20. Arnold Schering, "Die expressionistische Bewegung in der Musik," in *Einführung*, 156.

21. Bücken, *Führer und Probleme*, 169–71.

22. Johannes Wolf, "Altniederländische Kunst und Chormusik von Krenek und Hindemith," *Der Auftakt* 8 (1928): 114–20.

23. Hans Mersmann, "Die Musiksprache der Gegenwart," *Der Auftakt* 8 (1928): 1–3, and "Wege zum Verständnis gegenwärtiger Musik," *DTZ* 26 (1928): 1–2.

24. E.g., Hans Albrecht criticized the training of music teachers because it stressed

early music skills and ignored contemporary works. "Privatmusiklehrer und moderne Musik," *DTZ* 26 (1928): 5.

25. Manfred Bukofzer, "Erziehung zur neuer Musik," *Melos* 9 (1930): 465–69.

26. Alfred Orel, "Das Musikschaffen in unserer Zeit," *Literarischer Handweiser* 62 (1925): 1–8.

27. Karl Blessinger, "Zum Kapitel 'Zwölftonmusik,' " *DTZ* 26 (1928): 358–60.

28. Mersmann, *Musik der Gegenwart,* 12–13; Schering, "Die expressionistische Bewegung," 161.

29. Hans Scholz announced "Wir haben gerade erst die Hochblüte des sogenannten 'Atonalismus' hinter uns. Das war eine Unmusik, die weder dem Produzenten noch dem Verbraucher Freude machte und die in gesunden Zeiten undenkbar gewesen wäre." Scholz, "Die Intellektuellen der Musik," *Deutsche Zeitschrift* 47 (1933–34): 384.

30. Mersmann, *Musik der Gegenwart,* 54–55, 62–63.

31. Hans Joachim Moser, "Die Musik im Gefüge dieser Zeit," *Deutsche Rundschau* 233 (1932): 185–86. An atypical appeal to rescue modern music at the very beginning of the Third Reich was Hellmuth Christian Wolff's attempt to encourage modern music by revealing the Germanic-Nordic essence of dissonance. Hellmuth Christian Wolff, "Spielt zeitgenössische Musik!" *Melos* 12 (1933): 424–25.

32. Holtmeyer, "Schulmusik und Musiklehrer," 45, 50–52, 54, 59–60. On p. 45 is a quote of Kretzschmar's complaint regarding insufficient singing instruction, taken from his *Musikalische Zeitfragen,* 34, and on pp. 50–52 is a discussion of Abert's dismay with youth's alienation from music and the need for a sound music pedagogy, taken from his "Musik und Gymnasialunterricht," *Zeitschrift der Internationalen Musikgesellschaft* 1901–2, 87–92.

33. Hans Joachim Moser, "Zum Musikunterricht an den Volksschulen," *Mk* 20 (1928): 669–70; Bruno Stäblein, "Musikwissenschaftliches im Schulmusikunterricht," *Die Musikerziehung* 4 (1927): 389–97.

34. Moser, "Die äußere und innere Krisis in der Musikwissenschaft," 44–45.

35. Hans Joachim Moser, "Die Stellung der Musik im deutschen Geistesleben der Gegenwart," *DMJb* 2–3 (1925): 116–18, 121.

36. Georg Schünemann, "Gegenwartsfragen der Musikerziehung," *JbMP* (1928): 25–31; Schünemann, "Gebrauchsmusik und Erziehung," *Mk* 21 (1929): 434–36; Stäblein, "Musikwissenschaftliches im Schulmusikunterricht"; Müller-Blattau, "Grundsätzliches zur Musikerziehung," *Die Musikerziehung* 5 (1928): 3–12.

37. Most believed that this stratification began in the nineteenth century, but Fellerer contended that it had existed throughout the Middle Ages. Fellerer, "Gesellschaftsform und musikalischer Stil," *DTZ* 29 (1931): 206.

38. Fritz Jöde, "Musik und Volk," *Deutsches Volkstum* 1919–20: 139–43.

39. Orel, "Das Musikschaffen in unserer Zeit," 1–4.

40. Hermann Unger, "Volksbildnerische Aufgaben der Musik," *Österreichische Rundschau* 17 (1921): 950–52 and *AMz* 48 (1921): 791.

41. Wolf, "Musikwissenschaft und musikwissenschaftlicher Unterricht," 533; 179.

42. Hans Mersmann, "Volk und Musik," *AMz* 45 (1918): 511–12; Moser, "Stellung der Musik," 123–26.

43. Egon Wellesz, "Der Musiker und diese Zeit," *Melos* 8 (1929): 219–20.

44. Mersmann, "Volk und Musik," 511–13.

45. Egon Wellesz, "Die sozialen Grundlagen der gegenwärtigen Musikpflege," *Der Friede* 3 (1919): 300–301.

46. Holtmeyer, "Schulmusik und Musiklehrer," 86, 94–95.

47. Schünemann, "Gegenwartsfragen der Musikerziehung"; Leo Schrade, "Über das Bildungsethos in der Musikerziehung," *DTZ* 29 (1931): 157–59; Gurlitt, "Zur heutigen Musikerziehung," *DTZ* 28 (1930): 350–51; Müller-Blattau, "Grundsätzliches zur Musikerziehung."

48. Kretzschmar, *Musikalische Zeitfragen*, 126–27.

49. Egon Wellesz, "Die sozialen Grundlagen," 300–301.

50. Hans Joachim Moser, "Aus musikalischer Volksbildungsarbeit," *AMz* 50 (1923): 683–84.

51. Hans Joachim Moser, " 'Amateur' und 'Professional,' " *Mk* 20 (1928): 785–93.

52. Georg Schünemann, "Die Lage der Hausmusik," *Mk* 24 (1932): 561–62.

53. Karl Blessinger, "Repertoirebildung und Gebrauchsmusik," *AMz* 56 (1929): 311; Schünemann, "Lage der Hausmusik," 561.

54. Fritz Jöde, "Jugendmusikbewegung und Hausmusik," *Mk* 24 (1932): 568.

55. Rudolf Steglich, "Hugo Riemann als Förderer der Hausmusik durch Neuausgaben alter Tonwerke," *ZfM* 86 (1918): 178–81.

56. "Die Zeiten sind schwer und das Musikertum ist durch die Mechanisierung der Musik stark bedroht . . . so lange noch die Musik, vokale wie instrumentale, in der Schule hochgehalten wird, sind wir gewiß, daß die deutsche Musik ihre Weltgeltung behalten und ihre führende Stellung nicht verlieren wird." Johannes Wolf, "Hausmusik," *DTZ* 28 (1930): 215.

57. Eugen Schmitz, "Die Zukunft der Hausmusik," *Hochland* 17 (1919–20): 254–56.

58. Robert Treml, "Wie konnen wir Lauten und Gitarren erfolgreich in unser Musizieren einbeziehen?" *ZfH* 2/32, rpt. in *DJ* 358–60; "Österreichische Blockflöten- und Gambenspieltage, Ostern 1932," *ZfH* 5/32, rpt. *DJ* 361; Bruno Lehmann, "Abendspielwoche für Gitarre und Laute in Kassel," *Zeitschrift für Schulmusik* 1/31, rpt. in *DJ* 362–63; Herman Reichenbach, "Blasinstrument," *Der Kreis* 1932/33, rpt. in *DJ* 364–67; Fritz Reusch, "Von unseren Blockflöten," *Der Kreis* 7/29, rpt. in *DJ* 367–68; W. Kurka, "Blockflötentagung," *Der Kreis* 2/31, rpt. *DJ* 370–71; Karl Gofferje, "Blockflöten, die große Mode," *Die Singgemeinde* 5/31, rpt. *DJ* 371–74; Peter Harlan, "Bärenreitergamben und Bärenreiterfideln aus den Peter Harlan-Werkstätten, Markneukirchen," *Lied und Volk* 8/31, rpt. in *DJ* 375–76; idem, "Das Klavichord," *Die Singgemeinde* 6/27, rpt. *DJ* 377–79; Herbert Just, "Die Barockinstrumente in der Gegenwart," *Musik und Gesellschaft* 1/30, rpt. *DJ* 383; and Konrad Ameln, "Alte Musik auf alten Instrumenten," *Die Singgemeinde* 6/31, rpt. in *DJ* 384–86.

59. Schünemann, "Lage der Hausmusik," 561–64.

60. Hans Engel, "I. Kongreß für Chorgesangwesen in Essen, 8. bis 10. Oktober 1928," *DTZ* 26 (1928): 329–31.

61. See Hans Joachim Moser, "Noch ein Wort zur musikalischen Jugendbewegung," *AMz* 53 (1926): 381–82, and the response by Karl Hasse, "Zur Frage der Führung in der Jugendmusik," ibid., 527–28.

62. *DJ* 168–70, 323, 356, 393, 748, 752, 963–65, 895, 1009, 1016–18. Bukofzer is

not mentioned in this volume, but he, along with Besseler, Moser, and Mersmann, contributed to the movement's main periodical, *Die Musikantengilde.*

63. *DJ* 195, 318.

64. See the relevant discussion of Kurt Huber and Joseph Müller Blattau in chap. 6. Müller-Blattau also devoted a significant section of his 1932 monograph on German folk song to the history of the youth movement, praising its efforts as the salvation of an endangered folk tradition. Müller-Blattau, *Das deutsche Volkslied,* 121–36.

65. Prieberg mentions that Heinrich Besseler delivered a speech at the Musiktage der HJ in Erfurt in 1935 but does not clearly indicate his source for this information. Prieberg, *Musik im NS-Staat,* 255.

66. Müller-Blattau, "Collegium musicum" (introductory remarks to the first issue), rpt. in *DJ* 459–60; idem, "Viola, Bass und Geigen," *CM* 1 (1932): 61–64

67. See, e.g., Wilhelm Ehmann, "Die Liederstunde des Volkes," *ZfH* 5 (1936); Wilibald Gurlitt, "Unser Weihnachtssingen," *ZfH* 9 (1940); Joseph Müller-Blattau, "Cesar Bresgen Kantaten," *ZfH* 7 (1938); Hans Joachim Moser, "C. P. E. Bach und die Hausmusik," *ZfH* 7 (1938), "Hausmusik der Romantik," *ZfH* 8 (1939), "Innsbruck, ich muß dich lassen," *ZfH* 8 (1939), "Musikalische Formen," *ZfH* 10 (1941), "Lenze und Herbste der Musikepochen," *ZfH* 11 (1942), and "Genie und Talent, Groß- und Kleinmeister der Musik," *ZfH* 11 (1942). Walther Lipphardt also made several contributions on folk music repertoire.

68. Contributors included Johannes Wolf ("Aus der Geschichte großer Kantoreien," *MPf* 4 [1933–34]: 321–33), Friedrich Blume ("Bach und Händel, Zum Gedenkjahr," *MPf* 5 [1934–35]: 74–79; "Der Chor als Träger der städtischen Musikpflegens," *MPf* 7 [1936–37]: 250–58; "Individuum und Gemeinschaft im Chorgesang," *MPf* 9 [1938–39]: 45–58), and Ernst Bücken ("Das rheinische Volkslied," *MPf* 8 [1937–38]: 104–7), and there were several contributions by Moser and Fritz Stein.

69. Gotthold Frotscher, "Laientum und Dilettantismus," *VME,* 2 (1936): 209–13; Scholz, "Die Intellektuellen der Musik," 383–85; Karl Blessinger, "Künstler, Kenner und Liebhaber," *Volk und Welt* 5 (January 1937): 71–74.

70. Fritz Stein, "Das einheitliche deutsche Chorgesangwesen," *MPf* 4 (1933): 12.

71. Friedrich Blume, "Hausmusik heute und zur Zeit Luthers," *DTZ* 31 (1933): 140–141.

72. Friedrich Blume, "Hausmusik," *ZfH* 2 (1933): 62–69.

73. Gotthold Frotscher, "Hausmusik und Gegenwart," *VME* 3 (1937): 377–79; Karl Gustav Fellerer, "Das Klavier und seine Vorfahren in der Hausmusik," *Der Musikerzieher* 38 (1941–42): 21–23.

74. Hermann Halbig, "Altdeutsche Hausmusik," *VME* 4 (1938): 453–65; Gurlitt, "Unser Weihnachtssingen"; Gotthold Frotscher, "Hausmusik in Vergangenheit und Gegenwart," *MJV* 3 (1940): 225–32.

75. Georg Schünemann, "Klassische Hausmusik," *DTZ* 34 (1938): 26–27; Moser, "Hausmusik der Romantik"; Hans Engel, "Hausmusik um Goethe," *VME* 6 (1940): 206–9 and "Klavierkonzert und Hausmusik," *Der Musikerzieher* 36 (1940): 45–47, 65–67; Herbert Birtner, "Erschöpft sich die Aufgabe der Hausmusik im Musizieren leichter Spielmusik?" *Der Musikerzieher* 37 (1941): 169–71.

76. Peter Epstein, "Neue Forschungs- und Darstellungsmethoden der Musikge-

schichte," *Melos* 8 (1929): 360–63. When the Nazi Education Ministry commissioned Heinrich Besseler to reorganize the *Denkmäler deutscher Tonkunst,* Besseler called attention to the heightened public interest in early music that followed World War I: "Das deutsche Musikleben hatte nach dem Kriege immer stärker auf die Schätze der Vergangenheit zurückgegriffen, um aus dem Werk der Ahnen neue Kraft und Ausrichtung für die Zukunft zu gewinnen. Die Empfangsbereitschaft war groß." Heinrich Besseler, "Die Neuordnung des musikalischen Denkmalwesens," *Deutsche Wissenschaft, Erziehung und Volksbildung: Amtsblatt des Reichs- und Preußischen Ministeriums für Wissenschaft, Erziehung und Volksbildung und der Unterrichtsverwaltung der anderen Länder* 1 (1935): 188. On the occasion of Hugo Riemann's seventieth birthday in 1918, Rudolf Steglich held Riemann up as a model musicologist who showed sensitivity toward the musical needs of the general public in his scholarly editions. Rudolf Steglich, "Hugo Riemann als Wiedererwecker älterer Musik," *ZfMw* 1 (1918–19): 605–7.

77. Wilhelm Altmann, "Die Not der Musikwissenschaft," *DMJb* 2–3 (1925): 154–55.

78. Potter, "German Musicology and Early Music Performance," 97–99.

79. Blessinger, "Repertoirebildung und Gebrauchsmusik," 310–11.

80. Hans Joachim Moser, "Die Gegenwartsbedeutung der Liebhaberorchester," *DTZ* 29 (1931): 3–5.

81. "Mitteilungen der DGMW," *ZfMw* 17 (1935): 374.

82. Ibid., 372–73.

83. Ibid., 370–71.

84. Holtmeyer, "Schulmusik und Musiklehrer," 122, 165.

85. ZStA REM Nr. 2176, Bl. 5–8.

86. Karl Gustav Fellerer, "Musikerziehung und Musikwissenschaft," *VME* 8 (1942): 2–3.

87. Alfred Quellmalz, "Volksliedkunde und Musikerziehung," in Stumme, ed., *Musik im Volk,* 2d ed., 378–83.

88. Erich Valentin, "Musikgeschichte als Bildungsfaktor. Ein Beitrag zum musikalischen Erziehungsproblem," *AMz* 62 (1935): 195–96.

89. Fritz Stein, "Musikkultur und Musikerziehung. Gedanken und Erfahrungen aus dem Bereich einer Hochschule für Musik," *DMK* 1 (1936): 18–24.

90. Walter Wiora, "Volk und Musik," *Melos* 12 (1933): 269–76; idem, "Volk und musikalische Hochkultur," *Melos* 13 (1934): 2, 4.

91. Goslich, "Musikerziehung im Deutschen Volksbildungswerk," in Stumme, ed., *Musik im Volk,* 2d ed., 183, 185; Werner Korte, "Bildungs- und Ausbildungsfragen der Musik," *Mk* 28 (1936): 348.

92. Gotthold Frotscher, "Begriff und Aufgabe der musikalischen Bildung," *MJV* 4 (1941): 33–37.

93. Korte, "Bildungs- und Ausbildungsfragen der Musik," 348–56, Blessinger, *Judentum und Musik,* 1–16.

94. Hermann Halbig, "Hermann Kretzschmar als Musikerzieher," *VME* 4 (1938): 109–15.

95. Jöde, "Jugendmusikbewegung und Hausmusik," 565–66.

96. Hans Gansser and Karl Hasse, "Notwendige Betrachtungen zu den Ausführungen

von J. Steinle, Reutlingen über 'Die musikalische Erneuerungsbewegung vor der deutschen Revolution,' " *Der deutsche Erzieher* 3 (1935): 440–41.

97. Stein, "Musikkultur und Musikerziehung," 19.

98. Siegfried Goslich, "Arbeitsfeld und Methode einer neuzeitlichen Volksmusikerziehung," in Goslich, *Musikalische Volksbildung,* 11–12, 14–15.

99. Siegfried Goslich, "Musikschulwerk," *Mk* 31 (1939): 444–45. Paragraph 20 of the Nazi Party Program (first presented in February 1920) reads: "The State must consider a thorough reconstruction of our national system of education (with the aim of opening up to every able and hard-working German the possibility of higher education and of thus obtaining advancement). The curricula of all educational establishments must be brought into line with the requirements of practical life. The aim of the school must be to give the pupil, beginning with the first sign of intelligence, a grasp of the notion of the State (through the study of civic affairs). We demand the education of gifted children of poor parents, whatever their class or occupation, at the expense of the State." Trans. in Noakes and Pridham, *Nazism,* 14–15.

100. Goslich, "Arbeitsfeld," 20–22.

101. Goslich, "Musikerziehung im Deutschen Volksbildungswerk," 184–91.

102. See Hans Boettcher, "Zur Gegenwartslage der Berufsorganisation des 'Reichsverbandes Deutscher Tonkünstler und Musiklehrer,' " *DTZ* 29 (1931): 173–75, and other contributions in the same issue.

103. Karl Blessinger, "Musik und Politik," *Der Auftakt* 12 (1932): 1–6.

104. Hans Albrecht, "Zur 'Musikpolitik,' " *DTZ* 31 (1933): 1–2.

105. See Alfred Morgenroth, "Peter Raabe und sein Weg," in Morgenroth, ed., *Von Deutscher Tonkunst,* 9–22.

106. His speech "Stadtverwaltung und Chorgesang" is dated 1928 and appears in his *Kulturwille im deutschen Musikleben,* 26–41.

107. Fellerer, "Musik—Ethos politikon," *DTZ* 31 (1933): 103.

108. Fellerer, "Liberalismus und Antiliberalismus im Musikleben," *Schweizerische Rundschau* 34 (1933–34): 540.

109. Herbert Birtner, "Musikwissenschaft auf der 58. Philologentagung in Trier 1934," *ZfMw* 17 (1935): 60.

110. Walter Wiora referred to the strict interdependence and "unity" of music and everyday life to serve as a contrast to the "free, purposeless, self-governing art, 'art for its own sake.' " His point was to draw a parallel between the current situation and the era following the Peloponnesian wars, in which the active, communal "griechische Volksmusikkultur" ceased to exist, and in its place came "a new, subjective, individualized art, the Volk stopped singing and creating, and the virtuoso embarked on his road to victory." Wiora, "Altgriechische Volksmusikkultur," *DTZ* 25 (1927): 201–2. In 1928, as a response to reforms in the Prussian music education system, Walther Vetter alluded to the Greek "humanistic principle of education" to encourage the study of musicology for achieving a well-rounded humanistic education and for serving the needs of the youth through general education. Vetter, *Der humanistische Bildungsgedanke,* 13–30, 37–38. See also Hans Joachim Moser, "Die Bedeutung der Musik als Erziehungsfaktor im Geistesleben," *Die Musikerziehung. Vorträge* (1928); Müller-Blattau, "Grundsätzliches zur

Musikerziehung"; Schünemann, "Gegenwartsfragen der Musikerziehung"; and Schrade, "Bildungsethos."

111. See, e.g., Bannes, *Hitlers Kampf.*

112. For a detailed account of the circumstances, see Potter, "Deutsche Musikgesellschaft," and for a more complete description of the other papers featured at the meeting, see Potter, "Wissenschaftler im Zwiespalt."

113. Rudolf Steglich, "Die Elemente des musikalischen Ausdrucks im Umbruch," presumably the same as his published article "Die musikalischen Grundkräfte im Umbruch," *DMK* 3 (1938–39): 345–55; and Gerhard Pietzsch, "Staat und Musik," presumably the same as his published article "Die Betreuung der Musik durch den Staat," *DMK* 3 (1938–39): 464–69.

114. Fellerer, "Musik — Ethos politikon," 103.

115. Pietzsch, "Betreuung," 469.

116. Steglich, "Elemente," 346.

117. Korte, "Bildungs- und Ausbildungsfragen," 349–50. An interesting revelation to the lack of progress in solving this problem can be found in Peter Burkholder's recent article which also compares the concert hall to a museum for contemporary art music (Burkholder, "Museum Pieces," 115–34.)

118. Alfred Orel, "Zeitgenössische Musik in der Ostmark," *Die Pause* 4 (1939), Heft 4–5: 166; Eugen Schmitz, "Mut zur Einfachheit," *AMz* 67 (1940): 201–02.

119. See, e.g., his "Eine Lanze für Schoenberg!" *Mk* 27 (1934): 87–91; "Die Unterhaltungsmusik im Rundfunkprogramm," *Mk* 26 (1933) 13–18; "Die leichte Musik und der Rassegedanke," *NSM* 7 (1936); and "Was ist mit der Jazzmusik?" *Mk* 30 (1938): 686. The last two articles are excerpted in Wulf, *Musik im Dritten Reich,* 360, 387–88.

120. In his articles "Musicology in the Third Reich," 349–64, and "Nazi Musicologist," 649–65, Meyer refers to Friedrich Welter as "influential" ("Musicology in the Third Reich," 358) and "a musicologist of repute" ("Nazi Musicologist," 655) and to Walter Abendroth as "the authoritative Nazi musicologist" ("Nazi Musicologist," 654). He likewise designates the authors of legal tracts on the RMK, Karl Friedrich Schreiber, attorneys Willi Hoffmann and Wilhelm Ritter, and others, as "musicologists" (Nazi Musicologist," 657–58; "Musicology in the Third Reich," 356).

121. Karl Blessinger, "Mechanisierung der Musik," *AMz* 59 (1932): 397–99.

122. Irmgard Otto, "Tonfilm — ein Problem?" *Mk* 28 (1935): 111–17.

123. Karl Gustav Fellerer, "Musik und Technik," *Mk* 32 (1940): 397–401.

124. Joseph Müller-Blattau, "Die Anfänge der Musik," *Die Sendung* 8 (1931): "1. Vom Schall zum Ton," 36–37; "2. Arbeit und Rhythmus," 71–72; "3. Musik und Sprache," 89–90; "4. Musik und Tanz," 105–6; and "5. Musik und Gesellschaft," 139–40.

125. Herbert Gerigk, "Die Unterhaltungsmusik im Rundfunkprogramm," *Mk* 26 (1933): 13–18, and "Musik im Rundfunk," *Mk* 29 (1936): 241.

126. Peter Raabe, "Über den Mißbrauch des Rundfunks," *AMz* 65 (1938): 761–62.

127. Friedrich Blume, "Musikforschung und Musikpraxis," in Hoffmann and Rühlmann, *Festschrift Fritz Stein,* 20–25.

128. Gotthold Frotscher, "Musikwissenschaft und Gegenwart," *VME* 4 (1938): 116–18.

129. "Eine solche isolierte Stellung der Musikwissenschaft führt zur Krise, wenn es sich

um ihre Aufgaben gegenüber der *Gegenwart* handelt. Man hat der Musikwissenschaft mit Recht den Vorwurf machen können, daß sie oft versäumt hat, zu wichtigen Gegenwartsproblemen Stellung zu nehmen. Kaum einer ihrer Vertreter hat einst seine Stimme erhoben gegenüber den Verfalls- und Zersetzungserscheinungen in der Musik der Systemzeit, die Wissenschaft hat vielmehr dem Marktgeschrei der Journaille das Feld überlassen, und gerade durch deren pseudowissenschaftlich getarnte Agitation konnte das destruktive Neutönertum so rasch in weiteste Kreise dringen. Noch jetzt findet die Musikwissenschaft erst zögernd die Beziehung zu Problemen, die für unsere völkische Kultur entscheidend sind. Während sie in der Erforschung der Musik fremder Völker zu greifbaren Ergebnissen gelangt ist, hat sie sich bisher nur selten mit der eignene Volksmusik beschäftigt; während sie in der frühesten Vergangenheit so ziemlich alles Erschließbare erhellt hat, hat sie kaum je zu Ereignissen unserer Zeit das Wort ergriffen und Fragen der Gegenwart die Richtung gewiesen." Gotthold Frotscher, "Die Aufgabe der Musikwissenschaft," in Stumme, ed., *Musik im Volk*, 2d ed., 356–57.

130. Wilhelm Ehmann, "Das Musikleben an den deutschen Universitäten," in Stumme, ed., *Musik im Volk*, 2d ed., 159–61.

131. "Die deutsche Musikwissenschaft hat eines der edelsten Güter der deutschen Kultur zu hüten. Von ihr ist die Musik eine der lebendigsten und eigenartigsten Prägungen des deutschen Geistes gewesen. Das deutsche Volk hat sich und seinem Schicksal in der Musik seit Jahrhunderten eine 'Siegesallee' großartigster Denkmale gesetzt. Mit dieser Tatsache ist einer Musikforschung, die es mit ihren Pflichten gegen Volk und Staat ernst nimmt, die Ausrichtung vorgezeichnet. Das Erbe der deutschen Musik diktiert seinen Auftrag. Wenn eine frühere Forschung oftmals in unfruchtbarer Zersplitterung die lebendige Verbundenheit mit dem Artgegebenen der Jagd nach dem Außergewöhnlichen aufopferte, so kann eine nationalsozialistische Musikwissenschaft nur von der Lebensmitte der deutschen Musik ausgehen und um sie die weiteren Ringe legen, die entferntere Probleme um diese Mitte ordnen." Friedrich Blume, "Deutsche Musikwissenschaft," *Deutsche Wissenschaften*, 16.

132. Hans Engel, "Die Leistungen der deutschen Musikwissenschaft," *Geistige Arbeit* 6 (1939): 7.

133. "Der einzelne Musikhistoriker kann und darf nicht mehr abseits stehen und seinen eigenen Forschungsneigungen nachgehen. Die Stunde ist da, wo die Gesamtheit der deutschen Musikwissenschaft und der ihr Nahestehenden Hand anlegen muß, um das 'Erbe der deutschen Musik' vollständig und im wissenschaftlichen Sinne zu erfassen und es in seinen charakteristischen Leistungen dem Volk zugänglich zu machen." Rudolf Gerber, "Die Aufgaben der Musikwissenschaft im Dritten Reich," *ZfM* 102 (1935): 500.

Chapter 3. The Organization and Reorganization of Musicological Scholarship

1. Seiffert, *Ein Archiv für deutsche Musikgeschichte*, 6–16.

2. The trustee and director were both appointed by the court's Hofmarschallamt; the prince named a secretary, who, along with two elected members from the scholarly community, composed the senate. Additionally there was a body of thirty appointed voting members and a number of voteless foreign members. "Fürstliches Institut für

musikwissenschaftliche Forschung zu Bückeburg" [charter, 1919], Sandberger Papers (NStA); Rau to Freiherr von Feilitsch, 1 October 1917, NStA L4/7355 1; "Fürstliches Institut für musikwissenschaftliche Forschung i.E. zu Bückeburg" [printed prospectus], NStA L4/7355 2.

3. Rau to Fürstliches Ministerium, 16 August 1918, NStA L4/7355 3; "Bericht Nr. 2 an die ordentlichen Mitglieder," 10 August 1918, Sandberger Papers (NStA).

4. "Mit jähem Blitzstrahl zerschmetterte der Ausbruch des unseligen Weltkrieges diesen 15 Jahre hindurch gehegten träumerischen Wahn; von allen Seiten gellte der Schimpfruf 'Hunnen' in unser Ohr, aus Paris und London, von deren Kongressen wir kaum heimgekehrt waren." Quoted in Max Schneider, "Bericht über die erste Vollversammlung der Mitglieder des Fürstlichen Instituts für musikwissenschaftliche Forschung zu Bückeburg, 19. bis 20. Juni 1919," *AfMw* 2 (1919–20): 5.

5. The Fürst Adolf Prize was designated exclusively for Germans contributing to German music history. Schneider, "Bericht über die erste Vollversammlung," 7.

6. "Bericht Nr. 1 an die ordentlichen Mitglieder," 11 April 1918, item 8, Sandberger Papers (NStA).

7. The Editors, "Zum Geleit," *AfMw* 1 (1918–19): 2.

8. Seiffert, "Denkschrift betr. Umwandlung des Instituts für Musikforschung in Bückeburg in ein 'Reichsinstitut für deutsche Musikforschung' (gegründet als Fürst Adolf Institut)," 6–7, SIM.

9. "Protokoll der Sitzung am 20. Juni 1921," item 4, Sandberger Papers (NStA).

10. Hermann Matzke, "Bericht über die zweite Jahresversammlung der Mitglieder des des Fürstlichen Instituts für musikwissenschaftliche Forschung zu Bückeburg, 19. bis 21. Juni 1920," *AfMw* 2 (1919–20): 435–36; "Protokoll der Sitzung am 20. Juni 1921," item 5.i; "Protokoll der 6. Jahresversammlung," meeting on 20 June 1922, item 4, Sandberger Papers (NStA).

11. Quoted in Matzke, "Bericht über die zweite Jahresversammlung," 444–45.

12. Schneider, "Bericht über die erste Vollversammlung," 4.

13. "Bericht Nr. 1 an die ordentlichen Mitglieder," item 2.

14. "Bericht Nr. 2 an die ordentlichen Mitglieder," item 2, Sandberger Papers (NStA).

15. He originally envisioned the archive as consisting of a bibliographic division, an archive for German music history, a department for the study of musical instruments, and a department of iconography. The bibliographic division would catalogue all music manuscripts, printed music, and literature on music in the Reich, listing them both by author and by subject, with perhaps a special collection of samples of composers' handwriting and notation for purposes of identification. The archive for German music history was to include transcripts of all music-related documents in German state, municipal, and church archives, arranged geographically, with name and subject indices compiled to facilitate use. Seiffert, *Ein Archiv für deutsche Musikgeschichte,* 13–14.

16. Musikgeschichtliche Kommission zur Herausgabe der Denkmäler Deutscher Tonkunst, "Außerordentliche Sitzung, Mittwoch den 15. Mai 1918 . . . ," Sandberger Papers (NStA). A correspondence between Sandberger (Bavaria) and Seiffert, March 1918 to December 1919, Sandberger Papers (NStA), includes Seiffert's draft of an agreement with Sandberger's objections in the margins, the signed agreement (10 May 1918), and Sandberger's request for reimbursement for half the expenses for research trips of his col-

leagues Kroyer and Wallner (31 December 1919). Agreement signed by Seiffert, Kretz-schmar (Berlin Commission), and Sandberger, 8 April 1918; "Sitzung in Berlin 10. Mai 1918," Sandberger Papers (NStA). In addition, the institute drew up separate agreements with each of the commissions, with Sandberger securing more financial promises from Bückeburg and retaining more authority over the operation of the inventory than his Prussian counterparts. Agreement between the Denkmäler der Tonkunst in Bayern and the institute, 10 May 1918; agreement between the Prussian Commission and the in-stitute, 1 May 1918, Anlage B, Musikgeschichtliche Kommission zur Herausgabe der Denkmäler Deutscher Tonkunst, "Außerordentliche Sitzung, Mittwoch den 15. Mai 1918," Sandberger Papers (NStA).

17. Seiffert to Schaumburg-Lippische Landesregierung, 25 February 1922, 11 May 1928, 27 November 1928, 5 September 1930, 11 March 1932, and 29 January 1933, NStA L4/7355 35, 66, 68, 72, 74, 77.

18. Seiffert to Landesregierung, 11 March 1932, NStA L4/7355 74.

19. Fachausschüsse were established for ancient music (Abert, Riemann, Wolf), medi-eval music (Kroyer, Ludwig, Wolf), music since 1800 (Balling, Sahla, Schiedermair), opera history (Abert, Sandberger, Stieger), oratorio history (Kretzschmar, Schering, Schneider), history of song (Bolte, Friedländer, Kretzschmar), bibliography (Altmann, Schultz, Schwartz), instrumental music (Schering, Schiedermair, Schneider), Catholic church music (Kroyer, Müller, Weinmann), Protestant church music (Herold, Smend, Türnau), fourteenth- to seventeenth-century secular music (Ludwig, Sandberger, Schwartz), the score collection (Müller, Riemann, Wolf), the university writings col-lection (Friedländer, Riemann, Sandberger), and aesthetics (Schmitz, Stumpf, Volkelt). "Bericht Nr. 3 an die ordentlichen Mitglieder," 7 December 1918, items 1 and 3, Sand-berger Papers (NStA). Additional committees for fifteenth- to sixteenth-century music, for seventeenth- to eighteenth-century music, for comparative musicology, and for local German history were operating by 1921. "Protokoll der Sitzung am 20. Juni 1921," item 4, Sandberger Papers (NStA).

20. "Bericht Nr. 1 an die ordentlichen Mitglieder," item 9.

21. Rau to Sandberger, 25 November [1918], Sandberger Papers (NStA).

22. Handwritten transcript of "Stiftungs-Urkunde," drafted 8 February 1918, with addenda of 23 February 1919 and 23 February 1920, final approval dated 20 March 1920, NStA L4/7355 5–10; printed version also in Sandberger Papers (NStA), undated. This document named the prince as patron, listed the institute's assets as the present and future endowments from the prince and a yearly subsidy from the Hofmarschallamt, placed the supervision of the books under the Fürstliche Hofkammer, and left the certifi-cate to the approval of the state in accordance with political developments to come.

23. Rau to Schaumburg-Lippische Landesregierung, 9 September 1921, NStA L4/7355 24. The new charter entitled Prince Adolf to hold the position of trustee (*Kurator*), formerly held by the Hofmarschall; extended the assets to include contributions from the Reich, provinces, communities, and private interests; made specific provisions for the annual Founder's Day and members' meeting, at which the director and the senate were required to give reports; provided that upon the dissolution of the foundation, the in-stitute and its possessions should be handed over entirely to the musicology department of a German university; and stipulated that any changes in the charter required the

approval of the Schaumburg-Lippe government. It added the clause "ihre Wirksamkeit ist räumlich nicht beschränkt" to the paragraph describing the purpose of the foundation, perhaps to deemphasize its earlier, more provincial focus. Satzung des Fürstlichen Institutes für musikwissenschaftliche Forschung zu Bückeburg (abgeänderte Fassung vom 3. Juni 1921), NStA L4/7355 26–30.

24. Emphasizing the international stature of the institute, Rau quoted words of praise from Swiss musicologist Peter Wagner and from Spanish musicologist Pedrell, who had written to him: "Mit wahrer Ergriffenheit habe ich den Bericht (des Instituts) gelesen, in dieser Zeit so schwer von Hasz [sic] und Unverständnis tut uns solch ein erhebendes Beispiel not, wir können fernerhin an den deutschen Geist glauben, das geht alle Menschen an über alle Staatsgrenzen, und das ist ein groszer [sic] Trost." The Reich ministry had expressed its willingness to provide a substantial subsidy if the local government were to take the initiative. Rau to Schaumburg-Lippische Landesregierung, 26 February 1921, NStA L4/7355 13–15.

25. Telegram from Fürst Schaumburg Lippe, 9 October 1921; Seiffert to Landesregierung, 8 October 1921; certification from Landesregierung, NStA L4/7355 31–33.

26. Rau to Schaumburg-Lippische Landesregierung, 3 June 1921, NStA L4/7355 23; "An unsere Fachgenossen" (a plea to musicologists to support the Friends' Society and to subscribe to the journal), *AfMw* 4 (1922): 392; "Protokoll der ordentlichen Mitgliederversammlung der Gesellschaft der Freunde des Institutes für musikwissenschaftliche Forschung zu Bückeburg im Buchgewerbehaus zu Leipzig am 13. Januar 1922," *AfMw* 4 (1922): 117–18.

27. Theodor Werner, "Musikwissenschaftliche Tagung in Bückeburg," *AfMw* 5 (1923): 332.

28. "Protokoll der 6. Jahresversammlung," 20–21 June 1922, Sandberger Papers (NStA); Seiffert to Landesregierung, 25 February 1922 (requesting a subvention of 25,000 marks) and 18 November 1922 (reporting that inflation had incurred a deficit of 50,000 marks); Landesregierung to Institut, 23 May 1922 (doubling requested amount to 50,000) and 25 May 1923 (raising subvention tenfold to 500,000 marks); NStA L4/7355 35, 38, 39, 41; "Fürstliches Institut für Musikwissenschaftliche Forschung zu Bückeburg. Achte Jahresversammlung 20-6-1924," Sandberger Papers (NStA).

29. Schreiber, *Die Not der deutschen Wissenschaft,* 84–94.

30. Reichsministerium des Innern to Schaumburg-Lippische Landesregierung, 16 March 1925, Schaumburg-Lippische Landesregierung to Reichsministerium des Innern, 8 April 1925, Reichsministerium des Innern to Schaumburg-Lippische Landesregierung, 2 May 1925, NStA L4/7355 43–45.

31. Rau to Schaumburg-Lippischer Landtag, 26 February 1921, NStA L4/7355 14.

32. Preußische Akademie der Wissenschaften to Ministerium für Wissenschaft, Kunst und Volksbildung, 27 July 1925, NStA L4/7355 49–51.

33. Seiffert to Schaumburg-Lippische Landesregierung, 27 January 1926 and 9 January 1927, NStA L4/7355 48, 58.

34. Seiffert to Schaumburg-Lippische Landesregierung, 22 April 1927, [Landesregierung] to Institut, 28 May 1927, NStA L4/7355 60, 61.

35. Theodor Werner, "Zehnter Stiftungstag des Bückeburger Instituts für musikwissenschaftliche Forschung," *AfMw* 8 (1926): 486–87.

36. Theodor Werner, "Stiftungstag des Instituts für musikwissenschaftliche Forschung zu Bückeburg," *ZfMw* 8 (1925–26): 645–47.

37. "In der Tat haben Musik und Musikwissenschaft in Deutschland trotz der durch den Heeresdienst verminderten Arbeitskräfte und trotz der zahlreichen schmerzlichen Lücken, die der Krieg auch in ihre Reihen gerissen hat, emsig und im alten Geiste weitergearbeitet, ja der Krieg hat uns auch auf diesem Gebiete vor eine ganze Reihe neuer Aufgaben, vor allem nationalen Charakters gestellt und uns daran erinnert, daß unser im eigenen Hause noch sehr viel ungetane Arbeit harrt, an der wir früher zugunsten internationaler Beziehungen und nicht immer zum Vorteil unserer nationaler Musikkultur vorübergegangen sind." "Aufruf zur Gründung der Deutschen Musikgesellschaft," 1 December [1917], Sandberger Papers (BSB).

38. "Aufruf zum Eintritt in die Deutsche Musikgesellschaft," Sandberger Papers (BSB).

39. "Es darf auch nicht der Schatten eines Verdachtes aufkommen, daß ihre Beschränkung auf das engere Vaterland die Absicht des Ausschlusses der Ausländer bedeute. Gerade Deutschland, das mit den Werken seiner großen Tonkünstler seit 200 Jahren unbestritten und unbestreitbar für die Produktion des Auslandes vorbildlich ist, hat keinerlei Ursache, seine Grenzen hermetisch abzuschließen unter dem Vorwande, eine schädigende 'Ausländerei' abzuwehren." Riemann, *Altertum und Mittelalter*, xi.

40. For a detailed discussion of the society's conflicting purposes and increasing tendency toward isolation, see Potter, "Deutsche Musikgesellschaft."

41. Alfred Einstein, "Geleitwort," *ZfMw* 1 (1918–19): 3–4.

42. "Amtliche Mitteilungen der Deutschen Musikgesellschaft," *ZfMw* 4 (1921–22): 321 and *ZfMw* 5 (1922–23): 289.

43. Hermann Abert, "Eröffnungsrede," *Bericht über den I. Musikwissenschaftlichen Kongreß, Leipzig*, 5.

44. Abert, "Amtliche Mitteilung," *ZfMw* 5 (1922–23): 642 and *ZfMw* 8 (1925–26): 609.

45. "Mitteilungen der Deutschen Musikgesellschaft," *ZfMw* 14 (1931–32): 127.

46. Schiedermair to Sandberger, 2 July 1933, Sandberger Papers (BSB).

47. Draft of Sandberger's response to Schiedermair, 21 July 1933, Sandberger Papers (BSB).

48. Wolf, Schering, Schneider, and von Hase to Einstein, 24 June 1933, folder 1038, Einstein Papers.

49. Wolf to Einstein, 25 June and 29 October 1933, folder 1038, Einstein Papers.

50. Einstein to Kroyer, 16 October 1932, folder 568, Einstein Papers.

51. Einstein to Kroyer, 21 January 1933, folder 568, Einstein Papers

52. Schering to Sandberger, 21 September 1933, Sandberger Papers (BSB).

53. Schering to members, 6 October 1933, Ursprung Papers.

54. "Arbeitsordnung der Deutschen Gesellschaft für Musikwissenschaft (früher 'Deutsche Musikgesellschaft')," Ursprung Papers.

55. Schering to Sandberger, 23 December 1936, Sandberger Papers (BSB).

56. The group for regional studies (*Landeskunde*) headed by Max Seiffert set out to accumulate information on the local holdings in all musicology department libraries. The group for preservation (*Denkmalsschutz*) under Wilibald Gurlitt would similarly call the attention of state, municipal, and church facilities to the value of their respective musical

treasures, such as instruments, manuscripts and old printed matter. The group for university matters (*Universitätswesen*) under Schiedermair collected faculty data from universities, teachers colleges, and music conservatories. The group for publication (*Verlagswesen*) under Hellmuth von Hase concerned itself with the techniques of Denkmäler editions, copyright questions, and state funding. The press office (*Presseamt*) under Rudolf Steglich was to collect and distribute newspaper clippings and articles of interest to the society. Moser's plans for the folklore (*Volkskunde*) group included better coordination among the various folk music research facilities, better methods for cataloguing materials, more communication with related disciplines, and a bibliography, all naturally restricted to "German soil." The groups for comparative musicology (*vergleichende Musikwissenschaft*) and for radio and phonograph recordings (*Rundfunk, Schallplatte*), both headed by Georg Schünemann, concentrated on recording and transcription techniques, travel for field research, cataloguing of existing recordings (according to *Land, Volk,* and *Rasse*), and included questions on pedagogy (Schünemann's own specialty), music psychology, race studies (*Rassenkunde*) and its application to comparative musicology, and radio broadcasting. Other groups were devoted to bibliography and library science, music pedagogy (Fritz Stein), Protestant church music (Friedrich Blume), Catholic church music (Otto Ursprung), opera (Alfred Lorenz), criticism, publishing, and concert management (Alfred Heuss), musicological publications (Heinrich Besseler), and the planning of a German musicological conference. "Sammelrundschreiben Nr.1," Schering to members, December 1933, and "Arbeitsordnung der deutschen Gesellschaft für Musikwissenschaft," Ursprung Papers.

57. "Dem Herrn Reichsminister für Volksaufklärung und Propaganda senden die in Leipzig zur Neuorganisation der 'Deutschen Gesellschaft für Musikwissenschaft' versammelten Vertreter der Musikwissenschaft von 18 deutschen Universitäten und Hochschulen Treugelöbnis und ehrerbietigen Gruß. Sie bekunden den freudigen Willen, weiterhin mit dem Einsatz ihrer ganzen Kraft am Neuaufbau der deutschen Kultur mitzuarbeiten, und sind sich der hohen Verantwortung bewußt, die ihnen zu ihrem Teil an der Verwaltung und Mehrung der unvergänglichen musikalischen Kulturgüter unseres Volkes auferlegt ist." Schering to Goebbels, 26 November 1933, BA R 55/1141 184.

58. Herder (Propaganda Ministry) to DGMW, 30 November 1933, BA R 55/1141 185.

59. Eggers, "§16 Bildungswesen," 969.

60. Landesregierung to Institut, 23 December 1933; 7 May 1934, NStA L4/7355 82, 140–42.

61. Reichsstatthalter to Landespräsident, 11 September 1933; Reichsstatthalter to Landesregierung, 8 December 1933; and handwritten note dated 9 December 1933, NStA L4/7355 79, 81a.

62. Seiffert to Schaumburg-Lippische Landesregierung, 5 January 1934, NStA L4/7355 84.

63. Seiffert, "Denkschrift," 3–5.

64. Seiffert, "Denkschrift," 8–9.

65. Stein to Minister für Wissenschaft, Kunst und Volksbildung, 27 July 1933, SIM.

66. Meyer (Reichsstatthalter) to Hess, 24 May 1934, NStA L4/7355 173.

67. Von Keudell (Propaganda Ministry) to Reichsstatthalter, 12 June 1934, NStA L4/7355 199.

68. Sunkel (Education Ministry) to Meyer, 1 June 1934; Meyer to Dreier, 8 June 1934; [Dreier] to Seiffert, 12 June 1934, NStA L4/7355 185–87; NSDAP Gaukulturwart Meyer to Gauleitung Münster (Westfalen), 16 July 1934, NStA L4/7356 17–18.

69. Rust to Reichsstatthalter, 23 July 1934; Rust to Landespräsident, 4 October 1934, NStA L4/7356 11–12, 24–25.

70. Letters from August and October 1934, NStA L4/7356 13–16, 20–25.

71. "Auf das Schreiben vom 11.Oktober d. Js. . . . bestätige ich hiermit, daß die Aufsicht über das bisherige Fürstliche Institut für musikwissenschaftliche Forschung zu Bückeburg auf Grund der abgeänderten Satzung nunmehr durch mich ausgeübt wird." Rust to Landesregierung, 3 November 1934, NStA L4/7356 33.

72. "Staatliches Institut für Deutsche Musikforschung, Stand vom Juni 1939," Schiedermair Papers.

73. REM to Seiffert, 6 April 1936, SIM and BDC Seiffert.

74. Stein to Seiffert, 15 March 1932, SIM.

75. The intentions for the institute expressed in this letter were not only to move it to Berlin but also to create a musicological center, bringing all ongoing projects and institutions under one roof. Other plans included "cleaning up" the Jugendmusikbewegung; reforming GEMA (Gesellschaft für musikalische Aufführungs- und mechanische Vervielfältigungsrechte), the organization responsible for royalties of performed works; creating of a "chamber" for professionals, perhaps something along the lines of the RMK; and some action — one can assume a takeover or restriction — taken toward Jewish concert managers, some of whom were very influential in Berlin. It is not entirely clear whether these suggestions were Seiffert's. They parallel the points described in Stein's letter to the education minister of 27 July, which accompanied Seiffert's Denkschrift and commented on a proposal submitted by the Preußische Akademie der Künste. Taking the two letters together, it is possible that Seiffert's letter is a summary of the academy's proposals for Stein and does not necessarily represent his own plans. Seiffert to Stein, 27 March 1933, SIM.

76. Landespräsident to Reichsstatthalter, 13 March 1934, NStA L4/7355 139.

77. Seiffert, "Denkschrift," 10–11.

78. REM to Seiffert, 6 April 1936, SIM and BDC Seiffert.

79. The Freiburg archive later competed with the institute and hoped to take over its folk music division after World War II. Quellmalz to Leiter des Staatlichen Instituts für Deutsche Musikforschung, 27 February 1941; Meier to Albrecht, 4 January 1943 and 5 May 1944, BA NS 21/220; and letter of John Meier (director, Deutsches Volkliedarchiv Freiburg) to Rektor (University of Freiburg), 8 June 1943, UAF PA Meier.

80. Fürst Adolf zu Schaumburg-Lippe to Reichsminister für Wissenschaft, Erziehung und Volksbildung, 6 October 1934, NStA L4/7356 29–30.

81. Stein to Reichs-und Preußischer Minister für Wissenschaft, Erziehung und Volksbildung, 26 January 1935, Reichs-und Preußischer Minister für Wissenschaft, Erziehung und Volksbildung to Stein, 22 February 1935; Stein to Reichs- und Preußischer Minister für Wissenschaft, Erziehung und Volksbildung, 20 March 1935; and Stein and Kreich-

gauer (director of instrument collection) to Ganse (hired as instructor), 27 November 1935, SIM.

82. Moser, *Das musikalische Denkmälerwesen,* 20–22.

83. Heinrich Besseler and Adolf Sandberger to Reichs- und Preußischer Minister für Wissenschaft, Erziehung und Volksbildung, n.d., SIM.

84. Besseler to all participants in the "Reichsdenkmalunternehmen," 19 February 1935, SIM.

85. Besseler and Sandberger to Reichs- und Preußischer Minister für Wissenschaft, Erziehung und Volksbildung, n.d., 3, SIM. For example, in the detailed instructions for Baroque works, editors were told only to use conventional clefs (treble, bass, and "idiot" clef) and received explicit rules for realizing figured bass. "Richtlinien für die Herausgabe von Musik des 'Generalbaßzeitalters' im 'Erbe deutscher Musik,' " SIM.

86. "Mit dem neuen Titel ist eine bestimmte Grundauffassung angedeutet, aus der das Ziel und die organisatorischen Einzelheiten des Reichsunternehmens einheitlich zu verstehen sind. Die deutsche Musikwissenschaft bekennt sich zu der wesentlichsten Aufgabe, die ihr — soweit sie Geschichtsforschung ist — im völkischen Lebensraum erwächst: sie trägt die Verantwortung für das Erbe. Sie will das Überkommene nicht als monumentalen Besitz aufspeichern, sondern seine lebendige Aneignung fördern, die aus der Vergangenheit wirkenden Kräfte nutzbar machen und für die Gestaltung der Zukunft einsetzen. So liegt, wenn hier vom Erbe deutscher Musik gesprochen wird, der Ton auf dem ' . . . Erwirb es, um es zu besitzen.' " Besseler, "Die Neuordnung des musikalischen Denkmalwesens," *Deutsche Wissenschaft, Erziehung und Volksbildung: Amtsblatt der Reichs- und Preußischen Ministeriums für Wissenschaft, Erziehung und Volksbildung und der Unterrichtsverwaltung der anderen Länder* 1 (1935): 187.

87. "Das neue Denkmalunternehmen hat den überlieferten Titel 'Denkmäler deutscher Tonkunst' als mißverständlich und nicht voll zutreffend abgelegt. Nicht zutreffend deshalb, weil die Beschränkung auf Ton'kunst' zu Unrecht das einstimmig-lebensverbundene Musizieren (Volkslied und -tanz, Trompeterfanfaren, Gregorianik und ihre Eindeutschung) beiseite läßt. Aber nur die Gesamtheit der Musik, die auf unserem Boden gewachsen ist und Jahrhunderte hindurch das Leben der Nation erfüllt und verklärt hat, bildet das 'Erbe' im vollen Sinne." Besseler, "Das Erbe deutscher Musik," *DMK* 1 (1936–37): 16.

88. Besseler and Sandberger to Reichs- und Preußischer Minister für Wissenschaft, Erziehung und Volksbildung, n.d., SIM.

89. Ibid., 2.

90. Besseler, "Neuordnung des musikalischen Denkmalwesens," 188.

91. Besseler and Sandberger to Reichs- und Preußischer Minister für Wissenschaft, Erziehung und Volksbildung, n.d., 2–4, SIM.

92. Moser, *Das musikalische Denkmälerwesen,* 24–26, 32–33.

93. "Mitteilungen," *AfMf* 3 (1938): 502.

94. Engel to Sandberger, 20 September 1933, Sandberger Papers (BSB).

95. Schering to Sandberger, 30 December 1933, Sandberger Papers (BSB).

96. Schneider to Ursprung, 27 January 1936; Besseler to colleagues, 11 February 1936, Ursprung Papers.

97. Besseler to colleagues, July 1935, SIM.

98. The Editors, "Zum Beginn," *AfMf* 1 (1936): title page.

99. Schneider to Ursprung, 27 January 1936, Ursprung Papers.

100. "Die deutsche Musikwissenschaft benötigt zur Durchführung ihrer Aufgaben zwei verschiedene Organe: eine Fachzeitschrift, die über das gesamtdeutsche Gebiet und die kulturverwandten Länder zu wirken hat, und eine Musikzeitschrift, die im national-sozialistischen Deutschland die Verbindung von Wissenschaft und Leben herstellt. . . . Es handelt sich um eine musikwissenschaftlich geführte, kulturpolitisch aktive deutsche Musikzeitschrift, deren Bezieherkreis sich zusammensetzt (1) aus den deutschen Fach-genossen, (2) aus den im Beruf stehenden 'praktischen Musikwissenschaftlern' als natür-lichem Bindeglied zwischen Forschung und Leben, (3) aus den vom gegenwärtigen Tief-stand der Musikzeitschriften unbefriedigten Liebhabern." Besseler to colleagues, July 1935, SIM.

101. Besseler, report of a meeting regarding the publication of *Deutsche Musikkultur* on 14 October 1937, SIM.

102. Besseler to Seiffert, 29 January 1939, BDC Besseler.

103. Theodor Werner, "Jahrestagung des Fürstlichen Instituts für musikwissenschaft-liche Forschung (Bückeburg)," *ZfMw* 16 (1934): 381.

104. Werner, "Zehnter Stiftungstag des Bückeburger Instituts für musikwissenschaft-liche Forschung," 486–87.

105. "Mitteilungen," *AfMf* 1 (1936): 383.

106. Besseler to Ursprung, 1 October 1936, Ursprung Papers. The schedule included workshops led by Kurt Huber ("Volksliedforschung und Volksliedpflege"), Marius Schneider ("Fragen und Aufgaben der vergleichenden Musikwissenschaft"), and Wilhelm Ehmann ("Die Musik in der neuen akademischen Lebensgemeinschaft"); speeches by invited officials Werner Weber (Education Ministry), Eugen Bieder (director of the Hoch-schule für Musikerziehung), Alfons Kreichgauer (director of the instrument collection), and Peter Raabe (president of the RMK); and reports by a number of participants (includ-ing Engel, Müller-Blattau, Blume, Steglich, and Fellerer) addressing practical questions of musicology in society ("Plan der Musikwissenschaftlichen Arbeitswoche Frankfurt/ Oder, 4.–9. Oktober 1936"; "Teilnehmer und Gäste der Musikwissenschaftlichen Ar-beitswoche Frankfurt/Oder, 4.–9. Oktober 1936," BA NS 15/149a).

107. "Alle vier Herren [Moberg, Bartha, Pulikowski, Georgiades] sind an deutschen Universitäten ausgebildet, arbeiten an deutschen Zeitschriften mit und stehen dem neuen Deutschland freundlich gegenüber." Besseler to Education Minister, 23 June 1936, ZStA REM Nr. 2909, Bl. 90.

108. "Mitteilungen," *AfMf* 2 (1937): 503.

109. Rudolf Steglich, "Mitteilungen," *AfMf* 3 (1938): 380.

110. "Den Preis erhält nicht der junge Nationalsozialist, der etwas wagt und neue Wege sucht, sondern der Mann mit gutem Sitzfleisch und methodisch geschulter Schläue. Ich zweifle, ob das die Absicht des Herrn Ministers war. . . . Bei der gegenwärtigen Zusam-mensetzung dieses Gremiums genügt es offenbar *nicht,* daß nur ein Parteigenosse, der zufällig dabei ist, für seine Person die geschilderte Ansicht vertritt." Besseler to Miederer, 13 April 1939, BDC Besseler.

111. "Zum zehnjährigen Bestehen des Staatlichen Instituts für deutsche Musikfor-

schung" (speech probably written and delivered by Fritz Stein, 1945), 6–8, SIM. Willem De Vries asserts, incorrectly, that *MGG* started out as a project under the aegis of the Rosenberg Bureau (De Vries, *Sonderstab Musik*, 79–84).

112. Schering, "Mitteilung an die Mitglieder der Deutschen Gesellschaft für Musikwissenschaft," *ZfMw* 17 (1935): 481.

113. "Geld ist noch keins vorhanden. Die Behörden wissen noch nicht einmal, welcher Spitzenorganisation oder Kammer für uns M.-wissenschaftler zuordnen sollen." Schering to Sandberger, 30 December 1933, Sandberger Papers (BSB).

114. Schiedermair to Sandberger, 5 January 1937, Sandberger Papers (BSB).

115. Schiedermair to Sandberger, 3 February 1937, Sandberger Papers (BSB).

116. Whereas formerly at least a few marks from subscriptions had gone toward running the society, the new contract enabled the publisher to take the entire amount received from subscribers, and the society was left to cover the shipping costs, an amount which Schering had paid out of his own pocket. According to Schiedermair's analysis of the situation, Breitkopf & Härtel then tried to levy a special membership fee for the operation of the society, which at that point required minimal funding. Whatever was left over would go toward the 5,000 mark debt to Breitkopf & Härtel that Schering had run up. Schiedermair to Sandberger, 15 March 1938, Sandberger Papers (BSB).

117. Schiedermair to Sandberger, 2 March 1938, Sandberger Papers (BSB).

118. Reported in *Der Mittag*, 28 May 1938.

119. Complete program in "Mitteilungen," *AfMf* 3 (1938): 254–55 and BA NS 15/149a.

120. Although no conference report has been located, many of the papers appeared as separate articles, allowing for a partial reconstruction of the conference. These include H. J. Therstappen, "Die Musik im großdeutschen Raum," *DMK* 3 (1938–39): 425–28; W. Vetter, "Volkhafte Wesensmerkmale in Mozarts Opern," *ZfM* 105 (1938): 852–56; G. Pietzsch, "Die Betreuung der Musik durch den Staat," *DMK* 3 (1938–39): 464–69; R. Steglich, "Die musikalischen Grundkräfte im Umbruch," *DMK* 3 (1938–39): 345–55; W. Korte, "Die Grundlagenkrisis der deutschen Musikwissenschaft," *Mk* 30 (1938): 668–74; W. Danckert, "Von der Stammesart im Volkslied," *Mk* 32 (1940): 217–22; G. Frotscher, "Aufgaben und Ausrichtung der musikalischen Rassenstilforschung" in Waldmann, ed., *Rasse und Musik,* 102–12; H. Schultz, "Volkhafte Eigenschaften des Instrumentenklanges," *DMK* 5 (1940): 61–64; and F. Blume, "Musik und Rasse," *Mk* 30 (1938): 736–48. For a more detailed description of these contributions, see Potter, "Wissenschaftler im Zwiespalt."

121. Quoting Alfred Rosenberg, he demonstrates how Handel could never be considered an English composer, and consequently Mendelssohn, the Jew, can never be considered German: "Entsprechendes gilt für Mendelssohn: Er ist Jude, und da die Musik noch mehr als jede andere Kunstgattung Ausdruck des Nationalcharakters und der Volksseele ist, so kann Mendelssohn unmöglich ein hervorragender deutscher Komponist sein." Similarly, the fact that Mozart chooses an Italian text does not at all diminish the "Germanness" of the musical style. In this context, Vetter alludes once again to the Handel-Mendelssohn contrast: "Ich erinnere noch einmal an Händel und Mendelssohn: die fremdsprachlich textierte Musik braucht nicht undeutsche, die auf unsere Mutterlaute komponierte Musik nicht deutsch zu sein." Vetter, "Volkhafte Wesensmerkmale," 852–53.

122. Peter Seifert, "Musik und Rasse," *Düsseldorfer Nachrichten*, 23 May 1938, rpt. in Dümling and Girth, eds., *Entartete Musik*, 115.

123. The most extensive is his monograph, *Das Rasseproblem*.

124. BDC Kreichgauer; Dekan to Rektor, 27 June 1939, UAB PA Kreichgauer.

125. "Die deutsche Musikgesellschaft ist völlig eingeschlafen, und ich erwarte von Schiedermair in dieser Hinsicht auch nichts mehr." Gerigk to Osthoff, 13 August 1940, BA NS 15/26; Also Kreichgauer to Dekan, 23 January 1946, UAB PA Kreichgauer.

126. Frey (REM) to Schiedermair, 16 June 1941, UABonn PA Schiedermair.

127. BA R 21/11058.

128. Wilhelm Merian, "Begrüßungsrede," in *Bericht über den Musikwissenschaftlichen Kongreß in Basel*, 3.

129. Hermann Abert, "Der Internationale Musikwissenschaftliche Kongreß der Union Musicologique in Lübeck am 23. und 24. Juni 1926," *ZfMw* 8 (1925–26): 642–43.

130. Adler, "Internationalismus in der Tonkunst," in *Bericht über den Musikwissenschaftlichen Kongreß in Basel*, 36–48. Trans. as "Internationalism in Music," *Musical Quarterly* 11 (1925): 281–300.

131. Johannes Wolf, "Die Gründung der Internationalen Gesellschaft für Musikforschung," *ZfMw* 10 (1927–28): 116–17.

132. Wilhelm Merian, "Internationale Gesellschaft für Musikwissenschaft," *ZfMw* 11 (1928–29): 47.

133. "Mitteilungen," *ZfMw* 1 (1918–19): 376.

134. See Forman, "Scientific Internationalism," 158n.

135. Alfred Einstein, "Der Musikwissenschaftliche Kongreß in Basel," *ZfMw* 7 (1924–25): 108.

136. REM to Besseler, 23 March 1936, ZStA REM Nr. 2909, Bl. 40–42.

137. "Anderseits galt es, den auch auf dem Kongreß erscheineneden Emigranten ein Gegengewicht entgegenzusetzen. Ich gab der Anregung von Professor Besseler statt." Ursprung to Dean, 26 April 1936, Ursprung Papers.

138. Anglès to Ursprung, 28 February 1936, Ursprung Papers.

139. Ursprung to the Generalvikariat in Munich, 28 August 1936, Ursprung Papers.

140. "Vertraulich möchte ich Ihnen noch sagen, daß wir an Stelle Wolfs einen anderen deutschen Vertreter setzen müssen. Wolf hat die deutschen Interessen schlecht gewahrt, was umso bedauerlicher ist, als wir ein erheblicher Gegenfront von Juden und Emigranten gegenüberstehen. Mir scheint nun Kroyer die besten Aussichten zu haben, von einem internationalen Gremium gewählt zu werden." Besseler to Ursprung, 28 January 1936, Ursprung Papers.

141. Besseler to Weber (REM), 10 January 1936, Bl. 5; Besseler to Weber, 31 January 1936, Bl. 11; Besseler to REM, 22 March 1936, Bl. 50, all in ZStA REM Nr. 2909.

142. Besseler to Weber, 31 January 1936, ZStA REM Nr. 2909, Bl. 11.

143. Köcher (Deutsches Generalkonsulat für Spanien) to Auswärtiges Amt, 28 March 1936, ZStA REM Nr. 2909, Bl. 70.

144. Besseler to Huber, 31 January 1936, UAM PA Huber; Besseler to REM, 15 March 1936, ZStA REM Nr. 2909, Bl. 52.

145. Besseler, "Bericht über den III. Kongreß der Internationalen Gesellschaft für Mu-

sikwissenschaft, Barcelona, 18.-25. April 1936," dated 18 May 1936, ZStA REM Nr. 2909, Bl. 82–83.

146. REM to Dahnke, 10 December 1938, ZStA REM Nr. 2909, Bl. 104.

147. "Unabhängig hiervon ersuche ich um Prüfung der Frage, inwieweit im Zuge der von mir angestrebten Neuordnung der internationalen wissenschaftlichen Zusammenarbeit in den internationalen wissenschaftlichen Verbänden der praktische Einsatz der deutschen Musikwissenschaft zur Vorbereitung und Sicherung eines stärkeren deutschen Einflusses auf die internationale Zusammenarbeit auf dem Gebiete der Musik gegeben ist. . . . Bei dieser Anregung leitet mich auch die Auffassung, daß sich das Großdeutsche Reich in seinem Machtbereich für die Fortführung der wissenschaftlichen Zusammenarbeit und die Förderung der wissenschaftlichen Erkenntnis während des Krieges in gleicher Weise verantwortlich fühlen muß wie für den Neubau der wirtschaftlichen und politischen Ordnung Europas." Lamberts (REM) to Besseler, 13 October 1941, ZStA REM Nr. 3117, Bl. 7.

148. Besseler to REM, 20 May 1938, UAH Besseler file. Following Herbert Gerigk's characterization in his article "Eindrücke aus Florenz" (*Mk* 32 [1937]: 642–44) and Besseler's information, officials in the Ministry thereafter referred to the Maggio Musicale Fiorentino as a "Jewish meeting" and recommended that musicologists no longer attend. Frey to Dahnke, 20 January 1940, ZStA REM Nr. 2909, Bl. 105.

149. The Jews he names were Sachs, Adler, Prunières, and Egon Wellesz; their sympathizers Carlton Sprague Smith, Knud Jeppesen, Edward Dent, and John Brande Trend. Besseler to REM, 9 December 1938, ZStA REM Nr. 2909, Bl. 102.

150. Besseler to REM, 14 October 1941, ZStA REM Nr. 3117, Bl. 13.

151. See letter from Besseler, 17 July 1936, and the lengthy correspondence between Ursprung, who withdrew a contribution at the last minute, and *Acta* editor Knud Jeppesen (Ursprung Papers). For a description of the circumstances and repercussions of this boycott, see Potter, "Deutsche Musikgesellschaft."

152. Reichsministerium des Innern to Landesregierungen, 30 August 1934, Sandberger Papers (BSB).

153. REM to rectors of universities, 5 January 1935, Sandberger Papers (BSB).

154. "Wir haben keine Gelegenheit zum drucken mehr. Mehrere Zeitschriften sind unterdrückt, für neuere fehlt uns die Beglaubigung als 'zuverlässig' — welches bitterstes moralisches Unrecht wird uns da angetan! — und in ausländischen Zeitschriften werden deutsche Arbeiten und damit auch die unseren boykottiert." Ursprung to Gottron, 22 March 1939, Ursprung Papers.

155. The 1943 volume includes contributions by Moser ("Von der Steuerung des deutschen Musiklebens," "Von der Tätigkeit der Reichsstelle für Musikbearbeitungen," and "Das Mozart-Bild in unserer Zeit"); Frotscher ("Hitler-Jugend musiziert!"); and Eugen Schmitz ("Deutsche Musikforschung im Kriege").

Chapter 4. Musicology in the University

1. Ringer, *Decline,* 35–36.
2. Fallon, *German University,* 33, 35.
3. Ibid., 33–44.
4. Ringer, *Decline,* 35–36.

5. Ibid., 53–55; Fallon, *German University,* 46–47.

6. Ringer, *Decline,* 3–13. See also chap. 2.

7. Abendroth, "Die deutschen Professoren," 12, 17–18. Abendroth asserts that Mann's essay was one of the most popular works among professors; also Laqueur, *Weimar,* 188

8. Ringer, *Decline,* 83–84, 87.

9. Heiber, *Universität unterm Hakenkreuz,* 32.

10. Bleuel, *Deutschlands Bekenner,* 162–66

11. Laqueur, *Weimar,* 188.

12. *Chronik der Rheinischen Friedrich-Wilhelms-Universität zu Bonn* (1918–19), 69–70, UABonn; Dekan to REM, 19 November 1942, UABonn PA Schiedermair (Phil. Fak.).

13. Philosophische Fakultät to Senat, 8 September 1919 and 4 June 1920, UAF Reg. Akten V 1/159; letter of 17 July 1929, UAF PA Gurlitt.

14. UAH B–7559 and PA Kroyer.

15. UAH PA Moser.

16. Bücken to Philosophische Fakultät, 25 April 1922, Geh. Justizrat Franz Gaul (Bücken's uncle) to Rektor, 7 October 1925, UAK.

17. Letter from Dekan, 7 May 1930, UAK.

18. Dekan der Philosophischen Fakultät to Kultusministerium (Dresden), 20 December 1919, UAL PA 272, 12–18; Kroyer to Ursprung, 20 July 1932, Ursprung Papers.

19. [Krueger] to Philosophische Fakultät, 27 July 1931, UAL PA 661, 14–15; Sächsisches Ministerium für Volksbildung to Philosophische Fakultät Leipzig, 25 April 1932, and Dekan der Philosophischen Fakultät to Ministerium, 12 May 1932, UAL PA 661, 21–23; Sächsisches Ministerium für Volksbildung to Philosophische Fakultät Leipzig, 25 November 1932, UAL B2/20²¹, 71.

20. Dekan der Philosophischen Fakultät to H. Hinrichson, 4 January 1933, UAL B1/14²⁷ Bd.1, 12–17.

21. Sächsisches Ministerium für Volksbildung [to Dekan], 25 March 1933, UAL B2/20²¹, 166–67.

22. Sächsisches Ministerium für Volksbildung to Philosophische Fakultät, 26 July 1933, UAL PA 260, 43; Sächsisches Ministerium für Volksbildung to Philosophische Fakultät, 28 October 1932, UAL PA 260, 26.

23. Dekan to Kroyer, 20 January 1933, UAL B2/20²¹, 112–15; Dekan to Minister, 13 February 1933, UAL B2/20²¹, 156–57a.

24. Engel to Sandberger, 20 September 1933, Sandberger Papers (BSB). Sandberger confirmed that the feelings about the Leipzig situation were unanimous. Draft of answer to Engel, 22 September 1933, Sandberger Papers (BSB).

25. Report of discussion with dean on 25 January 1939, UAL PA 260, 59; Schultz to Dekan, 21 January 1941, UAL PA 260, 75–76; report of discussion with Minister, 7 February 1941, concluding that Schultz's request for promotion to Ordinarius could not be honored because of financial conditions in wartime, UAL PA 260, 83.

26. Karl Gustav Fellerer, "Hochschule, Musik und Musikwissenschaft," *DTZ* 26 (1928): 287–89.

27. Willibald Nagel, "Die Aufgabe der Musikwissenschaft an der Musikhochschule," *Die Musikerziehung. Vorträge* (1928): 73–76.

28. Dekan to H. Hinrichson, 4 January 1933, UAL B1/14²⁷ Bd.1, 12–17.

29. Joseph Müller-Blattau, "Collegium musicum" CM 1 (1932): 3–4.

30. Philosophiche Fakultät to Kultusministerium, 21 June 1915, UAL PA 925, 35.

31. Dekan to Kultusministerium, 20 December 1919, UAL PA 272, 17.

32. Krueger (Psychologisches Institut der Universität Leipzig) to Philosophische Fakultät, 27 July 1931, UAL PA 661, 14.

33. Birtner, "Lebenslauf" and "Darstellung über die wissenschaftliche Arbeit," 17 February 1938, BDC Birtner.

34. Lebenslauf, UAM FA Engel.

35. Luise Gutzeit, "Das Collegium musicum der Albertus-Universität Königsberg und seine Fahrt ins Baltikum," CM 1 (1932) 56–58.

36. Chronik der Rheinischen Friedrich-Wilhelms-Universität zu Bonn (1919–20), 70.

37. Ludwig Unterholzner, "Um das musikwissenschaftliche Seminar der Universität Erlangen," AMz 56 (1929): 478.

38. Müller-Blattau, "Collegium musicum," 4; Wilhelm Ehmann "Collegium Musicum der Universität Freiburg i. Br.," CM 1 (1932) 17–18.

39. Wilibald Gurlitt "Collegia Musica," DTZ 25 (1927): 309–10.

40. Gutzeit, "Collegium musicum der Albertus-Universität," 56–58.

41. Frotscher, "Lebenslauf," 23 May 1939, UAB PA Frotscher.

42. Bücken to Kuratorium, 20 June 1922, Bücken to Philosophische Fakultät, 25 April 1922, and Bücken to Eckert (Kuratorium), 20 December 1922, UAK.

43. Bücken to "Herr Geheimrat," 25 April 1922, UAK.

44. Pulzer, Jews and the German State, 108–11.

45. Ibid., 271, 276–78.

46. Mosse, Crisis of German Ideology, 271.

47. Ringer, Decline, 136–37.

48. Quoted in Bleuel, Deutschlands Bekenner, 189.

49. Pulzer, Jews and the German State, 109.

50. This figure is derived from an unpublished list compiled by Bruno Nettl and Lawrence Gushee.

51. Transcript of letter from Dekan, 14 January 1925, on possibility of replacing Fleischer with a systematic musicologist, UAB Phil. Fak. 1471.

52. Friedländer to Dekan, 19 January 1925, UAB Phil. Fak. 1471.

53. Sachs to Moser, 9 April 1949 (copy sent to Einstein), folder 812, Einstein Papers.

54. In 1915, Einstein was asked to contribute an essay to a Festschrift honoring Sandberger and flatly refused to pay tribute to the man whose anti-Semitic character defamation nearly destroyed his career. He was, however, willing to contribute money to the Festschrift anonymously, especially if his gift was going to make or break the project: "Es macht mir sogar einen gewissen Spaß, durch meine 'Noblesse' die Ehrung eines Mannes zu ermöglichen, der mir in antisemitischer Absicht zuweitgehende finanzielle Ansprüche öffentlich unter die Nase getrieben hat" (Einstein to Kroyer, 4 March 1915, folder 568, Einstein Papers). Ten years later, Einstein was still painfully aware of Sandberger's anti-Semitic feelings, reporting to Kroyer of a chance meeting with Sandberger: "Wir stehen äußerlich recht gut, aber Sie wissen, er vergißt nichts. Und ich bin Jude!" (Einstein to Kroyer, 17 February 1925, folder 568, Einstein Papers).

55. "Er war es, der genau vor 15 Jahren mir meine Wahl zum Schriftl. mitteilte, weil er

das Unrecht fühlte, das er mir angetan hatte" Einstein to Kroyer (draft), 7 July 1933, folder 568, Einstein Papers.

56. A priest named Decker wrote to fellow priest and musicologist Otto Ursprung in 1930 that it was common knowledge that Sandberger denied Einstein the opportunity to do his Habilitation "in any case because of his Judaism" (2 June 1930, Ursprung Papers). Curt Sachs recalled in 1949 that everyone knew that Sandberger had treated Einstein "like a dog" and bemoaned the fact that in those times when so many mediocre scholars could succeed, Einstein could not even do his Habilitation because he belonged to the wrong religion (Sachs to Moser, 9 April 1949, folder 812, Einstein Papers).

57. Kurt Heumann to A. L. Tietz, 11 July 1930, UAK.

58. Einstein to Kroyer, 12 May 1927, folder 568, Einstein Papers.

59. Moser to Kroyer, 28 May 1927, Kroyer Papers.

60. "Star of Knowledge."

61. Protokoll, 2 March 1927, UAW PA Lach; Fischer indicates in his curriculum vitae that he was born Jewish ("von Geburt mosaischer Religion") and converted to Catholicism in 1911. UAW PA Fischer.

62. Report of meeting on 14 December 1918, UAW PA Lach.

63. Adler also recommended Kurth, Rietsch, Ludwig, Schering, Nettl, and Einstein, in addition to the Austrians Ficker, Fischer, Haas, Orel, and Wellesz. He was oppposed to Lach (Protokoll, 2 March 1927, Kommissionsbericht, UAW PA Lach). The committee, in considering Adler's list, stated: "Der Vorschlag stellt hinter den Ordinarius der Berliner Universität [Abert] durchwegs österreichische Gelehrte, die wenigstens nach der Mehrheit der Kommission an Umfang und Wert der bisher geleisteten Arbeiten Prof. Lach sehr beträchtlich nachstehen." Mehrheitsgutachten (1927), UAW PA Lach.

64. *Neues Wiener Journal,* 30 September 1927 (copy in UAW PA Lach).

65. Kater, *Studentenschaft,* 19–24, 43–58, 103–9.

66. Kater, *Studentenschaft,* 173–97; Giles, "Rise of the National Socialist Students' Association," 162–63.

67. Giles, "Rise of the National Socialist Students' Association," 163–69.

68. Bracher, "Gleichschaltung der deutschen Universität," 137–38; Lundgreen, "Hochschulpolitik und Wissenschaft," 11–12.

69. Kater, *Studentenschaft,* 154–57; idem, "Studenten auf dem Weg," 34.

70. Giles, "Rise of the National Socialist Students' Association," 168.

71. Bücken to Dekan, 14 January 1929; Dekan to A. Schmitz, 27 May 1930; Kurator to Riezler (University, Frankfurt am Main), 16 January 1933; letter from Wolf, 7 October 1930, UAK.

72. Kroyer to Siepp (Dekan), 27 May 1931, UAK.

73. Kuratorium to Bürgermeister, 7 July 1931, UAK.

74. Kroyer to Kurator, 9 March 1932 and 29 July 1932, UAK.

75. Eichmann, Zaun, Raskin, and Wolters to REM [November 1933?], UAK.

76. Two identical letters ("Bescheinigung") from Obersturmbahnführer, Sturmbahn I/236, 20 November 1933; "Bericht betr. Ausschuss der Studierenden phil. Käte Knott und phil. Gottfried Wolters" [November 1933], UAK.

77. Kroyer to Dekan, 13 November 1933, Bücken to Krämer (lawyer), 15 November 1933, UAK.

78. Giles, *Students and National Socialism,* 197–201; idem, "Rise of the National Socialist Students' Association," 174.

79. "Urteil des Kreisgerichts Heidelberg der NSDAP: Begründung," 17 November 1939; Besseler to REM, 21 July 1941, BDC Besseler.

80. Emil Zirkel, "Eidesstattliche Erklärung," 2 July 1948, UAH PA Besseler.

81. Besseler to Rektor, 5 July 1948, UAH PA Besseler.

82. "Urteil des Kreisgerichts Heidelberg der NSDAP: Begründung," 17 November 1939, BDC Besseler.

83. Reimann, "Die 'Selbst-Gleichschaltung' der Universitäten," 43–46.

84. Geoffrey Giles, *Students and National Socialism,* 155.

85. Olszewski, *Zwischen Begeisterung und Widerstand,* 61–66.

86. Noakes and Pridham, *Nazism,* 444.

87. See chap. 2.

88. Alfred Lorenz, "Musikwissenschaft und Ahnenforschung," *ZfM* 105 (1938): 1372–73, and idem, "Musikwissenschaft und Judenfrage," *Mk* 31 (1938): 177–79.

89. "Kulturwacht e.V.," *Bayerische Staatszeitung,* 15 May 1931; Dekan to Rektor, 26 September 1939, UAM PA Schmidt.

90. Schmidt, "Lebenslauf" and "Verzeichnis der Schriften"; Schmidt to Dekan, 7 January 1939, UAM FA Schmidt.

91. Noakes and Pridham, *Nazism,* 223–25; Maier, "Nationalsozialistische Hochschulpolitik," 81–82.

92. Maier, "Nationalsozialistische Hochschulpolitik," 81–82.

93. REM to Sachs, 6 September 1933, and to Hornbostel, 24 September 1933, UAB 1478.

94. File card from RSK, 10 December 1941, BDC research files; Minister des Kultus, des Unterrichts und der Justiz to Rektor, 28 November 1933, UAF PA Gurlitt.

95. Olszewski, *Zwischen Begeisterung und Widerstand,* 78–79. A parallel situation for doctors is described in Kater, *Doctors under Hitler,* 185–92.

96. Noakes and Pridham, *Nazism,* 535–36.

97. Rektor to Engel (REM), 27 October 1936, UAF Reg. Akten V 1/159.

98. Rektor to Hufer (Intendant), 27 October 1936, UAF Reg. Akten V 1/159.

99. Anrich, *Universität als geistige Grenzfestungen.*

100. Rektor to REM, 28 October 1936, UAF Reg. Akten V 1/159.

101. Müller-Blattau [to Rektor?], 28 October 1936, UAF PA Gurlitt; Müller-Blattau to "Herr Kollege" [Dekan of Phil. Fak.], 1 April 1937, UAF Reg. Akten V 1/159.

102. Minister des Kultus und Unterrichts to Rektor, 25 June 1937, and Rektor to Minister des Kultus und Unterrichts, 25 September 1937, UAF PA Gurlitt.

103. Gurlitt to Badisches Ministerium des Kultus und Unterrichts, 8 August 1945, UAF PA Gurlitt.

104. Rektor to Minister des Kultus und Unterrichts (Baden), 30 June 1937, UAF Reg. Akten V 1/159.

105. Oppermann (Phil.Fak.) to Badisches Ministerium des Kultus und Unterrichts, 28 July 1937, UAF Reg. Akten V 1/159.

106. Schiedermair to REM, 31 January 1935, UABonn PA Schrade (Phil. Fak.).

107. Deutsche Botschaft to Auswärtiges Amt, 13 July 1935; REM to Universitätskurator, 10 August 1935, UABonn PA Schrade (Kuratorium).

108. Rektor to Dekan, 20 May 1937, UABonn PA Schrade (Phil. Fak.).

109. REM to Schrade, 25 June 1937; Dekan to REM, 4 December 1937, UABonn PA Schrade (Phil. Fak.).

110. Dekan to Rektor, 16 August 1937, UABonn PA Schrade (Phil. Fak.).

111. Schiedermair to Dekan, 28 January 1937 and 3 June 1937; Schiedermair to Rektor, 12 April 1940, UABonn PA Schiedermair (Phil. Fak.). Dekan to Kurator, 12 November 1941; Schiedermair to Kurator, 12 December 1941, 2 February 1942, and 20 October 1943, UABonn PA Schiedermair (Kuratorium). "Gutachten," 23 October 1945, UABonn PA Schiedermair (Rektorat).

112. Preußischer Minister für Wissenschaft, Kunst und Volksbildung to Moser, 4 June 1933, UAB PA Moser; to Wolf, same date, UAB PA Wolf.

113. Preußischer Minister für Wissenschaft, Kunst und Volksbildung to Moser, 30 August 1927 and 15 September 1934, UAB PA Moser.

114. Moser to Sandberger, 25 September 1933, Sandberger Papers (BSB).

115. UAB PA Schumann; Schumann to Dekan, 22 May 1941; Ministerialdirektor to Schumann, 31 July 1943, BDC Schumann.

116. Bose, "Lebenslauf," 25 November 1941, UAB PA Bose.

117. Danckert was active in the Rassenpolitisches Amt, the Reichsstelle zur Förderung des deutschen Schrifttums, and the Hohe Schule der Partei, and he was working on a project for Rosenberg. Letter from Danckert, stamped 9 February 1942, UAB PA Danckert.

118. Dekan to Rektor, 1 October 1945, UAB PA Danckert.

119. He became NSDAP Schulungsleiter in 1935 and Amtsleiter der NSDAP in 1937, and he was director of the organ task force in the Reich Youth Leadership. Frotscher, "Lebenslauf," 23 May 1939, and Fragebogen, UAB PA Frotscher.

120. Frotscher, Schriftenverzeichnis, UAB PA Frotscher.

121. Schering to Dekan, 25 July 1935, UAB PA Frotscher.

122. Dekan to REM, 24 January 1935, UAB PA Wolf.

123. Schering to REM, 1 July 1935, UAB PA Wolf.

124. Dekan to REM, 3 July 1935 and 6 September 1935, UAB PA Wolf; Weber to Hinz, 16 September 1935, BDC Wolf.

125. Letter from Vahlen (REM), 5 December 1935; Wolf to Dekan, 26 December 1935, UAB PA Wolf.

126. Oppermann (Phil. Fak.) to Badisches Ministerium des Kultus und Unterrichts, 28 July 1937, UAF Reg. Akten V 1/159.

127. Müller-Blattau to Badisches Ministerium des Kultus und Unterrichts, 19 May 1938; [Phil. Fak.] to REM, 26 July 1941, UAF Reg. Akten V 1/159.

128. Schiedermair, "Bericht über den Dozenten Dr. Leo Schrade," 23 May 1937, UABonn PA Schrade (Phil. Fak.).

129. *Chronik der Rheinischen Friedrich-Wilhelms-Universität zu Bonn,* Jg.59 (1933–34): 50, UABonn.

130. ZStA REM Nr. 2176, Bl. 13.

131. Gesellschaft der Musikfreunde to Landeskulturleitung der NSDAP, 26 March 1938, Archive of the Gesellschaft der Musikfreunde Exh. Nr. 101.

132. Gesellschaft to Geiringer, 31 March 1938; Notice, 1 April 1938; Gesellschaft to Geiringer, 13 April 1938, Archive of the Gesellschaft der Musikfreunde Exh. Nr. 103.

133. Bleuel, *Deutschlands Bekenner,* 8; Gallin, *Midwives to Nazism.*

134. Maier, "Nationalsozialistische Hochschulpolitik," 74–75, Olszewski, *Zwischen Begeisterung und Widerstand,* 68.

135. Hartshorne, *German Universities,* 48–52; Olszewski, *Zwischen Begeisterung und Widerstand,* 80; Maier, "Nationalsozialistische Hochschulpolitik," 80.

136. Hartshorne, *German Universities,* 50–51, 69.

137. Olszewski, *Zwischen Begeisterung und Widerstand,* 80–81.

138. Franz Hofer to Ministerpräsident Sieber, 26 June 1935, UAM PA Ficker.

139. UAM PA Ficker; Havemann (RMK) to Bayerisches Kultusministerium, 23 March 1934, UAM PA Sandberger.

140. Letter from Rektor, 5 May 1934, UAM PA Sandberger.

141. Hartshorne, *German Universities,* chap. 5.

142. Letters from Ursprung, 2 April 1938 and 29 April 1938, UAM PA Ursprung.

143. Rektor to Dekan, 20 October 1941, UAM PA Sandberger.

144. Dekan to Rektor, 10 December and 19 December 1941; Rektor to REM, 12 December 1941, UAM PA Sandberger.

145. Dekan to REM, 13 May 1941 and 27 January 1942, UAB PA Schering.

146. Dekan (Berlin) to Dekan (Kiel), 14 July 1941; Buddenbrock-Hettersdorf to Engelke (Kiel), 10 July 1941, UAB PA Schering.

147. Blume testimony, 20 October 1940, BDC Blume.

148. Dekan to Frey (REM), 13 May 1941, UAB PA Schering.

149. "Die jetzt notwendige Besetzung des 1. musikwissenschaftlichen Ordinariats an der Universität Berlin gibt Gelegenheit, mit der Wahl des neuen Mannes den heute maßgeblichen kulturpolitischen Grundsätzen verstärkte Geltung zu verschaffen. Diese Forderung dürfte kaum erfüllt sein, wenn man diesen Lehrstuhl mit einer Persönlichkeit besetzt, deren Hauptleitung auf dem Gebiet der evangelischen Kirchenmusik liegt, welcher obendrein der arteigene Ursprung aberkannt wird." NSD-Dozentenbund (Gaudozentenführer) to NSD-Dozentenbund (University of Berlin), 18 June 1941, UAB PA Schering.

150. NSD-Dozentenbund (Gaudozentenführer) to NSD-Dozentenbund (University of Berlin), 18 June 1941; "Abschrift! Prof. Dr. Freidrich Blume (Universität Kiel)," UAB PA Schering.

151. Gaudozentenbundführer, "Stellungnahme," 20 October 1941, UAB PA Schering.

152. "Mit Schreiben vom 29. Juli 1944 waren Sie bereits gebeten worden, an Stelle von Professor Blume-Kiel, Professor Osthoff-Frankfurt/Main den Lehrstuhl für Musikwissenschaft an der Universität Berlin zu übertragen. Es wird erneut um Mitteilung gebeten, aus welchen Gründen hiervon abgesehen und lediglich eine Abordnung vorgesehen wurde." Looft (Partei-Kanzlei) to REM, 8 March 1945, GStA Rep. 76/254.

153. Bücken to Krämer, 30 October 1934, UAK.

154. Trienes, "Stellungnahme zur Akte Bücken-Kroyer, Universität Köln," 2 June 1936; "Bericht betr. Ausschuss der Studierenden phil. Käte Knott und phil. Gottfried Wolters" [November 1933]; Bücken to H. Unger (Dozentenbund), 27 June 1938, UAK.

155. Krämer to Kurator, 2 November 1934, UAK.

156. Rektor to Dekan, 23 June 1936, UAK.

157. Trienes, "Stellungnahme zur Akte Bücken-Kroyer, Universität Köln," 2 June 1936, UAK.

158. Dekan to Rektor, 19 June 1936, UAK.

159. Dekan to REM, 13 January 1936; Dekan to Rektor, 19 June 1936; Rektor to Dekan, 23 June 1936, UAK.

160. Trienes to Kurator, 2 December 1938, UAK.

161. Eggers, "§16 Bildungswesen," 968–70, 981–83; Maier, "Nationalsozialistische Hochschulpolitik," 87–92.

162. Rektor to Munich Professors, 17 December 1934, Sandberger Papers (BSB).

163. Maier, "Nationalsozialistische Hochschulpolitik," 85–97.

164. Von der Leyen to Dekan, 9 December 1934, UAK.

165. Dehns (Education Ministry, Mecklenburg) to REM, 3 April 1934, ZStA REM Nr. 933, Bl. 2.

166. Ficker to Dekan, 31 January 1939, UAM FA Ficker; Ficker to Bayerisches Staatsministerium für Unterricht und Kultus, 20 November 1938, UAM FA Musikwissenschaftliches Seminar.

167. "Anzeige," lists Lorenz's NSDAP membership since December 1931, NSV, NSLB, and RMK; Lorenz to Rektor, 4 July 1935; Dozentenschaft to Rektor, 18 May 1936; Dekan to Rektor, 16 September 1938; Dozentenschaft to Rektor, 26 September 1938, UAM PA Lorenz.

168. "Vorlesungen über Musik an Hochschulen: Sommersemester 1933," *ZfMw* 15 (1932–33): 324; "Vorlesungen über Musik an Hochschulen: Wintersemester 1933/34," "Vorlesungen über Musik an Universitäten und Technischen Hochschulen: Sommersemester 1934," *ZfMw* 16 (1934): 47, 378; "Vorlesungen über Musik an Universitäten und Technischen Hochschulen," *ZfMw* 17 (1935): 51, 310.

169. "Die Neuheit der methodologischen Verbindung von Stilkritik und geisteswissenschaftlicher Einstellung fand in der Fachwelt einen großen Widerhall, der beispielsweise auch daraus zu erkennen ist, dass das erst zu einem Teile erschienene Handbuch der Musikwissenschaft bereits auf die 10. Auflage — zehntausend Bezieher — erhöht werden musste." Bücken to Dekan, 14 January 1929, UAK.

170. Fellerer established the Kölner Musikarchiv and centered a large number of research projects in the institute around the music history of Cologne. Karl Gustav Fellerer, "Das Kölner Musikarchiv," [1942/43] newspaper clipping (no source or date given); Fellerer to Kuratorium, 6 August 1943, UAK.

171. REM to Generalbevollmächtigten für die Reichsverwaltung, 18 April 1940, 1–4 and Anlage, BA R 21/209.

172. NSDAP-Partei-Kanzlei to REM, 27 March 1944, BA R 21/464.

173. Draft of REM response to Partei-Kanzlei, 5 April 1944, BA R 21/464.

174. Protokoll, 15 December 1938, UAW Dekanat 240.

175. "Wenn so also durch die ganzen vergangenen sieben Jahre seit 1931 wegen der äußerst beschränkten Mittel des Staates der vorhin erwähnte Mißstand nicht beseitigt werden konnte, so ist es nunmehr umso dankbarer zu begrüssen, daß jetzt — nach Uebernahme der Ostmark in das Reich — dieses Versäumnis nachgeholt und die Stelle des Extraordinarius mit einer geeigneten Kraft definitiv besetzt werden soll." "Bericht über die Kommissionssitzung am 15 December 1938," UAW Dekanat 240.

176. They had recommended Haas, but the Ministry expressed its intention to hire Schenk, noting it would consider Haas as Ordinarius to replace Lach in the coming year

(or vice versa, with Haas as Extraordinarius and Schenk as Ordinarius). The main reasons for the Ministry's decision seem to be the relevance of their work for an Austrian university. Ministerialrat Schaller to Dekan, 7 June 1939, UAW Dekanat 240.

177. Dekan to Ministerium für innere und kulturelle Angelegenheiten, 5 January 1939, UAW Dekanat 240.

178. Lach, "Besetzungsvorschlag für das Ordinariat der Musikwissenschaft," 29 June 1939, UAW Dekanat 240.

179. "Bericht über die Kommissionssitzung am 15 December 1938," Lach, "Besetzungsvorschlag," 19 June 1939; Haas curriculum vitae, UAW Dekanat 240.

180. Ministerialrat Schaller to Dekan, 7 June 1939; Protokoll, 15 December 1938, UAW Dekanat 240.

181. While conducting my research in this archive, I came across empty folders bearing the information "eingelangt von Prof. Erich Schenk." These included items from the personnel file of Alfred Orel (Dekanat file 680, 1939–40: "Gutachten über Prof. Orel 2.III.1940"), who was dismissed from the university after the war because of his Nazi party affiliation, and a file entitled "Wiener Mozartwoche: Klärung des Verhältnisses Gemeinde (Prof. Orel) und Universität (Prof. Schenk)" (Dekanat file 314, 1941–42). Missing altogether are Schenk's personnel files and a file possibly dealing with the seizure of Adler's library (file 172, 1942–43: "Einstellung einer Kriegsersatzkraft für die Bestandaufnahme der Adler-Bibl."). There is no documentation regarding Adler's fate after 1938 in the university files.

182. Hauptstelle Musik to Schenk, 21 March 1941, BA NS 15/21; Schenk to Gerigk, 31 March 1941, and Gerigk to Schenk, 28 December 1944, BA NS 15/21a. See chap. 5 for other aspects of their relationship.

183. Schenk to Obersturmführer Sievers (SS-"Ahnenerbe"), 29 August 1942, BDC Schenk.

184. Gmelin (REM), file transcript, 16 November 1942, UAB PA Frotscher.

185. REM to Reichsstatthalter in Österreich; Ministerium für innere und kulturelle Angelegenheiten, 16 September 1939, UAW Dekanat 240.

186. Rektor (Frankfurt/Main) to REM, 16 November 1935, ZStA REM Nr. 1782.

187. Rektor (Königsberg) to REM, 29 November 1941; "Denkschrift über die Errichtung einer Fakultät der Künste bei der Universität Königsberg," GStA I/76: 880.

188. "Auf der anderen Seite ist die Pflege der Musikwissenschaft an der Universität Königsberg bei dem Fehlen jeder musikwissenschaftlichen und musikpädagogischen Einsätze im deutschen Osten ein dringendes kulturpolitisches Erfordernis, so daß wir unsere sehr schweren Bedenken gegen diese Lösung zurückzustellen genötigt sind." Rektor (Königsberg) to REM, 28 September 1943, GStA I/76: 880.

189. Rektor (Kiel) to REM, 11 October 1937, BDC Blume. The dean of the Philosophische Fakultät in Kiel also sent his own appeal to the Education Ministry, pointing out the importance of music to the total educational task of National Socialism, the importance of Blume's work for the outlying northern district, and the fact that Blume had been appointed by the Education Ministry as "Director for the Collection and Cultivation of Musical Monuments in the Border Region Schleswig-Holstein, Hamburg and Lübeck." Dekan (Phil. Fak. Kiel) to REM, 11 November 1937, BDC Blume.

190. Zschintsch (REM) to Krebs (Oberbürgermeister, Frankfurt/Main), 24 August 1938; REM to Blume, 6 February 1938, BDC Blume.

191. Ehmann, "Das Musikleben an den deutschen Universitäten," 157–58

192. "Studenten musizieren," 6 July 1939, BDC Besseler.

193. Lach, "Besetzungsvorschlag," 29 June 1939, UAW Dekanat 240.

194. Birtner, "Darstellung über die wissenschaftliche Arbeit," 17 February 1938, BDC Birtner.

195. Drux, *Kölner Universitätskonzerte*, 63–65.

196. Wilhelm Ehmann, "Collegium musicum in der Wehrbetreuung," *DMK* 7 (1942): 14–19.

197. Gurlitt to Rektorat, 1 October 1935, UAF Reg. Akten V 1/159.

198. Ehmann, "Entwurf einer Neuordnung der musikalisch-praktischen Aufgaben innerhalb des Freiburger Universitätslebens," 22 December 1935, UAF Reg. Akten V 1/159.

199. Gurlitt to Dekan, 21 December 1935, UAF Reg. Akten V 1/159.

200. Dragendorff (Phil. Fak.) to Rektor, 30 January 1936; Dekan to Rektor, 2 May 1936, 2, UAF Reg. Akten V 1/159.

201. Studentenschaft to Gurlitt, 19 December 1935, UAF PA Gurlitt.

202. Giles, "German Students and Higher Education Policy," 331–32.

203. Rust, Transcript, "Totaler Kriegseinsatz," 20 September 1944, BA R 21/625.

204. The military allowed students to be released from service to prepare for exams. It also set up a very popular system of university extension that included correspondence courses; special courses on the front by professors eager to demonstrate their contribution to the war effort; and offered "extension matriculation," by which soldiers could enroll at universities without being on campus. Giles, "German Students and Higher Education Policy," 333–37.

205. Schünemann to Dekan, 19 June 1944, UAB PA Schünemann.

206. Schiedermair to Rektor, 2 February 1942; [Rektor] to Schiedermair, 12 May 1942 and 21 May 1942, UABonn PA Schiedermair (Rektorat). The lecture was published in 1942, as indicated in Gerigk's evaluation from the Amt Rosenberg, 4 March 1943, BA NS 15/101.

207. REM to Osthoff, 1 November 1937, 5 September 1938, 16 January 1939, 9 December 1944, Osthoff to Dekan, 21 December 1944, Dekan to Frotscher, 27 December 1944, UAB PA Osthoff; REM to Dekan, 25 January 1945, UAB PA Schering.

208. Dekan to Rektor, 1 October 1945, UAB PA Danckert.

209. Frotscher to Körner (Hochschule für Musikerziehung), 19 November 1943; Director, Staatliche Hochschule für Musikerziehung to Frotscher, 23 May 1944, BDC Frotscher.

210. UAK; Schiedermair to Universitäts-Präsident (Bonn), 1 August 1945, UABonn PA Schiedermair (Kuratorium); letter to Schiedermair, 21 February 1944, UABonn PA Schiedermair (Rektorat).

211. Dekan to Fellerer's unit, 6 April 1944, UAK.

212. REM to Besseler, 15 November 1941, [University] to Badisches Kultusministerium, 16 March 1944, UAH PA Besseler; Rektor to Besseler, 10 November 1942, UAF Reg. Akten V 1/159; REM to Besseler, 15 November 1941 and 21 April 1942, BDC Besseler.

213. Maurer (for the rector) to Ministerialrat Elsass, 2 November 1944, UAF PA Zenck; Besseler to REM, 3 January 1945, BDC Besseler.

214. Petry, *Studenten aufs Schafott,* 16, 138, 153; Giles, *Students and National Socialism,* 293, 303n.

215. Hans Eckhardt to REM, 26 April 1933, ZStA REM Nr. 1475, Bl. 259.

216. "Auszugsweise Abschrift eines Briefes von Besseler an Professor Weber-Berlin v.16.10.35," BDC Wolf.

217. BDC Wolf.

218. REM to Wolf, 20 March 1940, BDC Wolf.

219. "Die Musikwissenschaft hatte wie viele andere geistige Disziplinen die Schäden des großen Krieges noch nicht völlig überwunden, als die Pflicht zu neuer Abwehr jäh erstand, und das Erstarken rassischen Empfindens führte zur Ausscheidung von Kräften, die kurzer Hand nicht zu ersetzen waren." Wolf, "Musik und Musikwissenschaft," in Morgenroth, ed., *Von deutscher Tonkunst,* 39.

220. Petry, *Studenten aufs Schafott,* 153.

221. Volksgerichtshof Sch. 264, BDC Schmorell.

222. Von Staa in Amt V[olksbildung] to Amt W[issenschaft] in Education Ministry, 5 March 1937, ZStA REM Nr. H663, Bl. 38; "Vermerk," 19 March [1937], Bl. 39.

223. Petry, *Studenten aufs Schafott,* 44–47.

224. Dumbach and Newborn, *Shattering the German Night,* 114. I have called the authors' attention to the inaccuracies.

225. Von Staa in Amt V[olksbildung] to Amt W[issenschaft] in Education Ministry, 5 March 1937, ZStA REM Nr. H663, Bl. 38.

226. Philosophische Fakultät (University of Berlin) to REM, 21 May 1937, ZStA REM Nr. H663, Bl. 41.

227. Amt V to Amt W, 17 August 1937, ZStA REM Nr. H663, Bl. 42.

228. Frey to Miederer, 7 February 1938, ZStA REM Nr. H663, Bl. 47–48.

229. Miederer to Frey, 24 February 1938, ZStA REM Nr. H663, Bl. 47 verso.

230. "Professor Huber scheidet demgemäß auf seine eigene Rücksprache mit dem Sachbearbeiter meines Ministeriums, Regierungsrat Dr. Miederer, mit Wirkung vom 1. Oktober 1938 aus dem Staatlichen Institut aus." Zschintzsch (REM) to Institut, 30 August 1938, ZStA REM Nr. H663, Bl. 55–56.

231. Sachse (NSDAP-Reichsleitung, Hauptamt für Volkswohlfahrt) to Broemser (Rector, University of Munich), 27 July 1939, UAM PA Huber.

232. "Die *politischen* Gutachten über Huber führen zu dem Schlusse, daß seine Stellung zum neuen Staate einige Zeit nicht ganz eindeutig war, doch ist die nationale Gesinnung nie in Zweifel gezogen worden. . . . Es verdient Anerkennung, dass Huber sich seit 1934 den Gliederungen der Partei im Rahmen seiner volksmusikalischen Arbeit zur Verfügung gestellt hat. . . . Am 17. Januar 1939 erklärt Huber in einer Zuschrift an das Dekanat, er habe dem Herrn Referenten im Reichserziehungsministerium ausdrücklich die Erklärung abgegeben, dass er, sobald die Partei wieder geöffnet sei, sein Aufnahmegesuch einreichen werde (emphasis in original)." Wüst to Rektor, 10 October 1939, ZStA REM Nr. H663, Bl. 60 and UAM PA Huber.

233. Volksgerichtshof Sch. 264, BDC Schmorell.

234. See, e.g., his widow's description of his disillusionment from 1942 in Huber, ed., *Kurt Huber zum Gedächtnis,* 15–16.

235. I am grateful to Professor Klaus Schwabe (Aachen) for sharing this observation with me.

236. I am grateful to Professor Peter Fritzsche (Illinois) and his graduate students for providing me with these insights.

237. Giles, *Students and National Socialism in Germany,* 299–305.

Chapter 5. New Opportunities outside the University

1. "Aufruf zur Gründung der Deutschen Musikgesellschaft," 1 December [1917], Sandberger Papers (BSB).

2. In 1920, the Prussian Ministry for Science, Art and Public Education no longer required that doctoral dissertations be published, and many students found themselves spending time on a dissertation topic only to learn that it had already been done (Einstein, "Mitteilungen der Deutschen Musikgesellschaft," *ZfMw* 4 [1921–22]: 254). In 1925, the ministry withdrew the 1920 decision and required publication once again, waiving the requirement only when the doctoral student could demonstrate extreme financial need ("Mitteilungen," *ZfMw* 7 [1924–25]: 445), but by then most students were living in reduced circumstances, and the outlets for publishing theses were diminishing. For a limited time, the Bückeburg Institute published a few qualified Habilitationsschriften, but many publishers were having financial difficulties and required publication subsidies, which the young scholars were unable to provide (Bücken to Sandberger, 21 May 1921, Sandberger Papers [BSB]). Financial difficulties in the DMG's Publikationen älterer Musik series (established at the 1925 Leipzig conference under the direction of Theodor Kroyer's Department for the Publication of Early Music) threatened to close off another publication option for Habilitationsschriften ("Mitteilungen der Deutschen Musikgesellschaft," *ZfMw* 13 [1930–31]: 504–5).

3. Feldman, *The Great Disorder,* 547–48.

4. Besseler, "Lebensbeschreibung," 26 July 1945, UAH PA Besseler.

5. Wilhelm Trittenhoff [*sic;* elsewhere name appears as Twittenhoff], "Der Student der Musikwissenschaften," *DTZ* 29 (1931): 107.

6. In response to a proposal to form a central career placement organization for musicologists, Hans Engel cynically retorted that it would make more sense to set up an organization that would discourage students from going into musicology in the first place. Kurt Rasch, "Musikwissenschaft und Beruf: Ein Versuch zu einem organisatorischen Abriß," *ZfMw* 15 (1933): 69–67; Hans Engel, "Miszellen," *ZfMw* 15 (1933): 275.

7. Abert, "Kunst, Kunstwissenschaft, und Kunstkritik," 8–10.

8. Trittenhoff, "Student der Musikwissenschaften," 107–8.

9. Leichtentritt, "Vom Wesen der Kritik," *DMJb* 1 (1924): 46, 49.

10. Arnold Schering, "Aus der Geschichte der musikalischen Kritik in Deutschland," *JbMP* 35 (1928): 23.

11. Werner to Kroyer, 7 May 1923, Kroyer Papers.

12. Einstein to Kroyer, 12 May 1927, folder 568A, Einstein Papers.

13. Dekan to REM, 7 July 1925, UAF PA Müller-Blattau.

14. Blume to Philosophische Fakultät, 26 April 1923, UAL Phil. Fak. Promotionsakte 1350.

15. Heinrich Husmann, "Musikkultur und Volksbildungswesen," *AMz* 60 (1933): 309–10.

16. Siegfried Goslich, "Studium und Beruf des jungen Musikwissenschaftlers," *Mk* 27 (1935): 283, 285.

17. Karl Gustav Fellerer, "Praktische Musikwissenschaft," *ZfM* 103 (1936): 27–31. See also his "Entrümpelung und Musikwissenschaft," *Mk* 30 (1937): 100–101; and "Historische und systematische Musikwissenschaft," *Mk* 29 (1937): 340–43.

18. Friedrich Brand, "Musikdezernent oder Musikpolitiker?" *Mk* 30 (1937): 102.

19. Erich Valentin, "Existenzfragen der Berufskritik. Ein Vorschlag zur Neuorganisation des deutschen Musiklebens," *ZfM* 100 (1933): 1022–24.

20. In line with his portrayal of Goebbels as a champion of the artist, Steinweis suggested to me that the *Kritikverbot* may have been one more measure to protect the trained professional from the amateur, here in the form of eliminating journalistic attacks.

21. Prieberg proposed that the effects of the ban were greatly exaggerated after 1945, and Lovisa pursues this supposition, claiming that most journals had already "censored" themselves before the ban went into effect and highlighting the anti-Semitic symbolism in the wording of the measure (Prieberg, *Musik im NS-Staat,* 284–85; Lovisa, *Musikkritik im Nationalsozialismus,* 197–207). It seems that the measure was largely symbolic, cited in conjunction with the injustices against "true German" musicians in the past that would henceforward cease to destroy careers, and making obvious references to the elimination of "parasitic" (Jewish) critics who had victimized Germans and swayed public opinion. See, e.g., Gilliam, "Annexation of Bruckner," 592–93, 607.

22. Erich Valentin, "Seminar für Musikkritik," *ZfM* 104 (1937): 280–84.

23. Gerigk, "Die Musik im Jahre 1938," BA NS 15/99.

24. Paschen-Friedrich von Flotow, "Die Entwicklung der Musikberichterstattung in den 'Münchner Neuesten Nachrichten' nach dem Weltkrieg bis zum Jahre 1939," 53–57, condensed and quoted in Wulf, *Musik im Dritten Reich,* 186–88.

25. I. M. Otto, "Programmzettel, wie wir sie wünschen!" *AMz* 63 (1936): 163–64.

26. Reported in Richard Petzoldt, "Heutige Berufsziele der Musikwissenschaftler," *AMz* 63 (1936): 467–68.

27. "Auszug aus dem Schreiben von Dr. Alfred Orel vom 28.12.1938," folder 121, UNL; Albrecht (Staatliches Institut) to REM, 17 June 1944, BA R 21/11058; and BA NS 21/220.

28. This collection, never published, is in the Moser Papers, with a provisional title "Die deutsche Musik und ihre Nachbarn." The document is described in detail in Potter, "Musicology under Hitler."

29. Drewes to Sandberger, 15 March 1938, Sandberger Papers (BSB); letter of 5 September 1938, UAB PA Schering.

30. Moser, "Von der Tätigkeit der Reichsstelle für Musikbearbeitungen," in von Hase, *Jahrbuch der deutschen Musik 1943,* 78–82; Drewes, "Die Reichsstelle für Musikbearbeitungen," *AMz* 70 (1943): 25–27.

31. Moser, "Tätigkeit," 80, 82.

32. "Ausserdem erscheint mir die Heraushebung [Mosers] Stellung durchaus berechtigt, da es sich um die Durchführung eines Führerauftrags handelt, der vom Führer persönlich fortlaufend mit grösstem Interesse verfolgt wird." Drewes to personnel division, 7 March 1942, and Leiter M [Drewes] to Abteilung H (in Propaganda Ministry), 10 September 1942, BA R 55/240.

33. Schünemann to Dekan, 7 July 1938, UAB PA Schünemann.

34. Stumme, ed., *Musik im Volk,* 2d ed., and BDC Frotscher.

35. "Anlage 3: Beispiele unvollkommener kultupolitischer und weltanschaulicher Führung . . . " 2, BA NS 15/189.

36. Bracher, *German Dictatorship,* 351–52.

37. Kogon, *Der SS-Staat,* chap. 2.

38. Kater, *Das "Ahnenerbe" der SS,* 17–37.

39. Koehl, *RKFDV,* 28.

40. Kater, *Das "Ahnenerbe" der SS,* 66.

41. Questionnaire on Nazi party affiliations, signed 27 April 1939, UAB PA Bose; application form for RuSHA, signed 11 January 1942, BDC Quellmalz.

42. Kater, *Das "Ahnenerbe" der SS,* 38–46, 58–65.

43. Ibid., 66–67, 340–41. Quellmalz's application to join in 1942 may have been part of some of the RuSHA plans in the same year, which Kater discusses (e.g., the establishment of a Germanic research institute in Norway and a research facility for German rights in the East).

44. Ibid., 50–51.

45. Ibid., 74.

46. Sievers to Himmler, 15 March 1939; Sievers to Schottländer, 15 March 1939; Sievers to Schottländer, 17 April 1939, BDC Schottländer.

47. Fritz Bose, "Das Rassische in der Musik," *Unser Wille und Weg* 4 (1934): 111.

48. Eckardt to Rust, 26 April 1933, accusing the institute's director Doegen of Social Democratic leanings and professional indiscretions, ZStA REM Nr. 1475, Bl. 259; Doegen to REM, defending himself against accusations of discriminating against National Socialists, Bl. 265–66; Doegen's removal by Paragraph 6, Bl. 296; suggestion to attach the division to the university, Bl. 393; description of the new institute's three divisions (linguistic-phonetic, experimental-phonetic, and musical) with suggestion to appoint Bose as assistant for the musicological division, Bl. 444ff.

49. Bose to REM, 31 March 1934, ZStA REM Nr. 1475, Bl. 480.

50. Sievers to Himmler, 16 February 1940, BDC Bose.

51. Ibid.

52. "Ahnenerbe" to Heinitz, 14 January 1943, BDC Heinitz.

53. Einstein, *Geschichte,* 14; Moser, *Lehrbuch,* 15; *New Grove,* 2d. ed., s.v. "Lur."

54. Fleischer, "Die Luren," *Die Sonne: Monatsschrift für nordische Weltanschauung und Lebensgestaltung* 7 (1930): 556–59.

55. Eichenauer, *Musik und Rasse,* 74–93. The lur was featured in a 1941 issue of Alfred Rosenberg's *Nationalsozialistische Monatshefte* dedicated to music (Georg Karstädt, "Entwicklung und musikalische Bedeutung der altgermanischen Bronzeluren," *NSM* 12 [1941]: 596–604).

56. Bose to Himmler, 23 February 1937, BA NS 21/717.

57. Sievers to Himmler, 13 March 1941, BDC Bose; Quellmalz to Sievers, 6 January 1941, BA NS 21/220; Wüst to Himmler, 28 July 1941, BDC Quellmalz.

58. Bose to Weisthor, 26 June 1937, BA NS 21/717.

59. Weisthor to Himmler, 1 July 1937, BDC Bose.

60. Wüst to Himmler, 22 July 1937; Sievers to Galke, 31 May 1938, BDC Bose. Bose's name appears as "Mitarbeiter," under a space left blank for Leiter in a "Stellenbeset-

zungsplan" (n.d.), BDC. The document lists Himmler as "Präsident" and Wüst as "Kurator," which would place the date of the document no earlier than March 1937 and no later than January 1939 (see Kater, *Das "Ahnenerbe" der SS,* 58ff., 91ff.).

61. Kater, *Das "Ahnenerbe" der SS,* 104–10.

62. Sievers to Wüst ("Ahnenerbe"), 24 March 1938; Sievers to Widukind Verlag, 4 April 1938; Widukind Verlag to Sievers, 11 April 1938, BDC Müller-Blattau.

63. Sievers to Vieweg Verlag, 24 August 1938; "Betr.: Müller-Blattau," n.d., BDC Müller-Blattau.

64. See also Potter, "Musicology under Hitler," 94–97.

65. Plaßmann-Moser correspondence, September 1938 to June 1940, BDC Moser.

66. [Trathnigg] to Moser, 22 September 1938, BDC Moser (the article appeared as "Sudetendeutsche Musik," *Gn* 10 [1938]: 361–68).

67. [Plaßmann] to Moser, 21 October 1939, BDC Moser; Hans Joachim Moser, "Aus Danzigs musikalischer Vergangenheit," *Gn* 12 (1940): 18–23.

68. Hans Joachim Moser, "Sudetendeutsche Musik," *Gn* 10 (1938): 361–68, rpt. in Plaßmann and Trathnigg, eds., *Deutsches Land kehrt heim,* 128–35; idem, "Österreichs Musik und Musiker," *Gn* 11 (1939): 161–68, rpt. in Plaßmann and Trathnigg, eds., *Deutsches Land kehrt heim,* 84–91.

69. Moser to Plaßmann, 2 May 1940, BDC Moser.

70. "Über den Aufsatz von den flämisch-niederländisch-deutschen Musikbeziehungen wollen wir uns demnächst einigen; zur Zeit wird in dieser Hinsicht von amtlichen Stellen Kurztreten empfohlen." Plaßmann to Moser, 27 May 1940, BDC Moser.

71. BDC Moser; Moser to Hartung, 11 April 1941, UAB PA Schering.

72. Plaßmann to Moser, 20 June 1939; Moser to Plaßmann, 20 March 1940, BDC Moser.

73. File memo, 22 May 1940, BDC Moser.

74. "Wolfram" [Sievers] to Plaßmann, 20 May and 22 May 1940 (ordering that Moser's collaboration be terminated); Plaßmann to Moser, 27 May 1940 and 29 June 1940 (asking Moser to contribute more articles after the "Ahnenerbe" had officially banned him); file memo written by Plaßmann, 1 June 1940 (suggesting that Moser continue to contribute under the pseudonym "Heinz Hagebruch"), BDC Moser.

75. Kater, *Das "Ahnenerbe" der SS,* 145–97.

76. Ibid., 149–54.

77. Sicherheitspolizei to Himmler [August 1940], BDC Quellmalz.

78. Hohenhauer (REM) to Staatliches Institut, 25 September 1940, BA NS 21/220.

79. Quellmalz to Albrecht, 27 February 1941, BA NS 21/220; Quellmalz, "Bericht über das Phonogrammarchiv Warschau und dessen Leiter Dr. Julian von Pulikowski," 15 August 1941; Sievers to Sicherheitsdienst, 26 November 1941, BDC Quellmalz.

80. Sievers to Himmler, 16 February 1940, BDC Bose.

81. Bose to Sievers, 22 February 1940, BDC Bose.

82. Quellmalz to REM, 15 October 1940, BDC Quellmalz.

83. Kater, *Das "Ahnenerbe" der SS,* 159–163.

84. Seiffert to Sievers, 9 April 1940, BDC Quellmalz.

85. Quellmalz to REM, 15 October 1940, BDC Quellmalz.

86. "Leider ist damit nichts, da vertraglich zwischen Deutschland und Italien abge-

macht ist, daß über die Kulturarbeit in Südtirol nichts in der Presse erscheinen darf, solange diese noch im Gange ist. . . . Eine Zuwiderhandlung würde unweigerlich KZ eintragen." Quellmalz to Wiora, 15 October 1940, BA NS 21/220.

87. Quellmalz to Seiffert, 20 February 1941, BDC Quellmalz. Similarly, Himmler's office impressed upon the Education Ministry the patriotic importance of the project and the necessity to release Quellmalz from his obligations while continuing to pay his regular salary, a condition with which the Education Ministry was not happy to comply. RKF to REM and Reichsfinanzministerium, 26 March 1941, BDC Quellmalz.

88. "Bericht über den Abschluß der Arbeiten der Gruppe Volksmusik in der Deutschen Kulturkommission Südtirol, 11 December 1942," BA NS 21/220.

89. Oesterle, "Office of Ancestral Inheritance," 211–12, 218, 225–27, 230–32.

90. Quellmalz to Sievers, 25 January 1941, BDC Quellmalz.

91. Schenk to Sievers, 29 August 1942, BDC Schenk.

92. "Der Reichsführer SS bat uns festzustellen, wie lange man das Lied 'es ist ein Reis [sic] entsprungen' zurückverfolgen kann, und ob die Melodie vielleicht einmal einen anderen Text getragen hat." Plaßmann to Moser, 19 January 1940, BDC Moser. For a discussion of the possible reasons for Himmler's peculiar musicological interests, see Potter, "Did Himmler *Really* Like Gregorian Chant?" 45–68.

93. "Der Reichsführer-SS hat ein besonderes Interesse an den Fragen des gregorianischen Chorals und das 'Ahnenerbe' deshalb beauftragt, sich damit zu befassen." Sievers to Schenk, 7 September 1942; Sievers to Quellmalz, 2 October 1942, BDC Schenk.

94. Quellmalz to Sievers ("Betrifft: Beteiligung des musikwissenschaftlichen Seminars der Universität Wien an den Forschungen des 'Ahnenerbe' in Italien"), 14 October 1942, BDC Quellmalz.

95. Sievers to Wüst, 18 November 1942; Sievers to Schenk, 26 October 1942, BDC Schenk.

96. Sievers to Wüst, 18 November 1942; Schenk to Sievers, 26 November 1942; Sievers to Schenk, 5 January 1943, BDC Schenk.

97. Sievers to Quellmalz, 26 October 1942, BDC Quellmalz.

98. Quellmalz to Reichssicherheitshauptamt, 12 June 1943, BA NS 21/220.

99. Quellmalz to Kallmeyer Verlag, 1 June 1943; Quellmalz to Reichssicherheitshauptamt, 12 June 1943; Kallmeyer to Quellmalz, 3 August 1943 and 18 October 1943, BA NS 21/220.

100. Quellmalz, "Plan zur Erforschung der germanisch-deutschen Musik," 28 May 1941; "Ahnenerbe" to Reichssicherheitshauptamt, 14 August 1942, BDC Quellmalz.

101. Kater, *Das "Ahnenerbe" der SS,* 168–69.

102. "Ahnenerbe" to Reichsführer-SS, 14 July 1941; Quellmalz to Sievers, 24 June 1942, BDC Quellmalz.

103. Quellmalz to Sievers, 2 August 1944; Sievers to Gauleiter, Steiermark, 12 August 1944, BDC Quellmalz.

104. Kater, *Das "Ahnenerbe" der SS,* 21–24; Bollmus, *Das Amt Rosenberg,* chap. 5.

105. Bollmus, *Das Amt Rosenberg,* 17–28.

106. Rothfeder, "Rosenberg's Organization," 55–77; Bollmus, *Das Amt Rosenberg,* 45–60.

107. Bollmus, *Das Amt Rosenberg,* 71–85.

108. Rothfeder, "Rosenberg's Organization," 218–19.

109. Schroth to Gerigk, 31 January 1938, BA NS 15/59; Gerigk to Schenk, 4 August 1939, BA NS 15/26.

110. Bollmus, *Das Amt Rosenberg,* 107–8.

111. Rothfeder, "Rosenberg's Organization," 136–38, 217–21. The other was the *Verzeichnis jüdischer Autoren,* issued by the Amt Schrifttumspflege.

112. Kater, *Twisted Muse,* 84–85; De Vries, *Sonderstab Musik,* 64–66.

113. Bury (Reichsorganisationsleiter, NSDAP) to Hahnefeld, 11 January 1941, BA NS 15/21.

114. Hauptstelle Musik to Schenk, 21 March 1941, BA NS 15/21; Schenk to Gerigk, 31 March 1941, BA NS 15/21a; Gerigk to Rosen (ProMi) regarding Paumgartner (information supplied by Schenk), 11 July 1942, BA NS 15/99; Gerigk to Schenk, 28 December 1944, BA NS 15/21a.

115. Gerigk to Rassenpolitisches Amt der NSDAP, 2 May 1944, BA NS 15/21.

116. Blessinger to Gerigk, 30 April 1940, BA NS 15/21.

117. Gerigk to Schenk, 4 August 1939 and 4 May 1940, NS 15/26.

118. Gerigk to Payr (head of Hauptamt Schrifttum), 11 April 1944; Payr to Gerigk, 20 April 1944, concerning the possibility of publishing Werner Danckert's study of Debussy during the war, BA NS 15/73. The title pages of two publications in the series, Schenk's *Johann Strauss* and Fellerer's *Edvard Grieg,* list those musicologists as collaborators and Gerigk as general editor but give no indication that the series had any connection with the Rosenberg Bureau.

119. "Betrifft: Hauptstelle Musik — Aufgaben und Arbeiten laut Schreiben des Reichsleiters vom 14.5.1940," 2–3, BA NS 15/189.

120. "Hauptstelle Musik," 8 March 1939, BA NS 15/189.

121. Folders 109, 113, 120, 125, 127, 130, 142, 144, 145, and 157, UNL; BA NS 15/101, BA NS 15/185.

122. Rothfeder credits the Abteilung Schrifttumspflege with allowing Rosenberg to achieve "his most notable success" ("Rosenberg's Organization," 161), while Bollmus, omitting a detailed discussion of it from his study, claims that it was relatively ineffective (*Das Amt Rosenberg,* 104).

123. Rothfeder, "Rosenberg's Organization," 143–47, 161–74, 248–67.

124. Michaelis on Schering, "Franz Schuberts Symphonie in H-moll ("Unvollendete") und ihr Geheimnis," BA NS 15/101; Schenk on Reimann, "Untersuchungen zur Formgeschichte der Französischen Klavier-Suite," 2 August 1942, folder 157, UNL.

125. Boetticher on Zimmermann, "Um Anton Bruckners Vermächtnis: Ein Beitrag zur rassischen Erkenntnis germanischer Tonkunst," BA NS 15/101.

126. Danckert on Wiora, "Die deutsche Volksliedweise und der Osten," 2 July 1941, BA NS 15/101.

127. Boetticher on Schering, "Beethoven und die Dichtung," 27 January 1939; Boetticher on Schering, "Johann Sebastian Bach und das Musikleben Leipzigs im 18. Jahrhundert"; Michaelis on Schering, "Franz Schuberts Symphonie in H-moll ("Unvollendete") und ihr Geheimnis," BA NS 15/101.

128. Gerigk to PPK, 13 July 1938; Hauptstelle Musik to PPK, 22 September 1938 (both on Moser's "Kleine deutsche Musikgeschichte"); Gerigk to PPK, 10 December

1938 (on Lach, "Die Musik der Gegenwart"), BA NS 15/38; Gerigk on Riezler, "Beethoven," 21 March 1939, folder 126, UNL.

129. Killer (Kulturpolitisches Archiv) to Amt Musik, 4 and 19 August 1942, 23 February 1943, and 12 March 1943, BA NS 15/131.

130. Schroth (Reichsstudentenführung) to Gerigk, 31 January 1938, and Gerigk to Schroth, 19 February 1938, BA NS 15/59 (on Pfitzner and Fortner); Killer to Amt Musik, 26 October 1942, BA NS 15/131 (on Bach); Gerigk to Rassenpolitisches Amt der NSDAP, 26 July 1944, BA NS 15/153 (on Liszt).

131. "Betrifft: Hauptstelle Musik — Aufgaben und Arbeiten laut Schreiben des Reichsleiters vom 14.5.1940," 4, BA NS 15/189.

132. Rothfeder, "Rosenberg's Organization," 238.

133. The Abteilung Wissenschaft was later designated as "Hauptstelle" in 1936, "Amt" in 1938, and "Hauptamt" in 1941, as it grew in importance. Rothfeder, "Rosenberg's Organization," 151–54, 206–15.

134. Gerigk to Bäumler, 10 July 1940, BA NS 15/24.

135. BA NS 15/74.

136. Ibid.

137. Gerigk to Payr, 19 May 1944, BA NS 15/73.

138. Kurator (Kiel) to REM, 12 July 1937, BDC Blume.

139. Rothfeder, "Rosenberg's Organization," 96–107.

140. Bollmus, "Zum Projekt," 125–52; Rothfeder, "Rosenberg's Organization," 327–56.

141. Gerigk to Otto, 18 October 1944, BA NS 15/73; "Betrifft: Hauptstelle Musik — Aufgaben und Arbeiten laut Schreiben des Reichsleiters vom 14.5.1940," BA NS 15/189.

142. Gerigk to Amt Rosenberg (central administration), 10 May 1940, 28 May 1940, and 7 August 1940, BA NS 15/24.

143. "Betrifft: Hauptstelle Musik — Aufgaben und Arbeiten laut Schreiben des Reichsleiters vom 14.5.1940," BA NS 15/189; Gerigk to Gerber, 10 August 1939, 28 February 1940, 8 July 1940, and Gerber to Gerigk, 3 March 1940 and 13 July 1940 BA NS 15/25; Gerigk to Fellerer, 28 February 1940, 31 May 1940, and 30 June 1940, BA NS 15/24; Gerigk to Danckert, 11 August 1939, and Gerigk to Verwaltungsamt, 10 May 1940, BA NS 15/24; Gerigk to Schenk, 4 August 1939, Gerigk to Osthoff, 11 August 1939, and Osthoff to Gerigk, n.d., BA NS 15/26. In 1939, Gerigk sent out confidential inquiries to the Gestapo and the foreign office of the Nazi party inquiring into the advisability of including Johannes Wolf, Ewald Jammers, Oskar Kaul, and Swiss musicologist F. Gysi, but a 1940 report on the activities of the Music Bureau mentions only Danckert, Gerber, Fellerer, Schenk, H. Schole (Greifswald), and Erich Schumann as scholarly consultants who were assisting in "close collaboration" in Hohe Schule tasks. Letters from Gerigk, dated 4 August 1939, BA NS 15/25; "Betrifft: Hauptstelle Musik — Aufgaben und Arbeiten laut Schreiben des Reichsleiters vom 14.5.1940," BA NS 15/189.

144. Gerigk to Bäumler, 10 June 1940, BA NS 15/24.

145. Rothfeder, "Rosenberg's Organization," 357–61.

146. Bollmus, *Das Amt Rosenberg,* 145–51; De Vries, *Sonderstab Musik,* 91–93, 103–6.

147. Gerigk to Boetticher, 9 February 1942, BA NS 15/24.

148. Two certifications, 7 October 1940; Gerigk to head of Einsatzstab task forces, 9 August 1941; Einsatzstab to Commander of Waffen-SS, 29 November 1941; Boetticher to Verwaltungsamt, 22 January 1942; Gerigk to Boetticher, 9 February 1942, BA NS 15/24.

149. Petropoulos, *Art As Politics,* 133–37.

150. Robert Scholz, "Bericht über die 1. Sitzung im Reichsministerium für Volksaufklärung und Propaganda betreffend Rückforderung von Kulturgut aus den westlichen Ländern," 24 August 1940; Gerigk to Goebbels, 18 November 1942, BA NS 15/99. See also De Vries, *Sonderstab Musik,* 126–30.

151. "Sonderstab Musik Abrechnung für das Reichspropaganda-Ministerium," 16 August 1941, BA NS 15/99; Gerigk to Gerber, 8 May 1942, and Gerigk to Hohe Schule planning commission, 16 December 1942, BA NS 15/25; Gerigk to Bäumler (Hohe Schule planning commission), 17 September 1942, BA NS 15/24.

152. De Vries, *Sonderstab Musik,* 175.

153. Rosenberg to Goebbels, 7 September 1940, BA NS 15/190. For a detailed account of all music acquisitions from the Western occupation (France, Holland, and Belgium) see De Vries, *Sonderstab Musik,* chap. 3.

154. Gerigk to Gerber, 8 May 1942, BA NS 15/25.

155. "Mitteilungen" (signed by "A.E."), *ZfMw* 1 (1918–19): 566.

156. Martin Breslauer (book dealer) to Eckert (Kuratorium, University of Cologne), 14 December 1926, UAK.

157. Seiffert, "Denkschrift," 5, SIM.

158. "Planstelle," n.d., BDC.

159. Boetticher, "Lebenslauf," 4 January 1943, UAB PA Boetticher; Boetticher to Mittendorfer, 14 January 1944, BDC Boetticher; Boetticher, application for position in Haupstelle Musik, 3 November 1938, BA NS 15/24.

160. NSDAP Treasurer to Boetticher, 8 March 1939, Partei-Kanzlei to Boetticher, 9 November 1942, and Boetticher, "Lebenslauf," 4 January 1943, UAB PA Boetticher; Gerigk to Kerksiek (Verwaltungsamt, Amt Rosenberg), 18 January 1939, and Boetticher, list of NSDAP activities, 11 November 1939, BA NS 15/24. De Vries includes detailed accounts of Boetticher's activities in France, Holland, and possibly Belgium (139–43, 160–61, 175) and includes a general discussion of Boetticher's involvement with the Nazis (181–202).

161. Boetticher, list of scholarly publications, 4 January 1943; Schünemann, "Gutachten über die Habilitationsschrift Dr. Wolfgang Boettichers," 18 March 1943, UAB PA Boetticher.

162. Schünemann, "Gutachten über die Habilitationsschrift Dr. Wolfgang Boettichers," 18 March 1943, UAB PA Boetticher.

163. Boetticher to Dekan, 29 February 1944, UAB PA Boetticher.

164. Weinberg, *World at Arms,* 20–25.

165. Burleigh, *Germany Turns Eastwards.*

166. Item 1, Gerigk to Boetticher, 9 February 1942, BA NS 15/24. A transcription of this document appears in the appendix to Potter, "Musicology under Hitler."

167. Item 7, Gerigk to Boetticher, 9 February 1942, BA NS 15/24.

168. Einsatzstab Reichsleiter Rosenberg für die besetzten Gebiete to Reichsminister für die besetzten Ostgebiete, 7 May 1942, BA NS 15/25.

169. See Potter, "Musicology under Hitler," 91.

170. Gustav Becking, "Die Lage der sudetendeutschen Musik," *ZfM* 105 (1938): 574–76.

171 Gustav Becking, "Kleiner Beitrag zur musikalischen Kultur und Stammeskunde der Sudetendeutschen," *Der Ackermann aus Böhmen* 6 (1938): 457–62.

172. Hans Joachim Moser, "Deutsche Musik im polnischen Raum," *DMK* 4 (1939–40): 155–57; Gotthold Frotscher, "Stätten deutscher Musikkultur: Danzig," *DMK* 4 (1939–40): 152–55.

173. Hans Joachim Moser, "Die alte Ostfront der deutschen Musikkultur," *AMz* 66 (1939): 547–48; Gotthold Frotscher, "Die Bedeutung der deutschen Musik im Osten," *MJV* 4 (1941): 2–3; idem, "Deutsche Kulturleistungen im Osten," *MJV* 5 (1942): 102–5.

174. Walther Vetter, "Aus dem Posener Musikleben," *Wartheland: Zeitschrift für Aufbau und Kultur im deutschen Osten* 3/4–6 (1943): 23–24.

175. Hans Heinz Stuckenschmidt, "Joseph Keilberths Weg und Aufgabe," *Böhmen und Mähren* 2 (1941): 329–31; idem, "Musik in Böhmen und Mähren," *Ostland* 21 (1940): 194–98.

176. Albrecht (Staatliches Institut) to REM, 12 November 1943, BA R21/11058.

177. Schünemann to Dekan der Philosophischen Fakultät (Univ. Berlin), 22 January 1944, UAB PA Schünemann; Boetticher to Mittendorfer, 14 January 1944, BDC Boetticher.

178. Kurator (Königsberg) to REM, 20 July 1942; Rektor (Königsberg) to REM, 28 September 1943, GStA I/76: 880.

179. "Leiter M" (Drewes, with corrections by Moser) to Goebbels, 21 March 1941, Moser Papers. This letter, dated 21 March 1941, is one of only three extant letters in the catalogued portions of the Moser papers written before 1945. There is one other dated 1941 and one from 1932, followed by letters from 1946 on. The rest, Moser explains in later correspondence, were lost in a fire in his office. A transcription of the letter is included in Potter, "Musicology under Hitler."

180. "Mitteilungen," *AfMf* 3 (1938): 502; Quellmalz, "Arbeitsbericht der Abteilung II: Volksmusik, im Staatlichen Institut für Deutsche Musikforschung," 31 March 1944, p. 3; and a report from the "Gauausschüsse für Volksmusik in den Donau und Alpengauen," 1 January 1940 to 31 March 1943, BA NS 21/220.

181. "Auszug aus dem Schreiben von Dr. Alfred Orel vom 28.12.1938," folder 121, UNL.

182. Gerigk, "Betrifft: Salzburg," 7 October 1941, folder 147, UNL.

183. Rudolf Steglich, "Zentralinstitut für Mozart-Forschung," *AfMf* 4 (1939): 256; "Die wissenschaftliche Arbeiten der Deutschen Akademie," 4, BA R 51/8; Schiedermair to Kurator (Univ. Bonn), 12 December 1941 and 2 February 1942, UABonn PA Schiedermair (Kuratorium). Georg Schünemann was also called in as a consultant for a very high fee; see Wagner, *Das Mozarteum,* 223.

184. Memo of Ministerium für innere und kulturelle Angelegenheiten (Vienna), 24 October 1939, BA R21/10185. The position in Vienna is discussed in chap. 4.

185. Dekan (Graz) to Ministerium für innere und kulturelle Angelegenheiten, 22 July 1938, BA R21/10185.

186. Schenk to Dekan (Vienna), 31 March 1941, UAW Dekanat 78.

187. "Staatliches Institut für Deutsche Musikforschung, Stand vom Juni 1939," Schiedermair Papers.

188. "Mitteilungen," *AfMf* 4 (1939): 320.

189. Quellmalz, "Arbeitsbericht der Abteilung II," 3–6, BA NS 21/220.

190. "The Political Activity of the Deutsche Akademie," BA R 51/9.

191. BA R 51/8.

192. "Staatliches Institut für Deutsche Musikforschung, Stand vom Juni 1939," Schiedermair Papers.

193. Besseler to Seiffert, 29 January 1939, BDC Besseler.

194. Quellmalz to Sievers, 6 January 1941, BA NS 21/220.

195. Quellmalz to Volksdeutsche Mittelstelle, 18 January 1944; Quellmalz, "Arbeitsbericht der Abteilung II," 7–8; Quellmalz to Stumme (Hauptkulturamt), 20 April 1944; Quellmalz to Albrecht, 26 January 1943, BA NS 21/220.

196. Albrecht (Staatliches Institut) to Cerff (Hauptkulturamt) and Sievers to Albrecht, 5 February 1943; Albrecht to Kallmeyer Verlag, 7 October 1943; Quellmalz to Frotscher, 23 December 1942, BA NS 21/220.

197. Quellmalz to Meier, 23 December 1942; Meier to Albrecht, 4 January 1943, BA NS 21/220.

198. REM to Seiffert, 6 April 1936, SIM; Quellmalz, "Arbeitsbericht der Abteilung II," 6, transcript of agreement; Meier to Albrecht, 5 May 1944, and Albrecht to Meier, 11 May 1944, BA NS 21/220.

199. Quellmalz to Albrecht, 27 February 1941, BA NS 21/220.

200. Quellmalz to Sievers, 24 June 1942, BDC Quellmalz.

201. Quellmalz to Albrecht, 26 January 1943, BA NS 21/220.

202. Meier to Rektor (Freiburg), 8 June 1943, UAF PA Meier (Phil. Fak.).

203. An undated document among the Amt Rosenberg files bears the title "Die vordringlichsten Veränderungen unter den [B]erliner Musikwissenschaftlern" and states with regard to Huber's recent appointment: "Huber ist ein Mann der Katholischen Aktion und wissenschaftlich durchaus nicht für den Posten qualifiziert, den er jetzt einnimmt. Hier müsste eine möglichst umgehende Lösung des Vertrages angestrebt werden, damit an Hubers Stelle der unbestritten beste Volksliedkenner unter den deutschen Musikwissenschaftlern, Prof. Dr. Werner Danckert, Jena, gebracht werden kann." BA NS 15/149a.

204. Gerigk to Schroth, 22 October 1937 and 19 November 1937, BA NS 15/59; Frey to Amt V, 26 October 1937, ZStA REM Nr. H663, Bl. 45.

205. "Vermerk," 19 March [1937]; Miederer to Frey, 24 February 1938; NSDAP-Stellverteter des Führers, Braunes Haus, München, to REM, 23 June 1938, ZStA REM Nr. H663, Bl. 39, 48, 53; BA NS 15/59.

206. NSDAP-Stellverteter des Führers to REM, 28 February 1940, ZStA REM Nr. H663, Bl. 68.

207. Gerigk (Kulturpolitisches Archiv) to Gaustudentenführung Baden, 28 October 1937, BA NS 15/59.

208. "Beurteilung aus Amt Rosenberg," n.d., UAK; Besseler to Seiffert, 13 October 1938; Besseler, "Stellungnahme zu Anlage 2 (Schreiben vom 29.4.39)"; Besseler to Miederer, 26 May 1939; "Urteil des Kreisgerichts Heidelberg der NSDAP: Begründung," 17 November 1939, BDC Besseler.

209. Besseler to REM, 21 July 1941, BDC Besseler.

210. Seiffert to REM, 10 September 1941, BDC Besseler.

211. REM to Minister des Kultus und Unterrichts [Baden], 7 October 1941, BDC Besseler.

212. Besseler files, UAL PA 2926 and UAH.

213. Schroth (Reichsstudentenführung) to Gerigk, 31 January 1938, BA NS 15/59; Gerigk to Osthoff, 13 August 1940, BA NS 15/26.

214. Kümmel (Staatliche Museen) to REM, 30 July 1943, BA R 21/11058.

215. Gerigk to Hauptamt Wissenschaft, 4 January 1944 and 10 March 1944, BA NS 15/74; Partei-Kanzlei to REM, 29 April 1944 and 20 December 1944, BA R 21/11058.

216. Schmidt-Römer (Partei-Kanzlei) to Miederer, 24 April 1944, p. 2, BA R 21/11058.

217. Miederer to Albrecht, 20 June 1944; Albrecht to REM, 17 June 1944, BA R 21/11058.

218. "Mitteilungen," *ZfMw* 16 (1934): 256.

219. Engel to Sandberger, 15 February 1937 and 20 February 1937, Sandberger Papers (BSB).

220. Engel to Sandberger, 9 November 1937, Sandberger Papers (BSB).

221. Gerigk to Schroth, 19 February 1938, BA NS 15/59.

222. Schiedermair to Sandberger, 3 February 1937, Sandberger to Schiedermair, 24 February 1937, Sandberger Papers (BSB).

223. Sandberger to Rektor (draft), September 1937; Deutsche Akademie to Sandberger, 4 November 1937; Sandberger to von den Leyen, 6 November 1937 and 17 November 1937, Sandberger Papers (BSB).

224. Moser to Plaßmann, 20 March 1940, BDC Moser; "Anlage 3: Beispiele unvollkommener kulturpolitischer und weltanschaulicher Führung . . ." BA NS 15/189.

225. "Betrifft: Hauptstelle Musik — Aufgaben und Arbeiten laut Schreiben des Reichsleiters vom 14.5.1940," BA NS 15/189.

226. "Weiter wird für die Reichsstelle die Redaktion eines von mir angeregten Mehrmännerbuches besorgt, das demnächst im Max [H]esse Verlag erscheinen wird und den Einfluß der deutschen [M]usik auf die Nachbarländer zusammenfassend schildert; es wird sich so — der Wahrheit endlich die Ehre gebend — ein vielfach anderes Bild der europäischen Musikgeschichte als ehedem herausschälen." Drewes, "Die Reichsstelle für Musikbearbeitungen," 26.

227. Gerigk, "Betrifft: Europäische Musikgeschichte," 21 February 1942, BA NS 15/99.

228. Gerigk to Hohe Schule planning office, 16 December 1942, BA NS 15/25.

229. "Stand der Angelegenheiten der wissenschaftlichen Abteilungen und Länderausschüsse," 15 (file page no. 0203086), and "Tätigkeitsbericht, 1943," 49 (file page no. 0203148), BA R 51/8.

230. "Zum zehnjährigen Bestehen des Staatlichen Instituts für deutsche Musikforschung," 2, SIM.

231. Moser to Hartung, 11 April 1941, UAB PA Schering.

Chapter 6. The Shaping of New Methodologies

1. Iggers, *German Conception of History,* 506.

2. Ibid., 124–44.

3. Maren-Grisebach, *Methoden der Literaturwissenschaft*, 23–25, 29–30.

4. Ringer, *Decline*, 103, 253–54, 295.

5. Hermand, *Literaturwissenschaft und Kunstwissenschaft*.

6. A description of the methodological "crisis as never before" is succinctly outlined by Otto Gombosi, where he endorses style criticism for ending the crisis. Otto Gombosi, "Stilkritik," *Melos* 8 (1929): 354–58.

7. Egon Wellesz, "Die Grundlagen der musikgeschichtlichen Forschung," *AfMw* 1 (1919): 446.

8. Curt Sachs, "Kunstgeschichtliche Wege zur Musikwissenschaft," *AfMw* 1 (1919): 451–64.

9. Ernst Bücken, "Grundfragen der Musikgeschichte als Geisteswissenschaft," *JbMP* 34 (1927): 19, 29–30; Arnold Schering, "Das Problem einer Philosophie der Musikgeschichte," in *Bericht über den Musikwissenschaftlichen Kongreß in Basel*, 311–14.

10. Adler, *Der Stil in der Musik* and *Methode der Musikgeschichte*; Alfred Orel, "Ein Jubiläum Wiener musikwissenschaftlicher Arbeit," *ZfMw* 6 (1924): 177.

11. Hans Mersmann, "Zur Geschichte des Formbegriffs," *JbMP* 36 (1930): 32–47.

12. Wilibald Gurlitt, "Hugo Riemann und die Musikgeschichte," *ZfMw* 1 (1918–19): 584.

13. Hans Mersmann, "Zur Stilgeschichte der Musik," *JbMP* 28 (1922): 67–78. The style approach was received much more favorably than a history of form approach. For one, it resolved some of the problems that the history of form had posed for historical study dealing with the changing meanings of such formal designations as "symphony" (Gombosi, "Stilkritik"). Mersmann ("Zur Geschichte des Formbegriffs") also found fault with the form approach but falsely attributed it to Kretzschmar. He praised Riemann's work as a fusion of history of style and history of form, and he considered Kretzschmar's treatment as suspect. He identified Kretzschmar's series inaccurately as "Handbücher der Musikgeschichte nach Formen und Gattungen" and proceeded to criticize the limitations of Kretzschmar's supposed concentration on form (rather than genre, which was his actual focus in the series), owing to the variability of form such that "every work has its own individual form," rendering it far less reliable than style as a constant for historical investigation.

14. Einstein, *Geschichte*, 33, 35, 99–100.

15. Einstein, "Vorwort zur zweiten Auflage" (September 1919), *Geschichte*, 4.

16. Mersmann, "Zur Stilgeschichte der Musik," 70, 78; Adler, "Internationalism in Music," 282.

17. Bekker, *Musikgeschichte*, 6–7.

18. Ibid., 16–19, 80–82. Bekker would classify a period as dominated by the profane category if, for instance, composers use traditionally secular genres for church music, and vice versa.

19. Mersmann, "Zur Stilgeschichte der Musik," 71–78.

20. Arnold Schering, "Historische und nationale Klangstile," *JbMP* 33 (1927): 31–43.

21. Lorenz, *Abendländische Musikgeschichte*.

22. "[Die] Vollzugswirklichkeit des gültigen musikalischen Kunstwerkes zu erforschen, gesellt sich den älteren Betrachtungsweisen der Stil-, Kultur- und Heroengeschichte der Musik gleichberechtigt eine die Trägerschichten des Musizierenden und Hörenden er-

forschende Gesellschaftsgeschichte der Musik." Wilibald Gurlitt, "Der gegenwärtige Stand der deutschen Musikwissenschaft," *Deutsche Vierteljahrsschrift für Literaturwissenschaft und Geistesgeschichte* 17 (1939): 3.

23. Wiora, "Altgriechische Volksmusikkultur"; Arnold Schering "Geschichte und Bedeutung der deutschen Musikfeste" *DTZ* 28 (1930): 261–63; Karl Gustav Fellerer "Musik und Feier," *Mk* 31 (1939): 433–37; Schünemann, *Geschichte der deutschen Schulmusik;* Karl Gustav Fellerer "Häusliches Musizieren im Wandel der Zeit," *DTZ* 36 (1939): 13–14; Gotthold Frotscher, "Hausmusik in Vergangenheit und Gegenwart," *MJV* 3 (1940): 225–32; Hans Joachim Moser, "Die Anfänge städtischer Musikbetreuung," *MPf* 10 (1939): 67–76; Karl Gustav Fellerer, "Geschichte der Musik — Geschichte des Musizierens," *Mk* 29 (1937): 759–61; idem, "Von alter Kriegmusik," *Mk* 32 (1940): 80–81; idem, "Musikalische Kriegspropaganda," *Mk* 32 (1940): 162–63; Alfred Quellmalz "Von der Geschichte des Soldatenliedes bis zum Weltkrieg," *MJV* 2 (1939): 414; Moser series on history of military music in *Gn* 12 (1940) and in *Deutsche Militär-Musiker Zeitung* 65 (1943); idem, "War der deutsche Orchestermusiker in alter Zeit Proletarier?" *Orchester* 4 (1927): 49.

24. Hinton, *Idea of Gebrauchsmusik,* 5–14.

25. Bekker, *Deutsche Musikleben;* Berten, *Musik und Musikleben;* Bücken, *Musik der Deutschen.*

26. Peter Epstein, "Neue Forschungs- und Darstellungsmethoden der Musikgeschichte," *Melos* 8 (1929): 358–65; Gurlitt, "Der gegenwärtige Stand," 4.

27. Alfred Schnerich, "Musik als Kunst und als Wissenschaft," *Neue Zeitschrift für Musik* 85 (1918): 61–64.

28. Kretzschmar, *Einführung,* 15.

29. Wolf, "Musikwissenschaft und musikwissenschaftlicher Unterricht."

30. Schering, "Musikwissenschaft und Kunst der Gegenwart."

31. Guido Adler, "Umfang, Methode und Ziel der Musikwissenschaft," *Vierteljahrsschrift für Musikwissenschaft* 1 (1885): 5–20.

32. Riemann came up with his own classification for musicology that regarded music history as only one of five major subdisciplines and considered systematic musicology just as important as history. Riemann, *Grundriß der Musikwissenschaft.*

33. Gurlitt, "Hugo Riemann und die Musikgeschichte."

34. Schneider, "Germany and Austria," 78–80.

35. Ibid., 83–84, and idem, "Musikwissenschaft in der Emigration," 189–90.

36. Schneider, "Germany and Austria," 81–88.

37. Georg Schünemann, "Über die Beziehungen der vergleichenden Musikwissenschaft zur Musikgeschichte," *AfMw* 2 (1919–20): 175, 177–78, 180, 183–93.

38. Wilhelm Heinitz, "Vergleichende Musikwissenschaft," *ZfM* 92 (1925): 435.

39. Heinitz, "Vergleichende Musikwissenschaft," 437.

40. Johannes Wolf, "Zum Geleit," *Zeitschrift für vergleichende Musikwissenschaft* 1 (1933): 1.

41. Fritz Bose, "Neue Aufgaben der vergleichenden Musikwissenschaft," *ZfMw* 16 (1934): 229–31.

42. Karl Gustav Fellerer, "Historische und systematische Musikwissenschaft," *Mk* 29 (1936–37): 340–43.

43. Ernst Bücken, "Aufgaben und Ziele der deutschen Musikwissenschaft," *AMz* 65 (1938): 65–66; Blume, "Musikforschung und Musikpraxis," 24.

44. Alfred Lorenz, "Musikwissenschaft im Aufbau," *ZfM* 106 (1939): 369.

45. Joseph Müller-Blattau, "Gegenwartsfragen der Musikwissenschaft," *Musik und Volk* 4 (1936–37): 86.

46. Schneider, "Germany and Austria," 85; idem, "Musikwissenschaft in der Emigration," 192–97.

47. Sontheimer, *Antidemokratisches Denken,* 244–59.

48. Katz, *From Prejudice to Destruction,* 303–11.

49. Mosse, *Crisis of German Ideology,* 302–4.

50. Robert Lach, "Das Rassenproblem in der vergleichenden Musikwissenschaft," *Berichte des Forschungsinstituts für Osten und Orient* 3 (1923): 107–22.

51. He recognizes explicit "racial" elements in the "proclivities" for rhythm (including the attraction to "Niggerjazz"), and the "inborn predisposition for irony, satire, and the grotesque" of French music. In Eastern Europe, what the author considers racial may be more commonly understood as nationalist: he describes Mussorgsky's "unshakable racial feeling" as coming forth in his use of Russian folk music, or Bartók's and Kodaly's music as representing an "expression of race." Adolf Weissmann, "Rasse und Nation in der Musik," in Heinsheimer and Stefan, eds., *25 Jahre Neue Musik,* 88, 94–95, 97, 98–99.

52. Weissmann, "Rasse und Nation," 86, 101.

53. Schering, "Klangstile," 31.

54. Lorenz, *Abendländische Musikgeschichte,* 22–23.

55. BDC Eichenauer.

56. Eichenauer, *Musik und Rasse,* 16–42, 55, 74–112.

57. Ibid., 135–69.

58. Ibid., 170–263.

59. Ibid., 59–73.

60. Ibid., 280–303 (quote on p. 302).

61. Fritz Bose, "Zur Methodik einer musikalischen Rassenkunde," *DTZ* 31 (1933): 177.

62. Fritz Bose, "Das Rassische in der Musik," 111.

63. Irmgard Leux-Henschen, "Biologie und Musikwissenschaft," *DMK* 1 (1936–37): 330.

64. Prieberg, *Musik im NS-Staat,* 365.

65. Siegfried Günther, "Musikalische Begabung und Rassenforschung im Schrifttum der Gegenwart: Eine methodologische Untersuchung," *AfMf* 2 (1937): 309–16, 327, 336–38.

66. Siegfried Günther, "Rassenseelenkundliche Beiträge zur musikalischen Stilforschung," *AfMf* 3 (1938): 385–427.

67. Hans Engel, "Die Bedeutung Konstitutions- und psychologischer Typologien für die Musikwissenschaft," *AfMf* 7 (1942): 129–53.

68. Bücken, "Aufgaben und Ziele," 65–66.

69. Alfred Lorenz, "Musikwissenschaft und Ahnenforschung," 1372–73.

70. The Jew's lack of originality had allegedly been demonstrated in synagogue music by the "rabbi" A. Z. Idelssohn, "recognized in the *Systemzeit* [Weimar Republic] as a

diligent music researcher." Such was also the case with Salamone Rossi, who, as Lorenz claims in self-contradiction, did nothing more than imitate Marini and nevertheless was one of the first trio sonata composers. Lorenz cites another Jewish scholar to validate Mendelssohn's Jewishness: Mendelssohn's Jewish traits are difficult to detect, but a fellow Jew (philosopher Hermann Cohen) discovered them in 1915. From his quote of Cohen one senses that the philosopher is perhaps equally to blame for reading Jewish characteristics into Mendelssohn's music in order to claim him as a Jewish composer. Alfred Lorenz, "Musikwissenschaft und Judenfrage," 177–79.

71. "Musik und Rasse," *Der Mittag,* 28 May 1938, and Peter Seifert, "Musik und Rasse."

72. H. Relsbach, "Musik wissenschaftlich betrachtet," *Düsseldorfer Tageblatt,* 19 May 1938.

73. Compare with his "Volkslied und Stammesart," *VME* 5 (1939): 305–16, and "Von der Stammesart im Volkslied," *Mk* 32 (1939–40): 217–22.

74. Helmut Schultz, "Volkhafte Eigenschaften des Instrumentenklanges," *DMK* 5 (1940): 61–64;

75. Compare with his "Aufgaben und Ausrichtung der musikalischen Rassenstilforschung."

76. "Das Problem dieser völkischen Musik ist kein ästhetisches Problem, sondern ein rassisches, in dem Sinne, daß nach den Worten des Führers Blut und Rasse wieder zur Quelle der künstlerischen Intuition werden." Frotscher, "Aufgaben und Ausrichtungen," 112.

77. "Musik und Rasse," *Mk* 30 (1938): 736–48.

78. The lecture series is mentioned in Blume, *Das Rasseproblem,* 85.

79. Whereas post-1945 biographical entries in the *New Grove* and *MGG* frequently leave gaps in the publication lists of many prominent musicologists for the years 1933 to 1945, Blume's *Das Rasseproblem in der Musik* appears in both reference works.

80. "Studien zur musikalischen Volks- und Rassenkunde," published by Kallmeyer and including his own *Das Rasseproblem in der Musik,* Walter Wiora's *Die deutsche Volksliedweise und der Osten,* and Ewald Jammers's *Die völkische Zugehörigkeit des gregorianischen Chorals.* Wiora's book was named as part of Blume's seris in an evaluation for the Rosenberg Bureau by Werner Danckert, 2 July 1941, BA NS 15/101. The publication of Jammer's book as part of Blume's series was discussed in a correspondence between the SS and Kallmeyer, June 1943, BA NS 21/220.

81. "Hier stellt die nationalsozialistische Ausrichtung der Musikforschung die eindeutige Aufgabe, den Grund zu legen, auf dem das Gebäude einer musikalischen Rassenforschung errichtet werden kann." Blume, "Deutsche Musikwissenschaft," 18.

82. Blume, *Das Rasseproblem,* 3.

83. Ibid., 5.

84. Ibid., 6, 9.

85. Ibid., 15–19.

86. Ibid., 20–23.

87. Ibid., 37–40, 46–57.

88. Ibid., 60, 63; Riemann, *Das Generalbaßzeitalter,* 489, 492–93; *Die Musik des 18. und 19. Jahrhunderts,* 104–5.

89. Blume, *Das Rasseproblem,* 60.

90. Ibid., 63.

91. Ibid., 5, 45.

92. Ibid., 9, 78–79.

93. ". . . sie darf sich auf das Bewußtsein stützen, daß eben dieses rassische Moment, das nordische, es ist, das uns Heutige an Bach so gewaltig ergreift, dem wir das 'Et incarnatus,' das 'Cruxifixus' der h-moll Messe, aber auch ihr 'Et resurrexit' und ihr 'Sanctus' verdanken, die gewaltige Entladung nordischen Geistes und nordischer Lebenskraft." Blume, *Das Rasseproblem,* 78–79.

94. Ibid., 10, 65.

95. See criticisms of Eichenauer, ibid., 6, 53, 72, and of Clauß, ibid., 11.

96. Ibid., 82–83.

97. "Der Musikwissenschafter ist außerstande, in die Schädelmessung hineinzupfuschen." Ibid., 83.

98. Ibid., 84–85.

99. Boetticher, "Volkskunde und Musikwissenschaft. Zur Erkenntnis von Rasse und Volkstum in der Musik," in Stumme, ed., *Musik im Volk,* 1st ed., 227.

100. Engel, "Die Bedeutung Konstitutions- und psychologischer Typologien," 129–53.

101. BDC Blessinger.

102. Blessinger, *Judentum und Musik,* 7–8, 15–17; Eichenauer, *Musik und Rasse;* Wagner, "Das Judentum in der Musik."

103. Blessinger, *Judentum und Musik,* 8, 16–17.

104. Ibid., 18–26.

105. Ibid., 28–35.

106. Ibid., 94–97.

107. Ibid., 120–28. Blessinger makes some amazingly far-fetched connections between jazz and Jewish music, describing a rendition of Offenbach's "Barcarolle" that he heard performed on the radio in Prague as a model for jazz singing: "Die Art und Weise, wie damals zwei fette jüdische Frauenstimmen die bekannte Melodie in der Art eines Synagogalgesanges von Ton zu Ton gezogen haben, ist nicht zu beschreiben; sie war einfach widerlich und enthüllte in grellster Weise die wahre, uns ewig fremde Art des Juden. Aber sie bildete das Muster der Vortragsart, wie sie eben auch im Jazz die typische geworden ist" (127).

108. Joachim Beck, "Um die Einheit der deutschen Musik," *Das deutsche Podium* 7 (1939): 1–2; Walter Vetter, "Zur Erforschung des deutschen in der Musik," *DMK* 4 (1939–40): 106; Alfred Lorenz, "Musikwissenschaft und Judenfrage," *Mk* 31 (1938): 178.

109. Karl Blessinger, "Der Weg zur Einheit der deutschen Musik," *Deutschlands Erneuerung* 25 (1941): 80.

110. Katz, *From Prejudice to Destruction,* 191–93.

111. Gerber, "Die Aufgaben der Musikwissenschaft im Dritten Reich."

112. Bücken, "Aufgaben und Ziele," 66.

113. Mosse, *Crisis of German Ideology,* 280–93.

114. *MGG,* 1st ed., s.v. "Volksgesang, Volksmusik, Volkstanz," 1924–27.

115. Hans Mersmann, "Gegenwartsfragen der Volksliedkunde," *Musik und Volk* 3 (1935–36): 222–27.

116. "Der gute Geist der deutschen Jugendbewegung, der sich den von allen 'guten Bürgern' gefürchteten, widerspenstigen 'Zupfgeigenhansl' ersang, hat auch einer jungen Generation von Musikwissenschaftlern die ersten starken Antriebe zu einer nationalen Musikforschung gegeben." Kurt Huber, "Der künftige Aufbau der Volksmusikforschung," *Deutsche Wissenschaft Erziehung und Volksbildung: Amtsblatt des Reichsministeriums für Wissenschaft, Erziehung und Volksbildung und der Unterrichtsverwaltungen der Länder (Nichtamtlicher Teil)* 3 (1937): 127.

117. Müller-Blattau, "Gegenwartsfragen der Musikwissenschaft," 83–84.

118. Fritz Bose, "Neue Arbeitsgebiete des Institutes für Lautforschung," *Forschungen und Fortschritte* 10 (1934): 269–70.

119. Suppan, *Volkslied*, 8–10.

120. Kurt Huber, "Wege und Ziele neuer Volksliedforschung und Volksliedpflege," *Deutsche Zeitschrift* 48 (1934–35): 424–38.

121. Kurt Huber, "Der Aufbau deutscher Volksliedforschung und Volksliedpflege," *DMK* (1936): 65–73.

122. "Die vordringlichste dieser Aufgaben heißt: Reinerhaltung des echten deutschen Volksgutes! Es läuft beispielloser Schund in unseren Volksliedsammlungen und Volksliedarchiven mit unter. Natürlich Lied, das 'im Volke lebt oder einmal lebte.' Als ob im Volke nicht gänzlich Unvölkisches leben, ja das schönste Parasitenleben leben und die Wurzeln echten Volkstums anfressen könnte! Hinaus mit den bänkelsängerischen Schauerballaden und Moritaten einer Volkshefe, die nicht mehr völkisch fühlen konnte, aus unserer Volksliedpflege! Fort mit den elenden 'Mutterl-' und 'Waisenliedern,' den faulen Zoten (man läßt sich recht derbe Volkskost gerne gefallen, wenn sie echt ist!), sinnlosen Schlagern, die das Volk, das natürlich keine Stilkritik treibt, auch singt, wenn man sie ihm hunderte- und tausendemale vorsetzt!" Huber, "Aufbau deutscher Volksliedforschung," 69.

123. Huber, "Der künftige Aufbau," 129–31.

124. For one critique of Pulikowski, see Moser, "Zum Volksliedbegriff," *Jahrbuch für Volksliedforschung* 4 (1934): 134–37. Mersmann's work prompted a detailed response from Kurt Huber ("Die volkskundliche Methode in der Volksliedforschung," *AfMf* 3 [1938]: 257–76). Danckert responded to his critics in " 'Entwicklungsgeschichtliche' und organische Volkslied-Betrachtung," *AfMf* 6 (1941): 70–93.

125. Frotscher went a step further than the others in attempting to derive racial characteristics from a comparative study of versions of a folk song. He based his approach on the byzantine argument that folk song is an expression of life activities, and one must study its customary practice (*Brauchtum*) rather than its style, because Brauchtum is an expression of ideology (*Weltanschauung*), and since every Weltanschauung must be determined by race, Brauchtum is also an expression of race. Gotthold Frotscher, "Rassenstil und Brauchtum," *VME* 3 (1937): 3–10.

126. See Siegfried Goslich, "Ist alle Volksmusik wertvoll?" *Der Musikerzieher* 38 (1942): 65–67, and idem, " 'Volksmusik' als Wertbegriff," *DMK* 3 (1938): 283–91; Wilhelm Ehmann, "Volksmusik und Musikwissenschaft," *MJV* 1 (1937–38): 193–96;

Gotthold Frotscher, "Aufgabe und Weg der musikalischen Volkskunde," *MJV* 4 (1941): 66–71; Alfred Quellmalz, "Die Bedeutung der Volksliedkinde für die Musikerziehung," in Stumme, ed., *Musik im Volk,* 1st ed., 235–44.

127. Wilhelm Ehmann, "Musikwissenschaft und musikalische Volkskunde," *DMK* (1938): 3–14; Huber, "Die volkskundliche Methode."

128. Gotthold Frotscher expresses this view with a heavy reliance on the biological metaphor of the foreign influence "infecting the organism" of the Volk: "Es ist die Aufgabe der musikalischen Volkskunde, hier Urtümliches von Artfremdem zu scheiden. In der Erfüllung dieser Aufgabe wird die Volkskunde zur Kulturpolitik. Es muß ihr in Erkenntnis, Lehre und Auswirkung darum gehen, zersetzende und überfremdende Mächte zu überwinden, die in den Organismus der völkischen Kunst eingedrungen sind, das Erbgut der völkischen Kunst zum tätigen Besitztum des Volkes zu machen und eine lebendige Gegenwart mit einer lebendigen Vergangenheit zu verknüpfen. Es muß darauf ankommen, daß Bewußtsein für die Sinnhaftigkeit der Kunst im Lebenskreise unseres Volkes zu stärken und einer gesunden volksständigen Überlieferung zum Durchbruch zu verhelfen, damit einem lebensbezogenen Musizieren die Kräfte bereitet werden und aus den Lebensformen der Gegenwart völkisches Brauchtum neu erwachsen kann. Auch die musikalische Volkskunde trägt die Verantwortung dafür, daß aus der Weltanschauung eines bodenständigen, starken Volkstums ein volksständiges Liedgut emporsteigt, das die Kraft besitzt, Erleben und Haltung der völkischen Gemeinschaft zu gestalten und zu befruchten." Frotscher, "Aufgabe und Weg," 71.

129. See Lixfeld, *Folklore and Fascism,* 61–120; Oesterle, "Office of Ancestral Inheritance," 189–246.

130. Reported in *Der Mittag,* 28 May 1938.

131. Werner Korte, "Die Aufgabe der Musikwissenschaft," *Mk* 27 (1935): 338–40, 341.

132. Korte, "Grundlagenkrisis," 669–70.

133. Lorenz, "Musikwissenschaft im Aufbau," 368.

134. Siegfried Goslich, "Gedanken zur geisteswissenschaftlichen Musikbetrachtung," in *Festschrift Arnold Schering,* 90–91, 95.

135. Boetticher, "Zur Erkenntnis von Rasse und Volkstum in der Musik," 217–18, 221–22.

136. The Geistesgeschichte debate in its watered-down version gradually faded into oblivion. In 1939, Hans Engel reported on the achievements of musicology as a Geistesgeschichte (Engel, "Die Leistungen der deutschen Musikwissenschaft," 7–8); and in the same year Gurlitt emerged from his persona non grata status with a defense of its methods (Gurlitt, "Der gegenwärtige Stand," 1). In 1941 the term was used one more time in a pejorative sense: a report on the state of musicology refers to a study on Pfitzner as describing the composer's lied compositions in an outmoded geisteswissenschaftlich manner of examining style (Michael Alt, "Musikwissenschaft," *Zeitschrift für deutsche Geisteswissenschaft* 4 (1941–42): 72.

137. Gerber, "Die Aufgaben der Musikwissenschaft im Dritten Reich," 498, 500–501.

138. Blume, "Deutsche Musikwissenschaft," 18. See also his "Erbe und Auftrag," *DMK* 4 (1939–40): 1–11.

139. Gurlitt, "Der gegenwärtige Stand," 22–23, 30–31, 34.

140. Ibid., 44.

Chapter 7. *Attempts to Define "Germanness" in Music*

1. Scheibe, *Critischer Musicus*, 15th issue, 141–50.

2. Scheibe, *Critischer Musicus,* 1st issue, p. 9; 6th issue, pp. 55–65; 16th issue, pp. 151, 156; 59th issue, pp. 544–45; and 77th issue, pp. 701–2.

3. Such opinions were expressed by Marpurg in the 5th issue, 43rd issue, and 44th issue of *Des critischen Musicus an der Spree,* 33–40, 344–48, 356–57; and in "Vermischte Gedanken," vol. 2, no. 61 (1756), 3rd issue of *Historisch-Kritische Beyträge,* 220. Mizler also criticized the German public's attraction to all that was foreign in his *Neu eroeffnete musikalische Bibliothek,* vol. 1, pt. 3, p. 9.

4. See Pedersen, "On the Task of the Music Historian."

5. Plantinga, *Schumann As Critic,* 16–22.

6. See Applegate, "What Is German Music?"

7. Richard Wagner, "Was ist deutsch?" (1865–78), in *Wagner Dichtungen und Schriften,* vol. 10, p. 100.

8. Wagner [K. Freigedank, pseud.], "Das Judenthum in der Musik," *Neue Zeitschrift für Musik* 17 (September 3 and 6, 1850): 111–12; also in *Wagner Gesammelte Schriften,* vol. 5, pp. 84–85.

9. Wagner, "Was ist deutsch?," 88–91, 93, 95–98, 101, 103.

10. Moser, *Geschichte der deutschen Musik,* 2d ed., vol. 3, pp. 467, 469–70.

11. This lack of musicological engagement with the Germanness question was seen as a disadvantage even as late as 1938. Michael Alt, "Die deutsche Musikbegabung," *Zeitschrift für deutsche Geisteswissenschaft* 1 (1938–39): 69, 77.

12. He related the reworking of Netherlandic stylistic traits by Agricola, Hofhaimer, Isaac, and other "Germans" to Schütz's reworking and improvement of styles borrowed from both Gabrieli and Monteverdi as well as to Bach's borrowings from Couperin and Vivaldi. Riemann, *Das Generalbaßzeitalter,* 489–95, idem, *Die Musik des 18. und 19. Jahrhunderts,* 104–5.

13. Riemann, *Das Generalbaßzeitalter,* 492–93.

14. Einstein, *Geschichte,* 9, 12, 14.

15. Ibid., 58.

16. Ibid., 21, 29–30.

17. Ibid., 62.

18. Ibid., 79, 94–95.

19. Müller-Blattau, *Einführung in die Musikgeschichte.*

20. Schering, *Deutsche Musikgeschichte im Umriß.*

21. Moser, *Geschichte der deutschen Musik,* 3d ed., vol. 1, p. ix.

22. Moser, *Geschichte der deutschen Musik,* 3d ed., vol. 1, pp. 141, 295; vol. 2, pt. 2, pp. 492, 504–6.

23. He describes this as "kuhnsicheres Ausgreifen in weiten Schritten" rather than "scheinbar ängstliches kriechen in kleinsten Tondistanzen," because "Unsere Rasse besitzt eben die seelische Fähigkeit, in einer Art von souveränem Raumgefühl die Tondimensionen sprungweise zu durchmessen, sowie nach der Höhe und Tiefe zu erweitern." Moser, *Geschichte der deutschen Musik,* 3d ed., vol. 1, pp. 9–10.

24. Moser, *Geschichte der deutschen Musik,* 3d ed., vol. 1, pp. 6–7, 10, 12. These come through later in German sources of Gregorian chant that feature horn call sounds,

in medieval folk songs that employ the leading tone, and in an overall attraction to major tonality, which Moser claims to have determined as a constant feature of German music at the end of his survey. Moser, *Geschichte der deutschen Musik,* 3d ed., vol. 1, pp. 295, 298, 340–341; vol. 2, pt. 2, pp. 504–5.

25. Moser, *Geschichte der deutschen Musik,* 3d ed., vol. 1, pp. 6–7, 10–13; vol. 2, pt. 1, pp. 26, 129, 283, 399. He attributes masculinity and sincerity to all of the major composers with slight variations: Handel's "freie Männlichkeit," Haydn's "frische Männlichkeit," Beethoven's "herbfrische Männlichkeit," Weber's "straffe Männlichkeit," Handel's "Innigkeit," Mozart's "eingeborene Süße und Innigkeit," Beethoven's "scheue Innigkeit," and Schumann's "deutsche, bräutliche Innigkeit." Moser, *Geschichte der deutschen Musik,* 3d ed., vol. 1, pp. 12ff., 505; vol. 2, pt. 1, pp. 305, 445, 451; vol. 2, pt. 2, pp. 19, 25, 105, 171.

26. Moser, *Geschichte der deutschen Musik,* 3d ed., vol. 1, pp. 12–14, 19–39, 424, 461; vol. 2, pt. 1, pp. 17, 195–96. German Minnesang had a more religious and reforming quality than French court music, church music was always more important than secular music, and German opera was more Christian than Italian opera, accounting for the German revulsion against castrati. Moser can then point to the religious dedication of individual composers as a manifestation of their Germanness: Bach's oratorios commemorate events "regarded important by the Germanic tribes," Handel's Germanness comes through in his "Gottempfinden," Pfitzner is "christlich-germanisch," and the problems of modern German society lie not in the conflicts between the bourgeoisie and the proletariat but rather in the conflict between the relgious/idealistic and the nonreligious/materialistic. Moser, *Geschichte der deutschen Musik,* 3d ed., vol. 1, pp. 195–96; vol. 2, pt. 1, pp. 13ff., 34, 180, 224; vol. 2, pt. 2, pp. 372, 496, 519–20.

27. Although he acknowledges the strength and self-assuredness of German composers and their resistance to being "obsequious" to foreign masters by balancing the foreign with their own German features (such as with Hasler, Schütz, and Handel), he notes the importance of foreign influence for the realization of German potential. Gregorian chant never would have led to harmonic innovation without the Germans, but the Germans never would have progressed beyond yodeling and cow calling without the melodic culture of chant. Similarly, by transfering their admiration from the Italians to the French, Germans were led to their own "national style" and "sensitivity." Moser characterizes Wagner, the icon of German musical nationalism, not as a revolutionary but as a reformer. Moser, *Geschichte der deutschen Musik,* 3d ed., vol. 1, pp. 18, 68, 498; vol. 2, pt. 1, pp. 58–59, 292, 318.

28. Moser, "Über die Eigentümlichkeit der deutschen Musikbegabung," *JbMP* 30 (1924): 35–45.

29. Moser, *Geschichte der deutschen Musik,* 3d ed., vol. 2, pt. 2. pp. 153 and n4, 390, 404–8.

30. In addition to Moser, *Geschichte der deutschen Musik,* 3d ed., vol. 2, pt. 2, pp. 501–17, see also Hermann Unger, "Das Deutschtum in der Musik," *Akademische Blätter* 43 (1928): 49–50.

31. For a summary of the Pfitzner-Busoni-Bekker debates, see chap. 1 of Weiner, *Undertones of Insurrection.*

32. Sachs, "Aspects of Musical Politics," 74–95.

33. Peter Raabe, "Deutsches Musikwesen und deutsche Art," *AMz* 53 (1926): 737–38.

34. Hermann Unger, "Die musikalische Emanzipation der Völker," *Deutsches Volkstum* 1927: 39–43.

35. Unger, "Das Deutschtum in der Musik."

36. Gurlitt, "Vom Deutschtum in der Musik," *Die Kirchenmusik* 14 (1933): 167–69. He opens with the following: "Was von jedem Volksgenossen gefordert und geleistet werden muß, der sich zu dem großen Geschehen und Grundgedanken der deutschen Erhebung unter unserem Volkskanzler Adolf Hitler bekennt, nämlich: Selbsterziehung zum Deutschtum, gilt notwendig auch für den Musiker, den Kenner und Liebhaber der Musik. Auch ihn, der sich gern hinter die liberalistische Rede verschanzt, daß Musik mit Politik nichts zu tun habe, trifft der Ruf des Führers zur Neubesinnung auf deutsches Wesen und zu bewußter, verantwortlicher Mitarbeit am Neubau unseres nationalen und sozialen Lebens."

37. Karl Gustav Fellerer, "Musik und Volkstum," *ZfM* 100 (1933): 819–20.

38. Hans Mersmann's *Eine deutsche Musikgeschichte* considers German music in relation to other arts, sociological and political developments, and the music of Europe. Mersmann makes no attempts to isolate specific German musical tendencies but rather frames Germany's musical developments as entirely dependent on outside influence, albeit sometimes in the nature of a "struggle." Mersmann acknowledges the difficulty of defining "German" and locates the beginnings of an identifiable German music no earlier than the eighteenth century, and he makes no attempt to isolate or denigrate prominent Jews in German music. The work bears no publication date but must have appeared shortly after 1933: in speaking of the "national revolution of 1933," Mersmann comments that the event was too close to determine its effects on music and culture. (Mersmann, *Eine deutsche Musikgeschichte*, 505–6). Walther Berten's *Musik und Musikleben* is mostly concerned with sociological issues, and Otto Schumann's *Geschichte der deutschen Musik* devotes an entire chapter to the Jewish Question in modern times.

39. Alt, "Deutsche Musikbegabung," 70–83.

40. Karl Hasse, "Vom Wert und Sinn deutscher Musik," *Volk und Welt* (April 1936): 51–53; Hans Engel, "Das Deutsche in der Musik," *DMK* 3 (1938): 193–94.

41. Moser stated that the rejection of Romanticism was a mistake, which was thankfully rectified within the Jugendmusikbewegung. Moser, *Kleine deutsche Musikgeschichte*, 317.

42. Hans Engel, "Das Deutsche in der Musik," 185–205.

43. Hans Joachim Moser, "Was ist das 'Deutsche' an der deutschen Musik?" *Forschungen und Fortschritte* 10 (1934): 3–4 (also published in *Sächsische Schulzeitung* 102 [1934]: 59–61); idem, "Das innere Reich der deutschen Musik," *Das Innere Reich* 1 (1934–35): 779–88; Herbert Gerigk, "Von der Einheit der deutschen Musik," *NSM* 9 (1938): 629–34; Karl Blessinger, "Der Weg zur Einheit der deutschen Musik," *Deutschlands Erneuerung* 25 (1941): 75–84.

44. "Dieses Buch darf sich daher eine Gegenwartswertung der deutschen Musik und *des Deutschen in der Musik* nach unseren wesentlichen *heutigen* Forderungen und Gesichtspunkten nennen." Bücken, *Deutsche Musikkunde*, 5.

45. One can infer that Bücken found Riemann to be weak in his commitment to recognizing the superiority of German music. Bücken downplays the importance of musi-

cal forms and criticizes Riemann, the "Hanslick disciple," for accepting Hanslick's empty, architectural conception of form. In promoting the idea of German inventiveness, he finds it necessary to reject Riemann's classification of the Mannheim composers as "Bohemian and not German." Bücken, *Deutsche Musikkunde*, 63, 81–82.

46. Ibid., 11–14, 41–42, 62–70.

47. Ibid., 81–83.

48. Ibid., 105–16.

49. Müller-Blattau, *Geschichte der deutschen Musik*, 9, 16–17, 35–36, 76–77. Müller-Blattau also consistently employs the term "Erbe" both generally to describe the continuity of compositional practices from one master to another (146), and specifically to refer to the proximity of German composers to folk music (198), giving his reader the option of accepting or overlooking the biological implications of the term. Moreover, rather than ironing out the musical details of Germanness, he concentrates on creating a periodization unique not only to music history but to German music history: the Germanic era, the German Middle Ages (up to the death of Luther and Senffl), the era of the "great war" (from Hassler to Bach), the Goethe era, and the "Decline and Rise of German Music" from 1830 to the present.

50. Moser, *Kleine deutsche Musikgeschichte*. This work shows more interest in proposing a new schematization for the history of music (not limited to German music history) that treats monophony and polyphony as two separate realms and uses German music history as the ground on which to test this new organization. With a systematic segmentation of history reminiscent of Lorenz's rigid periodization by generations, Moser divides his presentation into two parts, one dealing exclusive with "monophony" but including accompanied folk songs of the present, and the significantly longer part dealing with polyphonic music from 1350 to the present.

51. Moser, *Kleine deutsche Musikgeschichte*, 322–23.

52. Walther Vetter, "Zur Erforschung des Deutschen in der Musik," *DMK* 4 (1939–40): 101–7.

53. Moser, *Kleine deutsche Musikgeschichte*, 244–47, 296–97, 313.

54. Bücken, *Musik der Nationen*. He sets out with presumptions to which he cannot hope to adhere: that the Germanic peoples have a natural tendency to penetrate to the innermost essence of all things, a tendency that manifests itself in music in their "conquest" of the harmonic realm (2), and he cites melody and rhythm as the strong points of the Latin and Slavic peoples, respectively. Beyond that, however, his claim loses credibility as his definition of "German" gets confused with "Germanic," "Nordic," and "Northern": he refers to the "Nordic" reaction against Gregorian chant; the "Germanic principle of four stresses (*germanisches Vierhebigkeitsprinzip*)" of Minnesang, a "Germanic feeling for major mode," and the "Germanic-Scandinavian" origins of polyphony (31–35, 37). Parallel organum in fourths, fifths, and octaves, he claims, was never in practice but was purely a theoretical attempt to conform the "Germanic-Scandinavian parallel singing" to the systematic principles of church music (38). By placing England and the Netherlands in the complex of Germanic peoples alongside the "Deutschen" and Scandinavians, Bücken evades the problem of having to explain the relative international insignificance of German music for at least the duration of the fifteenth century. Then, in his chapter on the "Germanic Nations" in the sixteenth century, the ambiguities become

more complex as the boundaries fall between German composers and composers in Germany (187). He claims, like so many of his contemporaries, that even German composers writing in an Italian style were nonetheless thoroughly German, yet he goes further by insisting first that Hasse is more German than one had previously assumed (196), and second by claiming Clementi as a German composer not only for his contribution to the "classic-German" sonata but also on the basis of his "German blood" from his mother's side (278).

55. E.g., Moser's treatment of the Minnesänger takes up more than four pages and follows a coverage of the troubadours and trouvères that barely fills a page. Moser, *Lehrbuch*, 42–47.

56. Moser, *Lehrbuch*. He still regards the "victory" of the interval of a third as a consonance as due to the "popular Nordic two-part polyphony" (9) and gives several pages over to his section on "Nordic antiquity," but he dismisses the possibility that the lur represents the earliest example of polyphonic performance (15). He also questions the assumption that the major scale is inherently Germanic and could be considered the "racial dialect" of the "Dinaric race" ("ebenso ist noch umstritten, ob das Dursystem die uransässige Volkstonart und die Kirchentonarten die Musiksprache des Mittelmeers darstellen, oder ob eher umgekehrt letztere als nordische, Dur aber als 'dinarische' Rassesprache anzusehen ist," p. 19). He continues to adhere to the notion of constancy of some German character traits, but does not necessarily regard them as assets. Romanticism is "Nordic openness, if not muddled, then certainly intricate [and] distant," (211) and German traits, even when present in their purest form, such as in the example of Schumann, come across as "Nordic-chaotic" and "irrational" and in the "Nordic style of confusion" (230–31).

57. Moser, "Ziele und Wege der musikalischen Lokalforschung," in *Bericht über den I. Musikwissenschaftlichen Kongress, Leipzig*, 381–82. As stated in a contribution to the Festschrift for Adolf Sandberger, "the summons to turn increased attention to local research was strongly emphasized at the last conference of the Deutsche Musikgesellschaft in Leipzig, Spring 1925." Max Herre, "Eine Augsburger Trompetenordnung," in *Adolf Sandberger, den hochgeschätzten Gelehrten und verehrten Lehrer zu seinem 60. Geburtstag, überreicht von seinen dankbaren und getreuen Schülern* (unpublished), Sandberger Papers (BSB).

58. Hans Engel, "Organisationsfragen der Musikwissenschaft." *ZfMw* 14 (1931–32): 272–76.

59. "Mitteilungen," *ZfMw* 12 (1929–30): 645; *ZfMw* 14 (1931–32): 384; *ZfMw* 15 (1932–33): 191–92, 288.

60. "Mitteilungen der Deutschen Musikgesellschaft," *ZfMw* 7 (1924–25): 604.

61. Ludwig Schiedermair, "Rheinische Musik und Musikforschung," *AMz* 65 (1938): 331.

62. This conclusion is based on data derived from Schaal, *Schrifttum zur musikalischen Lokalgeschichtsforschung*.

63. Gustav Becking, "Das Problem der nationalen Musikgeschichte," *Logos* 12 (1923–24): 282.

64. "So sehr wir vom Standpunkt deutscher Einigkeit solchen Zwiespalt beklagen dürfen, so verdanken wir ihm doch auch wieder jene fabelhafte Spannweite der tonkünst-

lerischen Sprachen, die im gleichen Jahrhundert und im gleichen Volkstum die Welten Bachs und Händels sowie die der Wiener Klassiker nebeneinander ermöglicht hat." Moser, *Geschichte der deutschen Musik*, 3d ed., vol. 2, pt. 1, p. 33.

65. Bücken, *Deutsche Musikkunde*, 16–23, 71–92.

66. Moser, *Geschichte der deutschen Musik*, 3d ed., vol. 2, pt. 1, pp. 4–6.

67. Wellek, *Typologie der Musikbegabung*, 255–82.

68. Müller-Blattau, *Das deutsche Volkslied*; idem, "Musikalische Studien zur altgermanischen Dichtung," *Deutsche Vierteljahrsschrift* 1926; and Müller-Blattau's contribution to Nollau, *Germanischer Wiedererstehung* (the last two items are cited in Hans Joachim Moser, "Die Entdeckung der Germanenmusik," *Gn* 12 (1940): 407.

69. Müller-Blattau, *Germanisches Erbe*.

70. Moser, "Die Entdeckung der Germanenmusik."

71. Oskar Fleischer, "Vor- und frühgeschichtliche Urgründe des Volksliedes," *Die Sonne* 5 (1928): 193–200 (quote on p. 199).

72. Hans Joachim Moser, "Die Entstehung des Durgedankens: ein kulturgeschichtliches Problem," *Sammelbände der Internationalen Musikgesellschaft* 5 (1913–14): 271–95 (quote on p. 291).

73. Jón Leifs, "Isländische Volksmusik und germanische Empfindungsart," *Mk* 16 (1923): 45.

74. Ibid., 48.

75. Ibid., 46, 51.

76. Danckert, "Altnordische Volksmusik," *Mk* 30 (1937): 4–12; idem, "Die ältesten Spuren germanischer Volksmusik," *Zeitschrift für Volkskunde* 47 (1938): 137–80.

77. "Die Tonalität und melodische Struktur des nordischen Volksliedes," cited in Prieberg, *Musik im NS-Staat*, 361.

78. Fritz Metzler, "Dur, Moll und 'Kirchentöne' als musikalischer Rassenausdruck," in Waldmann, ed., *Zur Tonalität*, 1–27.

79. Georg Schünemann, "Zur Tonalitätsfrage des deutschen Volksliedes," in Waldmann, ed., *Zur Tonalität*, 28–42.

80. Joseph Müller-Blattau, "Tonarten und Typen im deutschen Volkslied," in Waldmann, ed., *Zur Tonalität*, 42–49b.

81. Guido Waldmann, "Tonalitätsfragen im Volkslied der deutschen Sprachinseln," in Waldmann, ed., *Zur Tonalität*, 61–72.

82. Kurt Huber, "Wo stehen wir heute?," in Waldmann, ed., *Zur Tonalität*, 73–87.

83. Walter Wiora, "Die Tonarten im deutschen Volkslied," *DMK* 3 (1938–39): 428–40.

84. Riemann, *Die Musik des 18. und 19. Jahrhunderts*, 215, 231–32.

85. Moser, *Lehrbuch*, 120ff., 134–37.

86. Ibid., 118, 145.

87. Fellerer, *Deutsche Gregorianik*, 9–13.

88. Ibid., 32.

89. "Die Germanen haben nicht nur stärksten Anteil an der Ausbildung neuer Entwicklung der Gregorianik, zu denen sie die volkstumgebundene Vortragsweise drängte, sie wurden die eigentlichen Schöpfer der überlieferten Fassungen." Ibid., 33.

90. Ibid., 59–76.

91. Ibid., 76–85.

92. These included *Berühmte Musiker* (Berlin: Schlesisches Verlagsanstalt), *Musiker-reihe in auserlesenen Einzeldarstellungen* (Olten: Verlag Walter), *Zeitgenössische Komponisten* (Munich: Drei-Masken-Verlag), *Klassiker der Musik* (Berlin: Hesse; Stuttgart: Deutsche Verlagsanstalt), *Musikergestalten* (Wolfenbüttel: Kallmeyer); and *Breitkopf und Härtels kleine Musikerbiographien* (Leipzig: Breitkopf & Härtel).

93. A biography, according to Abert, can only be written by one who can collect historical documentation, sort out the important from the unimportant, and personally "experience" (*erleben*) the works of the master. Furthermore, it is necessary to consider the master in his context: historical events, national customs, interaction with others, and even climate and nature, but one must always keep in mind the special personality of the genius, in contrast to lesser known composers. The genius composes because his soul compels him, and in his work he is driven to surpass all that came before. For this reason, Abert chooses to downplay the notion of influence, for geniuses do not imitate, rather they "feel themselves drawn to" particular predecessors. Hermann Abert, "Über Aufgaben und Ziele der musikalischen Biographie," *AfMw* 2 (1919–20): 417–33.

94. Moser took care to point out that the "popularity" (*Volkstümlichkeit*) of Bach, Handel, Beethoven, Mozart, Weber, Wagner, Haydn, Brahms, Schubert, Strauss, Reger, and Pfitzner was not to be confused with the empty entertainment of contemporary popular music (*Unterhaltungsmusik*). Hans Joachim Moser, "Das Volkstümliche bei unseren großen Meistern," *Skizzen* 12/4 (1938): 4–6.

95. Hermann Reichenbach, "Unsere Stellung zu Bach," *Musikantengilde* 7/25, rpt. in *DJ* 330–34; Felix Messerschmid, "Von Johann Sebastian Bach, unserem Meister," *Die Schildgenossen* 6/24, rpt. in *DJ* 335–37.

96. Hans Joachim Moser, "Bach und wir," *Mk* 27 (1935): 330–35.

97. "Unsere Gegenwart stellt andere und neue Forderungen an eine Forschung, die ihr das große Musikerbild unserer Zeit darbieten soll, Forderungen nicht nur um der Wissenschaft willen, sondern gerade solche der Verbundenheit vom einstigen und heutigen Leben und Erleben." Ernst Bücken, "Die Erneuerung der großen Musikerbiographie aus dem Geiste von heute," *AMz* 66 (1939): 597.

98. Projected works included volumes on Gluck, Chopin, Puccini, and Tchaikovsky.

99. Bücken included two of his own studies (Beethoven and Wagner) and called upon colleagues Fritz Stein, Karl Geiringer, Robert Haas, Joseph Müller-Blattau, Rudolf Steglich, Walther Vetter, and Herbert Gerigk (whose Verdi book, ironically, was the only work on a non-German composer). Gerigk's Unsterbliche Tonkunst appeared in much smaller and less expensive volumes and actually had more works on non-German composers than Bücken's series. Contributors included Engel, Fellerer, Gerber, Korte, Müller-Blattau, and Schenk. Other ongoing series, such as Klassiker der Musik, depended far less on contributions from musicologists.

100. Riemann, *Die Musik des 18. und 19. Jahrhunderts,* 109–12.

101. Wolf even goes so far as to say that Germany lagged behind in the development of polyphony. Johannes Wolf, *Geschichte,* vol. 1, p. 71.

102. Ibid., vol. 2, pp. 67–68.

103. Ibid., 2d ed., vol. 3.

104. Hugo Leichtentritt's monumental study of 1924 viewed Handel in the context of

political and artistic developments during his lifetime. Leo Schrade characterized Handel's life as an unrelenting drive for world fame and for achieving an international musical ideal, a goal which was unattainable in the limited cultural outlets of Germany. Leichtentritt, *Händel*, 7–8; Schrade "Georg Friedrich Händels Lebensform," *Zeitschrift für deutsche Bildung* 10 (1934): 529–41.

105. Werner, " 'Das Fest unserer Zeit,' " 675–87.

106. Leichtentritt, *Händel*, 7–8, 262–64.

107. "Händels Musik ist aber mehr als gesellschaftbildend, sie ist — ohne Einschränkung — gemeinschaftbildend. Und daher kann sie wirklich einen Weg zeigen aus dem allzu individuell gelösten Leben in ein neues, gemeinschaftlich-geistig-gefestigtes." Rudolf Steglich, "Händel und die Gegenwart," *ZfM* 92 (1925): 336.

108. Friedrich Blume, "Bach und Händel. Zum Gedenkjahr," *MPf* 5 (1934–35): 403; Hans Joachim Moser, "Georg Friedrich Händel," *Das Innere Reich* 1 (1934–35): 1434; Karl Blessinger, "Georg Friedrich Händel," *Volk und Welt* (1935): 56; Steglich, "Händel und die Gegenwart," 335.

109. "Hätte Deutschland während des Krieges hinter der Front in diesem Sinne gewirkt, so wäre der Ausgang ein anderer gewesen. Wie erinnert aber diese Säuberung an die innerpolitische Arbeit der heutigen deutschen Regierung im letzten Jahr! Man setze an Stelle des im Werk gebrauchten Wortes 'Deutschland' und höre: 'Denn Zion, unser Zion, Gottes Sitz, es liegt in Staub, von Heidendienst entstellt. All' die Entweihung ruft zur Rache auf, soll ja im Kampfe Israels Glück erstehn.' (Mit Israel meint der Engländer in diesen nationalen Oratorien immer sich selbst.) Man erkennt, wie staatspolitisch dies alles gedacht ist. Der kriegerische Sieg erhält erst Bedeutung, wenn im Lande selbst ein sauberer gesunder Geist herrscht. Keines ohne das andere." Alfred Heuss, "Händel und Bach als zwei Seiten deutschen Wesens. Zum 175. Todestag Händels am 14. April 1759," *ZfM* 101 (1934): 492.

110. "Und noch etwas mutet in diesem Werk ganz zeitgemäß an. Das Volk hat seine besonderen Sprecher in als solchen namenlosen Vertretern, keine, sagen wir es so, parlamentarischen Zwischenglieder zwischen den Führern und dem Volk machen sich bemerkbar, frei äußern sie sich, die Namenlosen aus dem Volk, ein Mann und eine Frau. Und gewichtige Worte haben sie zu sagen und Herrliches zu singen. Wie gesagt, ein Oratorium, geradezu wie aus unserer Zeit geschaffen." Heuss, "Händel und Bach," 492.

111. Julius Kopsch, "Mut zu Händel," *NSM* 5 (1934): 381–84.

112. "Die in ihm zu Reife und Entscheidung gelangten Kämpfe aber waren primär Fragen englischer Art und englischer Geschichte und blieben es so lange, bis auch im deutschen Volke nationale Besinnung und nationale Sammlung zum Durchbruch gelangten." Blume, "Bach und Händel. Zum Gedenkjahr," 403. "Wo Individualismus und Liberalismus den Geist beherrschen, da bleibt kein Platz für eine wahrhaft heroische Kunst." Herbert Gerigk, "Händel. Bemerkungen aus Anlaß der 250. Wiederkehr seines Geburtstages," *NSM* 6 (1935): 303.

113. Heuss, "Händel und Bach"; Blume, "Bach und Händel"; Hans Joachim Moser, "Bach und Händel," *Forschungen und Fortschritte* 11 (March 1935): 109–10; Karl Hasse, "Bach und Händel," *Der deutsche Erzieher* 3 (1935): 114–15; Gerigk, "Händel," and Moser, "Georg Friedrich Händel," 1430.

114. Leichtentritt, *Händel*, 844. Müller-Blattau's Handel biography, published in

Bücken's Die grossen Meister der Musik series in 1933, similarly shows no signs of overstating Handel's Germanness. Müller-Blattau does, however, portray Handel as a victor "conquering" opera in Italy: "Händel hatte die Italiener auf ihrem eigensten Felde, der Oper, gewonnen." Müller-Blattau, *Georg Friedrich Händel*, 45.

115. Moser, "Georg Friedrich Händel," 1434.

116. Blessinger, "Georg Friedrich Händel," 56; Müller-Blattau, *Händel,* 57; Moser, "Georg Friedrich Händel," 1429, 1433, 1435 and idem, *Lehrbuch,* 152; Heuss, "Händel und Bach," 490; Kopsch, "Mut zu Händel," 383; and Gerigk, "Händel," 303.

117. Gerigk, "Händel," 304–5. While Blessinger claimed to discover elements of Handel's Germanic "love of nature" in the pastoral operas (Blessinger, "Georg Friedrich Händel," 56), Moser was almost alone in insisting that Handel's Germanness was just as pervasive in his Italian output and shone through the luster of Italian style, transforming what would be mere "treats for the ears" and vehicles for "castrati and prima donnas" in the hands of Scarlatti, Bononcini and Hasse into a "penetrating human experience" that was "uniquely German" (Moser, *Lehrbuch*, 151–52). He also insisted on the similarities between the operas and the oratorios and explained that Handel as "Germanic individualist" achieved a full, human development of his opera characters in a manner unmatched by Italian composers (Moser, "Georg Friedrich Händel," 1440–42).

118. Moser, "Georg Friedrich Händel," 1440. Gerigk devised the notion of the Nordic political drive expressed in Handel's music: "Das hohe Ethos des nordischen Menschen, die auf machtpolitischen Gebiet staatenbildende und erhaltende Kraft, das sind die Elemente, die aus der Musik Händels sprechen und deren Wirkung jetzt wie ehemals ungebrochen ist." Gerigk, "Händel," 303.

119. Gerigk, "Händel," 302, 304.

120. Müller-Blattau, *Georg Friedrich Händel,* 153–56; Blume, "Bach und Händel," 404–5; Moser, "Georg Friedrich Händel," 1439.

121. "Mit Jüdischem und Judentum haben sie, außer den Namen ihrer Gestalten und der Stoffquelle, in Wirklichkeit nicht das Geringste zu tun. Schon daß das Stoffliche des Alten Testaments durch völlige dichterische Neuschöpfung in unmittelbare Zeitnähe gerückt ist, läßt alles Fremdrassiges versinken." Arnold Schering, "Die Welt Händels," [lecture delivered at the Handel festival in Halle in 1922] *Händel Jahrbuch* 5 (1932), rpt. in Schering, *Von großen Meistern*, 68.

122. Günther Baum, "Über die Berechtigung der Aufführung von Händel-Oratorien," *MPf* 11 (1940): 153; RSK application, 29 January 1941, BDC Stephani.

123. Reported in Moser, "Georg Friedrich Händel," 1438.

124. Heuss, "Händel und Bach," 492; Moser, "Georg Friedrich Händel," 1437–38; Blessinger, "Georg Friedrich Händel," 56

125. Rosenberg, *Georg Friedrich Händel,* 13.

126. "Händel hat in seinen Oratorien meist biblische Stoffe vertont. Alfred Rosenberg hat in seiner Rede zur Eröffnung der Händel-Feier des deutschen Volkes in Halle die Haltung des neuen Deutschlands zu dieser Frage endgültig klargestellt." Gerigk, "Händel," 304.

127. He encapsulates Handel's Germanness in Beethoven's admiration for him and in the clarity that uncovered an inner struggle that could be traced throughout his life. Rosenberg, *Georg Friedrich Händel,* 7–9, 14.

128. "Gerade dieser objektivere deutsche Charakter Händels stand übrigens dem stammverwandten englischen Wesen viel näher als jeder einseitig zeitbedingte, subjektivere deutsche Charakter" (Steglich, "Händel und die Gegenwart," 335). "Und die große Wandlung geschieht. Geschieht mit der Rückkehr zum germanischen Norden. Das Land Shakespeares taut aufs neue seine deutsche Poetennatur auf. Das ist das Herrliche und zugleich Rätselhafte an diesem Manne, daß er vermochte, die nie verlorene Unergründlichkeit germanischer Gemütstiefe mit der Formklarheit der Romanen reibungslos zu verbinden" (Schering, "Die Welt Händels," 14). "Zudem zog ihn die Freiheit und Weltoffenheit des geist- und stammverwandten Volkes dorthin" (Müller-Blattau, *Georg Friedrich Händel,* 56). "Ohne seine deutsche Abstammung aber wäre ihm Form und Geist dieser englischen Tonkunst wohl verschlossen geblieben" (Müller-Blattau, *Georg Friedrich Händel,* 123).

129. Müller-Blattau, *Georg Friedrich Händel,* 56; Moser, "Georg Friedrich Händel," 1433–34, 1438.

130. *MJV* 4/10 (1941): "Händels deutsche Sendung" (ending with the quote from Rosenberg), unpaginated; Johann Adam Hiller, "Georg Friedrich Händel," 215–21; Rudolf Steglich, "Vom Leistungscharackter der Musik Georg Friedrich Händels," 222–26; Richard Eichenauer, "Händel und das alte Testament," 227–31; Gotthold Frotscher, "Händel und die Engländer," 232–34; and Frotscher, "Kleine Beiträge: Entzauberte Händel-legenden," 239–40.

131. "Händel ist weder in England zum Engländer geworden noch durch England einer der größten Komponisten seiner Zeit und aller Zeiten, sondern vielmehr trotz England und im Kampfe mit den Engländern." Frotscher, "Händel und die Engländer," 232–34. At the end of the issue, Frotscher followed up by deflating several common myths about Handel, some of which were "characteristic of the typical English drive to degrade greatness and to perpetuate an emotional cult with superficialities." Referring to the legend that Handel dedicated an aria to a blacksmith in Whitchurch who gave him shelter during a rainstorm, and the subsequent erection of a monument to the fictitious blacksmith, Frotscher remarks: "Der ganze Legendenkranz ist charackteristisch für die typisch englische Sucht, Großes zu verniedlichen und mit Äußerlichkeiten einen empfindsamen Kult zu treiben." Frotscher, "Kleine Beiträge," 240.

132. Moser, *Georg Friedrich Händel,* 26–27, 29.

133. "Trotzdem bleibt für manchen deutschen Volksgenossen, der nicht erläuternde und beschwichtigende Fußnoten mithören will und kann, die doppelte störende Schranke zwischen ihm und der Seele dieser Händelschen Oratorienkunst bestehen: der Wall des jüdischen Stoffs und der Wall des englischen Imperialanspruchs, die beide uns nach Erlebnissen des letzten Halbjahrhunderts unerträglich sind." Moser, *Georg Friedrich Händel,* 51.

134. Moser, "Zusammenschau," in Moser, ed., "Die Deutsche Musik und ihre Nachbarn," 34, Moser Papers.

135. Karl Blessinger, "Englands rassischer Niedergang im Spiegel seiner Musik," *Mk* 32 (1939): 37–41.

136. Karl Gustav Fellerer, "England und die Musik," *VME* 7 (1941): 186–88.

137. Ibid., 188–89.

138. Moser, "Zusammenschau," 34, 36–38.

139. Bankier, *Germans and the Final Solution,* 69–75, 87–88.

140. "Es ist geradezu widernatürlich, zwischen Kunst und Leben so zu scheiden, daß man zwar tagtäglich sich gegenseitig versichert, das Judentum sei der Weltfeind, daneben aber in den frömmsten, echtesten Tönen, die deutsche Meister jemals gefunden haben, Texte erklingen läßt, die samt und sonders auf eine Verherrlichung des jüdischen Volkes und seines Privatgottes Jahwe hinauslaufen." Eichenauer, "Händel und das alte Testament," 229.

141. Ibid., 230.

142. "Und ähnlich wird man (wenigstens als Zwischenlösung) so lange auch mit anderen Händelschen Oratorien verfahren müssen, bis wir Deutsche das Judenproblem hoffentlich derart weit in der Ferne hinter uns liegend sehen können, daß man die Originalstoffe Händels wie assyrisch-babylonische, chinesische oder indianische Legenden als 'exotisch' und 'altgeschichtlich schlechthin' neutralisiert empfinden wird." Moser, *Georg Friedrich Händel,* 52. See also pp. 65–66 and 72.

143. For a more detailed discussion of this literature, see Potter, "Musicology under Hitler," 87–104.

144. Einstein, *Geschichte,* 15.

145. Bücken, *Musik der Nationen,* 46–47.

146. Moser insisted that both of Liszt's parents were Austrian (*Lehrbuch,* 247) and referred to the "German-blooded Cesar Franck" (277).

147. Bücken, *Musik der Nationen,* 344–45.

148. Werner Danckert, "Deutsches Lehngut im Lied der skandinavischen Völker," *NSM* 12 (1941): 575–96.

149. Werner Danckert, "Deutsche Lieder und Tänze in Böhmen," *Böhmen und Mähren* 1 (1940): 90–94; idem, "Deutsches Lehngut im norwegischen Volkslied," *Deutsche Monatshefte in Norwegen* 3 (1942): 2; Walter Wiora, "Das Fortleben altdeutscher Volksweisen bei den Deutschen in Polen und im polnischen Lied," *DMK* 4 (1939–40): 182–83, 186–87; idem, "Die Molltonart im Volkslied der Deutschen in Polen und im polnischen Volkslied," *Mk* 32 (1940): 158–59, 161–62; Gotthold Frotscher, "Volksbräuche und Volkslieder der Deutschen in Polen," *MJV* 2 (1939): 399.

150. Robert Lach, "Die großdeutsche Kultureinheit," in *Die Anschlußfrage,* 286–95; idem, "Die großdeutsche Kultureinheit in der Musik," *Deutsche Welt. Monatshefte des Vereins für das Deutschtum im Ausland* 8 (1931): 27–31; idem, "Das Österreichertum in der Musik," *AMz* 65 (1938): 529–31.

151. Müller-Blattau went back to Oswald von Wolkenstein ("Vom Anteil Österreichs am Erbe deutscher Musik," *MJV* 1 [1937–38]: 218–26). Moser went back to the late sixteenth century ("Das deutsche weltliche Chorlied Altösterreichs," *MPf* 9 [1938]: 148, and "Österreichs Musik und Musiker," 86–87.) Other contributions celebrating the Anschluss include Andreas Liess, "Das deutsch-österreichische Musikschaffen der Gegenwart," *AMz* 65 (1938): 532; H. Strobel, "Österreichs Beitrag zur deutschen Musik," *Neues Musikblatt* 17 (1938): 1; and Therstappen, "Die Musik im großdeutschen Raum."

152. Rudolf Gerber, "Die Musik der Ostmark: Eine Wesensschau aus ihrer Geschichte," *Zeitschrift für deutsche Geisteswissenschaft* 2 (1939–40): 56–59, 63, 69, 72–74, 77–78.

153. Moser, "Sudetendeutsche Musik," 368; rpt. in Plaßmann and Trathnigg, eds., *Deutsches Land kehrt heim,* 135; idem, "Böhmen-Mähren in der deutschen Musikgeschichte," *AMz* 66 (1939): 383, 385. Additional publications by musicologists acknowl-

edging the annexation of the Sudetenland and appearing in 1938 and 1939 include Becking, "Kleiner Beitrag zur musikalischen Kultur- und Stammeskunde der Sudetendeutschen"; Karl Blessinger, "Die Musik im sudetendeutschen Raum," *Musik-Woche* 6 (1938): 629; Ernst Bücken, "Sudetendeutsche Musiker und die deutsche Klassik," *Rheinische Blätter* 15 (1938): 765; and Guido Waldmann, "Volkslieder der Sudetendeutschen," *Volksdeutsche Forschung* 2 (1938): 415.

154. Oskar Kaul, "Von alten sudetendeutschen Komponisten," *ZfM* 106 (1939): 9–13; Karl Michael Komma, "Die Sudetendeutschen in der 'Mannheimer Schule,'" *ZfM* 106 (1939): 13–15.

155. Komma, "Sudetendeutschen," 13–16; idem, *Johann Zach,* 6–7.

156. Frotscher, "Stätten deutscher Musikkultur: Danzig"; Moser, "Aus Danzigs musikalischer Vergangenheit"; Georg Schünemann, "Danziger Straßenrufe," *Mk* 32 (1940): 77–80. One particularly sharp attack invoked Hugo Riemann's name to discredit Polish musical creativity, since Riemann had allegedly determined the polonaise to have been imported into Poland from Spain via Germany. Kurt Hennemeyer, "Vom deutschen Geist in der polnischen Musik," *Mk* 31 (1939): 796.

157. Hans Joachim Moser, "Musiklandschaft Vlandern," *Niederdeutsche Welt* 16 (1941): 71; Karl Gustav Fellerer, "Holland in der europäischen Musik des 19. Jahrhunderts," *Musik im Kriege* 1 (1943): 49–50.

158. Fellerer, *Edvard Grieg;* file memo by Gerigk, 21 February 1942, BA NS 15/99.

159. The unpublished proofs exist among the Moser Papers. A detailed description of its contents and its genesis is in Potter, "Musicology under Hitler."

160. Engel, *Deutschland und Italien;* idem, "Deutsche und italienische Musik im Austausch," in Moser, ed., "Die Deutsche Musik und ihre Nachbarn."

161. "So wird auch die gesteigerte Aufnahme deutscher Musik und deutscher Opern seit 1940 in germanischer Kultureinheit gefördert." Fellerer, "Holland und Deutschland in der Musikgeschichte," in Moser, ed., "Die deutsche Musik und ihre Nachbarn," 85.

162. "Eine starke Ausweitung deutscher Konzerttätigkeit ergab sich mit der 1941 erforderlichen Besetzung des ehemaligen Jugoslawien, besonders des serbischen Raumes. Im Gefolge des deutschen Soldaten schritt auch der deutsche Künstler und hat seither eine Fülle von Veranstaltungen bewirkt, die der deutschen Tonkunst viele dankbare Freunde zuführten." "Die deutsche Tonkunst in Südslawien," in Moser, ed., "Die Deutsche Musik und ihre Nachbarn," 167a.

163. "Die Besetzung Frankreichs durch deutsche Truppen 1940 dämmte die weitere Ausbreitung jüdischen Musikgeistes kräftigst ein. Dafür hat eine verstärkte Pflege deutscher Musik planmäßig eingesetzt." Zimmermann, "Deutsche Musik im französischen Sprachbereich," in Moser, ed., "Die Deutsche Musik und ihre Nachbarn," 239.

164. Becking, "Das Problem der nationalen Musikgeschichte."

165. "Was ist Deutsch? Ich geriet vor dieser Frage in immer größere Verwirrung." Also quoted in Herbert Gerigk, "Von der Einheit der deutschen Musik," 629.

Chapter 8. Denazification and the German Musicological Legacy

1. Clipping from "Nachtausgabe" of 22 January 1944 sent from Hans Albrecht to REM, 27 January 1944, BA R 21/11058.

2. Craig, *Germany,* 758–62; Herzstein, *War That Hitler Won,* 391–400; and Weinberg, *World at Arms,* 782–83.

3. See Friedrich Blume, "Bilanz der Musikforschung," *Die Musikforschung* 1 (1948): 9–10, and Hans Engel, "Die Entwicklung der Musikwissenschaft, 1900–1950," *ZfM* 111 (1950): 21.

4. Kroyer to Dekan (Cologne), 27 May 1931, UAK; Engel to Sandberger, 20 September 1933, Sandberger Papers (BSB); Spanke to Ursprung, 28 September 1936, and Ursprung to H. Förster (recommendations for a musicology position in Fribourg, Switzerland), 6 May 1939, Ursprung Papers. Spanke complained about the watering down of German scholarship with the "fictional prose" of the Geisteswissenschaft trend, while scholars abroad were forging ahead with the old German traditions. Ursprung also approved only of those young scholars who, in his opinion, came out of the " 'good old' schools of scholarship" and evaded the "shallow aestheticization or flat historicization" prevalent after World War I.

5. Gottron to Ursprung, 15 January 1946, Ursprung Papers.

6. Military Government Fragebogen, 25 July 1945, UAH PA Besseler.

7. Blume, "Bilanz," 3–8.

8. Schiedermair, "Die Gegenwartslage der deutschen Musikforschung," *Allgemeine Kölnische Rundschau,* 29 October 1949, p. 154.

9. Blume, *Denkschrift,* 10–15, Moser Papers.

10. Blume, "Bilanz," 6–9.

11. Ibid., 3–4, 9–10, 14–16.

12. Benz, "Postwar Society and National Socialism," 1–12; see also Kater, "Problems of Political Reeducation in West Germany, 1945–1960," 101.

13. Osthoff, Fragebogen, UAL Phil. Fak. B 2/22[46].

14. Frotscher, Fragebogen, BDC Frotscher.

15. Erdmann, *Das Ende des Reiches,* 112–22.

16. Ericksen, "Religion und Nationalsozialismus," 83–101.

17. Husmann, "Lebenslauf," 12 June 1939; testimony of Klinger (dean at Leipzig), 21 November 1946, UAL PA 5.

18. Written evaluation of Zenck; Dekan to Gouvernment Militaire de Fribourg, 27 May 1946, UAF PA Zenck.

19. Engel to Dekan (Köln), 5 December 1945, UAK.

20. Lach to Dekan, 15 April 1946, UAW PA Lach.

21. Kreichgauer to Dekan, 23 January 1946, UAB PA Kreichgauer.

22. Lach to Dekan, 15 April 1946, UAW PA Lach.

23. Kater, "Carl Orff im Dritten Reich," 26ff.

24. Ursprung Papers.

25. Besseler to Ursprung, 1 December 1946, Ursprung Papers.

26. Lebenslauf, July 1945, UAM FA Engel.

27. Fragebogen, signed 23 May 1946, UABonn PA Schiedermair (Rektorat).

28. Lach to Dekan, 15 April 1946, UAW PA Lach.

29. Dekan to Rektor, 26 June 1941, UAH PA Besseler.

30. Philosophische Fakultät to Rektor, 29 December 1937, and letter from Dozenten-

bund, 27 December 1937, UAH PA Besseler; Weber (REM) to Frey, 9 September 1937, BDC Besseler.

31. Ministerium des Kultus und Unterrichts to Rektor, 15 January 1938, UAH PA Besseler.

32. Letter from Dozentenbund, 25 June 1941; Ministerium des Kultus und Unterrichts to Rektor, 10 December 1941, UAH PA Besseler.

33. Besseler to Dekan, 4 July 1944, UAH PA Besseler; Dekan to Miederer (REM), 14 August 1944, BDC Besseler.

34. REM to Dekan (Phil. Fak. Heidelberg), 9 October 1944, BDC Besseler.

35. Moser, "Lebenslauf," UAL Phil. Fak. B 2/22[46].

36. Moser to Hartung, 11 April 1941, UAB PA Schering.

37. Partei-Kanzlei to Miederer, 13 February 1945, forwarded by Miederer to Kummer, 20 February 1945; Kummer to Miederer, 15 March 1945, ZStA REM Nr. 12307, Bl. 3.

38. Moser, "Lebenslauf," UAL Phil. Fak. B 2/22[46].

39. Moser to Hartung, 11 April 1941, UAB PA Schering.

40. Moser, "Lebenslauf," UAL Phil. Fak. B 2/22[46].

41. Moser to Abteilung H, 23 June 1943, BA R 55/240.

42. Moser, "Lebenslauf," UAL Phil. Fak. B 2/22[46].

43. "Lebensbeschreibung," 26 July 1945, UAH PA Besseler.

44. Berghahn, *Modern Germany,* table 47, p. 307.

45. Tent, *Mission on the Rhine,* 67–68.

46. Bower, *Blind Eye to Murder,* 183–86.

47. Willis, *French in Germany,* 147–63.

48. Grohnert, *Die Entnazifizierung in Baden,* 136–43.

49. Tent, *Mission on the Rhine,* 58–62, 88.

50. Ibid., 65–66, 84.

51. Letter from SA Sturm 7/110, 21 July 1937; Besseler to Rektor, 17 January 1939 and 12 December 1942, UAH PA Besseler.

52. Judgment, Spruchkammer Heidelberg, 25 March 1947, UAH PA Besseler.

53. Rektor of University of Freiburg to Reich Education Ministry, 28 October 1936, UAF Reg. Akten V1/159; Frotscher to Dekan (Berlin), 11 February 1938; NS-Dozenten-führer to Rektor (Berlin), 8 June 1938, UAB PA Frotscher.

54. Frotscher to Rektor, 18 March 1938, UAB PA Frotscher.

55. Besseler to REM, 27 July 1942, UAH PA Besseler.

56. "Lebensbeschreibung," 26 July 1945; Besseler to Militär-Regierung Heidelberg, 18 December 1945, UAH PA Besseler.

57. Spruchkammer Heidelberg, 25 March 1947, UAH PA Besseler.

58. Berufungskammer VII Karlsruhe, 12 March 1948, UAH PA Besseler.

59. Blume to Rektor, 23 May 1947; Blume and Schmitz (Mainz) to Landespräsidium Karlsruhe, 6 August 1948; Affadavit signed by Blume, Gerber, Wolf, Schmidt-Görg, Engel, Kahl, Mahrenholz, Stäblein, Reichert, Heinitz, and Noack, 10 April 1947, UAH PA Besseler.

60. Besseler to Rektor, 5 July 1948, UAH PA Besseler.

61. Welsh, *Revolutionärer Wandel auf Befehl?* 83.

62. Tent, *Mission on the Rhine,* 107.

63. Ibid., 65–66, 80–86.

64. Rektor to Dekan, 9 September 1947; Dekan (Rudolf von Ficker) to Rektor, 19 September 1947, UAM PA Lorenz.

65. Recommendations of University of Bonn, 24 July 1945 and 23 October 1945, UABonn PA Schiedermair (Rektorat).

66. University of Cologne to Kultusministerium des Landes Nordrhein-Westfalen, 4 February 1949, UAK.

67. Connor, "Denazification in Post-War Germany," 398.

68. Berghahn, *Modern Germany,* 192–93.

69. Tent, *Mission on the Rhine,* 66.

70. "Fragebogen," UAB PA Danckert.

71. Dekan to Rektor, 1 October 1945, UAB PA Danckert.

72. Decision of Deutsche Verwaltung für Volksbildung, 23 February 1948, UAB PA Danckert.

73. Brockhaus, "Konzeptionen zur Musikgeschichte," 21.

74. Moser, "Lebenslauf," UAL Phil. Fak. B 2/22⁴⁶ and Moser Papers.

75. Moser to "Frau Ministerin" (Thuringia), 23 September 1947; Moser to Blume, 25 June 1948, Moser Papers.

76. Moser to Blume, 25 June 1948, Moser Papers; Senff (Land Thüringen Ministerium für Volksbildung) to Ministerium für Volksbildung in Saxony, 5 January 1948, UAL Phil. Fak. B 2/22⁴⁶.

77. Laux (Ministerium für Volksbildung, Saxony) to Moser, 17 February 1948; Hoffman und Campe Verlag to Moser, 9 March 1948, Moser Papers.

78. Letter from University of Jena, 18 December 1948, UAL PA 2926.

79. Moser to Blume, 25 June 1948, Moser Papers.

80. Welsh, *Revolutionärer Wandel auf Befehl?* 84–85.

81. Fragebogen, 15 April 1949, "Lebenslauf," 15 March 1950, UAL PA 2926.

82. "Lebenslauf," 26 August 1948, UAL PA 2926.

83. Judgment of Herstenberger, Personnel Division, UAL PA 2926.

84. Vetter to Dekan (Leipzig), 12 August 1948, UAL Phil. Fak. B 2/22⁴⁶.

85. Blume, *Denkschrift,* 8–9.

86. Gurlitt to Phil. Fak. Leipzig, 26 April 1946, UAL Phil. Fak. B 2/22⁴⁶.

87. Blume to Moser, 19 June 1948; Moser to Blume, 25 June 1948, Moser Papers.

88. Schiedermair Papers.

89. Ichthys Verlag to Moser, 1 March 1956, Moser Papers.

90. Moser to Plaßmann, 20 March 1940, BDC Moser ("Ahnenerbe" file).

91. Plaßmann to Kaiser, 6 April 1940; Sievers to Plaßmann, 13 May 1940 and 20 May 1940, BDC Moser ("Ahnenerbe" file); Moser to Hartung, 11 April 1941, UAB PA Schering.

92. "Der Vorstand der Gesellschaft für Musikforschung hat beschlossen, von einer Besprechung des oben genannten Buches in der Zeitschrift 'Die Musikforschung' Abstand zu nehmen, weil er sich von den das Judentum betreffenden Bemerkungen des Buches in aller Form zu distanzieren wünscht." "Besprechungen," *Die Musikforschung* 10 (1957): 334; see also Moser's reply, p. 463.

93. Moser to Hamel (editor of *Musica*), 18 June 1957, Moser Papers.

94. Moser to Mersmann, 2 May 1958, Moser Papers.

95. Deutsche Verlag für Musik to Moser, 24 May 1957, Moser Papers.

96. "Mein Vater hatte als Militärarzt eine Menge von Kameraden, die Juden waren, die aber zumindest ebensogute 'Antisemiten' waren, wie er selbst. Worauf es ankommt ist doch schließlich, ob ein Mensch anständig ist. . . . Wir im alten Österreich mit seiner galizischen Infiltration hatten alle Ursache zu unserer inaggressiven Abwehrstellung. Aber ich denke, wir beiden verstehen uns in dieser Hinsicht." Orel to Moser, 21 September 1958, Moser Papers.

97. [Geraldine de Courcy] to Moser, 24 August 1964, Moser Papers.

98. Gerigk to Moser, 11 January 1958, Moser Papers.

99. Paul Henry Lang, "Editorial," *Musical Quarterly* 43 (1957): 517.

100. Richard Freymann, review of Friedrich Blume, *Wesen und Werden deutscher Musik* (Kassel: Bärenreiter, 1944), *Music and Letters* 28 (1947): 279–80.

101. "Das ist eine Ehrenpflicht. Wir Deutsche haben in der Not einen Trost und einen Stolz: das ist die Musik, welche uns und der Welt die Meister aller Zeiten, einer Gegenwart, einer nahen und fernen Vergangenheit, aus diesem widerspruchsvollen, aber reich begnadeten, aus unserem Volke heraus geschenkt haben. Ihre Werke zu erforschen und ihre Pflege zu fördern, ist mehr als nur Deutschland zugute kommende Pflicht!" Engel, "Die Entwicklung der Musikwissenschaft, 1900–1950," 22.

102. Blume, "Bilanz," 19.

103. Ibid., 7–8.

104. For example, biographical entries on musicologists active in the Third Reich in both the *New Grove* and *MGG* notably omitted numerous biographical details and works falling between 1933 and 1945. See, e.g., the entry on Müller-Blattau, which leaves out his book *Germanisches Erbe in deutscher Tonkunst* and never mentions his position in Strasbourg.

105. Lewis, "Facing the Music."

106. Wolff, "Die Hand eines Handlangers."

107. Dümling, "Wie schuldig sind die Musikwissenschaftler." Dümling enumerates Moser's transgressions, including many which constitute little more than guilt by association: publishing in "nonneutral" periodicals, such as *Das innere Reich, Die Zeitwende,* and *Volkstum und Rasse;* being cited in works on music and race; and being involved in the rewriting of operettas by removing the stories from their Polish settings, thereby "falsifying history" and "excluding Poland from the arena of high culture." Dümling also designates Boetticher as the "director" of the music division of the Rosenberg Bureau since 1939. That position remained in Gerigk's hands from its creation until its dissolution. Boetticher was named "Stellenleiter" of the "Hauptstelle Musik" in 1939 at age twenty-five, but documentary evidence clearly shows that he received all his orders from Gerigk (NSDAP Treasurer to Boetticher, 8 March 1939, Partei-Kanzlei to Boetticher, 9 November 1942, and Boetticher, "Lebenslauf," 4 January 1943, UAB PA Boetticher; Gerigk to Kerksiek [Verwaltungsamt, Amt Rosenberg], 18 January 1939, and Boetticher, list of NSDAP activities, 11 November 1939, BA NS 15/24).

108. De Vries, *Sonderstab Musik,* 199–200.

109. Edward Lowinsky, "Heinrich Besseler (1900–1969)," *Journal of the American Musicological Society* 24 (1971): 501.

110. Christoph Wolff, Letter to the Editor, *Journal of the American Musicological Society* 37 (1984): 208–9. I was able to view the files in question five years later in 1988.

111. Brockhaus, "Konzeptionen zur Musikgeschichte," 2–21.

112. Eckhard John, "Vom Deutschtum in der Musik," in Dümling and Girth, eds., *Entartete Musik: Eine kommentierte Rekonstruktion,* 52.

113. Riethmüller, "German Music from the Perspective of German Musicology after 1933," 183–84.

114. Letters from Apel, 10 August 1959 and 25 April 1960, Moser Papers.

115. Gerstenberg to Einstein, 21 February 1949, folder 379; Einstein to Slonimsky, 30 March 1949, folder 851; and draft of letter to Internationale Stiftung Mozarteum Salzburg, 16 December 1949, folder 13, Einstein Papers.

116. Einstein to Mark Brunswick, 7 December 1948, folder 197; Einstein to Kroll, 16 August 1948, folder 567, Einstein Papers.

117. Einstein to Eric Blom, 25 August and 10 October 1948, folder 167, Einstein Papers.

118. Einstein to Blom, 10 October 1948, folder 167; Einstein to Slonimsky, 6 July 1949, folder 851, Einstein Papers.

119. Einstein to Kroll, 16 August 1948, folder 567; Einstein to Slonimsky, 15 December 1947, folder 851, Einstein Papers.

120. "Die Herren sehen nicht daß zwischen dem stramm-nationalen Mann und dem Henker von Auschwitz eine gerade Linie geht, auch we[n]n noch ein paar Posten dazwischen stehen. Kennen Sie Goethes Zauberlehrling? . . . Auch Sie, wie soviele andere Wissenschaftler, haben mitgeholfen die Mentalität vorzubereiten die schließlich zu den Schlachthäusern und Gaskammern der nationalen Konzentrationslager geführt hat. . . . [p. 2] Aber denen, die die geistigen Führer Deutschlands sein sollten, muß vorg[e]halten werden daß das fürchterliche Unglück das über die Welt gekommen ist und das auch von Ihnen soviel persönliche Opfer gefordert hat, nicht die Tat einiger weniger Fanatiker ist sondern die Explosion eines Zündstoffs der von Generationen betrügerischer Pseudo-Wissenschaftler wie Chamberlain, Woltman oder Günther (über die die ausländische Wissenschaft nur lacht) gelegt und von Generationen von Lehrern und Professoren genährt worden ist. Erst wenn der Deutsche lernen wird seine Heimat zu lieben ohne jedem von der Deutschen Seele und dem Deutschen Menschen in die Ohren zu brüllen, erst wenn er einsieht daß Nationalexhibitionismus keine Tugend sondern ein Laster ist erst dann kann es Frieden geben — für Deutschland und f[ü]r die andern [original punctuation]." Sachs to Moser, 9 April 1949 (copy to Einstein), folder 812, Einstein Papers.

121. Einstein to Slonimsky, 11 March 1951, folder 851, Einstein Papers.

122. Einstein to Kroll, 16 May 1948, folder 567, Einstein Papers.

123. Kerman, *Contemplating Music,* 26; Harrison, "American Musicology and the European Tradition," 56–57. Harrison lists the émigrés Willi Apel, Manfred Bukofzer, Hans David, Alfred Einstein, Karl Geiringer, Otto Gombosi, Erich Hertzmann, Edward Lowinsky, Hans Nathan, Paul Nettl, Dragan Plamenac, Curt Sachs, Leo Schrade, and Emmanuel Winternitz.

124. Hugo Leichtentritt is mentioned in addition to all of those included in Harrison's list of émigrés. German-trained scholars include Warren Dwight Allen, Theodore Baker, Henry Cowell, George Dickinson, Carl Engel, Charles Warren Fox, Glen Haydon,

George Herzog, Otto Kinkeldey, Paul Henry Lang, Oscar Sonneck, Albert Stanley, and Oliver Strunk. Steinzor, *American Musicologists*.

125. A lengthy description is to be found in chaps. 3 through 6 in FitzGibbon, *Denazification*. See also Tent, *Mission on the Rhine*, 50–57.

126. Meyer's 1970 dissertation "Assumptions and Implementation of Nazi Policy toward Music" was followed by two articles on Nazi musicology: "The Nazi Musicologist as Myth-Maker in the Third Reich" and "Musicology in the Third Reich: A Gap in Historical Studies."

127. Meyer, "The Musicologist as Myth Maker: Jews and Germans as Ideal Types," in *Politics of Music in the Third Reich*, 256–81.

128. Hubert Kolland, "Wagner-Rezeption," 498.

129. In the course of conducting research in Germany on musicology in the Third Reich, I interviewed at least one prominent musicologist who adamantly adhered to this position, and I confronted similar attitudes among archivists. Upon further inquiry, I found that German musicologists who had attempted projects such as mine found their efforts hindered by the musicology establishment in Germany. They encouraged me in my work, believing that only an outsider such as myself could successfully investigate this topic.

130. Spruchkammer Heidelberg, 25 March 1947, UAH PA Besseler.

131. See Bohlman, "Musicology As a Political Act."

Bibliography

Unpublished Documents

Archive of the Gesellschaft der Musikfreunde. Exh. Nrs. 101, 103.

Berlin Document Center. Files for Heinrich Besseler, Herbert Birtner, Karl Blessinger, Friedrich Blume, Wolfgang Boetticher, Fritz Bose, Richard Eichenauer, Gotthold Frotscher, Wilibald Gurlitt, Alfons Kreichgauer, Hans Joachim Moser, Joseph Maria Müller-Blattau, Alfred Quellmalz, Erich Schenk, Alexander Schmorell, Johann Wolfgang Schottländer, Erich Schumann, Max Seiffert, Hermann Stephani, and Johannes Wolf.

Bundesarchiv Koblenz. NS 15/21–21a, NS 15/24–26, NS 15/38, NS 15/59, NS 15/153, NS 15/73–74, NS 15/99, NS 15/101, NS 15/131, NS 15/149a, NS 15/185, NS 15/189–90, NS 21/220, NS 21/717, R 21/209, R 21/464, R 21/625, R 21/11058; R 21/10185, R 51/8–9, R 55/240, R 55/1141.

Einstein, Alfred. Papers. Memorabilia, Music Library, University of California at Berkeley.

Geheimes Staatsarchiv Preußischer Kulturbesitz, Berlin. I/76: 880; Rep. 76/254.

Kroyer, Theodor. Papers. Handschriften- und Inkunabelabteilung, Bayerische Staatsbibliothek, Munich.

Moser, Hans Joachim. Papers. Musikabteilung, Staatsbibliothek Preußischer Kulturbesitz, Berlin.

Niedersächsisches Staatsarchiv Bückeburg. L4/7355, L4/7356.

Sandberger, Adolf. Papers. Handschriften- und Inkunabelabteilung, Bayerische Staatsbibliothek, Munich.

Sandberger, Adolf. Papers. Niedersächsisches Staatsarchiv Bückeburg.

Schiedermair, Ludwig. Papers. Musikwissenschaftliches Seminar, Universität Bonn.

Staatliches Institut für Musikforschung, Preußicher Kulturbesitz, Berlin. Copies of archival materials.

Universitätsarchiv Berlin. Files for Wolfgang Boetticher, Fritz Bose, Werner Danckert, Max Friedländer, Gotthold Frotscher, Alfons Kreichgauer, Hans Joachim Moser, Helmut Osthoff, Arnold Schering, Erich Schumann, Georg Schünemann, and Johannes Wolf. Philosophische Fakultät, file 1471. Professoren, file 1478.

Universitätsarchiv Bonn. Faculty files for Adolf Bauer, Ludwig Schiedermair, and Leo Schrade. Curator files for Ludwig Schiedermair and Leo Schrade. Rector file for Ludwig Schiedermair.

Universitätsarchiv Freiburg. Personnel files for Wilibald Gurlitt, John Meier, Joseph Maria Müller-Blattau, and Hermann Zenck. Reg. Akten V 1/159 (Die ausserordentliche Professur für Musikwissenschaft und das musikwissenschaftliche Seminar).

Universitätsarchiv Heidelberg. Personnel files for Heinrich Besseler, Theodore Kroyer, and Hans Joachim Moser. File B–7559 (Plm. Extraordinariat für Musikwissenschaft). File B–6633/1 (Musikwissenschaftliches Seminar).

Universitätsarchiv Köln. Files on musicologists and the musicology department.

Universitätsarchiv Leipzig. B1/14[27] Bd.1, B2/20[21], B2/22[46], PA 5, PA 260, PA 272, PA 661, PA 925, and PA 2926. Philosophische Fakultät Promotion file 1350.

Universitätsarchiv München. Personnel files for Rudolf Ficker, Kurt Huber, Alfred Lorenz, Adolf Sandberger, Gustav Friedrich Schmidt, and Otto Ursprung. Faculty files for Hans Engel, Rudolf Ficker, and Gustav Friedrich Schmidt. Faculty file for Musikwissenschaftliches Seminar.

Universitätsarchiv Wien. Personnel files for Robert Lach and Wilhelm Fischer. Dekanat files 78, 172, 240, 314, 680.

University of Nebraska–Lincoln. University Archive/Rosenberg Collection.

Ursprung, Otto. Papers. Handschriften- und Inkunabelabteilung, Bayerische Staatsbibliothek, Munich.

Zentrales Staatsarchiv Potsdam. Reichsministerium für Wissenschaft, Erziehung und Volksbildung (49–01) Nr. 933, 2176, 2909, 3117, 1782, 1475, 12307, H663.

Contemporary Periodicals and Serials

Akademische Blätter

Der Ackermann aus Böhmen

Allgemeine Kölnische Rundschau

Allgemeine Musikzeitung

Amtliche Mitteilungen der Reichsmusikkammer

Archiv für Musikforschung

Archiv für Musikwissenschaft

Der Auftakt

Bayerische Staatszeitung

Berichte des Forschungsinstituts für Osten und Orient

Berliner Tageblatt

Der Blockflötenspiegel: Arbeitsblatt zur Belebung historischer Instrumente in der Jugend- und Hausmusik
Böhmen und Mähren
Bundeszeitung des Deutschen Mandolinen- und Gitarrenspieler-Bundes
Collegium Musicum
Der deutsche Erzieher
Deutsche Militär-Musiker Zeitung
Deutsche Monatshefte in Norwegen
Deutsche Musikkultur
Das deutsche Podium
Deutsche Rundschau
Deutsche Tonkünstler-Zeitung
Deutsche Vierteljahrsschrift für Literaturwissenschaft und Geistesgeschichte
Deutsche Welt. Monatshefte des Vereins für das Deutschtum im Ausland
Deutsche Wissenschaft, Erziehung und Volksbildung: Amtsblatt des Reichs- und Preuß-ischen Ministeriums für Wissenschaft, Erziehung und Volksbildung und der Unter-richtsverwaltung der anderen Länder
Deutsche Zeitschrift
Deutsches Musikjahrbuch
Deutsches Volkstum
Deutschlands Erneuerung
Düsseldorfer Nachrichten
Düsseldorfer Tageblatt
Forschungen und Fortschritte
Der Friede
Geistige Arbeit
Germanien
Germanische Wiedererstehung
Die Gitarre: Zeitschrift zur Pflege des Gitarren- und Lautenspiels und der Hausmusik
Händel Jahrbuch
Hochland
Die Hochschule
Das Innere Reich
Jahrbuch der Musikbibliothek Peters
Jahrbuch für Volksliedforschung
Journal of the American Musicological Society
Die Kirchenmusik
Die Laute: Monatsschrift zur Pflege des deutschen Liedes und guter Hausmusik
Lauten-Almanach: Ein Jahr- und Handbuch für alle Lauten- und Gitarrenspieler
Der Lautenspieler
Literarischer Handweiser
Logos
Melos
Der Mittag
Mitteilungen der Internationalen Gesellschaft für Musikwissenschaft

Münchner Zither-Zeitung: Fachblatt für Zitherspiel
Muse des Saitenspiels: Fach- und Werbe-Monatsschrift für Zither-, Gitarren- und Schoss-
    geigenspiel
Music and Letters
The Musical Quarterly
Die Musik
Musik im Kriege
Musik in Jugend und Volk
Musik und Volk
Die Musikantengilde
Der Musikerzieher
Die Musikerziehung
Die Musikforschung
Die Musikpflege
Musik-Woche
Nationalsozialistische Monatshefte
Niederdeutsche Welt
Neue Zeitschrift für Musik
Neues Musikblatt
Neues Wiener Journal
Orchester
Österreichische Rundschau
Ostland
Die Pause
Rheinische Blätter
Sächsische Schulzeitung
Sammelbände der Internationalen Musikgesellschaft
Schallkiste: Illustrierte Zeitschrift für Hausmusik
Die Schildgenossen
Schweizerische Rundschau
Die Sendung
Signale für die musikalische Welt
Skizzen
Die Sonne: Monatsschrift für nordische Weltanschauung und Lebensgestaltung
Unser Wille und Weg
Vierteljahrsschrift für Musikwissenschaft
Volk und Welt
Völkische Musikerziehung
Volksdeutsche Forschung
Die Volksmusik
Wartheland: Zeitschrift für Aufbau und Kultur im deutschen Osten
Zeitschrift der Internationalen Musikgesellschaft
Zeitschrift für deutsche Bildung
Zeitschrift für deutsche Geisteswissenschaft
Zeitschrift für Hausmusik

Zeitschrift für Volkskunde
Zeitschrift für Musik
Zeitschrift für Musikwissenschaft
Die Zupfmusik

Primary Books

Adler, Guido. *Methode der Musikgeschichte.* Leipzig: Breitkopf & Härtel, 1919.

———. *Der Stil in der Musik.* 2d ed. Leipzig: Breitkopf & Härtel, 1929.

Anrich, Ernst. *Universität als geistige Grenzfestungen.* Stuttgart: Kohlhammer, 1936

Die Anschlußfrage in ihrer kulturellen, politischen und wirtschaftlichen Bedeutung als europäisches Problem. Vienna: Universitäts-Verlags Buchhandlung, 1930.

Bannes, Joachim. *Hitlers Kampf und Platons Staat: Eine Studie über den ideologischen Aufbau der nationalsozialistischen Freiheitsbewegung.* Leipzig, 1933.

Bekker, Paul. *Das Deutsche Musikleben.* Berlin: Schuster & Loeffler, 1916.

———. *Musikgeschichte als Geschichte der musikalischen Formwandlungen.* Stuttgart: Deutsche Verlags-Anstalt, 1926.

Bericht über den I. Musikwissenschaftlichen Kongress der Deutschen Musikgesellschaft in Leipzig vom 4. bis 8. Juni 1925. Leipzig: Breitkopf & Härtel, 1926.

Bericht über den Musikwissenschaftlichen Kongreß in Basel. Leipzig: Breitkopf & Härtel, 1925.

Berten, Walther. *Musik und Musikleben der Deutschen.* Hamburg: Hanseatische Verlagsanstalt, 1933.

Blessinger, Karl. *Mendelssohn, Meyerbeer, Mahler: Drei Kapitel Judentum in der Musik als Schlüssel zur Musikgeschichte des 19. Jahrhunderts.* Berlin: Hahnefeld, 1939.

———. *Judentum und Musik. Ein Beitrag zur Kultur- und Rassenpolitik.* Berlin: Hahnefeld, 1944.

Blume, Friederich. *Das Rasseproblem in der Musik. Entwurf zu einer Methodologie musikwissenschaftlicher Rasseforschung.* Wolfenbüttel: Kallmeyer, 1939.

———. *Zur Lage der deutschen Musikforschung. Denkschrift dem Herrn Bundepräsidenten der Bundesrepublik Deutschland, der Regierung der Bundesrepublik Deutschland, dem Bundesrat der Bundesrepublik Deutschland, dem Bundestag der Bundesrepublik Deutschland, den Regierungen der westdeutschen Länder, dem Deutschen Städtetag, der Evangelischen Kirche Deutschlands und den deutschen evangelischen Landeskirchen sowie den Bischöfen der römisch-katholischen Kirche in Deutschland vorgelegt von der Gesellschaft für Musikforschung.* Kassel: Bärenreiter, 1952.

Bücken, Ernst. *Führer und Probleme der neuen Musik.* Cologne: Tonger, 1924.

———. *Deutsche Musikkunde.* Potsdam: Akademische Verlagsgesellschaft Athenaion, 1935.

———. *Die Musik der Nationen.* Leipzig: Kröner, 1937.

———. *Musik der Deutschen.* Cologne: Staufen Verlag, 1941.

Deutsche Wissenschaften. Arbeit und Aufgabe. Dem Führer und Reichskanzler zum 50. Geburtstag. Leipzig, 1939.

Eichenauer, Richard. *Musik und Rasse.* 2d ed. Munich: Lehmann, 1937.

Einstein, Alfred. *Geschichte der Musik.* Leipzig: B. G. Teubner, 1920.

Engel, Hans. *Deutschland und Italien in ihren musikgeschichtlichen Beziehungen*. Regensburg: Bosse, 1944.

Fellerer, Karl Gustav. *Deutsche Gregorianik im Frankenreich*. Kölner Beiträge zur Musikforschung, ed. Karl Gustav Fellerer. Regensburg: Bosse, 1941.

———. *Edvard Grieg*. Potsdam: Akademische Verlagsgesellschaft Athenaion, 1942.

Festschrift Arnold Schering zum sechzigsten Geburtstag. Berlin: Glas, 1937.

Festschrift Hermann Kretzschmar zum 70. Geburtstag. Leipzig: Peters, 1918.

Gerigk, Herbert, and Theophil Stengel, eds. *Lexikon der Juden in der Musik*. Veröffentlichungen des Instituts der NSDAP zur Erforschung der Judenfrage, no. 2. Berlin: Hahnefeld, 1940.

Goslich, Siegfried, ed. *Musikalische Volksbildung*. Volksmusikalische Werkreihe Serie 3: Lehrwerk für den Lehrer. Hamburg: Hanseatische Verlagsanstalt, 1943.

Hase, Hellmuth von, ed. *Jahrbuch der deutschen Musik 1943*. Leipzig: Breitkopf & Härtel, and Berlin: Hesse, [1943].

Heinsheimer, Hans, and Paul Stefan, eds. *25 Jahre Neue Musik. Jahrbuch 1926 der Universal-Edition*. Vienna: Universal, [1926].

Hinkel, Hans, ed. *Handbuch der Reichskulturkammer*. Berlin: Deutscher Verlag für Politik und Wirtschaft, 1937.

Hoffmann, Hans, and Franz Rühlmann, eds. *Festschrift Fritz Stein zum 60. Geburtstag*. Braunschweig: Litolff, 1939.

Hübbenet, Anatol von. *Die NS.-Gemeinschaft "Kraft durch Freude": Aufbau und Arbeit*. Schriften der Hochschule für Politik, 27/28, ed. Paul Meier-Benneckenstein. Berlin: Junker & Dünnhaupt, 1939.

Kestenberg, Leo. *Jahrbuch der deutschen Musikorganisationen 1931*. Berlin: Max Hesse, [1931].

Komma, Karl Michael. *Johann Zach und die tschechischen Musiker im deutschen Umbruch des 18. Jahrhunderts*. Studien zur Heidelberger Musikwissenschaft, no. 7. Kassel: Bärenreiter, 1938.

Kretzschmar, Hermann. *Musikalische Zeitfragen*. Leipzig: C. F. Peters, 1903.

———. *Einführung in die Musikgeschichte*. Vol. 7 of Kleine Handbücher der Musikgeschichte nach Gattungen, ed. H. Kretzschmar. Leipzig: Breitkopf & Härtel, 1920.

Leichtentritt, Hugo. *Händel*. Stuttgart: Deutsche Verlags-Anstalt, 1924.

Lorenz, Alfred. *Abendländische Musikgeschichte im Rhythmus der Generationen*. Berlin: Hesse Verlag, 1928.

Marpurg, Friedrich Wilhelm. *Des critischen Musicus an der Spree*. 5th issue (1 April 1749); 43rd issue (23 December 1749); and 44th issue (30 December 1749). Berlin, 1750; rpt. Hildesheim: Georg Olms Verlag, 1970.

———. *Historisch-Kritische Beyträge zur Aufnahme der Musik*. Berlin, 1754–78; rpt. Hildesheim: Georg Olms Verlag, 1970.

Mersmann, Hans. *Musik der Gegenwart*. Berlin: Julius Brand, 1924.

———. *Eine deutsche Musikgeschichte*. Potsdam: Sanssouci, n.d..

Mizler, Lorenz. *Neu eroeffnete musikalische Bibliothek*. Leipzig, 1739–54.

Morgenroth, Alfred, ed. *Von deutscher Tonkunst: Festschrift zu Peter Raabes 70. Geburtstag*. Leipzig: C. F. Peters, 1942.

Moser, Hans Joachim. *Geschichte der deutschen Musik: Von den Anfängen bis zum Beginn des Dreißigjährigen Krieges*. 3d ed., vol. 1. Stuttgart: Cotta, 1923.

———. *Geschichte der deutschen Musik: Vom Beginn des dreißigjährigen Krieges bis zum Tode Joseph Haydns.* 2d and 3d eds., vol. 2, pt. 1. Stuttgart and Berlin: Cotta, 1923.

———. *Geschichte der deutschen Musik. Vom Auftreten Beethovens bis zur Gegenwart.* 2d ed., vol. 3. Berlin: Cotta, 1928; 3d ed., vol. 2, pt. 2. Stuttgart and Berlin: Cotta, 1924.

———. *Lehrbuch der Musikgeschichte.* Berlin: Hesse, 1936.

———. *Kleine deutsche Musikgeschichte.* Stuttgart: Cotta, 1938.

———. *Georg Friedrich Händel.* Kassel: Bärenreiter, 1941.

———. *Die Musik der deutschen Stämme.* Vienna: Wancura Verlag, 1957.

Müller-Blattau, Joseph. *Das deutsche Volkslied.* Berlin: Max Hesse, 1932.

———. *Einführung in die Musikgeschichte.* Berlin: Vieweg, [1932].

———. *Georg Friedrich Händel.* Die Grossen Meister der Musik, ed. Ernst Bücken. Potsdam: Akademische Verlagsgesellschaft Athenaion, 1933.

———. *Germanisches Erbe in deutscher Tonkunst.* Berlin: Vieweg, 1938.

———. *Geschichte der deutschen Musik.* Berlin: Vieweg, 1938.

Plaßmann, J. O., and G. Trathnigg, eds. *Deutsches Land kehrt heim: Ostmark und Sudetenland als germanischer Volksboden.* Deutsches Ahnenerbe Serie C: Volkstümliche Schriften, no. 3. Berlin: Ahnenerbe-Stiftung, [1939].

Raabe, Peter. *Kulturwille im deutschen Musikleben.* Von deutscher Musik, no. 49. Regensburg: Bosse, 1936.

Riemann, Hugo. *Altertum und Mittelalter (bis 1300).* 3d ed. Vol. 1. of *Handbuch der Musikgeschichte.* Leipzig: Breitkopf & Härtel, 1923.

———. *Das Generalbaßzeitalter: Die Monodie des 17. Jahrhunderts und die Weltherrschaft der Italiener.* 2d. ed. Vol. 2, pt. 2 of *Handbuch der Musikgeschichte.* Leipzig: Breitkopf & Härtel, 1922.

———. *Die Musik des 18. und 19. Jahrhunderts: Die großen deutschen Meister.* 2d. ed. Vol. 2, pt. 3 of *Handbuch der Musikgeschichte.* Leipzig: Breitkopf & Härtel, 1922.

———. *Grundriß der Musikwissenschaft.* 4th ed. Leipzig: Quelle & Meyer, 1928.

Rosenberg, Alfred. *Georg Friedrich Händel. Rede bei der Feier des 250. Geburtstages Händels am 22. Februar 1935 in Halle.* Schriftenreihe des Händelhauses in Halle, no. 1. Wolffenbüttel: Kallmeyer, 1937.

Scheibe, Johann Adolf. *Critischer Musicus.* 1st issue (5 March 1737); 6th issue (14 May 1737); 15th issue (17 September 1737); 16th issue (1 October 1737); 59th issue (13 October 1739); and 77th issue (16 February 1740). Leipzig: Breitkopf, 1745.

Schenk, Erich. *Johann Strauss.* Potsdam: Akademische Verlagsgesellschaft Athenaion, 1940.

Schering, Arnold. *Deutsche Musikgeschichte im Umriß.* Leipzig: Siegel, 1917.

———. *Einführung in die Kunst der Gegenwart.* Leipzig: E. A. Seemann, 1919.

———. *Von großen Meistern der Musik.* Leipzig: Koehler & Amelang, 1940.

Schreiber, Georg. *Die Not der deutschen Wissenschaft und der geistigen Arbeiter. Geschehnisse und Gedanken zur Kulturpolitik des Deutschen Reiches.* Leipzig: Quelle & Meyer, 1923.

Schumann, Otto. *Geschichte der deutschen Musik.* Leipzig: Bibliographisches Institut, 1940.

Schünemann, Georg. *Geschichte der deutschen Schulmusik.* Handbücher der Musikerziehung. 2d. ed. Leipzig: Kistner & Siegel, 1931.

Seiffert, Max. *Ein Archiv für deutsche Musikgeschichte. Rede gehalten bei der Feier des allerhöchsten Geburtstages seiner Majestät des Kaisers und Königs am 27. Januar 1914.* Berlin: Mittler, [1914].

Stenographische Berichte über die öffentlichen Sitzungen der Stadtverordnetenversammlungen der Stadt Berlin.

Stumme, Wolfgang, ed. *Musik im Volk: Grundfragen der Musikerziehung.* Berlin: Vieweg, 1939; 2d. ed. *Musik im Volk: Gegenwartsfragen der deutschen Musik.* Berlin: Vieweg, 1944.

Vetter, Walther. *Der humanistische Bildungsgedanke in Musik und Musikwissenschaft.* Langensalza: Beyer, 1928.

Wagner, Richard. *Richard Wagner Gesammelte Schriften,* ed. Wolfgang Golther. Leipzig: Deutsches Verlagshaus Bong & Co., 1913.

———. *Richard Wagner Dichtungen und Schriften,* ed. Dieter Borchmeyer. Frankfurt/Main: Insel, 1983.

Waldmann, Guido, ed. *Zur Tonalität des deutschen Volksliedes. Herausgegeben im Auftrage der Reichsjugendführung.* Wolfenbüttel: Kallmeyer, 1938.

Wellek, Albert. *Typologie der Musikbegabung im deutschen Volke: Grundlegung einer psychologischen Theorie der Musik und Musikgeschichte.* Munich: C. H. Beck'sche Verlagsbuchhandlung, 1939.

Wolf, Johannes. *Geschichte der Musik in allgemeinverständlicher Form.* 3 vols. plus *Sing und Spielmusik aus älterer Zeit.* Leipzig: Quelle & Meyer, 1930; 2d ed. Leipzig: Quelle & Meyer, 1934.

Ziegler, Hans Severus. *Entartete Musik: Eine Abrechnung.* 2d ed. Düsseldorf: Völkischer Verlag, 1939.

Secondary Works

Abendroth, Wolfgang. "Die deutschen Professoren und die Weimarer Republik." Pages 11–25 in *Hochschule und Wissenschaft im Dritten Reich,* ed. Jörg Tröger. Frankfurt/Main: Campus, 1986.

Amzoll, Stephan. "Aufstieg und Verfall: Unterhaltungsmusik im Rundfunk der Weimarer Republik." *Musik und Gesellschaft* 37 (1987): 196–202.

———. "Zur Rolle des Rundfunks der Weimarer Republik als ästhetische Avantgarde." Pages 110–24 in *Studien zur Berliner Musikgeschichte: Musikkultur der zwanziger Jahre,* ed. Klaus Mehner and Joachim Lucchesi. Berlin: Henschel, 1989.

Applegate, Celia. "What Is German Music? Reflections on the Role of Art in the Creation of a Nation." *German Studies Review: Special Issue, German Identity* (winter 1992): 21–32.

Bair, Henry. "National Socialism and Opera: The Berlin Opera Houses, 1933–1939." *Opera* 35 (1984): 17–23, 129–37.

Bankier, David. *The Germans and the Final Solution: Public Opinion under Nazism.* Oxford: Blackwell, 1992.

Benz, Wolfgang. "Postwar Society and National Socialism: Remembrance, Amnesia, Rejection." *Tel Aviver Jahrbuch für deutsche Geschichte* 19 (1990): 1–12.

Bergen, Doris. *Twisted Cross: The German Christian Movement in the Third Reich.* Chapel Hill: University of North Carolina Press, 1996.

Berghahn, Volker R. *Modern Germany: Society, Economy and Politics in the Twentieth Century.* 2d ed. Cambridge: Cambridge University Press, 1987.

Bleuel, Hans Peter. *Deutschlands Bekenner. Professoren zwischen Kaiserreich und Diktatur.* Bern: Scherz, 1968.

Blume, Friedrich. "Musicology in German Universities." *Current Musicology* 9 (1969): 52–64.

Bohlman, Philip. "Musicology As a Political Act." *Journal of Musicology* 11 (1993): 411–36.

Bollmus, Reinhard. *Das Amt Rosenberg und seine Gegner: Zum Machtkampf im nationalsozialistischen Herrschaftssystem.* Studien zur Zeitgeschichte herausgegeben vom Institut für Zeitgeschichte. Stuttgart: Deutsche Verlags-Anstalt, 1970.

———. "Zum Projekt einer nationalsozialistischen Alternativ-Universität: Alfred Rosenbergs 'Hohe Schule'." Pages 125–52 in *Erziehung und Schulung im Dritten Reich. Teil 2: Hochschule, Erwachsenbildung,* ed. Manfred Heinemann. Stuttgart: Klett-Cotta, 1980.

Bower, Tom. *Blind Eye to Murder: Britain, America and the Purging of Nazi Germany— A Pledge Betrayed.* London: Andre Deutsch, 1981.

Bracher, Karl Dietrich. "Die Gleichschaltung der deutschen Universität." Pages 126–42 in *Universitätstage 1966: Nationalsozialismus und die deutsche Universität.* Berlin: DeGruyter, 1966.

———. *The German Dictatorship: Origins, Structure, and Effects of National Socialism.* Trans. Jean Steinberg. New York: Praeger, 1970.

Brockhaus, Heinz Alfred. "Konzeptionen zur Musikgeschichte." *Wissenschaftliche Zeitschrift der Humboldt-Universität zu Berlin: Gesellschafts- und Sprachwissenschaftliche Reihe* 29 (1980): 15–24.

Bunge, Fritz. *Musik in der Waffen-SS.* Osnabrück: Munin, 1975.

Burkholder, Peter. "Museum Pieces: The Historicist Mainstream in Music of the Last Hundred Years." *Journal of Musicology* 2 (1983): 115–34.

Burleigh, Michael. *Germany Turns Eastwards: A Study of* Ostforschung *in the Third Reich.* Cambridge: Cambridge University Press, 1988.

Connor, Ian. "Denazification in Post-War Germany." *European History Quarterly* 21 (1991): 397–402.

Craig, Gordon. *Germany 1866–1945.* New York: Oxford University Press, 1980.

De Vries, Willem. *Sonderstab Musik: Music Confiscations by the Einsatzstab Reichsleiter Rosenberg under the Nazi Occupation of Western Europe.* Trans. UvA Vertalers, Lee K. Mitzman. Amsterdam: Amsterdam University Press, 1996.

Dower, Catherine, ed. *Alfred Einstein on Music: Selected Music Criticisms.* Contributions to the Study of Music and Dance, no. 21. New York: Greenwood, 1991.

Drechsler, Nanny. *Die Funktion der Musik im Deutschen Rundfunk, 1933–1945.* Pfaffenweiler: Centaurus, 1988.

Drux, Herbert. *Kölner Universitätskonzerte, 1939–1970.* Cologne, 1970.

Dumbach, Annette, and Jud Newborn. *Shattering the German Night: The Story of the White Rose.* Boston: Little, Brown, 1986.

Dümling, Albrecht, and Peter Girth, eds. *Entartete Musik: Eine kommentierte Rekonstruktion.* Düsseldorf: Kleinherne, 1988.

——. "Wie schuldig sind die Musikwissenschaftler: Zur Rolle von Wolfgang Boetticher und Hans-Joachim Moser im NS-Musikleben." *Neue Musikzeitung* 39/5 (October-November 1990): 9.

Düwell, Kurt. "Kultur und Kulturpolitik in der Weimarer Republik." Pages 64–79 in *Weimarer Republik: Eine Nation im Umbruch,* ed. Gerhard Schulz. Freiburg: Verlag Ploetz, 1987.

Eggers, Philipp. "§16 Bildungswesen." Pages 966–87 in *Deutsche Verwaltungsgeschichte. Band 4: Das Reich als Republik und in der Zeit des Nationalsozialismus.* Stuttgart: Deutsche Verlags-Anstalt, 1985.

Ellis, Donald Wesley. "Music in the Third Reich: National Socialist Aesthetic Theory as Governmental Policy." Ph.D. diss., University of Kansas, 1970.

Elste, Martin. "Zwischen Privatheit und Politik: Die Schallplatten Industrie im NS-Staat." Pages 107–14 in *Musik und Musikpolitik im faschistischen Deutschland,* ed. Hanns-Werner Heister and Hans-Günter Klein. Frankfurt/Main: Fischer, 1984.

Erdmann, Karl Dietrich. *Das Ende des Reiches und die Entstehung der Republik Österreich, der Bundesrepublik Deutschland und der Deutschen Demokratischen Republik.* Vol. 22 of Handbuch der deutschen Geschichte. 9th ed. Munich: DAV, 1980.

Ericksen, Robert P. "Religion und Nationalsozialismus im Spiegel der Entnazifizierungsakten der Göttinger Universität." *Kirchliche Zeitgeschichte* 7 (1994): 83–101.

Evans, Joan. "Die Rezeption der Musik Igor Strawinskys in Hitlerdeutschland." *Archiv für Musikwissenschaft* 55 (forthcoming, 1998).

Fallon, Daniel. *The German University: A Heroic Ideal in Conflict with the Modern World.* Boulder: Colorado Associated University Press, 1980.

Feldman, Gerald D. *The Great Disorder: Politics, Economics, and Society in the German Inflation.* New York: Oxford University Press, 1993.

Fischer, Georg, and Harald Scholtz. "Stellung und Funktion der Erwachsenenbildung im Nationalsozialismus." Pages 153–69 in *Erziehung und Schulung im Dritten Reich. Teil 2: Hochschule, Erwachsenenbildung,* ed. Manfred Heinemann. Stuttgart: Klett-Cotta, 1980.

Fischer-Defoy, Christine. *Kunst Macht Politik: Die Nazifizierung der Kunst- und Musikhochschulen in Berlin.* [Berlin:] Elefanten, [1987].

FitzGibbon, Constantin. *Denazification.* London: Michael Joseph, 1969.

Forman, Paul. "Scientific Internationalism and the Weimar Physicists: The Ideology and Its Manipulation in Germany after World War I." *Isis* 64 (1973): 151–80.

Freeden, Herbert. *Die jüdische Presse im Dritten Reich.* Frankfurt/Main: Jüdischer Verlag bei Athenäum, 1987.

Gallin, Alice. *Midwives to Nazism: University Professors in Weimar Germany 1925–1933.* Macon, Ga.: Mercer University Press, 1986.

Gay, Peter. *Weimar Culture: The Outsider As Insider.* New York: Harper & Row, 1968.

Giles, Geoffrey. "The Rise of the National Socialist Students' Association and the Failure of Political Education in the Third Reich." Pages 160–85 in *The Shaping of the Nazi State,* ed. Peter D. Stachura. London: Croom Helm; New York: Barnes & Noble, 1978.

———. "German Students and Higher Education Policy in the Second World War." *Central European History* 17 (1984): 330–53.

———. *Students and National Socialism in Germany*. Princeton: Princeton University Press, 1985.

Gilliam, Bryan. "The Annexation of Anton Bruckner: Nazi Revisionism and the Politics of Appropriation." *Musical Quarterly* 78 (1994): 584–609.

———. "Stage and Screen: Kurt Weill and Operatic Reform in the 1920s." Pages 1–12 in *Music and Performance during the Weimar Republic*, ed. Bryan Gilliam. Cambridge Studies in Performance Practice. Cambridge: Cambridge University Press, 1994.

Grohnert, Reinhardt. *Die Entnazifizierung in Baden 1945–1949: Konzeption und Praxis der "Epuration" am Beispiel eines Landes der französischen Besatzungszone*. Veröffentlichungen der Kommission für Geschichtliche Landeskunde in Baden-Württemberg. Series B, no. 123. Stuttgart: W. Kohlhammer, 1991.

Guttsman, W. L. *Workers' Culture in Weimar Germany: Between Tradition and Commitment*. New York: Berg, 1990.

Hailey, Christopher. "Rethinking Sound: Music and Radio in Weimar Germany." Pages 13–36 in *Music and Performance during the Weimar Republic*, ed. Bryan Gilliam. Cambridge Studies in Performance Practice. Cambridge: Cambridge University Press, 1994.

Harrison, Frank Ll. "American Musicology and the European Tradition." Pages 1–85 in *Musicology*, by Frank Ll. Harrison, Mantle Hood, and Claude V. Palisca. Englewood Cliffs, N.J.: Prentice Hall, 1963.

Hartshorne, Edward Yarnall. *The German Universities and National Socialism*. Cambridge: Harvard University Press, 1937.

Heiber, Helmut. *Universität unterm Hakenkreuz. Teil i: Der Professor im Dritten Reich*. Munich: K. G. Saur, 1991.

Hermand, Jost. *Literaturwissenschaft und Kunstwissenschaft*. Stuttgart: Metzlersche Verlagsbuchhandlung, 1971.

Herzstein, Robert Edwin. *The War That Hitler Won: The Most Infamous Propaganda Campaign in History*. New York: Putnam, 1978.

Hinton, Stephen. *The Idea of Gebrauchsmusik: A Study of Musical Aesthetics in the Weimar Republic (1919–1933) with Particular Reference to the Works of Paul Hindemith*. Outstanding Dissertations in Music from British Universities, ed. John Caldwell. New York: Garland, 1989.

Holtmeyer, Gerd. "Schulmusik und Musiklehrer an der höheren Schule. Ein Beitrag zur Geschichte des Musikpädagogen in Preußen." Ph.D. diss., Universität zu Köln, 1975.

Huber, Clara, ed. *Kurt Huber zum Gedächtnis: Bildnis eines Menschen, Denkers und Forschers*. Regensburg: Habbel, 1947.

Iggers, George. *The German Conception of History: The National Tradition of Historical Thought from Herder to the Present*. Rev. ed. Middletown, Conn.: Wesleyan University Press, 1983.

Jarausch, Konrad. *The Unfree Professions: German Lawyers, Teachers, and Engineers, 1900–1950*. New York: Oxford University Press, 1990.

Jelavich, Peter. *Berlin Cabaret*. Cambridge: Harvard University Press, 1993.

John, Eckhard. "Vom Deutschtum in der Musik." Pages 49–55 in *Entartete Musik: Eine kommentierte Rekonstruktion,* ed. Albrecht Dümling and Peter Girth. Düsseldorf: Kleinherne, 1988.

——. "Musik und Konzentrationslager: Eine Annäherung." *Archiv für Musikwissenschaft* 48 (1991): 1–36.

Karbaum, Michael. *Studien zur Geschichte der Bayreuther Festspiele (1876-1976).* Regensburg: Bosse, 1976.

Kater, Michael. *Das "Ahnenerbe" der SS 1935–1945: Ein Beitrag zur Kulturpolitik des Dritten Reiches.* Studien zur Zeitgeschichte herausgegeben vom Institut für Zeitgeschichte. Stuttgart: Deutsche Verlags-Anstalt, 1974.

——. *Studentenschaft und Rechtsradikalismus in Deutschland 1918–1933.* Hamburg: Hoffmann und Campe, 1975.

——. "Bürgerliche Jugendbewegung und Hitlerjugend in Deutschland von 1926 bis 1939." *Archiv für Sozialgeschichte* 17 (1977): 127–74.

——. "Die Studenten auf dem Weg in den Nationalsozialismus." Pages 26–37 in *Hochschule und Wissenschaft im Dritten Reich,* ed. Jörg Tröger. Frankfurt/Main: Campus, 1986.

——. "Problems of Political Reeducation in West Germany, 1945–1960." *Simon Wiesenthal Center Annual* 4 (1987): 99–123.

——. *Doctors under Hitler.* Chapel Hill: University of North Carolina Press, 1989.

——. *Different Drummers: Jazz in the Culture of Nazi Germany.* Oxford: Oxford University Press, 1992.

——. "Carl Orff im Dritten Reich." *Vierteljahrshefte für Zeitgeschichte* 43 (1995): 12–35.

——. *The Twisted Muse: Musicians and Their Music in the Third Reich.* New York: Oxford University Press, 1997.

Katz, Jacob. *From Prejudice to Destruction: Anti-Semitism, 1700–1933.* Cambridge: Harvard University Press, 1980.

Kerman, Joseph. *Contemplating Music: Challenges to Musicology.* Cambridge: Harvard University Press, 1985.

Kershaw, Ian. *The Nazi Dictatorship: Problems and Perspectives of Interpretation.* 3d ed. London: Edward Arnold, 1993.

Klönne, Arno. *Jugend im Dritten Reich. Die Hitler-Jugend und ihre Gegner.* Düsseldorf: Diederichs, 1982.

Koehl, Robert L. *RKFDV: German Resettlement and Population Policy 1939–1945.* Cambridge: Harvard University Press, 1957.

Kogon, Eugen. *Der SS-Staat: Das System der deutschen Konzentrationslager.* 18th ed. Munich: Heyne, 1974.

Kolland, Dorothea. *Die Jugendmusikbewegung. "Gemeinschaftsmusik" — Theorie und Praxis.* Stuttgart: Metzler, 1979.

Kolland, Hubert. "Wagner-Rezeption im deutschen Faschismus." Pages 494–503 in *Bericht über den internationalen musikwissenschaftlichen Kongreß Bayreuth 1981,* ed. Christoph-Hellmut Mahling and Sigrid Weismann. Basel: Bärenreiter, 1984.

Lämmert, Eberhard. "Germanistik — eine deutsche Wissenschaft." Pages 76–91 in *Nationalsozialismus und die deutsche Universität.* Universitätstage 1966: Veröffentlichungen der Freien Universität Berlin. Berlin: De Gruyter, 1966.

Lange, C. F. *Groß-Berliner Tagebuch 1920–1933*. Berlin: Berlinische Verlagsbuchhandlung, 1951.

Laqueur, Walter. *Young Germany: A History of the German Youth Movement*. New York: Basic Books, 1962.

———. *Weimar: A Cultural History 1918–1933*. New York: Putnam, 1974.

Lewis, Anthony. "Facing the Music." *New York Times,* 18 February 1982, p. A23.

Lixfeld, Hannsjost. *Folklore and Fascism: The Reich Institute for German Volkskunde.* Ed. and trans. James R. Dow. Bloomington: Indiana University Press, 1994.

Lovisa, Fabian R. *Musikkritik im Nationalsozialismus: Die Rolle deutschsprachiger Musikzeitschriften 1920–1945.* Neue Heidelberger Studien zur Musikwissenschaft, no. 22. Laaber: Laaber Verlag, 1993.

Lundgreen, Peter. "Hochschulpolitik und Wissenschaft im Dritten Reich." Pages 9–30 in *Wissenschaft im Dritten Reich,* ed. P. Lundgreen. Frankfurt/Main: Suhrkamp, 1985.

Maier, Hans. "Nationalsozialistische Hochschulpolitik." Pages 71–102 in *Die deutsche Universität im Dritten Reich.* Munich: Piper, 1966.

Maren-Grisebach, Manon. *Methoden der Literaturwissenschaft.* 6th ed. Munich: Francke Verlag, 1977.

Meyer, Michael. "Assumptions and Implementation of Nazi Policy toward Music." Ph.D. diss., University of California at Los Angeles, 1970.

———. "The Nazi Musicologist as Myth-Maker in the Third Reich." *Journal of Contemporary History* 10 (1975): 649–65.

———. "Musicology in the Third Reich: A Gap in Historical Studies." *European Studies Review* 8 (1978): 349–64.

———. *The Politics of Music in the Third Reich.* American University Studies. Series 9, History; no. 49. New York: Peter Lang, 1991.

Moser, H. J. *Das musikalische Denkmälerwesen in Deutschland.* Kassel: Bärenreiter, 1952.

Mosse, George. *The Crisis of German Ideology: Intellectual Origins of the Third Reich.* New York: Grosset and Dunlap, 1964.

Muck, Peter, ed. *Einhundert Jahre Berliner Philharmonisches Orchester: Darstellung in Dokumenten.* Tutzing: Schneider, 1982.

Newhouse, Martin J. "Artists, Artisans, or Workers? Orchestral Musicians in the German Empire." Ph.D. diss., Columbia University, 1979.

Noakes, J., and G. Pridham, eds. *Nazism: A History in Documents and Eyewitness Accounts, 1919–1945. Volume 1: The Nazi Party, State and Society, 1919–1939.* New York: Schocken Books, 1990.

Oellers, Norbert. "Dichtung und Volkstum: Der Fall der Literaturwissenschaft." Pages 232–54 in *Literatur und Germanistik nach der 'Machtübernahme': Colloquium zur 50. Wiederkehr des 30. Januar 1933,* ed. Beda Allemann. Bonn: Bouvier, 1983.

Oesterle, Anke. "The Office of Ancestral Inheritance and Folklore Scholarship." Pages 189–246 in *The Nazification of an Academic Discipline: Folklore in the Third Reich,* ed. and trans. James R. Dow and Hannsjost Lixfeld. Bloomington: Indiana University Press, 1994.

Olszewski, Henryk. *Zwischen Begeisterung und Widerstand: Deutsche Hochschullehrer und der Nationalsozialismus.* Posen: Instytut Zachodni, 1989.

Pedersen, Sanna. "On the Task of the Music Historian: The Myth of the Symphony after Beethoven." *Repercussions* 2 (1993): 5–30.

Petropoulos, Jonathan. *Art As Politics in the Third Reich*. Chapel Hill: University of North Carolina Press, 1996.

Petry, Christian. *Studenten aufs Schafott: Die Weiße Rose und ihr Scheitern*. Munich: Piper, 1968.

Plantinga, Leon. *Schumann As Critic*. New Haven: Yale University Press, 1967.

Potter, Pamela M. "Wissenschaftler im Zwiespalt." Pages 62–66 in *Entartete Musik: Eine kommentierte Rekonstruktion,* ed. Albrecht Dümling and Peter Girth. Düsseldorf: Kleinherne, 1988.

———. "The Deutsche Musikgesellschaft, 1918–1938." *Journal of Musicological Research* 11 (1991): 151–76.

———. "German Musicology and Early Music Performance, 1918–1933." Pages 94–106 in *Music and Performance during the Weimar Republic,* ed. Bryan Gilliam. Cambridge Studies in Performance Practice. Cambridge: Cambridge University Press, 1994.

———. "Did Himmler *Really* Like Gregorian Chant? The SS and Musicology." Special Issue on Fascism and Culture, Part One, *Modernism/Modernity* 2/3 (1995): 45–68.

———. "The Nazi 'Seizure' of the Berlin Philharmonic, or the Decline of a Bourgeois Musical Institution." Pages 39–66 in *National Socialist Cultural Policy,* ed. Glenn R. Cuomo. New York: St. Martin's, 1995.

———. "Musicology under Hitler: New Sources in Context." *Journal of the American Musicological Society* 49 (1996): 70–113.

Prieberg, Fred K. *Musik im NS-Staat*. Frankfurt/Main: Fischer, 1982.

Pulzer, Peter. *Jews and the German State: The Political History of a Minority, 1848–1933*. Oxford: Blackwell, 1992.

Reimann, Bruno W. "Die 'Selbst-Gleichschaltung' der Universitäten 1933." Pages 38–52 in *Hochschule und Wissenschaft im Dritten Reich,* ed. Jörg Tröger. Frankfurt/Main: Campus, 1986.

Riethmüller, Albrecht. "Die Bestimmung der Orgel im Dritten Reich." Pages 28–69 in *Orgel und Ideologie. Bericht über das fünfte Colloquium der Walcker-Stiftung für orgelwissenschaftliche Forschung 5.-7. Mai 1983 in Göttweig,* ed. Hans Heinrich Eggebrecht. Murrhardt: Musikwissenschaftliche Verlags-Gesellschaft, 1984.

———. "German Music from the Perspective of German Musicology after 1933." *Journal of Musicological Research* 11 (1991): 177–87.

———. "Musik, die 'deutscheste' Kunst." Pages 91–103 in *Verfemte Musik: Komponisten in den Diktaturen unseres Jahrhunderts,* ed. Joachim Braun, Vladimir Karbusický, and Heidi Tamar Hoffmann. Frankfurt: Peter Lang, 1995.

———. *Die Walhalla und ihre Musiker*. Laaber: Laaber Verlag, 1993.

Ringer, Fritz. *The Decline of the German Mandarins: The German Academic Community, 1890–1933*. Cambridge: Harvard University Press, 1969.

Robinson, J. Bradford. "Jazz Reception in Weimar Germany: In Search of a Shimmy Figure." Pages 107–34 in *Music and Performance during the Weimar Republic,* ed. Bryan Gilliam. Cambridge Studies in Performance Practice. Cambridge: Cambridge University Press, 1994.

Rothfeder, Herbert P. "A Study of Alfred Rosenberg's Organization for National Socialist Ideology." Ph.D. diss., University of Michigan, 1963.

Sachs, Joel. "Some Aspects of Musical Politics in Pre-Nazi Germany." *Perspectives of New Music* 9 (1970): 74–95.

Schaal, Richard. *Das Schrifttum zur musikalischen Lokalgeschichtsforschung.* Kassel: Bärenreiter, [1947].

Schnauber, Cornelius. "Introduction." Pages vii–xxii in *NS-Literaturtheorie: Eine Dokumentation,* ed. Sander L. Gilman. Frankfurt/Main: Athenäum, 1971.

Schneider, Albrecht. "Germany and Austria." Pages 77–94 in *Ethnomusicology: Historical and Regional Studies,* ed. Helen Meyers. Norton/Grove Handbooks in Music. New York: W. W. Norton, 1993.

———. "Musikwissenschaft in der Emigration." Pages 187–211 in *Musik im Exil: Folgen des Nazismus für die internationale Musikkultur,* ed. Hanns-Werner Heister, Claudia Maurer Zenck, and Peter Petersen. Frankfurt/Main: Fischer, 1993.

Scholtz, Wilhelm, and Waltraut Jonas-Corrieri, eds. *Die deutsche Jugendmusikbewegung in Dokumenten ihrer Zeit von den Anfängen bis 1933.* Wolfenbüttel: Möseler, 1980.

Schwarz, Boris. *Music and Musical Life in Soviet Russia, 1917–1970.* New York: W. W. Norton, 1972.

Schwerter, Werner. "Heerschau und Selektion." Pages 111–26 in *Entartete Musik: Eine kommentierte Rekonstruktion,* ed. Albrecht Dümling and Peter Girth. Düsseldorf: Kleinherne, 1988.

Sontheimer, Kurt. *Antidemokratisches Denken in der Weimarer Republik: Die politischen Ideen des deutschen Nationalismus zwischen 1918 und 1933.* 2d ed. Munich: Nymphenburger Verlagshandlung, 1968.

Sponheuer, Bernd. "Musik auf einer 'kulturellen und physischen Insel': Musik als Überlebensmittel im Jüdischen Kulturbund 1933–1941." Pages 108–35 in *Musik in der Emigration 1933–1945: Verfolgung — Vertreibung — Rückwirkung,* ed. Horst Weber. Stuttgart: Metzler, 1994.

Stachura, Peter D. *The German Youth Movement, 1900–1945.* New York: St. Martin's, 1981.

"A Star of Knowledge." *Time,* 24 April 1950.

Steinweis, Alan. *Art, Ideology, and Economics in Nazi Germany: The Reich Chambers of Music, Theater, and the Visual Arts.* Chapel Hill: University of North Carolina Press, 1993.

Steinzor, Curt Efram, comp. *American Musicologists, c. 1890–1945: A Bio-Bibliographical Sourcebook to the Formative Period.* Music Reference Collection, no. 17, ed. Donald L. Hixon. New York: Greenwood, 1989

Suppan, Wolfgang. *Volkslied.* Sammlung Metzler, Realienbücher für Germanisten Abt. E: Poetik. Stuttgart: Metzler, 1966.

Tent, James F. *Mission on the Rhine: Reeducation and Denazification in American-Occupied Germany.* Chicago: University of Chicago Press, 1982.

Treziak, Ulrike. *Deutsche Jugendbewegung am Ende der Weimarer Republik: Zum Verhältnis von Bündischer Jugend und Nationalsozialismus.* Frankfurt/Main: dipa-Verlag, 1986.

Voßkamp, Wilhelm. "Kontinuität und Diskontinuität. Zur deutschen Literaturwissenschaft im Dritten Reich." Pages 140–62 in *Wissenschaft im Dritten Reich,* ed. Peter Lundgreen. Frankfurt/Main: Suhrkamp, 1985.

Wagner, Karl. *Das Mozarteum: Geschichte und Entwicklung einer kulturellen Institution.* Innsbruck: Edition Helbling, 1993.

Weinberg, Gerhard. *A World at Arms: A Global History of World War II.* Cambridge: Cambridge University Press, 1994.

Weiner, Marc A. *Undertones of Insurrection: Music, Politics, and the Social Sphere in the Modern German Narrative.* Lincoln: University of Nebraska Press, 1993.

Welsh, Helga. *Revolutionärer Wandel auf Befehl? Entnazifizierungs- und Personalpolitik in Thüringen und Sachsen (1945–1948).* Schriftenreihe der Vierteljarhshefte für Zeitgeschichte, no. 58. Munich: R. Oldenbourg, 1989.

Werner, Michael G. "'Das Fest unserer Zeit': Händel-Inszenierungen in den 1920er Jahren und ihre Implikationen für das nationalsozialistische Thingspiel." Pages 675–87 in *"Und Jedermann erwartet sich ein Fest." Fest, Theater, Festspiele. Gesammelte Vorträge des Salzburger Symposions 1995,* ed. P. Csobáldi, G. Gruber, J. Kühnel, U. Müller, O. Panagl and F. V. Spechtler. Salzburg: Müller-Speiser, 1996.

Williams, Peter. "The Idea of *Bewegung* in the German Organ Reform Movement of the 1920s." Pages 135–39 in *Music and Performance during the Weimar Republic,* ed. Bryan Gilliam. Cambridge Studies in Performance Practice. Cambridge: Cambridge University Press, 1994.

Willis, F. Roy. *The French in Germany, 1945–1949.* Stanford: Stanford University Press, 1962.

Wolff, Christoph. "Die Hand eines Handlangers. 'Musikwissenschaft' im Dritten Reich." *Frankfurter Rundschau* 168, 24 July 1982, "Zeit und Bild" (weekend supplement), p. 2. Rpt., pages 93–94 in *Entartete Musik: Eine kommentierte Rekonstruktion,* ed. Albrecht Dümling and Peter Girth. Düsseldorf: Kleinherne, 1988.

Wulf, Joseph. *Musik im Dritten Reich: Eine Dokumentation.* Berlin: Ullstein, 1966, 1983.

Index